T0213007

Lecture Notes in Computer Science   10507

Commenced Publication in 1973
Founding and Former Series Editors:
Gerhard Goos, Juris Hartmanis, and Jan van Leeuwen

Nagisa Munekata · Itsuki Kunita
Junichi Hoshino (Eds.)

Entertainment Computing – ICEC 2017

16th IFIP TC 14 International Conference
Tsukuba City, Japan, September 18–21, 2017
Proceedings

 Springer

Editors
Nagisa Munekata
Kyoto Sangyo University
Kyoto
Japan

Itsuki Kunita 🆔
University of the Ryukyus
Okinawa
Japan

Junichi Hoshino
University of Tsukuba
Tsukuba
Japan

ISSN 0302-9743   ISSN 1611-3349 (electronic)
Lecture Notes in Computer Science
ISBN 978-3-319-66714-0   ISBN 978-3-319-66715-7   (eBook)
DOI 10.1007/978-3-319-66715-7

Library of Congress Control Number: 2017952385

LNCS Sublibrary: SL3 – Information Systems and Applications, incl. Internet/Web, and HCI

Printed on acid-free paper

This Springer imprint is published by Springer Nature
The registered company is Springer International Publishing AG
The registered company address is: Gewerbestrasse 11, 6330 Cham, Switzerland

Preface

This volume collects all contributions accepted for ICEC 2017, the International Conference on Entertainment Computing. ICEC 2017 was the 16th event in a series of successful conferences on entertainment computing, previously held in São Paulo, Brazil (2013); Sydney, Australia (2014); Trondheim, Norway (2015); and Vienna, Austria (2016).

This year's event was held in Tsukuba, Japan on September 18–21, 2017. ICEC 2017 was hosted by the Special Interest Group on Entertainment Computing (SIG-EC) of the Information Processing Society of Japan (IPSJ), and the Entertainment Computing Lab (ECL) of the University of Tsukuba.

The papers brought together in this edited volume span a variety of topics pertaining to different aspects of entertainment computing, including but not limited to games for health and learning, player behavioral analysis, and technological aspects. This once again shows that entertainment computing is a diverse and thriving research area bringing together experts from a wide range of disciplines. In this regard, ICEC 2017 served as a lively forum for multidisciplinary exchange to advance our understanding of this exciting field.

Overall, we received 52 submissions by authors from 15 countries across Europe, North and South America, and Asia. Eventually, 14 submissions were accepted as full papers, and 23 as short papers. In addition, 32 posters and demonstrations, three workshops, two tutorials, and a doctoral consortium were held during the conference.

The conference program was further complemented by three invited keynotes, held by Driancourt Remi and Miyake Yoichiro from the Advanced Technology Division, Square Enix Co., Ltd. and STUDIO 4°C Co., Ltd., and Toshimasa Yamanaka from the University of Tsukuba.

Finally, we would like to thank all members of the Program Committee and all external reviewers for their commitment and contribution to making ICEC 2017 a success. We also would like to thank our sponsor, Rakuten, Inc.

July 2017

Yoshinari Takegawa
Jannicke Baalsrud Hauge
Itaru Kuramoto
Yuta Sugiura
Junichi Hoshino

Organization

General Chair

Junichi Hoshino — University of Tsukuba, Japan

Vice General Chair

Soh Masuko — Rakuten Institute of Technology, Japan

Program Chairs

Jannicke Baalsrud Hauge — KTH-Royal Institute of Technology, Sweden
and Bremer Institut für Produktion und Logistik, Germany

Yoshinari Takegawa — Future University Hakodate, Japan

Vice Program Chairs

Kuramoto Itaru — Osaka University, Japan
Yuta Sugiura — Keio University, Japan

Publication Chairs

Nagisa Munekata — Kyoto Sangyo University, Japan
Itsuki Kunita — University of the Ryukyus, Japan

Poster/Demo Chair

Taku Hachisu — University of Tsukuba, Japan

Workshop Chairs

Letizia Jaccheri — Norwegian University of Science and Technology, Norway
Erik van der Spek — Eindhoven University of Technology, The Netherlands

IPSJ Liaison Chair

Kuramoto Itaru — Osaka University, Japan

Accounting Chair

Hiroshi Mori — Utsunomiya University, Japan

Publicity Chair

Masanori Ishida   Tin Machine Creative, Japan

Local Chairs

Nobumitsu Shikine   University of Tsukuba, Japan
Hirotaka Osawa   University of Tsukuba, Japan

Doctoral Consortium

Esteban Clua   Fluminense Federal University, Brazil

Steering Committee Members

Rainer Malaka   University of Bremen, Germany
Artur Lugmayr   Curtin University, Australia, University of Cape Coast,
                               Ghana
Hyun-Seung Yang   Korea Advanced Institute of Science and Technology,
                               South Korea
Helmut Hlavacs   University of Vienna, Austria
Esteban Clua   Fluminense Federal University, Brazil
Letizia Jaccheri   Norwegian University of Science and Technology,
                               Norway
Ryohei Nakatsu   Kyoto University, Japan
Matthias Rauterberg   Eindhoven University of Technology, The Netherlands

Sponsoring Institutions

Rakuten, Inc., Tokyo, Japan

Program Committee Members

Alexander Hofmann   University of Applied Science Technikum Wien,
                               Austria
Anton Nijholt   University of Twente, Netherlands
Antonio J. Fernández Leiva   Universidad de Málaga, Spain
Artur Lugmayr   Curtin University, Australia
Börje Karlsson   Microsoft Research Asia, China
Chris Geiger   University of Applied Sciences Düsseldorf, German
Christopher Helf   University of Vienna, Austria
Daniel Martinek   University of Vienna, Austria
Elpida Tzafestas   University of Athens, Greece
Esteban Clua   Universidade Federal Fluminense, Brazil
Ewald Hotop   University of Vienna, Austria
Flavio S. Correa Da Silva   Universidade de São Paulo, Brazil

Guenter Wallner	University of Applied Arts Vienna, Austria
Hannes Wagner	University of Vienna, Austria
Haruhiro Katayose	Kwansei Gakuin University, Japan
Helmut Hlavacs	University of Vienna, Austria
Hyun Seung Yang	KAIST, Japan
Ines Di Loreto	UTT - Université de Technologie de Troyes, France
Irene Mavrommati	Hellenic Open University, Greece
Jannicke Baalsrud Hauge	Bremer Institut für Produktion und Logistik, University of Bremen, German
Jerome Dupire	CNAM - CEDRIC, France
Joaquim Madeira	Universidade de Aveiro, Portugal
Johanna Pirker	Graz University of Technology, Austria
Junghyun Han	Korea University, Korea
Junichi Hoshino	University of Tsukuba, Entertainment Computing Lab, Japan
Kendra Cooper	UT-Dallas, USA
Konrad Peters	University of Vienna, Austria
Luca Chittaro	HCI Lab, University of Udine, Italy
Luis Carriço	University of Lisbon, Portugal
Maic Masuch	University of Duisburg-Essen, German
Manuel Oliveira	Sintef, Norway
Marc Herrlich	TZI, University of Bremen, German
Marc Cavazza	University of Teesside, England
Margarida Romero	Université Laval, Canada
Maria Letizia Jaccheri	University of Trondheim, Norway
Matthias Rauterberg	Eindhoven University of Technology, Netherlands
Michail Giannakos	Norwegian University of Science and Technology, Norway
Monica Divitini	IDI-NTNU, Norway
Nikitas Sgouros	University of Piraeus, Greece
Owen Noel Newton Fernandon	NTU, Singapore
Paolo Ciancarini	University of Bologna, Italy
Pedro González Calero	Complutense University of Madrid, Spain
Rafael Bidarra	Delft University of Technology, Netherlands
Rainer Malaka	University of Bremen, German
Rebecca Wölfle	University of Vienna, Austria
Ryohei Nakatsu	National University of Singapore, Singapore
Sander Bakkes	University of Amsterdam, Netherlands
Simone Kriglstein	Vienna University of Technology, Austria
Sobah Abbas Petersen	Norwegian University of Science and Technology, Norway
Staffan Björk	University of Gothenburg, Sweden
Sung-Bae Cho	Yonsei University, Korea
Teresa Romão	DI/FCT/UNL, USA
Tim Marsh	Griffith University, Australia

Valentina Nisi   Carnagie Mellon/Portugal, University of Madeira,
                            Portugal
Walt Scacchi   University of California, Irvine, USA
Werner Gaisbauer   University of Vienna, Austria
Zlatogor Minchev   IICT-BAS, Bulgaria

Contents

Serious Games

Education

Reality

Game Understanding

Game Design

Poster and Interactive Session

Workshops and Tutorials

Art and Music

Genesis: New Media Art Created as a Visualization of Fluid Dynamics

Naoko Tosa[1(✉)], Pang Yunian[2], Liang Zhao[2], and Ryohei Nakatsu[3]

[1] Institute for Information Management and Communication, Kyoto University, Kyoto, Japan
`tosa@media.kyoto-u.ac.jp`
[2] Shishukan, Kyoto University, Kyoto, Japan
`pang.yunian.87r@st.kyoto-u.ac.jp`, `liang@gsais.kyoto-u.ac.jp`
[3] Design School, Kyoto University, Kyoto, Japan
`ryohei.nakatsu@design.kyoto-u.ac.jp`

Abstract. We have been working on the creation of media art utilizing technologies. As an extension of our previous research, this time we have focused on the visualization of behaviors of fluid. This area has been named as "fluid mechanics" or "fluid dynamics" and there have been various researches in this area. As some of the fluid motion look beautiful, there is another research area called "visualization of fluid motion."

However most of these results show only stable fluid behaviors and lacks of unstable or in other words unpredictable behaviors that would be substantial for the creation of art. Therefore, to create various unstable or unpredictable fluid behaviors in trials to create artworks, we have introduced several new methods such as usage of dry ice, injection of paints into fluid, and usage of air gun to create an explosive effect. This paper proposes the basic concept of new video art called "Genesis" based on the visualization of fluid dynamics, describes details of the above mentioned three ideas that were introduced to create unpredictable fluid dynamics based phenomena, and then describes details of new media art we have created combining these ideas.

Keywords: Fluid dynamics · High speed camera · Air gun · Dry ice · Media art

1 Introduction

We have been creating media art where new technologies play an essential role. Recently we have been interested in the usage of a high speed camera by using which we have found that hidden beauty in various physical phenomena could be revealed. Based on this methodology we have been trying to create new type of media art [1]. In our previous trial, we used viscous fluids such as paints with various colors, gave vibration to the fluids, and made them jumping up. Jumping up paints created beautiful forms that change in a very short time which were shot by a high speed camera and then based on editing of the obtained video a new type of media art was created [2]. Also some of such media art were exhibited in the form of projection mapping [3]. Figures 1 and 2 illustrate several

N. Munekata et al. (Eds.): ICEC 2017, LNCS 10507, pp. 3–13, 2017.
DOI: 10.1007/978-3-319-66715-7_1

scenes of the artwork called "Sound of Ikebana" we have created and also a scene of its projection mapping held at ArtScience Museum in Singapore in 2014.

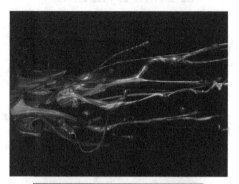

Fig. 1. Several shots of "Sound of Ikebana."

Fig. 2. A scene of the projection mapping of "Sound of Ikebana" carried out at ArtScience Museum in Singapore.

As an extension of our previous research, this time we have focused on the visualization of behaviors of fluid. This area has been considered as "fluid mechanics" or "fluid dynamics" and there have been various researches in this area [4, 5]. As some of the fluid motion look beautiful, there is an another research area called "visualization of fluid motion" [6]. One of such beautiful fluid motions is well known "milk crown" [7].

However most of these results show only stable fluid behaviors and lacks of unstable or in other words unpredictable behaviors that would be substantial for the creation of art. Therefore, to create various unstable or unpredictable fluid behaviors in trials to create artworks, we have introduced several new ideas such as usage of dry ice, injection of paints into fluid, and usage of air gun to create an explosive effect. This paper proposes the basic concept of new video art based on the visualization of fluid dynamics, describes details of the above mentioned three ideas that were introduced to create unpredictable fluid dynamics based phenomena, and then describes details of new media art we have created combining these ideas. This paper consists of the following contents. In Sect. 2, the basic concept of visualization of fluid dynamics as a method to create artworks will be described. In Sect. 3, the detailed description of three physical phenomena introduced in the visualization process of fluid dynamics to create new artworks will be described. In Sect. 4, the details of actual art creation process based on the combination of these three physical phenomena will be described. And in Sect. 5 conclusion and future work of the paper will be discussed.

2   Visualization of Fluid Dynamics as a Method to Create Media Art

Study of behaviors of fluid, especially in an environment where several obstacles exist in the pathway of fluid has been a long time research topic in physics and this area has been called as "fluid dynamics" [4, 5]. In physics, fluid dynamics is a sub-discipline of fluid mechanics that deals with fluid flow – the science of fluid (liquids and gases) in motion. It has several sub-disciplines itself, including aerodynamics (the study of air and other gases in motion) and hydrodynamics (the study of liquids in motion). Fluid dynamics has a wide range of applications including calculating forces and moments on aircraft, determining the mass flow rate of petroleum through pipelines, predicting weather patterns, understanding nebulae in interstellar space and modeling fission weapon detonation. How to explicitly show the behavior of fluid is another research area called "visualization of scientific phenomena" [6]. Based on this visualization process it became possible for people to watch the actual process of fluid behavior and it has been recognized that various beautiful fluid motion can be created depending on various conditions. As beauty is the fundamental concept of art, utilizing fluid dynamics as a method to create artworks has been one of the key concepts of art creation. There are various artworks that utilize the concept of fluid dynamics. These approaches can be classified into two ways.

One is an approach from purely scientific side. Fluid motion, especially when there are obstacles in the pathway of the fluid, look beautiful and sometimes the visualized result of such fluid motion are considered as art. Figure 3 shows a result of visualization of a stable flow called "laminar flow." As the ratio between inertia and viscosity, called

"Reynolds number," increases, the laminar flow changes into unstable flow called "turbulence." In turbulence frequently various types of vortex occur, some of which look beautiful. Figure 4 shows one example of such vortex. Other examples are special types of fluid behaviors. One of such behaviors is a well-known phenomenon called "magnetic fluid" or "ferrofluid" which forms itself in specific and beautiful way when it is placed near magnet [7]. Inspired by the beauty of such magnetic fluid several artists have been trying to create artworks. Figure 5 shows an example of the phenomenon of magnetic fluid.

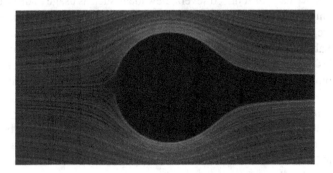

Fig. 3. An example of laminar flow.

Fig. 4. An example of vorlex.

Fig. 5. An example of magnetic fluid.

Although various types of beautiful forms can be created based on such approaches, created forms based on such approaches are not considered as pure art. The reason is that these phenomena or created forms are still too much physics-based and it is difficult to include in the form creation process "intention of artists." There is a clear distinction between physical phenomenon and art works and the border is how much intention of the artists to create artworks is involved in the created work. If there is no intention or such intention is too weak, created forms are considered physical phenomenon rather than art works. In other words, forms created as physical phenomenon are controlled by laws of physics and there is only a small space where something unexpected happens. And this unexpectedness is very important core part of art works.

On the other hand, there is different approach from art side. Here the usage of fluid is strongly controlled by artists and unexpected phenomena or chance phenomena that happen in the process of fluid usage is utilized by the artists to include something unexpected into their art works. One representative such art creation processes is "Action Painting" [10] led by Jackson Pollock [11]. Action painting is a form of art creation in which, instead of drawing paintings using paintbrush, artists throw or draw paints on a campus. Basically artists have intentions of what kind of paints they use and where on the campus they throw or draw pains. Therefore, in addition to the intensions of artists, a kind of contingency caused by thrown or drawn paints influence the final form of the created artwork. Figure 6 shows one of the representative artwork of Jackson Pollock. Although he is highly evaluated and appreciated in modern history of art, a problem with his art works is that the lack of pure beauty, which has been long time a core concept of great art, and therefore which has confused many people.

Fig. 6. One of Jackson Pollac's drawings.

Based on the problems included in these two approaches, we think that there should be another way of new art creation somewhere in between these two approaches. We have started from the former approach but tried to include more unexpectedness in created forms. In the next Section several methods to realize this will be described.

3 Physical Phenomena Introduced to Realize Unexpected Behavior of Fluid

We have introduced three new methods into fluid dynamics to realize unexpected behaviors of fluid; namely "injection of paints into fluid," "usage of dry ice as obstacles in fluid pathway," and "usage of air gun to generate explosive effect."

3.1 Injection of Paints into Fluid

As a basic material to observe behaviors we chose color paints. In our previous work to create artworks also we chose color paints and succeeded in creating various types of beautiful and mysterious forms by giving vibrations to them [1–3]. And therefore we are familiar with behaviors of color paints. This time, instead of giving them sound vibrations, we tried to inject them into water. Based on various preliminary experiments we found that color paints injected into water from droppers can create interesting forms that resemble the phenomenon of volcano eruption or something similar (Fig. 7).

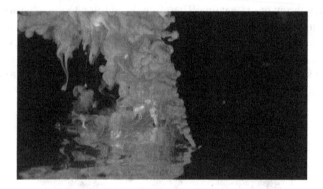

Fig. 7. Injection of color paints into fluid. (Color figure online)

As water and color paints even in the case of oil-based pains there is some affinity and therefore injected paints and water are mingled rapidly and the whole water became a kind of "colored water" rapidly. As what we want to create is interesting behaviors of injected paints, this rapid mingling process is not preferable. Then we tried to add agar into water to increase its viscosity. And we have found that in the case of water with certain amount of viscosity has the effect of delaying such mingling process. Also we have found that level of viscosity based on the amount of added agar plays an important role by changing the mingling time to some extent. This finding was important to create interesting behavior of injected paints. However, basically behaviors of injected paints are based on diffusing process and, as the time passes, water and paint are mixed based on one-way process. Therefore it is difficult to generate something unexpected based on this basic method. Therefore, some new mechanism of creating unexpected phenomenon should be introduced. To realize this, we have introduced the usage of dry ice which is described in next subsection.

3.2   Usage of Dry Ice as Obstacles in Fluid Pathway

Based on fluid dynamics study we have learned that the existence of obstacles in the pathway of fluid motion is the key to generate beautiful and mysterious forms. At the same time, we have learned that such obstacles should not be fixed ones. Fixed obstacles gives fixed effects to the behaviors of fluid and this process is not effective in generating something unexpected. Therefore, such obstacles should move around. Also it is preferable that the moving patterns of such obstacles would be unstable or even unexpected. In addition, it would be preferable if forms of the obstacles would change unexpectedly. We have carried out various kinds of experiments to find out such obstacles and finally found that the use of dry ice is very effective to be used as obstacles to be interacted with injected paints.

Dry ice is the solid form of carbon dioxide. It is used primarily as a cooling agent. Its advantages included lower temperature than that of water ice and not leaving residue. At the same time, dry ice has been frequently used as a material to create mysterious stage effect, as it creates huge amount of fog when it is put into water. People have been focusing on the effect of fog generation when they use dry ice. However, we have focused on the early process of fog generation. When dry ice is put into water, based on the temperature difference between water and dry ice, rapid vaporization process of dry ice occurs. Many small bubbles, each of which contains carbon dioxide fog, are generated as the result of vaporization and these small bubbles rise from dry ice at bottom to water surface and finally create fog. Watching this process by using a high speed camera, we have found that such bubbles have interesting forms with each bubble having a different form. And during the process of its rising up to water surface the bubble always changes its form. This phenomenon gives us an impression that each bubble is a kind of living creature (Fig. 8). Then we had an idea that the combination of these bubbles and injected paints described in the previous subsection would be ideal to generate a new type of phenomenon based on fluid dynamics. Therefore, we have adopted the usage of dry ice as an obstacle material in the pathway of injected fluid.

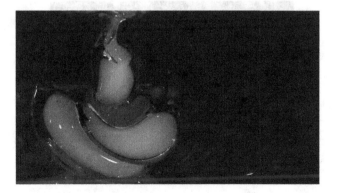

Fig. 8. Bubbles generated by dry ice.

3.3 Usage of Air Gun to Generate Explosive Effect

Based on our observation we have found that each of the two described effects and especially their integration could create really new fluid dynamics based effect that would be described in detail in the next section. At the same time, we have found that it would be important and necessary for us to have another phenomenon that can create surprising effect such as an explosive effect. In our previous work we used an air gun to explode frozen flowers and this could create really beautiful and at the same time surprising effect [3]. Based on our experience we have decided to use again an air gun to realize a new effect. Based on various kinds of experiments, we have found that shooting an air gun bullet into water could create a surprising phenomenon. By being shot into water with relevant speed, firstly an air gun bullet creates a big hollow ball with nothing inside. Then the ball crashes itself quickly by intriguing surrounding water as if there is an internal waterfall in water. This process is difficult to watch by our naked eye but is observable once the process is shot by a high speed camera. This process is shown in Figs. 9 and 10 and because of an amazing effect it can create, we have decided to adopt it in combination with the above mentioned two methods.

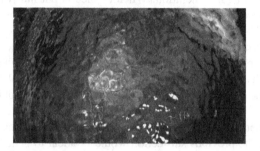

Fig. 9. Effect of an air gun bullet shot into fluid.

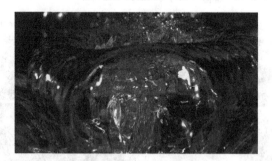

Fig. 10. Break down of a bubble created by an air gun bullet.

4   Physical Phenomena Introduced to Realize Unexpected Behavior of Fluid

By combining three types of new effect creation methods described in the previous Section, we tried to create new type of physical phenomena. As a first step, we have combined two methods described in Subsects. 3.1 and 3.3. The actual process is as follows. Firstly, combination of color paints is selected. Of course single color is acceptable. But combination of several colors is more effective as it can generate beautiful and deep effect. At the same time, an air gun bullet is shot into water aiming the injected color paints. As this whole process occurs in a very short time, this process can become visible only by being shot using a high speed camera. Several examples of obtained images are shown in Fig. 11. We have found that the water falling effect, that occurs when a hollow bubble created by a shot bullet, gives us the feeling that comic dust is being drawn into a black hall. This is the main reason that we have decided to call our new artwork as "Genesis" which means the end and also reborn of our cosmos, life, etc.

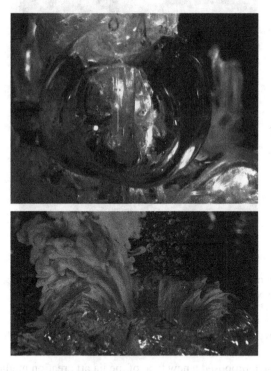

Fig. 11. Several examples of interaction between a bubble created by an air gun bullet and injected color paints. (Color figure online)

As a next step we tried to integrate two methods described in Subsects. 3.1 and 3.2. Firstly, we put a small block of dry ice into water letting it generate bubbles with carbon dioxide fog inside. Then a combination of several color paints is injected into water.

Without dry ice based bubbles, the injected color paints quickly diffuse making the whole water as a colored water. There are two ways to avoid this somewhat boring event to happen. One is that, as is described in Subsect. 3.1, we have used agar to increase water viscosity to some extent. Based on several experiences we have found that there is a certain range of viscosity in which the diffusion of color paint into water occurs slowly. Then under such condition we added dry ice into water. As described in Subsect. 3.2, various dry ice bubbles are generated as the result of vaporization process of dry ice where forms of dry ice bubbles are different each other and even their forms change continuously while rising up in water to water surface. Then injected color paints interact with these various bubbles and create various complex forms as shown in Fig. 12. These created forms are beyond the forms we often see as the result of scientific visualization and look very artistic. Combining images obtained in the first step and the second step can become sophisticated media art that has never been created.

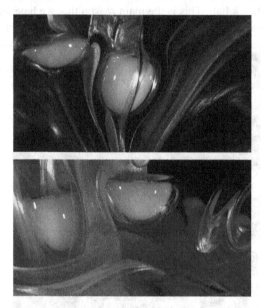

Fig. 12. Several examples of interaction between bubbles created by dry ice and injected color paints. (Color figure online)

5   Conclusion

In this paper we have proposed a new type of media art creation method and described its details. As an extension of our previous experience of creating media art based on the movement of color paints that are vibrated and jumped up forming various types of surprising and mysterious forms, we have tried to explore different type of fluid dynamics based phenomenon. This time we have decided to explore the behavior of color paints in water. To give people different type of sense of surprise and mystery we have introduced three methods to create new fluid dynamics phenomenon. One is an effect obtained by injecting color paints into water with various viscosity. Second is to use dry ice as obstacles that would interact with the flow of injected paints and based on this to create surprising and mysterious liquid forms. In addition to these phenomena, we have decided to use an air gun and we have found that an air gun bullet shot into water could create a new type of explosive effect. By integrating these three methods in a relevant way and also by using a high speed camera to shoot and visualize generated phenomena that occur in very short time, we have tried to create various kinds of new phenomena. Interestingly enough what we could create is something beautiful, noble, and inspiring that never existed and that is somewhere between existing two types of art creation process. One is a purely scientific process and its aim is to find out beauty in the process of liquid motion as a physical phenomenon. Another is the usage of liquid as a basic material for creating drawing. Here the basic idea of art creation is controlled by an artist but in the final art making process of paint throwing and dropping a randomness, that is one of basic natures of physical phenomena, is included to add values to the created artwork.

We have found that our proposed method situates somewhere in between these two different processes. Its feature is that on one hand it can keep pure beauty included in physical phenomenon that is something missing in the art creation process called Action Painting. On the other hand, our method can get rid of a feeling associated with too scientific phenomena which we would have when watching works created purely based on uncontrolled physical phenomenon. Therefore, we believe that we succeeded in creating a new type of artwork. We are going to exhibit our newly created artworks at various exhibitions over the worlds to know responses from people in different countries and cultures. We hope and expect that our new artwork would be welcomed by people in various countries with different cultures.

References

1. Chen, F., Sawada, T., Tosa, N.: Sound based scenery painting. In: 2013 International Conference on Culture and Computing. IEEE Press (2013)
2. Pang, Y., Tosa, N.: New approach of cultural aesthetic using sound and image. In: 2015 International Conference on Culture and Computing. IEEE Press (2015)
3. Tosa, N., Nakatsu, R., Yunian, P., Ogata, K.: Projection mapping celebrating RIMPA 400th anniversary. In: 2015 Conference on Culture and Computing. IEEE Press (2015)
4. Munson, B.R., et al.: Fundamentals of Fluid Mechanics. Wiley, Hoboken (2012)
5. Peter, S.: Bernard: Fluid Dynamics. Cambridge University Press, New York (2015)
6. Smits, A.J., Lim, T.T. (eds.): Flow Visualization: Techniques and Examples. Imperial College Press, London (2012)
7. Krechetnikov, R., Homsy, G.M.: Crown-forming instability phenomena in the drop splash problem. J. Colloid Interface Sci. **331**(2), 555–559 (2009)
8. Odenbach, S. (ed.): Colloidal Magnetic Fluids: Basics, Development and Applications of Ferrofluid. Lecture Note in Physics. Springer, Heidelberg (2009)
9. Kodama, S.: Dynamic ferrofluid sculpture: organic shape-changing art forms. Commun. ACM **51**(6), 79–81 (2008)
10. Fleck, R., et al.: Action Painting. Hatje Cantz, Ostfildern (2008)
11. Ellen, G.: Landau: Jackson Pollock. Harry N. Abrams, New York (2010)

Bubble Clouds: 3D Display Composed of Soap Bubble Cluster

Yuki Kubo[1]([✉]), Hirobumi Tomita[1], Shuta Nakamae[1], Takayuki Hoshi[2], and Yoichi Ochiai[3]

[1] University of Tsukuba, 1-1-1 Tennodai, Tsukuba, Ibaraki 305-8573, Japan
{kubo,tomita,nakamae}@iplab.cs.tsukuba.ac.jp
[2] The University of Tokyo, 7-3-1 Hongo, Bunkyo-ku, Tokyo 113-8658, Japan
star@star.rcast.u-tokyo.ac.jp
[3] University of Tsukuba, 1-2 Kasuga, Tsukuba, Ibaraki 305-8550, Japan
wizard@slis.tsukuba.ac.jp

Abstract. We examine Bubble Clouds composed of a bubble cluster for a three-dimensional display. A bubble cluster is flexible in that its shape can be modified and it can float in the air with helium gas confinement of the bubbles. By varying the density of the bubble clusters, we project images onto the bubbles without requiring fog confinement or use of special equipment. Moreover, we investigate whether a soap bubble cluster can become interactive by electrifying it.

Keywords: Bubble display · Soap bubbles · Ephemeral user interfaces

1 Introduction

Previously, bubble displays have been achieved as singular [9], multi-layered [10], or multiple bubble surfaces [6]. A single bubble surface cannot display three-dimensional (3D) structures. Although a multi-layered bubble surface can show a semblance of 3D assemblies, they cannot display a complete range of the same.

Bubble displays have several limitations in their size, structure, and projection methods. This motivated us to use a soap bubble cluster as a display system (Fig. 1). We can express 3D objects by reshaping the bubble clusters without fog confinement, and can project images onto the bubbles. In this study, we present Bubble Clouds [5], as displays that use a bubble cluster (Fig. 1). A bubble cluster is flexible in that its shape can be modified. In this regard, we examined five shapes of a bubble cluster. Furthermore, it can float in the air by helium gas confinement of the bubbles and adjustment of the bubble density. We can project images on the bubble clouds without requiring fog confinement or special equipment, and by confining helium in the bubbles. We can provide the utility of bubble clusters when producing a bubble display. For example, we can project images onto a bubble cluster without fog confinement, as shown in Fig. 2.

© IFIP International Federation for Information Processing 2017
Published by Springer International Publishing AG 2017. All Rights Reserved
N. Munekata et al. (Eds.): ICEC 2017, LNCS 10507, pp. 14–23, 2017.
DOI: 10.1007/978-3-319-66715-7_2

2   Related Work

Research on bubble cluster displays is related to studies that involve bubble displays and ephemeral user interfaces.

2.1   Bubble Display

Some research studies have proposed displaying images by using soap bubbles. For example, Bubble Cosmos [9] provides tangible interactions with bubbles, and a sound is played when a user bursts a bubble. Bubble Cosmos is a single-bubble display that projects an image onto a bubble with fog confinement. FRAG-WRAP [7] encapsulates fragrances in a bubble confined with fog, so that when the bubble bursts, the fragrance is released to the user. SensaBubble [13] is a display system that uses the fog confinement of the bubbles to deliver information to users by using a projector and fragrances. Colloidal Displays [10,11] project images onto a soap film by using the ultrasound waves emitted from an ultrasonic-phased array. The reflectance can be varied by vibrating the film using the phased array. Similar to this work, we also used an ultrasonic-phased array as one of the methods to project images on a bubble cluster. Liquids, Smoke, and Soap Bubbles [14] form bubble display that consists of bubbles, a soap liquid, and fog, and can be made to interact by moving or blowing bubbles over a dark surface. Sahoo et al. [12] proposed a method that could alter the trajectory of a bubble by confining an electrostatically charged fog in the bubble and applying an electric field. In comparison with these displays that utilize single soap bubbles or a soap film, our proposed Bubble Clouds utilize a bubble cluster.

An example of a display that uses multiple soap bubbles is Shaboned Display [4]. This display consists of an array of soap bubbles, and each soap bubble works as a pixel of an image. Flogos [3] is a device that can form characters

Fig. 1. A bubble cluster.

Fig. 2. Dense Bubble Cloud.

and logos that can float by utilizing soap clusters. Bubble Clouds can combine multiple bubbles into a single bubble cluster, and can express 3D objects by reshaping the bubble cluster. Furthermore, Bubble Clouds can project images onto the bubble cluster.

2.2 Ephemeral User Interfaces

A soap bubble display is a type of an ephemeral user interface [2]. Similarly, several displays using ephemeral materials such as water, smoke, and fog have been previously proposed. For example, Barnum et al. [1] proposed a display that projected images on multi-layered water drops. Cloud Display [16] is a space filling display composed of smoke rings. Tangible Sound [18] uses fluid water as an input of a musical instrument. By adjusting the flowing water, a sound is produced. HydroMorph [8] is a water display that can vary the shape by sensing the users input by camera. Cool Interaction with Calm Technologies [17] is a multi-touch screen built from an ice-wall, that can detect the palm of a user and achieve multi-touch by using an infrared camera. Cloud Interface [15] is a mid-air display that can move in the air. It consists of a blimp, a gondola, and a projector. Bubble Clouds use soap bubbles as the ephemeral material.

3 Implementation

We use a bubble generator to produce the bubbles that comprise the bubble cluster (Fig. 3). The bubble generator consists of a helium cylinder, a pressure gage, an air tube, a bucket containing soap solution, and an acrylic case with five holes. To generate bubbles that can float, helium gas is passed through the soap solution that passes through the holes in the acrylic case. A floatable bubble cluster is generated by separating the bubbles from the bucket by using an air tube having an inner diameter of 3 mm. The pressure gage regulates the pressure inside the air tube. We place an acrylic panel on the bucket with a 25 cm square hole at its center from which the bubbles escape from the bucket. To hold the soap bubble solution and store bubbles, we use a bucket with a diameter of 45 cm and height of 15 cm. The solution should generate bubbles that do not burst easily, and we use a solution mixture of water, a detergent that includes a surfactant, and laundry starch that includes polyvinyl alcohol in a ratio of 5:1:5.

An ultrasonic-phased array with 283 ultrasonic transducers is shown in Fig. 4. Ultrasound waves, generated from an ultrasonic-phased array and emitted to the bubbles, change the reflectance of the soap film, and thereby produce vibrations and project images onto the film. An ultrasonic-phased array generates an ultrasonic wave front to stimulate the entire surface of the bubble cluster.

4 Bubble Clouds

4.1 Dense Bubble Cloud

When the bubbles are small, they seem to appear as if they are pixels of a projected image, as shown in Fig. 2. Dense Bubble Cloud allows each bubble to function as an individual pixel, and hence does not require fog confinement or additional material to project images.

4.2 Sparse Bubble Cloud

Images cannot be projected onto bubbles when their diameter is extremely large because the soap film permeates light. However, we can project images onto such bubbles by using ultrasonic waves, and we call this Sparse Bubble Cloud.

In Colloidal Display, a method of projecting images by changing the reflection properties of the film by ultrasonic wave was introduced. We investigated whether this method can work effectively for bubble clusters. Figure 5a shows a state when the film is not vibrating. The image is not projected by light; it is permeated. Figure 5b depicts the bubble cluster when the reflectance is varied by applying an ultrasonic wave to the soap film via an ultrasonic-phased array. Compared with Fig. 5a, the reflectance changes in Fig. 5b. We attempted to project images onto a bubble cluster by using an ultrasonic-phased array (Fig. 4). The image projected was slightly clear compared with a bubble cluster without ultrasonic waves (Fig. 6).

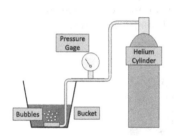

Fig. 3. Bubble generator.

Fig. 4. Ultrasonic-phased array.

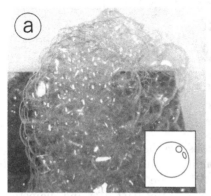 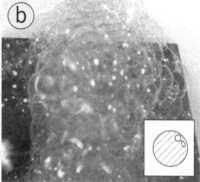

Fig. 5. Variation of the reflectance of a bubble by controlling ultrasound waves. (a) non-vibrating soap film. (b) vibrating soap film.

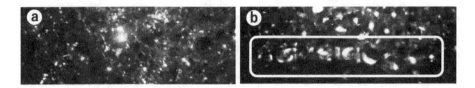

Fig. 6. Sparse Bubble Cloud using an ultrasonic-phased array: (a) non-vibrating bubbles with projection, and (b) vibrating bubbles with projection (projection characters: "ACM SIGGRAPH").

5   Evaluation of Bubble Generator

We evaluated the effect of the pressure and diameter of the holes of the acrylic case. We conducted this experiment to evaluate whether these conditions meet the smallest diameter requirement of the bubbles that enables the display to float. The pressure was measured by using a pressure gage. In our experiment, we applied the following values: 0.02, 0.04, and 0.06 MPa. We consider two diameter sizes for the acrylic cases: 0.02 and 0.04 mm, and there are five holes in each case, positioned at the same distance from each other (Fig. 7). The diameter of a bubble cluster is measured by a ruler. The bubbles cannot be uniform in size, and thus, we measured the diameters of numerous bubbles and averaged the result.

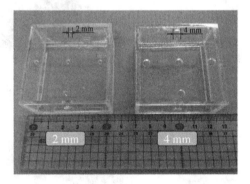

Fig. 7. Acrylic cases with five holes (scale is $54 \times 54 \times 24$ mm). Left: hole diameter of 2 mm. Right: hole diameter of 4 mm.

The results are shown in Table 1. We observe that higher pressures or larger holes produce larger bubbles. These conditions satisfy the smallest diameter requirement enabling a bubble to float. We chose the following conditions to generate the smallest bubbles possible: pressure of 0.02 MPa and diameter of 2.0 mm.

Table 1. Effect of hole diameter and pressure on the bubble diameter.

Holes diameter (mm)	Pressure (MPa)		
	0.02	0.04	0.06
2.0	10 mm	15 mm – 20 mm	20 mm – 30 mm
4.0	15 mm – 25 mm	25 mm – 30 mm	30 mm – 35 mm

6 Shape of Bubble Cluster

We investigated the shapes that could be generated with a bubble cluster. In this experiment, we formed five shapes with the bubble cluster, namely, cube, quadrangular pyramid, sphere, mountain, and two mountains. Figure 8 shows the different cluster shapes. Bubble cluster reshaping was performed by using a 5 × 30 cm plate. We poured the soap bubble solution into a bucket and fixed an acrylic case to the bottom. A helium cylinder was connected to the acrylic case by an air tube. Helium gas was released at a constant rate from the acrylic case into the soap bubble solution. The reason helium gas was confined is because it is easy to process and maintain the shape of the bubble cluster without being influenced by gravity. Bubble clusters escaped from a 25 × 25 cm hole on a plate that was placed on the bucket. Thus, the user could reshape the bubble cluster to any shape.

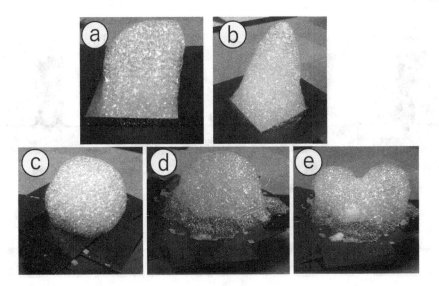

Fig. 8. Five shapes of bubble cluster: (a) cube, (b) quadrangular pyramid, (c) sphere, (d) mountain, and (e) two mountains.

Figure 8 shows the five shapes of the bubble cluster we produced. The cube shown in Fig. 8a was formed by placing a cubic mold on the top of the hole. The cubic mold was made from five plates, and we separated each plate individually to create a cube. The quadrangular pyramid shown in Fig. 8b was formed by sharpening the tip by scraping the bubble cluster using a plate. The sphere and mountain shown in Fig. 8c and d, respectively were generated by adjusting the hole with the plates. The two mountains shown in Fig. 8e were formed by scraping the middle of the bubble cluster.

7   Interaction with Electrified Bubble Cluster

We investigated whether an electrified soap bubble cluster could be interactive. This was verified in an indoor still air environment. To electrify the bubble clusters, we used a polyvinyl chloride pipe and tissue paper. Static electricity was generated by their friction that was charged by touching the bubble cluster with the polyvinyl chloride pipe in the air. After that, we examined how the bubble cluster behaved when a user placed a hand near the bubble cluster. Consequently, we could observe a bubble cluster being tracked by the hand of a user. As shown in Fig. 9, the bubble cluster moves in the same direction as the hand. We believe that this occurs owing to the Coulomb force between the hand of a user and the bubble cluster. Therefore, we can manipulate the soap bubble cluster in mid-air. We also noticed that the tracking was lost once the Coulomb force ceased to exist.

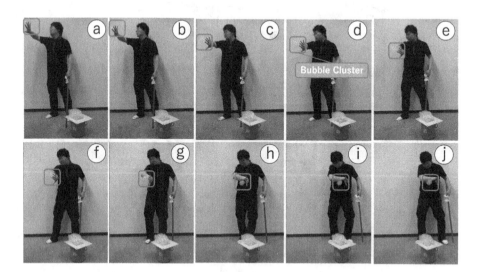

Fig. 9. Time-lapse of interaction between user and bubble cluster.

8   Example Application

8.1   Bubble Characters

We propose that characters could be generated by using a Bubble Cloud. A user could then interact with the characters using his/her hands and with objects. For example, we could formulate a game in which a user could use a toy sword to attack the generated characters (e.g., monsters). Each character could be projected differently, and thus, a user would be able to classify each character.

9   Discussion and Future Work

We attempted to project images onto a Sparse Bubble Cloud in mid-air by using an ultrasonic-phased array. However, this Sparse Bubble Cloud moved because of the ultrasonic wave emitted from the phased array. This suggests that if we project images onto Sparse Bubble Cloud in mid-air, we must track the movement of the bubble cluster and counter the effect of the ultrasonic wave to prevent the movement.

In our experiment, we observed the phenomenon of a bubble cluster tracking hand of a user. However, it was unable to track when its size was extremely large. Our results showed that the Coulomb force between the hand of the user and bubble cluster was not sufficiently strong. It is to be noted that we electrified the bubble cluster by using a simple method in this experiment. For this reason, we believe that the bubble cluster could be moved if it was strongly electrified by a specific equipment. Moreover, this interaction was easily affected by wind.

Dense Bubble Cloud is a type of Bubble Cloud that could project an image to the surface of a bubble cluster. In addition, we found that we can utilize an entire soap bubble cluster including the bubbles inside, as pixels and use it as a 3D display (Fig. 10). This is possible apparently because each of the bubbles in the bubble cluster reflects and permeates light. In the future, to achieve 3D projection on a bubble cluster, we will investigate conditions such as the diameter of the bubbles that compose the bubble cluster. We will also examine if we can realize a true 3D display by using multiple planes because presently our display only has a single plane.

In this work, we used panels to reshape the bubble cluster. However, this method has a poor reproducibility in terms of shape because the process of reshaping is different for different users. The reproducibility of shape can be ensured by a method that uses an ultrasonic-phased array. In the future, we will reshape the bubble cluster automatically to ensure shape reproducibility by using an ultrasonic-phased array.

Furthermore, in the future, we plan to conduct quantitative evaluations such as how long the bubble cluster lasts, and character recognition rate. Additionally, we aim to conduct quantitative evaluation such as the user perception of the applicability of the display for entertainment purposes.

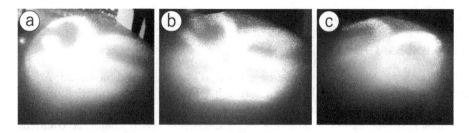

Fig. 10. 3D form display composed of bubble cluster. Photo from the (a) left,(b) front,(c) right (projecting the inverted ace2016 logo).

10   Conclusion

In this study, we presented Bubble Clouds using bubble cluster as displays. A bubble cluster is flexible because its shape can be varied and it can float in the air by helium confinement. We introduced two types of Bubble Clouds, namely, Dense Bubble Cloud and Sparse Bubble Cloud. By changing the density of the bubble cluster, images could be projected onto it without fog confinement or use any special equipment. We formed five shapes with the bubble clusters: cube, quadrangular pyramid, sphere, mountain, and two mountains. Moreover, we also explored whether an electrified soap bubble cluster could be interactive.

In the future, to realize 3D projection on a bubble cluster, we will investigate conditions such as the diameter of the bubbles that compose the bubble cluster. Furthermore, we plan to explore reshaping the bubble clusters automatically to ensure shape reproducibility by using an ultrasonic-phased array.

References

1. Barnum, P.C., Narasimhan, S.G., Kanade, T.: A multi-layered display with water drops. ACM Trans. Graph. **29**(4), 76:1–76:7 (2010). doi:10.1145/1778765.1778813
2. Döring, T., Sylvester, A., Schmidt, A.: A design space for ephemeral user interfaces. In: Proceedings of the 7th International Conference on Tangible, Embedded and Embodied Interaction, TEI 2013, pp. 75–82. ACM, New York (2013). doi:10.1145/2460625.2460637
3. Global special effects Flogos (2008). http://globalspecialeffects.com/flogos.aspx
4. Hirayama, S., Kakehi, Y.: Shaboned display: an interactive substantial display using soap bubbles. In: ACM SIGGRAPH 2010 Emerging Technologies, SIGGRAPH 2010. ACM (2010). doi:10.1145/1836821.1836842
5. Kubo, Y., Tomita, H., Nakamae, S., Hoshi, T., Ochiai, Y.: Bubble cloud: projection of an image onto a bubble cluster. In: Proceedings of the 13th International Conference on Advances in Computer Entertainment Technology, ACE 2016, pp. 41:1–41:4. ACM, New York (2016). doi:10.1145/3001773.3001815
6. Kwon, H., Jaiswal, S., Benford, S., Seah, S.A., Bennett, P., Koleva, B., Schnädelbach, H.: FugaciousFilm: exploring attentive interaction with ephemeral material. In: Proceedings of the 33rd Annual ACM Conference on Human Factors in Computing Systems, CHI 2015, pp. 1285–1294. ACM, New York (2015). doi:10.1145/2702123.2702206

7. Kyono, Y., Yonezawa, T., Nozaki, H., Nakazawa, J., Tokuda, H.: FRAGWRAP: fragrance-encapsulated and projected soap bubble for scent mapping. In: Proceedings of the 2013 ACM Conference on Pervasive and Ubiquitous Computing Adjunct Publication, UbiComp 2013 Adjunct, pp. 311–314. ACM (2013). doi:10.1145/2494091.2494187

8. Nakagaki, K., Totaro, P., Peraino, J., Shihipar, T., Akiyama, C., Shuang, Y., Ishii, H.: HydroMorph: shape changing water membrane for display and interaction. In: Proceedings of the TEI 2016: Tenth International Conference on Tangible, Embedded, and Embodied Interaction, TEI 2016, pp. 512–517. ACM (2016). doi:10.1145/2839462.2856517

9. Nakamura, M., Inaba, G., Tamaoki, J., Shiratori, K., Hoshino, J.: Mounting and application of bubble display system: bubble cosmos. In: Proceedings of the 2006 ACM SIGCHI International Conference on Advances in Computer Entertainment Technology, ACE 2006. ACM (2006). doi:10.1145/1178823.1178879

10. Ochiai, Y., Oyama, A., Hoshi, T., Rekimoto, J.: The colloidal metamorphosis: time division multiplexing of the reflectance state. IEEE Comput. Graph. Appl. **34**(4), 42–51 (2014)

11. Ochiai, Y., Oyama, A., Hoshi, T., Rekimoto, J.: Theory and application of the colloidal display: programmable bubble screen for computer entertainment. In: Reidsma, D., Katayose, H., Nijholt, A. (eds.) ACE 2013. LNCS, vol. 8253, pp. 198–214. Springer, Cham (2013). doi:10.1007/978-3-319-03161-3_14

12. Sahoo, D.R., Martinez Plasencia, D., Subramanian, S.: Control of non-solid diffusers by electrostatic charging. In: Proceedings of the 33rd Annual ACM Conference on Human Factors in Computing Systems, CHI 2015, pp. 11–14. ACM, New York (2015). doi:10.1145/2702123.2702363

13. Seah, S.A., Martinez Plasencia, D., Bennett, P.D., Karnik, A., Otrocol, V.S., Knibbe, J., Cockburn, A., Subramanian, S.: SensaBubble: a chrono-sensory mid-air display of sight and smell. In: Proceedings of the 32nd Annual ACM Conference on Human Factors in Computing Systems, CHI 2014, pp. 2863–2872. ACM, New York (2014). doi:10.1145/2556288.2557087

14. Sylvester, A., Döring, T., Schmidt, A.: Liquids, smoke, and soap bubbles: reflections on materials for ephemeral user interfaces. In: Proceedings of the Fourth International Conference on Tangible, Embedded, and Embodied Interaction, TEI 2010, pp. 269–270. ACM (2010). doi:10.1145/1709886.1709941

15. Tobita, H.: Cloud interface: designing aerial computer environment for novel user interface. In: Proceedings of the 8th International Conference on Advances in Computer Entertainment Technology, ACE 2011, pp. 57:1–57:8. ACM, New York (2011). doi:10.1145/2071423.2071495

16. Tokuda, Y., Suzuki, Y., Nishimura, K., Tanikawa, T., Hirose, M.: Cloud display. In: Proceedings of the 7th International Conference on Advances in Computer Entertainment Technology, ACE 2010, pp. 32–35. ACM (2010). doi:10.1145/1971630.1971640

17. Virolainen, A., Puikkonen, A., Kärkkäinen, T., Häkkilä, J.: Cool interaction with calm technologies: experimenting with ice as a multitouch surface. In: Proceedings of ACM International Conference on Interactive Tabletops and Surfaces, ITS 2010, pp. 15–18. ACM (2010). doi:10.1145/1936652.1936656

18. Yonezawa, T., Mase, K.: Tangible sound: musical instrument using fluid water. In: Proceedings of International Computer Music Association, ICMC 2000. Citeseer (2000)

A Literary Analysis of Poems Automatically Produced by *Peter's Haiku Generator*

Vinicius Carvalho Pereira[(✉)] and Cristiano Maciel

Universidade Federal de Mato Grosso, Cuiabá, MT, Brazil
viniciuscarpe@gmail.com, crismac@gmail.com

Abstract. The development of computer technologies gives rise to a revolution in all socio-cultural practices, including arts and literature. In terms of poetry, for example, readers have now access to new lyrical experiences either through emerging poetic genres or through so-far unimagined approaches to traditional ones. Lots of research has been done in the field of Computer Science on technical issues of computer-generated poetry, but little on the aesthetic impacts of having poems produced by machines. Therefore, we herein propose a multidisciplinary literary analysis of poems produced by the tool Peter's Haiku Generator, in order to discuss how software design decisions can affect literary aspects and the aesthetic effects of those poems.

Keywords: Literature and new technologies · Text generators · Computer-based poetry · Peter's haiku generator

1 Introduction

The development of computer technologies gives rise to a revolution in socio-cultural practices, including arts and literature. Along with a subversion of the literary system, in which the roles of authors and readers become blurry, in a prosumer paradigm Kim et al. [11], the materiality of poetic works is also altered, since the digital and the printed media develop increasingly distinct aesthetic resources. Analyzing the research area of entertainment computing in industry and academy, Nakatsu and Rauterberg [16] highlight "art and entertainment" as one of the seven active working groups in TC14 (Entertainment Computing) by IFIP, where an interdisciplinary approach is highly desired.

The printing press revolutionized the literary art of the Modern Age, providing it with agile circulation and effective reproducibility. The emergence of the novel as a longer literary genre, due to the invention press, is one of the most noticeable effects of how technology influences much more than the contents of a literary text. McLuhan [14] agrees with that in his most famous quoting: "the medium is the message".

Likewise, the new information and communication technologies radically affected the symbolic practices of our increasingly digital society, which is immersed in what Lévi [12] calls cyberculture. Like any other field, such paradigm affects also literature, which causes the emergence of new genres, some of which compose an exclusively virtual poetics. That is the case of computer-generated poetry (grouped under the wider

N. Munekata et al. (Eds.): ICEC 2017, LNCS 10507, pp. 24–31, 2017.
DOI: 10.1007/978-3-319-66715-7_3

term "Generative Literature"), which consists of poems produced by automatic recombination of elements of different granularity, following algorithms that consider natural language processing.

To Zhang and Lapata [25], automated poetry generation has been a popular research topic over past decades, but we herein discuss how software design decisions can affect literary aspects and the aesthetic effects of those poems. To do so, we chose the tool *Peter's Haiku Generator*, among others available online, because the genres of poem it produces (haiku and tanka), in comparison to most poetic forms in the West, are very short and and rely on sometimes fragmented visual images, which are features easier to meet in passable quality by computer-generated poems. Besides, different from most other online haiku generators, this tool produces haiku in English, instead of Japanese, which makes it easier for a broader audience to follow the discussions herein presented.

This paper is structured as follows: after the introduction, we present in Sect. 2 a brief theoretical discussion about generative literature and a review of related works about haiku generators. Section 3 presents an overview of Peter's Haiku Generator and a close reading of two of its poems. Section 4 contains the final remarks of the paper and is followed by the references section.

2   Algorithmic Literature: Computer-Generated Haiku

In the area of Literature Studies, research on computer-generated literature is still scarce, since the idea of machines producing poems deconstructs some of the most traditional understandings of poetry as an emotional expression that comes from inspiration. Therefore, before we move to a literary analysis of the poems generated by *Peter's Haiku Generator*, it is necessary to specify what notions of language and literature are at stake when discussing computer-generated poems.

An analysis of literary texts generated by computers must be grounded in the assumption that language itself is an algorithmic phenomenon, as proposed in Structural Linguistics [21], Generative Grammar [3] and Computational Linguistics [15]. According to those approaches, every language is formed by a grammar, that is, a set of associative and restrictive principles that command the selection and ordering of lexical items, similarly to the data a computer processes following combination rules [13]. Furthermore, as in the digital information cryptography into binary systems, every natural language also operates by means of opposite relations, according Saussure [21].

As to the definitions of literature herein adopted, Barthes [2] considered that literature is a cheating within language rules, thus deconstructing traditional forms of perception and representation. To do so, literature brings linguistic systems to limit situations, forcing new word associations that are possible according to language rules, but not commonly used in daily communication. Such understanding of literature supports the idea that a machine, equipped with the structures and the lexicon of a language, can form verses by combinatory rules, since it will operate within the limits imposed by language itself and coded by the software programmer. And, if the verses formed seem sometimes unfit, or even nonsensical, this does not make their aesthetic value null, since these awkward formations can be read as the cheatings within language argued for by Barthes.

Considering that estrangement is a formalist category associated with literariness [10], an awkward verse produced by the machine could be read not only as an accidental malformation, but as a token of what makes a text literary: the capacity to make people think about language, denaturalizing the relationship between things and words. Besides, as computer-generated poems frequently lead to somewhat disjointed verses, it is important to highlight that Eco [5] stated that semiosis comes not only from respecting, but also from disrespecting established codes, so there is meaning even in noise. This is why Manurung et al. stated that "poetry generation is different from traditional informative generation due to poetry's unity, which essentially means the satisfying of interdependent constraints on semantics, syntax and lexis." [14].

Accepting the hypothesis that texts randomly produced by machines can be poetic, Generative Literature must be read and analyzed considering the characteristics of this emerging genre, imposed by its enunciation format: instead of a poetic product whose full message is a logical product, coherent in its parts, as in more traditional literary texts, fragmentation is inherent to this virtual poetic.

Another problem that this genre poses to the traditional literary system has to do with authorship. Far beyond the death of the author professed by Barthes [1], who defended people should read texts ignoring authorial intention, Generative Literature goes further: it dissolves notions of authorship as understood in the area of Literature Studies. In summation, who is the author of a software-generated poem? The reader that unchains the poem's random composition by simply clicking a button? The software engineer who also wrote a text - the system code -, which allows the functioning and artistic operation of the machine? Or the author of the original verses recombined by the software, in the case of machines that work with this feedstock? Among other software programs of this kind, the group ALAMO (Atélier de Littérature Assistée par les Mathématiques et les Ordinateurs) developed the software Alexandrins au greffoir [19], which forms sonnets from the random recombination of halves of alexandrine verses by famous French poets, such as Nerval, Valéry and Baudelaire.

The problem is that none of these agents knows the final poetic product before the automatic recombination happens. If authorship is decentralized among agents who do not know the final product of their work, it is because software-generated poems make language itself speak, minimizing the effects of authorial intention. Thus, what is poetic is the process through which the poems are generated, rather than each generated text itself, since each of them is nothing but one among countless combinations the machine could generate. Furthermore, they vanish forever by means of a single click if they are not saved in a separate file, in case some reader wants to perpetuate a poetic moment.

Whereas the romantic tradition and the 19th century criticism valued the image of the author as that of a person touched by inspiration, away from the common people and master of the meanings of his text, Generative Literature deconstructs all these parameters, leading us to re-think the act of writing itself. Compared to a text engineer, the poet is no longer someone who works guided by the muses' whispers, but an individual that operates linguistic (and computer-based) algorithms, aiming at an aesthetic effect. Surprised with a machine's random combinations, the system developer who created the algorithms becomes a common reader of the poems. And other readers who click the refresh button generate new poems, so they play a physical part in the poetic production, thus contributing as co-authors. But who is the writer and who is the reader then? Maybe, such aesthetic claims for a new paradigm: that of the wreader [8].

Among different poetic genres that can be produced by automated text generators, haikus tend to have more effective aesthetic results in comparison to most poetic forms in the West, since haikus are very short and and rely on visual images, which are features easier to meet in passable quality by computer-generated poems. According to Obara, Tosa and Minoh [18], haiku is a "Japanese classical poem style with minimal length of 5-7-5 characters" and "it is a story that generates context – the shortest story in the world". In English, as in any other Indo-European languages, haikus are composed of three verses, with 5-7-5 syllables respectively.

Tools to produce software-generated poems are not new. The first of them, created by Theo Lutz in 1959 [13], did not allow any input from users. More recent tools, on the other hand, allow users to interact with the system, such as *Hitch Haiku* (2007 - 25) and its developments [22, 23]; others use Word Associations Norms, such as *Gaiku* [17]. There are also systems that combine traditional poetry culture and mobile messaging technology, such as *Poetry Mix-up* [6] and others which use word occurrences in the WWW and grammar templates, as proposed by [20].

Recently, Hreskova and Machová [24] carried out research comparing two different approaches to the automated generation of haiku poetry. Their first approach consists of evolutionary algorithms and human as a fitness function in the evolution. The second approach consists in generating poems based on haiku models that were extracted from haiku database. The goal is to create poems, considered by humans as understandable and with aesthetic value. In this research, when comparing poems generated by both systems, generating haiku poetry with poem models created better poems both in terms of form and content. According to the authors, one of the reasons is that it is easier to combine words than whole verses.

3   *Peter's Haiku Generator* and Two of its Poems

Peter's Haiku Generator is a system programmed in Flash that generates haikus and tankas automatically whenever a user clicks the refresh button. The system does so through a series of algorithms that rule the combination of words registered in its data-base. These words are categorized according to their parts of speech. The initial step taken by the software, after the user's click, is the random selection of a syntactic structure for each verse (there are 3 in a haiku, or 5 in a tanka). Although the software initially works with a predefined set of basic sentence patterns, those can also be enriched by the user, as long as he or she has some knowledge of Linguistics and Flash.

In linguistic terms, Howard opted for a generative model, where a structure called "simple sentence" can be divided into two substructures, called noun phrase and verb phrase, also breakable into even smaller substructures, and so on, until minimal non-breakable structures. Table 1 shows the basic syntactic structures and the respective substructures that can be employed by *Peter's Haiku Generator*. Brackets indicate that a certain substructure is optional, depending on the number of syllables of the selected words, so as to meet the requirements of 5-7-5 syllables per verse, respectively:

Table 1. Parsing rules processed by *Peter's Haiku Generator* [9]

Structures	Substructures
\<sentence>	\<clause > [< linking word > < clause >]
\<clause>	[< gerund utterance >] < clause>
\<clause>	1. < noun phrase > [< adverb phrase >] < intransitive verb > [< preposition > < noun phrase> 2. < noun phrase > < intransitive verb > [< preposition > < noun phrase >] [< adverb phrase >] 3. [< adverb phrase >] < noun phrase > < intransitive verb > [< preposition > < noun phrase >] 4. < noun phrase > < transitive verb phrase > < noun phrase>
\<noun phrase>	1. < definite article > [< adjective phrase >] < common noun> 2. [< adjective phrase >] < noun> 3. < indefinite article > [< adjective phrase >] < common singular noun>
\<gerund utterance>	1. [< adverb phrase >] < gerund verb>
\<adverb phrase>	1. [< adverb >] < adverb>
\<transitive verb phrase>	1. [< adverb phrase >] < transitive verb>
\<adjective phrase>	1. < adjective > [",", < adjective >]
\<adjective>	1. < adjective > [< adjective >] 2. [< adverb >] < adjective>

After the random selection of the underlying syntactic structure, the system randomly selects words in its database to fill the previously defined syntactic substructures, which obey the standard English grammar. Furthermore, to warrant isotopies [7], i.e., coherence produced by words with meanings from similar areas, the words in the database are tagged according to the semantic field to which they belong. Before clicking the refresh button, the user can choose the semantic field of the poem to be generated; he or she can also add new words to the database, in case he or she has some knowledge about programming in Flash. Finally, an algorithm related to the metrics of the verses is triggered: only verses with seven and five syllables are formed according to the traditional versification of haikus and tankas.

Such idiosyncrasies of the machine's "writing" process, if compared to the way how poems are traditionally produced also demand particular methods for literary analysis. For example, it is not possible to exhaustively read the whole poetic production generated by the software, as it is frequently done in researches on human poets and their writings. The only methodological option, so to speak, is to randomly generate some poems and make a *close reading* of them, which means disregarding elements like authorial intention, literary period, social context and other features frequently considered in literary analyses.

For the sake of the literary analysis herein proposed, we chose the semantic field noir in the interface and clicked the refresh button twelve times before we reached the haiku below transcribed:

Yellow winds waste streets.
Fear turns however heat turns.
Tepid heaven burns [9].

The choice for that specific semantic field justifies the presence of words associated to the notions of destruction and suffering, such as *waste, fear* and *burns*. The same meaning is conveyed in the phonetic layer of the verses by the assonance (vowel repetition) of the central vowel followed by the voiced alveolar trill, in *fear, turns, however* and *burns*. In those words, the sound resonates in the mouth cavity with little movement of the lips and tongue; they are inert as the desolate landscape described in the haiku. Also regarding stylistic phonetics, the alliteration of the semivowel/w/(produced by the gliding movement of the lips) suggests the waves of warm wind that ravage the images described in the poem.

A poem *coldly* written by a machine, and not by an inspired author, paradoxically describes a warm scene, both in the phonological and in the lexical layers, as seen in the phrase "*tepid heaven burns*". That paradox is analogue to the one that connects programming and random in the construction of a haiku by a machine. Another paradox is produced by the synesthesia in the phrase "yellow winds", which describes winds that sweep the images of the poem just like the electric currents that erase each new haiku when the user clicks the refresh button.

But how can one make a literary interpretation of software generated by a machine? If each haiku is only the fortuitous product of chance, is it pertinent to search for different layers of meaning in their reading? Eco [4] defends a literary analysis based on the work's intention, rather than the author's intention or the reader's intention. According to that paradigm, every literary text is provided with an immanent intention and significance, which the analysis herein carried out tries to retrace.

4   Final Remarks

If Remington type-writers once revolutionized the way people write, today poetry generators revolutionize the way to understand writing itself: in generative literature, who writes? Who reads? What is the work of art: the software or the poem? In this sequence of questions, the definitions of literature and poetry are at stake, especially because the concepts of reader and writer do not really apply to generative literature.

Poems automatically produced by a machine require specific analytical procedures, which must understand poetry as a product of systems (both linguistic and computational ones) rather than inspiration. Therefore, we have opted for a close reading approach in this paper.

A new aesthetics paradigm is brought forth by generative literature, which requires new understandings of literature. In that context, some of the haikus produced by Peter's Haiku Generator can be read as metapoems, whose noise from awkward images is not a communication break. Rather than that, it is meaning formed by random word association, which should be read as the work's intention, and not as the author's.

References

1. Barthes, R.. A morte do autor. In: Barthes, R. (ed.) O rumor da língua. Martins Fontes, São Paulo (2004)
2. Barthes, R.. Aula. Cultrix, São Paulo (1994)
3. Chomsky, N.: Language and Mind. Harcourt Brace & World, New York (1986)
4. Eco, U.: Interpretação e superinterpretação. Martins Fontes, São Paulo (2005)
5. Eco, U.: The Open Work. University Press, Harvard (1989)
6. Fernando, O.N.N., et al.: Poetry mix-up: a poetry generating system for cultural communication. In: Proceedings of the International Conference on Advances in Computer Entertainment Technology. ACM (2009)
7. Greimas, A.J., Courtès, J.: Sémiotique; dictionnaire raisonné de la théorie du langage. Hachette, Paris (1993)
8. Hayles, N.K.: Electronic Literature: What is it? V.1.0., Januay 2007. https://eliterature. org/pad/elp.html
9. Howard, P.: Peter's Haiku Generator. http://www.peterhoward.org/flash/haikugen.html
10. Jakobson, R.: Linguística e comunicação. Cultrix, São Paulo (1995)
11. Kim, W., Jeong, O.R., Lee, S.W.: On social web sites. Inf. Syst. **35**(2), 215–236 (2010)
12. Lévy, P.: Cibercultura. Editora, São Paulo, vol. 34 (2009)
13. Lutz, T.: Stochastische text. Augenblick **4**(1), 3–9 (1959)
14. Mcluhan, M.: Os meios de comunicação como extensões do homem. Cultrix, São Paulo (2000)
15. Mitkov, R.: The Oxford Handbook of Computational Linguistics. Oxford University Press, New York (2005)
16. Nakatsu, R., Rauterberg, M.: Entertainment computing: inaugural editorial. Entertainment Comput. **1**(1), 1–7 (2009)
17. Netzer, Y., et al.: Gaiku: Generating haiku with word associations norms. In: Proceedings of the Workshop on Computational Approaches to Linguistic Creativity. Association for Computational Linguistics (2009)
18. Obara, H., Tosa, N., Minoh, M.: Hitch haiku: an interactive generation system of haiku. In: Proceedings of the International Conference on Advances in Computer Entertainment Technology. ACM (2007)
19. Pereira, V.C., Maciel, C.: The user's and the designer's role and the aesthetic experience of generative literature. In: Proceedings of the 12th Brazilian Symposium on Human Factors in Computing Systems, pp. 188–197. Brazilian Computer Society, October 2013
20. Rzepka, R., Araki, K.: Haiku generator that reads blogs and illustrates them with sounds and images. In: Proceedings of 24th International Joint Conference on Artificial Intelligence (IJCAI 2015) (2015)
21. Saussure, F.: Cours de linguistique générale. Payot, Lausanne (1955)
22. Tosa, N., Obara, H., Minoh, M.: Hitch Haiku: An interactive supporting system for composing haiku poem. In: Stevens, Scott M., Saldamarco, Shirley J. (eds.) ICEC 2008. LNCS, vol. 5309, pp. 209–216. Springer, Heidelberg (2008). doi:10.1007/978-3-540-89222-9_26
23. Wu, X., Tosa, N., Nakatsu, R.: New hitch haiku: An interactive renku poem composition supporting tool applied for sightseeing navigation system. In: Natkin, S., Dupire, J. (eds.) ICEC 2009. LNCS, vol. 5709, pp. 191–196. Springer, Heidelberg (2009). doi: 10.1007/978-3-642-04052-8_19

24. Hruskova, M., Machova, K.: Interactive evolution and poem models in haiku poetry generation. In Bieliková, M., SRBA, I., Použitie transformačnej regresnej techniky pre dolovanie v údajoch. In: 11TH Workshop on Intelligent and Knowledge Oriented Technologies, pp. 103–108 (2016)
25. Zhang, X., Lapata, M.: Chinese poetry generation with recurrent neural networks. In: EMNLP (2014)

RoughON: A Portable Music Sketch Production System by Real Time Input of Melody

Kazuhisa Akimoto[✉] and Junichi Hoshino

Graduate School of Information and Engineering, University of Tsukuba,
Tsukuba-shi 305-8577, Japan
akimoto.kazuhisa@entcomp.esys.tsukuba.ac.jp

Abstract. In order to produce a music sketch (a combination of melody and accompaniment) in the beginning of musical composition, it is effective to use a composition means with high portability capable of inputting a melody in real time. In this paper, we propose a system that enables a beginner of musical composition or instrument easily and readily to create a music sketch by constructing a system capable of inputting a natural melody on a smartphone in real time in concert with accompaniment. In addition, we implemented the proposed system as an application to evaluate the proposed system through extensive use experiments by releasing it to the general public, showing the effectiveness of the proposed system in musical composition.

Keywords: Making music · Real-time · Production system · Portable

1 Introduction

In recent years, smartphone composing applications and music posting sites are well-supported [1–3]. As the environment in which composing activities can be easily done has become improved, novice musical composers and instrument users begin to occupy a part of users who use composition tools. In this paper, we propose a system to support novice musical composers.

For a novice musical composer or instrument user who is not easy to play, it is difficult "to produce a natural combination of melody and accompaniment" such as accompaniment production and the harmony of melody and accompaniment. Musical compositing support research thus far has realized a system to produce a combination of melody and accompaniment (hereinafter referred to as "music sketch") by automatic musical composition such as automatic accompaniment generation [4] and automatic lead sheet generation [5]. However, for users such as who want to publish a produced song, because they have a main purpose of self-expression, it is desirable to be able to directly and easily input the composing elements of a melody such as a rhythm, tones and a chord. Furthermore, portability is also necessary to form their inspiration. Portable systems [2,3] are also available, but their support is not enough compared to the existing composition support researches.

© IFIP International Federation for Information Processing 2017
Published by Springer International Publishing AG 2017. All Rights Reserved
N. Munekata et al. (Eds.): ICEC 2017, LNCS 10507, pp. 32–37, 2017.
DOI: 10.1007/978-3-319-66715-7_4

Therefore, in this paper, we propose a portable system that allows users to input a melody in real time during automatic playing of accompaniment, thereby enabling to directly and easily enter the composition elements of a melody. In this system, we use a smartphone to generate a corrected melody so as to be able to input a natural melody even on the small screen so that it is consistent with the accompaniment and the melody up to the time of input. It also outputs musical score and MIDI, enabling to coordinate with instrument playing and DTM. In this paper, in order to verify its usefulness, we released it to the general public as iOS and Android applications [6] to conduct extensive use experiments.

2   System Overview

We show the system outline in Fig. 1 to illustrate the flow of the proposed system following the numbers in the Figure.

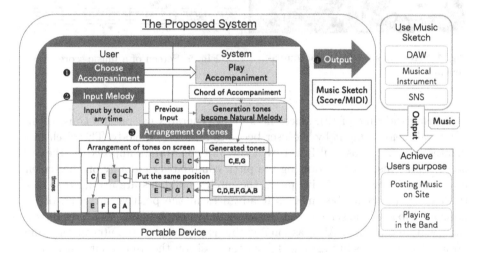

Fig. 1. Schematic chart of the proposed system.

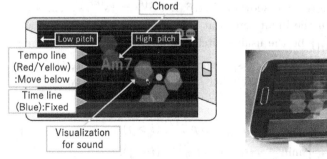

Fig. 2. Illustration of input screen.

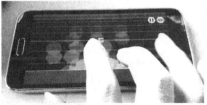

Fig. 3. Input screen of application.

The user produces a music sketch by (1) Selecting one out of 12 kinds of accompaniments prepared in advance, and (2) Inputting an melody extemporarily in real time during the automatic playing. The input screen at this time is shown in Figs. 2 and 3 and the select screen in shown in Fig. 4. As it is difficult to input it in real time in concert with the accompaniment at sight reading, display of a line showing the tempo(Tempo line and Time line), addition of percussion, and quantization of sound to reproduce were implemented as simplifying functions.

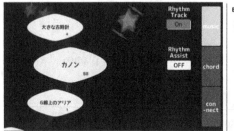

Fig. 4. Screen of selecting an accompaniment.

Fig. 5. Screen of a music score.

During the time of (2), since the system generates (3) pitches constituting a natural melody, input by the user becomes a natural melody. The pitch candidates to generate is multiplied by a key and constraints imposed by the last user's input. Instead of arranging the pitch candidates randomly on the screen, in order to follow the relative pitch, the pitch candidates are arranged so that the higher the sound becomes as it advances in the positive direction of the horizontal axis of the screen, and the lower the sound becomes as it advances in the negative direction. Also, as long as the user continues to enter at the same position, the pitches are arranged from the position the user input last so that the same pitch is played.

This pitches arrangement can be defined by a recurrence formula starting from i as follows. The algorithm is shown in Fig. 6. Let $S^{(k)} = \{s_1^{(k)}, s_2^{(k)}, ..., s_{|N|}^{(k)}\}$ be the pitch sequence on the input screen at the time of input number k and $P^{(k)} = \{p_1^{(k)}, p_2^{(k)}, ..., p_{|M|}^{(k)}\}$ be the usable pitch candidate array. $P^{(k+1)}$ is generated depending on the input pitch $s_i^{(k)}$ and chord. At that time, the pitch sequence $S^{(k+1)}$ at the time of input number $k + 1$ becomes as follows.

$$
s_j^{k+1} = \begin{cases} s_i^k & (i = j) \\ \max_{m, s_{j+1}^{(k+1)} > p_m^{(k+1)}} p_m^{(k+1)} & (i > j) \\ \min_{m, s_{j-1}^{(k+1)} < p_m^{(k+1)}} p_m^{(k+1)} & (i < j). \end{cases} \tag{1}
$$

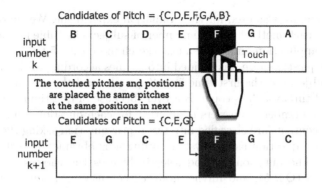

Fig. 6. The algorithm of arranging pitches.

After inputting the melody, the system edits the input melody, and (4) outputs the music sketch in the form of music score or MIDI. The score screen is shown in Fig. 5.

3   Experiment

We implemented the system as a smartphone application "RoughON" [6] to release it to the general public. As of January 27, 2017, the number of unique users of the application reached 4300. In addition, the cumulative number of music sketch productions exceeds 10,000 (music: 9800, chord: 3500), and the cumulative output number in MIDI format reaches 3300. Furthermore, even now it is used about 100 times every day.

Table 1. Questions for evaluation.

Question	Method	Number of subjects
Subjects' Experience		
Q1. Do you have any experience in musical composition?	choices	84
Q2. Can you compose with a musical instrument?	choices	84
System Evaluation		
Q3. Is RoughON useful in supporting the early stage of composition?	points	46
Q4. Which would you like to use: RoughON or other applications?	choices	84
Q5. Could a music sketch become a clue to music production?	points	38
Q6. Do you want to use a music sketch in the future?	choices	37

A questionnaire was used for the evaluation experiment. We show the questionnaire, the each method and the number of subjects in Table 1. The user who installed the application and made music sketch more than 5 times was the subject, and the questionnaire was divided into 2 times according to the period. The number of subjects at the first time was 46 people, and the number of subjects at the second time was 38 people. However, because of questionnaire by public disclosure, the number of answers is different for each question item.

Question contents are classified into two types: question asking the attributes of subjects and question asking system evaluations obtained by subjects using "RoughON". The question method selectively uses the choices (Q1, 2, 4, 6) and the points (Q3, 5), and furthermore a free answer column was provided. In the scoring system, we made a 5-point evaluation with 1 step (5: very good evaluation, 1: very bad evaluation). The results of the evaluation experiment are shown in Fig. 7.

In Q1 and 2, we asked the subjects' experience in musical composition and instrument. In question Q1 asking the experience in musical composition, those who have no experience in musical composition and beginners accounted for about 80%. For Q4 asking the difficulty of music composition by musical instruments, about 40% answered that musical composition using musical instruments was possible, but nearly all of the respondents felt difficulty in musical composition using musical instruments.

Q3 and Q4 are questions concerning the evaluation as a system for supporting the music composition. Q3 asked the support of initial music composing, which is the purpose of the proposed system, having gotten 3.57 with a 5-point score evaluation. Compared to the score evaluation, in the free description column, many favorable opinions were obtained, saying that "the operation was intuitive and easy." Besides, there are also answers: "we can compose a music with a game feeling," "it is difficult to compose a music from the beginning, but we can easily take the first step if we use RoughON." When Q4 asked which one would you like to use: RoughON or other composition applications?, and 47 people out of 57 people who had use experience of other music composition applications answered that they want to use RoughON. As a reason for that, there were many answers: "simple and easy to use compared to other applications," similarly in Q3. In addition, there was also an answer that "Although other applications inhibit the pleasure of making a music because of a full automatic system, RoughON reasonably supports the composer." Besides, favorable answers for the

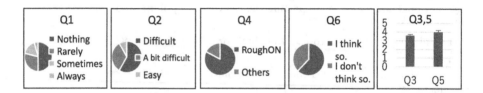

Fig. 7. Graph of experimental results.(Q3, Q5 show the average and SE.)

accompaniment function, such as "it is easier to do if accompaniment is available at first" and "it can superimpose a sound easily" were obtained. In Q3 and 4, it was shown that the proposed system is useful for supporting the early stage of music composition.

Q5 and 6 are questions about the sufficiency of music sketch to develop it into a music. In the score evaluation conducted in Q5 asking whether music sketch would become a clue to complete a music, the average value was 4.0. Also, in Q6 asking if you would like to actually use music sketch, there were 23 subjects who answered that they would use it. They answered various uses, such as "they make use of it to their own song" as a place to use and "they use for the BGM of radio, game and movie." Q5 and 6 showed that the music sketch produced by the proposed system plays a role of helping to complete a music.

4 Conclusion

In this paper, we proposed a portable system for music composition and instrument novices to produce a music sketch with real time input. In addition, the proposed system was implemented, released to the general public, and evaluated as a smartphone application: "RoughON." As a result, it was shown that the proposed system played a role of supporting the first step of music composition, revealing that its output, music sketch, is suitable as an intermediate product for completing a music.

A wide range of experiments were carried out by public questionnaire, so many subjects were able to be obtained. However, problems such as not being able to confirm the detailed operation of the examinee, not being able to confirm whether the subject used the music sketch produced by the proposed system or not occurred. In the future, we will acquire operation history and plan to investigate more detailedly for users who use the proposed system frequently.

References

1. Christopher, C.: The youtube effect: how youtube has provided new ways to consume, create, and share music. Int. J. Educ. Arts **12**(6), 1–30 (2011)
2. Garage Band. Apple Computer (2011). http://www.apple.com/jp/ilife/garage band/
3. Music Memo. Apple Computer (2016). http://www.apple.com/jp/music-memos/
4. Simon, I., Morris, D., Basu, S.: MySong: automatic accompaniment generation for vocal melodies. In: Proceedings of the SIGCHI Conference on Human Factors in Computing Systems, pp. 725–734 (2008)
5. Papadopoulos, A., Roy, P., Pachet, F.: Assisted lead sheet composition using flow-composer. In: Rueher, M. (ed.) CP 2016. LNCS, vol. 9892, pp. 769–785. Springer, Cham (2016). doi:10.1007/978-3-319-44953-1_48
6. Akimoto, K.: RoughON (2016). https://peraichi.com/landing_pages/view/x2sow

InvisibleSound: An App Enabling Blind People to Compose Music

Maximilian Stolze and Helmut Hlavacs[✉]

Research Group Entertainment Computing, University of Vienna, Vienna, Austria
maxstolze@yahoo.de, helmut.hlavacs@univie.ac.at

Abstract. InvisibleSound is a mobile application software developed for blind people to compose music. The app's handling is adapted to the needs and requirements of blind people. As a control mechanism to navigate through the app's functions we tested two modes: a common swipe control and an interactive motion control by moving the phone. Also publishing and sharing the composed songs on a shared server is possible. The app was created with Unity and is available for Android and iOS.

Keywords: Blind · Compose music · Creativity tool

1 Introduction

Nowadays there are hundreds of music apps and hundreds more that support to create, edit and publish own songs. All of these apps have one thing in common: their complexity. They mostly provide a huge amount of functions, controlled and used by numerous buttons and sliders. This is especially true for many popular music apps, which often provide interfaces not fit to be used for people with bad eye sight or even being blind. The latter usually depend on screen readers, which in the presence of the above GUIs cannot be used by them at all. So the Question was: How could a music composing app be designed to be accessible for blind and low-vision users?

In order to answer this question we created the music composing app InvisibleSound. The app's handling is adapted to the needs and requirements of blind people. Two different control mechanism to navigate through the apps functions are provided: a common screen swipe control and an interactive motion control by moving the phone (see below). With two different control techniques, the app gives blind and low vision users the opportunity to choose their individual favourite handling for apps.

2 Related Work

As mentioned there are a lot of composing apps and software and also a few with some support for screen readers. But by now there is no composing app for blind

© IFIP International Federation for Information Processing 2017
Published by Springer International Publishing AG 2017. All Rights Reserved
N. Munekata et al. (Eds.): ICEC 2017, LNCS 10507, pp. 38–43, 2017.
DOI: 10.1007/978-3-319-66715-7_5

users in particular. Nevertheless the field of entertainment computing focused a lot on accessibility features and human computer interaction for people with disabilitiesfocusing on game design and educational games [4]. There are some guidelines for that, helping to design software for people with disabilities and give the developers some assistance [5,7].

It is possible to categorize the different types of Impairments [9]: 1. hearing impairment, 2. motor impairment, 3. cognitive impairment and 4. visual impairment, including bad eye sight, complete blindness and color blindness. This paper we focus on the last impairment, including all three types. Also there are already some music games for blind users like Finger Dance [3] and a blind version of the game Guitar Hero, called Blind Hero [8].

In some cases it is possible to replace visual components with audio, haptic or just enhance visuals (if the user is not totally blind) [9, Table 4]. But there is still a small market for accessibility games because there are still two main arguments: "The cost of implementing accessibility features isn't worth the return" [10] and "There isn't a wide-enough audience to make accessibility development worthwhile" [10]. But these arguments are outdated, nowadays it is worth to invest in accessibility features and also the costs decreased over the last years [6,10].

There are several ways to make such games. One way is to create new platforms like the "Blindstation" [2] that was realized by the "TiM Project" (tacticle Interactive Multimedia) [1]. This project was formed by the European commission and tries to make games accessibly for children between 3 and 10 years old with vision rates "less than 0.05" [1].

3   Handling and Control

The app provides two selectable types of handling: a screen swipe handling and a motion handling. The swipe control provides all options by swiping horizontal and vertical over the screen.[1] Swiping horizontal changes between the different options in every single menu. Every time the option will be announced verbally to the user. Swiping vertical offers the option to go back to the menu before. So the user does not have to do unnecessary swipes vertically, just to get the *back option*. A single click on the screen confirms the active selected option. When an option is selected also a haptic feedback in form of a short vibration is given, so the user knows that his click was successfully recognized by his device.

The motion control the user needs an image that can be downloaded from http://homepage.univie.ac.at/a1308624/invisiblesound/index.html, and seen in Fig. 1.

This target image is used by the app with Vuforia, an augmented reality SDK. Once the camera records this target image, Vuforia is able to detect it automatically, and with it, any motion of the mobile phone. Moving the mobile phone now up or down, left or right then triggers the same control actions as would be triggered by swipe moves, as described above.

---

[1] https://youtu.be/1HbfuwVbFWM.

Fig. 1. Picture an Android Device running the app with the focusing on the Vuforia reference image and showing the augmented reality objects

InvisibleSound is grouped into three *modes*. the first is the *move mode*, the second the *swipe mode* and third is the *network mode*. Move and swipe mode have the same main functions that are required to compose and edit own songs. They just differ in their handling (*swiping* and *moving the phone*), as described in Sect. 3.

The network mode is responsible for all online components of the app, for example publishing a song on the server. The users can choose between these three modes in the first menu directly after starting the app. It is always possible to change the mode by just going back to the *first start menu*.

3.1   The Composing Process

A song (Fig. 2) has a playback speed, called *beats per minute (bpm)*. The bpm declares the delay time of a note. For example in a song with 60 bpm the delay time of a quarter note is exactly one second. This can be resolved with the following formula:

$$time = (60/bpm) \times 4\,\mathrm{s}$$
$$noteTime = (time/toneLength)$$

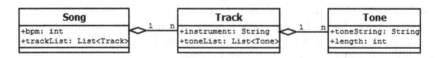

Fig. 2. Class diagram: song

Here, *time* denotes the delay time of a full note with the current bpm in seconds, *noteTime* is the actual time of the tone in seconds, *toneLength* can have the values of 1 (full note), 2 (half note), 4 (quarter note) and, 8 (eighth note) Example 1: Song with 60 bpm and a quarter note (*toneLength* = 4):

$$time = (60/60) \times 4\,\mathrm{s} = 4\,\mathrm{s}$$
$$noteTime = (4\,\mathrm{s}/4) = 1\,\mathrm{s}$$

Example 2: Song with 120 bpm and a quarter note (*toneLength* = 4):

$$time = (60/120) \times 4\,\mathrm{s} = 2\,\mathrm{s}$$
$$noteTime = (2\,\mathrm{s}/4) = 0.5\,\mathrm{s}$$

A song has also a list with objects of the class Track. A track object needs two attributes: an instrument and a list with all tones this instrument plays in the song. So each track represents an instrument in the song. A tone object then represents a note, played by the instrument. The *toneString* is the sound itself saved as a string. The *length* is the type of the note (whole note, half note, etc.).

Therefore, a song has its bpm, its list of tracks, each track representing exactly one instrument and having a list of tones, with relative duration, depending on the bpm of the song. Songs are saved as text-files in the *application persistent data path*.

After selecting the *move- ore swipe mode* and with this the kind of handling the user wants to create a song, the next menu is the *start menu* of the mode itself. Here the user has three options: Play the song, edit the song, a create a new song.

Selecting **create song** brings the user to the first step in the composing process:

Song Menu: In the *song menu* all options to edit the specifications for the whole song are provided: Change bpm, play the song, add a new track, edit a track, save the song, and go back.

Instrument Menu: In the composing process the next step is to add a track to the new song. When picking this option the user comes to the *pick instrument menu*. Here the instrument for the track needs to be selected. The next menu is the *Instrument menu*. Here the user has all functions and options to create and edit a single track. A track needs tones and so the next option in the process is to add tones. This happens in the *add tone menu*.

The user can go through all available tones and sounds of the instrument and can add them to the track. After every tone selection the user needs to declare the type of the note (full, half, quarter, eighth). As mentioned is there a *back* option in every menu, so the user just needs to go back to the upper menu. To save the created song, the user picks the *save song* option and comes to the *select- memory slot menu.* Is the selected memory slot already in use the user is asked to overwrite. If not, he can pick another memory slot. The last version of the app provides ten memory slots to save songs locally on the device. After saving the song, the user is back in the *start menu.*

Network Menu. The *network menu* will be entered from the first *start menu* when selection the *network mode.* This menu has all functions that are necessary to upload own songs, listen to songs of other users and also to own uploaded songs. To enter the *network mode* and the *network menu* an Internet connection is required. This mode is controlled with the swipe handling. When a user enters the mode the first time the app creates a connection to an online database and the user gets a unique ID. With this ID the user can be identified in the network. When this process is done the user has the following five options: announce an ID, upload a song, play newest song, search for a song id, or play own online songs. Now the most important design choices have been explained and also this menu layout was tested successfully at the second user test (see Sect. 4).

4   Evaluation

By now the app was tested two times by blind children at the Bundes-Blinden-erziehungsinstitut in Vienna, first together with one blind expert, in a second test with 10 blind children in a workshop setting.

For blind people it is easier and more in common to manage a space directly in front of them, for example the half square meter in front of them on a table. The image target should now be placed on a table in front of the user. So since the first evaluation the objects needed to be replaced to fit to the moves from left to right instead of up and down. The second big innovation that resulted form this first test was the swipe control. We learned that blind users are very in common with swipe moves and switching between options with this kind of handling.

For the second test all options were provided with both control mechanism and the network functions. Here we could see how some blind people use their phone in general: holding the device with the speakers on their ear with very quiet sound setting and swiping through the options. For this they hold the device in in one hand and upright. So we need to block the apps auto rotation, otherwise the app will rotate and the swipe direction would change.

All in all the students were very excited and agreed to test the app again when the bugs are fixed.

5   Conclusion

The app is something new on the market. Till now there is no composing app only for blind people. So there was no specific app to get some ideas for InvisibleSound. Only the main structure of creating a song is similar to common composing apps:

A song has tracks, representing instruments and a track has tones. Also the first prototype had only the motion control and after a first user test the idea and the motivation for an alternative swipe control was developed.

References

1. Archambault, D.: The TiM project: overview of results. In: Miesenberger, K., Klaus, J., Zagler, W.L., Burger, D. (eds.) ICCHP 2004. LNCS, vol. 3118, pp. 248–256. Springer, Heidelberg (2004). doi:10.1007/978-3-540-27817-7_38
2. Archambault, D., Olivier, D.: How to make games for visually impaired children. In: Proceedings of the 2005 ACM SIGCHI International Conference on Advances in Computer Entertainment Technology, ACE 2005, pp. 450–453. ACM, New York (2005). doi:10.1145/1178477.1178578
3. Miller, D., Parecki, A., Douglas, S.A.: Finger dance: a sound game for blind people. In: Assets 2007: Proceedings of the 9th International ACM SIGACCESS Conference on Computers and Accessibility, pp. 253–254 (2007)
4. Hughes, K.: Adapting audio/video games for handicapped learners: part 1. Teach. Except. Child. **14**, 80–83 (1981)
5. Siebra, C., Gouveia, T., Macedo, J., Correia, W., Penha, M., Silva, F., Santos, A., Anjos, M., Florentin, F.: Usability requirements for mobile accessibility: a study on the vision impairment. In: Proceedings of the 14th International Conference on Mobile and Ubiquitous Multimedia, MUM 2015, pp. 384–389. ACM, New York (2015). doi:10.1145/2836041.2841213
6. Torrente, J., del Blanco, Á., Serrano-Laguna, Á., Vallejo-Pinto, J.Á., Moreno-Ger, P., Fernández-Manjón, B.: Towards a low cost adaptation of educational games for people with disabilities. Comput. Sci. Inf. Syst. **11**(1), 369–391 (2014)
7. W3C: Web content accessibility guidelines 2, 09 July 2016. https://www.w3.org/TR/WCAG20
8. Yuan, B., Folmer, E.: Blind hero: enabling guitar hero for the visually impaired. In: Assets 2008: Proceedings of the 10th International ACM SIGACCESS Conference on Computers and Accessibility, pp. 169–176 (2008)
9. Yuan, B., Folmer, E., Harris, F.C.: Game accessibility: a survey. Univ. Access Inf. Soc. **10**(1), 81–100 (2011). doi:10.1007/s10209-010-0189-5
10. Zahand, B.: Making video games accessible: business justifications and design considerations, 09 July 2016. https://msdn.microsoft.com/en-us/library/ee415219.aspx

Device

SofTouch: Turning Soft Objects into Touch Interfaces Using Detachable Photo Sensor Modules

Naomi Furui[✉], Katsuhiro Suzuki, Yuta Sugiura, and Maki Sugimoto

Keio University, Hiyoshi 3-14-1, Yokohama, Kanagawa 223-8522, Japan
furui@imlab.ics.keio.ac.jp

Abstract. We propose a system that turns everyday soft objects, such as cushions, into touch interfaces in a non-intrusive manner. The belt type sensor modules developed in this study, which can be attached to the outside of soft objects, comprise several photo reflective sensors to measure the reflection intensity from an object by emitting infrared light (IR LED). When the light is irradiated to a material with the same reflection coefficient, a reflection intensity that is inversely proportional to the square of the distance can be obtained. Our method uses the sensor modules to measure the change in distance from the sensor to the surface of the soft object, and the touch position is estimated using a Support Vector Machine (SVM). To evaluate our method, we measured the accuracy when touching nine points on a cushion. Using existing everyday soft objects, it is possible to create interfaces that not only blend into the living space naturally but also match the preferences of each user.

Keywords: Soft user interface · Photo reflective sensor · Touch interface

1 Introduction

People closely interact with soft objects such as cushions, plush toys, and pillows that exist in our everyday living space. By measuring the interaction between people and these soft objects, we can construct a user interface that blends the everyday environment [9], recognizes the users' behavior in their daily lives, and provides services according to the users' condition [2, 11, 14].

Many researchers have attempted to construct soft user interfaces. For example, Tominaga et al. and Vanderloock et al. developed soft user interfaces consisting of conductive fibers and soft material such as wool [12, 13], and Hiramatsu et al. developed a soft ball interface by placing an atmospheric pressure sensor inside a soft ball to sense the deformation of the ball [1]. However, these studies focused on creating original soft interfaces rather than developing techniques to use existing soft objects as interfaces.

There are several advantages to using an existing soft object as an interface. First, using soft objects with which people are already used to having in their living space makes it possible to measure users' usual movements. Second, since it eliminates the need to purchase soft objects with built-in sensors, costs can be reduced. Third, it is possible to create an interface using soft objects that match the users' preferences.

© IFIP International Federation for Information Processing 2017
Published by Springer International Publishing AG 2017. All Rights Reserved
N. Munekata et al. (Eds.): ICEC 2017, LNCS 10507, pp. 47–58, 2017.
DOI: 10.1007/978-3-319-66715-7_6

Because existing approaches [9, 15] place sensors inside of soft objects, it is difficult to insert the sensors without damaging the users' favorite soft objects.

We thus propose a system that turns a soft object into a touch interface in a non-intrusive manner (Fig. 1). Our system measures the shape of deformations of a soft object and estimates the touch position using detachable photo sensor modules. To prove the concept, we conduct an experiment to evaluate the estimation accuracy of the touch positions using the developed module.

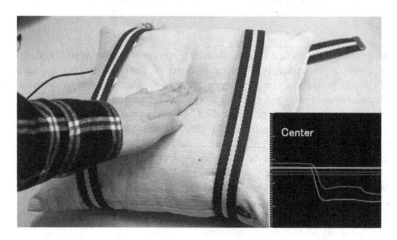

Fig. 1. Detecting a touch position using photo sensor modules.

2   Related Work

2.1   Soft Sensors and Soft User Interfaces

Previous studies have developed soft sensors to detect haptic interactions using various sensing devices such as a phototransistor and multiple IR LEDs [3], conductive rubber [16], gel [17], and fabric [18]. As those methods require creating a dedicated soft element for sensing, we propose a method to turn existing soft object surfaces into sensors.

Kamiyama et al. proposed a camera-based method for detecting deformations of a soft material by tacking positions of embedded markers [4]. The method allows accurate three-dimensional force vector detection using their GPGPU technique. Sato et al. proposed an alternative camera-based detection method based on polarization [8]. However, it is difficult to apply these methods to existing soft object surfaces available in people's daily lives due to spatial restrictions and shielding issues.

To overcome these restrictions, Sugiura et al. proposed a method to enable people to interact with soft objects without changing their softness by embedding a photo sensor module inside a soft object containing cotton [9]. However, for soft objects that cannot be opened, such as cushions, it is necessary to cut open the object to insert the sensor module, thus damaging the object. To avoid this damage, our proposed method turns soft objects into interfaces without causing any damage by attaching the module to the outside of a soft object.

Yagi et al. developed a system that measures the state of the cushion by sewing an acceleration sensor, photo sensors, and touch sensors to the back of the cushion cover [14]. This system can estimate the user's behavior and intention from the cushion state and can thus be used to control the environment, such as the lighting and sound. However, since the touch sensor is sewn near to the surface of the cushion, the user might feel the hardness of the sensor when touching the cushion. We therefore construct a system that allows touch sensing without eliminating any of its softness.

Sugiura et al. developed a ring-type device that can convert existing plush toys into interactive robots [10]. The device, which has a built-in sensor and motor, can drive plush toys while attached to the arms, legs, and tail. Because there is no need to cut open the plush toys, they are not damaged. However, since this device uses sensors to measure the joint angles of the plush toys, it cannot be attached to an object that has no joints. It is thus difficult to attach it to soft objects such as cushions and pillows.

2.2 Detecting Shape Deformation Using Photo Reflective Sensors

Photo reflective sensors measure the reflection intensity of emitted light, which can be changed by the distance and reflection properties of a reflective object. Considerable research has been conducted to estimate the deformation of soft objects caused by human skin making contact with the surface of the sensor. Nakamura et al. proposed a device that intuitively controls augmented reality information according to eyebrow movement. The system, which has one photo reflective sensor, detects eyebrow movements by the amount of reflected light [5]. Ogata et al. developed a system to use skin as a soft interface through a band-type device [6]. Photo reflective sensors are installed on the back of this device, and the sensor measures a change in the distance to the skin and estimates deformations in the skin. In this paper, we estimate the deformation of a soft object by measuring the distance between the soft surface and the photo reflective sensors.

3   Detecting Touch Position Using Photo Sensors

Photo reflective sensors consist of an infrared light (IR LED) and a phototransistor, which senses the light transmitted by the IR LED. When an object is placed near to the photo reflective sensor, the light from the IR LED is reflected by the object and detected by the phototransistor. Hence, a photo reflective sensor is an effective tool for measuring distances between objects. Since the reflection intensity of the IR LED varies depending on the distance between the photo reflective sensor and the object, the distance to the object can be measured. When the object is deformed, the distance between the sensor and the object changes; thus, the deformation of the object can be estimated from the change in the sensor values.

We develop a belt type sensor module that can be attached to the outside of soft objects. Figure 2 shows the principle of the proposed sensing method. Several photo reflective sensors are placed on the back of the belt of the sensor module. The shape deformation of the soft object is estimated by measuring changes in the distance between the soft object and the photo reflective sensors. When the surface of the soft object is touched, the elasticity of the periphery of the touched position becomes deformed, and the touched position can be estimated, even if it is positioned away from the sensor module.

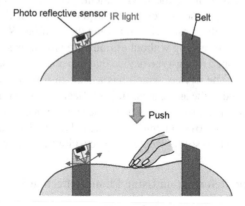

Fig. 2. Principle of touch sensing using photo reflective sensor modules attached to the soft object.

4   Implementation

4.1   Overview of Our System

Figure 3 shows a system overview of our touch sensing system. In this system, the photo sensor modules obtain sensor values from a deformable object and label the touch positions as a training dataset. After learning the training dataset, classifiers can estimate the current touch point from the inputted sensor values. We used Support Vector Machine (SVM) to train the classifiers. The sensor values are transmitted and used to make the classifiers on the PC.

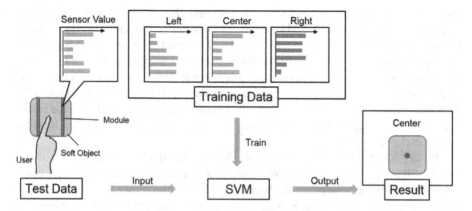

Fig. 3. Overview of the sensing system.

4.2 Hardware

Figure 4 shows an overview of our prototype of the photo reflective sensor module, which consists of multiple photo reflective sensors (KODENSHI SG - 105) and a microcontroller (Arduino Micro). Resistances of 300 Ω for the IR LED of the photo reflective sensor and 10 k Ω for the phototransistor were attached to the sensor module. Three optical sensors were installed on the belt, 7 cm apart. Since photo reflective sensors are not sensitive at a distance shorter than the minimum measurement distance, a tiny donut-shaped plastic isolator (0.3 cm thickness) is attached to each sensor to keep the deformable surface at a sensible distance. As the AT mega 328 microcontroller has a 10-bit A/D converter, the output of the photo reflective sensor is between 0 and 1,023. To detect the positon of touch on the cushion, two belt type sensor modules were constructed and attached.

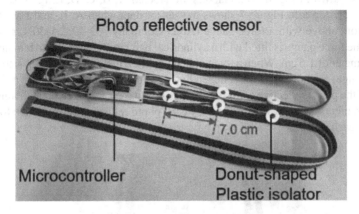

Fig. 4. Prototyped belt type module.

Figure 5 shows how the module is attached to the cushion. The cushion is filled with polyester cotton and covered with cotton fabric (30 cm × 30 cm). The actual size after filling the cotton was 24 cm (length) × 24 cm (width) × 10 cm (height). The sensors of the belt attached to the left side of the cushion are S1, S2, and S3 in order from the side

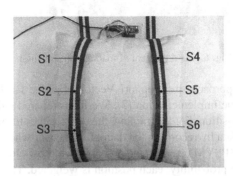

Fig. 5. A cushion equipped with two photo reflective sensor modules.

closest to the microcontroller, and the sensors of the belt attached to the right side are S4, S5, and S6 in the same order. Six sensor values are used as sensor data.

4.3   Method of Estimating the Touch Position

4.3.1   Filtering Photo Reflective Sensor Value

Since a photo reflective sensor is affected by ambient light, it is necessary to use a filter to reduce noise. Before estimating the touch position using the machine learning technique, we applied an IIR low-pass filter(cutoff frequency: 1.7 Hz).

4.3.2   Estimating the Touch Position Using SVM

The area between the two modules was divided into nine areas, and markers were attached as shown in Fig. 6. The markers are labeled A, B, C, D, E, F, G, H, and I in order from the top left. Figure 7 shows the sensor data when A, E, and I are touched directly from above with a force gauge (A&D Company AD-4932A-50N, resolution: 0.01N). The force gauge is fitted with a cylindrical part similar in shape to human fingers with a diameter of 1.5 cm. When a force of 7N is applied in different positions, the sensor values change, as shown in Fig. 7, depending on the position touched. We normalized a range of the photo reflective sensors from 0 to 1 based on averaged data obtained from 10 measurements, which were recorded by each photo reflective sensor when force was applied in each place.

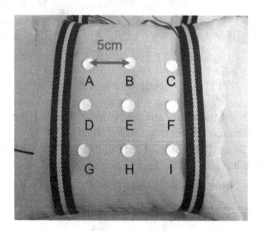

Fig. 6. Arrangement of markers on a cushion.

Using the SVM approach, the Support Vector Machine for Processing (PSVM) library was used for the implementation [7]. We first prepared a direction dataset for estimating the touch position. For the training, the user touches the soft object and accumulates the learning data by recording the data of the sensor when touching nine areas on the soft object. The PSVM provides the probability of how close the input is to each position. Based on the probability, each position is weighted. This enables the system

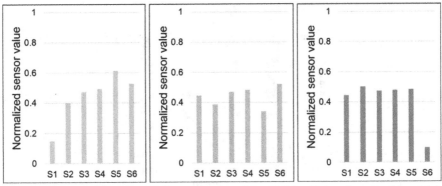

Data when touching A   (a).Data when touching E (b).   Data when touching I (c).

Fig. 7. Sensor data when touching each position.

to not only recognize the basic nine areas, but also calculate a position on the 2D plane to which the force is applied.

5   System Evaluation

To evaluate this system, we conducted an experiment to validate the classification accuracy in ten touching conditions (non-touch and touch conditions at marked locations on the cushion). To investigate the classification accuracy in various touching conditions, we conducted the experiment by changing the touch force in four conditions (1N, 3N, 5N, and 7N).

5.1   Conditions

To control the touch force to the cushion, a force gauge (A&D Company AD-4932A-50N, resolution: 0.01N) with 1.5-cm-diameter cylinder parts attached at the tip was used. Sensor values were measured when touched for each force of 1N, 3N, 5N, and 7N. The cushion used is the same as that described in Sect. 4.3. The arrangement of the markers was set as shown in Fig. 6. The captured dataset was divided into two: training data in the first half and test data in the second half.

5.2   Result

5.2.1   Accuracy of Training Each Force Data When Applying the Same Force
Figure 8 shows the accuracy when using the same force data during training and testing. The average accuracy is 93.7%.

As shown in Fig. 8, higher force conditions showed higher accuracy except for in the 7N condition. However, the lowest accuracy (83.9%) was achieved in the 1N condition. Table 1 shows the confusion matrix of the result in the 1N condition.

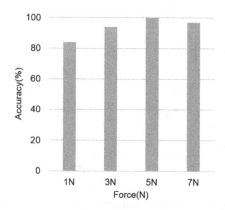

Fig. 8. The accuracy of using the training data for each force.

Table 1. Confusion matrix of the result when touching with IN.

Result\ Input	Non-Touch	A	B	C	D	E	F	G	H	I
Non-Touch	52.0	0.0	27.0	0.0	0.0	0.0	0.0	0.0	21.0	0.0
A	0.0	100.0	0.0	0.0	0.0	0.0	0.0	0.0	0.0	0.0
B	5.0	0.0	82.0	0.0	0.0	13.0	0.0	0.0	0.0	0.0
C	10.0	0.0	0.0	75.0	0.0	0.0	0.0	0.0	15.0	0.0
D	0.0	0.0	0.0	0.0	100.0	0.0	0.0	0.0	0.0	0.0
E	8.0	0.0	6.0	0.0	0.0	86.0	0.0	0.0	0.0	0.0
F	0.0	0.0	0.0	0.0	0.0	0.0	100.0	0.0	0.0	0.0
G	0.0	0.0	0.0	0.0	0.0	0.0	0.0	100.0	0.0	0.0
H	33.0	0.0	20.0	0.0	0.0	3.0	0.0	0.0	44.0	0.0
I	0.0	0.0	0.0	0.0	0.0	0.0	0.0	0.0	0.0	100.0

Table 1 shows that confusion occurs between non-touch, B, and H. The locations of B and H are furthest from the sensor modules in the experimental conditions. In the 1N condition, the intensity and the spatial size of the deformation were small. Therefore, when touching those points with a weak force, the deformation might not be enough to be classified.

It is thought that the accuracy increased as the touching force became larger because the range in which the deformation of the cushion propagated became wider and the change in the sensor value became relatively large. To improve the accuracy in a weak force condition, it is necessary to shorten the distance between the modules.

5.2.2 Accuracy of Training Each Force Data When Applying Different Forces

Table 2 shows the accuracy when training each force data and applying different forces. An accuracy of 80% or more is displayed in bold letters.

Table 2. Accuracy with training each force data and applying each force (%)

		Test Data			
		1N	3N	5N	7N
Training Data	1N	**83.9**	58.2	50.4	40.0
	3N	18.9	**93.8**	73.0	75.0
	5N	10.1	70.6	**100.0**	**98.0**
	7N	13.4	43.3	**83.6**	**97.0**

The test dataset in the 1N force condition showed a low accuracy when we applied the training datasets of the other conditions. Table 3 presents a confusion matrix of 1N test dataset, which shows the average accuracy of the 3N, 5N, and 7N training dataset conditions.

Table 3. Confusion matrix (Test data: 1N, Training data: 3N, 5N, 7N).

	Non-Touch	A	B	C	D	E	F	G	H	I
Non-Touch	63.3	0.0	36.7	0.0	0.0	0.0	0.0	0.0	0.0	0.0
A	0.0	0.0	100.0	0.0	0.0	0.0	0.0	0.0	0.0	0.0
B	22.0	0.0	78.0	0.0	0.0	0.0	0.0	0.0	0.0	0.0
C	51.0	0.0	38.3	0.0	0.0	0.0	0.0	0.0	10.7	0.0
D	90.0	0.0	0.0	0.0	0.0	10.0	0.0	0.0	0.0	0.0
E	62.0	0.0	38.0	0.0	0.0	0.0	0.0	0.0	0.0	0.0
F	0.0	0.0	0.0	0.0	0.0	78.0	0.0	0.0	22.0	0.0
G	71.7	0.0	28.3	0.0	0.0	0.0	0.0	0.0	0.0	0.0
H	66.0	0.0	34.0	0.0	0.0	0.0	0.0	0.0	0.0	0.0
I	60.0	0.0	14.0	0.0	0.0	0.0	0.0	0.0	26.0	0.0

According to Table 3, confusion occurs between non-touch and B, and most of the results are concentrated in these two classes. In other words, when the training data involves all data other than 1N data, if the user touches with 1N, it is likely to be determined as a non-touch. For the system to detect a weak force such as 1N, it is necessary to prepare training data of the same force.

5.2.3 Accuracy of Training All Force Data When Applying Different Forces

To check the possibility of a universal classifier among the force conditions, we applied all the training datasets (1N, 3N, 5N, and 7N) and made a classifier. Figure 9 shows the accuracies when testing all of the test data; the average accuracy is 79.0%. As shown in

Fig. 9, the accuracy when touching with 1N force is the lowest. As described above, it is considered that a 1N input is identified as non-touch.

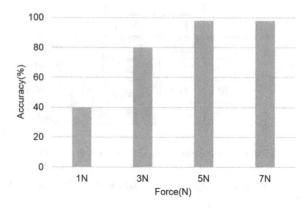

Fig. 9. The accuracy of all training data.

The accuracy when touching with a force of 3N is lower than when training 3N force data only. However, the accuracy when touching with forces of 5N and 7N is 98.0%, which is almost the same as when training the force of only 5N or 7N data.

When we excluded the test data of the 1N condition, it showed a 92.0% classification accuracy. Thus, a force of >3N shows a good performance among the different force conditions.

6 Application

We developed a prototype of our proposed system (Fig. 10), which enables the user to interact dynamically with the content shown on a screen by crushing a plush toy. When the user touches the plush toy, soap bubbles are displayed on the screen. The content also changes depending on the strength of the user's applied force. The user can use their favorite plush toy as the user interface. This system has the potential to use dynamic

Fig. 10. Example application.

and emotional gestures such as hitting, stroking, and hugging as an input method. This system could thus be used in applications such as entertainment, therapy, and rehabilitation.

7 Limitations and Future Work

This research study has several limitations, which we incorporate in our plans for future work. We tested the recognition rate in a deformable object. Future works could thus examine the recognition rate with different materials, shapes, sizes, and softness levels.

While we detected the touch positions in this study at nine points on a cushion, in future studies, we aim to recognize gestures on soft objects using continuous recognition results.

The photo reflective sensors were found to be affected by ambient light such as from an electric lamp or sunlight. We thus plan to implement a filtering system using light modulation that separates IR light emitted by the LEDs in the photo reflective sensors from ambient light.

Our proposed sensor module is wrapped around a soft object such as a cushion; however, the position of the module gradually shifts when using it. We therefore plan to add clips or safety pins to fix the sensor module in place.

Furthermore, deformable objects show hysteresis over long-term use. Future work should thus test the repeatability over a long time frame.

8 Conclusion

In this paper, we proposed a sensing system to turn soft objects into soft touch interfaces using belt type photo reflective sensor modules. In our proposed system, the change in reflected intensity due to the deformation of the surface is captured by the reflective optical sensor modules placed on the deformable object. The touch position is estimated using an SVM machine learning technique.

To evaluate the estimation accuracy of the touch position to the deformable object, we measured the recognition rates by touching nine points on the cushion with various touch forces (1N–7N). When using a training and test dataset with the same touch force, the estimated touch position achieved an accuracy of 93.7%. Furthermore, by excluding the dataset of the weakest force (1N), the average recognition rate was 92.0%, even when mixing the test dataset. It is considered that the proposed method shows a good performance at certain force conditions (3N-7N).

References

1. Hiramatsu, R.: Puyo-Con. In: ACM SIGGRAPH ASIA 2009 Art Gallery & Emerging Technologies: Adaptation (SIGGRAPH ASIA 2009), p. 81. ACM, New York (2009)
2. Ikeda, K., Koizumi, N., Naemura, T.: FunCushion: a functional cushion interface that can detect user's push and display iconic patterns. In: IEICE-MVE2016-42, IEICE Technical report, 116; 412, pp. 347–352 (2017). (in Japanese)

3. Kadowaki, A., Yoshikai, T., Hayashi, M., Inaba, M.: Development of soft sensor exterior embedded with multi-axis deformable tactile sensor system. In: RO-MAN 2009 - The 18th IEEE International Symposium on Robot and Human Interactive Communication, Toyama, pp. 1093–1098 (2009)
4. Kamiyama, K., Vlack, K., Mizota, T., Kajimoto, H., Kawakami, N., Tachi, S.: Vision-based sensor for real-time measuring of surface traction fields. IEEE Comput. Graph. Appl. 25(1), 68–75 (2005)
5. Nakamura, H., Miyashita, H.: Control of augmented reality information volume by glabellar fader. In: Proceedings of the 1st Augmented Human International Conference (AH 2010), 3 p. ACM, Article 20, New York (2010)
6. Ogata, M., Sugiura, Y., Makino, Y., Inami, M., Imai, M.: SenSkin: adapting skin as a soft interface. In: Proceedings of the 26th Annual ACM Symposium on User Interface Software and Technology (UIST 2013), pp. 539–544. ACM, New York (2013)
7. PSVM: Support Vector Machines for Processing. http://makematics.com/code/psvm/
8. Sato, T., Mamiya, H., Koike, H., Fukuchi, K.: PhotoelasticTouch: transparent rubbery tangible interface using an LCD and photoelasticity. In: Proceedings on the 22nd Annual ACM Symposium on User Interface Software and Technology (UIST 2009), pp. 43–50 (2009)
9. Sugiura, Y., Kakehi, G., Withana, A., Lee, C., Sakamoto, D., Sugimoto, M., Inami, M., Igarashi, T.: Detecting shape deformation of soft objects using directional photoreflectivity measurement. In: Proceedings of the 24th Annual ACM Symposium on User Interface Software and Technology (UIST 2011), pp. 509–516. ACM, New York (2011)
10. Sugiura, Y., Lee, C., Ogata, M., Withana, A., Makino, Y., Sakamoto, D., Inami, M., Igarashi, T.: PINOKY: a ring that animates your plush toys. In: Proceedings of the SIGCHI Conference on Human Factors in Computing Systems (CHI 2012), pp. 725–734. ACM, New York (2012)
11. Tsuruoka, H., Koyama, K., Shirakashi, Y., Yairi, I.: Ambient system for encouraging autonomous learning using cushion shaped device. In: The 30th Annual Conference of the Japanese Society for Artificial Intelligence (2016). (in Japanese)
12. Tominaga, Y., Tsukada, K., Siio, I.: FuwaMonyu interface. In: Interaction 2010, pp. 665–668 (2011). (in Japanese)
13. Vanderloock, K., Vanden Abeele, V., Suykens, J.A.K., Geurts, L.: The skweezee system: enabling the design and the programming of squeeze interactions. In: Proceedings of the 26th Annual ACM Symposium on User Interface Software and Technology (UIST 2013), pp. 521–530. ACM, New York (2013)
14. Yagi, I., Kobayashi, S., Kashiwagi, R., Uriu, D., Okude, N.: Media cushion: soft interface to control living environment using human natural behavior. In: ACM SIGGRAPH 2011 Posters (SIGGRAPH 2011), 1 p. ACM, Article 46, New York (2011)
15. Yonezawa, T., Clarkson, B., Yasumura, M., Mase, K.: Context-aware sensor-doll as a music expression device. In: CHI 2001 Extended Abstracts on Human Factors in Computing Systems (CHI EA 2001), pp. 307–308. ACM, New York (2001)
16. Shimojo, M., Ishikawa, M., Kanayama, K.: A flexible high resolution tactile imager with video signal output. In: Proceedings of the 1991 IEEE International Conference on Robotics and Automation, pp. 384–391 (1991)
17. Tajima, R., Kagami, S., Inaba, M., Inoue, H.: Development of soft and distributed tactile sensors and the application to a humanoid robot. Adv. Robot. 16(4), 381–397 (2002)
18. Hoshi, T., Shinoda, H.: Tactile sensing using nonlinear elasticity. In: Proceedings of SICE Annual Conference 2005, pp. 2978–2981 (2005)

Understanding User Experience with Game Controllers: A Case Study with an Adaptive Smart Controller and a Traditional Gamepad

Guilherme Gonçalves[✉], Érica Mourão, Leonardo Torok, Daniela Trevisan, Esteban Clua, and Anselmo Montenegro

Instituto de Computação, Universidade Federal Fluminense,
Niterói, RJ 24210-310, Brazil
{galves,emourao,ltorok,daniela,esteban,anselmo}@ic.uff.br
http://www.ic.uff.br

Abstract. Evaluating digital games is challenging since success is defined by enjoyment and gameplay experience, two factors that are hard to measure. While several works presented methods to analyze these factors, it is rare to find studies that evaluate the impact that the input methods (gamepads, touch, keyboards) have on the experience. We now introduce an exploratory user experience and usability study that compares two radically different game controllers: a mobile touch-based controller and a traditional gamepad, using subjective and objective user data. Results of this exploratory study indicate that while the general user experience and usability were similar with both controllers, the physiological measures indicate that the emotions differ between interfaces. In our final thoughts, we provide insights about how to evaluate and compare the experience with game controllers.

Keywords: UX · AttrakDiff · Emotion analysis · Game controllers · Adaptive interfaces

1 Introduction

Digital games are an extremely varied set of applications with a rich range of experiences offered to players. This diversity makes it difficult to devise a unique approach to their conceptualization and measurement. Terms such as fun, flow and gameplay are widely used to explain the user experience in game design [4]. However, there is an open discussion to include other relevant factors. Fluency on the gamepad and the game controls [27] as well as emotion [14] are often cited as key elements of the user experience. Emotions in digital games act as a motivator for the cognitive decisions players make during gameplay and they drive user experience in digital games [19]. The success of the gaming experience is determined by the positive aspects of the gameplay experience and by the quality of the input method used to control it. The game controls are not just

© IFIP International Federation for Information Processing 2017
Published by Springer International Publishing AG 2017. All Rights Reserved
N. Munekata et al. (Eds.): ICEC 2017, LNCS 10507, pp. 59–71, 2017.
DOI: 10.1007/978-3-319-66715-7_7

related to the hardware used to play: it includes learning how to manipulate the game, move the avatar and memorize the mappings of in-game actions to the gamepad. While there is plenty of works about evaluating the experience provided by the game, we have a limited literature about how the game controller can interfere with the experience and performance of a user [15, 20, 28, 30].

We propose a method to evaluate the game in an exploratory user experience and usability study that investigated a commercial joystick as input device compared to a novel adaptive touch-based controller (the Smart controller [22, 26, 27]). Our goal is to advance the theoretical understanding of how game controllers can affect the user experience, focusing on the measurement of user experience, usability, and physiology. One limitation of current psychophysiological studies is that they cannot precisely classify UX in games since many aspects of the experience lack standardized quantitative measurements [16, 18]. Hence, another purpose of this study is to determine if there is a correlation between subjective player experience (with AttrakDiff questionnaire) and objective physiological data (collected with electroencephalography (EEG) sensors), in an attempt to determine which measures are more adequate to evaluate game controllers. While not the focus of this research, we will report any interesting finding relative to evaluating the game itself, to stimulate further research about the topic.

2   How to Evaluate UX in Games

The current ISO definition on user experience focuses on a person's perception and the responses resulting from the use or anticipated use of a product, system, or service. User experience includes all the users' emotions, beliefs, preferences, perceptions, physical and psychological responses, behaviors and accomplishments that occur before, during and after use [9]. In the literature, there are many works that perform user experience evaluations in games [4], however, very few focus on the evaluation of the players' experiences with game controllers.

2.1   User Experience Questionnaires

Some questionnaires use a broader approach, looking to evaluate all aspects of gaming experience [7, 12] while others try to determine more specific aspects, such as immersion [13] or motivation [24]. Brown et al. [6] explored the experience, functionality, and usability through different controllers (gamepads, keyboard, racing wheel). Subjective Mental Effort Questionnaire (SMEQ) [3] and Consumer Product Questionnaire (CPQ) [17] were used to respectively measure effectiveness and satisfaction.

Attractiveness has been used to measure UX in games [8, 14], being described as a set of four dimensions: (1) Pragmatic Quality (PQ), (2) Hedonic Quality - Stimulation (HQS), (3) Hedonic Quality - Identity (HQI) and (4) Attractiveness (ATT) [11, 25]. The first one (PQ) focuses on task-related design aspects and indicates if the users reached their goals on an interaction. The Hedonic Quality dimensions (HQS and HQI) describe quality aspects, like originality and beauty. The Attractiveness (ATT) represents a global value of the product, based on quality perception. AttrakDiff is a usability questionnaire that analyzes all these dimensions. It has 28 questions (7 per dimension) with a semantic differential scale [25] (integer values from −3 to 3).

Lankees et al. [14] applied the AttrakDiff questionnaire to understand how emotional stimuli (facial expressions by Embodied Conversational Agents and emotion-eliciting situations) in interactive systems affect the user experience. Christou [8] applied the AttrakDiff questionnaire to explore the connection between the players' perceptions of usability and appeal of massively multiplayer role-playing games using World of Warcraft. Findings pointed that the relationship between usability and the general quality of the experience is reaffirmed in the realm of video and computer games. Different cases were successfully evaluated with AttrakDiff: iTV [4], user interface for business management system [25] and games [8,14].

2.2 Psychophysiological Measures and Its Correlation with Subjective User Data

The use of objective data, like physiological measures (e.g. galvanic skin response, muscles contraction, respiratory and cardiovascular signals), are widely employed in the literature to evaluate UX and user engagement in digital games [16,18,19]. Basically, these methods seek to obtain objective data to measure factors that are normally subjective, like the emotional state.

Some works have focused on studying the correlation between subjective user response and objective physiological data while measuring the player experience. Mandryk et al. [16] collect galvanic skin response (GSR), electrocardiography (EKG), electromyography of the jaw (EMG) and respiration. In their first experiment, they found many inconsistent correlations across participants. They observed that participants were responding more to the experimental situation than the experimental manipulations. In a second experiment, they decided to maximize the user experience by adding a competition factor, with users testing two situations: playing against other player and against the computer. This time, they could correlate the data showing that the increases in subjective ratings corresponded increases in the physiological data.

3 Method

3.1 Research Goals and Hypotheses

Recently, Torok et al. [26,27] and Pelegrino [22] proposed a novel adaptive controller for digital games called Smart controller[1]. Smart controller is a mobile app available for Android and iOS that allows the player to use a mobile phone as a touch-based gamepad for PC games. This is not a regular gamepad: the game

---

[1] Smart controller: http://smartcontrollerapp.com/.

can configure which buttons will be shown, their position, size, and icons, being also able to change it anytime during the gameplay section. New UI elements, not present on traditional controllers, can also be used, creating a totally new experience. As a touch-based interface, it lacks any kind of tactile perception. To partially counter this issue, it dynamically changes the size and position of its buttons according to the user behavior, optimizing its ergonomics on-the-fly to improve the experience. Preliminary evaluation of that controller [26] demonstrated that players had better performance results with the intelligent adaptations turned on. Subsequent tests [22] showed that it provided a significantly different user experience to gamers than what a regular gamepad could offer.

The goal of our research is to propose a method to evaluate the user experience and usability aspects of game controllers. We decided to use two radically different interfaces, the Smart controller, and a traditional gamepad, to test our method, seeking to propose a way to compare any game controllers in different aspects, like user experience (e.g. attractiveness and emotions), usability factors, physiological and performance data. In more detail, we intend to address the following research question:

RQ1: How the user experience and usability (measured with both objective and subjective data) are perceived with the different controllers in digital games?

We are also looking for potentials correlations between AttrakDiff data and EEG data. For instance, here we are interested in answering questions such as:

RQ2: Which dimensions of user experience (measured with AttrakDiff questionnaire) correlate with user emotions (measured with physiological EEG data) for the different controllers?

3.2   Evaluation Criteria

Our approach is based on the capture and analysis of subjective and objective user data. We applied two methods: the AttrakDiff questionnaire [1,11] and collection of EEG data [2]. User satisfaction is captured with the System Usability Scale (SUS) [5] questionnaire and player performance is analyzed with a game log (text file). The SUS questionnaire was designed to evaluate user satisfaction during a software system interaction. Its score is calculated from all answers and a mean score below 68 indicates usability problems. The in-game performance when using both controllers was measured with 2 metrics: time to complete a stage in seconds and number of deaths in each stage.

Raw EEG signals were recorded with the Emotiv EPOC+ device [2], using the Xavier software platform. The device has 16 electrodes (14 for data capture, 2 for reference and positioning). The Xavier software process the EEG signal and exports metrics for different emotional states (Engagement, Excitement, Interest, Relaxation, Stress and Focus) [23]. During a test section, Xavier will collect all emotions as real values between 0 and 1. After the test, the software generates an average value, that will be used in our analysis.

(a) Playing with the Smart controller   (b) Xbox 360 gamepad

Fig. 1. Input devices used in the user's sessions: Smart controller (a) and a Microsoft Xbox 360 controller (b).

4 Experiment

4.1 Participants and Procedure

Data were recorded from 10 volunteers, students invited on the university campus, with varying levels of experience with video games. No financial compensation was given. Their age ranged from 18 to 30 years. Six participants were male and none had previous experience with the testing game. 70% of the volunteers played frequently on their smartphones. 40% played games on a console at least twice a week, 20% up to six days a week and 40% do not play on game consoles. Furthermore, we also collected their game genre preference resulting in (70%) Adventure, (50%) Strategy, (40%) Casuals, (40%) Simulation, (30%) Fight. Other genres were cited with percentages lower than 20%. We performed three pilot tests in order to improve the experiment.

After signing a standard agreement term, each user filled the profile mapping questionnaire, used to obtain the previously mentioned statistics. The user would then, with our help, put the Emotiv Epoc+ helmet (as shown in Fig. 1a). Before the experiment, the participant was requested to close his eyes and concentrate his attention on a relaxing music during two minutes, so we could measure a neutral mental state to calibrate the EEG device. After that, the participant received brief instructions about the game and the controllers. The user would play for 10 min with each controller. At the end, the participants filled the SUS and AttrakDiff questionnaires for each controller experience. To avoid any bias due to learning the game mechanics, half the users started with the touch controller while half started with the traditional gamepad.

4.2 The Game

Pelegrino [22] developed a game, called Guardians of Eternity, to test the Smart controller. Figure 2 shows the different levels of the game. We decided to use the same game in our evaluation since it explored well the new functions of the novel controller while also being compatible with a Xbox 360 gamepad. Adding support to the Smart controller involves altering the source code of a game and

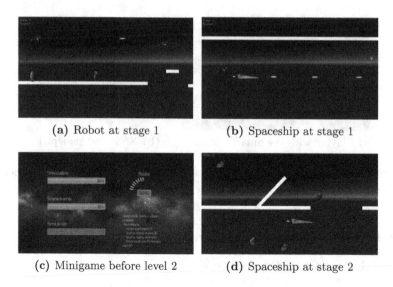

(a) Robot at stage 1   **(b)** Spaceship at stage 1

(c) Minigame before level 2   **(d)** Spaceship at stage 2

Fig. 2. Game screens for both stages. Stage 1 has two gameplay modes: platforming as robot (a) and dual-stick shooter with the spaceship (b). After finishing this level, the player enters a minigame (c) that precedes the second stage (d)

adding the correct API calls to configure the controller and gather input, while the game must be developed in Unity. Performing significant changes to games (that would have to be open source and made in Unity) is out of our scope, so we decided to use Guardian of Eternity. Keeping the game choice consistent also allow future works to compare our findings with the previous study by Pelegrino. As the source code is available, we could also slightly alter it to add routines to log the performance data. The game has two simple stages. The first one is mainly a platforming game, with the player controlling a robot and traversing different platforms while defeating or avoiding enemies. The main character can also transform in a spaceship and the gameplay becomes more similar to a dual-stick shooter. With the adaptive controller, the interface changes as the player alternates forms (see Fig. 3. With the 360 controller, only the key mappings are altered. In the end of the stage, the robot is severely damaged and the player must disable several subsystems: the Smart controller presents a screen similar to a control panel, while the regular gamepad maps these actions to its buttons. As the robot lost its transforming power as well as its weapons, level 2 is a maze to escape the planet. The player must avoid colliding with walls or asteroids. The layout in the touch controller is unusual: one hand controls the vertical level while the other controls the horizontal movements (as for the 360 gamepad, each analog stick controls one level).

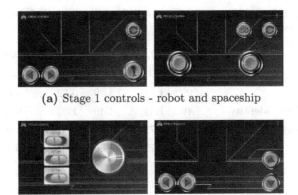

(a) Stage 1 controls - robot and spaceship

(b) Stage 2 controls - minigame and spaceship

Fig. 3. The layout displayed by the Smart controller during the different stages of the game.

5   Results

For numeric results, we extensively used the Wilcoxon signed-rank test [29], a non-parametric statistical test, to compare the data for both controllers and determine if the difference was statistically significant. The significance level was 0.05 and we performed a paired test since the samples are dependent (same users). If the resulting p-value for any test is lower than 0.05, the difference is significant. The Wilcoxon test was used because it does not depend on the distribution of the data (while a t-test demands a normal distribution, for instance) and has a high precision [10]. For correlation results, we applied the Pearson correlation [21]. The Pearson correlation returns a p-value (that also must be lower than 0.05) and a correlation score between -1 and 1. Values closer to 0 indicate that the data is not correlated or that the correlation is weak. Values closer to -1 or 1 show a strong correlation. While positive values are a direct correlation (i.e. if A increases, B also increases), negative values are the opposite (if A increases, B decreases).

5.1   Attractiveness and Satisfaction

Table 1 shows the results for the AttrakDiff questionnaire. While the means for all qualities were slightly higher with the physical gamepad, none of these differences were statistically significant. As the two interfaces are radically different, this could mean that the AttrakDiff evaluation was more affected by the game itself than by the controllers.

The SUS results seemed to indicate a lower satisfaction with the Smart controller (64.8, below the desirable mean of 68) than with the traditional controller (74.0). However, the p-value for all participants was 0.853 (not-significant). The SUS scores were apparently too subjective, with hugely different answers that did not provide any definitive conclusion.

Table 1. Comparison of the scores for the different qualities of AttrakDiff. SD = Standard Deviation.

	Xbox gamepad		Smart controller		Wilcoxon test
Qualities	Mean	SD	Mean	SD	p-value
Pragmatic	3.99	1.21	3.89	0.72	0.661
Hedonic quality - identity	4.49	1.47	4.40	1.03	0.556
Hedonic quality - stimulation	4.91	1.72	3.79	0.81	0.989
Attractiveness	3.93	0.71	3.86	0.91	0.743

5.2 Performance

The stage duration for level 1 was slightly lower with the traditional controller (M = 145.4) when compared to the adaptive one (M = 158.7). In Stage 2, the opposite happens (traditional controller averages 268.3 s while the adaptive averages 243.9 s). The p-value for both stages was, respectively, 0.375 and 0.444, both non-statistically significant. The number of player deaths in stage 1 is higher with the adaptive controller (M = 3.7) than with the traditional (M = 1.8). Stage 2 resulted in an apparent draw (M = 1.6 with the 360 gamepad and M = 1.5 with the Smart controller). With p-values of 0.188 and 0.930, respectively, we confirm that no significant difference in game performance was caused by either controller.

5.3 Emotion Analysis

Our findings show that all emotions reach higher levels with the Smart controller (see Fig. 4). Excitement (p-value = 0.0141) and Focus (p-value = 0.0245) emotions resulted in significant differences. This presents an interesting evidence that the Smart controller increased the excitement and allowed players to focus more intensively on the gameplay experience.

Table 2. Emotions versus deaths in stage 1. Only statistically significant (p < 0.05) results are reported.

Emotion versus stage duration in seconds			
Emotions	Controller	p-value < 0.05	Pearson correlation
Excitement	Traditional	0.0065	0.73
	Adaptive	0.0161	0.78
Interest	Traditional	0.0242	0.69

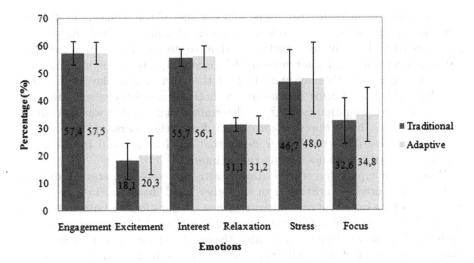

Fig. 4. Emotions in Smart controller and traditional controller - mean and standard deviation.

5.4 Insights About Interrelations Between Emotions, Performance and Usability

We also evaluated how emotions changed accordingly to in-game performance. While stage 2 did not have any correlation between emotions and deaths, during stage 1 we had a strong positive correlation between excitement with in-game deaths (when $0.7 \leqslant r < 0.9$, as seen in Table 3), for both controllers. All results are significant. The interest emotion was moderately correlated with deaths only with the traditional controller (when $0.5 \leqslant r < 0.7$), with the adaptive one resulting in a p-value higher than 0.05 (not-significant). This difference could indicate that the new experience of the Smart controller had an impact on the interest of users, but more in-depth evaluations would be necessary to determine if it was a significant factor and if it was positive or negative.

Table 3. Emotions versus stage duration in seconds. Only statistically significant ($p < 0.05$) results are reported.

Emotion versus stage duration in seconds			
Emotions	Controller	p-value < 0.05	Pearson correlation
Excitement	Traditional	0.0016	0.85
	Adaptive	0.0044	0.81
Interest	Traditional	0.0466	0.64
	Adaptive	0.0322	0.67

This seems to indicate that users who considered the game more difficult were more interested in the experience and were also more excited. As the test game tended to be easy and short (according to user feedback after our tests and consistent with user interviews in Pelegrino [22]) when compared to most commercial games. This may indicate that the most skilled players probably considered the game boring because it was not a reasonable challenge to their abilities. Future evaluation could try to determine if a game that was excessively hard could result in an opposite correlation, frustrating users and resulting in a lack of interest. This result also shows that EEG data could be useful for developers to balance games and maximize interest.

When we compare the stage duration with the emotions, stage 1 did not result in any correlation. Stage 2 in the other hand, had moderate or strong correlations for excitement and interest with stage duration for both controllers (see Table 2). This level differs from the first one since it lacks enemies, so it is harder to die. The challenge is on beating the maze and users that took longer to complete the task had more difficulties, so it seems to indicate that, once more, a higher challenge was considered more exciting and interesting.

Our first research question (**RQ1**), intended to discover the difference in usability and user experience with both controllers. There was not a significant difference in game performance. Attractiveness was also similar. The Smart controller had a lower than ideal SUS score, which indicates usability problems. However, the difference between both interfaces in satisfaction was not significant. The user experience evaluations shows a different scenario, with the Smart controller increasing significantly both excitement and focus, improving the user experience and showing that innovative interfaces, even with a slight loss in performance, can provide a better experience to users.

In order to answer **RQ2**, we looked for correlations between emotions and attractiveness, comparing the results from AttrakDiff dimensions and the EEG data. The correlation between the Pragmatic Quality dimension and the Interest emotion was strong (0.7894 with p-value = 0.0066), showing that one of the dimensions was indeed directly linked to physiological data, answering the aforementioned question. This seems to indicate that the users' interest is higher when they consider that a game experience has a good usability and learnability, showing a direct correlation between subjective and objective data. In the other hand, the SUS data was correlated to neither emotion results or AttrakDiff dimensions.

6   Conclusion and Future Works

The evaluation of game controllers is a relatively unexplored area. With this work, we intended to verify which approaches to measure the user experience of gamepads were effective by comparing two different game controllers. The AttrakDiff and SUS results were similar for both interfaces, creating doubt about their efficiency to compare game controllers. The users seemed to have difficulties to separate which usability aspects were correspondent to the game itself and which were related to the controllers, a finding consistent with the work of Pelegrino [22]. It is not surprising that objective data, that does not rely on the user's capacity to separate different interaction facets, was a better fit to evaluate game controllers. The EEG data showed that the new interface, the Smart controller, resulted in a significantly more exciting experience and increased the focus in the game. When evaluating game controllers, it seems that objective data, like our EEG results, is much more reliable than subjective data provided by user feedback.

While not directly related to game controllers, we also observed that users that died more on stage 1 or demanded more time to complete stage 2 were more interested in the game and were generally more excited. As the test game tended to be excessively easy, the absence of challenge may have bored the most skilled players. As a side result, we believe that EEG data can be a promising method to determine if a game is correctly balanced and provides an adequate challenge to its players. An interesting finding was the correlation between the Pragmatic Quality dimension and the "Interest" emotion. This may indicate that the interest measured by the Epoc raises when the quality and usability of a game improves, showing that developers could benefit from monitoring this emotion with EEG during usability tests.

Clearly, these results are the first step in order to fully understand user experience with game controllers. As future developments, it would be relevant to perform in-depth tests to determine if the non-significant correlation between interest and in-game deaths for the Smart controller was a result of the impact that the interface itself had on that emotion, especially because the traditional controller did not seem to interfere at all with the level of interest. Another possibility is to repeat the tests with a game that is significantly harder since we found a correlation between difficulty and interest/excitement. This could confirm if an increased difficulty, even to the point of frustration, could revert this correlation. In this case, maybe EEG is a viable option for balancing the difficulty of games, seeking to maximize positive emotions like interest and excitement.

Acknowledgments. We would like to express our gratitude to Adriel Araújo, Bruno Olímpio and José Santos for helping in this study. We also would like to thank all our participants. Finally, we would like to thank CAPES, CNPQ and FAPERJ for the financial support.

References

1. Attrakdiff. http://attrakdiff.de/index-en.html
2. Emoti. https://www.emotiv.com/
3. Arnold, A.G.: Mental effort and evaluation of user-interfaces: a questionnaire approach. In: Proceedings of HCI International (the 8th International Conference on Human-Computer Interaction) on Human-Computer Interaction: Ergonomics and User Interfaces-Volume I-Volume I, pp. 1003–1007. L. Erlbaum Associates Inc. (1999)

4. Bernhaupt, R., Desnos, A., Pirker, M., Schwaiger, D.: TV interaction beyond the button press. In: Abascal, J., Barbosa, S., Fetter, M., Gross, T., Palanque, P., Winckler, M. (eds.) INTERACT 2015. LNCS, vol. 9297, pp. 412–419. Springer, Cham (2015). doi:10.1007/978-3-319-22668-2_31

5. Brooke, J., et al.: Sus-a quick and dirty usability scale. Usability Eval. Ind. **189**(194), 4–7 (1996)

6. Brown, M., Kehoe, A., Kirakowski, J., Pitt, I.: Beyond the gamepad: HCI and game controller design and evaluation. In: Bernhaupt, R. (ed.) Game User Experience Evaluation, pp. 263–285. Springer, London (2015). doi:10.1007/978-1-84882-963-3_12

7. Calvillo-Gámez, E.H., Cairns, P., Cox, A.: Assessing the core elements of the gaming experience. In: Bernhaupt, R. (ed.) Game User Experience Evaluation, pp. 37–62. Springer, London (2015). doi:10.1007/978-1-84882-963-3_4

8. Christou, G.: Exploring player perceptions that contribute to the appeal of world of warcraft. In: Proceedings of the 4th International Conference on Fun and Games, pp. 105–108. ACM (2012)

9. Dis, I.: 9241–210: 2010. ergonomics of human system interaction-part 210: Human-centred design for interactive systems. International Standardization Organization (pISO). Switzerland (2009)

10. Fay, M.P., Proschan, M.A.: Wilcoxon-mann-whitney or t-test? on assumptions for hypothesis tests and multiple interpretations of decision rules. Stat. Surv. **4**, 1 (2010)

11. Hassenzahl, M.: Hedonic, emotional, and experiential perspectives on product quality. In: Encyclopedia of Human Computer Interaction, pp. 266–272. IGI Global (2006)

12. IJsselsteijn, W., Van Den Hoogen, W., Klimmt, C., De Kort, Y., Lindley, C., Mathiak, K., Poels, K., Ravaja, N., Turpeinen, M., Vorderer, P.: Measuring the experience of digital game enjoyment. In: Proceedings of Measuring Behavior, pp. 88–89. Noldus Information Tecnology Wageningen, Netherlands (2008)

13. Jennett, C., Cox, A.L., Cairns, P., Dhoparee, S., Epps, A., Tijs, T., Walton, A.: Measuring and defining the experience of immersion in games. Int. J. Hum Comput Stud. **66**(9), 641–661 (2008)

14. Lankes, M., Bernhaupt, R., Tscheligi, M.: Evaluating user experience factors using experiments: expressive artificial faces embedded in contexts. In: Bernhaupt, R. (ed.) Evaluating User Experience in Games, pp. 165–183. Springer, Cham (2010). doi:10.1007/978-3-319-15985-0_6

15. Malfatti, S.M., Dos Santos, F.F., Dos Santos, S.R.: Using mobile phones to control desktop multiplayer games. In: 2010 Brazilian Symposium on Games and Digital Entertainment (SBGAMES), pp. 230–238. IEEE (2010)

16. Mandryk, R.L., Inkpen, K.M., Calvert, T.W.: Using psychophysiological techniques to measure user experience with entertainment technologies. Behav. Inf. Technol. **25**(2), 141–158 (2006)

17. McNamara, N., Kirakowski, J.: Measuring user-satisfaction with electronic consumer products: the consumer products questionnaire. Int. J. Hum Comput. Stud. **69**(6), 375–386 (2011)

18. Nacke, L.E., Grimshaw, M.N., Lindley, C.A.: More than a feeling: measurement of sonic user experience and psychophysiology in a first-person shooter game. Interact. Comput. **22**(5), 336–343 (2010)

19. Nacke, L.E., Lindley, C.A.: Affective ludology, flow and immersion in a first-person shooter: measurement of player experience. arXiv preprint (2010). arXiv:1004.0248

20. Natapov, D., Castellucci, S.J., MacKenzie, I.S.: ISO 9241–9 evaluation of video game controllers. In: Proceedings of Graphics Interface 2009, pp. 223–230. Canadian Information Processing Society (2009)

21. Pearson, K.: Note on regression and inheritance in the case of two parents. Proc. Royal Soc. London **58**, 240–242 (1895)

22. Pelegrino, M.: Um Controle Virtual Dinmico para Jogos Adaptado ao Gameplay e ao Usurio. Master's thesis, Universidade Federal Fluminense (2016)

23. Ramirez, R., Vamvakousis, Z.: Detecting emotion from EEG signals using the emotive epoc device. In: Zanzotto, F.M., Tsumoto, S., Taatgen, N., Yao, Y. (eds.) BI 2012. LNCS, vol. 7670, pp. 175–184. Springer, Heidelberg (2012). doi:10.1007/978-3-642-35139-6_17

24. Ryan, R.M., Rigby, C.S., Przybylski, A.: The motivational pull of video games: a self-determination theory approach. Motiv. Emot. **30**(4), 344–360 (2006)

25. Schrepp, M., Held, T., Laugwitz, B.: The influence of hedonic quality on the attractiveness of user interfaces of business management software. Interact. Comput. **18**(5), 1055–1069 (2006)

26. Torok, L., Pelegrino, M., Lessa, J., Trevisan, D.G., Vasconcelos, C.N., Clua, E., Montenegro, A.: Evaluating and customizing user interaction in an adaptive game controller. In: Marcus, A. (ed.) DUXU 2015. LNCS, vol. 9188, pp. 315–326. Springer, Cham (2015). doi:10.1007/978-3-319-20889-3_30

27. Torok, L., Pelegrino, M., Trevisan, D.G., Clua, E., Montenegro, A.: A mobile game controller adapted to the gameplay and user's behavior using machine learning. In: Chorianopoulos, K., Divitini, M., Hauge, J.B., Jaccheri, L., Malaka, R. (eds.) ICEC 2015. LNCS, vol. 9353, pp. 3–16. Springer, Cham (2015). doi:10.1007/978-3-319-24589-8_1

28. Vajk, T., Coulton, P., Bamford, W., Edwards, R.: Using a mobile phone as a wii-like controller for playing games on a large public display. Int. J. Comput. Games Technol. **2008** (2007)

29. Wilcoxon, F.: Individual comparisons by ranking methods. Biometrics Bull. **1**(6), 80–83 (1945)

30. Zhang, Z.: Microsoft kinect sensor and its effect. IEEE Multimedia **19**(2), 4–10 (2012)

InsTangible: A Tangible User Interface Combining Pop-up Cards with Conductive Ink Printing

Yan Zhao[1](✉), Yuta Sugiura[2](✉), Mitsunori Tada[3], and Jun Mitani[1]

[1] University of Tsukuba, Tsukuba, Ibaraki 305-0006, Japan
yanzhao.npal.tsukuba@gmail.com, mitani@cs.tsukuba.ac.jp
[2] Keio University, Yokohama, Kanagawa 223-8521, Japan
sugiura@keio.jp
[3] National Institute of Advanced Industrial Science and Technology (AIST),
Tokyo 135-0064, Japan
m.tada@aist.go.jp

Abstract. We propose a tangible user interface combining pop-up cards with conductive ink printing technique. To fulfill our purpose, we developed software that can automatically calculate the circuit layouts on the pop-up card. The circuit layout is made to have the shortest path by considering the thickness of the layout, the space between circuit lines, and that the layout should not crossover cut lines. The crease pattern and layouts are printed separately when the layouts are calculated. By attaching electronic elements, we can make an interactive pop-up card. In a use trial, we confirmed that even novice could create original interactive pop-up card with our software and use such card to build an application. Furthermore, we demonstrated the effectiveness of our method by making and showing example applications using the interactive pop-up card interface.

Keywords: Interactive pop-up card · Tangible user interface · Rapid prototyping

1 Introduction

In recent years, directly printing circuits on paper with low cost, fast and accessible technology has been studied and commercialized [5]. By combining the features of paper and the interactive properties of electronics, a variety of applications that go beyond the conventional uses of paper are emerging. One important feature of paper is that it can easily be cut and folded into many shapes, as can be seen in paper-craft and origami. In our research, we have combined this feature of paper with the conductive ink printing technique to produce interactive devices (e.g., Fig. 1) that are new uses of paper.

Among the methods of using paper to construct shapes, we focused on the pop-up card, which is used in greeting cards and childrens picture books.

© IFIP International Federation for Information Processing 2017
Published by Springer International Publishing AG 2017. All Rights Reserved
N. Munekata et al. (Eds.): ICEC 2017, LNCS 10507, pp. 72–80, 2017.
DOI: 10.1007/978-3-319-66715-7_8

Fig. 1. A room layout design application in which the user can move the interactive pop-up card interface on the table to manipulate the furniture layout in a room.

There are several attractive aspects of pop-up cards: (1) it is easy to use them to make 3D shapes by using everyday tools and materials such as scissors, cutters, and paper; (2) the cost of creating a pop-up card is low; (3) A pop-up card can quickly change from flat to shaped, a feature that is important for its users as entertainment.

In our research, we devised a method to build a tangible user interface (TUI) by combining pop-up cards with the conductive ink printing technique without the user having to calculate the electronic circuit layout on the crease pattern of the pop-up card. The interactive property of this paper is that it can recognize whether and where the user touched the pop-up card and present such information to the user. We use electrostatic capacitance to recognize the touch and place electronic elements (e.g., microcontroller, LEDs) to handle and output the interactive information. In order to add interactive properties to paper, it is necessary to calculate the circuit layout on the paper to connect the touched place and the output. The user can connect electronic elements (e.g., LEDs) to microcontrollers and other sensors because the whole surface of the pop-up card is connected to the base sheet. However, calculating a circuit layout on a pop-up card with a complex 3D shape can be frustrating for a novice.

To make such calculations easier on paper with crease patterns, we developed software that calculates the circuit layout between user-specified start and end points on the crease pattern of the pop-up card [8]. The circuit layout is made to have the shortest path by considering the thickness of the layout, the space between circuit lines, and that the layout should not crossover cut lines. The layout data is then converted into data for printing.

The interactive pop-up cards made with our method can be used as greeting cards with a TUI expressing messages or music by touching the pop-up or be manipulated for various purposes, e.g., as miniatures that can be placed on a table top for room design applications (Fig. 1). In a user trial, we found that even novice could use our software to build an interactive pop-up card and application with a pop-up card interface. We also devised our own example applications to demonstrate the effectiveness of our concept.

2   Related Work

2.1   Paper with Electronics

A number of studies have tried combining paper with electronics to produce interactive media. Kawahara et al. presented an approach to inkjet printing flexible circuits on paper using commodity inkjet printers; it has been commercialized in the form of AgIC[1]. Olberding et al. proposed a printed capacitive multi-touch sensor that is robust against cuts, damages and removed areas [9]. Kato et al. proposed a striped pattern sticker called ExtensionSticker that allows a touch input to be transferred from an external source by simply attaching the sticker to a touch panel [4]. Koizumi et al. proposed "Animated Paper", which combines paper, shape memory alloy (SMA), retro-reflective material, and copper foil. In Animated Paper, paper-craft actuated by the SMA can be made to move with a high-power laser pointer [6]. Qi et al. developed a dynamic interactive pop-up book that integrates pop-up mechanisms with thin, flexible, paper-based electronics [11]. Zhu et al. proposed "AutoGami", which allows users to explore the design space of automated paper craft in a low-cost way [1]. Ramakers et al. proposed "PaperPulse", which enables designers to produce standalone interactive paper artifacts by augmenting them with electronics [10]. Olberding et al. proposed "Foldios", which combines the advantages of folding for thin, lightweight and shape-changing objects with the strengths of thin-film printed electronics for embedded sensing and output [3]. In our research, our contribution is to provide an automatically circuit layout calculation software for calculting circuit layout on complex pop-up card. Such software is expect to support user to design the circuit layout on complex pop-up card.

2.2   Support for Circuit Layouts

Many optimizations for supporting circuit layouts have been incorporated in standard libraries or tools in electronic circuit design software. The Eagle[2] which is an easy graphical layout editor for circuit layout design, and its algorithm calculates optimal layouts among electronic components. There is also a research to support the circuit layout calculation on a particular model. Savage et al. imported the model shape by photograph and build a software to define the desired shape, layout, and type of touching sensitive areas, routing obstacles and calculate the circuit layout [12]. Comparing to these existing researches, we focus on the optimization for making circuit layout on pop-up card.

---

[1] AgIC. http://agic.cc/ja.
[2] Eagle. http://www.cadsoftusa.com/.

2.3 Support for Pop-up Card Fabrication

Several studies have been undertaken on making interactive pop-up cards. Mitani proposed a method and developed commercial software to design pop-up cards and export the crease patterns to be printed on a single sheet of paper [8]. Li et al. proposed an algorithm for generating pop-up paper architecture from a user-specified 3D model [7]. Iizuka et al. developed software to support pop-up card designs using multiple sheets of paper [2]. In our research, our motivation is to add interactive property to the pop-up card in order to give new experience to the user.

3 Software of Circuit Layout on Pop-up Card

First, we import the crease pattern of the pop-up card designed by Mitani's software (Fig. 2(a)). The crease pattern is on one piece of paper with cut lines and folding lines (i.e., mountain and valley folding lines). The 3D object rises when the pop-up card is opened 90 degrees. Such pop-up card is widely known as the folding architecture whose feature is that it can be easily created. As there are various pieces of software for designing pop-up cards besides Mitani's, we import the crease pattern, instead of the 3D shape of the pop-up card itself, into our system for general and further use of our software.

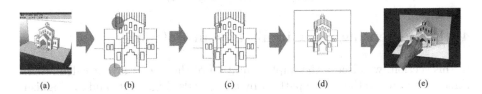

(a)   (b)   (c)   (d)   (e)

Fig. 2. Overview of our method: (a) a pop-up card designed by the user, (b) the user specifies the start and end points, (c) the circuit layout is calculated automatically, (d) data is converted into printable form, (e) the model made by user.

Then, as shown in Fig. 2(b), our software automatically calculate and render the circuit layout when the user specifies the start and end points by clicking the mouse on crease pattern (discussed in Sect. 4). The resulting circuit layout is the shortest path avoiding cut lines (Figs. 2(c) and 3) and has space between it and different layouts (Fig. 3). The user can increase the thickness of the circuit layout to make it capable of containing capacitance-type sensors but should avoid interference from other circuits. Furthermore, the user can modify the circuit layout by dragging the start or end point, or even specifying a new middle point. Such modifications can be made in real-time and always maintain the constraints for calculating the circuit layout. When circuit layouts are calculated, the next one does not cross over the region of the previous one.

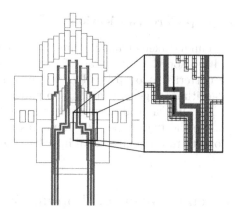

Fig. 3. Individual circuits never crossover the cut lines, and the space separating the circuits is maintained.

Finally, when the circuit layouts are completed, the user exports the crease pattern and the circuit layouts in PDF format and prints them separately (Fig. 2(d)). In our research, we used a printer to print the crease pattern with normal ink and the circuit layouts with conductive ink. The user then makes the pop-up card by cutting and folding the crease pattern and attaching electronic elements to add interactive properties on it (Fig. 2(e)).

4   Implementing the Circuit Layout Software

In this section, we discuss the implementation of the circuit layout calculation. First, we discretize the crease pattern by using grids (Fig. 4 left) and distinguish the grids that are incapable of being part of the circuit layout because they contain cut lines or other circuits (Fig. 4 right). The user can adjust the size of the grid to approximate the crease pattern while controlling the search cost. Specifically, it is hard to represent a crease pattern when the grid is too big. On the other hand, it is difficult to modify one circuit layout in real time as the calculation cost rises drastically when the grid is too fine.

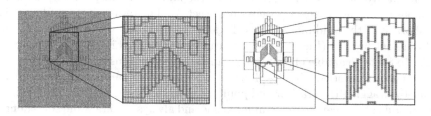

Fig. 4. Discrete crease pattern with grids (left), and grids distinguished as capable or incapable of being used in the circuit layout (right).

Then, our software recognizes the grids which are capable of being circuit layout nodes as defined in graph theory. We applied Dijkstra's algorithm to find the shortest layout between the user specified start and end points. The calculated layout satisfies the constraints, which the circuits should not crossover cut lines and maintain space between individual layouts.

Furthermore, the start or end point of one circuit layout can be moved by dragging with the mouse, and the constraints will be maintained. When we drag the end points (Fig. 5 left), the circuit layout around the end point stays parallel to the boundary of the pop-up card. Such circuit layouts are inconvenient for connecting outer electronic elements such as alligator clips. To refine the circuit layout, we insert a middle point in such a layout to divide one circuit layout into two parts and then find the shortest path of the two parts separately. The middle point can be moved by dragging and thus the user can move the middle point to let the circuit layout around end point be perpendicular to the boundary of the pop-up card (Fig. 5 right).

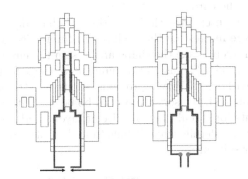

Fig. 5. Drag the end point (left), and insert one middle point to refine the circuit layout (right).

Our circuit layout software can handle complex 3D models. Figure 6 illustrates an example of circuit layouts on a pop-up card, called Block Castle?, designed by the fourth author. Such a 3D model is complex, and the work of making the layouts manually is time-consuming and could soon become frustrating for novices. However, by using our software, we only took about three minutes to complete the circuit layout work.

5   User Trial

We conducted a user trial on one novice to demonstrate that our system can help users build a TUI system. The procedure of the user trial is: first, the user make a pop-up card by the software of Mitani [8]. Second, the user creates circuit layouts using our software. Finally, the user prints the crease pattern and the

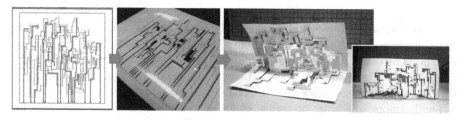

Fig. 6. Example of circuit layouts on pop-up card.

circuit layouts and attaches the provided electronic elements to make an original interactive pop-up card. After the user trial, we interview the user to obtain the comments on our software.

The user successfully designed the pop-up card (Fig. 7(a)) and used our software to design the circuit layouts on the crease pattern (Fig. 7(b)). Figure 7(c) and (d) shows the user and his interactive pop-up card, respectively. The designed pop-up card is named Tower and could emit red light by LED when touching the edge of the card.

We interviewed the user after the trial. He said that, designing the pop-up card by myself is more interesting than selecting commercial interactive pop-up cards, because I can freely make the shape and design the circuit layouts to add interactive properties to it. The user also commented: the software can calculate the circuit layouts without me having to consider its constraints. On the other hand, the user complained, the software would be better if it had some patterns of electronic elements for calculating the circuit layout and the software would be better if it gave more details when it fails to find a path. Such comments will help us to refine our software.

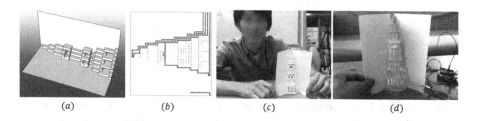

     (a)   (b)   (c)   (d)

Fig. 7. The pop-up card designed by the user in a user trial.

6 Example Applications

In this section, we display two example applications. The first application (Fig. 1) is a TUI based on an interactive pop-up card interface displayed on the table. We export designs of objects such as desks, chairs, and stairs to the interactive pop-up card interface and place them on the table. The application recognizes the positions of pop-up cards on the table when a user touches it. Unique IDs made by different conductive layout patterns are assigned to the pop-up cards.

When moving the interactive pop-up card interface on the table, the user can intuitively manipulate the furniture layout in a room. We also developed an application to play music on a pop-up card (Fig. 8). This application shows that our circuit layout software can handle curved cut lines on the pop-up card. We place the start point of the circuit layout on the middle of each stage. The application play notes corresponding to the location of the touched stage.

Fig. 8. A musical instrument application which plays a musical note corresponding to the location of the touched stage.

7   Conclusion and Future Work

We proposed a method to combine the pop-up card, which can easily generate a 3D shape, with the conductive ink printing technique to build a TUI. To fulfill our purpose, we built software to calculate circuit layouts on the crease patterns of pop-up cards. We conducted a user trial on one novice and obtained feedback for refining our software. Finally, we displayed two applications to show the advantages of the TUI based on pop-up cards.

There are limitations to the method: (1) the pop-up card made of paper is rather flimsy. In the application (Fig. 8), the pop-up card was heavily deformed when it was touched by the user; (2) although pop-up cards can express 3D shapes, they can't express whole surfaces; (3) the 3D shapes of pop-up cards can degenerate to 2.5D ones.

As future work, three aspects of our work can be improved: (i) inviting more participants for user test to evaluate the result in terms of entertainment or usability, (ii) using flexible and stretchable conductive ink as an alternative material, since we notice that the circuit layouts printed on the crease pattern were cut several times during the process of making the pop-up card, (iii) adding interactive properties not only for pop-up cards but also for paper-craft and origami.

References

1. Zhu, K., Zhao, S.: AutoGami: a low-cost rapid prototyping toolkit for automated movable paper craft. In: Proceedings of the SIGCHI Conference on Human Factors in Computing Systems (CHI 2013), pp. 661–670. ACM, New York (2013)
2. Iizuka, S., Endo, Y., Mitani, J., Kanamori, Y., Fukui, Y.: An interactive design system for pop-up cards with a physical simulation. In: Proceedings of Computer Graphics International 2011, vol. 27(6), pp. 605–612 (2011)
3. Olberding, S., Soto Ortega, S., Hildebrandt, K., Steimle, J.: Foldio: digital fabrication of interactive and shape-changing objects with foldable printed electronics. In: Proceedings of the 28th Annual ACM Symposium on User Interface Software and Technology (UIST 2015), pp. 223–232. ACM, New York (2015)
4. Kato, K., Miyashita, H.: A proposal for a striped pattern sticker to extend touch interfaces and its assessment. In: Proceedings of the 33rd Annual ACM Conference on Human Factors in Computing Systems (CHI 2015), pp. 1851–1854. ACM, New York (2015)
5. Kawahara, Y., Hodges, S., Cook, B.S., Zhang, C., Abowd, G.D.: Instant inkjet circuits: lab-based inkjet printing to support rapid prototyping of UbiComp devices. In: Proceedings of the 2013 ACM International Joint Conference on Pervasive and Ubiquitous Computing (UbiComp 2013), pp. 363–372. ACM, New York (2013)
6. Koizumi, N., Yasu, K., Liu, A., Sugimoto, M., Inami, M.: Animated paper: a toolkit for building moving toys. Comput. Entertain. (CIE) 8(2), 1–16, Article 7 (2010)
7. Li, X.Y., Shen, C.H., Huang, S.S., Ju, T., Hu, S.M.: Popup: automatic paper architectures from 3D models. In: ACM SIGGRAPH 2010 papers (SIGGRAPH 2010), Article 111, 9 p. ACM, New York (2010)
8. Mitani, J., Suzuki, H.: Computer aided design for origamic architecture models with polygonal representation. In: Proceedings of Computer Graphics International 2004, pp. 93–99. IEEE (2004)
9. Olberding, S., Gong, N.W., Tiab, J., Paradiso, J.A., Steimle, J.: A cuttable multi-touch sensor. In: Proceedings of the 26th Annual ACM Symposium on User Interface Software and Technology (UIST 2013), pp. 245–254. ACM, New York (2013)
10. Ramakers, R., Todi, K., Luyten, K.: PaperPulse: an integrated approach for embedding electronics in paper designs. In: Proceedings of the 33rd Annual ACM Conference on Human Factors in Computing Systems (CHI 2015), pp. 2457–2466. ACM, New York (2015)
11. Qi, J., Buechley, L.: Electronic popables: exploring paper-based computing through an interactive pop-up book. In: Proceedings of the Fourth International Conference on Tangible, Embedded, and Embodied Interaction (TEI 2010), pp. 121–128. ACM, New York (2010)
12. Savage, V., Zhang, X., Hartmann, B.: Midas: fabricating custom capacitive touch sensors to prototype interactive objects. In: Proceedings of the 25th Annual ACM Symposium on User Interface Software and Technology (UIST 2012), pp. 579–588. ACM, New York (2012)

Design and Implementation of a Voice Feedback Device for Voice Loudness Control

Fumiya Hara[✉], Yoshinari Takegawa, and Keiji Hirata

Future University Hakodate, Hakodate, Hokkaido 041-8655, Japan
{g2117040,yoshi,hirata}@fun.ac.jp
http://www.hiratakelab.jp

Abstract. In recent years, wearable devices such as Google Glass and Apple Watch are spreading in society. However, their devices cannot be used the following types of situations. In the case of user wants to quieten children being noisy in a public place, the user wants to speak clearly in a presentation despite being nervous. Therefore, wearable devices are important for the user to control his/her actions. This research aims to achieve involuntary and non-perceptual control of the user's actions, without inflicting mental stress. The first stage of the research is to design and implement a voice feedback system for voice control. This device is composed of an environmental sound measurement microphone, a speaking voice input microphone, a switch for the white noise function, a minicomputer, and a volume amplifier circuit. A first function of the device change the user's voice feedback from earphones by the user's voice loudness. Moreover, a second function of the device that output white noise add in order to consciously increase the use's voice loudness. In this paper, I describe the proposed vocal volume control and the implementation method of the proposed system.

Keywords: Loudness feedback system · White noise system · Wearable device · Involuntarily

1 Introduction

In recent years, information provision techniques that consider the user's situation are attracting notice in the field of wearable computing. Google Glass and Apple Watch are such wearable devices that provide beneficial information for the user. For example, navigation to a destination, and health management based on number of steps and heart rate. These information provision techniques present information for choices of action and promote specific actions. However, there are situations in which we cannot immediately control our own actions, even when it is vital. For example, in the case of user wants to quieten children being noisy in a public place, user wants to speak clearly in a presentation despite being nervous, a disaster or other unexpected event. Therefore, wearable devices are important for the user to control his/her actions. This research aims

© IFIP International Federation for Information Processing 2017
Published by Springer International Publishing AG 2017. All Rights Reserved
N. Munekata et al. (Eds.): ICEC 2017, LNCS 10507, pp. 81–87, 2017.
DOI: 10.1007/978-3-319-66715-7_9

to achieve involuntary and non-perceptual control of the user's actions, without inflicting mental stress. The first stage of research is to design and implement a voice feedback system for voice control.

This research applies the effect by which humans involuntarily speak in a loud voice in a noisy environment [1]. Moreover, changes the voice loudness that the user hears (hereafter: Heard voice loudness) according to the environment sound and controls the voice loudness at which the user speaks (hereafter: Speaking voice loudness).

2   Relevant Research

Since many years ago, a great amount of research on human vocalization models has been conducted. Speech Chain [2] is a major example of this. Humans control voice loudness according to auditory information, such as ambient sound, and visual information, such as the distance between oneself and the listener. Also, Lombard Effect is a voice model specialized in auditory feedback. We naturally tend to use loud voices in noisy environments, and listening to this noise not only causes the voice to become loud but is also known to change a variety of acoustic features, for example by causing the fundamental and formant frequency to rise. There are various research results relating to Lombard Effect [1]. For example, Hodoshima, Arai, Kurisu [3] surveys clarity of voice in a silent environment, a noisy environment, and a reverberant environment. Our research differs from existing research in that it surveys the effects of providing user voice feedback in real time. On the other hand, there are many existing research cases on control of user's action by wearable devices.

Various approaches to involuntary control of action exist, including control of appetite by visual presentation by VR (Virtual Reality) [4], and control of action by vibrating motor [5,6].

Kurihara, Tsukada [7] developed a system called SpeechJammer which inhibits speech, without imposing physical pain, by using Delayed Auditory Feedback to artificially delay when the speaker hears his own speech. SpeechJammer is closely related to our research in terms of control of speech. The approach of this research is different in that in aims for involuntary and non-perceptual control of user's speech.

3   Designs

3.1   Principle of Control of Voice Loudness

It is thought that the user's voice loudness can be changed by controlling the information the user can obtain from sound and sight. One of the reasons that voice control depends on auditory information is thought to be the relationship between environmental sound and one's own voice loudness. For example, our voices are louder than usual when we talk in a noisy place such as a concert hall or construction site. This phenomenon is called Lombard Effect [1]. Conversely, our voices are quieter than usual when we are in a quiet place such as library. In other words, we compare voice loudness with environmental noise and appropriately control voice loudness to maintain the difference between the loudnesses of the two sounds. In the case of noisy places, a person compares environmental noise and their ordinary voice loudness, and finds the voice loudness to be low, as a result of which voice loudness increases. In the case of quiet places, voice loudness becomes low because it is found to be louder than environmental sound.

Following on, it is thought that perspective is involved as a visual approach. Our voice loudness increases when we want to talk to a person who is far away. In contrast, our voice loudness decreases when we want to talk to a person who is nearby. Using this, this research designs and implements a basic voice loudness control system and system structure.

3.2   Voice Loudness Control System

To propose our voice loudness control system, we built the hypothesis that speaking voice volume becomes quiet when heard voice volume is loud, and, inversely, speaking voice volume becomes loud when heard voice volume is quiet. The reason for this is described below.

Amplification of Voice Loudness. To amplify the user's voice loudness, first, it was considered that the current heard voice volume is made quieter than the normal heard voice loudness. Second, the user will increase speaking voice loudness in order to make the level of the current heard voice loudness the same as the normal heard voice loudness. Therefore, we must make the current volume of environmental noise louder than the usual volume of environmental noise that the user hears with their own ears, in order to attenuate heard voice loudness. Accordingly, we considered that, in the situation where heard voice loudness is amplified, attenuating heard voice loudness will result in amplification of speaking voice loudness.

Attenuation of Voice Loudness. To attenuate the user's voice loudness, we must invert voice loudness amplification. That is to say, we considered that the current heard voice loudness is amplified the current speaking voice volume will be involuntary attenuated.

3.3   Usage Scenarios

In the Case of Increasing Voice Loudness. There are few people who do not feel stress during interviews for job hunting and part-time jobs, examinations. In particular, stress gets worse as the importance of the interview increases. By preventing this problem and controlling the voice loudness transmitted to the user, it is possible to eliminate the issues of what the interviewer is saying being inaudible or not understood. Also, by inducing appropriate voice loudness in the same manner as in the interview scenario, a presenter can use this system to efficaciously make a presentation to listeners.

In the Case of Decreasing Voice Loudness. It is poor manners to speak loudly when other people are nearby, such as during a party at someone's house, in a library or on an aeroplane. However, we sometimes forget to be considerate when having an exciting conversation. It is expected that our system, which causes the user to control voice volume involuntarily, can reduce voice loudness, even when the user has forgotten to can considerate and without altering the user's consciousness.

3.4 Design Policy

Involuntariness and Non-perception. There are some situations in which we consciously change voice loudness. For example, when a presenter speaking quietly while making a small-scale presentation is told to speak more loudly, or when someone talking loudly in a library is warned to become quieter. After receiving such a warning, we attempt to change voice loudness, but tend gradually to return to the former voice loudness so that there is no change. The system proposed by this research provides the user with heard voice loudness, as mentioned in Sect. 3.1, in order to resolve these problems.

This system needs to be a designed in such a way that the user does not notice changes to heard voice loudness, so that they may speak without perception. Thereby, the user is given heard voice loudness matched to environmental sound. Also, when the degree of amplification changes it is not changed suddenly, but at such a speed that the user does not notice.

Response to Continually Changing Situation and Environment. Environments and situations in which the proposed system can be used include quiet environments, such as a library, and noisy environments, such as a party. The system must constantly acquire environmental sound and return voice feed-back appropriate for the environmental sound at each moment. Therefore, it is necessary to consider the validity of the stages of amplification, in order to give appropriate heard voice loudness.

Also, when giving a presentation, the system feeds back white noise when the user consciously wishes to increase speaking voice loudness. This is because, by the Lombard Effect [1], the user's speaking voice loudness increases when the loudness of white noise increases. Accordingly, it is thought that the system can be utilized in situations such as public speaking. As a result, this research implements a switcher that changes between a feed-back function and a white noise function.

Miniaturization and Weight Reduction. The wearable device created in this research is supposed to be used in as many different situations and environments as possible, thus miniaturization and weight reduction are essential. Therefore, this wearable device only focuses on heard voice loudness and does not use visual recognition, enabling the system to be constructed from only microphone, earphones, and a minicomputer such as Arduino.

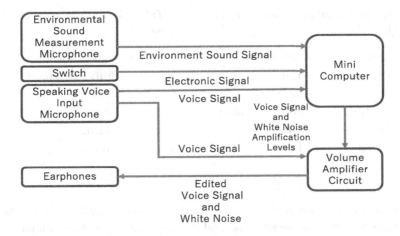

Fig. 1. System configuration

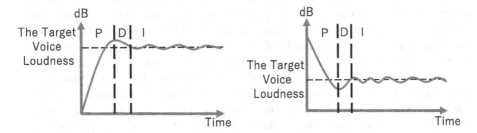

Fig. 2. For example of amplification of voice loudness

Fig. 3. For example of attenuation of voice loudness

3.5   Implementation

The system[1] configuration of our wearable device is shown in Fig. 1. This device is composed of an environmental sound measurement microphone, a speaking voice input microphone, a switch, earphones, a minicomputer, and a volume amplifier circuit. First, the system decides the amplification level of the volume amplifier circuit based on the environmental sound, the user's voice loudness and the target voice loudness programmed in advance using the minicomputer. These ranks are shown in Table 1.

To establish target voice volume, we established five ranks of amplification of loudness. These ranks are shown in Table 2. PID (Proportional-Integral-Differential) control [8] is used as a control model of an amplification of loudness depending on environment sound. Moreover, the reason for establishing five ranks for amplification of loudness is to inspect how much speaking voice loud-

---

[1] You can watch a demonstration video at https://1drv.ms/f/s!AqUbzynYF8M8ij k0JOORnx3p4AAp.

Table 1. Amplification of voice volume feed-back

Levels	Pulse volume	Amplification
1	550 μs	−12 dB
2	1050 μs	−6 dB
3	1500 μs	0 dB (basic point)
4	1950 μs	+6 dB
5	2400 μs	+12 dB

Table 2. Amplification of white noise

Levels	Amplification
1	0 dB (basic point)
2	+2 dB
3	+8 dB
4	+12 dB
5	+16 dB

ness changes in relation to heard voice loudness. First, −12 dB is the state in which voice feed-back is the smallest, and is close to the level of an ordinary conversation. However, as explained in Sect. 3.2, speaking voice loudness increases when heard voice loudness decreases, and speaking voice loudness decreases when heard voice loudness increases. To prove that speaking voice becomes quieter, we first give heard voice loudness level 3 when using our device. The system switches to amplification level 2 when the user wants to increase speaking voice loudness in a loud environment by decreasing heard voice loudness. If the user wants to speak even more loudly, the amplification level switches to 1. The control model of an amplification voice loudness is shown in Fig. 2. First, the user is given the heard voice loudness for the user's voice loudness to reach the target voice loudness. An amplification voice loudness is equivalent to a proportional control(P). Moreover, an integral control(D) is to perform voice loudness control that does not exceed the target voice loudness. Finally, a differential control(I) is to perform voice volume control so as to eliminate the difference from the target voice loudness. Next, amplification switches to level 4 when the user wants to decrease speaking voice loudness in a quiet environment. If the user wants to speak even more quietly, the amplification level switches to 5. The control model of an attenuation voice loudness is shown in Fig. 3. A proportional control(P) with relation to an attenuation voice loudness is shows the opposite effect to an amplification voice loudness.

Also, we implemented an additional function that plays white noise to make speech louder when users want to increase voice loudness by themselves. This function sends a signal from the microcomputer and increases white noise when a switch is pressed. At this time, voice loudness feed-back is not output. We have established five levels of white noise amplification, and the level increases each time the switch is pressed. The amplification levels are shown in the Table 2 below. The control model is as same as Fig. 1 and the heard voice loudness takes the place of white noise. When the user is using this functions but does not speak, white noise is not output, so as not to impede the speech of others. We will design a wearable system as described in this paper, and conduct an evaluation experiment.

References

1. Lane, H., Tranel, B.: The Lombard sign and the role of hearing in speech. J. Speech Hear. Res. **14**, 677–709 (1971)
2. Denes, P., Pinson, E.: The Speech Chain, 2nd edn. W.H Freeman and Co., New York (1993)
3. Hodoshima, N., Arai, T., Kurisu, K.: Intelligibility of speech spoken in noise and reverberation. In: Proceedings of 20th International Congress on Acoustics, ICA 2010, pp. 3632–3635 (2010)
4. Narumi, T., Ban, Y., Kajinami, T., Tanikawa, T., Hirose, M.: Augmented perception of satiety: controlling food consumption by changing apparent size of food with augmented reality. In: Proceedings of the SIGCHI Conference on Human Factors in Computing Systems, pp. 109–118 (2012)
5. Rekimoto, J.: Traxion: a tactile interaction device with virtual force sensation. In: Proceeding of Annual ACM Symposium on User Interface Software and Technology, UIST 2013, pp. 427–432 (2013)
6. Junji, W., Ando, H., Maeda, T.: Shoe-shaped interface for inducing a walking cycle. In: Proceedings of the 2005 International Conference on Augmented Tele-existence, ICAT 2005, pp. 30–34 (2005)
7. Kurihara, K., Tsukada, K.: SpeechJammer: a system utilizing artificial speech disturbance with delayed auditory feedback. In: Proceedings of the 8th Workshop on Interactive Systems and Software, pp. 77–82 (2010)
8. Avery, P.: Introduction to PID control. http://www.machinedesign.com/sites/machinedesign.com/files/datasheets/gated/IntroToPIDControl.pdf. Accessed 19 June 2017

e2-Mask: Design and Implementation of a Mask-Type Display to Support Face-to-Face Communication

Akino Umezawa$^{(\boxtimes)}$, Yoshinari Takegawa, and Keiji Hirtata

Department of System Information Science, Future University Hakodate,
Hakodate, Hokkaido 041-8655, Japan
{p4417001,yoshi,hirata}@fun.ac.jp
http://hiratakelab.jp/

Abstract. In Face-to-Face communication, his or her face is an important part that decides the impression of a person because a person estimates the personality of the interlocutor from the features of the face of the interlocutor. Therefore, we made a hypothesis own impression and personality of giving to others by changing the own face freely. Then we proposed the e2-Mask that a mask-type display that synchronizes with facial expressions and substitutes an avatar for a human face.

Keywords: Face-to-Face communication · Avatar · Cognitive psychology · Display

1 Introduction

There is a relationship between people's visual appeal and the impression of their inner personality [1]. In particular, this relationship is strong in the initial stage of interpersonal relationships [2]. The psychologist Mehrabian mentioned that first impressions are formed from 7% language information, 38% auditory information and 55% visual information [3]. Also, Secord mentioned that people estimate a person's character from the characteristics of his or her face [4]. Therefore, the better the impression of a person's face, he or she can have a positive character such as being kind and friendly to interlocutor. Also, people change the impression of the face according to the situation, such as making up makeup or shaving a beard. In conventional research, there are some systems that change face virtually. Yamamoto et al. implemented a system to enable people to relax during public speaking by substituting the audience's faces with an avatar of a smiley pumpkin [5]. However, this system aims to change the face of the audience and cannot change the user's own face when the audience sees the user's face. Then we think that if we can change the face of the user seen by an unspecified number of others, we can operate the impression and atmosphere of the user more flexibly and strongly.

© IFIP International Federation for Information Processing 2017
Published by Springer International Publishing AG 2017. All Rights Reserved
N. Munekata et al. (Eds.): ICEC 2017, LNCS 10507, pp. 88–93, 2017.
DOI: 10.1007/978-3-319-66715-7_10

Therefore, we proposed the system that a mask-type display that substitutes a person's face with an avatar. We call the proposed system the e2-Mask. The user's face is substituted with the avatar synchronously with the facial expression. Also, the e2-Mask can show the motion of the user's eyes. We think that using the e2-Mask cannot only operate the impression of the user's face but also support face-to-face communication. In a conversation with the user and an interlocutor, the impression of the using's looks can be improved by using the e2-Mask. Then interlocutor can assume that the user is positive character. Therefore, the e2-Mask will have effects that relax and increase the number of utterances. In addition, eye contact will be easier because the user talks through the avatar.

2   Related Research

In conventional research, there are some systems that change people's face virtually. Here we will introduce the three such systems. The first system is the ChameleonMask, used for telepresence [6]. The ChameleonMask shows the face of remote user on a display. In telepresence, an agent can act on behalf of a remote user by wearing the ChameleonMask. Therefore, the ChameleonMask gives a sense of presence to a conversation between a remote user and interlocutor. In contract, the e2-Mask shows the avatar on the display and is used in FTF communication. The second system is the Agencyglass, which is a system, in the form of sunglasses, that acts as a substitute for the user's eyes [7]. The Agencyglass a liquid crystal plate of the same size as the eye is placed on the lens of the sunglasses, then the motion of the user's eyes, recorded in advance, is shown on the liquid crystal display. The Agencyglass shows the prerecorded motion of the user's eyes. However, the e2-Mask shows an avatar synchronized with expressions in real time. The third system is a support system for presentations [5]. This system proposed a method of overlapping positive responses on audiences, and implemented a system which overlaps an image of a smiling pumpkin on each audience member using see-through HMD. This system is used in presentations. However, the e2-Mask is used in FTF communication such as a conversation by turns.

3   System Structure

We design and implement a mask-type display that substitutes a person's face with an avatar[1]. FTF communication involves scenarios such as a daily conversation, a meeting and an interview. As a situation in which the e2-Mask can be used, there is an interview. For example, an interviewee is nervous by the atmosphere of interview and an interviewer who look craggy. Therefore, the interviewee cannot speak own opinion and understand interviewer fs questions. We think that the interviewer uses e2-Mask to substitute the face of the interviewer with an impressive avatar for the interviewee, so that the interviewee can ease tension and make it easy to talk. The e2-Mask is assumed for use in FTF communication as mentioned above. Therefore, we set up two design policies.

---

[1] https://drive.google.com/open?id=0B5YrczXNVwFVRkVSbDVMSl9QZHM.

(1) Transmissibility: The e2-Mask usage scenario is FTF communication such as a daily conversation, a meeting or an interview. Therefore, we need to design the mask so that the user and the interlocutor can visually recognize each other's gestures, figures and expressions. Especially, facial expression is an effective means to transmit and read feelings such as joy or surprise [8]. Thus the e2-Mask changes the expression of the avatar in real time based on the user's expression, to transmit the user's feeling to the interlocutor at once. In addition, by covering the entire head like a costume, the voice of the e2-Mask user and the voice of the interlocutor are not heard. Therefore, we should consider that each other's voice is transmitted to the other.

(2) Wearability: The e2-Mask is used in various situations, as described above. In improving the wearability, we should consider how to prevent the user's daily activity, such as shaking hands, holding luggage, moving up and down stairs and walking, from being impeded when wearing the e2-Mask. Thus it is important that the user can use the e2-Mask hands-free and that the e2-Mask is small and lightweight.

We implemented the prototype of the e2-Mask based on these two design policies. Figure 1 shows the appearance of someone wearing the e2-Mask. Figure 2 shows the structure of the system. The weight of the e2-Mask is 3.9 kg. Table 1 shows the manufacturer's name, specifications and number of the devices used. The reason for using this display is that the size fits people's faces and it is light. The reason for using this web camera is that it is small and it recognize even if the distance between the lens and the face is short. The following is an explanation of the composition of the e2-Mask (Fig. 3).

(1) The facial expression output unit: The e2-Mask uses the Facerig to substitute an avatar for a human face. The Facerig is software that can reflect a person's face recognized by the web camera onto an avatar and stream facial expressions to synchronize with the avatar (Fig. 2). Also, it is possible to select the avatar according to the preference of the user and interlocutor because the Facerig has over the 55 kinds of avatar. The display shows picture of avatar that attached user's expression obtained from the facial expression recognition camera to the avatar by using the Facerig.

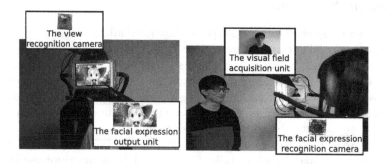

Fig. 1. Wearing the prototype of the proposed system

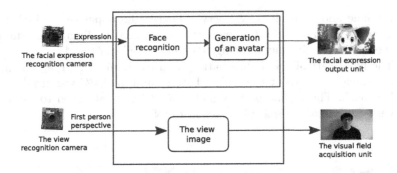

Fig. 2. System configuration

(2) The visual field acquisition unit: The e2-Mask uses the display and the web camera to secure the user's view. The display for securing visual field shows the image from the visual recognition camera.

(3) Each fixed part: Fig. 4 shows each fixed part of the e2-Mask.

  (a) The fixing of the facial expression output unit and the visual field acquisition unit: The facial expression output unit and the visual field acquisition unit were put into display cases (the upper left in Fig. 4). After that, the two displays were combined back to back. Also, the lower part of the display case of the facial expression output unit was fixed the facial expression recognition camera. The upper part of the display case of the visual field acquisition unit was fixed the visual recognition camera.

  (b) The fixing of arm: Between the facial expression output unit and the visual acquisition unit is fixed an acrylic board with a hole of a size through which the arm can pass. We fixed to the arm, the facial expression output unit and the visual acquisition unit by passing the arm through

Table 1. Information on the devices used in the prototype of the proposed system

Device	Manufacture name	Spec	Number
Display	IGZO-LCD panel	7 in., 41 g	2
The Facial expression recognition camera	ELP-USB500WO5G-L170	170° degree megapixel fisheye lens	1
The view recognition camera	ELP-USBFHD01M-L21-J	Wide angle full HD, 2.1 miri lens	1
The mobile battery	Poweradd 23000 mAh mobile battery	Maximum output: DC 9/12/16/19/20 V, 4.5 A, USB1 5 V/2.5 A, USB2 5V1A	1
The mini PC	IntelBOXNUC6I5SYK	Number of USB port: 4 Speed of CPU: 2.8 GHz	1
The display case	SHARP 7 in. IGO-LCD Acrylic panel kit	Only for IGZO-LCD panel, panel protection	2
The fixing arm	HANGNBTS	1.3 m length	1

the hole and fixing it to the acrylic board (the upper center in Fig. 4). Then the arm and the backpack were connected by fixing the arm and the backpack with metal fittings (the upper right in Fig. 4).

(c) The fixed part of the mobile battery and the mini PC: An acrylic plate of sufficient size to fit the mobile battery and mini PC was fixed to the backpack. The mobile battery and mini PC were attached to the plate with double-sided tape (the lower in Fig. 4).

Fig. 3. Facial expression recognition

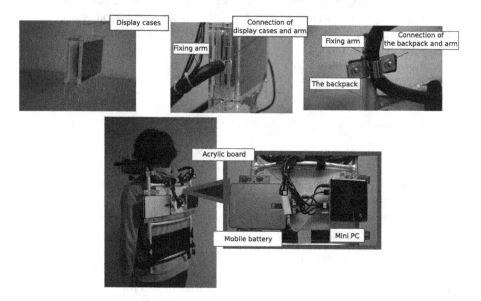

Fig. 4. Each fixed part of the system

4   Conclusions

We proposed the e2-Mask that a mask-type display to support FTF communication. At this stage, we set up design policies and implemented the prototype of the e2-Mask. We are going to evaluation experiment.

References

1. Dion, K., Berscheid, E., Walster, E.: What is beautiful is good. J. Pers. Soc. Psychol. **24**, 285–290 (1972)
2. Fiske, S.T., Cox, M.G.: Person concepts: the effects of targets familiarity and descriptive @purpose on the process of describing others. J. Pers. **47**, 136–161 (1979)
3. Mehrabian, A.: Nonverbal betrayal of feeling of feeling. J. Exp. Res. Pers. **5**, 64–73 (1971)
4. Secord, P.F.: Facial features and inference processes in interpersonal perception. In: Tagiuri, R., Petrullo, L. (eds.) Person Perception and Interpersonal Behavior. Stanford University Press, Stanford (1958)
5. Yamamoto, K., Kassai, K., Kuramoto, I., Tsujino, Y.: Presenter supporting system with visual-overlapped positive response on audiences. Advances in Affective and Pleasurable Design, pp. 87–93. Springer, Florida (2016)
6. Misawa, K., Rekimoto, J.: ChameleonMask: Embodied physical and social telepresence using human surrogates. https://lab.rekimoto.org/projects/chameleonmask. Accessed 8 Apr 2018
7. Moore, C.: Mass Appeal -Hirotaka Osawa's Glasses Give a Fuck Even If You Don't (2014). https://massappeal.com/hirotaka-osawas-glasses-give-a-fuck-even-if-you-dont. Accessed 8 Apr 2018
8. Ekman, P.: Facial expressions of emotion; new findings, new questions. Am. Psychol. Soc. **3**, 34–38 (1992)

Serious Games

Serious Games for Cognitive Assessment with Older Adults: A Preliminary Study

Helio C. Silva Neto[1]([⊠]) [iD], Joaquim Cerejeira[2] [iD],
and Licinio Roque[1] [iD]

[1] Department of Informatics Engine, University of Coimbra, Coimbra, Portugal
helio.hx@gmail.com, lir@dei.uc.pt
[2] Faculty of Medicine, University of Coimbra, Coimbra, Portugal
jcerejeira@netcabo.pt

Abstract. One of the strategies proposed by the World Health Organization to promote a healthy aging, also known as "Active Aging", where the maintenance of health and Independence in old age is identified as a good quality of physical, mental and social life, are the relevant factors concerning the preservation of the potential of achievement and development in this stage of life. Due to the common occurrence of mental disorders in older people, which are caused by many factors, the neuropsychological assessments form a part of the psychological clinical studies, where new approaches and techniques are resulting in tests that have been significantly progressing, although the principles in which these tests are based remain unchanged. In order to make those tests less tiring, and more relaxing and engaging, the Serious Games appeared, aiming to adapt the current neuropsychological tests to the context of videogaming and Digital Games, in order to achieve a better performance of the participants during the assessment and to enable a better data collection to the medical evaluation Thus, the aim of this study was to evaluate whether a serious game can be a useful instrument to be used in cognitive assessment and stimulation, and which gameplay indicators could be potential proxies of cognitive measurement.

Keywords: Serious games · e-health · Aging · Cognitive assessment

1 Introduction

Increased longevity of the population is a worldwide phenomenon with profound implications for society. The ageing process, which is only partially related with chronological age, is a heterogeneous group of health and functional states experienced by older people and determined by a range of genetic, biologic, social environmental, psychological and cultural factors [4]. Although with a significant diversity, the aging process is characterized by a gradual impairment in many body systems and an increased risk for disease. The Central Nervous System is affected by changes in neurotransmitter levels and neuronal function, brain atrophy, reduction in oxygenation and cerebral blood flow among others [1]. Some deterioration in memory, information processing speed, inductive reasoning, numerical abilities as well as impairment in motor and visuoperceptive functions are commonly found in older persons. Yet, age

© IFIP International Federation for Information Processing 2017
Published by Springer International Publishing AG 2017. All Rights Reserved
N. Munekata et al. (Eds.): ICEC 2017, LNCS 10507, pp. 97–112, 2017.
DOI: 10.1007/978-3-319-66715-7_11

associated cognitive changes are not irreversible and improvements can be achieved with adequate training [1].

Thus, cognitive stimulation is a component of "active aging", a term that was adopted by the World Health Organization (WHO) to promote a better quality of life and improved autonomy and independence of older people. There is evidence that regular engagement in moderate physical and cognitive activity can delay functional decline and the onset of chronic disorders in older subjects [19]. This not only stimulates neuronal plasticity [12] but also makes use of the "cognitive reserve" as additional brain regions are recruited during the task to compensate the reduced functional capacity [2, 5]. Optimizing cognitive function is an important objective since cognitive decline is associated with adverse outcomes in mental and physical health as well as in longevity [8, 18]. Stimulation and monitoring of cognitive performance can potentially be implemented with Serious Games, a class of games often simulating practical daily-life situations for professional training in critical conditions as well as for educational purposes targeting a diversity of users [20]. The increase utilization of Serious Games in immersive environments and the adoption of non-conventional devices has strengthened the relation with Digital Games. The possibility of generating virtual scenarios can increase motivation of users during the learning process. Previous research demonstrated that Digital Games are beneficial to old age users [10] specifically in visual perception [9], spatial orientation, reaction time [3], eyehand coordination and quality of life [11]. Green and Bavalier [14] suggested that these benefits are related to increased dopamine levels in the brain, (which decline with age,) that, when elicited by digital games, have an important role in cognitive performance following the training session.

Serious Games share some characteristics with other methods of cognitive stimulation, as defined by Franco and Orihuela [9]. These games involve a task which is continuous, systematic, stimulating and providing reinforcement, avoiding the routine and repetition. The task can also stimulate specific cognitive domains, especially attention-concentration, facilitating the stimulation of other domains. In addition, Serious Games fulfil the criteria proposed by Thompson and Foth [17] for cognitive stimulation in older persons: easy accessibility, not too expensive and user-friendly.

The aim of this study was to develop and test a serious game (Counting Sheep) to be applied in cognitive stimulation of older subjects, while providing, at the same time, a useful indicator about the cognitive performance of the player, which could be useful for healthcare professionals. Thus, our main question is: which game play indicators and metrics could be used as a good proxy for predicting (a correlate) evaluation with a rapid screening instrument, such as that obtained with Montreal Cognitive Assessment (MoCA)?

In the second section of this study, we will present the idea of the Serious Game and its functioning in comparison to the traditional methods of cognitive assessment. In the third section, we will present the methodology and the samples used in the research. Next we will present the results of testing this game with the sample population, together with the results of a MoCA. The analyses of the research are outlined in the fifth section. Finally, we will present the conclusions of this paper and future works.

2 Design Proposal

2.1 The Counting Sheep Game

Since a significant proportion of older subjects have mobility problems this game was developed for mobile technology (Smartphones or Tablets), to make the solution easily available everywhere. Thus, even the user with mobility problems can have access to the game on a variety of places including in hospitals, nursing homes or their own residence. Thus the choice of mobile technology was considered convenient to meet availability needs of the players [15, 16]. In this game the player will be asked to identify the number of Sheep that will appear in the Enclosure.

During the game, sheep and wolve representations are presented during short periods (Fig. 1). To identify the number of sheep, the player needs to focus on the screen and process the visual stimuli. To increase stimulation and challenge attention wolves will also be randomly generated, and the player will be asked to identify the number of these animals [7]. The operation of the game goes through the following steps: (1) When the game starts, the player will have one second to view the number of Sheep and/or Wolves in the Enclosure; (2) Sheep and/or Wolves will be moving; (3) After one second, the player will have to answer with the number of Sheep and/or Wolves in the enclosure; (4) The player will be asked randomly about the number of Wolves; (5) In case the answer about the number of Wolves is not correct the player will not be penalized; (6) If the player provides a correct answer the difficulty level of the game will rise; (7) If the player gives a wrong answer, the difficulty level of the game will be reduced and the player can only miss two more times, i.e., the player will only be entitled to three attempts.

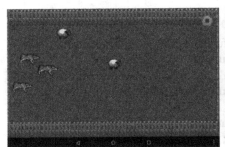

Fig. 1. The counting sheep game challenge and response interface.

Counting Sheep is culturally adapted to the target population (with a rural scenario and familiar animals) which is important to obtain reliable performances and assessments. The game variables are described in Table 1.

The game level was designed such that, when the player hits the correct number of sheep, the game gets harder, and when there is an error on the response on the number of sheep, there is a decrease in the number of sheep and wolves. Therefore, two stacks were implemented in order to store the number of sheep and wolves in each level, and

Table 1. Variables of the Game Counting Sheep.

Variable	Description
Highest level	Variable that is related to recording the maximum level reached by the player in his attempt at the game, for example: 3 (the maximum level of the player was three)
Number Score Wolves	Variable that stores the number of wolves hits the player correctly made
Number Errors Sheep	Stores the total amount of errors the player committed when reporting the quantity of sheep
Time spent in the game opening	Stores the time (in seconds) that the player spent on the launcher screen by attempts.
Time spent in the game tutorial	Time in seconds spent in the tutorial screen

both randomly draw a value between zero and three to add to the existing number of sheep and wolves. The same happens when the player misses the quantity of sheep, although the random draw will instead reduce the number of wolves and sheep. The total stack of wolves and sheep is limited to a minimum of one and a maximum of fifteen.

By means of experimental analysis, we wanted to compare the performance of the players in the game with the results obtained in the MoCA and thus, validate if the game could serve as a rapid cognitive stimulation and evaluation instrument. With this purpose, we wanted to collect gameplay data that could help us identify possible game performance variables that could serve as proxy for the MoCA evaluations.

2.2 The Montreal Cognitive Assessment (MoCA)

This is a brief screening test for cognitive function which can discriminate between normal and cognitive impairment in older adults [9]. This test has a one-page protocol and takes 10 to 20 min to apply. It doesn't have adaptations for education level, sensorial impairment and it lacks a ludic component. It is not particularly sensitive to assess some cognitive domains.

Executive functions are assessed by the part B of Trail Making Test (the subject has to link letters and numbers in alternate order); Phonemic Verbal Fluency (also included in Language); Verbal Abstraction (also included in Abstraction). Visuo-spatial assessment consists in the Clock Drawing Test (circle, numbers and hands) and copying a cube. "Attention, Concentration and Working Memory" are assessed with digit span test in direct and reverse orders. A Sustained Attention task (target detection) consists in identifying the letter "A" during the pronunciation of a series of letters. Finally, in the Serial Sevens subtractions the subject has to consecutively sub-tract 7 starting from 100. Language tasks consist in naming 3 animals, repetition of 2 sentences with complex syntax, and phonemic verbal fluency in which the subject is asked to generate as many words starting with "p" as possible (excluding proper names). For verbal abstraction the subject must think and verbalize the similarity between two objects (e.g. banana and orange being fruits). Differed memory recall is tested 5 min after retention of 5 words (short term memory). The subject has two trials to recall the words after completing other tasks (attention, language and abstraction). The Orientation domain is assessed questioning the subject about the time (e.g. date, month) and location. Each task has a score as follows: Executive Function/Visio-spatial (5 points); Naming (3 points); Attention (6 points); Abstraction (2 points); Memory (5 points) and Orientation (6 points).

The sum of each individual score provides a total score (max. 30 points) which can be compared with standardized values according to age and educational level.

2.3   Relation Between MoCA Domains and Counting Sheep

Table 2 presents the expected overlap of cognitive competences, in a comparison between the cognitive domains assessed by MoCA, and the demands of the Counting Sheep game, from the perspective of a trained Psychiatrist. The level of overlap is classified as strong (+++), moderate (++), weak (+) and none (−).

Table 2. Expected relation between MoCA evaluations and Counting Sheep overall test.

	Counting Sheep
Executive Function	+
Visuo-spacial function	++
Attention, Concentration and Working Memory	+++
Abstraction	−
Memory	+++
Language	+
Orientation	++

From Table 2 we would expect, as our initial conjecture, to find an empirical relation between the performance within the current Counting Sheep game and a cognitive assessment, especially relevant along the visuospatial, attention-concentration, and memory functions.

3   Methodology

Group 1 was composed with subjects with high cognitive performance attending a cultural Academy (Academia de Convívio e Cultura da Casa Cor de Rosa) and a senior University (Universidade Sénior Nova Acrópole). Group 2 consisted in subjects with cognitive impairment recruited in the Old Age Psychiatric Unit of Centro Hospital Universitário de Coimbra. All subjects with age ≥ 50 years were eligible to enter the study. The final sample consisted of 55 subjects in Group 1 and 51 subjects in Group 2 (Table 3).

Table 3. Group 1 and Group 2.

	Group 1 (Gr.1)	Group 2 (Gr.2)	p-value
Age	64.8 ± 9.2 [50–85]	76.5 ± 7.6 [53–89]	<0.001
Gender (fem. %)	80%	74.1%	<0.001
Education level (%)	None (0.0%)	None (24.07%)	<0.001
	1–12 years (45.46%)	1–12 years (70.37%)	
	Specialization /University (54.54%)	Specialization /University (5.55%)	
Occupation (%)	Active worker (29.09%)	Active worker (0.0%)	<0.001
	Retired (67.27%)	Retired (77.78%)	
	Household work (3.64%)	Household work (22.22%)	

After explaining the purpose and details of the study to each participant, all participants gave consent and agree to participate in the study; the research was conducted with the following steps: (1) Baseline cognitive assessment (MoCA); (2) Demonstration of the game (rules and how to play); (3) Game play during 10 min; and (4) Administering post-test questionnaire.

4 Results

4.1 Cognitive Assessment and Game Performance

This section aims to analyze the results found in groups in both the MoCA test in the Counting Sheep game. By applying the nonparametric Mann-Whitney test to the MoCA results belonging to samples "Group 1 and 2" (Table 4), we can conclude that the samples showed different results in the variables (Executive Function, Naming, Attention, Language, Abstraction, Memory, Orientation and Total Score). The reason for the choice of two distinct groups was to analyze the behavior and performance of the game as a mechanism of stimulation and evaluation in aged people who receive hospital follow-up and in aged people that, in principle, did not need hospital follow-up, that is, they were two possibly disjoint samples or population regions from which we would expect clearly diverse results.

The sample "Group 1" (Table 5) achieved higher levels in comparison with "Group 2" (Table 5), since the average number of levels completed by "Group 1" was 11.67, while "Group 2" completion average was of 5.61. It is known that the maximum amount of errors allowed in the indication of number of sheep is three, but if the player hits the right quantity of wolves he recovers a lost attempt, so sample "Group 1" committed an average of 6.69 errors in reporting the number of sheep, while "Group 2" made an average number of 4.65 errors.

Table 4. MoCA evaluation results with Group 1 and Group 2.

	Group 1 (Gr.1)	Group 2 (Gr.2)	p-value
Executive Function	3.95 ± 1.32 [1–5]	1.87 ± 1.31 [0–5]	<0.001
Naming	2.75 ± 0.51 [1–3]	1.65 ± 0.97 [0–3]	<0.001
Attention	5.11 ± 1.10 [2–6]	2.37 ± 1.60 [0–6]	<0.001
Language	2.07 ± 0.95 [0–3]	0.85 ± 0.97 [0–3]	<0.001
Abstraction	1.96 ± 0.18 [1, 2]	1.15 ± 0.85 [0–2]	<0.001
Memory	2.33 ± 1.29 [0–5]	0.94 ± 1.48 [0–5]	<0.001
Orientation	5.84 ± 0.50 [3–6]	4.69 ± 1.52 [1–6]	<0.001
Total Score	24.3 ± 3.39 [14–29]	13.5 ± 6.18 [4–29]	<0.001

Table 5. Performance variables in Game selected from 127 logged items, based on the correlations identified - Groups 1 and 2.

	N	Gr.1	N	Gr.2	p-value
Maximum Level (ML)	55	11.7 ± 4.90 [2–29]	51	5.61 ± 4.10 [0–19]	<0.001
Number Score Wolves (NSW)	55	11.67 ± 4.95 [2–29]	51	5.61 ± 4.14 [0–19]	<0.001
Number Errors Sheep (NES)	55	6.69 ± 2.97 [3–18]	51	4.65 ± 1.84 [3–12]	<0.001
Time spent in the game opening (TGO)	55	8.29 ± 7.41 [2–49]	51	8.35 ± 9.10 [2–62]	.740
Time spent in the game tutorial (TGT)	55	2.20 ± 0.83 [1–3]	51	1.92 ± 0.85 [1–3]	.090

By applying the nonparametric Mann-Whitney test to the game results belonging to samples "Group 1" and "Group 2" (Table 5), we can conclude that different results were achieved in the variables "Maximum Level", "Number Scores Wolves" and "Number Errors Sheep". Variables "Time spent in the game opening" and "Time spent in the game tutorial" showed similar results in both samples. This is relevant to identify which performance variables could distinguish between the groups' performance and be possible candidates for approximating the MoCA based evaluations.

We concluded that, by the results achieved in MoCA, there is a higher incidence of people with cognitive impairment in sample "Group 2", compared to sample "Group 1". "Group 1" presented a more skillful behavior in the game in regards to the behavior shown by group "Group 2". Finally, "Group 1" is characterized as a better qualified sample in what regards the cognitive context, which is shown by its participants achieving a higher score in both the game and MoCA compared with those of the sample of "Group 2".

4.2   Correlations Between Game and MoCA

This section is intended to explain the choice of the correlation method used and verify if there was a correlation between the MoCA assessment and the performance in the game. To do so, the correlation method adopted was Spearman's ®, because of its characterization as a nonparametric correlation measure [17]. Once r, the sample correlation coefficient, is calculated, it is necessary to determine whether there is sufficient evidence to decide whether the population correlation coefficient ρ (significance) is conclusive in a designated level of significance α [14].

Present below are the results of the correlations between the MoCA and the Counting Sheep game, used in both samples. By the performance of players of "Group 1" and "Group 2" with the MoCA (Table 6), we get (C: correlation; S: significance and N: sample):

Table 6. Correlation MoCA evaluations and game performance variables for Group 1 and 2 (showing only meaningful variables out of 127 logged and calculated game play metrics).

		Executive Function		Naming		Attention		Language		Abstraction		Memory		Orientation		Total Score	
		Gr.1	Gr.2	Gr.1	Gr.2	Gr.1	Gr.2	Gr.1	Gr.2	Gr.1	Gr.2	Gr.1	Gr.2	Gr.1	Gr.2	Gr.1	Gr.2
ML	C	.085	.581	.258	.491	.380	.700	.329	.346	-.025	.091	.150	.229	-.063	.478	.300	.633
	S	.535	.000	.058	.000	.004	.000	.014	.013	.859	.527	.275	.106	.650	.000	.026	.000
	N	55	51	55	51	55	51	55	51	55	51	55	51	55	51	55	51
NSW	C	.085	.581	.258	.491	.380	.700	.329	.346	-.025	.091	.150	.229	-.063	.478	.300	.633
	S	.535	.000	.058	.000	.004	.000	.014	.013	.859	.527	.275	.106	.650	.000	.026	.000
	N	55	51	55	51	55	51	55	51	55	51	55	51	55	51	55	51
NES	C	.138	.418	.008	.326	-.064	.410	.140	.193	-.084	.083	.041	.101	-.141	.265	.051	.410
	S	.316	.002	.952	.020	.644	.003	.308	.175	.542	.562	.766	.481	.303	.061	.713	.003
	N	55	51	55	51	55	51	55	51	55	51	55	51	55	51	55	51
TGO	C	.185	.044	-.005	.074	.195	-.010	-.257	.020	-.089	-.268	-.103	-.052	-.127	-.073	-.027	-.059
	S	.177	.760	.969	.608	.153	.942	.058	.892	.517	.057	.454	.719	.356	.611	.844	.681
	N	55	51	55	51	55	51	55	51	55	51	55	51	55	51	55	51
TGT	C	-.218	.346	-.011	.157	-.103	.323	.007	.455	.036	-.235	-.176	.149	.147	.239	-.143	.295
	S	.110	.013	.937	.270	.453	.021	.958	.001	.793	.097	.198	.297	.284	.092	.299	.035
	N	55	51	55	51	55	51	55	51	55	51	55	51	55	51	55	51

The performance of the players of "Group 1" and "Group 2" with the variables "Education" (the values adopted were the following: 0 – No formal education, 1 – Until 12th year and 5 – Technical Expertise/Higher Education), "Age" and "Occupation" (the values adopted were the following: 1 – Active Worker, 2 – Retired and 3 – Domestic Worker) (Table 7) showed that (C: correlation; S: significance and N: sample):

Table 7. Correlation Group 1 (N = 55) and Group 2 (N = 51) with selected game play indicators.

		Education		Age		Occupation	
		Gr.1	Gr.2	Gr.1	Gr.2	Gr.1	Gr.2
ML	C	.099	**.459**	−**.383**	−**.429**	.131	−.062
	S	.470	**.001**	**.004**	**.002**	.342	.667
	N	55	51	55	51	55	51
NSW	C	.099	**.459**	−**.383**	−**.429**	.131	−.062
	S	.470	**.001**	**.004**	**.002**	.342	.667
	N	55	51	55	51	55	51
NES	C	.044	**.422**	−.266	−**.386**	.088	−.049
	S	.749	**.002**	.050	**.005**	.524	.735
	N	55	51	55	51	55	51
TGO	C	−.013	−.049	.017	−.095	-.291	.230
	S	.926	.733	.899	.507	.031	.104
	N	55	51	55	51	55	51
TGT	C	−.081	**.328**	.025	−.177	.013	−.002
	S	.558	**.019**	.858	.214	.927	.991
	N	55	51	55	51	55	51

4.3   Feedback from Users

As mentioned beforehand, after participating in the experimental phase of the research, players were asked to answer a questionnaire to evaluate their views and level of satisfaction with Counting Sheep game.

In Table 8, we show the results of "Group 1" and "Group 2". It is noticeable that in both samples, players understood the game (rules and gameplay) (96.36% "Group 1" and 96.08% "Group 2"). 96.36% of "Group 1" and 94.12% of "Group 2" found the

Table 8. Reception of the Game by Groups 1 and 2.

	Group 1	Group 2	p-value
Did you understand how to play? (%)	Yes (96.36%)	Yes (96.08%)	.090
Would you play the game at home? (%)	Yes (96.36%)	Yes (94.12%)	.081
Could you see the game well? (%)	Yes (98.18%)	Yes (98.04%)	.070
Gameplay? (%)	Finger (100%)	Finger (100%)	1.000
	Pen (0%)	Pen (0%)	

game as a valid practice as a daily exercise at home. 98.18% of "Group 1" and 98.04% of "Group 2" had no difficulty in recognizing and viewing the animals and the buttons of the game (1.96% of the sample of "Group 2" had vision problems such as cataracts). Finally, both groups used the finger to perform the operations (100% "Group 1" and 100% "Group 2").

5   Discussion

For "Group 1", the "Attention" was the cognitive domain that presented the highest correlation coefficient with the maximum level that the player obtained and with the other variables of correctness or error in the quantity response of the animals. This is a game that demands more attention from the player to observe the quantity of animals exposed during the attempts and, consequently, to answer the quantity of the respective animals correctly.

The cognitive domain "Language" is activated in the context of understanding the rules and gameplay of the game. It is also possible to notice a pattern with time-related variables of the game. Players from the "Group 1" sample with high scores in the "Language" domain tend to spend less time answering questions in the game. The greatest amount of correlations occurred in the declaration of wolf numbers. Unfortunately, it was not possible to understand why the higher incidence of correlation in the response time of the wolves. We emphasize that, with the increase of the player's attempts to answer the number of the respective animals, the correlation strength increases. For the variable "Total Score", there is a correlation because players that present high performance in MoCA, that is, absence of cognitive deficit, tend to reach higher levels.

For the "Group 1" sample, the cognitive domain of "Naming" is activated to respond to the number of sheep (goal of the game). With the increase of the player's attempts to answer the number of the respective animals, the correlation strength increases. Therefore, the level of perception to name the animals might be important for the players during the attempts to answer the challenge.

The "Orientation" domain (Group 1) was correlated during the response time (not shown in the table) more often present in the response time for the number of wolfs. Unfortunately, it was not possible to know why the higher incidence of correlations in the response time of the wolves. With the increase of the player's attempts to answer the number of the respective animals, the correlation strength increased. For the players in "Group 2", "Attention" was correlated to the activity of responding to the number of sheep (goal of the game) and the time used to respond to the animals, thus, this cognitive domain was important for response performance and, the higher the player's attention scoring in the MoCA, the less time the player took to respond. We emphasize that, with the increase in the player's attempts to answer the number of the respective animals, the correlation coefficient increases.

In "Group 2", the cognitive domain "Naming" exhibited a similar behavior to that of "Executive Function", that is, the level of perception for naming animals seems important for players during answering attempts. Throughout the results, across game levels, we noticed that the correlation coefficients between these cognitive domains and the answering variable remain constant.

Thus, for the "Group 2" sample, some domains are important for a player's best performance, such as "Language" (understanding the rules and gameplay of the game), "Naming" (perceiving which is the animal, processing the question and answering, e.g. "three wolves" and "two sheep"), "Orientation" (spatial orientation of how many animals are exposed), "Executive Function" (in answering the questions of the quantity of each animal). The "Attention" is the cognitive domain that presented the highest correlation coefficient with the Maximum Level that the player obtained. Therefore, this is a game that demands a greater attention from the player to observe the amount of the animals exposed in the attempts. For the variable "Total Score", there is a correlation because players who perform high at MoCA. That is, lack of cognitive deficit, tend to reach higher levels and make more attempts to inform the number of the respective animals.

The "Education" of the players of both samples presented a similar behavior in the correlation coefficient. "Group 1", is a sample composed of people with schooling and, in "Group 2" there were some members who did not have schooling. So, results of "Group 1", presented a correlation, also common in the results of "Group 2". The players who presented better performances had a higher level of schooling. It can be concluded that, for the Game, a minimum is required in the concept of schooling (counting animals and number recognition).

The age of the players in both samples allowed to conclude that players with less age presented the greater amount of correct answers to inform the number of wolves, compatible with a generally healthier situation. This makes it possible for the younger group to miss the number of sheep more often and thus not reaching the amount of errors that the game allows. As expected, another characteristic factor for player profile is that the higher the age, the lower the probability of reaching higher levels (inversely proportional correlation). These are important aspects relevant for the calibration of the game as a screening instrument for target groups.

Finally, the Occupation of the players did not present significant correlations, that is, the occupation of the players was not an important factor for the performance in the Game, or the characterization of occupation was not adequate for this purpose. Through results in Table 9 it was possible to notice that the game environment did not present major difficulties in the context of usability for the target population. There was encouragement of the players in particular of those in "Group 2", to play the game.

Table 9. Evaluation of the players in the sample Group 1.

Age	Education level			
	None	1–12 years	Special/University	All education level
50–65	none	13.00 ± 3.84	13.61 ± 5.63	13.37 ± 4.92
N	0	12	18	30
> 65	none	9.77 ± 5.48	9.50 ± 2.50	9.64 ± 4.23
N	0	13	12	25
All Ages	none	11.32 ± 4.95	11.97 ± 5.01	11.67 ± 4.95
N	0	25	30	55

Table 10. Evaluation of the players of the sample Group 2.

Age	Education level			
	None	1–12 years	Special/University	All education level
50–65	none	8,67 ± 4,04	6.00 ± 0	8.00 ± 3.56
N	0	3	1	4
> 65	2.62 ± 1.85	6.59 ± 4.41	4.50 ± 2.12	5.40 ± 4.16
N	13	32	2	47
All Ages	2.62 ± 1.85	6.77 ± 4.36	5.00 ± 1.73	5.61 ± 4.14
N	13	35	3	51

As a tool to help health professionals interpret players' results, normative tables of player performance have been constructed (Tables 9 and 10). In the context of cognitive assessment, Table 9 shows the performance "Group 1" in the game and makes it possible to evaluate the performance of the sample players against their population profile. The table was assembled with "Highest Level", the most efficient variable in the evaluation criterion of player performance and the other variables chosen are profiles such as "Age" (important variable to indicate cognitive decline) and "Education level" of the player (Second important variable to indicate cognitive decline) [6].

Similar to the table above presented in the context of cognitive assessment, Table 10 exposes the "Group 2" profile in the game.

The results of the investigation also allowed us to conclude that the game presents a challenge better calibrated to screen the performance of "Group 2" than for "Group 1". This is because "Group 2" contains players with cognitive limitations (some with cognitive pathology), the opposite occurs in "Group 1" (people without diagnosed

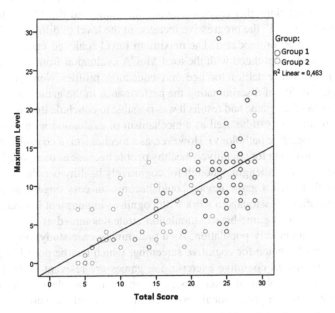

Fig. 2. Total Score (MoCA) and Maximum Level (Game) by Group 1 and 2.

cognitive pathologies or significant deficits). This calibration is confirmed by the clear number of correlations between the MoCA and several game play indicators, where "Group 2" presented a significant amount of correlations compared to "Group 1".

When we put together both sample groups, still not a representative random sample, we gain a perspective that we can notice a promising trend line correlating performance in the MoCA screening test with game performance (Max Level achieved), thus justifying the need and usefulness of further investment in testing this approach (Fig. 2).

6   Conclusions

Our research had the goal of preparing a preliminary case study on the development of a serious game, which aims to cognitively stimulate its users and allow further study a possible relation between gameplay metrics and the assessment of cognitive abilities with the MoCA instrument. The prototype was tested with two groups that met the sample inclusion criteria of the senior target population. In order to contribute to the development of applications that could evaluate the cognitive performance of the senior public against a model for the target population profile, we carried out a preliminary study, with the aim to find game play indicator variables that could present a relationship between the cognitive stimulation and the cognitive assessment of the player. The research used a cognitive screening mechanism validated in the local population (MoCA), in order to enable a comparison with performance gameplay metrics recorded by the game, seeking a possible correlation with the cognitive domains presumably being activated.

The particular game design has shown to be better adjusted (rules, gameplay and difficulty) to the sample of "Group 2" (a clinical sample). This fact can be confirmed by the number of correlations that existed between the game and the MoCA for sample "Group 2". For "Group 1" the progressive increase in the level of difficulty of the game seems to have been accommodated. The maximum Level achieved variable showed to be a promising proxy correlated with the total MoCA evaluation from a screening test. Normalized performance tables for age and education profiles were presented that showed the plausibility of discriminating the performance in the game for each profile.

In the analysis of the game and results it was possible to conclude that the game in the current conceptual form can be used as a mechanism of evaluation with elderly public (with or without cognitive pathology). However, as a mechanism of cognitive exercise, It can be quite demotivating for cognitively healthy people because as mentioned, the game does not appear to be challenging enough for cognitively healthy people.

We found that such a game device could become an easy engagement tool that would allow health professionals to work with cognitive impairment indicators of their patients, and implement game-based stimulation strategies aimed at ensuring a better quality of life to the elderly population. As a preliminary case study, this exemplifies the development of a game for cognitive screening, which can be used independently by players repeatedly as cognitive exercise, i.e. games are relevant tools that can be used as a stimulus supplement (exercises), assessment of the players and may offer useful information to the professionals involved in the care of the patients.

In order to improve the prototype, and therefore obtain data to better address the object of study, other studies must be carried out, such as: (1) Create a variable to store the amount of each animal, even in case of hits or errors. This will benefit the analysis of the results reached by each player. (2) In order to avoid the infinite *"loop"* of errors and/or hits of the players, a new rule will be added: When a player commits three errors in a row when reporting the amount of each animal, the game will end, even if there are attempts still available (to solve the cases of players that only remark one kind of animal). (3) Deal with lack of skill in handling the device, nervousness, or anxiety that can result of a cognitive disease or a dislike for gaming.

References

1. Albert, M.S., Killiany, R.J.: Age-related cognitive change and brain-behavior relationships. In: Birren, J.E., Schaie, K.W. (eds.) Handbook of the Psychology of Aging, 5th edn., pp. 161–185. Academic Press, San Diego (2001)
2. Barreto, J.: A reserva cognitiva e a prevenção da demência. Trabalho apresentado nas VI Jornadas de Saúde Mental do Idoso. Faculdade de Medicina da Universidade do Porto (2007)
3. Bialystok, E.: Effect of bilingualism and computer video game experience on the Simon task. Can. J. Exp. Psychol. **60**(1), 68–79 (2006)
4. Ferrari, M.A.C.: O envelhecer no Brasil. O mundo da saúde, São Paulo **23**(4), 197–203 (1999)
5. Franco-Martín, M.A., Orihuela-Villameriel, T.: A reabilitação das funções cognitivas superiores na demência. In: Firmino, H., Pinto, L.C., Leuschner, A., Barreto, J. (eds.). Psicogeriatria. Coimbra: Psiquiatria Clínica, pp. 471–487 (2006)
6. Freitas, S., Simões, M.R., Alves, L.: Montreal cognitive assessment (MoCA): normative study for the portuguese population. J. Clin. Exp. Neuropsychol. (2011)
7. Gamberini, L., et al.: Cognition, technology and games for the elderly: an introduction to ElderGames Project. PsychNology J. **4**(3), 285–308 (2006)
8. Ghisletta, P., McArdle, J.J., Lindenberger, U.: Longitudinal cognition-survival relations in old and very old age: 13-year data from the Berlin aging study. Eur. Psychol. **11**, 204–223 (2006)
9. Green, C.S., Bavelier, D.: Action-video-game experience alters the spacial resolution of vision. Psychol. Sci. **18**(1), 88–94 (2007)
10. Lager, A., Bremberg, S.: Health effects of video and computer game playing: a systematic review. Swedish National Institute of Public Health, Estocolmo (2005)
11. Leung, L., Lee, P.S.N.: Multiple determinants of life quality: the roles of Internet activities, use of new media, social support, and leisure activities. Telematics Inform. **22**, 161–180 (2005)
12. Mahncke, H.W., Bronstone, A., Merzenich, M.M.: Brain plasticity and functional losses in the aged: scientific bases for a novel intervention. Prog. Brain Res. **157**, 81–109 (2006)
13. Nasreddine, Z., Phillips, N.A., Bédirian, V., Charbonneau, S., Whitehead, V., Collin, I., Cummings, J.L., Chertkow, H.: The montreal cognitive assessment, MoCA: a brief screening tool for mild cognitive impairment. Am. Geriatr. Soc. **53**, 695–699 (2005)
14. Pontes, A.C.F., Corrente, J.E.: The use of nonparametric contrasts in one-way layouts and random block designs. J. Nonparametric Stat. **17**(3), 335–346 (2005)

15. Silva Neto, H.C., Roque, L.: Senior care clinic - modeling a cognitive assessment system. Anais do Simpósio Brasileiro de Jogos e Entretenimento Digital - SBGames (2014)
16. Silva Neto, H.C., Roque, L.: Experiências dos Videojogos aplicados ao Envelhecimento Ativo. Anais do Simpósio Brasileiro de Jogos e Entretenimento Digital - SBGames (2014)
17. Thompson, G., Foth, D.: Cognitive-training programs for older adults: what are they and can they enhance mental fitness? Educ. Gerontol. **31**(8), 603–626 (2005)
18. Vinters, H.V.: Aging and the human nervous system. In: Birren, J.E., Schaie, K.W. (eds.) Handbook of the Psychology of Aging, 5th edn., pp. 135–160. Academic Press, San Diego (CA) (2001)
19. WHO - World Health Organization. Envelhecimento ativo: uma política de saúde. Brasília (2015)
20. Zyda, M.: From Visual Simulation to Virtual Reality to Games, vol. 38(9), pp. 25–32. IEEE Computer Society Press, California, September 2005

Designing Game-Based Interventions
for Subverting Normative Attitudes

Mikel Polzer and Helmut Hlavacs[(✉)]

Entertainment Computing Research Group, Faculty of Computer Science,
University of Vienna, Vienna, Austria
m.polzer@gmx.net, helmut.hlavacs@univie.ac.at

Abstract. The present study explores persuasive and interventional strategies for designing and evaluating low-threshold browser games that adequately aim for affording prejudice-reducing social impact in everyday life scenarios. Our investigation was guided by the premise that a covert persuasion approach is suited for also reaching out to otherwise adverse attitude holders. Building on a framework for embedding change-related messages into games by their design, and in combination with rhetorical techniques and subversive strategies from queer-theoretical philosophy and social psychology, we modified an existing impactful game about *Coming Out* so as to obfuscate its change-related content, and make it more approachable for a not-queer audience. The evaluation of the modified prototype suggests the efficacy of the employed strategies for facilitating and elevating emotional engagement based on group membership effects, which is linked to a greater potential for attitude change and prejudice reduction.

Keywords: Social impact games · Prejudice reduction · Embedded persuasion · Activist games · Queer game design

1 Introduction

1.1 Background

As digital technologies are becoming increasingly advanced, available and affordable around the globe [1], digital entertainment systems are gaining popularity and prevalence among a variety of users, too. Correspondingly, the rising consumption of entertainment media has increased their "significant role as socializing agents" [2] especially that of digital games, which are superseding non-interactive media [3]. Aside from these quantitative aspects, another indicator for the social impact of games results from the unique quality of their consumption, especially in the light of unprecedented technological possibilities for social interaction, self-representation and identity (re-)construction [4]. On the one hand, character-based online gameplay scenarios are a showcase for the transference of persisting social norms into virtual environments. On the other hand,

© IFIP International Federation for Information Processing 2017
Published by Springer International Publishing AG 2017. All Rights Reserved
N. Munekata et al. (Eds.): ICEC 2017, LNCS 10507, pp. 113–124, 2017.
DOI: 10.1007/978-3-319-66715-7_12

these environments seem to enable counter-normative behavior, as seen in the phenomenon of online gender-swapping (assigning a different gender identity to ones online avatar than ones 'offline' gender) [5]. From a queer-theoretical point of view, these acts can be said to constitute a performative transgression of the conceptual boundaries that regulate and maintain one of the most fundamental social categories: in 'real life', perceived deviations from norms regarding gender and sexuality face societal repression [6], as do individuals based on categorizations by 'race' or 'ability'. Such sanctions can be directly or implicitly enacted in the form of hostile and aversive attitudes towards non-conforming individuals, frequently expressed subtly in everyday interaction [7].

1.2 Motivation

Considering the prevalence and persistence of normative attitudes, these emergent trends emphasize the social dimension of games and the responsibility for their design: games seem to bear the potential to reinforce, but also to transform social normativity and the structures of inequality resulting from it. These possibilities and challenges have motivated the development of "serious games for social change" [8], which exploit the cognitive and affective affordances of gameplay for pro-social persuasive purposes, such as prejudice reduction and prosocial attitude change. While many game-based interventional systems have been successfully deployed, research on their systematic design is still in its early stages. For one thing, many of these games were developed outside an academic context and hence without a scientific framing. On the other hand, as has been noted by G. Kaufman and M. Flanagan [9], much work relies on an explicit persuasive strategy that focuses on providing propositional information and factual content. However, as has been shown by research on social cognition and psychology, overt persuasive approaches often run the risk to fail especially in the context of prejudice reduction, where a high perception of psychological threat and the resulting activation of defense mechanisms are often encountered. Moreover, an educational appeal might impair the quality of gameplay, and consequently reduce its interventional efficacy or transformative impact. In addition, overt approaches are methodologically problematic in the context of attitude assessment and thus for the evaluation of social intervention games. For these reasons, this work focuses on the investigation of subtle design and evaluation strategies for implementing the premise that "serious games must look like casual games" [10]. Extending the *Embedded Design Model* developed by G. Kaufman, M. Flanagan and M. Seidman [11] with additional persuasive strategies on the basis of queer theory and digital gameplay affordances, we argue, is suitable for addressing subtle manifestations of internalized norms related to gender, sexuality, race and related social group concepts that manifest as daily prejudiced and stereotyped attitudes.

2 Attitude Persistence and Change

2.1 Attitudes

In basic terms, an attitude is "an evaluation of an object of thought", i.e. of the mental representations of "things, people, groups, and ideas" [12]. This evaluative mechanism plays a crucial role in regulating the dynamics within interactive systems: on the basis of an attitudes positive or negative valence, individuals will decide which entities to avoid, and which objects to approach or engage with [13]. According to dual-processing theories, attitudes are formed based on propositional and associative learning processes. Similarly, their adaptation is typically induced by the acquisition of novel information about the attitude object, e.g. due to new significant encounters with representatives of a concept, which revise the validity of previous beliefs about and/or emotions towards it.

2.2 Prejudice and Stereotype

Prejudiced and stereotypical attitudes are negative evaluations that are formed prior to actual encounters or reasoning, and instead based on societal norms about concepts referring to social groups [14]. Despite their fallacious cognitive structure and unjustified affective nature, stereotype and prejudice are particularly resistant against modification through learning. Researchers have attributed this persistence to a strong association of normative beliefs with ones central self-concept and worldviews [15]. Therefore, any transformative attempt be-comes fundamentally psychologically threatening, which further triggers a number of defensive resistance mechanisms to prevent relevant normative attitudes from being updated. In the context of designing prejudice-reducing interventional games, the consideration and circumvention of such mechanisms thus poses a core challenge.

2.3 Resistance Mechanisms

Avoidance and Selective Exposure. The principle of avoidance strategies is simple: the recipient prevents her/his/their attitudes from being updated by evading any exposure to counter-attitudinal information [16], i.e. information that would presumably force her/him/them to modify beliefs or feelings about or towards a topic, group or (other) ideological constructs. Such behavior has also been linked to aversive racism [17], a form of internalized racist prejudice which leads to the unconscious avoidance of certain social groups. Moreover, the attitude holder is mostly unaware of their prejudice, which makes it even more difficult to address. In the context of the present work, avoidant behavior could prevent potential recipients from playing a game if it is perceived to contain a counter-attitudinal message. In the case of strong prejudice, knowing that the game features prejudice-targeted social group member(s) might even be sufficiently repellent. This effect was prevented by applying the obfuscation strategy.

Reactance. The phenomenon of reactance results when an individual feels forced to preserve their freedom and independence in view of a persuasive attempt [18]. Moreover, this effect even occurs when the attitude holder actually agrees with the position or message transported in the course of the persuasion. Therefore, this effect is another instance that was considered in the present context, by refraining from any persuasive appeals when framing the game. It was therefore not framed as a game with a different interventional target.

3   Related Work

3.1   Embedded Design Model

In view of these psychological responses, G. Kaufman, M. Flanagan and M. Seidman have developed a general model for covertly embedding change-related messages into interventional games for prosocial attitude shifts. This framework offers broad guidelines that are applicable to a variety of different game genres, including digital, character-based interactive fiction. The model specifies three guidelines, for which the authors provide example techniques regarding their implementation.

Intermixing. This technique consists in balancing 'on-message' and 'off-message' content, whereas the developers suggest that an unbalanced ratio with *less* on-message content leads to *more* transformative impact than a reversed ratio of overloaded message-content.

Obfuscating. The obfuscation strategy consists in diverting the players attention away from the games persuasive intention, by employing genre, framing language or similar devices for distraction. One variant of this technique consists in the gradual introduction of message-related content: in non-interactive fiction, for example, the delayed revelation of a characters outgroup membership has been linked to higher effects of *experience-taking*, which enable the reduction of outgroup bias.

Distancing. This principle seeks to provide a sufficient degree of safety so as to allow for a transgression of normative boundaries despite their association with ones self-concept. Consequently, this is done by increasing the "psychological gap" be-tween in-game experience and 'real-life', thereby allowing for the players *narrative transportation* and emotional engagement [19]. This can be achieved by employing fiction and metaphor, and the suggestion of hypotheticality.

These techniques have been successfully tested and applied to non-digital multi-player games of party-game genres by the developers. Despite suggestions, the model itself does not contain any detailed specifications regarding the mes-sage-unrelated content (for the intermixing strategy), genre choices (for the obfuscating strategy), or the narratological introduction of a characters outgroup membership (for the distancing strategy). These were added on the basis of further persuasive strategies and in consideration of the defense effects that normative attitudes are accompanied by.

3.2 Performativity and Embodied Persuasion

Procedural Rhetoric. The notion of procedural rhetoric, as suggested by I. Bogost [20], refers to the "practice of persuading through processes", especially those of computational nature. As an argumentative practice, it is helpful for both the designer and the player, as suggested by the author. Games, by virtue of their "procedurality" and interactivity, afford the employment of arguments in a procedural way, e.g. the embodiment of ideologies and normativity, and the revelation of the dynamics they result in. As such, games can function as an analogy, or even as a parody.

Parody as Subversive Strategy. The argumentative power and function of embodied imitation has also been analyzed in the context of societal norms and the possibility their transformation. As expressed by philosopher J. Butler: "*In imitating gender, drag implicitly reveals the imitative structure of gender itself-as well as its contingency.*" [21]. In this sense, gender swapping, as facilitated in digital games, might work to implicitly subvert gender norms and related ideologies.

3.3 Psychotherapy-Informed Prejudice Reduction

As noted by M. Birtel and R. Crisp [22], the cognitive and affective biases that characterize stereotype and prejudice show phenomenological similarities to symptoms of pathological anxiety, e.g. patterns of distorted thinking and irrational fear. This has motivated the employment of techniques adopted from cognitive-behavioral therapy for the purpose of prejudice-reduction. One of the adopted strategies builds on the principle of exposure therapy, in which a patient is confronted with an instance of the feared concept in order to reduce anxiety and distress triggered by it. [23] This intervention requires a sufficiently safe and unthreatening environment or framing, which can be achieved by mentally simulating an encounter.

Imagined Intergroup Contact. As has been theorized by G.W. Allport [24], meaningful intergroup contact can effectively reduce prejudiced attitudes towards social groups. In order to evade potentially adverse effects related to persuasive pressure, the technique of imagined intergroup contact [25] relies on the safe affordances and therapeutic effects of mental simulation for prejudice reduction. The successful deployment of this interventional strategy suggests a promising efficacy when combined with the engaging, interactive and yet fictional, 'casual' appeal of gameplay.

4   Design and Implementation

Based on these assumptions, the *Embedded Design Model* was extended and applied for the modification of an existing social impact game, which was targeted for a queer or queer-friendly audience and did therefore not rely on a covert strategy, with the goal to conceal its interventional attempt while preserving its prosocial message.

4.1   Original Game

The open-source browser game *Coming Out Simulator* developed by game designer N. Case [26] is a semi-autobiographic dialogue-based fiction about a queer game developer's coming out experience. The protagonist Nick appears as non-player character in the first scene, and becomes playable as the user jumps into Nicks simulator in order to interactively experience the story from first-person perspective. The player interacts with the system by making choices among several answers and action options. The story has different endings, and the user is given the freedom to make the crucial choice whether to come out to the parents as gay/bisexual or stay 'closeted'. In the end, the user returns, talking to the NPC-version of Nick again (see Fig. 1).

Game Principles and Mechanics. Since the game is framed as a story, it does not specify a goal or score metrics there are no 'right' or 'wrong' answers. This is a crucial part of the games em-bodied rhetoric: the system does not correct the player. While this is a beneficial aspect e.g. with regard to the aforementioned backfiring effect, it also poses a difficulty when re-framing the game in the sense of the *Obfuscation* strategy defined by the *Embedded Design Model*.

Narratological Design and Structure. The games conceptualization as 'story within a story' interestingly embodies a sort of pathway for narrative transportation: by introducing another layer of hypotheticality, the game suggests a further step away from 'real-life', in the sense of the *Distancing* strategy described in the *Embedded Design Model*. In addition, the shift of narrative perspective along with the concept of 'simulation' encourages experience-taking. Furthermore, the games slogan 'a half-true story about half-truths' can be viewed as an ironic handling of the contradiction between telling a story and playing a game which changes the story, as faced in the con-text of interactive fiction writing. At the same time, it can be interpreted as a critical commentary on essentialist constructions of heteronormative ideologies and the fallacies of stereotype and prejudice.

Graphical Design and Interface. The graphical interface, which reminds of text messaging applications, supports the games focus on dialogue and communication. The cartoonish style further-more facilitates an innocent and casual appeal, which works in the sense of *Distancing* again.

4.2   Modification

The modification attempted to retain the beneficial aspects the original game design affords, on the premise that these didn't reveal the message beforehand. The game mechanics and graphical interface were therefore kept. The narratological structure was employed as well, with one exception: this game version does not feature multiple endings, but 'forces' the user to come out to the parents. This design choice was made with regard to the evaluation, for the sake of comparability. On the other hand, it embodies the lack of power to escape or correct unjustified prejudice, which is also the case for some choices in the original game and makes up an important part of the procedural rhetoric of the game. The greatest change was made to the content and framing of the story, both of which in the case of the original game intentionally reveal its purpose before-hand. In order to refrain from giving it a moralizing tone, the game was not re-designed as a puzzle or learning game which would've included an instance for the correction of 'wrong' answers or choices made by the player. Also, the presence of a controlling and evaluating dimension might have impacted the players ability for experience-taking and narrative transportation. For these reasons, the game was framed as a message-driven interactive story; however, not in an activist and topic-related, but in a 'personal' and thus less threatening sense.

Target Audience. The modified version is designed for a non-queer (heterosexual) audience which might have moderately explicit or implicit prejudiced attitudes towards queer (not heterosexual) individuals or topics. However, the persuasive effects are expected to be highest in players who share salient characteristics with the protagonist that are of significance with regard to the conflicts. In this version of the game, those features are the characters educational background and, as in the original game, the characters sexual orientation. In this work, we were most interested in players who shared the first group membership with the character, but not the second.

Synopsis. The interactive fiction, titled *The Imitation Game*, is framed as a metaphorical story about a difficult day in the life of a computer-science student, on which he faces two situations of stereotype-based rejection. The first conflict occurs at a job interview, based on the interviewers stereotypical belief that computer geeks are the opposite of 'creative'. The conflict is followed by the characters coming out as gay to the parents, for which he is rejected following the same logic of prejudice. Before returning, the player makes one last positive encounter with an NPC. His little brother asks him for help with his computer-science homework.

Narratological Structure. The structure of the game was retained: the player has an encounter with the NPC, who then becomes playable, however with a different motivation: instead of offering the player to experience a simulation, the NPC asks the player to help them (re-)write their story in real-time. The player now has the chance (the task) to create a 'true' story about the NPC, even if it is not the story others might like to hear.

Persuasive Effects. The game relies on appeals to empathy, sympathy and identification effects due to *ingroup bias*, which hypothetically also affect *experience-taking* and *narrative transportation* in players who identify with the protagonists initially revealed group membership (computer science students, game designers, geeks, gamers). The first conflict, in which the antagonistic NPC invokes negative stereotypes towards this group, should generate more emotional engagement in players who identify with this group. If this effect is strong enough, it should maintain those players engagement also in the following scene and conflict, where the characters outgroup membership (gay, bisexual, queer) is revealed. In this sense, the order of the events serves in the sense of an *affective* strategy of persuasion, and polarizes the players attitudes. Moreover, this procedural aspect also embodies a *propositional* argument: the first conflict has the same fallacious structure as the second one. Hence, it serves as an *analogy* that reveals the flaws of prejudiced logic. This forces a player to reach the same conclusions in the second conflict as in the first conflict, also on a level of affect. If a player felt a sense of injustice and anger in the first case, these implicit evaluations should also hold for the second case. The positive encounter in the last scene is meant to reinvoke and appeal to the first group membership (ingroup bias) again, and to *procedurally* implicate and encourage a similar positive and affirmative reaction towards members from the second group. As the player returns, and the PC becomes an NPC again, the player both had an *imaginary encounter with* and also *took the perspective of* an out-group member (regarding the second group concept) (see Fig. 2).

5   Evaluation

We implemented a semi-quantitative study for in-game and post-game subjective assessment of gameplay experience. Participants were asked to test-play the prototype game and report their experiences qualitatively (providing answers to open-ended questions) as well as quantitatively (indicating their level of agreement with subjective statements on a 7-point Likert scale). These reports were obtained in written form, for which a questionnaire was used.

5.1   Experimental Setup

Participants. The study was conducted with 10 participants, 8 of them male, all of which were between 23 and 28 year-old university students. Each participant completed the test individually and voluntarily after written consent was obtained. The study was conducted in a controlled environment, using the same infrastructure and prototype version of the game. In order to facilitate mental involvement, participants were made aware that the study did not depend on psychometric measures or other objective performance (e.g. reaction time,

Fig. 1. Screenshot of the original game's coming out scene.

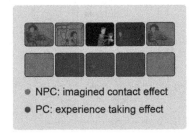

- NPC: imagined contact effect
- PC: experience taking effect

Fig. 2. Storyboard and effects related to narrative perspective.

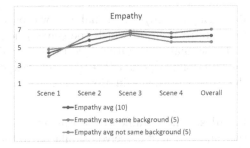

Fig. 3. Levels of empathy reported in and post gameplay.

reading speed or similar), but relied on experiential data subjectively reported by them only. Each run-through had a duration of about 30–40 min (20–25 min for gameplay and 10–15 min for completing the questionnaire). The questionnaire used for obtaining subjective data consisted of two parts: one for in-game evaluation, and one for post-game evaluation as well as obtaining demographic data.

Part I – In-game. Part one consisted of a series of three scales ranging from 1 (low) to 7 (high), indicating the level of *empathy*, *sympathy*, and of *identification*, respectively, that the participant had felt towards the main character Nick during gameplay. This series was answered immediately at the end of each scene (except for the last scene, where the second part of the questionnaire was provided).

Part II – Post-game. The same scales were used once again after gameplay, to indicate the overall levels of felt empathy, sympathy and identification, referring to the gameplay experience in general. Additionally, participants were asked to report their levels of narrative transportation using the 6-item narrative transportation scale, short form [27]. In order to assess whether the game was perceived as an educational, interventional or persuasive game, participants were asked to describe what the game was about in an open-ended question.

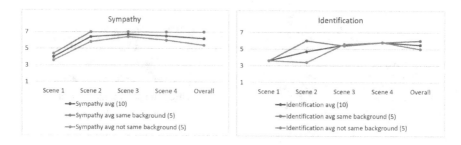

Fig. 4. Levels of sympathy and identification reported in and post gameplay.

Demographic and/or personal data was partly obtained indirectly, by asking participants to indicate which (perceived) demographic characteristics they share with the character. Other questions regarded interaction possibilities, technical/functional aspects of the game-play experience, as well as feedback regarding the game and the evaluation itself.

Results. The obtained data was analyzed by grouping participants based on their indication of perceived similarity to the character with regards to five characteristics: educational/professional background/study field, age, gender, sexual orientation/sexuality, and interest in gaming/computer games. We were especially interested in the impact a perceived shared educational/professional background and/or interest in computer games has on the levels of empathy, sympathy and identification felt towards the character during each scene (scene 1–scene 4) and overall. Narrative transportation levels on average were higher for same-background individuals as compared to not-same background individuals. Results are seen in Figs. 3 and 4.

6   Discussion

The experimental results suggest the occurrence of ingroup bias effects with correspondingly elevated levels of sympathy, empathy and identification report-ed during the introductory scene and first conflict by members who share the group membership (computer-related background) that was made salient there. Empathy and sympathy levels continue to be elevated in the second conflict even if players didn't share the group membership (queer sexual orientation) that was made salient at this point of the interactive fiction. More importantly, the levels for all three items raised after gameplay, as reflected in the overall evaluation of the game. An interesting observation was made regarding the identification of and with the characters study field (background): two participants ascribed a different background to the main character than the rest, namely the one they each identified with. This suggests a potential inclination and flexibility in the perception of characteristics that could be exploited when designing games for a large audience. Character design could aim at ambiguity in order to be appealing for different, maybe even contradictory reasons. None of the participants answers regarding the game itself indicated that they perceived the game as an educational, interventional or social change game, while all participants were aware of the characters sexual orientation, and experienced the conflict related to it with high levels of empathy and sympathy towards the character during their coming out. This suggests the successful implementation of an embedded design and evaluation strategy.

7   Conclusion

This exploratory study demonstrates a possible application of the general guidelines offered by the *Embedded Design Model*, combined with prejudice-reduction techniques, to the design of small-scale character-based games. The findings are rather to be regarded as a stepping stone for further research and iteration - both on the level of design and implementation. Probably the greatest shortcoming the current design strategy poses, lies in the conditionality of its efficacy, which requires the message to stay hidden to the users until they 'play' it. This poses a limitation to a games' (re-)usability, especially for activist purposes that seek to reach a wide audience. Also, its effect is currently restricted to one gameplay session. This aspect could be refined with the aid of narratological devices such as cliffhanger situations [28]. These techniques could motivate further confrontation with the game and topic once the player is involved, and thereby enhance the games efficacy and impact.

References

1. International Telecommunication Union (ITU): Measuring the Information Society (MIS) Report (2015). http://www.itu.int/pub/D-IND-ICTOI-2015
2. Prot, S., Anderson, C.A., Gentile, D.A., Warburton, W., Saleem, M., Groves, C.L., Brown, S.C.: Media as agents of socialization. In: Grusec, J., Hastings, P.D. (eds.) Handbook of Socialization, pp. 276–300. Guilford Press, New York (2015)
3. Entertainment Software Association (ESA): Essential Facts About the Computer and Video Game Industry (2016). http://essentialfacts.theesa.com
4. Nakamura, L.: Race in/for cyberspace: identity tourism and racial passing on the internet. In: Trend, D. (ed.) Reading Digital Culture, pp. 226–235. Blackwell, Malden (2001)
5. Hussain, Z., Griffiths, M.D.: Gender swapping and socializing in cyberspace: an exploratory study. CyberPsychology Behav. **11**, 47–53 (2008)
6. Bosson, J.K., Taylor, J.N., Prewitt-Freilino, J.L.: Gender role violations and identity misclassification: the roles of audience and actor variables. Sex Roles **55**, 13–24 (2006)
7. Chambers, S.A.: An incalculable effect': subversions of heteronormativity. Polit. Stud. **55**, 656–679 (2007)
8. Klimmt, C.: Serious games and social change. Why they (should) work. In: Ritterfeld, U. (ed.) Serious Games: Effects and Mechanisms, pp. 247–270. Routledge, New York (2009)

9. Kaufman, G., Flanagan, M.: A psychologically "embedded" approach to designing games for prosocial causes. Cyberpsychology J. Psychosoc. Res. Cyberspace **9**(3) (2015)

10. Hlavacs, H.: Serious games must look like casual games. In: Entertainment in Serious Games and Entertaining Serious Purposes Workshop at ICEC 2014, Australia, Sydney (2014)

11. Geoff, K., Mary, F., Max, S.: Creating stealth game interventions for attitude and behavior change: an "embedded design" model. Divers. Play Games Cult. Identities **2**(3), 173–193 (2016)

12. Bohner, G., Dickel, N.: Attitudes and attitude change. Annu. Rev. Psychol. **62**, 391–417 (2011)

13. Bodenhausen, G., Gawronski, B.: Attitude change, pp. 957–969. Oxford Unversity Press (2013)

14. Brown, R.: Prejudice: Its Social Psychology. Wiley-Blackwell, Chichester (2010)

15. Greenwald, A.G., Banaji, M.R., Rudman, L.A., Farnham, S.D., Nosek, B.A., Mellott, D.S.: A unified theory of implicit attitudes, stereotypes, self-esteem, and self-concept. Psychol. Rev. **109**(1), 3–25 (2002)

16. Frey, D.: Recent research on selective exposure to information. In: Advances in Experimental Social Psychology, pp. 41–80. Elsevier BV (1986)

17. Dovidio, J.F.: Prejudice, Discrimination, and Racism. Academic Press, Orlando (1986)

18. Brehm, J.W.: Control, its loss, and psychological reactance. In: Weary, G., Gleicher, F., Marsh, K.L. (eds.) Control Motivation and Social Cognition, pp. 3–30. Springer, New York (1993)

19. Green, M.C., Brock, T.C.: The role of transportation in the persuasiveness of public narratives. J. Pers. Soc. Psychol. **79**(5), 701–721 (2000)

20. Bogost, I., Games, P.: The Expressive Power of Videogames (MIT Press). The MIT Press, Cambridge (2007)

21. Butler, J.: Gender Trouble. Routledge Press, New York (1999)

22. Birtel, M.D., Crisp, R.J.: Psychotherapy and social change: utilizing principles of cognitive-behavioral therapy to help develop new prejudice-reduction interventions. Front. Psychol. **6**, November 2015

23. Turner, R.N., Hewstone, M., Voci, A.: Reducing explicit and implicit outgroup prejudice via direct and extended contact: the mediating role of self-disclosure and intergroup anxiety. J. Pers. Soc. Psychol. **93**(3), 369–388 (2007)

24. Allport, G.W.: The Nature of Prejudice. Doubleday Anchor, Garden City (1958)

25. Stathi, S., Tsantila, K., Crisp, R.J.: Imagining intergroup contact can combat mental health stigma by reducing anxiety, avoidance and negative stereotyping. J. Soc. Psychol. **152**, 746–757 (2012)

26. Case, N.: Coming Out Simulator (2014). ncase.me

27. Appel, M., Gnambs, T., Richter, T., Green, M.C.: The transportation scale–short form (TS-SF). Media Psychol. **18**, 243–266 (2015)

28. Lugmayr, A., Suhonen, E.S.J., Sendano, C.I., Hlavacs, H.: Serious Storytelling and Serious Entertainment - A Survey and Definition (2017). Accepted by Multimedia Tools and Applications

Evaluating a Serious Game for Cognitive Stimulation and Assessment with Older Adults: The Sorting Sheep Game

Helio C. Silva Neto[1]([✉]) [iD], Joaquim Cerejeira[2] [iD],
and Licinio Roque[1] [iD]

[1] Department of Informatics Engine, University of Coimbra, Coimbra, Portugal
helio.hx@gmail.com, lir@dei.uc.pt
[2] Faculty of Medicine, University of Coimbra, Coimbra, Portugal
jcerejeira@netcabo.pt

Abstract. Active Ageing, the preservation of the potential for achievement and development in old age, is a societal concern and neuropsychological assessments are part of psychological clinical studies. Although approaches are based on stable principles, Serious Games with designs based on neuropsychological tests can enable data collection and analysis useful for medical evaluation. This study developed and tested a game (Sorting Sheep) to be applied in cognitive stimulation with older adults providing, at the same time, useful information about the performance of the player. Meaningful correlations have been found between aspects of performance and the standard MoCA test, when the game is calibrated for a population with cognitive conditions.

Keywords: e-health · Active aging · Cognitive assessment · Serious Games

1 Introduction

Increased longevity of the population is a worldwide phenomenon with profound implications for society. The ageing process, which is only partially related with chronological age, is a heterogeneous group of health and functional states experienced by older people and determined by a range of genetic, biologic, social environmental, psychologic and cultural factors [16]. Although with a significant diversity, the aging process is characterized by a gradual impairment in many body systems and an increased risk for disease. The Central Nervous System is affected by changes in neurotransmitter levels and neuronal function, brain atrophy, reduction in oxygenation and cerebral blood flow among others [1]. Some deterioration in memory, processing speed of information, inductive reasoning, numeric abilities as well as impairment in motor and visual-perceptive functions are commonly found in older persons. Yet, age-associated cognitive changes are not irreversible and can be improved with adequate training [16].

The original version of this chapter has been revised: The erratum to this chapter can be found at https://doi.org/10.1007/978-3-319-66715-7_73

N. Munekata et al. (Eds.): ICEC 2017, LNCS 10507, pp. 125–139, 2017.
https://doi.org/10.1007/978-3-319-66715-7_13

Thus, cognitive stimulation is a component of "active aging", a term was adopted by the World Health Organization (WHO) to promote a better quality of life and improved autonomy and independence of older people. There is evidence that regular engagement in physical and cognitive activity with moderate intensity can delay functional decline and the onset of chronic disorders in older subjects [16]. This not only stimulates neuronal plasticity [7] but also makes use of the "cognitive reserve" as additional brain regions are recruited during the task to compensate the reduced functional capacity [2, 16]. Optimizing cognitive function is an important objective since cognitive decline is associated with adverse outcomes in mental and physical health as well as in longevity [6, 15].

Cognitive stimulation and monitoring of cognitive performance can be implemented with Serious Games. These belong to a class of games simulating practical daily-life situations for professional training in critical conditions as well as for educational purposes targeting a diversity of users [5, 17]. The increase utilization of Serious Games in immersive environments and the adoption of non-conventional devices has strengthened the relation with Digital Games. The possibility of generating virtual scenarios can increase motivation of users during the learning process [18].

Previous research as Tong et al. [14] proposed to demonstrate the feasibility of cognitive assessment in the elderly populations based on mobile platform games. The methodology of the study was to study the viability of the game in an emergency department of the hospital of the University of Toronto [13]. The results of the players were correlated with a series of standard evaluations (MMSE, MoCA and CAM). The authors of the study concluded that this is the first time that a serious game is used for cognitive assessment in an elderly population, followed by a full battery of conventional cognitive assessment methods to correlate the results. The research developed by Boletsis and Mccallum [3] aims to design and develop a serious game for the cognitive health screening of the elderly, that is, evaluate the Smartkuber game and document its development design. The study follows a mixed methodological approach using the In-Game Experience Questionnaire to assess players' gameplay experience and a correlation study to examine the relationship between the Smartkuber and MoCA scores (the study sample was thirteen older adults). The study shows that Smartkuber is a promising tool for cognitive health screening, providing a fun and motivating gameplay experience for older players.

The study by Manera et al. [8], which aims to examine the acceptability of the Kitchen and Cooking game, is a serious mobile platform game developed in the context of VERVE (EU project available at http://www.verveconsortium.eu/), being a game designed for the elderly population. In this game, a list of activities is employed to evaluate and stimulate executive functions (such as planning skills). Kitchen and Cooking was used by a sample of 21 elderly people (with and without cognitive pathology) for a month. Finally, the author of the study could conclude that the game Kitchen and Cooking is adapted for the elderly population with or without cognitive pathology. The investigation by Robert et al. [10] intends to analyze the feasibility, advantages and disadvantages of using Serious Games in patients with Alzheimer's disease in order to provide practical recommendations for the development and use of Serious Games in these populations. The methodology adopted by the authors of the research was not clear, but the authors concluded that the results revealed that Serious

Games can offer very useful tools for professionals involved in the care of patients suffering from Alzheimer's.

The aim of this study was to develop and test a serious game (Sorting Sheep) in cognitive stimulation of older adults providing, at the same time, useful information about the cognitive performance of the player which could be used by healthcare professionals. For this purpose we aimed to establish a correspondence between performance in game and performance on a simple standard cognitive assessment test. Thus, our main question is: which game play indicators and metrics could be used as a good proxy for predicting (a correlate) evaluation with a rapid screening instrument, such as that obtained with MoCA?

In the second section of this study, we will present the serious game proposal and its functioning, with a comparison to a traditional method of cognitive assessment. Next we present the methodology and details of the samples used in the research. The analysis of results and reception of the game proposal are outlined in the fourth section. In the fifth section are discussed relevant points for research. Finally, we will present the conclusions and future work.

2 Methodology

2.1 The Sorting Sheep Design Proposal

Since a significant proportion of older subjects have mobility problems, this game was developed for mobile touch technology such as Tablets. Thus, the user can have access to this game in every place including hospitals, nursing homes or their own residence [11, 12]. In this game (Fig. 1) the objective is to separate all sheep according to their colour into the correspondent zone or field. Thus, black sheep should remain in the right-hand side whereas white sheep must be kept in the left-hand side. To achieve this goal, the player should use a finger to open (touch) and move the Gate (drag) allowing the sheep to transpose the field to the correct side.

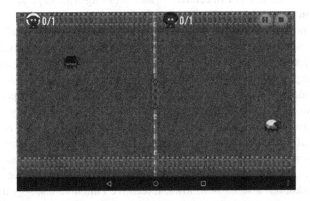

Fig. 1. Interface of Sorting Sheep.

The game has the following functioning mechanic: (1) the scenario consists of two fields separated by a gate. Sheep can move across the fields through the gate; (2) White and black sheep are randomly generated in the fields; (3) Sheep move randomly across the fields without any intervention from the user; (4) After the goal of separating black from white sheep is achieved, the difficulty level rises with the generation of one additional sheep of each colour.

Separating Sheep was culturally calibrated to the target population (with a rural scenario and familiar animals) which is important to obtain reliable assessments. A set of game play logging variables are recorded, as described in Table 1.

Table 1. Variables of the game Sorting Sheep.

Variable	Description
Highest level	Highest level played during the game
Nx (x = 1 to 4) completed	Accomplished level by the player (yes = 1 or no = 0)
Time Nx (x = 1 to 4)	Time in seconds to complete the respective level. If a level is not completed this variable is empty

2.2 The Montreal Cognitive Assessment (MoCA)

This is a brief screening test for cognitive function which can discriminate between normal and cognitive impairment in older adults [9]. This test has a one-page protocol and takes 10 to 20 min to apply. It doesn't have adaptations for education level, sensorial impairment and it lacks a ludic component. It is not particularly sensitive to assess some cognitive domains.

Executive functions are assessed by the part B of Trail Making Test (the subject has to link letters and numbers in alternate order); Phonemic Verbal Fluency (also included in Language); Verbal Abstraction (also included in Abstraction). Visuo-spatial assessment consists in the Clock Drawing Test (circle, numbers and hands) and copying a cube. "Attention, Concentration and Working Memory" are assessed with digit span test in direct and reverse orders. A Sustained Attention task (target detection) consists in identifying the letter "A" during the pronunciation of a series of letters. Finally, in the Serial Sevens subtractions the subject has to consecutively subtract 7 starting from 100. Language tasks consist in naming 3 animals, repetition of 2 sentences with complex syntax, and phonemic verbal fluency in which the subject is asked to generate as many words starting with "p" as possible (excluding proper names). For verbal abstraction the subject must think and verbalize the similarity between two objects (e.g. banana and orange being fruits). Differed memory recall is tested 5 min after retention of 5 words (short term memory). The subject has two trials to recall the words after completing other tasks (attention, language and abstraction). The Orientation domain is assessed questioning the subject about the time (e.g. date, month) and location. Each task has a score as follows: Executive Function/Visio-spatial (5 points); Naming (3 points); Attention (6 points); Abstraction (2 points); Memory (5 points) and Orientation (6 points).

The sum of each individual score provides a total score (max. 30 points) which can be compared with standardized values according to age and educational level [18].

2.3 Conjectured Relation Between MoCA Domains and Sorting Sheep

Table 2 presents the expected overlap of cognitive competences, in a comparison between the cognitive domains assessed by MoCA, and the demands of the Counting Sheep game, from the perspective of a trained Psychiatrist. The level of overlap is classified as strong (+++), moderate (++), weak (+) and none (−). We wanted to gather empirical data to corroborate, or not, this initial assessment.

Table 2. MoCA and Sorting Sheep.

	Sorting Sheep
Executive function	++
Visuo-spacial function	+++
Attention, Concentration and Working Memory	+++
Abstraction	−
Memory	+
Language	+
Orientation	+++

From Table 2 we would expect, as our initial conjecture, to find an empirical relation between the performance within the current Sorting Sheep game and a cognitive assessment, especially relevant along the visuo-spatial, attention-concentration, and orientation.

2.4 Procedure and Population

The study was previously validated by the University Hospital Ethics Comission. Concurrent validity for cognitive domains was tested against the Montreal Cognitive Assessment (MoCA). The game was tested with two groups with a distinct profile. Group 1 was composed with subjects with high cognitive performance attending a "Cultural Academy" (Academia de Convívio e Cultura da Casa Cor de Rosa) and a "Senior University" (Universidade Sênior Nova Acrópole). Group 2 consisted in subjects with cognitive impairment recruited in the Old Age Psychiatric Unit of Centro Hospital Universitário de Coimbra. All subjects with age ≥ 50 years were eligible to enter the study. The final sample consisted in 55 subjects in Group 1 (Gr.1) and 54 subjects in Group 2 (Gr.2).

Although a high proportion of participants in Gr.1 used internet-based mobile services, the majority is not familiar with digital games on mobile devices. Gr.2 is characterized by low internet usage and no knowledge of digital games (Table 3).

After explaining the purpose and details of the study to each subject and obtaining the informed consent, the research was conducted with the following steps:

Table 3. Groups characteristics.

	Group 1 (Gr.1)	Group 2 (Gr.2)	p-value
Age	64.8 ± 9.17 [50–85]	76.5 ± 7.59 [53–89]	<0.001
Gender (female, %)	80%	74.1%	<0.001
Education level (%)	None (0.0%)	None (24.07%)	<0.001
	1–12 years (45.46%)	1–12 years (70.37%)	
	Special/University (54.54%)	Special/University (5.55%)	
Occupation (%)	Active worker (29.09%)	Active worker (0.0%)	<0.001
	Retired (67.27%)	Retired (77.78%)	
	Household work (3.64%)	Household work (22.22%)	
Social network use (%)	Yes (61.82%)	No (98.15%)	<0.001
Email (%)	Yes (70.91%)	No (96.30%)	0.010
Text message (%)	Yes (72.73%)	No (92.59%)	0.044
Mobile Internet (%)	Yes (52.73%)	No (98.15%)	<0.001
Mobile Gaming (%)	No (61.82%)	No (100%)	<0.001

1. Baseline cognitive assessment (MoCA);
2. Demonstration of the game (rules and how to play);
3. Game play during 10 min;
4. Post-test questionnaire.

3   Results

3.1   Cognitive Assessment and Game Performance

The two groups differed in respect to baseline cognitive performance in all assessed cognitive domains (Table 4). The proportion of subjects completing each level correlated negatively with level difficulty; game performance was higher in Gr.1 (Table 5).

In Group 1 the variables Highest Level correlated positively with "Language" and MoCA total score suggesting that comprehension of the game rules and global cognitive function are important in achieving higher game performance (Table 6) (C:

Table 4. MoCA Group 1 and Group 2.

	Group 1 (Gr.1)	Group 2 (Gr.2)	p-value
Executive function	3.95 ± 1.32 [1–5]	1.87 ± 1.31 [0–5]	<0.001
Naming	2.75 ± 0.51 [1–3]	1.65 ± 0.97 [0–3]	<0.001
Attention	5.11 ± 1.1 [2–6]	2.37 ± 1.60 [0–6]	<0.001
Language	2.07 ± 0.95 [0–3]	0.85 ± 0.97 [0–3]	<0.001
Abstraction	1.96 ± 0.18 [1–2]	1.15 ± 0.85 [0–2]	<0.001
Memory	2.33 ± 1.29 [0–5]	0.94 ± 1.48 [0–5]	<0.001
Orientation	5.84 ± 0.5 [3–6]	4.69 ± 1.52 [1–6]	<0.001
Total score	24.3 ± 3.39 [14–29]	13.5 ± 6.18 [4–29]	<0.001

Table 5. Performance in Game Group 1 and 2.

	N	Gr.1	N	Gr.2	p-value
Highest Level (HL)	55	5.75 ± 1.60 [2–9]	54	3.44 ± 1.30 [1–6]	<0.001
Completed Level 1 (CL1)	55	1.00 ± .00 (100%)	54	.91 ± .29 (90.7%)	<0.001
Time on Level 1 (TL1)	55	45.42 ± 45.7 [9–284]	49	83.16 ± 79.9 [16–379]	<0.001
Completed Level 2 (CL2)	55	.96 ± 0.19 (96.4%)	54	.76 ± .43 (75.9%)	<0.001
Time on Level 2 (TL2)	53	78.55 ± 50.7 [11–269]	41	134.2 ± 81.3 [29–357]	<0.001
Completed Level 3 (CL3)	55	0.89 ± 0.32 (89.1%)	54	0.52 ± 0.51 (51.9%)	<0.001
Time on Level 3 (TL3)	49	96.53 ± 48.94 [28–246]	28	169.0 ± 90.3 [56–390]	<0.001
Completed Level 4 (CL4)	55	.80 ± .40 (80%)	54	.24 ± .43 (24.1%)	.632
Time on Level 4 (TL4)	44	126.93 ± 71.7 [44–385]	13	169.5 ± 67.3 [72–337]	0.018

correlation; S: significance and N: sample). Language correlated negatively with the time spent in level 1, with the presence of 3 extreme outliers (Fig. 2).

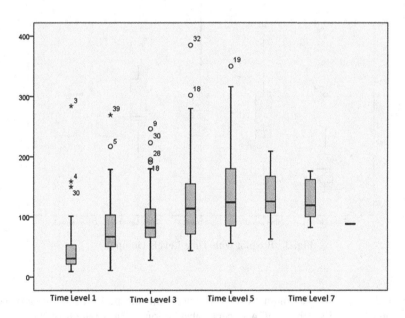

Fig. 2. Boxplot with Time Levels Group 1.

In Gr.1, Memory, Language and Total MoCA score correlated with Completed Level 2, 3 and 4.

The outliers and extreme outliers (as shown in Fig. 2) can be justified by:

(1) Players with low scores on cognitive domains correlated, i.e., Time on Level2 ("Player39" and "Player5"), Time on Level3 ("Player18", "Player28" and "Player30").

(2) There was a break in the linearity of time spent by the player when completing the levels. This was caused by the random and independent movement of 6 sheep changing the speed and direction every 20 s. In level 3 one or more sheep don't reach the gate before their speed or direction changes inducing an increased player-independent waiting time. This game design problem explains why the correlation between time measure and completed level disappeared in level 4. i.e., Time on Level 3 ("Player 9"), Time on Level 4 ("Player18" and "Player32") and Time on Level 5 ("Player 19"). Therefore, these are players with an absence of cognitive impairment according to the normative rules of MoCA performed by Freitas et al. [4].

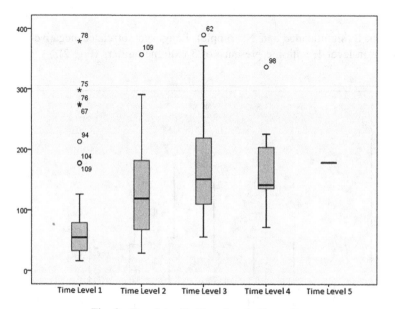

Fig. 3. Boxplot with Time Levels Group 2.

In Gr.2 (Table 6) Maximum Level correlated with the performance in most cognitive domains assessed by MoCA except "abstraction". The strength of these correlation increases in higher levels suggesting that cognitive performance is increasingly important as the difficulty increases. It is apparent that in Level 1 there was no correlation suggesting that this level is a stage of learning. "Orientation" is recruited during this level as the learning process includes spatial orientation of the player into the game. The decreased strength of correlations with cognitive performance observed in Level 4 and might be explained by the loss of game linearity with excessive waiting time (Fig. 3).

As in Gr.1, subjects in Gr.2 with higher cognitive performance spend less time to complete the game stages.

Table 6. Correlation MoCA and game Group 1 and 2.

		Executive function		Naming		Attention		Language		Abstraction		Memory		Orientation		Total score	
		Gr1	Gr2	Gr1	Gr2	Gr1	Gr2	Gr1	Gr2	Gr1	Gr2	Gr1	Gr2	Gr1	Gr2	Gr1	Gr2
HL	C	.204	**.600**	.086	**.427**	.132	**.538**	**.396**	**.305**	-.175	.159	.195	**.415**	.122	**.672**	**.309**	**.688**
	S	.135	**.000**	.533	**.001**	.338	**.000**	**.003**	**.025**	.202	.251	.154	**.002**	.374	**.000**	**.022**	**.000**
	N	55	54	55	54	55	54	55	54	55	54	55	54	55	54	55	54
CL1	C	–	**.282**	–	.171	–	.173	–	-.060	–	.053	–	.054	–	**.326**	–	.226
	S	.	**.039**	.	.216	.	.210	.	.667	.	.705	.	.699	.	**.016**	.	.100
	N	55	54	55	54	55	54	55	54	55	54	55	54	55	54	55	54
TL1	C	.065	-.298	.025	-.336	.060	-.351	-.334	-.160	.190	-.038	-.176	-.378	-.021	-.345	-.140	-.387
	S	.640	**.038**	.858	**.018**	.663	**.013**	**.013**	.271	.165	.795	.199	**.007**	.878	**.015**	.306	**.006**
	N	55	49	55	49	55	49	55	49	55	49	55	49	55	49	55	49
CL2	C	.007	**.547**	.123	**.386**	.089	**.437**	**.282**	.056	-.038	**.343**	**.315**	**.303**	.212	**.704**	**.274**	**.618**
	S	.962	**.000**	.369	**.004**	.516	**.001**	**.037**	.689	.784	**.011**	**.019**	**.026**	.121	**.000**	**.043**	**.000**
	N	55	54	55	54	55	54	55	54	55	54	55	54	55	54	55	54
TL2	C	-.11	-.215	-.061	-.053	.130	-.213	-.120	-.165	-.016	-.013	**-.274**	-.068	.142	-.076	-.104	-.187
	S	.435	.177	.662	.740	.355	.180	.394	.303	.908	.935	**.047**	.673	.312	.638	.459	.241
	N	53	41	53	41	53	41	53	41	53	41	53	41	53	41	53	41
CL3	C	.092	**.575**	.253	**.368**	.040	**.477**	.208	**.322**	-.068	.125	**.274**	**.391**	.232	**.614**	.248	**.623**
	S	.502	**.000**	.062	**.006**	.773	**.000**	.127	**.018**	.622	.368	**.043**	**.003**	.088	**.000**	.068	**.000**
	N	55	54	55	54	55	54	55	54	55	54	55	54	55	54	55	54
TL3	C	.005	-.067	-.008	-.048	.071	-.173	**-.335**	-.302	.277	-.162	-.235	-.257	.248	.081	-.137	-.250
	S	.972	.735	.957	.807	.629	.378	**.019**	.118	.054	.411	.103	.187	.086	.683	.348	.200
	N	49	28	49	28	49	28	49	28	49	28	49	28	49	28	49	28
CL4	C	.250	**.345**	.207	**.293**	.062	**.409**	**.351**	**.381**	-.097	-.039	**.283**	**.330**	.094	**.351**	**.329**	**.469**
	S	.066	**.011**	.129	**.032**	.653	**.002**	**.009**	**.005**	.481	.781	**.036**	**.015**	.494	**.009**	**.014**	**.000**
	N	55	54	55	54	55	54	55	54	55	54	55	54	55	54	55	54
TL4	C	.129	-.533	-.125	.048	-.022	-.425	-.135	-.023	.013	.090	-.053	-.091	.118	-.425	-.037	-.218
	S	.405	.061	.418	.876	.887	.148	.383	.940	.934	.771	.733	.767	.444	.148	.812	.474
	N	44	13	44	13	44	13	44	13	44	13	44	13	44	13	44	13

The outliers and extreme outliers of Time in Level1 ("Player109", "Player104", "Player94", "Player67", "Player76", "Player75" and "Player 78"), Time in Level 2 ("Player109"), Time in Level 3 ("Player62") and Time in Level 4 ("Player98"), are cases of players with some cognitive impairment according to the normative rules of MoCA performed by Freitas et al. [4].

In both groups the education level and occupation did not correlate with any game variable (Table 7) (C: correlation; S: significance and N: sample). Subjects with increasing age tend to spend more time in the game and not to reach the higher levels.

Table 7. Correlation of Group 1 and Group 2 profile with gameplay.

		Education		Age		Occupation	
		Gr.1	Gr.2	Gr.1	Gr.2	Gr.1	Gr.2
HL	C	.106	.227	−.506	−.500	.193	−.111
	S	.440	.098	.000	.000	.158	.422
	N	55	54	55	54	55	54
CP1	C	–	−.028	–	−.412	–	−.017
	S	.	.841	.	.002	.	.902
	N	55	54	55	54	55	54
TL1	C	.042	−.112	.167	.324	−.256	−.081
	S	.761	.444	.222	.023	.059	.579
	N	55	49	55	49	55	49
CP2	C	−.010	.085	−.178	−.316	.105	−.197
	S	.944	.541	.195	.020	.447	.154
	N	55	54	55	54	55	54
TL2	C	.047	−.107	.355	.085	−.223	.044
	S	.738	.505	.009	.599	.108	.784
	N	53	41	53	41	53	41
CP3	C	.131	.245	−.305	−.461	.188	−.069
	S	.342	.074	.023	.000	.168	.618
	N	55	54	55	54	55	54
TL3	C	.003	−.032	.322	.249	−.110	.010
	S	.982	.872	.024	.202	.450	.959
	N	49	28	49	28	49	28
CP4	C	.073	.213	−.427	−.342	.084	−.012
	S	.597	.123	.001	.011	.543	.934
	N	55	54	55	54	55	54
TL4	C	−.086	−.242	.239	.387	−.260	−.195
	S	.578	.426	.119	.192	.089	.523
	N	44	13	44	13	44	13

3.2   Feedback from Users

Globally, participants could understand the rules and how to play the game (100% in Gr.1 vs. 92.6% in Gr.2). The majority of participants in Gr.1 and 2 (87.3% and 72.2% respectively) considered the game a valid instrument to be used daily at home and did not find difficult to identify the animals, gate and game buttons (100% vs. 94.4%) (Table 8).

Table 8. Reception of the Game by Groups 1 and 2.

	Gr.1	Gr.2	p-value
Understood how to play? (%)	Yes (100%)	Yes (92.59%)	<0.001
Would you play at home? (%)	Yes (87,27%)	Yes (72.22%)	<0.001
Could you see well? (%)	Yes (100%)	Yes (94.44%)	<0.001
Did the sound affect your performance? (%)	Recognize gate is open (7%)	Motivated to play (25.93%)	.069
	Motivated to play (34%)	Familiar sounds (12.96%)	
	Familiar sounds (5.45%)	No (61.11%)	
	No (52.73%)		
Any critics on the game? (%)	Faster Sheep (10.91%)	Horses instead. (1.85%)	<0.001
	No (89.09%)	No (1.85%)	
Gameplay? (%)	Finger (63.64%)	Finger (11.11%)	<0.001
	Pen (36.36%)	Pen (88.89%)	

For 52.7% of players in Gr.1 and 61.1% in Gr.2 the sound during the game did not affect their performance while other participants (34.5% vs. 25.9%) reported increased motivation with sound and some (5.5% vs. 13%) considered that a familiar sound was an empathic element in the game. Increasing the speed of sheep (Gr.1) and replacing sheep with horses (Gr.2) were suggested although the majority of participants (89.1% vs. 98.1%) did not present any suggestion for changes. Most subjects preferred to play with a touch screen pen (63.6% vs. 88.9%).

4 Discussion

The Sorting Sheep Game for Gr.1 did not present correlations directly with the cognitive domains proposed by the game design (Table 2), but, it is noticed that some domains do not work in isolation, that is, they work together, for example, Language with Attention or Executive Function with Orientation.

Analyzing the results of the game for Gr.2, we can conclude that the game presented more calibration, thus, there were correlations predicted in the game development process, corresponding to the expectations of the game design (Table 2).

In the context of cognitive assessment, Table 9 shows the performance profile Gr.1 in the game and makes it possible to evaluate the performance of the sample players. The table was assembled with "Highest Level", the most efficient variable in the evaluation criterion of player performance and the other variables chosen are profiles such as "Age" (important variable to indicate cognitive decline) and "Education level" of the player (Second important variable to indicate cognitive decline) [4].

Similar to the table above presented in the context of cognitive assessment, Table 10 exposes the Gr.2 profile in the game.

Table 9. Evaluation of the players of the sample Gr.1.

Age	Education level			
	None	1–12 years	Special/University	All education level
50–65	None	6.67 ± 0.778	6.28 ± 1.227	6.43 ± 1.073
N	0	12	18	30
>65	Sem caso	4.62 ± 1.609	5.25 ± 1.913	4.92 ± 1.754
N	0	13	12	25
All Ages	Sem caso	5.60 ± 1.633	5.87 ± 1.592	5.75 ± 1.601
N	0	25	30	55

Table 10. Evaluation of the players of the sample Gr.2.

Age	Education level			
	None	1–12 years	Special/University	All education level
50–65	None	5.00 ± 1.000	5.00 ± 0	5.00 ± 0.816
N	0	3	1	4
>65	3.08 ± 1.115	3.37 ± 1.330	4.00 ± 0	3.32 ± 1.253
N	13	35	2	50
All Ages	3.08 ± 1.115	3.50 ± 1.371	4.33 ± 0.577	3.44 ± 1.298
N	13	38	3	54

Through the results, it was possible to perceive that the game environment did not present difficulties in the context of usability towards the target population. There was encouragement and evaluation of the players in particular to the Gr.2 players. As a tool to help health professionals interpret players' results, normative tables of player performance have been constructed (Tables 9 and 10).

The results of the investigation also allowed us to conclude that the game presents a challenge better calibrated for Gr.2 (Hospital), than for Gr.1 (Cultural Association/Senior University). Remember Gr.2 contains players with cognitive limitations (some with already diagnosed cognitive pathology), the opposite occurs in Gr.1 (people without diagnosed cognitive pathologies). Evidence for this calibration with Gr.2 is the number of correlations between the MoCA and some of the gameplay variables, where Gr.2 presented a significant amount of correlations when compared to Gr.1.

When we put together both sample groups, still not a random sample, we gain a perspective from which we can notice a promising trend line correlating performance in MoCA test with in game performance (Highest Level Achieved), thus justifying the need and usefulness of further investment in testing this approach (Fig. 4).

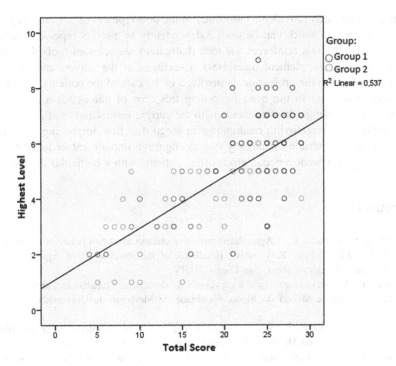

Fig. 4. Total score (MoCA) and Maximum Level (Game) by Group 1 and 2.

5   Conclusions

The objective of this research was to design and test a serious game to be used for cognitive stimulation and assessment with older adults (with and without cognitive impairment) using a mobile device.

The results suggest that this game is more calibrated to users from Group 2 profile (clinical sample). This is confirmed by the great number of correlations between MoCA variables (Executive Function, Attention, Orientation, Total Score) and game variables (Highest Level) in this sub-sample. In contrast, a ceiling effect occurred in Group 1 in which a higher level of difficulty was not associated with the performance in several cognitive domains. Thus, with healthy subjects, the game performance was, in addition to age, only dependent on the capacity to understand the rules. Additionally, the time for level completion didn't correlate with level difficulty. Thus, time was not useful to determine the player performance.

In the general analysis of the game and results it is possible to conclude that the game in the current conceptual form seems adequate to be used as an evaluation instrument, when compared with a screening test, with elderly population (with or without cognitive pathology), however, as a device for cognitive exercise, it can be quite demotivating for cognitively healthy people because as mentioned, the current game design does not appear to be challenging for cognitively healthy people.

Thus, this research provided a case study in the development of Serious Games for cognitive screening, which can be used independently by players repeatedly as cognitive exercise, and this reinforces the idea that games are relevant tools that can be used as a stimulus supplement (exercises), assessment of the players and may offer useful information to the professionals involved in the care of the patients. The design issues identified point to the need for tuning this type of games for a more linear progression of challenge. In accordance with the current results and limitations, future work should include removing randomness in sheep direction, improving game communication to compensate for anxiety due to cognitive impairment or lack of familiarity; Testing with homogeneous groups (e.g. patients with a particular diagnosis).

References

1. Albert, M.S., Killiany, R.J.: Age-related cognitive change and brain-behavior relationships. In: Birren, J.E., Schaie, K.W. (eds.) Handbook of the Psychology of Aging, 5th edn., pp. 161–185. Academic Press, San Diego (2001)
2. Barreto, J.: A reserva cognitiva e a prevenção da demência. Trabalho apresentado nas VI Jornadas de Saúde Mental do Idoso. Faculdade de Medicina da Universidade do Porto (2007)
3. Boletsis, C., Mccallum, S.: Smartkuber: A serious game for cognitive health screening of elderly players. Games Health J. 5(4), Mary Ann Liebert Publishers (2016)
4. Freitas, S., Simões, M.R., Alves, L.: Montreal Cognitive Assessment (MoCA): normative study for the Portuguese population. J. Clin. Exp. Neuropsychol. 33, 989–996 (2011)
5. Gamberini, L., et al.: Cognition, technology and games for the elderly: an introduction to ElderGames Project. Psychol. J. 4(3), 285–308 (2006)
6. Ghisletta, P., McArdle, J.J., Lindenberger, U.: Longitudinal cognition-survival relations in old and very old age: 13-year data from the Berlin Aging Study. Eur. Psychol. 11, 204–223 (2006)
7. Mahncke, H.W., Bronstone, A., Merzenich, M.M.: Brain plasticity and functional losses in the aged: scientific bases for a novel intervention. Prog. Brain Res. 157, 81–109 (2006)
8. Manera, V., et al.: Kitchen and cooking, a serious game for mild cognitive impairment and Alzheimer's disease: a pilot study. Front. Aging Neurosc. 7, article 24 (2015)
9. Nasreddine, Z., Phillips, N.A., Bédirian, V., Charbonneau, S., Whitehead, V., Collin, I., Cummings, J.L., Chertkow, H.: The Montreal Cognitive Assessment, MoCA: a brief screening tool for mild cognitive impairment. Am. Geriatrics Soc. 53, 695–699 (2005)
10. Robert, P.H., et al.: Recommendations for the use of Serious Games in people with Alzheimer's Disease, related disorder s and frailty. Front. Aging Neurosci. 6, 1–13 (2014)
11. Silva Neto, H.S., Roque, L.: Senior Care Clinic - modeling a cognitive assessment system. In: Anais do Simpósio Brasileiro de Jogos e Entretenimento Digital - SBGames (2014)
12. Silva Neto, H.S., Roque, L.: Experiências dos Videojogos aplicados ao Envelhecimento Ativo. In: Anais do Simpósio Brasileiro de Jogos e Entretenimento Digital - SBGames (2014)
13. Tong, T., et al.: Designing Serious Games for cognitive assessment of the elderly. In: International Symposium on Human Factors and Ergonomics in Health Care: Advancing the Cause (2014)
14. Tong, T., et al.: A Serious Game for clinical assessment of cognitive status: validation study. JMIR Ser. Games 4(1), e7, p. 1 (2016)

15. Vinters, H.V.: Aging and the human nervous system. In: Birren, J.E., Schaie, K.W. (eds.) Handbook of the Psychology of Aging, 5th edn., pp. 135–160. Academic Press, San Diego (2001)
16. WHO - World Health Organization. Envelhecimento ativo: uma política de saúde. Brasília (2015)
17. Zyda, M.: From Visual Simulation to Virtual Reality to Games, vol. 38(9), pp. 25–32. IEEE Computer Society Press, California, September 2005
18. Silva Neto, H.C., Neto, D.P.C., Leite, J.B., Cerejeira, J., Roque, L.: Cow milking game: evaluating a serious game for cognitive stimulation with an elderly population. In: ITAP '16, October 20–22, 2016, Kochi, Japan. ACM, New York (2016). https://doi.org/10.1145/2996267.2996272

An Interactive Digital Storytelling System with "What If" Functions

Nozomu Yahata[✉] and Kaoru Sumi

Future University Hakodate, 116-2 Kameda Hakodate-shi, Hokkaido, Japan
g2117049@fun.ac.jp, kaoru.sumi@acm.org

Abstract. We developed a system that generates stories from hypothetical questions. Specifically, the stories are expressed in a knowledge base of the form "If Then." The system allows users to create a story that has a synopsis different from the original story by changing the "If." For example, if the user changes the appearance and personality of a character, the outline of the story also changes. We think that this process can help increase the creativity of the users of the system. This system was developed to help users visualize written stories as images and allows users to experience stories interactively. Evaluation experiments conducted on 21 children of elementary school fifth grade children showed that there was improvement in the children's creative ability, demonstrating that the system is effective. Thus the system can be used as an idea creation tool for narrative generation as the process helps to increase the creativity of users.

Keywords: Story generation · Expanding storylines · "What If" functions

1   Introduction

In this study, we developed a digital storytelling system that generates stories from hypothetical questions. The digital storytelling system is capable of developing stories in a non-linear order, and users can actively experience the stories [1]. In this system, a story is represented by expressing it in a knowledge base in "If Then" format. Users can create a story with a synopsis different from the original story simply by changing the "If" part. For example, if the user changes the appearance and personality of a character, the outline of the story will change. It is therefore possible to generate different stories derived from the original story.

In the *What-If Machine* [2], a considerable amount of knowledge and fictitious ideas are necessary for story generation, and stories are generated by using questions and answers. By choosing the answer to a given question such as "What" or "Where," it automatically generates and displays the question "What If ~ then." For example, when the user sets Who (he) and Where (park), the trigger of the story of (play) is displayed. In this system, the user creates those settings, and then the subsequent deployment is also generated.

Scheherazade automatically generates continuing developments to the question. Scheherazade searches for answers to questions on the Internet and incorporates the

N. Munekata et al. (Eds.): ICEC 2017, LNCS 10507, pp. 140–146, 2017.
DOI: 10.1007/978-3-319-66715-7_14

answers into stories [3, 4]. In our proposed research, we do not use information on the internet but instead use commonsense knowledge offline.

In the proposed system, the user can generate various stories by setting and changing the "If." By so doing it is possible to improve the creativity of the user by creating patterns of various stories and imagining the future of the story.

Our objective is to realize a system that can help users to visually recognize the story as an image and allow the user to experience the story interactively. Therefore, in this system, we decided to add an animation as well as text information with generated story.

There is a research [5] to convert text information into animation by performing semantic analysis for each sentence using natural language processing. *Interactive e-Hon* [6] generates stories with animation by analyzing the meaning of text information and combines animation materials. In *WordsAnime* [7, 8], users can set the storyline by guiding the system according to the sentence construction method, and animation according to each storyline is displayed. By expressing hints for storyline creation, we support the user's story generation by knowledge base of the story connecting storylines and storylines. We adopted the method of assigning animation in this system from the text information in these studies.

In this study, we developed a digital storytelling system that generates stories from hypothetical questions, and verified that creativity is enhanced by using the developed system.

2   An Interactive Digital Storytelling System with "What If" Functions

In this system, the user defines the personality and appearance of characters based on the existing story. Based on that definition, a new story is generated by firing a knowledge base of behavior patterns of characters.

2.1   System Overview

In the system, the properties of the characters can be changed by using a production system called CLIPS. This system writes the execution history to a text file that can be read by an animation system called Unity. By so doing, the animation and narrative of the stories can be displayed on the screen. This process is repeated for every branch of the story.

2.1.1   What If Functions

In this section we explain What If functions. There are many branches where the flow of the story changes in advancing a story in this system. The user can change the definition of "If" of "If Then." In one branch, the story advances based on the definition of the character set for the user. In addition, the user can select and modify not only the characters but also the definitions of the objects related to the story.

For example, in Snow White, the user can change definitions such as "if the appearance is beautiful," "if the personality is evil," "if the poisoned apple is a poison banana." This function can result into multiple stories.

2.1.2   Story Development Using Commonsense Knowledge

In this system, the kinds of actions based on various properties are accumulated in the knowledge base. We set the behavior patterns of characters using this commonsense knowledge. Table 1 shows excerpts of the commonsense knowledge accumulated. Table 2 lists examples of what actions are actually taken based on Table 1. In order to point to what kind of character it is in the column of the rule, we define in advance what the character will be if the characters are pure, mean, or cowardly. The "If" part shows conditioning. The "Then" part defines what action to take in the case of "If." X and Y mentioned here also refer to the characters. Table 2 gives examples of behaviors that made the characters Snow White. From the above, a story is generated by applying multiple rules that define what kind of behavior to take depending on the character and appearance of the character.

Table 1. Commonsense knowledge

Rule		Pure	
if	Y hands A (food) to X	Y passes B (tool) to X	Y passes C (box) to X
then	X peacefully cat A	X uses B	X opens C

Table 2. Examples of behaviors that applied commonsense knowledge

Rule		Pure	
if	Princess hands apple to Snow White	The princess passes the broom to Snow White	Princess gives gifts to Snow White
then	Snow White cats apples	Snow White uses a broom	Snow White opens a gift

Fig. 1. System screen (Snow White)

In CLIPS, "defrule" allows the user to define the rules of actions according to the appearance and personality of characters. It is possible to display the execution history as a synopsis. In "assert," it is possible to add or change the definition of the character and save it to a text file. In the "rule" in Fig. 1, if the personality of a character is beautiful and its appearance is evil, it is a flow that shows a synopsis is shown with a "printout."

2.2 Example of Story Generation

We developed a system based on a story. "Snow White" is selected because it is famous worldwide in Grimm's fairy tale. It is easy to think of points in these stories where branching can occur.

We developed a system based on "Snow White" as a theme. Figure 1 shows the execution screen of this system. In the lower right corner there is an "Next" button. By pressing the button, text information is read and animation is given. In addition, in the window on the left side, it is possible to confirm the definition of characters currently selected by the user. Finally, the lower left side shows a synopsis in Japanese notation. For example, when the user encounters a branch, "The princess visited a house in Snow White," the user sets the definition of Snow White with "cautious character" and CLIPS. Then, based on the definition, it conducts actions that conform to the definition, and it is the trend that the story advances by taking action such as "close the door without getting an apple." When this sequence of flow is applied to the condition of "If then," the "If" part becomes "if Snow White is a prudent personality" and the "then" part becomes "close the door without accepting the apple." In addition, if Snow White's definition is "pure personality," actions such as "Open the door and eat apples from the woman and go into a coma" are selected. If this example also applies to the condition of "If then," the "If" part becomes "if Snow White is pure personality" and the "then" part becomes "she opens the door and gets an apple from the woman and eats it and enters a comatose state." The action of "then" obtained from commonsense knowledge is written out to a text file, its behavior is read in Unity, and animation is applied. There are multiple actions, but we applied only one this time. A new story is completed by repeating a branch point of such a story a plurality of times.

3   Experimental Evaluation

In this experiment, we asked 21 subjects of elementary school fifth graders to use this system and distributed a questionnaire in order to determine whether the system increases creativity. Creativity is increased by using the questionnaire. Creativity is defined by Ito as "the discovery of a new viewpoint that enables it to transform to a new theory, new combination of materials, solving problems" [9]. In this study, we defined that "Creating is to act of combining and expressing new ideas and perspectives as one's own" and used as evaluation indicators. By using these indicators, we verified how much creativity was enriched before and after the system was used. We first conducted a pre-test first, and then asked the subjects to observe images projected by a dome-type projector. A dome-type projector is a half-circle assembled with cardboard. We carried out a pre-test before using this system and carried out a post-test after using the system. The experiment took about 45 to 50 min in total. In the pre-test, it was assumed that the material of the creativity test [10] proposed by Yumino et al. (2001) was revised to ensure that it was consistent with the fairy tale. In the creativity test, the experimenter showed a picture, asked the subjects themselves to talk about the continuation of this picture, and then had them write it on paper. We taught the subjects that it is okay to create as many sentences as desired. The pre-test involved the continuation of the scene in which *Momotaro* was born. ("Momotaro" is a famous Japanese fairy tale.) The post-test involved the continuation of the scene in which Momotaro was born and the ant is working and the grasshopper is sleeping in *ants and grasshoppers* of Grimm 's fairy tale. In addition, the questionnaire contained seven questions asking about the contents of the system, such as whether it was interesting using this system or the system was easy to understand. Three to four of the subjects were in the dome at any one time, and they had this system using Snow White as their theme. All subjects selected What-If, and the experimenter manipulated this system while commenting.

4   Results

For the results of the experiment using "Snow White," we used the score in the creativity test to measure creativity. The average score for the first question in the pre-test was 1.33, and the average score of the first question in the post-test was 3.10: thus, the score increased significantly ($t = 4.15$, df = 20, $p < 0.05$). Because there was no pre-test in the second question, we compared points compared with the existing story. It was assumed that the average score of the pre-test is zero point. The average score of the post-test was 1.86 points and the score significantly increased compared with the existing story ($t = 5.83$, df = 20, $p < 0.05$). Further, in the system questionnaire, at least 90% of the subjects gave the highest grade, grade 5, to the questions, "Is this system was interesting?" "Do you want to do this system?" and stated that "Is this system easy to understand?"

5   Discussion

We developed a digital storytelling system that automatically generates narratives from hypothetical questions, and examined whether the creativity of children improved based on the experiments conducted with them as subjects.

The post-test of the average points on the creativity tests were improved by 1.77 points from post-test for the first question, and improved by 1.86 points from post-test for the second question. From this, it is considered that there is a possibility that this system will increase creativity.

In response to the creativity test, many of those who wrote responses applying the storylines displayed in this system were observed, and the effect of this system was considered. For example, the users chose "gentle personality" or "evil nature" in the system story. As a result, there were many cases in which subjects applied the character "gentle" or "evil" in the post-test, and created new stories using that personality.

In the questionnaire, "90% or more of the subjects gave the highest grade (5) to the questions," "Was the system interesting?" "Do you want to do it again?" and "Was this system easy to understand?" The reason cited by many subjects was the fact that "many different stories can be made." It is thought that it is interesting because the user to create his/her own favorite story. In addition, there were many statements that "Pictures and sentences are written and easy to understand." Based on this, it can be said that displaying the narrative of the story as well as the animation makes the system easier to understand.

We also asked the question, "When you tried using the system, what were the bad points?" The users indicated that as a good point that "a variety of stories can be made" were many, but also indicated that as a bad point such as "it is difficult to see with bugs or blurry options." It is may be necessary to separately adjust the layout of the screen to be displayed when projecting onto the dome-type screen. There is the opinion that "the screen is large and it was easy to see." It could be thought that it is easier to see when projected 180° with a screen or dome type than having the system on a personal computer screen. In addition, because some subjects thought that "the length of the story is short," we would like to take a long story into consideration. In future work, as there is still little commonsense knowledge in this system, we would like to increase the commonsense knowledge in the knowledge base.

6   Conclusion

In this study, we developed a system that generates and animates stories by the function of expanding stories from questions and definitions based on hypotheses. Users were able to create a story with a synopsis different from the original story by selecting and changing the definition of the story in the knowledge base system. In evaluation experiments conducted, children's creativity improved as a result of experience with system we developed.

References

1. Miller, C.-H.: Digital Storytelling: A Creator's Guide to Interactive Entertainment. Focal Press, Amsterdam (2008)
2. The What-If Machine, The What-If Machine Project. http://www.whim-project.eu/. Last accessed 2 Apr 2017
3. Li, B., Urban, S.-L., Johnston, G., Riedl, M.-O.: Story generation with crowd-sourced plot graphs. In: Proceedings of the 27th AAAI Conference on Artificial Intelligence, Bellevue, Washington, July 2013
4. Li, B., Riedl, M.-O.: Scheherazade: crowd-powered interactive narrative generation. In: The 29th AAAI Conference on Artificial Intelligence, Austin, Texas (2015)
5. Kengo, H., Takehiro, N., Toru, S., Hideji, E.: A trial of story comprehension simulation: through automatic generation of animation from story text. In: The 29th Annual Meeting of the Japanese Cognitive Science Society, pp. 1–7 (2012)
6. Sumi, K., Tanaka, K.: Automatic conversion from e-content into virtual storytelling. In: Subsol, G. (ed.) ICVS 2005. LNCS, vol. 3805, pp. 260–269. Springer, Heidelberg (2005). doi:10.1007/11590361_30

In.Line: A Navigation Game for Visually Impaired People

Laura Giarré[1]([✉]), Ilenia Tinnirello[2], and Letizia Jaccheri[3]

[1] DIEF, Università di Modena e Reggio Emilia, Modena, Italy
laura.giarre@unimore.it
[2] DEIM, Università di Palermo, Palermo, Italy
ilenia.tinnirello@unipa.it
[3] Department of Computer Science, NTNU, Trondheim, Norway
letizia@idi.ntnu.no

Abstract. In.line is a novel game based on a navigation system, called ARIANNA (pAth Recognition for Indoor Assisted NavigatioN with Augmented perception, [1]), primarily designed for visually impaired people permitting to navigate and find some points of interests in an indoor and outdoor environment by following a path painted or stuck on the floor. The aim of the game is twofold: (1) let the users learn and familiarize with the system, (2) improve blind people spatial skills to let them learn and acquire an allocentric spatial representation. The impact stands in the possibility of enhancing the social inclusion of a large part of the society that is increasing with the aging of the population by augmenting their autonomous mobility. The paper presents the concept design and preliminary evaluation of a game specifically designed for blind people. The evaluation has been performed via qualitative and quantitative tests.

Keywords: Navigation · Assistive technology · Game · Visually impaired people

1 Introduction and Related Work

Worldwide, 161 million people are visually impaired (according to the 2002 World Health Organization statistics), with an average of 3.4 low-vision patients for each blind person. Visual impairments pose a number of challenges related to mobility and hand-eye coordination. With technology we try to face the challenge of helping Visually Impaired Person to live a more independent life, working and socializing via autonomously and safely moving in an unknown environment and retrieving information about the places nearby. An important aspect of the

The authors acknowledge In.Sight s.r.l. (http:in.sight.srl) for developing the ARIANNA (patented) and In.Line; they also thank Prof. Lofti Merabet, Harvard Medical school, for very fruitful discussions.

design of assistive technology for Visually Impaired People, underlined in [2], is the possibility for the blind community to be taught and accompanied by the use of the novel device. A learning phase trough games is envisioned as a possible solution to let the blind community to accept such aids, by learning the use of them. This reasoning is the first motivation for the developing of In.line to let the blind people being familiar with the ARIANNA system and its use. The system permits to autonomously navigate and find some points of interests in an indoor and outdoor environment. A path stuck or painted on the floor is detected by the smartphone camera and a vibration signal providing a feedback to the user for correcting his/her direction is generated. Some special landmarks have been deployed for coding additional information, using Beacon technology or Qr codes. With ARIANNA, then, by following pre-determined paths located in the indoor and outdoor environment the visually impaired people can move independently in unfamiliar environments.

The accessibility of Internet to blind persons, and in particular the design of accessible game has been analyzed in the survey [3] where a large number of accessible games are listed for different types of impairments, across several game genres, from which a number of high- and low-level accessibility strategies are distilled for game developers to inform their design. In that analysis it has been stressed how the accessibility problems can be related to (a) not being able to receive feedback; (b) not being able to determine in-game responses; (c) not being able to provide input using conventional input devices. The design of our game is taking into account some of the suggestions presented here. Many blind persons, especially if young or adolescent, have a very high technological ability and many are the commercial games designed specifically for blinds. The pervasive presence of low-cost smart devices with increased computation ability allows the growth of innovative solution in several application fields. As [10] reports that for profoundly blind individuals navigating in an unfamiliar building represents a significant challenge, and investigated the use of an audio-based, virtual environment called Audio-based Environment Simulator that can be explored for the purposes of learning the layout of an unfamiliar, complex indoor environment, we were pushed towards the developing of our game. The highly interactive and immerse exploration of the virtual environment greatly engages a blind user to develop skills akin to positive near transfer of learning. Learning through a game play strategy appears to confer certain behavioral advantages with respect to how spatial information is acquired and ultimately manipulated for navigation.

2   Concept Design of In.Line

In.line is a game primarily designed for visually impaired people which is based on the navigation system ARIANNA.

2.1   ARIANNA System Description

ARIANNA system permits to navigate and find some points of interests in an indoor environment by following a path on the floor. Descriptions of the system were presented in [4,5], and the Patent [1]. The system works as follows: the camera of the smartphone continuously captures the scene in front of the person (see Fig. 1) and identifies the path by recognizing special colored strips painted or stuck on the floor. The users, then, receives a vibration signal through his cell phone. The vibration is related to the position and the direction of the user. In any installations of the system, the paths are marked with colored lines on the floor; QRcodes or beacon are also settled close to points of interest and they provide information on the right line to follow in order to get to the desired destination. The user interface employs tactile stimuli to receive feedback on the heading corrections to be employed, as better described in the following.

Fig. 1. The line captured by the phone

2.2   Aim of the Game

The aim of the game is twofold: (1) let the users learn and familiarize with ARI-ANNA (2) to improve blind people spatial skills. The latter is obtained with the design of some 'find short-cuts' task during the play, (navigate trough locations not linked by pathways directly experienced during the game) in order to let them learn and acquire an allocentric spatial representation instead of the ego-centric one. We recall that blind people have an egocentric spatial representation (based on themselves) while sighted people have also an allocentric representation, linked to a reference based on the external environment and independent of their current location in it. At first, we have started building up our game to fulfill the following scope: let the blind community play&learn. This will achieve also the secondary goal that is letting ARIANNA become a tool that the blind associations are happy with, by enforcing its use by the game helping blinds to familiarize with it. But learning trough games and amusement, is really the main scope of In.line because, as reported in a recent panel, [6], the use of games as an educational tool provides opportunities for deeper learning.

During the process of designing the game, we then asked ourselves if the game could be also a tool that could offer more to the blind community than a simple game to learn and be familiar with an app. Then, along what has been studied by [7], we have decided to use In.line to improve blind people spatial skills. To this aim, we design some 'find short-cuts' tasks during the play, (navigate trough locations not linked by pathways directly experienced during the game). While understanding the presence of short cuts may let them learn, acquire and improve an allocentric spatial representation. Egocentric type of representation is a route-based representation, while allocentric one is a survey-based one. For example, the reproduction of previously explored pathway only requires memory trace of the route, while finding shortcuts requires to build a survey representation and to compute a completely new pathway in the brain. Many have been the studies regarding whether the congenital blind individual prefers egocentric over allocentric spatial representation, [7] and references therein, but many studies are also suggesting the use of educational programs helping and training blind person in developing such an allocentric skill. Similar experiments have been already carried out, see [8–10].

2.3   The Game In.Line

The first prototype of In.Line was a game where a virtual line was projected on the floor. The person stands on the path and follows the line that is moving in front. During the projection of the line, some QR codes were also depicted and the blind (or blind folded) users had to catch it. Clearly, this previous release could be used only in a specific settings, with external teachers guiding the user trough the game. The line was projected on the floor, and the area was restricted so that no one could enter it and be an obstacle for the gamers. The aim of this first release was to teach the blind person how to use the system. We wanted to achieve the following: to be able to follow tactile indication from a common device such as a smartphone. The main objective of the game is to collect max possible scores in a precise time interval, start and the end of the game are reported by different audio signals. During the play, the ARIANNA path or line is projected in front of the player. During the game, the user is not walking on the path but the path flow moves in front of it. The game consists of following the line movements with the smartphone, the player tries to follow the movements of the line in front of him/her. If the line is captured the phone vibrates, the skill of the player is to predict the line changes and keeping on the smartphone vibration. The game has many levels of difficulty related to different paths, every level has a speed line runs and many changes direction different from other levels. The maximum score is reached when the player never looses the line, to all the game time, and consequently, the smartphone never stops the vibration. If the player obtains at least 3/4 of the maximum score, then it can move to the next level. Moreover, the player can intercept markers, such as QR code on the path. If this occurs further information about the point of interests are reported, with more scores and bonus to quickly go at next level.

The second release of the game was designed to be entirely developed on the smartphone. The Game is designed according to the second modalities of ARIANNA, that is the user is following the virtual line with the finger and the phone vibrates only if the finger captures the line. There is a virtual path on the smartphone screen, the finger is used to intercept the line; an on/off vibration feedback will tell the user if he/she gets the line or not. This second release could be used by the blind people in complete autonomy. The main objective of the game is to collect max possible scores during a session, no time limits are considered in a session. Every session is composed of three phases, during the first phase a line shape is shown on smartphone touch screen, the smartphone vibrates when the player finger intersects the line. The first phase consists of following the line shape with the player finger, from start point to end point and store the shape. In the second phase, the player must remember the line and uses the finger to reproduce the line on smartphone touch screen. If the reproduced line is completely matched with the original line shape, the player reaches the maximum score and it moves to the third stage. Otherwise, the player can retry unlimited time, any attempt produces a penalty and the total score is reduced.

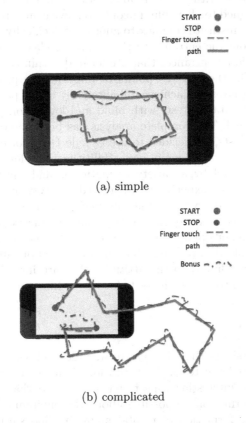

(a) simple

(b) complicated

Fig. 2. In.line virtual path in the second release of the game

In the third stage, the player must remember the start and stop line points, the player skill is to connect them together through a shortcuts path. Lower path enables additional scores for the player. The game has different levels with different difficulty related to paths shape. An example of the virtual path to follow is depicted in Fig. 2(a). To let the player acquire more points the virtual paths is intended to be followed in a more complicated way, in order to design also the shortcuts necessary for the developing of Allocentric vs. egocentric spatial perception (see Fig. 2(b)).

To let the player acquire more points the virtual paths is intended to be followed in a more complicated way, in order to design also the shortcuts necessary for the developing of Allocentric vs. egocentric spatial perception (see Fig. 2(b)).

3   Evaluation and Discussion

The game, in its first release, was tested during the smart city exhibition in Bologna. ARIANNA system has been deployed in various test environments, and also in real installations, such as in the Farm Cultural Park in Favara (AG) [12] and in the Blind Institute of Palermo Florio Salamone [13], (see [11]). The latter has been designed to allow blind people to move completely independently from one area of the institute complex to another. Specifically, the route crosses both courtyards, from the entrance to the computer classroom, and it enables to reach all the building entrances that are located within the perimeter of the three courtyards. On the way, 10 points of interests are placed allowing the users to orient themselves and achieve full autonomy in any part of the building. Qualitative and quantitative tests with blind and low vision people have been collected and analyzed. The complete analysis has been described in details in [15]. To design our tests, we decided to use Google Drive for our online survey, because it is compatible with many accessibility features for visually impaired people and is supported by a variety of platforms and smartphones. To get information on the user's experience, we created a survey where the scoring of the results provides an overview of the consumer satisfaction. The data can be analyzed and processed to verify the strengths and weaknesses of the system To determine the consumer opinions we use the Likert scale [14], a psychometric scale commonly involved in research that employs questionnaires. It consists of a series of statements linked to the attitudes that are investigated. A similar approach will be used to design the tests for the In-Line game.

4   Conclusions

Overall, the survey shows that the system was received with good enthusiasm and the users enjoyed the tests. They consider it a breakthrough and would definitely use it. An interesting aspect that emerged is that all users wish to obtain as much information as possible about the environment around them. A key aspect of the formation of mental maps in blind subjects is linked to the memory of the paths and the location of objects that they develop with repetition and practice. If a person follows in his mind a small-scale model of the external reality, he is able to think of various alternatives, choose the best among them, react to future situations before they happen The obtained results stimulate us to further develop the game and in particular to let the blind people at the Blind Institute use the game together with ARIANNA and then running more tests and collect qualitative and subjective feedback trough questionnaires.

References

1. Italian Patent N. BG2014A000054, Sistema di navigazione per non vedenti, presented 2015, patented (2017)
2. Elli, G., Benetti, S., Collignon, O.: Is there a future for sensory substitution outside academic laboratories. Multisens. Res. **27**, 271–291 (2014)
3. Yuan, B., Folmer, E., Harris, F.C.: Game accessibility: a survey. Univ. Access Inf. Soc. **10**(1), 81–100 (2011)
4. Croce, D., Gallo, P., Garlisi, D., Giarré, L., Mangione, S., Tinnirello, I.: ARIANNA: a smartphone-based navigation system with human in the loop. In: 22nd Mediterranean Conference of Control and Automation (MED), pp. 8–13 (2014)
5. Croce, D., Giarré, L., Rosa, F.G.L., Montana, E., Tinnirello, I.: Enhancing tracking performance in a smartphone-based navigation system for visually impaired people. In: 2016 24th Mediterranean Conference on Control and Automation (MED), Athens, pp. 1355–1360 (2016). doi:10.1109/MED.2016.7535871
6. Mackay, R.F.: Playing to learn Stanford Report, 1 March 2013. http://news.stanford.edu/news/2013/march/games-education-tool-030113.html
7. Cattaneo, Z., Vecchi, T.: Blind Vision: The Neuroscience of Visual Impairment. MIT Press, Cambridge (2011)
8. Halko, M.A., Connors, E.C., Snchez, J., Merabet, L.: Real world navigation independence in the early blind correlates with differential brain activity associated with virtual navigation. Hum. Brain Mapp. 2013 PMID: 24027192 (2013)
9. Connors, E., Yazzolino, L., Snchez, J., Merabet, L.: Development of an audio-based virtual gaming environment to assist with navigation skills in the blind. J. Vis. Exp. 2013 PMID: 23568182 (2013)
10. Connors, E., Chrastil, E., Snchez, J., Merabet, L.: Virtual environments for the transfer of navigation skills in the blind: a comparison of directed instruction vs. video game based learning approaches. Front. Hum. Neurosci. **8**, 223 (2014). doi:10.3389/fnhum.2014.00223
11. http://in.sight.srl/installations/
12. http://www.farmculturalpark.com/
13. http://www.istciechipalermo.it/
14. Likert scale: https://en.wikipedia.org/wiki/Likertscale
15. Deliverable Technical Report of the EU project FIC-3, SUB-GRANT AGREEMENT N CALL 2–28

Education

SikkerhetsLøypa - Knowledge Toward Sustainable and Secure Paths of Creative and Critical Digital Skills

Letizia Jaccheri[1(✉)], Deepti Mishra[2(✉)], Siv Hilde Houmb[3,4],
Aida Omerovic[5], and Sofia Papavlasopoulou[1]

[1] Department of Computer Science, Norwegian University of Science and Technology (NTNU),
Trondheim, Norway
{letizia.jaccheri,spapav}@ntnu.no

[2] Department of Computer Science, Norwegian University of Science and Technology (NTNU),
Gjøvik, Norway
deepti.mishra@ntnu.no

[3] Department of Information Security and Communication Technology, Norwegian University
of Science and Technology (NTNU), Gjøvik, Norway
siv.houmb@ntnu.no

[4] Secure-NOK AS, Stavanger, Norway
sivhoumb@securenok.com

[5] SINTEF Digital, Oslo, Norway
Aida.Omerovic@sintef.no

Abstract. Children spend numerous hours on the Internet daily. While online, they meet a great number of opportunities as well as risks. Of these risks, cyber bullying and privacy violations are of major concern, in addition to exploitation and child pornography. Our hypothesis is that the solution is not to keep children and teens away from the Internet, but to ensure that young citizens are empowered with the necessary knowledge and skill set to become critical consumers and creators of new secure and sustainable digital services and products. Our objective is to develop a knowledge and skill set base and offer learning through playful solutions for empowering children and young people with creative and critical digital skills, in an engaging and motivating way. The aim is to build on the method and lessons learns of Kodeløypa, one of the scientific offerings for children at the Norwegian University of Science and Technology (NTNU), and the related scientific efforts made to empower a new generation of online users to avoid risks in the modern digital society. The project, SikkerhetsLøypa, is highly inter-disciplinary and spans across the fields of information security, user experience, software engineering, and computer science education. The scientific results of this project aims at strengthen education methods and practices in secure and privacy-aware behavior in the digital world.

Keywords: Digital society · Online behavior · Video games · Security · Gender

© IFIP International Federation for Information Processing 2017
Published by Springer International Publishing AG 2017. All Rights Reserved
N. Munekata et al. (Eds.): ICEC 2017, LNCS 10507, pp. 157–168, 2017.
DOI: 10.1007/978-3-319-66715-7_16

1   Introduction

The digital literacy level of children and young adults has increased significantly in recent years. Unfortunately, their digital safety and privacy skills have not kept up with the digital literacy level. The wider use of the Internet to seek information, share ideas, consume entertainment and network using social media brings great opportunities, as well as larger risks to young users. Despite a growing body of rules and regulations implemented to enhance safe online behaviour, more efforts in this direction are still needed. Children require support to be aware of the potential risks and threats of Internet use for their online security. Staksrud and Livingstone [1] define online risks as a set of intended or unintended experiences that increase the likelihood of harm to the Internet user, and include encountering pornographic, racist or hateful content online, as well as inappropriate or potentially harmful contact via harassment and bullying. Online risks to children generally comprise a set of wanted or unwanted inappropriate activities by children (as actors, receivers, or participants) that are of concern [2]. Child pornography is addressed by the Cybersecurity SRA [3] as one of their list of serious cybercrimes and malware. Everyone, child or adult, has the right to the protection of their personal data, but many young people normalise the sharing of intimate details on social media without understanding the risks, and possibly with an overestimation of their governments ability to protect them from online risks.

Parents can play an important role in providing a safe Internet environment for their children. However, it is not easy for parents to engage effectively in an instructive mediation of their child's Internet use, and co-viewing is much less likely when it comes to Internet compared with other audio-visual mediums such as television. Therefore, proper training and teaching is crucial for imparting online security-related life skills. This is further supported by Reid and Van Niekerk [4], who assert that cyber security education is becoming a necessary precaution for individuals to protect themselves against the dangers of online technologies and resources. It has also been observed that learning activities that employ gamification [5] generally lead to better learning outcomes. However, gaming brings the gender challenge to the table, which needs to be considered when using gaming as a learning platform for online security-related life skills. Although women remain under-represented in cultural representations of gamers, in the design considerations of game producers, and in the production companies themselves, the percentage of girls and women playing and creating video games is continuing to increase. Female gamers tend to play as much as male gamers or longer online, per session and per week than males [6]. As women have become more present online and in the Internet economy, this brings challenges such as becoming the prey of cybercrime and bullying, arguably at a higher level of risk or different manner of risks than for men.

The paper describes work in progress. Initially a series of workshops were conducted in the framework of Koderløypa (see Sect. 3) with the aim to explore using gamification as a learning platform. With the above-mentioned motivations and the results of these workshops, the present study describes an ongoing project, SikkerhetsLøypa, with the aim to create new knowledge, methods, and tools that will lead to new services and products by gamifying education on online opportunities and risks with innovative gaming technologies for young online users.

The paper is organized as follows: Sect. 2 describes the challenges and concerns regarding digital safety and security of young users, along with gender issues in gaming. Section 3 provides a walk-through of the Kodeløpa workshop and method. The proposal to develop knowledge and offer playful solutions for empowering children and young people with creative and critical digital skills is discussed in Sect. 4. Section 5 provides discussion and conclusions.

2 Literature Review

A European study of 21 countries stated 75% of children are using the Internet [7]. Another study finds that more than 65% of Facebook and Myspace users are children [8]. This increasing Internet usage among children brings both opportunities and risks for those children [7]. This means that the more opportunities children gain online, the more likely they are to encounter increased risk [9].

2.1 Online Safety and Security Issues

A research network founded by the European Commission's Safer Internet Programme, known then as 'EU Kids Online' and now as 'Better Internet for Kids', developed a classification [10] of online risks comprising:

Content risks where the child is a recipient of unwelcome or inappropriate mass communication;

Contact risks where the child participates in risky peer or personal communication;

Conduct risks where the child themselves contributes to risky content or contact.

Lorenz *et al.* [11] identified that the challenges or concerns regarding digital safety and security are related to reputation (self-inflicted damage, outside damage), data (data loss, data exposure), fraud (dishonesty, money loss), health (physical and mental health factors), and freedom. Some major security risks in relation to online behaviour of children are as follows:

Children are trusting. The number of children believing everything they read on the Internet is significantly increased, according to an Ofcom study which has found that 'digital natives' are too trusting of what they find online [12].

Online grooming. Online grooming is another major problem in online communities where groomers often pretend to be children in order to become friends and establish a relationship with their young victims [13].

Unwanted exposure to sexual material. Children are more likely to experience unwanted exposure to pornography [2]. Furthermore, boys experienced more exposure to the risks compared to girls [2].

Unwanted exposure to violent content. Children are exposed to potential harmful risks such as seeing bloody movies or photos, seeing people being beaten up, and seeing hate messages [2].

Contact risks. This includes contacting someone online whom the child never met face-to-face, meeting someone face-to-face whom the child knows only online, meeting someone whom the child knows only online and being harassed [2].

Sharing personal details. Children may share and reveal personal data because they do not realize the possible consequences [14]. Minors are more likely than adults to give out personal information in order to receive an award [15]. Eight out of 10 adolescents who use social networks share personal information about themselves to a much greater extent compared to previous years [14], revealing sensitive information about their family and friends as well as themselves [16].

Online bullying/being bullied. According to Ktoridou *et al.* [17], one in three children have experienced Internet bullying. 38% of girls and 26% boys have faced online bullying [17].

Internet addiction. Overuse and addiction to the Internet among children has been examined by many researchers [18–20]. Several studies [18, 21, 22] have also investigated online gaming addiction among school-going adolescents.

Digital safety areas are scattered across every element defined in the above list, for example: understanding internet safety trends; choosing secure devices to surf online; recognize potential insecure behaviours or threats; knowing how to act when something bad happens or how to seek help when needed; perceiving and judging the dangers of your own and others' online behaviour; knowledge about account privacy and maintenance; helping students to learn how to interact online positively and with consideration for others [11].

There are also major differences in online behavior depending on the age of children and young people. Each of these demonstrable differences in experience of the Internet and online gaming, and it is critical to take this into consideration when developing tools and techniques to improve online security skills for children.

2.2 Gender Issues in Gaming

Gender issues in technology and specifically in computer games have been a research topic for many years. Twenty years have passed since Cassel and Jenkins wrote the groundbreaking "From Barbie to Mortal Kombat" that highlighted the ways gender stereotyping and related social and economic issues characterize digital game play. Kafai *et al.* [23] have recently edited a collection of contributions around the still-relevant question about women and gaming. Video games are an important part of the life of adolescents. According to Gorriz and Medina [24], boys reported playing an average of nearly 43 h per week, or over 6 h per day, and girls reported playing nearly 30 h per week, or over 4 h per day. According to Fron *et al.* [25], 88.5% of all game development workers are male; 83.3% are white; 92% are heterosexual.

Bryce and Rutter [26] have argued that 'the popularity of domestic and online gaming among females, and the development of female gaming clans, highlights that leisure activities and spaces are becoming less gendered, and can provide sites for resistance to societal notions of the gender appropriateness of leisure activities. In the years since that study was published, female video game players have long since ceased to be a negligible minority. Women are also actively creating video games- not only as employees of computer game production companies but in a few notable cases as the owners of those companies as well. Women-owned computer game companies include HerInteractive, Girl Games, Girltech, Purple Moon (developed by Brenda Laurel, who had established Purple Moon games with the explicit goal of designing products which reflected socio-logical and ethnographic research into young girls' play patterns). Gorriz and Medina [24] provides an excellent classification of games for girls from Barbie Fashion Designer to tools for boosting self-esteem such as Let's Talk About Me.

The gender aspect of Internet and online situational awareness is important, and is related to questions around users' age and maturity. It is important to understand these gender differences and to develop a training program that is both tailored to the gendered experience of learning (women learn differently than men) and the differences in the cyber situations that girls and boys (or women and men) could be exposed to.

3   Kodeløypa Workshop

Building upon several documented efforts [27, 28], we designed a one-day workshop program for 15-years old students in secondary schools in Trondheim, Norway. Students attended this five-hour workshop as part of their school day [29]. We adopted the constructionist approach as one of its main principles is learning by making. This approach was chosen because of the observation that young people of that age tend to rebel against concrete advice, and learn better through engaging with educational content in a creative and self-directed way. We have chosen to use Scratch (a digital learning environment) due to its ease of use for young students and its connection to the principles of constructionism. For a hardware platform, we selected Arduino due to its well-estab-lished and smooth integration with Scratch. We also used Scratch for Arduino (S4A), an extension of Scratch that provides extra modules for robot control.

Five teaching assistants facilitated the workshops and designed the process together with a researcher and an artist. In general, children who attended the workshop worked collaboratively in triads. Digital artifacts (robots) were placed next to each of the computers, and the students had the option to select the robot they wanted (Fig. 1).

Fig. 1. Kodeløypa workshop

The workshop was organized in the following two main sections.

3.1 Playing (and Learning) with Robots

At the beginning of the workshop, one assistant welcomed the students and presented the scope of the workshop to the students. Then, the assistant demonstrated the robots and advised students to keep their attention on the tutorial placed next to each of the computers. The tutorial contained instructions with examples and pictures similar to the robots they were using. Students were asked to investigate the robots and find the exact place of their sensors and lights, write the location of the LED lights and sensors while answering some questions. Examples were deliberately sparse of text and image-rich, with images demonstrating exactly what the students were asked to do. As students had no experience with programming we wanted a smooth start that would increase their motivation to engage, so they were first asked to do a series of simple tasks making the robot react to the environment through visual effects (for example, cause a light to switch on when there was less light on the sensors). The robots were built from recycled computer parts/materials. Students could touch and play with the robots but not change any parts of them, since those robots have been constructed to support computational thinking (CT) concepts (i.e. sequences, loops, parallelism, events, conditionals, operators, variables, and lists).

During this phase, students made simple loops that could control the robots. Through this activity, students understood the metaphors and interactions between the physical design elements and the Scratch environment. The first section lasted one and a half hours.

3.2 Create Games with Scratch

In the second part of the workshop, we wanted students to be creative and implement simple game development concepts using Scratch. The students were given another tutorial with the basic CT concepts, with images arranged in an order to help them with the development of their own game. This part lasted three hours and did not use the robots.

Students were able to create their own game structure and stories by designing and programming. It is very important that students had a plan for what kind of game they want to create. Therefore, they were asked to draft a storyboard first. In order to stimulate creativity, examples of different loops and existing game characters were given to students to be used as elements of the game. Examples and visualizations of the process helped students to ideate their own original project. Help was provided anytime students asked for it and the number of assistants was enough to provide sufficient help to all teams. More complex programming concepts were introduced on an individual level when the students asked for them and those concepts were relevant to their projects. Throughout the whole process, students were iteratively testing and trying to debug their games, and they worked collaboratively according to their own pace. At the end, each of the students' teams created a Scratch game based on their own preferences and ideas. Students' games were not presented formally, but all teams had the chance to play each other's games.

3.3 Participants

Seven KodeLøypa workshops took place during Autumn 2015, and students from four different schools participated. In total, 128 students attended, consisting of 60 male and 68 female students. All workshops followed the same structure as outlined above and each of the workshops had between 18 and 22 participants [29].

3.4 Data Collection and Measurements

A range of data was collected across the seven workshops, including surveys, photographs and observations. For the purpose of this study we focused on the quantitative data. To collect the quantitative data, we conducted a post-workshop survey based on questions adopted from similar studies in the literature. Students responded to the survey at the end of the workshop day. In summary, we collected 105 responses (53.3% males and 46.7% females). Each attitude (construct) consisted of three to four questions (items) and was measured using a seven-point Likert scale.

3.5 Lessons Learned

There were several lessons learned from the KodeLøypa workshop that form the basis for the planned SikkerhetsLøypa workshop series. In particular, the results showed that age and maturity heavily influence the learning capability. However, age and maturity level does not necessary align, which is an essential lessons learns when planning

SikkerhetsLøypa workshops. For example, while 14–16 year old's have an equal need for the same level and types of online security awareness and skills, their readiness to receive and understand the workshop's training modules varied significantly based on their age and inconsistently age-linked maturity levels. The workshop could ideally be tailored to match the learning styles and maturity of each student, but the wide variability and rapid pace of change in teenagers' development makes it difficult to make useful assumptions about their learning preferences and abilities ahead of meeting the individual learners themselves.

4   Towards an Intersectional Understanding of Online Security, Gender, Creative Careers and Learning Styles

This project SikkerhetsLøypa lies at the intersection between (a) the gamification of digital empowerment of children and young people and (b) user-centered and adaptive training in cyber security risks and online opportunities.

4.1   Objective of the Project

The objective of the SikkerhetsLøypa project is to: create new knowledge, methods and techniques that will lead to products and services of gamified education about online opportunities and risks. This will enhance the level and competitiveness of the Norwegian education system and at the same time open up market opportunities for Norwegian publishing, gaming and e-learning industries, both nationally- and internationally-facing. The targeted end users of these products and services are children at the level of the Norwegian middle school (Ungdomskole).

The gamification of security training for youth is cross-disciplinary and the main research challenge is in the intersection between cyber security, user experience and learning science. The challenge is two-fold: (1) Identify and dynamically update the most recent knowledge on online opportunities and cyber security risks, including documented guidance on how to deal with them; and (2) Design and empirically validate the SikkerhetsLøypa products and services so that, as well as efficiently conveying the abovementioned up-to-date knowledge, they are attractive, highly motivating and entertaining to the users, so that kids actually want to use them and the teachers and policy makers want to adopt them.

4.2   Research Questions

We aim to investigate the following research questions with the aim to offer playful solutions for empowering children and young people with creative and critical digital skills, in an engaging and motivating way:

How could we develop a security knowledge tale into a video game?
How could we evaluate the video game?

The second question can be separated into two sub-questions: How do we evaluate the game after production? And how do we evaluate the game during the design and production phase to create a game that better achieves the creators' goals? The literature review will identify papers that can most usefully serve as guidance for choosing an evaluation model and methodology. Papers of relevance include examinations of evaluation methods previously applied to education-oriented video games, as well as suggestions for future evaluations of both the learning outcomes and the quality of engagement with video games among diverse audiences. It is very likely that findings related to how best to evaluate the video game will inform the methods for developing (designing and producing) the game.

The proposed work will contribute to the knowledge, methods and tools needed for: (1) acquisition of the cyber security knowledge that needs to be communicated to the user groups, (2) storytelling around the knowledge to be communicated, (3) dynamic content update of the SikkerhetsLøypa products and services with most recent knowledge and corresponding stories, and (4) adaptive learning which customizes the SikkerhetsLøypa products and services to the level and learning pace of the user.

4.3 Main Activities, Objectives and Deliverables

The main activities, objectives and deliverables of SikkerhetsLøypa are as follows:

Knowledge management regarding online opportunities and risks: Develop an approach to the acquisition of knowledge of online opportunities and risks, as well as ways of dealing with online resources associated with both.

Serious game design and user experience: Develop an approach to interactive and motivating storytelling. Develop method and metrics for evaluation of usability. Develop an approach to updating the design of serious games with new content.

Pedagogical solutions for game-based learning: Develop an approach to knowledge transfer through storytelling as well as guidance for when and how to leverage the different learning means and mechanisms. Develop method and metrics for evaluation of learning effects. Develop a method for adaptive learning.

Empirical evaluation in pilot environments: Identify requirements for SikkerhetsLøypa products and services. Evaluate the feasibility of SikkerhetsLøypa early products and services for education about online opportunities and risks. Evaluate the effect of SikkerhetsLøypa products and services on user experience and learning. Conduct an overall evaluation of the final version of the SikkerhetsLøypa products and services.

Dissemination and internationalization. Open seminars, participation in social media, scholarly articles. The pilot at NTNU and in schools will generate attention in the media. We mention that Kodeløypa has been broadcasted at NRK News and other National media channels. Kodeløypa is one of the main case studies in Horizon 2020 Umi-Sci-Ed [30], and SikkerhetsLøypa will utilize existing relationships with the international partners and previous event/activity partners of Kodeløypa.

5 Conclusions

The rapid increase over recent years in the digital literacy level of children has not been equaled by a parallel increase in online situational awareness or digital security skills. This paper has provided a brief summary of statistics outlining increasing use of the Internet by young people, including girls. This paper has also explored in brief the awareness in the literature that the Internet ecosystem, and video games especially, are increasingly inhabited by girls and women, and that although women remain under-represented in depictions of and opportunities in the gaming industry, the percentage of girls and women playing and creating video games is continuing to increase. In summary, exposure to the Internet provides a wealth of opportunities to young people, and therefore, rather than preventing exposure to the commensurate risks and dangers by favoring restriction of access, it would be more beneficial to encourage young people to become aware of those risks and dangers, and to equip them with tools to improve their own digital safety.

A one-day workshop for school-age Norwegian children (age 15) was developed, taking a constructionist approach that used gamification to motivate students to learn about programming by playing with robots and designing their own simple video games. These "Kodeløypa" workshops were delivered to 128 students in total, with representative participation by different genders, and employed Scratch software as well as Arduino hardware. Quantitative feedback was effectively gathered from the majority of participants and can be used to improve workshop structure and learning outcomes of similar workshops in future. The Kodeløypa workshop model developed by our team is summarized here to provide evidence of the efficacy of this model of innovative learning, and to propose that a new workshop, called SikkerhetsLøypa, be developed based on the experiences and lessons learns from the Kodeløypa's workshops. The aim of the SikkerhetsLøypa workshop is to deal specifically with issues around online safety awareness and skills. The objective of the SikkerhetsLøypa project is to create new knowledge, methods and techniques that will lead to products and services of gamified education about online opportunities and risks.

To that end, we found that a number of building block studies will need to be developed in order to deliver a workshop that addresses the intersecting needs of school-age students of different genders, ages, maturities and learning styles. These studies, which will take the form of literature reviews, original research and iterative workshops, will deliver a new knowledge base that can be used to guide pedagogy, service creation and product development around teaching internet safety to young people.

References

1. Staksrud, E., Livingstone, S.: Children and online risk. Inf. Commun. Soc. **12**(3), 364–387 (2009). doi:10.1080/13691180802635455
2. Teimouri, M., Hassan, M.S., Griffiths, M., Benrazavi, S.R., Bolong, J., Daud, A., Adzharuddin, N.A.: Assessing the validity of western measurement of online risks to children in an Asian context. Child Indic. Res. (2015)

3. Cybersecurity Strategic Research Agenda – SRA, Produced by the European Network and Information Security (NIS) Platform. http://www.kowi.de/Portaldata/2/Resources/horizon2020/coop/cybersecurity-SRA-final-v0_96-ENISA.pdf

4. Reid, R., Van Niekerk, J.: Back to basics: information security education for the youth via gameplay. In: Dodge, R.C., Futcher, L. (eds.) WISE 2009. IAICT, vol. 406, pp. 1–10. Springer, Heidelberg (2013). doi:10.1007/978-3-642-39377-8_1

5. Stanescu, I.A., Stefan, A., Baalsrud Hauge, J.M.: Using gamification mechanisms and digital games in structured and unstructured learning contexts. In: Wallner, G., Kriglstein, S., Hlavacs, H., Malaka, R., Lugmayr, A., Yang, H.-S. (eds.) ICEC 2016. LNCS, vol. 9926, pp. 3–14. Springer, Cham (2016). doi:10.1007/978-3-319-46100-7_1

6. Hussain, Z., Griffiths, M.D., Baguley, T.: Online gaming addiction : classification, prediction and associated risk factors. Inf. Healthc. **6359** (2012)

7. Livingstone, S., Haddon, L.: Comparing children's online opportunities and risks across Europe (2009)

8. Lenhart, A.: Teens and sexting: how and why minor teens are sending sexually suggestive nude or nearly nude images via text messaging. Specialist **4**, 2010 (2009)

9. Livingstone, S., Mascheroni, G., Ólafsson, K.: Children's online risks and opportunities: comparative findings from EU Kids Online and Net Children Go Mobile Executive summary (2014)

10. Hasebrink, U., Görzig, A., Haddon, L., Kalmus, V., Livingstone, S.: Patterns of Risk and Safety Online. LSD, EU Kids Online Network, London (2011)

11. Lorenz, B., Kikkas, K., Laanpere, M., Laugasson, E.: A model to evaluate digital safety concerns in school environment. In: Zaphiris, P., Ioannou, A. (eds.) LCT 2016. LNCS, vol. 9753, pp. 707–721. Springer, Cham (2016). doi:10.1007/978-3-319-39483-1_64

12. Ofcom: Children Believe Everything they Read Online (2015)

13. Ashcroft, M., Kaati, L., Meyer, M.: A step towards detecting online grooming – identifying adults pretending to be children. In: Proceedings of the 2015 European Intelligence and Security Informatics Conference, EISIC 2015, pp. 98–104. IEEE Computer Society, Washington, DC (2015)

14. Tsirtsis, A., Tsapatsoulis, N., Stamatelatos, M., Papadamou, K., Sirivianos, M.: Cyber security risks for minors: a taxonomy and a software architecture. In: 2016 11th International Workshop on Semantic and Social Media Adaptation and Personalization (SMAP), Thessaloniki, pp. 93–99 (2016)

15. Implementing the Children's Online Privacy Protection Act: A Report to Congress, FTC, February 2007. http://www.ftc.gov/reports/coppa/07COPPA-Report-to-Congress.pdf

16. Marwick, A., Murgia-Diaz, D., Palfrey, J.: Youth, privacy and reputations. Berkman Center Research, Technical report 2010-5 (2010). http://papers.ssrn.com/sol3/papers.cfm?abstract_id=1588163

17. Ktoridou, D., Eteokleous, N., Zahariadou, A.: Exploring parents' and children's awareness on internet threats in relation to internet safety. Campus Wide Inf. Syst. **29**(3), 133–143 (2012)

18. Gentile, D.A., Choo, H., Liau, A., Sim, T., Li, D., Fung, D., Khoo, A.: Pathological video game use amongst youths: a two-year longitudinal study. Pediatrics **127**, 319–329 (2011)

19. Huang, X., Zhang, H., Li, M., Wang, J., Zhang, Y., Tao, R.: Mental health, personality, and parental rearing styles of adolescents with internet addiction disorder. Cyber Psychol. Behav. Soc. Netw. **13**(4), 401–406 (2010)

20. Kwisook, C., Hyunsook, S., Myunghee, P., Jinkyu, H., Kitai, K., Byungkoo, L., Hyesun, G.: Internet overuse and excessive daytime sleepiness in adolescents. Psychiatry Clin. Neurosci. **63**(4), 455–462 (2009)

21. Lemmens, J.S., Valkenburg, P.M., Peter, J.: Development and validation of a game addiction scale for adolescents. Media Psychol. **12**, 77–95 (2009)
22. Van Rooij, A.J., Schoenmakers, T.M., Vermulst, A.A., Van Den Eijnden, R.J.J.M., Van De Mheen, D.: Online video game addiction: identification of addicted adolescent gamers. Addiction **106**, 205–212 (2011)
23. Kafai, Y.B., Richard, G.T., Brendesha, M. (eds.) Diversifying Barbie and Mortal Kombat, Intersectional Perspectives and Inclusive Designs in Gaming. ETC Press (2016)
24. Gorriz, C.M., Medina, C.: Engaging girls with computers through software games. Commun. ACM **43**(1), 42–49 (2000)
25. Fron, J., Fullerton, T., Morie, J., Pearce, C.: The hegemony of play. In: Baba, A. (ed.) Situated Play: Proceedings of the Digital Games Research Association Conference, Tokyo, pp. 309–318, 24–28 September 2007
26. Bryce, J.O., Rutter, J.: Gender dynamics and the social and spatial organization of computer gaming. Leis. Stud. **22**(1), 1–15 (2003). Routledge, London
27. Giannakos, M.N., Jaccheri, L., Leftheriotis, I.: Happy girls engaging with technology: assessing emotions and engagement related to programming activities. In: Zaphiris, P., Ioannou, A. (eds.) LCT 2014. LNCS, vol. 8523, pp. 398–409. Springer, Cham (2014). doi: 10.1007/978-3-319-07482-5_38
28. Giannakos, M.N., Jaccheri, L.: What motivates children to become creators of digital enriched artifacts? In: Proceedings of the 9th ACM Conference on Creativity & Cognition. ACM (2013)
29. Papavlasopoulou, S., Giannakos, M.N., Jaccheri, L.: Creative programming experiences for teenagers: attitudes, performance and gender differences. In: Proceedings of the 15th International Conference on Interaction Design and Children, IDC 2016, pp. 565–570. ACM, New York (2016)
30. Exploiting Ubiquitous Computing, Mobile Computing and the Internet of Things to promote Science Education. http://umi-sci-ed.eu/

A Game System for Learning Mathematics with Pacing Considering Individual Motivation and Feeling

Nobumitsu Shikine[1]([✉]), Toshimasa Yamanaka[2],
and Junichi Hoshino[3]

[1] Graduate School of Integrative and Global Majors,
University of Tsukuba, Tsukuba, Japan
shikine-shikine@entcomp.esys.tsukuba.ac.jp
[2] Faculty of Art and Design, University of Tsukuba, Tsukuba, Japan
tyam@geijutsu.tsukuba.ac.jp
[3] Faculty of Engineering, Information and Systems,
University of Tsukuba, Tsukuba, Japan
jhoshino@esys.tsukuba.ac.jp

Abstract. In these days, there are many e-learning system for studying by yourself. In these systems, learner can make their own pacing in for each learning section. But many learner needs more shorter term pacing adjusted to individual motivation and feeling in one session. Many video learning system has lack of interaction. On the other hand, novel game type e-learning system can interact to learner. But, previous novel game system can not keep the prosody information. So this paper proposed new novel game system "NOVELICA" which segmented the lesson to conversation size. And you can easily see the head of conversation with no stress by using NOVELICA. We compared with NOVELICA to previous novel game system and video learning system. And we investigate how different in these 3 contents. Finally, we found that NOVELICA is tend to be less stressful and keeping arousal in learning mathematics.

Keywords: e-Learning · Remedial education · Math anxiety · Video learning · Novel game · Instructional pacing

1 Introduction

There are many students who are not good at or have anxiety towards math [1]. Many situations exist in math above the high school level that require cross-referencing of knowledge of various units, and depending on the student, there are those who are good at and those who are not, creating the need for instructional pacing that suits the individual. In recent years there have been many examples of adaptive learning that introduce an e-Learning system as a follow-up to the one-to-many lecture format, and various systems are being developed according to use. In particular, the self-study system for visual lessons is easy to match to a schedule and is often used in universities and corporate training. However, some issues that are raised concerning these systems

N. Munekata et al. (Eds.): ICEC 2017, LNCS 10507, pp. 169–176, 2017.
DOI: 10.1007/978-3-319-66715-7_17

is that they don't take into account the pace of students, there's no interaction with a teacher, and it is difficult to maintain the motivation to study [2], which leads to stress during learning. It is known that stress during studying puts pressure on working memory and has a negative effect on learning study contents, and importance is being placed on stress management in school and at home [3, 4]. Although stress comes from various sources, such as from a dislike of a subject or circumstances at home, either source negatively affects learning. There are numerous scales when speaking generally about instructional pacing, and we can even consider choosing what to study on a certain day based on a monthly study schedule as instructional pacing. Conventional systems split study into sections such as "trigonometric functions" and "differentials and integrals" according to a learner's comprehension and even use single lessons to keep up pace with the student. However, there has been no consideration made so far for attentive pacing corresponding to motivation and mood for studying in one lesson. To consider this, it will be necessary to review a new time structure that differs from that held by existing contents such as videos. Therefore, this study focuses on the time structuring of e-Learning systems and examines a statistical model of the time characteristics of comprehension of discussion contents within lessons by looking at how a majority of user utilize these systems. It also conducts a real-time appeal corresponding to the study situations of users and develops a system that assists in improving comprehension and maintaining concentration and study motivation. As a first step, this paper conducted a survey regarding how to split up time segments for study contents.

2   Our Propose "NOVELICA"

2.1   Time Structure of Existing System

The existing self-study e-Learning systems can be split up into the two types of automatic progression and manual progression when classifying it based on the pace of lesson progression, and each has their own issues.

The visual lesson system falls under automatic progression and basically progresses unilaterally without keeping pace with the student. Although it is possible to control it by changing playback speed, fast forwarding, or rewinding, it is difficult for listening again to speech when wanting to hear a part over again.

On the other hand, manual progression systems which primarily consist of text and illustrations are used quite often. This paper collectively refers to this type of system as the novel game format. Many of these systems which use study agents are also researched and are taken into consideration more so than visual lessons for their interactivity with students. But while they are tailored for carefully progressing through anxiety areas, there is the nuisance of the student being required to control progression all on their end. In addition, since contents with accompanying voices are often marked by separate speech units, the rhythms of pausing (intervals), speech speed, and pitch in voice conversations break down and don't allow for natural comprehension of voices (Figs. 1 and 2). The visual lesson system can be watched with comfort, and since the novel game system has the time structural advantage of being able to carefully read data, we examined a time segmenting method that allows us to incorporate both of these.

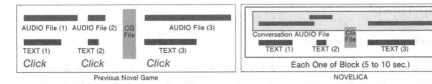

Fig. 1. Timing structure of novel game   **Fig. 2.** Timing structure of NOVELICA

2.2 Summary of Proposed System

NOVELICA is a novel game system which splits lessons into time segments of single response prompts of conversations in order to solve the aforementioned issues. These are referred to as "blocks". One block consists of a single voice file, and text and images are displayed in sync with the conversation from that voice file. One block therefore maintains prosodic information intended by the teacher (Fig. 1).

5 to 10 s is recommended for one block. Somewhere around this length is recommended since one response in a conversation can fit within this range. There is also no essential need for clicks in between each block, and a video experience is made possible by having the game automatically progress. A huge difference when compared with video is that the producer can insert click prompts (response prompts) in between blocks anywhere they choose. In other words, they can basically progress it automatically like a video while leaving it to the student to progress in situations where they want to put emphasis on speech or give the student time for deliberation. In addition, it is a semi-automatic type system that allows you to stop at the current block or jump to a block of your choice in the middle of automatic progression. Since speech can be cued for each block, listening back to topics can be carried out smoothly (Figs. 3 and 4).

NOVELICA can be developed with normal novel-game engine. (ex. kirikiri, AIR Novel, Utage)

If you use our NOVELICA framework, you will be able to compose a lesson program easily. We estimate that it is easier than developing usual novel-game or video-lesson.

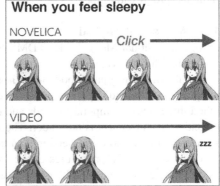

Fig. 3. System reaction difference between   **Fig. 4.** Advantage of semi-automatic progress
NOVELICA and videos

3 Experiment

3.1 Summary of Experiment

This paper used the differentials and integrals volume of the math study assistance novel game " AKAHONe! Prototype A" in order to study how mood and psychological state changes when studying with NOVELICA compared to when studying with existing systems (Fig. 5). This content was prepared as a novel game format with manual progression, the proposed method with semi-automatic progression, and a video format with automatic progression. The lesson contents including the characters and speech was exactly the same between these three conditions and only the progression type differed.

Fig. 5. AKAHONe! Prototype A

3.1.1 Subjects

21 men and women who had graduated high school and had at least somewhat weak at math cooperated as subjects for the experiment. They were chosen because high school graduates would have studied differentials and integrals in Math II B. Subjects were split into three groups consisting of (1) those receiving lessons using the novel game (manual progression type), (2) those receiving lessons using NOVELICA (semi-automatic progression type), and (3) those receiving lessons by watching videos (automatic progression type).

3.1.2 Assessment Method

A Two-Dimensional Mood Scale (TDMS-ST) [5], POMS [6], and a verification test were applied for assessment.

The Two-Dimensional Mood Scale is a psychological scale that measures psychological state (mood) upon response to eight questions. POMS is a questionnaire method that assesses temporary moods and emotional states that change depending on the conditions the subject is put under. There are 65 questions which are condensed to 30 questions in the shortened version, and this method has a high degree of reliability. In accordance with the procedures of the short version of POMS [6], the stress score was taken to be the Total Mood Disturbance (TMD) score which is the total amount of the 5-scale score except with energetic being taken away.

3.1.3 Experiment Procedure

After each participant answered the TMDS-ST a first time, they were asked to try out the contents and afterward respond a second time to the TMDS-ST as well as respond to the short version of POMS (Profile of Mood States) and a verification test. Through this the stress level during learning of all contents and change in mood was studied. In addition, after all items were responded to, they were asked to try out the remaining two contents and give their free opinion on how each compared to one another. Finally, subjects were asked to fill out a mathematical profile. The confirmation test consisted of questions like those in Table 1.

Table 1. Comprehension check test

Q1	Explain the "Takashi underestimation phenomenon (たかし過小評価現象)" (You may use the figure)
Q2	Which formula is the derivative of the function f (x)? 1. $f'(a) = \lim\limits_{h \to 0} \dfrac{f(a+h) - f(a)}{h}$ 2. $f'(x) = \lim\limits_{h \to 0} \dfrac{f(x+h) - f(x)}{h} = \lim\limits_{h \to 0} \dfrac{(x+h)^2 - x^2}{h}$ 3. $f'(x) = \lim\limits_{h \to 0} \dfrac{f(x+h) - f(x)}{h}$ 4. $\int x^n dx = \dfrac{1}{n+1} x^{n+1} + C$
Q3	Differentiate the constant C based on the definition of derivative

Table 2. Mathematical profile sheet

Questions about your math
· Do you feel math anxiety?
Very High, High, M-H, Moderate,   M-L, Low, Nothing
· What was the unit you were good at?
· What was the unit you were weak at?
· If you have impressions or memories about math, please describe.

3.2 Results and Consideration Concerning Stress

The TMD score of POMS was taken as the stress score (average of 4.6). While the score and dispersion of Group 2 was the smallest, no significant difference was found. There were participants in groups 1 and 3 whose stress scores largely exceeded from the average of 10 points. Upon checking their profiles, it was found that group 1 was good at differentials while group 3 was weak at (the range of study including) differentials (Tables 2 and 3).

After performing a morpheme analysis of the free opinions and searching for frequent vocabulary, many people in group 1 explained that they were able to progress on their own but they found the clicking to be bothersome, while many in group 3 explained that they couldn't keep up with the tempo of the videos. Upon performing a chi-square test, a statistically significant correlation ($p < .05$) was verified wherein group 1 expressed their displeasure of the system citing that they had to make a lot of clicks, while group 3 also expressed displeasure towards the system citing that it was too fast to keep up with. From the above, it was confirmed that if someone was studying something they were good at, they were displeased with having to progress through the manual progression type system in detail by themselves, while if someone was studying something they were weak at, they were displeased with advancing through the automatic progression type system without being able to keep up with understanding it. Through this we can surmise that there are situations where someone can't create a good pace for themselves and feel strongly stressed. Meanwhile, the stress score for all participants in group 2 using NOVELICA was lower than 10.

With NOVELICA you can just watch or skip areas that you already know or don't need to listen to without having to control anything, and you can dedicate more time to areas you want to listen to again or concentrate on. Due to this, participants were able to create their own pace regardless of whether they were good or weak at differentials, which helped prevent stress (Fig. 6).

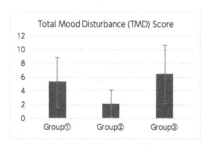

Fig. 6. Total mood disturbance score

Table 3. TMD Score and Mathematical Profile

	TMD Score	good at	weak at	Group
Partici-pant1	20	Differential and integral Vector Combinatorics	Numerical sequence Limit	①
P-3	21	Trigonometric functions Geometry	Mathematics II,B and later general	③
P-4	13	Differential Geometry	Integral Probability theory	①
P-9	23	Nothing	Overall	③

3.3 Results and Consideration Regarding Content Comprehension and Arousal Level

The ratio of correct answers for the confirmation test was as follows for questions 1 to 3. Question 1 was not too related to math and could be answered if someone understood the topic. Question 3 was an Advanced-level exercise and could not be answered except mainly by those who were good at differentials. Thus, the total score was only tallied for questions 1 and 2. Group 2 had the highest ratio of correct answers, suggesting they were able to keep up with the lesson discussions. The difference between groups 1 and 2 is thought to be due to natural understanding of voices through maintaining prosodic information. Although the ratio of correct answers for group 3 for whom the rhythm of natural voices should have been natural, the free opinions revealed that some couldn't get into watching a video, found the experience passive, or felt they were being left behind, which means that one-sided viewing without interactivity makes it not possible to maintain concentration. The ratio of correct answers is thought to be low due to the number of things not heard increasing when unable to concentrate (Figs. 7 and 8).

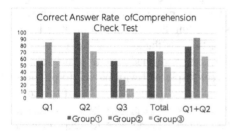

Fig. 7. Correct answer rate of check test

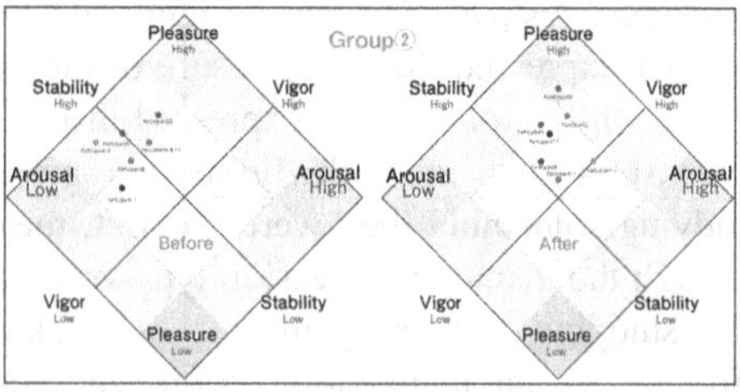

Fig. 8. TDMS-ST result Group②

We can estimate from the changes in arousal level whether the contents were faced head-on and an effort was made to study. Looking at the measurement results of the Two-Dimensional Mood Scale, we see that the arousal levels of all participants only rose for group 2. After studying with NOVELICA, six out of seven people changed to a normal mood state, and the remaining one person's mood changed to an area suitable for activity. NOVELICA has a time structure that differs from that of video or a novel game, and prompts can be inserted. This way it doesn't really feel like one-way viewing and a moderate arousal state can be maintained.

4 Conclusion

In this paper, we conducted a study concerning how to best split time segments for study contents that take into consideration attentive pacing corresponding to learning desire and mood during a lesson. The proposed system NOVELICA is a semi-automatic type novel game e-Learning system that segments lessons into conversation block that are 5 to 10 s long so that one may interactively cue conversations while maintaining the prosodic information of voices.

21 men and women who had graduated high school and were weak at math were split into three groups and an experiment was conducted that had them study by means of (1) manual progression type contents, (2) semi-automatic progression contents, and (3) automatic progression contents. It was understood from an assessment of stress scores using the POMS that with NOVELICA, it is possible to create a suitable pace for oneself regardless of whether someone is good or weak at the study units, and it is possible to study in a low-stress state. In addition, results of the change measured in mood with a Two-Dimensional Mood Scale showed that inserting prompts with NOVELICA maintained a moderate state of arousal and comprehension of the lesson contents was promoted together with maintaining the prosodic information of voices.

These results indicated that NOVELICA's segmentation makes it possible to create individually suited lesson paces and acts as a time structure that reduces stress during learning and assists with comprehension. In the future, we expect that if we can appeal to real-time from the system side in accordance with the block transition state of the user, we can implement e-Learning with interactivity.

References

1. Stoet, G., Bailey, D.H., Moore, A.M., Geary, D.C.: Countries with higher levels of gender equality show larger national sex differences in mathematics anxiety and relatively lower parental mathematics valuation for girls. PLoS ONE 11(4), e0153857 (2016). doi:10.1371/journal.pone.0153857. Published online 21 Apr 2016
2. Nakamura, R., Inoue, A., Ichimura, S., Okada, K., Matsushita, Y.: "Ghost-Tutor": a learning support system suggesting learning pace for on-demand learning. IPSJ 47(7), 2099–2106 (2006)
3. Vukovic, R.K., Kieffer, M.J., Bailey, S.P., Harari, R.R.: Mathematics anxiety in young children: Concurrent and longitudinal associations with mathematical performance. Contemp. Educ. Psychol. 38(1), 1–10 (2013)

Visual-Effect Dictionary for Converting Words into Visual Images

Shogo Hirai[✉] and Kaoru Sumi

Future University Hakodate, 116-2 Kameda, Hakodate-shi, Hokkaido, Japan
g2117041@fun.ac.jp, kaoru.sumi@acm.org

Abstract. This paper describes a visual effect dictionary that can visually express images of words used as modifiers, such as adjectives, onomatopoeia by adding 3D objects with a visual effect. This visual effect dictionary links words and visual effects for the target objects. The same modifier can have different meanings depending on the target object thus, an intelligent algorithm to select the visual effects is required. This dictionary can be used as communication support for images that are difficult to express only by modifier words such as adjectives, onomatopoeia. When multiple regression analysis was conducted in the questionnaire results, it was found that there are appropriate visual effects and inadequate visual effects depending on nouns.

Keywords: Visual effect · 3D object · Image words

1 Introduction

In this research, we have developed a visual effect dictionary that can visually express images of words as modifiers such as adjectives, onomatopoeias as visual effects for 3D objects. Onomatopoeia is a word that phonetically imitates, resembles or suggests the sound. This visual effect dictionary is a dictionary that links a word and a visual effect of the target object. Development of visual effect dictionary is difficult because the same modifier could have different meanings depending on the type of the target object; thus, an intelligent algorithm of selecting visual effects is required.

WordsEye [1] is a system in which "a yellow elephant" is displayed as a 3D object when text such as "Yellow elephant" is inputted. Our system is different from that in that it shows visual effects by specializing on modifiers. Tanaka et al. [2] developed Kairai which expresses audio information by animation using 3D objects. Kairai is a natural-language understanding system that emphasizes spoken words such as 3D space viewpoint. Therefore, Kairai expresses about distances and colors such as "far" and "blue" as adjectival expressions. Similarly, our research also expresses onomatopoeic words as adjectives, but differs from Kairai, our system is targeted for animation and effects. Anime de Blog is also available in which 3D animation is displayed by entering characters [3–5]. Anime de Blog creates 3D animation by matching the motion of a subject character to a verb. In our system, adjectives or onomatopoeias is defined as surfaces of things generated by textures, visual effects, and animation.

© IFIP International Federation for Information Processing 2017
Published by Springer International Publishing AG 2017. All Rights Reserved
N. Munekata et al. (Eds.): ICEC 2017, LNCS 10507, pp. 177–182, 2017.
DOI: 10.1007/978-3-319-66715-7_18

For developing the algorithms, we analyzed the impression of participants by questionnaires using subjects and examined the algorithm for developing the visual effect dictionary. We believe that this dictionary is useful for supporting communication via images when we express impressions which is difficult to express only by words.

2   Visual Effect Dictionary System that Visually Expresses Images of Words

A game development engine system that used Unity5 and C# was employed as a development language. In this system, the user provides audio information to the system. The system converts the given audio information into a visual effect and a 3D object. The speech recognition of this system uses the IBM Watson Speech to Text. The recognized speech information is classified into "modifier" and "noun" by morphological analysis using the NMeCab system. The classified part of speech is classified by the IBM Watson Natural Language Classifier(NLC). According to the classified information, the "modifier" is converted into a visual effect, and the "noun" is converted into a 3D object and displayed to the user.

The classification method uses NMeCab, which can be used in Unity. NMecab is a morphological analysis engine of the .NET library. This system classifies sentences into nouns and adjectives.

The noun classification uses IBM Bluemix NLC. The NLC classifies the contents inputted by the user into one of the classes prepared by using a previously trained classifier. The NLC automatically classifies the noun information entered by the user into these four classes with a possibility. For example, apple is classified in a class called "fruit" which is prepared in advance.

In this system, we classified the modifiers into seven categories with reference to "*E de manabu Giongo • Gitaigo Card*" (Onomatopoeia-mimetic word card studied with pictures) [6]. We created "glowing", "disturbed," "moisture," "dynamic," and "floating" as visual representation with visual effect. The 3D-prepared objects are "fruit," "food," "ball," and "car." The visual effect and 3D object classification method will be explained later. This system converts classified adjectives, onomatopoeias, into associated visual effects. The visual effects are of three types, namely, "visual effect around a 3D object", "visual effect modified texture", and "Movement to a 3D object itself."

The visual effect-modified texture expresses colors such as "red" and "blue". An example of a visual effect around a 3D object expresses abstract words such as "delicious", "beautiful." In the movement to a 3D object itself, the coordinates of the 3D object are varied to adapt to the expressions such as "fast" and "slow". Visual effects are created by imagining the aforementioned "glowing", "disturbed", "moisture," "dynamic," and "floating." We searched synonyms using Japanese WordNet and added the test data.

Nouns are displayed by importing the 3D object from the Asset Store of Unity. Currently available 3D objects are of five types, namely, "fruit", "warm food", "cold food", "car", "ball". First, we chose foods for many adjectives that we often use adjectives such as taste, tactile, and soon. In addition, we chose fruits whose characteristics can be easily understood, such as hard and soft. Even the system can be used with other foods; thus, we investigated whether we can use the same visual effect. Therefore, we chose food, in addition to fruit. The classification for food alone is too broad; hence, we divided the food into warm and cold foods. We selected a "ball" as that is similar shape of "apple" and an example of other than food. In addition to the above four types, we prepared a "car" as a classification that is likely to reflect many animated visual effects.

3   Experiment

We will introduce from the aspects of clustering classification, and multiple regression analysis based on the questionnaire according to the common points of visual effect, modifier word, and 3D object. In this experiment, the factors and groups were analyzed using clustering classification in order to obtain common items and unknown groups from the questionnaire result. Then, we conducted multiple regression analysis to investigate the correlation when we perform evaluation using common sense knowledge of objects.

3.1   Purpose of the Experiment

The purpose of this experiment is to investigate whether an image of a word can be correctly reflected by the visual effect and the 3D object. In this research, we assume that by investigating visual effects and 3D objects, we can explore new classification method that can be understood using visual effect.

3.2   Experimental Method

This experiment was conducted employing 30 male and female University students over the age of 18 years in December 2016. The questionnaires asked whether the subject that read the sentences consisting of "modifier & noun" from the combined animation of "3D object & visual effect" in order to investigate whether the subject can recall the modifier from the 3D object and visual effect. The questionnaire was created using Google Form. The questionnaire generated three classification types, namely, "fruit," "food" and "others." In each item, the "fruit" class is composed of 25 videos and 43 questions, the "food" class is composed of 23 videos and 37 questions, and the "others" class is composed of 28 videos, 42 questions. The subjects viewed the videos checked and answered the questions. For example, a subject watched a movie showing a combination of the glowing effect and a 3D-object representation of an apple. Next, the video presented a question of whether the subject can recall the "delicious apple." The subject selected appropriate answers from five levels of recollection, namely, "can recall," "can somewhat recall," "do not know," "cannot very much recall," "cannot recall."

3.3 Experiment Results

In the case of a combination of "*Oishii*" (delicious) apple and "glowing" effect, 60.50% of the subjects selected "can recall" or "can somewhat recall." The "glowing" effect represented a majority of the answers in both "*Oishii*" (delicious) and "*Atarashii*" (new) ratios of the apple recall. With regard to bananas and peaches, the proportion of "new" represented the majority of the answers. The majority answers of the two objects of "warm food" accounted for the proportion that can be recalled with the "steam" effect for both "*Oishii*" (delicious) and "warm" effects. Regarding the "cold food," more subjects cannot recall either effect. The evaluation of "ball" was dominated by a majority of the proportion in which "*Atarashii*" (new) can be recalled when using the glow effect was used. Majority of the subjects accounted for the proportion in which "cars" and "buses" can recall "*Atarashii*" (new) with the "glowing" effect.

3.4 Relationship of Common Sense Knowledge of Objects

We investigated the modifier "*Atarashii*" (new) from the common sense knowledge of the object. The common sense knowledge of the object cited common sense knowledge and general items that appeared as a result of searching each noun using a meaning dictionary called Japanese Wordnet. We conducted a multiple regression analysis. As a result, the decision coefficient (R2) was 0.989, which shows that it was significant at the 10% level. The significance of the regression equation as a whole was 0.00, which was significant at 1% level. The standardization factor that each item was significant at a significant probability of 0.01% of the warm food was 0.000. We found that the cold one was significant at 0.011 and food was significant at 0.034. The significant probability was at 0.1% level. we found that the normalization coefficient of the warm one was 0.932, and the positive correlation provided even greater influence. In other words, the combination of "steam" and "warm food" turned out to be appropriate to express the modifier "*Atarashii*" (new). The following is a summary of the "new" "steam" visual effects. (1) We focused on the common sense of objects. (2) The result showed a positive correlation among warm, and cold things and food as common sense of objects appropriate for "steam" visual effects. We also focused on "*Oishii*" (delicious) using the same visual effects as different modifiers, and performed multiple regression analysis. From the multiple regression analysis using the variable reduction method with the combination of "*Oishii*" (delicious) and glow, the common sense of all objects was excluded, and the significance probability could not be calculated. In other words, the data were not appropriate data for multiple regression analysis and no relationship was found. Finally, we observed the combination of "*Oishii*" (delicious) and steam. The coefficient of determination (R2) was 0.997 and turned out to be significant at the 10% level. The significance of the regression equation as a whole was 0.00, which was significant at the 1% level. The standardization factor of each item was significant at a significance probability of 0.01% level of the "warm food." The normalization coefficient also showed a positive correlation of 0.939. In other words, in expressing the modifier "*Oishii*" (delicious), we found that the combination of "steam" and "warm food" was appropriate.

4   Discussion

According to the questionnaire result, a majority of subjects recalled "*Oishii* (delicious) apple" with the "glowing" effect and the "apple". A majority of subjects recalled "*Atarashii* (new)" with the "glowing" effect and the "fruit". However, a majority of subjects didn't recall "*Atarashii* (new)" with the "glowing" effect and the "hot food" or "cold food". Therefore, only the "glowing" effect of the fruits in the food turned out to represent the adjective "new."

A majority of subjects recalled delicious, new and warm foods with the "steam" effect. In other words, "steam" can be remembered as delicious for expressing a new warm food.

As the multiple regression analysis, it was suggested that "hot food & steam" had a strong influence on the questionnaire result recall of "*Atarashii* (new)". Further, we found that the combination of "warm food & steam" was appropriate for the modifier "*Oishii*(delicious)". This analysis suggested that appropriate or inappropriate combinations are available for the visual effects, modifiers, and 3D objects. The modifiers are related to the common sense knowledge of 3D objects for visualizing. By examining this relationship in more detail, nouns can be classified into multiple classes, such as common sense knowledge of 3D objects. Thus, we could be concluded that we can visualize a modifier with multiple meanings by using common sense knowledge of the object. As a future work, we will increase the number of questionnaires, visual effects to use and nouns (Fig. 1).

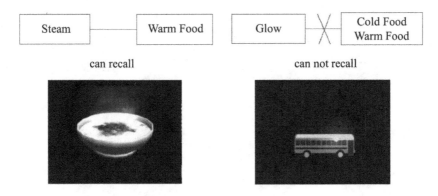

Fig. 1. Analysis summary

5   Conclusion

We have introduced the development of a dictionary that shows visual effects of adjectives, onomatopoeias that corresponding to 3D objects. According to the questionnaire result, it was suggested that "delicious" is easily recalled by giving a steam effect to warm food. Thus, by investigating from the common sense knowledge of the object, we found that it is possible to provide an appropriate visual effect to the modifier using the system.

References

1. Bob, C., Richard, S.: WordsEye: An automatic text-to-scene conversion system. In: Proceedings of the 28th Annual Conference on Computer Graphics, SIGGRAPH 2001. ACM, Los Angeles (2001)
2. Hozumi, T., Takenobu, T., Yusuke, S.: Animated agents capable of understanding natural language and performing actions. In: Prendinger, H., Ishizuka, M. (eds.) Life-Like Characters, pp. 163–187. Springer, Heidelberg (2004)
3. Sumi, K.: Anime de Blog: Animation CGM for content distribution. In: Proceedings of International Conference on Advances in Computer Entertainment Technology (ACE2008), SIGCHI, pp. 187–190. ACM (2008)
4. Sumi, K.: Animation-Based Interactive Storytelling System. In: Spierling, Ulrike, Szilas, Nicolas (eds.) ICIDS 2008. LNCS, vol. 5334, pp. 48–50. Springer, Heidelberg (2008). doi: 10.1007/978-3-540-89454-4_8
5. Kaoru, S.: Capturing common sense knowledge via story generation. In: Common Sense and Intelligent User Interfaces 2009: Story Understanding and Generation for Context-Aware Interface Design, 2009 International Conference on Intelligent User Interfaces (IUI2009), SIGCHI. ACM (2009)
6. Tomikawa, K.: Onomatopoeia/mimetic word card studied with pictures, 3anet (1997)

Design and Evaluation of a Cybersecurity Awareness Training Game

Duy Huynh$^{(\boxtimes)}$, Phuc Luong, Hiroyuki Iida$^{(\boxtimes)}$, and Razvan Beuran$^{(\boxtimes)}$

School of Information Science, Japan Advanced Institute of Science and Technology,
1-1 Asahidai, Nomi, Ishikawa 923-1211, Japan
{duyhuynh,luongphuc,iida,razvan}@jaist.ac.jp

Abstract. Serious games are becoming more popular because they provide an opportunity for learning in a natural environment. Although many concepts included in cybersecurity awareness training are universal, many forms of training fail because they are based on rote learning and do not require users to think about security concepts. The main objective of this study is to design a candidate cybersecurity awareness training tool which provides an environment for helping users to understand security concepts while playing a game. To reach our goal, we applied a newly developed model, which is Activity Theory-based Model of Serious Games (ATMSG), to design our own game. According to the design, we implemented a game demo and assessed its gameplay. The results indicated that the story gameplay can help players improve their understanding of cybersecurity problems and resolutions.

Keywords: Serious game · Sybersecurity · Game design · Activity theory · ATMSG

1 Introduction

Nowadays, the whole world is facing severe challenges posed by hackers, spammers and a large pool of attackers who are motivated by a variety of reasons. To prevent attacks from high-tech criminals, some organizations use a cybersecurity training tool to enhance its information assurance posture. However, creating an engaging training tool, which holds trainees' attention sufficiently long to impart awareness, is a considerable challenge. Moreover, many forms of training fail the studied concepts because the training is by rote learning and does not require users to think about and apply. Generally, to increase motivation and engagement of users, many trainers has designed their training tools as a serious game. A serious game is the combination between game learning sciences and digital entertainment. Similar to simulations, serious games present a virtual reality of varying fidelity that allows learners to explore, experiment, or simply engage in learning. Therefore, our research aims at designing a training tool, which helps users enhance their cybersecurity knowledge, by using a serious

© IFIP International Federation for Information Processing 2017
Published by Springer International Publishing AG 2017. All Rights Reserved
N. Munekata et al. (Eds.): ICEC 2017, LNCS 10507, pp. 183–188, 2017.
DOI: 10.1007/978-3-319-66715-7_19

game design model. Moreover, we also try to find a suitable gameplay which helps users understand the knowledge obviously. In this study, we use the Activity Theory-based Model of Serious Games (ATMSG) [1] and a story gameplay to design the training game. The details are shown in the next sections.

2   Theoretical Background

The learning effects of serious games in studies across educational contexts are inconclusive [10]. One of the recommendations is to ensure that game objectives and learning objectives correspond. It is really difficult to determine whether or not a game supports the learning of students because a learning objective and outcomes are unclear. There exist several models such as RETAIN [4], DODDEL [7], and the 5/10 method [6] which support to design serious games. However, in this study, we use ATMSG [1] to implement our game design idea. The ATMSG provides a comprehensive way to investigate, in detail, how a serious game is structured, and uses activity theory as the theoretical background.

In ATMSG, educational serious games are seen as used in the context of four activities: the gaming activity, the learning activity, the intrinsic instructional activity and the extrinsic instructional activity. There is a four-steps-approach that progressively guides the user in applying the ATMSG to the design or analysis of educational serious games. These steps take the user from a high-level understanding of the activities to the concrete components which implement those activities. The user identifies game components with the help of the taxonomy of serious game components. The details of the four-steps-approach are shown in [1].

In comparison to other models, ATMSG offers a more precise model for the analysis of the educational and gaming aspects of a game, allowing users to perform a more exhaustive decomposition of components as the game unfolds, and to link these components to the overall learning objectives [1]. Moreover, the design using ATMSG is expressed as tables and charts. That facilitates game developers to understand the designer's idea. That is a reason why we choose ATMSG. In our design, we use a gameplay in story games as our main gameplay. We call it a "story gameplay". The story gameplay uses storytelling technique to lead players to experience game events. Hence, we apply this gameplay into our game to support users in clearly understanding the given problem and its solution.

3   Design of Cybersecurity Awareness Training Game

Firstly, we introduce our game design idea. Our game design idea focuses on making a cybersecurity training game for users to learn and understand obviously cybersecurity concepts. We aim at giving them some reality situations of security attack. For example, "How to recognize phishing emails?", "How to protect your information at public locations?". In those situations, users will control their character and find the solution for given problems. We will lead users through a story step by step and they must make choices, which reflect their character's behavior. After each situation, a system will evaluate users' answer and gives them the right answer with its explanation. Following this idea, we design a game and describe it in detail by using the four-steps-approach of ATMSG. Critical points of each step are shown in the next discussion.

Step 1 - Describe the activities: In this step, we highlight the main aspects of activities to understand this game easily. Moreover, to make it convenient to the implementation, test and evaluation, we choose the topic "Cybersecurity awareness training in a university". It not only makes convenient for us but also players (university students) to be familiar with given situations in the game and to keep cybersecurity concepts in mind easily. As a result, the main subject of gaming and learning activities is university students who will gain knowledge by experiencing directly real cybersecurity problems and learning to avoid and solve them. Our game demo aims at providing the training tool for students in our university (JAIST). Therefore, game resources such as images, learning content or story reflect the daily life at JAIST.

Step 2 - Represent the game sequence: In this step, we provide a diagram to present our game sequence by using UML. The game includes two main activities: "Problem Solving" and "Practice". Both game activities have different gameplay. The Problem Solving will give players a new situation (story) to experience. Players must understand given situations and choose their behavior carefully to get a perfect score. If players choose a wrong answer, they cannot get a score in this event. An explanation and a right answer will be given after evaluation. While Practice gives players a quiz game, which contains questions about cybersecurity awareness. Players must answer them repeatedly and they will be punished if they choose a wrong answer. Whereas Problem Solving is commonly used to support players in understanding situations, Practice helps players remember cybersecurity concepts. Practice's gameplay is easy to understand, so in our demo, we only give an example. On the other hand, Problem Solving is more complicated than Practice, and our research tries to examine the effect of story gameplay at understanding of users. Thus, we only focus on designing Problem Solving for our game demo.

Step 3 - Identify actions, tools and goals: In order to understand a game sequence easily, we are going to identify components that are related to each node in the game sequence. Those nodes are composed from their actions, tools and goals. We first choose the relevant components directly from the taxonomy of serious games (Table 11 in [1]), and fill them into the three layers of each activity involved (gaming, learning, intrinsic and extrinsic instruction). The extrinsic instructional activity is performed outside by the teacher or instructor in the context of the overall learning setting. Our game purpose is not to create an open learning environment for a teacher to teach anything they want. We provide a training tool which helps players in enhancing their awareness about cybersecurity problems in a specific organization (e.g. university, company, etc.). Therefore, in our case, we do not consider an extrinsic instruction, but we simply fill nine layers in total. Almost all components were selected based on main gameplay in order to clearly show designer's ideas by the game actions, tools and goals. Therefore, this step can help game developers understand the designer's idea thoroughly.

Step 4 - Description of the implementation: In this step, we provide a more detailed description of our implementation. We explain what is being done, using which tool, and with what purpose in each block of a table. We also explain how the use of such components and characteristics support the achievement of the entertainment and/or pedagogical goals of the game.

The combination of the four steps described above provides a comprehensive view of the structure of our game, from its high-level purposes and general characteristics to its concrete implementation. In this study, we used Novelty [8] to implement our design. Novelty provides simple methods to create our own visual novel game. A visual novel game [9], also known as a story game, is an interactive game. Typically, the majority of players' interaction is limited to clicking to keep the text, graphics and sound moving on while making narrative choices along the way. Our detailed design and demo is available at [3].

4   Evaluation and Discussion

To collect players' feedback on the demo, we created a survey which is available at [2]. The survey requires players to evaluate the demo in multiple aspects of the gameplay and educational value. They must rate on a scale from 1 (worst) to 10 (best). We had 10 participants who filled out the questionnaire. Six of them are at the beginner level in cybersecurity knowledge and other participants are at intermediate level. The details of the survey question and its results are shown in Tables 1 and 2. The survey questions are categorized into three groups. The first group (Q1–Q6) is used to test abilities of the game demo such as clarity, game length, content, and enjoyment aspect. It helps us figure out a comfortable game setting in official implementation. The second group (Q7–Q9) aims at evaluating learning purposes and the effect of story gameplay on helping players understand cybersecurity concept. The last question is used to estimate how much this game improves players' motivation.

The responses to the survey show some advantages of the game. The first advantage is that the game is very easy to play for both groups of participants (Q4, the average in total is 9.6). Besides, the game is rated highly on two aspects that are what to do (Q1, the average in total is 8.7) and the story of the game (Q2, the average in total is 7.5). However, the interest of this game is rated not so high by beginners (Q3, the average is 6.0), but it is interesting for learners who are at intermediate level (Q3, the average is 7.3). The reason is that the game provides new materials to beginners more than intermediate learners (Q6, the averages are 7.8 and 7.0). That makes the beginners feel that the game length is quite long (Q5, the average is 6.5), so they become boring when playing this game. On the contrary, the game length is suitable for intermediate learners (Q5, the average is 5.5) so they feel more comfortable than the others. According to

Table 1. Survey questions.

ID	Question
Q1	Clarity on what to do
Q2	Clarity of story
Q3	How fun it is to play the game
Q4	How easy it is to play the game
Q5	Length of the game
Q6	The game provides you to new material
Q7	The game helps you to understand a situation of the problem
Q8	The game helps you to understand how to solve the problem
Q9	Improving your understanding in cybersecurity
Q10	Improving the motivation to learn more about cybersecurity

Table 2. Survey results: average score per question.

Level	Q1	Q2	Q3	Q4	Q5[a]	Q6	Q7	Q8	Q9	Q10
Beginner	8.8	7.3	6.0	9.8	6.5	7.8	8.8	8.0	8.0	6.7
Intermediate	8.5	7.8	7.3	9.3	5.5	7.0	7.8	7.5	7.0	6.8
Total	8.7	7.5	6.5	9.6	6.1	7.5	8.4	7.8	7.6	6.7

[a] This aspect is rated on a scale from 1 (short) to 10 (long)

the results of questions from 7 to 9, we have high ratings on the aspect of understanding a problem situation, how to solve the problem and improving students' understanding (Q7–Q9, the averages in total are 8.4, 7.8 and 7.6). However, those aspects are rated by beginner higher than by intermediate learners. The reason is that the game was designed to be a training tool for awareness raising for a beginner to obtain new knowledge. Therefore, this game is more helpful for beginner than intermediate learners. It seems that the game is not good at making enjoyment, so it improves the motivation of users not so well (Q10, the average in total is 6.7). In conclusion, the advantage is that the game can help the students improve their understanding of cybersecurity awareness. By giving a story, the game aims to lead players to understand cybersecurity problems and resolutions, even though it teaches an intermediate student nothing new in the material.

5   Conclusion

In this study, we presented the design of a security awareness training tool. By using the ATMSG paradigm, which offers a more precise model for the design of the educational and gaming aspects of a game, we present our game idea in detail. Moreover, the model ensures that game objectives and learning objectives correspond. The four-steps-approach helps game developers follow the idea of designer easily. To evaluate the suitability of the game structure and a story gameplay, we have built a game demo which is implemented by using the Novelty software. After the game was played and evaluated by university students, the result indicated that the game was rated well on the aspect of understanding cybersecurity problems and solutions. Therefore, the game which we developed by following this design help us avoid the rote learning of users when using the training tool. However, to improve the enjoyment of this game and the learners' motivation, we should add more game actions and game elements.

Although the game can help users in understanding the cybersecurity concept, it is not good at making enjoyment for players because it is simple to play by clicking and reading. Therefore, our future works aim at fairly changing in a gameplay which increases interaction of users such as control character, click on items, etc. to make the game more interesting. Moreover, the balance between tasks and rewards in a serious game is very important for its entertaining aspect, so we aim to find a suitable learning content structure in order to improve enjoyment in the designed game by applying some game theories on measuring the game enjoyment such as game refinement theory [5].

Acknowledgments. The authors wish to thank the anonymous referees for their constructive comments that helped to improve the article considerably, and the group of students who participated in the survey of this study.

References

1. Carvalho, M.B., Bellotti, F., Berta, R., De Gloria, A., Islas Sedano, C., Baalsrud Hauge, J.: An activity theory-based model for serious games analysis and conceptual design. Comput. Educ. **87**, 166–181 (2015)
2. CSAG Survey - Google Form. N.p. (2017). https://goo.gl/forms/jZUDRFcx8TMdfsTJ3. Accessed 5 Jan 2017
3. Cybersecurity Awareness Game Demo - Dropbox. N.p. (2017). https://www.dropbox.com/sh/xpzlfjmuqaljvxm/AAAGPRHfgZimUeWmQyx3QYiHa?dl=0. Accessed 5 Jan 2017
4. Gunter, G.A., Kenny, R.F., Vick, E.H.: Taking educational games seriously: using the RETAIN model to design endogenous fantasy into standalone educational games. Educ. Tech. Res. Dev. **56**, 511–537 (2008)
5. Iida, H., Takeshita, N., Yoshimura, J.: A metric for entertainment of boardgames: its implication for evolution of chess variants. In: Entertainment Computing Technologies and Applications, pp. 65–72 (2003)
6. Van Rooij, R.: The 5/10 method: a method for designing educational games. Masters thesis, Game and Media Technology, Utrecht University (2013)
7. McMahon, M.: Using the DODDEL model to teach serious game design to novice designers. In: Proceedings ASCILITE Auckland (2009)
8. Novelty - Visual Novel Maker. Visualnovelty.com. N.p. (2017). http://www.visualnovelty.com. Accessed 4 Jan 2017
9. Visual Novel. En.wikipedia.org. N.p. (2017). https://en.wikipedia.org/wiki/Visual_novel. Accessed 4 Jan 2017
10. Young, M.F., Slota, S., Cutter, A.B., Jalette, G., Mullin, G., Lai, B., Simeoni, Z., Tran, M., Yukhymenko, M.: Our princess is in another castle: a review of trends in serious gaming for education. Rev. Educ. Res. **82**(1), 61–89 (2012)

Sports Training System for Situational Judgment Improvement by Reliving First Person Viewpoint

Shunki Shimizu[✉] and Kaoru Sumi

Future University Hakodate, Kameda, Hakodate, 116-2, Japan
g2117025@fun.ac.jp, kaoru.sumi@acm.org

Abstract. Situational judgment in a ballgame is said to be more difficult to obtain than skills such as basic passing and shooting. However, by displaying the images seen by a player from a first person viewpoint, it is possible to have a user perform the actual sports action performed by the player and experience the same feeling. We developed a situational judgment training system for this purpose. In this research, we particularly aim to improve the user's situational judgment ability and focus on learning situations in ballgames in which the user does not know how to move to get the ball. The results of evaluation experiments conducted with six subjects indicate that the gameplay of users improved such that they were consciously able to move and get the ball better than they had before using the system.

Keywords: First person viewpoint · Situational judgment · Reliving

1 Introduction

It is said that judging the situation in ballgames is more important than basic skills like passing, shooting, and dribbling. One of the reasons why situational judgment skills is important is that the attacking sides' mistakes might instantly replace offense and defense because they play to directly force each other in goal-oriented ballgames, requiring instant situational judgment [1]. Another reason is spatial ability. It has been stated that one of the reasons is that players can find empty space or other players around whom there are no defenses when viewed from a third person viewpoint, but they lose empty space and the free player when they play in the court and watch from a first person viewpoint [1].

Various studies have been conducted on situational judgment and sports training. Further, we can experience a player's viewpoint through the use of Virtual Reality (VR) devices such as Head Mount Display (HMD). However, even though we can experience sports scenes from a player's viewpoint, the experience is not interactive as we cannot perform any action in the game or somewhat interact with the video.

Using JackIn [2], people's activities are shared and viewers can be assisted or guided by other people's expertise. It enables people to experience the viewpoint of professional players. With the first person viewpoint streaming from a person wearing a see-through HMD with a camera called JackIn Head, another person can share in the first person's

© IFIP International Federation for Information Processing 2017
Published by Springer International Publishing AG 2017. All Rights Reserved
N. Munekata et al. (Eds.): ICEC 2017, LNCS 10507, pp. 189–195, 2017.
DOI: 10.1007/978-3-319-66715-7_20

viewpoint. Covaci et al. [3] developed a VR-based free throw training system that is highly reliable.

A system that provides experiences from a first person viewpoint is useful for effectively and quickly learning motions and exercises [4]. It is also easier to remember first person images than third person images [5]. Nakagawa stated that situational judgment involves applying the most appropriate play from experience and memory [6]; thus, reliving experiences from a first person viewpoint leads to improved situational judgment.

Our aim is to develop a sports training system that enables situational judgment and spatial awareness from a third person viewpoint and relive interaction from a first person viewpoint. We focus on situations in which players have difficulty getting the ball and how to move and judge the situation in such scenarios. From the background that spatial awareness is difficult, first we discuss how to move to get the ball from a third person viewpoint. Then, we analyze the experience from a first person viewpoint.

2 Sports Training System for Situational Judgment by Reliving First Person Viewpoint

The proposed system comprises two subsystems: a whiteboard system and a reliving system. The system is similar to a strategy board used in games such as basketball or soccer. In this system, users set the situations they wish to learn by moving pieces and 3D images corresponding to each piece's position are displayed.

In the reliving system, images corresponding to each piece's position are displayed in the whiteboard system. First, the system visually teaches the manner in which the movement is executed in the various situations in videos from a third person viewpoint. Then, the user is asked to experience a virtual basketball by performing the actual basketball action from a first person viewpoint. The system teaches only movement and judgment to get the ball because our focus is on learning in a situation where the user does not know how to move to get the ball.

The system was developed in C# using Microsoft Visual Studio 2015 and the Unity development engine, developed by Unity Technology. In addition, Microsoft Kinect v2 for Windows is utilized. Kinect is a peripheral device that is able to sense body movements, gestures, and voice, and carry out face tracking, etc. We selected it to develop the interactive system owing to its many functions.

The system hardware comprises one Kinect, a projector, and fisheye lens in a dome made from cardboard, as depicted in Fig. 1. We project a video in a part of the dome's side and magnify the projection range via the fisheye lens. The Kinect is situated between the user and the projector. The dome is approximately 180 cm high and sufficiently wide that the user can move two or three steps. We conducted experiments in a limited space so as to simulate a system that users can use in their house.

Fig. 1. Implementation environment: the inside and outside of the dome.

2.1   Teaching from Third Person Viewpoint

In this study, the system teaches how to move to get a ball without dribbling so as to reduce the difference in individual ability. At this point, the system provides support for the following three skills (for which we made videos based on sports lessons from professional basketball players in Hokkaido, Japan)[1]. (1) Cutting and Back cut, (2) Pass and Run, (3) High or low speed movement.

Cutting is a movement in which players attempt to get the ball by shaking the defense. Back cut refers to cutting behind the defense. Tips for back cut are when the defense cannot observe; otherwise, the movement is read by the defense. The system teaches users these kinds of movements.

Pass and Run is a series of movements in which passes are thrown to make good use of empty space based on moving when they throw a pass. In Pass and Run, the player who threw the pass must move. In doing, if they are unable to get the ball, the space where the player used to stand is empty such that other players move to get the ball. Users repeat these movements.

Users don't have to run at full speed at all times. It is because defense would make it easy for the defense to follow. In that case, it can be easy to get the ball via high or low speed movement. By doing so, it is easy to get the ball because of the distance between offence player and defense player.

This system teaches how to get the ball with their three basic skills. First the system explains cutting, pass and run, and movement by high or low speed moving. Next it gives examples of these movements from third person viewpoint. Subsequently, it teaches them from a first person viewpoint and the user tries to relive the experience. Figure 2 is example of the scene used to teach the skills from third person viewpoint.

---

[1] NHK E Tele, Television Sports Classroom
"Let's learn basketball team style", 9/11, 2016 URL:https://www.levanga.com/news/11389.html.

An example of using back cut

To be moved by high or low speed moving

Fig. 2. Content of video from a third person viewpoint

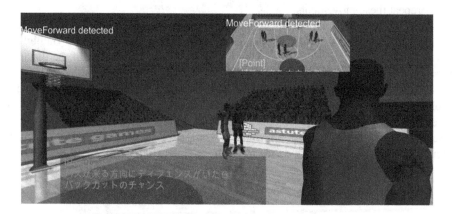

Fig. 3. Example of teaching content from a first person viewpoint

2.2 Reliving from First Person Viewpoint

First person viewpoint lets users relive the experience of a player. All videos in first person viewpoint shift from third person viewpoint to the player's eyes. Users can move the player in the video by moving back and forth and around because Kinect senses the user's movements and gestures. They move following arrows on the screen and voice teaching in this system. Figure 3 is example of reliving from first person viewpoint.

3   Experiment

We experimentally verified whether situational judgment skill to get the ball improved after using the system. Six male university students (two groups of three students) participated in the experiment: group 1 for 3 days and the group 2 for 2 days to determine the relationship to days. We played short three-minute games two times with three subjects and three basketball experiences we had collected in the gym of the same university on the first and final days. In that time, we established the following set of rules. (1) Three on three in a half court, (2) Three subjects play only offense, (3) No dribbling.

After playing on the first day, we carried out a questionnaire survey before using the system. Then, each participant used the system in the cardboard dome. In this system, we first displayed explanatory videos about "Back cut" and "Pass and Run" and a scene to use three skills to get the ball from a third-person viewpoint two times each. Next, they relived the experience two times each time from the first person viewpoint. Finally, we played the short games at the same place on the final day.

3.1   Experimental Results and Analysis

We assessed the system based on Game Performance Assessment Instrument (GPAI), developed Griffin et al. [7] to determine its learning effect. GPAI was developed to measure game performance behaviors that demonstrate tactical understanding, as well as the player's ability to solve tactical problems by selecting and applying appropriate skills. In this study, we analyzed "support" based on GPAI. "support" are defined that provides appropriate support for a teammate with the ball (or projectile) by being in a position to receive a pass so "support" are important off-the-ball movement skills.

We recorded all games played before and after using the proposed system using a video camera. Then, we analyzed the video and assessed how well subjects executed "support" movements. We assessed whether or not player movement is a "support" movement as follows and counted each instance as one.

4   Discussion

In group 1, the three subjects were consciously able to move to get the ball after using the system, but subjects A and C did not improve their situational judgment statistically. For subject B, we could always see his aggressiveness and his situational judgment improved by approximately 14% after using the system.

In group 2, there was growth little by little for each of the three subjects. Both subjects D and F improved by 10% or more compared to before system use, and subject E had a result of 50% or more before and after using system.

We conducted experiments for three days with group 1 and for two days with group 2, but group 2 produced better results. This is because subjects also involved factors such as differences in combinations and differences in sports ability. Two of the subjects had experience in soccer and handball, which are classified as games in which attack is directed toward the enemy's goal, like basketball. This resulted in similar movements and early recognition of sensation, and may have caused them to improve by 10% or more as a result. Subjects commented that "I've had similar practice during high school club activities," during the experiment. Therefore, although it seems to be individual differences, we believe that the improvement rate will change.

There were many instances where on-the-ball players missed to pass the ball. This system mainly supports the movement of off-the-ball players. Therefore, simulations in the case of a failure such as a pass mistake pattern were not conducted. However, if on-the-ball movement is supported, we believe that improvement of judgment can be expected for all subjects.

Also the participants said that most of them understood the contents that the system taught. However, there were many comments that the body does not move quickly when it comes to actual play. However, the subjects sufficiently understood the contents because they stated that they had the movement experience and that it is easy to understand the teaching content, which good points of this system. Therefore, we need to improve the system by judging how we can move the body instantaneously.

We cannot state definitively say that there is only a small improvement in judgment by using the system because the system is not yet perfect and this experiment was a short-term implementation. While evaluating this experiment, we focused only on the support movement in this research, and ignored the on-the-ball player. However, it is felt that if the players previously experienced sports in which they attack toward the enemy's goal, the improvement margin would increase.

5   Conclusion

In this study, we developed a sports training system that improves situational judgment by reliving the first person viewpoint. We focused on "judging to get the ball" and verified whether judgment improved after using the system. The experimental results obtained indicate that it is possible for players to further improve if they have prior experience with interstitial sports such as basketball or soccer.

References

1. Fujiwara, M.: Practice about "how to use space" in the lesson of basketball. Res. J. Sports Sci. **15**, 80–81 (2013). Nara Women's University
2. Kasahara, S., Rekimoto, J.: JackIn: integration the first person view with out-of-body vision generation for human-human augmentation. IPSJ J. **56**(4), 1–8 (2014)
3. Covaci, A., Olivier, A.-H., Multon, F.: Visual perspective and feedback guidance for VR free-throw training. In: Virtual Reality Software and Technology, pp. 79–82 (2015)
4. Ruby, P., Decety, J.: Effect of subjective perspective taking during simulation of action: a PET investigation of agency. Nat. Neurosci. **4**, 546–550 (2001)
5. Ryan, E.D., Simons, J.: Efficacy of mental imagery in enhancing mental rehearsal of motor skills. J. Sport Psychol. **4**, 41–51 (1982)
6. Nakagawa, S.: Some basic concepts for the study on situational judgment in ball games. Japan. Soc. Phys. Edu. **28**(4), 287–289 (1984)
7. Griffin, L., Takahashi, T., Okade, M., et al. (eds.) Teaching Sport Concepts and Skills, pp. 100–102. Taishukan Press, June 1999

Exploring Pervasive Entertainment Games to Construct Learning Paths

Jannicke Madeleine Baalsrud Hauge[1,2,3(✉)], Ioana Andreea Stefan[4], and Antoniu Stefan[4]

[1] BIBA – Bremer Institut für Produktion und Logistik GmbH, Hochschulring 20, 28359 Bremen, Germany
baa@biba.uni-bremen.de
[2] Royal Institute of Technology, Mariekällgatan 3, 15181 Södertälje, Sweden
jmbh@kth.se
[3] University of Bremen, Bibliothek Straße 1, 28359 Bremen, Germany
jmbh@uni-bremen.de
[4] Advanced Technology Systems, Str. Tineretului Nr 1, 130029 Targoviste, Romania
{ioana.stefan,antoniu.stefan}@ats.com.ro

Abstract. Digital Educational Games (DEGs) aim to provide motivating, personalized play experiences that blend learning and engagement, while addressing pedagogical requirements. The ultimate challenge is to enable and stimulate knowledge acquisition by creating rich environments that employ Entertainment Games (EGs) mechanics in order to accommodate learning objectives and support skills' development. In recent years, the gap between EGs and DEGs has started to close, with studies looking not only into lessons learnt from EGs, but also into how EGs can be used in learning settings. This research analyses the possibility to integrate EGs mechanics into the pedagogical flows, in order to potentate learning. The paper further outline the design of a learning path that will be used as a unit on logistics and production means. The unit will be used for letting high school students explore functions of logistics and production (as a recruitment tool during the Open University days), as well as for the first introductionary course on production logistics.

Keywords: Pervasive mechanics · Entertainment · Learning · Lesson path

1 Introduction

The massive success of Entertainment Games (EGs), such as Ingress and Pokemon GO, prove the games' capacity to act as a medium to motivate and engage individuals in various types of activities, ranging from strategizing, planning, and resource collecting to collaborating and socializing. Digital Educational Games (DEGs) aim to explore this potential in educational settings, in order to provide students with more attractive means to explore learning paths. In order to recruit new students to STEM subjects on activities like Open University days or to engage young museums visitors, several games have been used with great success, but often the games used for the classical course teaching, the focus on the pedagogical component has often altered the fun of DEGs or have

N. Munekata et al. (Eds.): ICEC 2017, LNCS 10507, pp. 196–201, 2017.
DOI: 10.1007/978-3-319-66715-7_21

prevented them from reaching their full engaging potential. Moreover, learning paths are individual and do not follow pre-defined scenarios, requiring in-depth levels of personalization.

The emergence of pervasive EGs has opened up new possibilities to explore user-personalized scenarios [1], balancing randomness, individually-driven play with pre-established game goals and rules. They are able to captivate users to willingly and repeatedly play for extensive periods. Therefore, EGs offer an excellent ground for defining best practices [2] and fundament the design of DEGs that stimulate learners [3]. This paper describes a way of how EG can be integrated in an introductory class or also as a stand- alone unit to be used for recruitment settings like Open University Days.

2   Approach for Constructing BEACONING Learning Paths

The shift towards more flexible learning implies the adoption of new methodologies and practices. The emergence of gamification and gaming technologies offer opportunities to construct new approaches to learning, giving learners more freedom, strengthening collaboration skills, and stimulating their creative mind [4]. Pervasive Learning is such new way of learning and is defined as "learning at the speed of need through formal, informal and social learning modalities" [5]. The BEACONING project aims to take advantage of this playful pervasive learning and integrate such informal ways of learning into curricula to provide personalized learning paths. The main focus is STEM and problem-based learning [6]. The BEACONING platform will provide the users (teachers, students) diverse applications, so that the teacher with support of the integrated authoring tool and learning analytics can personalize the learning units to the specific student's needs. In order to ensure the reusability of the different learning paths, a set of templates as well as a taxonomy have been developed. The constructed learning paths have similarities to lessons plans, and will therefore be easy to use for teachers since they can easily adapt. The templates and the taxonomy are described in [6], and Sect. 3 provides an overview on how such a path can look like.

3   Adapted Learning Path for Understanding Industry 4.0 Applications in Production Logistics

As described in the introduction, we have experienced that it is difficult for students to understand the technical systems and new concepts (like industry 4.0 and IoT) can support logistics operation [7, 9, 10], without experiencing how it works, specifically it they lack experience in logistics operations. This also makes it hard for future potential students to know what a study on production engineering and logistics is about. Based upon the long experience of the authors in game-based learning for the given application field, we decided to construct a new learning unit that can be used as an introduction part to a course on production logistics, as well as a single unit for workshops on open university days as the previous mentioned Open University Days.

Fig. 1. Experimental environment

The unit is designed as a part of the small scale pilot that the BIBA will have as a part of the BEACONING project (Fig. 1).

Table 1 describes the learning scenario. It is based on our experiences with Ingress and Pokemon, and uses the same mechanics [11]. Table 2 describes the missions that are implemented. The game environment for mission 1 is illustrated below. Different objects will comprise different information which the students need in order to solve their tasks efficiently. For this main introductionary session is the focus on awareness raising, motivation and engagement. We therefore use game mechanics like time, competitions and exploration more than if the main learning outcome should be specific knowledge about the different system components.

Table 1. Learning scenario on IoT in production logistics

A. Domain/Area/Subject: *Production logistics*
B. Topic: *IT tools for production logistics and warehousing systems*
C. Age Group/Key Stage/Year/Background   *Undergraduate students starting specialization in production logistics, high school students in the phase of deciding on what to study*
D. What is it about?/What's in your mind?/What's the matter?   *Concepts like Industry 4.0 and Internet of Things have an increased usage with logistics and production, especially in Germany. The improved possibility to support the logistics processes by allowing access to data and information throughout the whole chain gives rise to a lot of new possibilities, but the concept itself is often difficult to grasp for students hardly knowing how logistics operations are carried out and which tools currently used. In addition, there have been a rapidly development of new technologies. This unit will let the students experience different picking technologies (picking by light, by voice, digital etiquettes etc.) as well as the stock-in and out. The lesson is problem based and the students shall experience the differences with and without technology support.*

(continued)

Table 1. (*continued*)

E. Play - Lesson Path
The lesson path is divided in four missions presenting basic knowledge on the underlying concepts and technologies for Industrie 4.0. The lesson starts with a small (toy size) forklift able to move around move all around and to do stock-in and stock-out in a miniature warehouse. The forklift (see pict.) has sensors and actuators installed. Depending on which sensors (tilt, temperature, humidity, gravity etc.), the students will be able to carry out different operations. During the first small part the student does not get access to the data during operation, whereas these are provided in the second part. The data are collected and provided as feedback for analysis so that the students can use this experience in solving the next quests and challenges. This part is carried out in a safe environment in the gaming lab. The second part of the unit is organized as a treasure hunt with quests and challenges related to the equipment and tools (warehouse, large forklift, conveyer belt, picking tools) we have in different parts of the BIBA building. The students will get different challenges (i.e. on what material to store or to provide at the conveyer belt, lead times etc. relevant for production logistics tasks). With their mobile they will search for the right object to solve this tasks best (these objects are outside or in our production hall). When collected enough information on the real devices, the students will return to the lab and apply what they have learned by developing similar services equipping the miniature world with relevant sensors, actuators and define the interfaces between the PPC, ERP, etc. systems for ensuring the access to the right information. The students will test out if their application works.

Table 2. Mission descriptions

Mission A: Exploring how information from an IoT environment can support in- and out-stocking
Background: No prior knowledge on production and logistics
Skills: logical thinking

Quest 1
Discover the in- and out-stocking process in a warehouse

Brief overview of Quest 1 activities.

Time Frame	**Participants**	**Location(s)**	**Pedagogical Resources**
1 h of work in 1 session.	The teacher Their classmates	Gaming Lab BIBA hall Home	Introductionary (on line) Books, Websites Interactive mater
Evidence End result, Data from exercise (i.e. time used, tilt and numbers of errors etc.).	**Rewards** Points to have accessed/read the lesson material Points according to performance	**Beacons** The beacons will indicate the physical location of the students	

(*continued*)

Table 2. (*continued*)

Quest 2
Discover different equipment work
Reverse classroom style and learning by doing.

Brief overview of Quest 2 activities.

Time Frame	Participants	Location(s)	Resources
1 h in one session.	The teacher Their classmates	Lab and hall On their mobile	Information stored in the objects (technical data and description) Videos on usage
Evidence End result (analysis of collected information)	**Rewards** Points awarded in game are used for a class/school wide leaderboard	**Beacons** Will allow access to the game within building and around	

Quest 3
Equip the miniature truck with different sensors and actuators and combine into new services

Brief overview of Quest 3 activities.

Time Frame	Participants	Location(s)	Resources
2 h in one session.	The teacher The technicians Their classmates	Gaming and FabLab On their mobile On the lab PC	Sensor and actuator data Description of system and service components (in an LMS)
Evidence End result, how the different sensors can be used to provide different services	**Rewards** Points awarded in game are used for a leaderboard (Different points for performance, innovation, etc.)	**Beacons** Will allow access to the game at around the hall and outside the building	

4   Discussion and Next Steps

The design of the curricula and learning path, as well as of the game is now completed and we are currently adapting the game environment described in [12]. For the modding we use part of the ATMSG framework [13]. The digital part of the game is realized in Unity, and the real world data are imported into the unity scenario. (i.e. this part can be seen as a game in a game). This part is also used alone. The mini-games and the overall gamification (including the treasure hunting) are integrated as a part of the overall narrative. The small scale piloting starts in autumn 2017.

Acknowledgement. The work presented herein is partially funded under the Horizon 2020 Framework Program of the European Union, BEACONING – Grant Agreement 68676 and by Unitatea Executiva pentru Finantarea Invatamantului Superior, a Cercetarii, Dezvoltarii si Inovarii (UEFISCDI) in Romania, Contract no. 19/2014 (DESiG).

References

1. Costanza, R., et al.: Simulation games that integrate research, entertainment, and learning around ecosystem services. Ecosyst. Serv. **10**, 195–201 (2014). doi:10.1016/j.ecoser.2014. 10.001
2. Ham, E.: Tabletop Game Design for Video Game Designers. Focal Press, Oxon (2015)
3. Marsh, T., Champion, E., Hlavacs, H.: Special issue title: entertainment in serious games and entertaining serious purposes. Entertainment Comput. **14**, 15 (2016)
4. Ştefan, A., et al.: Approaches to reengineering digital games. In: Proceedings of the ASME 2016 International Design Engineering Technical Conferences & Computers and Information in Engineering Conference, IDETC/CIE 2016 (2016)
5. Pontefract, D.: Learning by Osmosis. http://www.danpontefract.com/learning-by-osmosis/
6. BEACONING project. D3.3 Learning Environment System Specification (2017)
7. Baalsrud Hauge, J., et al.: Deploying serious games for management in higher education: lessons learned and good practices. In: EAI Endorsed Transactions on Serious Games (2014)
8. Baalsrud Hauge, J., et al.: Study design and data gathering guide for serious games' evaluation. In: Connolly, T.M., Hainey, T., Boyle, E., Baxter, G., Moreno-Ger, P. (eds.) Psychology, Pedagogy, and Assessment in Serious Games. Advances in Game-Based Learning (AGBL) Book Series. USA. IGI Global (2013)
9. Riedel, J., Baalsrud Hauge, J.: Evaluation of simulation games for teach-ing production (Engineering). In: Cruz-Cunha, M., Varvalho, V., Tavares, P. (eds.) Computer Games as Educational and Management Tools: Uses and Approaches, pp. 263–279. Information Science Reference, Hershey, PA (2011)
10. Baalsrud Hauge, J.: An educational framework for supporting the implementation of the intelligent cargo concept. Int. J. Adv. Logistics **5**(2), 86–100 (2016)
11. Söbke, H., et al.: Prime example ingress reframing the pervasive game design framework (PGDF). Int. Jour on Serious games **4**(2) (2017). http://dx.doi.org/10.17083/ijsg.v4i2.182
12. Baalsrud Hauge J., et al.: Analysis on educating mechanical engineers through serious games using pervasive technologies. In: ASME, IDETC CIE Conference, Volume 1B: 36th Computers and Information in Engineering Conference, V01BT02A050 (2016). doi:10. 1115/DETC2016-59826
13. Carvalho, M.B., et al.: An activity theory-based model for serious games analysis and conceptual design. Comput. Educ. **87**, 166–181 (2015)

Reality

Virtual Scuba Diving System Utilizing the Sense of Weightlessness Underwater

Kazuma Nagata[✉], Denik Hatsushika, and Yuki Hashimoto

University of Tsukuba, 1-1-1 Tennodai, Tsukuba, Ibaraki 305-8573, Japan
nagata.kazuma@entcomp.esys.tsukuba.ac.jp,
d_hatsushika@vrlab.esys.tsukuba.ac.jp,
hashimoto@iit.tsukuba.ac.jp

Abstract. We propose a virtual scuba diving system using an underwater head mounted display (UHMD). This system has two advantages. First, a strong sense of reality is obtained by combining the weightlessness obtained by diving with a highly immersive image presented by a waterproof UHMD. Second, the system is very versatile, such that a user can experience the system in easily accessible waters such as swimming pools or shallow water. In this paper, we describe the design and implementation of the proposed system and the creation of underwater virtual reality (VR) content to provide a diving experience. The proposed system consists of the UHMD with a head tracking sensor, laptop PC, and a hose to protect the cables. The UHMD and laptop PC are connected by cables for power, communication, and video transmission. Each part is waterproof. The created VR content makes it possible to freely swim in the virtual undersea world by head tracking and operation of the controller. We conducted a pilot experiment to test the proposed system while users swam in a pool of about 4 m in depth. The UHMD was confirmed to have sufficient waterproofness at water depth of about 4 m. It is also suggested that it is possible to create the illusion that the water depth in the virtual underwater space is the user's own water depth.

Keywords: Scuba diving · Head Mounted Display · Underwater · Virtual Reality

1 Introduction

Scuba diving is an attractive sport that enables participants to enjoy a mysterious and beautiful underwater world. However, scuba diving cannot be enjoyed easily anytime. A license is required for free diving, and there is a limit to the depth of dives for safety. In addition, it is necessary to consider the appropriate location, time, and weather to do scuba diving.

Our goal is to realize a virtual scuba diving system so that anyone can enjoy a diving experience with high reality at any time in familiar waters such as pools.

Many systems to experience the underwater virtually have been proposed [1–4]. However, many of them present underwater images while the user is not in the water. Therefore, it is difficult for these systems to present weightlessness and water resistance.

© IFIP International Federation for Information Processing 2017
Published by Springer International Publishing AG 2017. All Rights Reserved
N. Munekata et al. (Eds.): ICEC 2017, LNCS 10507, pp. 205–210, 2017.
DOI: 10.1007/978-3-319-66715-7_22

In contrast, several virtual underwater experience systems in which the user is underwater have been proposed in recent years. DOLPHYN [5] is an underwater experience system equipped with sensors such as a webcam, GPS, thermometer, flowmeter, and tablet PC. Users can experience the virtual undersea world through the DOLPHYN display. However, this system has less immersion than a head mounted display (HMD). In addition, body movement is restricted because it is necessary to operate the equipment with both hands. AquaCAVE [6, 7] realizes the experience of swimming in the ocean by projecting images on the wall of the aquarium. However, the available places for experiencing this system are limited because of the necessity of preparing a dedicated aquarium. The movement of the user is also limited by the narrowness of the aquarium.

Hence, this research proposes a new virtual underwater experience system using an underwater HMD (UHMD). Several UHMDs have been proposed [8–10]. These systems use a smartphone with a waterproof case, and users can enjoy a virtual sea world synchronized with the movement of their head underwater. However, because of the limitations of smartphone performance, the quality of the computer graphics (CG) that can be provided is not high. Moreover, there is a possibility of virtual reality (VR) sickness due to insufficient head tracking performance. Furthermore, the feeling of immersion is lower than with a dedicated HMD. In contrast, we aim to design and implement a system to solve this problem.

In this paper, we report on the design and implementation of our system, its content production, and the result of a verification of the system's operation in a pool.

2   System Configuration

2.1   Design Principle

Our system is designed to be used at a depth of about 4 m, in which the whole body of a person can move freely in the water. For this reason, we decided to make the system waterproof enough to withstand a water depth of 4 m. According to Oculus best practices [11], we tried to render CG at 75 fps or higher, and selected a sensor so that the tracking delay would be less than 20 ms. To address portability, we decided to design the system to a weight and size that can be carried by one person.

2.2   Implementation

Our system consists of a UHMD with head tracking sensor, laptop PC, and a hose that protects cables. The UHMD and laptop PC are connected by cables for power, communication, and video transmission. The use of a laptop increases the system portability. The UHMD system is shown in Fig. 1.

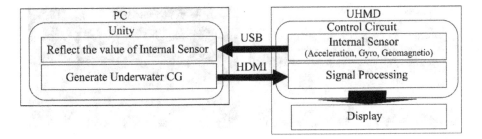

Fig. 1. Configuration of the UHMD system.

For the UHMD body, we disassembled an Oculus Rift DK 2 (Oculus VR, Inc.) and used the circuits and display. The cables were 10 m in length so that the system could move freely at a water depth of 4 m. For head tracking, the internal sensor of Oculus Rift DK 2 was used. The laptop GPU (NVIDIA, Geforce GTX 980M) was used for video output.

The UHMD was entirely covered with a circuit sealing agent. The connector was protected with a waterproof-type heat shrink tube. Hose was used to protect the wired cables. Further, to ensure close contact between the user and the UHMD, the frame of an underwater mask was joined with the HMD section (Fig. 2). We applied defogging liquid to the HMD's lenses.

Fig. 2. Image of the UHMD.

3   Production of Content

3.1   Scene Design

We produced underwater content using Unity, which can create high-quality CG and is easy to link with external equipment. To achieve a good VR experience, we adjusted the number of 3D objects and effects so that the frame rate did not fall below 75 fps. We produced two diving environments. One is a shoal (Fig. 3, left). The depth of this scene is 5 m. The user can watch seaweed, coral, and a school of fish. The other virtual environment is large vertical hole (Fig. 3, right). The depth and diameter of this scene is 40 m. The surroundings become darker as the water depth increases. To make the surroundings visible, even in deep water, we installed a light that illuminates the field of vision on the head of the user. The user can see various types of seaweed, various corals, and two whales.

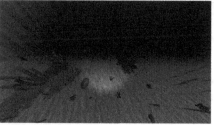

Fig. 3. Left: shallow water. Right: vertical hole

3.2 Interaction Design

The movement of the user's head is recognized by the sensor for tracking and fed back to the visual field of the CG in real time. A controller is used to move the user. The joystick is used to move in the planar direction, the trigger is used to change the depth, and buttons provide instantaneous movement to preset locations.

4 Pilot Study

4.1 Content of the Pilot Study

We conducted a pilot study using our system in an indoor pool (maximum water depth of 3.8 m) to confirm that the system operates normally in water and determine the immersion obtained by this system. In this study, participants dived completely into the water and looked around for as long as they could hold their breath (Fig. 4). Our system followed the rotation of the head, but could not acquire other movement. We instructed the participants not to move during diving and they did not use a controller. The vertical hole scene was used. The depth of the virtual underwater world was about 20 m.

Fig. 4. Diving while wearing the UHMD.

4.2 Result

As a result of the study, a visual presentation with high immersive feeling was achieved in the water, and the sensor for head tracking kept the same accuracy and refresh rate as it did on dry land. Therefore, it has been demonstrated that this system operates normally at a depth of about 4 m.

In the questionnaire that we distributed after the experiment, all participants commented that they felt like they were "in deep water even though it should feel like shallow water." This indicates that our system has the potential to provide underwater experiences of various depths despite being used in a pool.

5 Future Work

5.1 Intuitive Operation

Virtual movement in the current system is not intuitive because it uses joysticks, the trigger, and buttons. To achieve a more intuitive movement, it is necessary to sense the movement of the body. There are two ways to achieve this. One is to use an external sensor system such as a camera (Fig. 5, left). The other one is to use an internal sensor such as a bend sensor (Fig. 5, right). Currently, we are working toward achieving motion capture underwater using a stereo camera. We also track the walls and bottom of the pool using edge detection and markers to avoid allowing the user to bump against them.

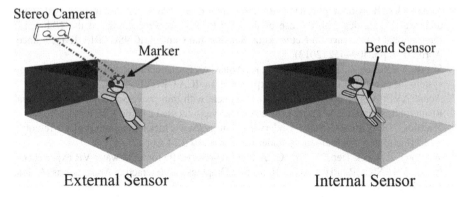

Fig. 5. Schematic of movement capture methods

5.2 Quality of the Content

For this study, we created content that would not fall below 75 fps. However, the reality was decreased somewhat. To achieve both high content quality and refresh rate, it is necessary to find ways to reduce the processing load such as adjusting the mesh of a 3D model, canceling undisplayed part rendering, or introducing single-pass stereo rendering.

6   Conclusion

In this paper, we proposed a virtual scuba diving system using a UHMD and attempted to realize an arbitrary underwater environment experience in familiar underwater areas such as a pool. Our aim is to achieve the overwhelmingly immersive feeling obtained with a dedicated HMD and enable the user to move freely. We developed a prototype of our system and created underwater content. The results of the pilot study confirmed that our system works well in water and has the potential to provide underwater experiences of various depths despite being in a pool. We will continue to improve image quality and pursue further immersive reality by improving the content so that it can be linked to user movement.

References

1. XL Catlin Seaview Survey. http://catlinseaviewsurvey.com. Accessed 24 Apr 2017
2. Sumsung Shark Dive VR. https://www.sammobile.com/2016/04/02/samsung-uploads-360-degree-shark-dive-video-to-youtube. Accessed 24 Apr 2017
3. Wevr theBlu. http://blog.wevr.com/acclaimed-vr-series-theblu-out-on-transport-oculus-touch-896. Accessed 24 Apr 2017
4. Dhruv, J., Misha, S., Jingru, G., Rodrigo, M., Raymond, W., Justin, C., Chris, S.: Immersive terrestrial scuba diving using virtual reality. In: Proceedings of the 2016 CHI Conference Extended Abstracts on Human Factors in Computing Systems, pp. 1563–1569 (2016). Amphibian
5. Abdelkader, B., Christophe, D., Samir, O., Samir, B., Alain, D.: Augmented reality for underwater activities with the use of the DOLPHYN. In: Proceedings of the 10th IEEE International Conference on Networking, Sensing and Control, ICNSC 2013, Evry, France, April 2013, pp. 409–412 (2013)
6. Shogo, Y., Xinlei, Z., Takashi, M., Jun, R.: AquaCAVE: an underwater immersive projection system for enhancing the swimming experience. In: ICAT-EGVE 2016 (2016)
7. AquaCAVE: Augmented Swimming Environment with Immersive Surround-Screen Virtual Reality. https://lab.rekimoto.org/projects/aquacave. Accessed 24 Apr 2017
8. Nautilus VR Virtual Reality Underwater. https://www.kickstarter.com/projects/remotte/project-nautilus-vr-virtual-reality-underwater. Accessed 24 Apr 2017
9. Wenlong, Z., Chek Tien, T., Tim, C.: A safe low-cost HMD for underwater VR experiences. In: SA 2016 SIGGRAPH ASIA 2016 Mobile Graphics and Interactive Applications, Article No. 12 (2016)
10. Experience Weightless VR With This Waterproof Headset. https://vrscout.com/news/experience-weightless-vr-waterproof-headset. Accessed 24 Apr 2017
11. Oculus Best Practices. https://static.oculus.com/documentation/pdfs/intro-vr/latest/bp.pdf. Accessed 24 Apr 2017

The Alteration of Gustatory Sense by Virtual Chromatic Transition of Food Items

Yuto Sugita[1], Keiichi Zempo[2,3]([envelope]), Koichi Mizutani[2], and Naoto Wakatsuki[2]

[1] Graduate School of Systems and Information Engineering, University of Tsukuba,
Tsukuba, Ibaraki 305-8573, Japan
[2] Faculty of Engineering, Information and Systems, University of Tsukuba,
Tsukuba, Ibaraki 305-8573, Japan
zempo@iit.tsukuba.ac.jp
[3] Artificial Intelligence Research Center, AIST, Tokyo, Japan

Abstract. When we visually recognize food items, their color influences the impression of their taste, because the gustatory sense is affected by other senses such as smell and eyesight. In this study, in order to control the gustatory sense of human beings, we examined the influence on gustatory sense by giving a virtual chromatic transition of food through Head-Mounted Display. The experiment was conducted under six conditions that changed three factors: "before or after eating", "viewing through HMD or naked eyes", "with virtual chromatic transition or without". As a result, we confirmed that the difference in the amount of visual information influenced the impression of food items before eating. It is expected to realize more applicative control of the gustatory sense by analyzing this difference.

Keywords: Gustatory sense · Virtual reality · Head-Mounted Display · Visual information

1 Introduction

The taste information obtained from the taste cells present in the tongue accounts for the majority of the human gustatory sense [1]. However, it is known that the gustatory sense is affected not only by taste information but also by other sensory information such as visual information [2,3]. Recently, studies have been increasingly being made to change dining experience by externally changing sensory information [4]. In particular, the influence of olfactory and visual information on taste sensation is large, therefore a lot of studies have been done by using this [5–8]. These effects are recognized also in psychological experiments [9]. For example, Meta Cookie gives a change to the feeling of human gustatory sense by changing both visual information and olfactory information [8]. It's also said that auditory information when chewing food, tactile information such as the texture of food and chewy feeling influences the feeling of taste [10–12].

N. Munekata et al. (Eds.): ICEC 2017, LNCS 10507, pp. 211–217, 2017.
DOI: 10.1007/978-3-319-66715-7_23

Previous research suggests that changes in sensory information from the outside can also change taste information. However, quantitative evaluation of how taste information is affected by changes given to sensory information has not yet been made. If a quantitative evaluation is possible, more applicative control of the gustatory sense becomes possible. Among the sensory information affecting the taste like this, the visual information can change most easily the feeling of the taste significant. Unlike other sensory information, the visual information can be separated three primary colors of light, therefore it is easy to present any visual information. Therefore, by changing the color of the food through the visual sensor and visually recognizing the food through the display, it is possible to change the visual information of the food. In addition, as the penetration rate of smartphones is increasing in recent years, there are many scenes of possessing visual sensors such as cameras. There are also many Head-Mounted Display (HMD) that can provide VR environment easily by wearing smartphones, therefore it is possible to impart real world to a chromatic transition of food.

Also, in recent years, content production related to dining experience has been actively performed [13, 14]. Dining experiences that are familiar to humans should be always new and enjoyable by adding such entertainment characteristics. It is expected that the control of the gustatory sense will greatly contribute to such content creation in the future.

In this research, we aim to verify the influence of a chromatic transition of food through a HMD on the impression of taste for food. For this purpose, we constructed a system that gives a chromatic transition to the color of food through HMD. In this research, we also examine the difference between visually recognizing food with the naked eye and the recognition it through HMD. Therefore, to control the impression of human taste by optimal color change, it is necessary to consider the difference between the case of visually recognizing with the naked eye and the case of seeing through the display.

2 VR System of a Chromatic Transition

In this research, smartphone and HMD were used as a color change presentation device. iPhone 7 Plus which iOS 10 introduced by Apple Co., Ltd. was introduced, and VOX + 3DVR goggle provided by VOX was used for HMD. We can really find the image which we acquired from the camera of the smartphone like the image actually in front of the eyes by attaching HMD which set the smartphone. By giving a color change to the image acquired from this camera and outputting it to the display, it is also possible to give a chromatic transition to the user. These devices are shown in Fig. 1.

And, we installed the application created in Xcode on iPhone 7 Plus and used it to detect target food and change color to that food. The source code of the application is written in Objective-C and introduced the OpenCV framework for image processing such as a color change to target food. A flow chart showing the flow of the created application is shown in Fig. 1, and detailed specifications are shown below.

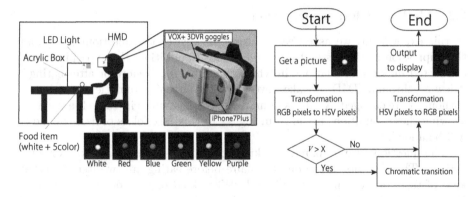

Fig. 1. Experiment environment and a virtual chromatic transition system (Color figure online)

1. Acquire an image from a camera mounted on a smartphone
2. Convert all the pixels in the image obtained from the camera from the original RGB color space to the HSV color space
3. Of the parameters of the HSV color space, make specified color change for pixels with V (Value, Brightness) above a certain value
4. Output the pixel on which the color change was made on the original image to the display

The food whose color has been changed by the above operation is outputted to the display and made to be visible to the human through the HMD.

3   Experiment of Verification

3.1   The Experimental Environment and Target Food Item

This experiment was conducted for 11 males and females in their twenties who are healthy with both visual and taste. The experimental environment is shown in Fig. 1. In this experiment, the application was carried out in a room that turned off the light, unifying the background to black so that the application can easily detect white food. A target food was placed on the inside of which processing was made by attaching a black felt fabric around an acrylic box which is a cube having one side of 300 mm and the front side does not exist, and this subject was visually recognized by the subject.

In this experiment, the self-made fizzing candy was used as the target food item. All of the ingredients were made equal in 0.1 g unit so that each of the fizzing candy had the same taste. Those colored by using coloring agents were prepared for each of them. The colors used this time are five types of red, blue, yellow, green and purple shown in Fig. 1. Experiments were carried out using a total of six kinds of color fizzing candies to which white of the reference color was added.

3.2 Method of Experimentation

In this experiment, we asked each subject to answer the questionnaire about
the impression of the taste of the target food. In addition, the experiment was
conducted under six situations in which three factors, "before or after eating,"
"viewing through HMD or naked eyes," "with Virtual chromatic transition or
without" were changed. A table summarizing these is shown in Table 1, a diagram
showing these conditions is shown in Fig. 2. To this "six colors of fizzing candy"
will be added.

The questionnaire prepared two kinds of contents different "before or after
eating". The contents of the questionnaire before eating are two items, "What
kind of taste do you think it is?," and "What kind of food do you imagine?".
Next, the contents of the questionnaire after eating are three items, "What kind
of taste did you feel?", "What kind of food did you imagine?", "Were there any
differences of impressions before eating?". The first questionnaire item evaluated
what kind of taste it felt before and after eating about five colors excluding
white, in 5 grades each of the five flavors. At this time, white was defined as the
evaluation value 3 in all the five flavors before and after eating, and it was used
as a standard.

Table 1. Situation of experiment

Experiment no.	Before or after	Viewing method	Chromatic transition
#1	Before	Naked eye	None
#2	After	Naked eye	None
#3	Before	HMD equipped	None
#4	After	HMD equipped	None
#5	Before	HMD equipped	Transitioned
#6	After	HMD equipped	Transitioned

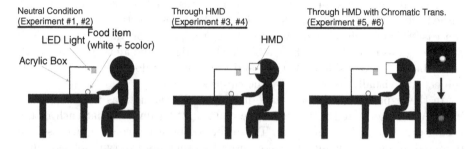

Fig. 2. Situation of experiment

3.3   Result

From the experimental results, evaluate how far away the impression was from the white fizzing candy received as a reference against the colored. At this time, we define the taste space as 5-dimensional space and evaluate the evaluation value of each basic taste answered by the subject to Euclidean distance when white is taken as the origin and evaluate.

First, in order to compare "before or after eating" and "viewing through HMD or naked eyes", we perform Analysis of variance using the result of experiment 1, 2, 3 and 4, as factors. Next, in order to compare "before or after eating" and "giving or not virtual chromatic transition", we perform an analysis of variance using the result of experiment 3, 4, 5 and 6, as factors. Graph showing these results is shown in Fig. 3.

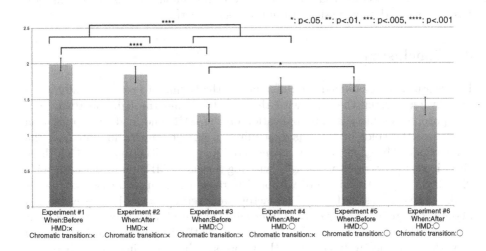

Fig. 3. Result of analysis of variance

The abscissa of Fig. 3 shows the six situations of experiment shown in Table 1, and the ordinate shows the average value of the Euclidean distance of the result calculated for each situation of the experiment.

Firstly, as a result of analyzing the experiment #1, #2, #3 and #4, the interaction of "before or after eating" and "viewing through the HMD or naked eyes" was superior at 5% level or less. It was also revealed that the impression before eating was different depending on the presence or absence of the HMD by the simple main effect test. It seems to be due to the difference in the amount of visual information obtained when comparing the state in which the food is viewed through the HMD and the state in which the food is visually recognized with the naked eye. The information acquired from the camera has a difference in information amount as compared with information obtained from the naked eyes due to various factors such as image quality and viewing angle. It seems that the difference in this amount of information affected the impression of the food before eating.

Next, as a result of analyzing the experiment #3, #4, #5 and #6, the interaction of "before or after eating" and "with virtual chromatic transition or without" was superior at 1% level or less. Moreover, it was revealed that the impression before eating is caused by the presence or absence of color change by examination of simple main effect. This seems to be related to the amount of visual information as well. The amount of visual information decreases if it passes through a display like a camera. The application used in this experiment was to add a chromatic transition from the top of the image acquired from the camera. In other words, when a chromatic transition is added by the application used in this experiment, it can be said that it is easier to obtain visual information because clear colors can be seen compared with the case where no chromatic transition. It is seemed that the difference in the amount of visual information has influenced the impression of the food before eating.

4   Conclusion

In this study, we examined the difference in the feeling of taste especially when visually recognizing the food with the naked eye and through the HMD. For this purpose, we installed an application on the HMD and made an application to change the color of the image acquired from the camera mounted on the smartphone. The experiment was conducted under six situations in which three situations, "before or after eating", "viewing through HMD or naked eyes", "with virtual chromatic transition or without" were changed. In each case, differences in the taste impression due to these factors were verified by subjective evaluation about the taste impression of the target food. The result of analysis revealed that "viewing through HMD or naked eyes," and "with virtual chromatic transition or without" respectively influence the impression before eating food. Therefore, the experiments suggested that the impression of food tastes were changed due to the difference in the amount of visual information between the naked eye and the screen. In other words, when giving a chromatic transition to a food through a screen such as HMD, it is possible that considering the difference in impression of the case of visual recognition with the naked eye leads to more advanced control of taste.

Moreover, verification experiments have revealed that there is almost no influence on the feeling of the taste of eating food merely by changing the visual information. Changes in olfaction, tactile sensation, and auditory information are thought to be useful for effecting this. From now on, we will investigate how they affect taste sensation by changing these, and also realize a taste control system by constructing a multimodal interface including these.

References

1. Yutaka, M.: Mechanisms for taste signaling in taste buds. In: The Japanese Association for the Study of Taste and Smell, vol. 15(1), pp. 5–10 (2008)
2. Tomomi, K.: Nippon jin no mikaku [Japanese taste]. Tamagawa sensyo, Tokyo (1980)
3. Keiji, U., Masao, O.: Mikaku, Kyukaku [Taste, Smell]. Asakura syoten, Tokyo (2008)
4. Marcelo, C.: DinnerWare: why playing with food should be encouraged. In: CHI Extended Abstracts, pp. 3505–3506 (2009)
5. Alley, R.L., Alley, T.R.: The influence of physical state and color on perceived sweetness. J. Psychol. Interdiscip. Appl. **132**, 561–568 (1997)
6. Bayarri, S., Calvo, C., Costell, E., Duran, L.: Influence of color on perception of sweetness and fruit flavor of fruit drinks. Food Sci. Technol. Int. **7**, 399–404 (2001)
7. Stillman, J.A.: Color influences flavor identification in fruit-flavored beverages. J. Food Sci. **58**, 810–812 (1993)
8. Takuji, N., Tomohiro, T., Takashi, K., Michitaka, H.: Meta cookie: pseudo - gustatory display based on cross - modal integration. Trans. Virtual Real. Soc. Jpn. **15**, 579–588 (2010)
9. Johnson, J.: The psychophysical relationship between color and flavor. Ph.D. thesis. University of Massachusetts at Amherst (1982)
10. Daichi, I., Takafumi, K.: Change of mouthfeel by means of cross-modal effect using mastication sound and visual information of food. In: IEICE Technical Report I.M.Q., vol. 114, pp. 83–86 (2014)
11. Tetsuro, M., Hiroaki, Y., Hiroo, I.: Research on sensory integration in a taste of food. Trans. Virtual Real. Soc. Jpn. **9**, 259–264 (2004)
12. Koizumi, N., Tanaka, H., Uema, Y., Inami, M.: Chewing jockey: augmented food texture by using sound based on the cross-modal effect. In: Proceedings of the 8th International Conference on Advances in Computer Entertainment Technology (ACE 2011), article 21, pp. 1–4 (2011)
13. Verchan Reality. http://www.awajikoku.com/
14. Project Nourished. http://www.projectnourished.com/

Hoverboard: A Leap to the Future of Locomotion in VR!?

Jan Smeddinck$^{(\boxtimes)}$, Dmitry Alexandrovsky, Dirk Wenig,
Michel Zimmer, Waldemar Wegele, Sylvia Juergens,
and Rainer Malaka

Digital Media Lab, TZI, University of Bremen, Bremen, Germany
{smeddinck,dimi,dwenig,mzimmer,waldemar,sjuergens,
malaka}@tzi.de

Abstract. Locomotion in virtual reality (VR) remains challenging due to limitations of common input methods. Sedentary input devices may endanger immersion, real-to-virtual world perception dissonance can lead to simulator sickness, and physical input devices such as framed walking dishes are often complex and expensive. We present a low-cost, easy to use, easy to manufacture, and easily portable device for locomotion in VR based on a *hoverboard* metaphor. Building on related work and our own iterative VR locomotion system designs we hypothesize that *hoverboarding* can provide a compelling and intuitive method for short- and long-distance locomotion in VR with a potential to reduce simulator sickness due to consistent and stable locomotion that corresponds well to the physical proprioception of the users while navigating VR. We discuss design iterations of our device prototypes, promising results from an early explorative evaluation, as well as ongoing continued work.

Keywords: Locomotion · Virtual Reality (VR) · Motion-based control · Natural user interface · Hoverboard · Leaning · Whole-body interface · Gaming

1 Introduction

Virtual reality (VR) is expected to play an important role as a key new interaction modality for mainstream applications in entertainment computing, education, computer-supported cooperative work, and beyond. Due to the strong notion of physical presence and location in VR, applications require novel physical locomotion interfaces for navigation in virtual worlds which allow the user to travel long distances that cannot be bridged in reality while using the system due to physical constraints as well as due to constraints with tracking technologies.

In VR applications that present larger spaces and invite users to change locations, for example in many simulators or games, using traditional controllers, such as gamepads, or keyboard and mouse, is often cumbersome and unintuitive, since the input does not map well the impression of first-person movement that player-view camera translations in VR induce [1]. In many cases, a disconnect between the input method which leads to a specific sensory experience (including the vestibular system)

© IFIP International Federation for Information Processing 2017
Published by Springer International Publishing AG 2017. All Rights Reserved
N. Munekata et al. (Eds.): ICEC 2017, LNCS 10507, pp. 218–225, 2017.
DOI: 10.1007/978-3-319-66715-7_24

for the user and the resulting displayed action can contribute to problems with VR sickness [2] and challenge immersion [3].

Modern VR systems offer "room-scale" tracking of physical motion (e.g., the HTC Vive), allowing the user to walk around in a small area. For traveling longer distances, there are approaches such as teleportation [4], walking-in-place (WIP) [5], or using walking dishes [6], treadmills [7], or spheres [8]. All of these approaches have specific advantages and disadvantages. They are either not fully immersive, or uncomfortable, or they require a complex or expensive hardware setup.

This motivated our iterative design exploration of further suspension devices following the original suspended walking system [5], targeting increased comfort, ease of use, lowered cost, immersion, reduced VR sickness, and facilitating faster and further locomotion. The resulting most favorable setup of a suspended wooden board (see Fig. 1, top) induced the emergence of the hoverboard metaphor and was integrated in a fully interactive VR locomotion prototype that was subjected to an early evaluation. The outcomes, while promising, indicated room for improvements, motivat-

Fig. 1. Intermediate prototype from the iterative design process for a range of suspended setups for locomotion in VR.

ing iterations towards a follow-up modified hoverboard concept that is not suspended and targets increased portability, stability, and control.

This work contributes to the development of full-body interfaces for locomotion in VR with use cases in gaming and beyond. The publication of these late-breaking developments is meant to inform researchers and developers that may currently pursue similar challenges in the booming area of VR.

2 Related Work

In the past, there have been commercial devices for body-based input that became popular for arcade of casual games. Instead of a VR setup the systems often realize visual output on a display, allowing users to reference the stationary environment around the display, thus motion sickness is not an issue. Sickness due to unconstrained movement in VR [3] is such a notable problem that most (even top-level) current VR games radically confine movement (e.g. *Space Pirate Trainer*) or use considerable workarounds, such as teleporting (e.g. *Rec Room*). Many acclaimed VR experiences (e.g. *Elite Dangerous*) are based on metaphors that match well with a seated computer desk setting and thus do not induce require physical locomotion. Some games use a "moving platform" (e.g. *Hover Junkers*), since standing on a surface that moves around the VR space matches better with actual proprioception if VR is used while standing, even if the floor is stable and does not move.

A considerable body of research explores the design space of traveling through virtual environments. Bowman et al. [3] provide a broad overview of techniques and devices. Stationary controls that are used in VR experiences with considerable loco-motion mainly result in visual cues disregarding vestibular perception/feedback. This negatively affects a user's sense of presence and spatial awareness and also contributes to the risk of simulator sickness [3, 9]. Involving a user's body in the interaction loop, providing multimodal feedback, can arguably help overcome these issues [1, 3, 9–12].

Hence, it is not surprising that a number of research projects have investigated interfaces that implement a walking metaphor. While many methods, such as walking in place [13], walking dishes and spheres [8], or treadmills [7] draw on walking motions that require users to actively carry their own weight, alternative suspended walking interfaces that utilize hanging harnesses have also been introduced [5]. Such walking-based methods offer an intuitive approach to locomotion in VR and can support immersive experiences [13, 14]. However, they suffer from shortcomings around latency, tracking accuracy, discomfort, restricted freedom of motion, or unnatural leg movements. Furthermore, they only work well with small virtual envi-ronments. Once a user is to explore large areas, techniques that involve walking, become exhausting [10]. Thus, other modalities, or mixed methods for traveling mark interesting venues for further exploration.

As one example, related work suggests the application of interfaces that rely on devices that are sensitive to weight shift, mapping a user's leaning motion to the direction and/or the speed of the device. Similar approaches have been discussed employing a "flying carpet" metaphor [3]. The *Joyman* [12] is an *isotonic* [3] VR locomotion interface that provides stability through resistive force that increases with displacement. A circular platform with a safeguard is connected via springs to a base. The inclination is measured with an inertia sensor. Along with the device the authors provide a translation model for the inclination of the device to a realistic control of virtual vehicles. Compared with a joystick, users completed navigation tasks signifi-cantly faster with the joystick, but had more fun and felt more present with *Joyman*. The interface encourages exaggerated leaning motions over the limit of balance. While this can be a fun way to navigate through some extreme sport games, such gestures appear inappropriate for regular navigation tasks. However, if the visual and auditory feedback presented in VR adequately corresponds to the movements that are enacted on the surface, such input schemes can provide close real-world-to-VR perceptive consistency.

Related work on vestibular feedback comparing a *Wii Fit Balance Board* as an *isometric* (i.e. non-displacing [3]) device with an *isotonic* device (the *Reebok Core Trainer Tilt Board*) found that, while no sig. diff. in performance between these two devices existed, participants preferred the isotonic interface, perceiving it as more joyful and realistic [1].

3 Hoverboard System Design

Based on related work and our own prior experience with suspension devices for locomotion in VR [5], an iterative design process was carried out to further investigate alternative suspended movement setups for locomotion in VR. The developments were motivated by the challenges around alternative techniques discussed above. Early informal evaluations with convenient subjects showed that the prototype devices pictured in Fig. 1 could support entertaining VR experiences, when test participants were asked to act out user generated gestures for direction control when using the setups while watching a VR video of moving down a rail that changed directions. In comparison, two alternative concepts of suspended walking and suspended flying were dismissed for reasons of discomfort and setup complexity when considering an interactive integration with a VR test application, and the third concept employing a hoverboard metaphor (Fig. 1) was chosen as first candidate for an interactive evaluation due to favorable ratings of comfort and ease of use.

3.1   Hardware Design

The hoverboard setup originally consisted of a wooden board attached by ropes to a roof-mounted hold, allowing for rotation around the horizontal or vertical axis. A smartphone was attached to the bottom of the board as a readily available integrated sensor device with wireless network connectivity. Although this could easily be replaced by a dedicated embedded device for further developments, this setup allowed rapid iteration, benefitting from the integrated accelerometer, gyro, and compass for a high accuracy rotation detection [15]. A belt at waist level was added for safety reasons prior to testing the setup with users.

3.2   Software Design

A small android app employs the acceleration sensors and transfers the orientation data via Wi-Fi. For a simple, low-cost, and replicable approach, the Unity game engine was chosen to drive a VR test application. The design of the VR environment was deliberately kept simple (Fig. 2). It contains a virtual representation of the board that moves along hovering above a corridor or track for depth reference at a constant speed that was set to approximate 25 km/h. The level contains a series of crosses that are placed along the

Fig. 2. Playful VR test application. Implemented in Unity3D.

virtual track and can be collected by the user to induce steering movements and to measure precision. When a cross is collected, the counter in the HUD increases and the user hears a jingle sound. The application also plays a simple background music tune for ambience.

Incoming rotation values are interpolated to avoid jitter in movements and mapped to the rotation around vertical or horizontal axis of the virtual board according to the physical manipulation of the real wooden board. The application allows for a forward, as well as for a sideways stance orientation. The system was used in conjunction with an Oculus DK2.

4 Evaluation

An exploratory evaluation was carried out to capture first impressions regarding the general usability, user experience, and acceptance of the suspended locomotion method. It included four trials with different stance orientation (sideways vs. forward stance) and different perspectives (first-person vs. third-person), lasting about three minutes per trial. The users participated in an interview comparing the conditions and discussing the perception of the general approach regarding aspects of fun, precision of control, the level of immersion, the occurrence of motion-sickness, and a comparison to the applicability of traditional input methods (such as keyboard and mouse) for controlling similar locomotion in VR.

4.1 Outcomes

Four convenient subject casual gamer participants with an average age of 23 years were recruited for the study. None had used a VR headset before. However, one participant immediately reported VR sickness, which is not a rare occurrence when working with translational movement in VR. The participant did not complete the study and is thus not considered in the following results and analysis. None of the remaining participants reported sickness. Problems due to latency in tracking and smoothing were not observed. The remaining three subjects (1 m, 2f) all reported the interactions to be a fun experience. P1 and P3 explicitly related their impression to the control modality. Although no common preference could be isolated regarding the stance, the individual favorites appeared to correspond to the stance of their favorite stance-related sports. The third-person perspective was noted to provide a better impression of the orientation of the board. All felt immersed noted that they find the game boring without the hoverboard control scheme. P2 and P3 highlighted the role of whole-body input. P1 and P3 noted that they felt they had precise control of the board (P3 collected most crosses). P3 also commented on the performance and showed notable increases across trials. P1 and P2 attempted to collect crosses with imaginary virtual representations of their real (untracked) body parts (e.g. hands). P2 showed very pronounced movement, at one time shouting "this is great; I would immediately buy this".

4.2 Discussion and Limitations

Overall, these exploratory evaluation results point towards a positive interaction experience. However, the evaluation is limited due to the low number of participants. Future evaluations should also consider using more immersive (real game) test applications, comparing to other control modalities, comparing the effect of controlling different objects that are not immediate representations of the input board, and controlling for the impact of first time VR experiences. In practical terms the most apparent limitation of the setup was a restricted portability, together with the need to provide hand holds due to fast rotations around the horizontal axis. This inspired the development of a follow-up prototype.

5 Updated Prototype

Although the interaction method discussed above appeared promising, the setup is not easily portable. Thus, we developed a smaller device that utilizes an isotonic hoverboard interaction metaphor. It consists of two identical wooden boards that are connected by springs (Fig. 3). Again, a smartphone attached to the bottom side of the top board provides the inclination data to the host computer. For this prototype, the springs are chosen to bear a 70–80 kg person allowing an inclination up to 10° in each direction. The springs can easily be swapped for different bodyweights and different maximum inclinations. One major advantage over the previous swing version is that it allows not only a leaning motion, but also to move freely on the board, which aims at facilitating improved tilting control.

Fig. 3. The updated springboard iteration of the hoverboard device.

6 Discussion and Future Work

The current prototype will be iterated to be fit for interactive demo use as well as to support further evaluations regarding the question of how the degrees of freedom can best be mapped to movement in VR, possibly combining velocity/speed and turning. Furthermore, a hydraulic suspension could support different weight ranges without requiring a manual swapping of the springs. We envision that the hoverboard concept can be used in entertainment computing applications as a simple and fun input device, tackling challenges of locomotion and travelling longer distances in virtual worlds. Hoverboard is as a simple, cheap, and easy to build device. As a physical input technique based on the user's body balance, it can be employed in fall prevention, for training core stability or a sense or space and time. It could also be used for spatial data exploration, e.g. traveling through detailed visualizations of the organs of a human body, or exploring large tags clouds or image collections, as well as to navigate geo-mapping environments such as Google Earth or StreetView. The hoverboard implements relative positioning (similar to a computer mouse or joystick) and, to allow for high immersion, it reacts to user input with dampened acceleration. This has advantages from the point of the user experience but presents problems regarding core usability metrics, such as time efficiency [12]. Therefore, we primarily envision application scenarios where efficiency is not a primary concern.

In many cases stationary controls are not well suited for immersive traveling in VR. Based on recent research we presented two iterations of full-body interfaces for locomotion in large virtual environments that are based on a hoverboard metaphor. First evaluation results promise a positive user experience and good control. Our latest prototype is a portable low-cost and easy to prepare device that promises to provide more precise control due to isotonic increasing resistance with increased stability, allowing for further explorations of the applicability of leaning for rotation and/or acceleration for long-range locomotion in VR.

Acknowledgments. This research is partially funded by the German Federal Ministry of Education and Research (BMBF). We thank the University of Bremen *Spiele AG* for support with the latest prototype.

References

1. Wang, J., Lindeman, R.W.: Comparing isometric and elastic surfboard interfaces for leaning-based travel in 3D virtual environments. In: 3DUI 2012, pp. 31–38. IEEE (2012)
2. Klatzky, R.L., Loomis, J.M., Beall, A.C., Chance, S.S., Golledge, R.G.: Spatial updating of self-position and orientation during real, imagined, and virtual locomotion. Psychol. Sci. **9**, 293–298 (1998)
3. Bowman, D.A., Kruijff, E., Laviola, J.J., Poupyrev, I.: 3D User Interfaces: Theory and Practice. Addison-Wesley, Boston (2004)
4. Teleporting. In: HTC Vive Support. https://www.vive.com/us/support/category_howto/ 839430.html. Accessed 11 Jan 2017
5. Walther-Franks, B., Wenig, D., Smeddinck, J., Malaka, R.: Suspended walking: a physical locomotion interface for virtual reality. In: Anacleto, J.C., Clua, E.W.G., Silva, F.S.C., Fels, S., Yang, H.S. (eds.) ICEC 2013. LNCS, vol. 8215, pp. 185–188. Springer, Heidelberg (2013). doi:10.1007/978-3-642-41106-9_27
6. Ohnishi, K., Shibata, M., Murakami, T.: Motion control for advanced mechatronics. IEEE ASME Trans. Mechatron. **1**, 56–67 (1996)
7. Iwata, H., Yano, H., Nakaizumi, F.: Gait master: a versatile locomotion interface for uneven virtual terrain. In: Proceedings of IEEE Virtual Reality 2001, pp. 131–137 (2001)
8. Medina, E., Fruland, R., Weghorst, S.: Virtusphere: walking in a human size VR "Hamster Ball". Proc. Hum. Factors Ergon. Soc. Annu. Meet. **52**, 2102–2106 (2008)
9. Ruddle, R.A., Lessels, S.: For efficient navigational search, humans require full physical movement, but not a rich visual scene. Psychol. Sci. **17**, 460–465 (2006)
10. Harris, A., Nguyen, K., Wilson, P.T., Jackoski, M., Williams, B.: Human joystick: Wii-leaning to translate in large virtual environments. In: VRCAI 2014, pp. 231–234. ACM (2014)
11. Kruijff, E., Marquardt, A., Trepkowski, C., Lindeman, R.W., Hinkenjann, A., Maiero, J., Riecke, B.E.: On Your Feet! enhancing self-motion perception in leaning-based interfaces through multisensory stimuli. In: SUI 2016, pp. 149–158. ACM (2016)
12. Marchal, M., Pettré, J., Lécuyer, A.: Joyman: a human-scale joystick for navigating in virtual worlds. In: 3DUI 2011, pp. 19–26. IEEE (2011)
13. Slater, M., Usoh, M., Steed, A.: Taking steps: the influence of a walking technique on presence in virtual reality. ACM Trans. Comput. Hum Interact. (TOCHI) **2**, 201–219 (1995)

14. Williams, B., Bailey, S., Narasimham, G., Li, M., Bodenheimer, B.: Evaluation of walking in place on a Wii balance board to explore a virtual environment. ACM Trans. Appl. Percept. **8**, 1–14 (2011)
15. Anjum, A., Ilyas, M.U.: Activity recognition using smartphone sensors. In: Proceedings of the 10th Consumer Communications and Networking Conference, pp. 914–919. IEEE (2013)

Masking Distracting Ambient Sound
in an Adaptive VR-Application
to Increase Presence

Felix Born[✉] and Maic Masuch

Entertainment Computing Group, University of Duisburg-Essen, Duisburg, Germany
{felix.born,maic.masuch}@uni-due.de

Abstract. The perception of disruptive outside sound while being inside a virtual reality simulation can break the experience of presence. Even with noise cancelling headphones external sound cannot be blocked completely. In this paper, we present an acoustic compensation method to sustain the virtual illusion. We developed a testbed VR prototype that allows to classify real-life sound and to adapt the virtual world accordingly by activating pre-defined playable content. The application analyzes and classifies outside sound in real time and triggers a suitable in-game object that matches the outside sound. Our implementation is a first approach, we want to use it to further examine the possibility of adaptive audio to mask external disruptive sounds resulting in an enhanced VR experience.

Keywords: Virtual reality gaming · Immersion · Presence · Adaptivity · Auditory immersion · Audio masking

1 Introduction

Being inside an immersive Virtual Reality (VR) simulation allows the user to fade out the real surrounding and focus on the presented virtual illusion. In full-immersive VR, visual stimuli of the real surrounding are blocked out and thus allow to create the experience of presence. Presence is often described as the feeling of being there [4], accompanied by fading out the real surrounding and experiencing the virtual world as the real world. Besides the importance of different visual aspects [1], a realistic auditory environment is also a major influence on presence in virtual worlds [5,11,17]. In contrast to visual perception, auditory cues of the reality can still reach the user and thus affect the user. Having two different sources of auditory information can lead to a problem due to human's nature of processing different input modalities. According to Wickens [15] this will lead to a conflict and to an increased cognitive demand to

We wish to thank D. Pohl for his participation and commitment in the development of the algorithms and virtual world.

N. Munekata et al. (Eds.): ICEC 2017, LNCS 10507, pp. 226–232, 2017.
DOI: 10.1007/978-3-319-66715-7_25

fade out the disruptive sound. This instance is a major problem for applications that mostly rely on the experience of the player being part of the virtual world, such as VR-systems that are used during local surgeries to distract the patient from potential stress inducing stimuli [7]. One solution would be to integrate the distracting sound elements in the VR world, maintaining the illusion by pretending there is a reason for the sound. This idea raises the question to what degree such a workaround would be beneficial to the immersion or presence? To answer this, we developed a testbed prototype that allows to recognize real-life sounds, and thus to adapt the visual environment accordingly. The virtual adaptive world is based on classification algorithms that allow an analysis of the auditory environment of the real world. Hence, the virtual world changes according to the classified sound in order to match the virtual visual elements with the real auditory surrounding. Offering this match of sensory information ought to help players experience presence and ignoring possible disruptive perceptions.

2 Related Work

2.1 Effects of Disruptive Audio

One of the main prerequisite for the experience of presence is sensory immersion [16]. Sensory immersion is defined by the ability of a system to deliver sensory cues that are close to real perceptions [13]. Thus, immersion can be described as an objective quality of a medium. The level of immersion increases if more senses and cognitions of the player are addressed. Hence, using modern VR-systems allows to create a high level of sensory immersion by presenting nearly photo-realistic stereoscopic images and thus creating a greater experience of presence. In-game sound is a core element of video games and modern VR-applications and a crucial factor for experiencing presence [5,11,17]. While modern VR-systems use head-mounted displays (HMD) that render the stereoscopic image and shield external visual cues from the user, intense sound of the real world can still reach the user and thus disrupt the presence of the player. Though this argument also applies for other sensory perception such as haptics, olfaction, or gustation, auditory perception and the experienced realism of the auditory cues are besides visual perception, the main influencing factors of a virtual experience [17]. In an experiment of Wharton and Collins [14] participants reported that the main reason for listening to additional music while playing games was to mask external sounds and therefore increase their immersion. This underlines the need for users to immerse with the virtual world and to fade out external stimuli. Furthermore, Wharton and Collins [14] examined, that the wrong selection of music can have an adverse effect and reduces the experienced immersion, especially if the music does not fit the visual content. Hence, non-matching visual and auditory cues can break the experience of presence.

2.2 Adaptive Audio

Active Noise Cancelling (ANC) Headphones are a common approach to fade out disruptive sounds. These headphones eliminate sound using destructive interference and are often used to shield the user from distracting ambient sound [9,12]. Due to different ear forms of every person and to the circumstance that sound is also transferred by the cranial bone, ANC Headphones can not eliminate the sound completely but rather reduce it. In addition, ANC headphones have a varying effectiveness according to the present sound pitches [3,9,10]. Furthermore, the use of ANC headphones can filter out important information that must be perceived, i.e. instructions during medical procedures, and are therefore not applicable in several fields of application. Hence disruptive sound can still reach the user. To counter the problem of disruptive sound, the approach of adaptive audio exists. Adaptive audio in games refers to the ability of a game to change the in-game sound or music according to the game play [2]. A well-known example for the first application of this technique can be found in the game "Super Mario Bros."[1], where the tempo of the music increases when the timer begins to run out. However, most of the digital games only consider the game state as a possible music changing event and do not include external auditory sources such as music or ambient sound of the real world. Nevertheless, games like "Audiosurf"[2], "Beat Hazard"[3] or "Audio Shield"[4] generate game content according to preselected music. These are first approaches to adapt the game world to external influences, however, the chosen music will be analyzed prior to the game. Hence, ambient sound changes in the real world are not considered. "The Polynomial"[5] takes this one step further and considers microphone input and thus manipulates the visual game world accordingly. This game world is adapted in real-time and is a first approach to match the visual impressions with the auditory cues of the surrounding. However, "The Polynomial" only changes the visual surrounding and does not adapt the gameplay according to the real-life sounds. So far, we could not find any application, that allows such a game play adaptation based on real-life ambient sound. Therefore, we have developed a fully functional testbed prototype of an adaptive VR-Game that generates games and regulates the visual surrounding based on real time classified auditory cues.

3   Development of an Adaptive VR Game

Based on the concept of an VR application that considers real-life sound and changes game world elements accordingly and thus integrate external sounds in a meaningful way into the virtual world, we examined the idea of an adaptive audio VR-game. Therefore, we developed a fully immersive VR-environment using the HTC Vive to display the rendered virtual world and an external microphone to analyze all auditory cues of the real-world. We created a scenario that allows to explore four different types of environments. Every environment is located in a different area, allows different kinds of playful interaction, and is activated

---

[1] Nintendo 1985, *Super Mario Bros.*
[2] Invisible Handlebar 2008, *Audiosurf.*
[3] Cold Beam Games 2009, *Beat Hazard.*
[4] Dylan Fitterer 2016, *Audioshield.*
[5] Dmytry Lavrov 2010, *The Polynomial.*

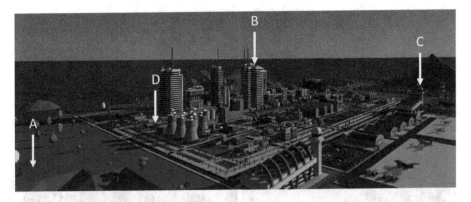

Fig. 1. Each environment and the according mini-game that can be activated is located in a different area in the virtual city. Based on the location, the dominant sound of the environment is different.

when the outside sound pitch is similar to the dominant sound of the according environment. Hence, we try to achieve a fit of the virtual environment and the real-world surrounding. The four different situations are a showcase for four discriminable tone pitches and are a first approach to integrate outside sound in a meaningful way. There is no interactive walkthrough possible since every environment is only active, if the real-life sound is present. Our development is a first approach of a testbed game that allows to examine how the perception of disruptive sound can be reduced and which tone pitches are of particular importance. The virtual world was implemented using the game engine Unity. The game is a 3D-Singleplayer game which takes place in a virtual city that consists of different buildings, railroads, airports, and a street system. The perspective of the player is a top-down view that allows an observation of the complete urban surrounding. The virtual city is located on an island that is surrounded by water. All assets are designed using a low-poly style, since we did not focus on a photo realistic setting but rather on a first testbed prototype. Besides activating virtual environments according to the real-life sound pitches, the volume of the ambient real-world sound regulates the dynamic of the city. Noisy surrounding leads to a high volume of traffic on the streets and in the air.

3.1 Adaptive Elements

The game incorporates two different adaptive approaches. On the one hand, mini-games are triggered according to the pitch of the real-world sound. On the other hand, an increase of the total real-world volume increases the city's traffic and thus leading to a higher traffic ambient sound.

Mini-games. There are four acoustic places that come along with a mini-game. Each of the mini-games is activated when the real-life sound is classified accordingly. The first mini-game (Game A) takes place in a park near the city

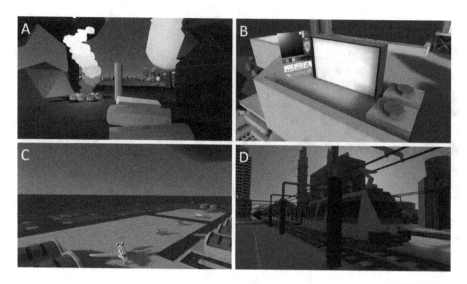

Fig. 2. Illustration of the location of the mini-games. Each mini-game is located in a different environment with ambient sound. Game A is located in a natural environment next to a bonfire with a medium-high sound pitch. Game B takes place on top of a building next to an AC system referring to a high sound pitch. Game C is located in the tower of an airport that is similar to medium-low sound pitches and game D sets the player next to rail station that represents low sound pitches.

and consists of a bonfire which is about to run out of wood. The player's task is to rapidly gather wood to increase the fire. The dominant sound in this environment consists of medium-high frequency sounds, such as bird cheeping. The second mini-game (Game B) is located on top of a building and allows the player to paint on a wall using the controller as spray can. The sound of the spray can as well as the sound of the air conditions system, that is installed next to the wall are high frequency sounds. In the third mini-game (Game C) the player is inside the airport tower and controls departing airplanes. The sound of the engines is situated in a medium-low frequency. The fourth mini-game (Game D) is near the central station and the player has to clean and repair incoming trains. Here the situation suggests a low frequency sound due to the mechanical surrounding. Every game will be activated when the corresponding sound is classified and only one game is playable at the same time. The surrounding of each mini-game matches a certain real-life tone pitch. If this tone pitch is recognized by the game, the according game is activated. A real-life surrounding that is similar to bird cheeping will lead to the bonfire game, whereas deep industrial noise will trigger the tram repair game.

Traffic. As a metaphor, outside sound is mapped to in-game traffic. This mechanism allows to manipulate the visual ambient environment and matches real-life sound to the sound of the driving cars and airplanes. Within the city, a street system with several parking lots exists. At the start of the game, all cars are parked. If the system recognizes a certain volume of the real-world sound, cars will start to drive a random route in the city. The higher the real-world volume is, the more cars are driving. The same principle applies for airplanes. If the real-world sound decreases, cars will park at the nearest parking lot and airplanes start to land.

4   Discussion and Future Work

Our goal is to improve immersion and presence in VR despite disturbing outside sounds. Hence, we developed a fully functional prototype that allows to analyze real-life ambient sound and to change game elements within the virtual world accordingly. We facilitate the possibility to integrate potential disruptive sounds of the surrounding in a meaningful way into the game world. Thus, we maintain the illusion and the experience of presence. Considering the works of Hoffman [6–8], who examined the use of VR to distract patients from painful and stress inducing medical procedures, our approach can be used to increase the distracting effect of the VR world by countering discomforting ambient sound in such situations. This field of application was our initial motivation for this investigation. Our development thus serves as a testbed game which we will further evaluate. We want to use our testbed game to examine which tone-pitches and sounds are specifically suitable for the adaptive approach. We hope to use the findings of our future research to examine guidelines how a diverse adaptive audio application should be implemented and which factors are crucial to increase presence. For further development, the site of operation should be considered when adapting the game. Thus, the sounds that will occur during the usage of our prototype can be estimated and result in game changes that are closer to the real-life sounds. For this instance, it is advisable to pre-analyze disruptive sounds of the site of operation and create acoustic fingerprints for each sound that might occur. These fingerprints can be used for a comparison at the run-time of the game. If a stored fingerprint matches the current sound, the game can instantly activate game content to match this specific sound. Thus, pre-defining situations as it is implemented in our prototype, would not be necessary. Ideally, such an adaptive virtual world could react to a great variety of outside sounds and generate a more persistent game experience. An extension to the existing idea would be the use of spatial sound. So far, the position of the sound source is not considered. Generating elements in the virtual world that match the real-life sound should be located at the same place in the virtual world as the sound source in the real world. Otherwise the visual representation does not match the acoustic surrounding and can therefore be a presence breaking problem. This research presents a first approach to improve presence and immersion despite disturbing outside sounds. Though shortcomings exist and the prototype has to be adapted for the according field of application the method can contribute to deliver a more compelling VR experience.

References

1. Cummings, J.J., Bailenson, J.N.: How immersive is enough? A meta-analysis of the effect of immersive technology on user presence. Media Psychol. **19**(2), 272–309 (2016)
2. Eladhari, M., Nieuwdorp, R., Fridenfalk, M.: The soundtrack of your mind: mind music-adaptive audio for game characters. In: Proceedings of the 2006 ACM SIGCHI International Conference on Advances in Computer Entertainment Technology, p. 54. ACM (2006)
3. Gan, W.S., Kuo, S.M.: An integrated audio and active noise control headset. IEEE Trans. Consum. Electron. **48**(2), 242–247 (2002)
4. Heeter, C.: Being there: the subjective experience of presence. Presence Teleoperators Virtual Environ. **1**(2), 262–271 (1992)
5. Hendrix, C., Barfield, W.: The sense of presence within auditory virtual environments. Presence Teleoperators Virtual Environ. **5**(3), 290–301 (1996)
6. Hoffman, H.G., Doctor, J.N., Patterson, D.R., Carrougher, G.J., Furness, T.A.: Virtual reality as an adjunctive pain control during burn wound care in adolescent patients. Pain **85**(1), 305–309 (2000)
7. Hoffman, H.G., Patterson, D.R., Seibel, E., Soltani, M., Jewett-Leahy, L., Sharar, S.R.: Virtual reality pain control during burn wound debridement in the hydrotank. Clin. J. Pain **24**(4), 299–304 (2008)
8. Hoffman, H.G., Seibel, E.J., Richards, T.L., Furness, T.A., Patterson, D.R., Sharar, S.R.: Virtual reality helmet display quality influences the magnitude of virtual reality analgesia. J. Pain **7**(11), 843–850 (2006)
9. Karalar, M., Keles, I., Doğantekin, E., Kahveci, O.K., Sarici, H.: Reduced pain and anxiety with music and noise-canceling headphones during shockwave lithotripsy. J. Endourol. **30**(6), 674–677 (2016)
10. Molesworth, B.R., Burgess, M., Gunnell, B., Löffler, D., Venjakob, A., et al.: The effect on recognition memory of noise cancelling headphones in a noisy environment with native and nonnative speakers. Noise Health **16**(71), 240 (2014)
11. Poeschl, S., Wall, K., Doering, N.: Integration of spatial sound in immersive virtual environments an experimental study on effects of spatial sound on presence. In: 2013 IEEE Virtual Reality (VR), pp. 129–130. IEEE (2013)
12. Riecke, B.E., Feuereissen, D.: To move or not to move: can active control and user-driven motion cueing enhance self-motion perception (vection) in virtual reality? In: Proceedings of the ACM Symposium on Applied Perception, pp. 17–24. ACM (2012)
13. Slater, M.: A note on presence terminology. Presence Connect **3**(3), 1–5 (2003)
14. Wharton, A., Collins, K.: Subjective measures of the influence of music customization on the video game play experience: a pilot study. Game Stud. Int. J. Comput. Game Res. **11**(2) (2011)
15. Wickens, C.: Processing resources in attention, dual task performance, and workload assessment (no. epl-81-3/onr-81-3). Illinois University at Urbana Engineering-Psychology Research Lab (1981)
16. Witmer, B.G., Singer, M.J.: Measuring presence in virtual environments: a presence questionnaire. Presence Teleoperators Virtual Environ. **7**(3), 225–240 (1998)
17. Wood, R.T., Griffiths, M.D., Chappell, D., Davies, M.N.: The structural characteristics of video games: a psycho-structural analysis. CyberPsychology Behav. **7**(1), 1–10 (2004)

Proposal of an Erasure-Oriented Drawing Style to Develop the Ability to Copy Images

Riho Kurotaki[1]([✉]), Yoshinari Takegawa[2], and Keiji Hirata[2]

[1] Department of Systems Information Science, Future University Hakodate, Hakodate, Hokkaido 041-8655, Japan
g2117019@fun.ac.jp
[2] Future University Hakodate, Hakodate, Hokkaido 041-8655, Japan
{yoshi,hirata}@fun.ac.jp
http://hiratakelab.jp/

Abstract. The purpose of this study is the proposal of an erasure-oriented drawing style to develop the ability to copy images. Possible erasable parts of an existing illustration were inferred and classified. As a result, the erasure processes were divided into two types and regarded as erasure patterns in this study. Then, we created an illustration drawing support system that makes use of erasure method. By automatically performing part of erasure, we made the drawing and erasure processes of illustration easier to memorize. Also, using drawing songs as models, we supported memorization of the procedures from auditory sense.

Keywords: Illustration · Drawing · Character · Drawing song

1 Introduction

There are various kind of picture, such as portraits, but we focus on pictures (illustrations) that are simplified versions of real things, like the image in Fig. 1. Illustrations are easier to convey than sentences when used to explain to others. For example, when making ideas with multiple people such as meeting, it becomes easier to concretely image by drawing illustrations. As a result, people will be able to smoothly progress discussions, so the skills to draw illustrations is important.

Copying is the basic practice for developing illustration drawing skills. In general, there are many ways to copy from a model image, but it takes time to develop skills, or monotonous repetition is necessary. Also, copying generally involves the drawing of auxiliary lines and guidelines to determine the composition and position of parts.

In this study, we adopt the approach that by assertively utilizing and increasing editing ability, we can also increase the ability to imitate an example image. As the first step, we focus on the editing operation of erasure. For example, the shape in Fig. 2 is an unfamiliar shape, unlike a circle or a rectangle. To draw this

N. Munekata et al. (Eds.): ICEC 2017, LNCS 10507, pp. 233–239, 2017.
DOI: 10.1007/978-3-319-66715-7_26

using an erasure method, two ellipses are aligned and the dotted line is erased, as shown in Fig. 3. Although it is difficult to accurately imitate unfamiliar figures in this way, by assertively introducing the erasure method, the threshold of the required drawing skill is lowered.

Therefore, we aim to propose an erasure-oriented drawing style to develop the ability to imitate model images.

The distinctive feature of this research is the drawing of illustrations on the premise of erasing. The proposed system has a function that automates a part of the erasure method to enable users to erase efficiently, a function that enables users to self-analyze the similarity between the model and their own illustrations, and a model, in the form of drawing song, to enable efficient memorization of drawing and erasing procedures. Through this study, we help people who are not good at drawing shapes and have a weak consciousness to draw shapes according to model.

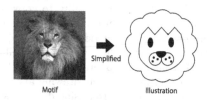

Fig. 1. Relationship between motif and illustration in this study

Fig. 2. Existing illustration   **Fig. 3.** Draw Fig. 2 using editing operation

2   Related Work

Murakami et al. [1] created a learning system for self-taught drawing of characters. An illustration drawn by the user is processed into evaluation images. After that, it is evaluated from three viewpoints and a score is given as feedback. However, when the evaluation result is low, this system does not show which parts should be modified. For example, if the evaluation is low when the centers of the evaluation image and the model are aligned, it is possible for the user to infer that the size and overall balance are bad. However, it is difficult to achieve deep understanding, because it is only the user's consideration.

3   Erasure Method

From 44 existing illustrations, we searched for examples where the erasure method works efficiently. As a result of analysis, the erasure processes were divided into two types. These two types were regarded as erasure patterns in this study. The details are as follows:

Fig. 4. Erasing all the lines of a diagram

Fig. 5. Erasing a single line of a diagram

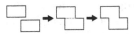

Fig. 6. Erasing multiple lines of diagrams

Fig. 7. Erasing overlapping edges

① Erasing all the lines of one diagram

   Diagrams are used as auxiliary lines, and the completed illustration does not include the initial diagrams. In Fig. 4, a circle and lines in the form of an asterisk are drawn. These diagrams are overlapped, then the intersections are connected to form a hexagon. Finally, the original circle and lines are erased.

② Erasing partially the lines of one diagram

   Part of the initial diagram is erased, while other parts are left. This method can be divided into three patterns:

   (a) Erasing a single line of a diagram

      In Fig. 5, an overlapped circle and rectangle are drawn. Then, only the line of the circle that overlaps the rectangle is erased.

   (b) Erasing multiple lines of diagrams

      In Fig. 6, a circle and rectangle are drawn, as in (a). Then, the lines of the circle and rectangle that are contained within the main outline are erased, to create a single shape.

   (c) Erasing overlapping edges

      In Fig. 7, two identical rectangles are prepared, and placed such that one side of each rectangle partially touches the other. Then, this adjoining line is erased.

4   Proposed System

4.1   System Requirements

Automation of Part of Erasure: The proposed method of adding erasure increases the processes involved when compared to existing drawing styles of simply drawing by adding more and more lines. In addition, the importance of learning in each process is different. For example, what the user should learn in erasing is the procedure of what part to erase with what timing. Therefore, the memory of the procedure has high importance. In contrast, the erasure of unnecessary lines by the user is simple and easy to learn, so it has low importance. As described earlier, it is necessary to separate the processes into two types: manual operations performed by the user, and automatic operations performed by the system.

Drawing Songs as Models: The metaphors of drawing songs are used to enable users to remember how to draw accurately in a short time. Drawing songs are one kind of Japanese play song, by which shapes, like that shown in Fig. 8, are drawn by following the lyrics, as shown in Table 1. By the end of the song the illustration is complete. The characteristic of drawing songs is to draw while listening to a song. Ron [2] cited the advantages of a memorization method using parody songs, stating that when recalling part of the rhythm and lyrics, one also recalls the thing related to them. In these parody songs, the lyrics are about the thing one wants to memorize, so the same effect can also be expected from drawing songs. In addition, Kinoshita et al. [3] have confirmed that the creation of drawing songs is effective in reducing awareness of one's lack of confidence regarding drawing and music. It is said that this is caused by experiencing returning to a childlike mentality and drawing, and singing a song, and we expected that the same effect would be obtained in our study as well.

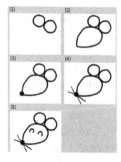

Table 1. Lyrics

(1)	After all it is two a dumpling
(2)	smartly I put one strawberry
(3)	I put only one bean
(4)	A lot of buds appear once again
(5)	squeaky It's a mouse

Fig. 8. An existing drawing song [4]

Using the Advantages of Existing Drawing Learning: One existing drawing learning methods is to attend drawing classes. This has the advantage that the learner can receive advice from the teacher on the spot. We aim to introduce this advantage into the proposed system.

4.2   Presented Contents

Figure 9 shows the proposed system [1]. It is supposed to be used on a tablet PC. Because it is easy to carry, the users can learn regardless of location and time. By using a touch pen, it is like drawing with analog tools. Details of the contents are given below. The numbering corresponds to the numbers in Fig. 9.

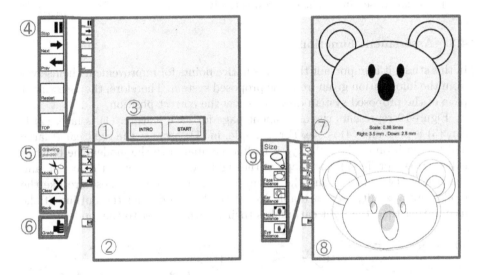

Fig. 9. Proposed system/(left)Top page, (right)Grading page

① **Model movie area**
   Plays the model movie selected using ③. Operated with button group ④.
② **Drawing area**
   To draw and erase.
③ **Model select button**
   Selects the model movie to be displayed in ①. INTRO is an explanation of the erasure method in this system. START is the drawing song.
④ **Model operation button**
   Operates model movie.
⑤ **Drawing support button**
   Provides drawing support by switching between drawing mode and erasure mode (Mode) etc. The user touches Mode to switch to erasure mode, and touches the line he/she wants to erase. Then, the system automatically erases that line.

---

[1] https://goo.gl/sXxdwc.

⑥ **Move to assessment button**
  Saves the drawing area as an image, and switches to the assessment page.
⑦ **Model area**
  Shows the model image. Under the model, the ratio between the model and a user's image is displayed. At the time of size assessment, the deviation from the center of the model is displayed.
⑧ **Assessment area**
  Shows the assessment result selected with ⑨.
⑨ **Assessment select button**
  From the top: Size superimposes the model image as it is. Face balance, Ear balance, Nose balance, and Eye balance are matched to the contours of face, right ear, nose, and right eye, respectively.

4.3   Assessment Function

In this study, it is important that users notice points for improvement themselves from the information given from the proposed system. Therefore, the assessment page of the proposed system does not show the correct position.

Figure 10 represents the assessment page for each feature. (1) is face, (2) is ear, (3) is nose and (4) is eye. For example, in (1), because the right ear is large and the position of the right eye is shifted compared to the model, the balance is bad. However, in (2), the shape of the right ear matches with the model, and the size of the right ear and the position of the eyes and the nose are like the model. As a result, users are able to notice that modifying the outline of the face, rather than the right ear, makes their drawing closer to the model.

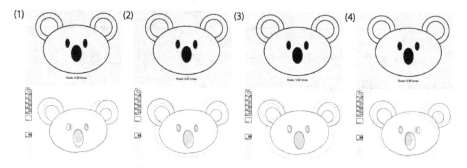

Fig. 10. Proposed system/Each assessment page

5   Conclusion

The purpose of this study is the proposal of an erasure-oriented style to develop the ability to copy images. We considered the places where erasure works, from existing illustrations, and established erasure patterns. Also, we created a system that can efficiently erase. By automating a part of the erasure process and using a drawing song as a model, we made it easier to memorize the illustration procedure. In the assessment function, we did not directly present the deviation from the example, but instead superimposed a model to make learners themselves aware of deviations and points for improvement.

Our future task is to increase the number of models. Currently, only one model is available, and even if users become able to draw one model perfectly, it cannot be said that it they have become able to draw illustrations. It is therefore essential also to learn combinations of erasure patterns and illustrations involving the drawing of varying shapes.

References

1. Murakami, R., Muranaka, N.: Grading evaluation method in character drawing study support system. In: IEEE 45th International Symposium on Multiple-Valued Logic, pp. 127–131 (2015)
2. Hale-Evans, R.: Mind Performance Hacks: Tips & Tools for Overclocking Your Brain. O'Reilly Media, Sebastopol (2006)
3. Kinoshita, N., Nishida, O.: A study on the creation of drawing songs -Practice examples in teacher training agencies-. Educational Practice Center, pp. 147–158 (2009)
4. Drawing Song of animals: Drawing Song of animals. https://youtu.be/j8ZXHw1aKG0. Accessed 20 Sep 2016

Game Understanding

Survey of How Human Players Divert
In-game Actions for Other Purposes:
Towards Human-Like Computer Players

Sila Temsiririrkkul[✉], Naoyuki Sato, Kenta Nakagawa, and Kokolo Ikeda

Japan Advanced Institute of Science and Technology, Asahidai 1-8, Nomi 923-1211, Japan
{temsiririrkkul,satonao,kokolo}@jaist.ac.jp

Abstract. Human-like behaviors are an important factor in achieving entertaining computer players. So far, the target of human-like behavior has been focused on actions in a game with the goal of winning. However, human behaviors might also be performed with other purposes not directly related to the game's main objective. For example, in FPS games, some human players create illustrations or graffiti with a weapon (i.e., gun). In co-operative online FPS, when chat is not allowed in-game, some players shoot the nearest wall to warn an ally about danger. This kind of action for an indirect purpose is hard to reproduce with a computer player, but it is very important to simulate human behavior and to entertain human players. In this article, we present a survey of the possible actions in a game that are not directly related to the game's main objective. Study cases of these behaviors are collected and classified by task and intention (i.e., warning, notification, provocation, greeting, expressing empathy, showing off, and self-satisfaction) and we discuss the possibility of reproducing such actions with a computer player. Furthermore, we show in experiments with multi-agent Q-learning that such actions with another purpose can emerge naturally.

Keywords: Human-likeness · Entertainment · Computer players · Q-learning · Multi-agent

1 Introduction

Nowadays, computer game players (game-AIs) are strong enough in term of performance to surpass human players in many domains, especially in classical board games such as chess or the game of Go [1]. In video games, which are more complex, DeepMind showed that a computer player was able to play 49 games, among which 29 were at the level or surpassing human record levels or scores [2, 3]. Game-AIs are now strong enough to be a human opponent or partner in terms of performance.

However, performance is not enough to entertain human players. In recent years, generating "human-like" behavior has become an important target among game researchers [4].

For example, one attempt to generate an entertaining game-AI by Ikeda and colleagues presented a method to entertain human players in the game of Go by letting them

© IFIP International Federation for Information Processing 2017
Published by Springer International Publishing AG 2017. All Rights Reserved
N. Munekata et al. (Eds.): ICEC 2017, LNCS 10507, pp. 243–256, 2017.
DOI: 10.1007/978-3-319-66715-7_27

win without allowing the players to notice their advantage, by choosing suboptimal actions but avoiding obviously bad ones [5].

Togelius and colleagues introduced the idea of "believability," which refers to the ability of a character or bot to make someone believe that the character is real or being controlled by a human being [6]. Many approaches were proposed to obtain believability and produce human-like behavior, such as in Fujii and colleagues, where a human-like computer player is obtained by simulating biological constraints. This approach considers human-likeness only in relation to the game's main objective [7].

In some games, the human player can perform actions "outside" of the game itself, such as bluffing or using facial expressions in poker games, or natural language communication via VOIP programs such as Skype. This communication is performed "outside" of the game itself in order to achieve the game's main objective. Such actions are also an important target for human-likeness.

However, sometimes, human player actions are not directly related to the game's main objective. For example, in FPS games, some players try to use their guns to create illustrations with bullet holes; in racing games, some players stop just before the goal, wait until another player comes closer, and then reach the goal. Such actions can be observed in many types of games, such as action games, RPGs, MMORPGs, puzzle games, and racing games. They are sufficiently frequent and significant to be a target (or even possibly a necessity) for obtaining human-likeness in computer agents.

In this research, we focus on human players' actions in-game that are not directly related to the game's main objective. We collect study cases from several types of games and classify them into seven types (i.e., warning, notification, provocation, greeting, expressing empathy, showing off, self-satisfaction). We also discuss the context in which these types of actions appear. In addition, we present an experiment that shows how multiple Q agents in an easy hunting game learn to divert game actions from their original goal in a way that we believe is similar to humans.

2   Human-Like Behavior: Previous Literature and Target Area

Recently, there are a number of approaches that aim for creating entertaining computer players. Specifically, computer players with human-like mannerisms are a very popular subject of interest among researchers. The idea of human-like AI was originally proposed by Alan Turing in the Imitation Game, which was the starting point of the Turing test [13]. Togelius and colleagues defined "believability" as the ability to make someone believe that the character/bot is being controlled by a human player [6]. So far, believability can be assessed by conducting a Turing test, which is mainly conducted by observing in-game behavior from a third person perspective.

Many computer players/bots in competitions were assessed according to believability assessment in order to indicate their performance in the believability aspect. For example, an assessment of the competition of computer players in an FPS (first person shooter) game was based on an Unreal tournament [9]; another assessment was based on competition in an action side-scrolling game, Super Mario Bros [10].

In an FPS game, finite state machine which represent state by information of combat and collected item, and another approach using behavior tree combine with Neuro Evolution, performed good performance to play game with human-like behavior [9]. In a Turing test tracking a Mario AI competition in 2012, top ranking human-like computer players used artificial neural network, influence map, and nearest neighbor methods [11]. Also, in recent years, Fujii and colleagues presented approaches to creating believable computer players by using biological constraints, which are applied to Q-learning and the A* algorithm [7]. These earlier methods are improved based on action/behavior in-game directly concerning the main objective of the game ((1) in Table 1) (e.g., Super Mario Bros: reach the goal at the right-most end of the screen). However, there are many behaviors that are produced which indirectly related to game main objective.

Table 1. Human player's action categories

	Directly concerned with main objective	Indirectly concerned with main objective
Inside a game	(1) Normal play	(3) provoking, reminding, etc.
Outside a game	(2) Bluff, Skype, etc.	(4) Screaming, leaning, etc.

Shiratori and colleagues showed another aspect of human-like behavior: communication outside the game, such as through facial expression and bluffing [8]. This behavior is important in some board games or card games such as poker and mahjong. They presented computer players in a fighting game with facial expressions outside the game that match the in-game state. Such "outside game" actions are related to a game's entertainment value, similar to shouting when a game character is being attacked ((2) in Table 1).

Current human-like behavior or believability research is focused on action in-game or outside the game that is mostly based on the intention to clear the game's main objective. However, human players also take some actions with intentions that are indirectly related to the main objective of the game. For example, outside the game, human players might scream when their characters get attacked in-game or may lean in the direction of their characters when turning in a racing game. Human players often take these unnecessary actions in order to immerse themselves in the game environment.

In-game, human players might show behaviors with intentions other than to clear the main objective ((3) in Table 1). For example, some players make illustrations using bullet holes in FPS games. These in-game actions are used for reasons other than reaching the game objective, for purposes such as provoking, reminding, or warning the other player (for example, punching when not in attack range to provoke the opponent in a fighting game).

We created Table 1 to briefly explain the behavior of human players in response to a game. These behavior have been widely discussed in the field of games and culture; for example, Tylor studied the behavior of players in the game World of Warcraft [12]. However, in the study of computer gaming AIs, these behaviors still receive less attention, especially (3), which is the main subject of discussion in this article.

3   Classification of Human Behavior not Directly Related to the Game's Main Objective

In Sect. 2, four types of action were presented. When playing a game, human players do not only aim to clear the game's main objective (such as getting high scores, clearing the stage, or defeating the enemy), but they also divert game actions for purposes not directly related to the game's main objective. In a game where cooperation with another player is necessary, some actions might be used to transmit a message, such as a notification or warning about something, or to provoke an enemy.

For human players, it is also possible to notify or warn about something with natural language by using an in-game chat system or VOIP programs such as Skype. However, in some situations, these communication channels are unavailable (e.g., chat is not available in the game or "too busy to chat, chat is difficult"), and in that case, actions inside the game itself can be diverted from their original use and used to represent different meanings or intentions.

In this chapter, 50 typical cases are introduced where human players seem to select their actions not to win, but for another purpose. We have viewed many videos of human gameplay and selected 50 typical cases. We do not claim that they are a complete or representative set of such behaviors; there might be other interesting and important examples, but we believe these 50 cases are valuable to show. These cases were then grouped into seven classes according to the purpose of the action, such as warning, provocation, or greeting. Some of these action types, such as the warning type, are highly related to the main objective of winning, and some of them, such as greeting, are less related. The following subsections explain the seven types of indirect action, from highly-related ones to less-related ones.

3.1   Warning

In cooperative games, warning is important for developing a strategy to clear the main objective of the game. Vocal warnings, alarms, or simple signals are part of some games. However, in cases where these functions are not available or the player is unavailable at that time, players often use other actions to transmit their messages. Actions with the intention of warning are strongly related to the main objective of the game. For humans, these actions facilitate a feeling of cooperation, so it is important for game-AI to produce and understand such actions in order to increase the satisfaction of human players with game-AI. We show two study cases of warning actions.

- Study case < 1 > (MOBA: League of Legends): Warning a team member about an incoming enemy or enemy action by using the "?" mark available in the game itself instead of the in-game chat, which can be used but consumes more time.
- Study case < 2 > (FPS: Sudden Attack): When the player notices a sniper, he/she shoots the nearest wall or corner in order to warn allied players (Fig. 1).

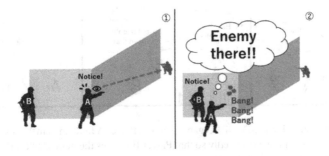

Fig. 1. Warning action in FPS Game: (1) Player A moves out from the corner of the building and finds an enemy, then (2) Player A tries to warn player B by shooting the nearest corner.

3.2 Notification

A notification action is defined as an action where the intention is to tell something to an opponent or ally, such as "Let's start the match!", "Please surrender!", or "Hey, come here!" Notification actions are strongly related to the game's main objective, thus the implementation of them in game-AI might be not difficult. The following study cases show some examples of the notification action.

- Study case < 3 > (MMO: Maple Story): To notify another player that there is a forgotten item on the floor, the player jumps repeatedly over an item with one hand over the item or in the direction of the other player. The intent of this action is to tell another player "there is an item here" and "please pick it up hurry" (Fig. 2.).
- Study case < 4 > (Action fighting: Super Smash Bros): In the character selection lobby in online matching, the match will start when all players press the ready button. In this phase, it is possible to press ready and cancel repeatedly to notify another player to "hurry up."
- Study case < 5 > (MMO: Dungeon & Fighter): In a dungeon while the team is co-operating, using attack actions at the door or passage that a player wants to explore indicates the destination to the other teammate.
- Study case < 6 > (Board Game: Go): In a situation where one player has an advantage on the other player, a clearly suboptimal move is chosen on purpose in order to transmit "I can beat you even if I choose this kind of suboptimal move. Surrender now!"

Fig. 2. Notification action in MMORPG game: (upper) Player A finds an item that Player B didn't notice; (mid) Player A jumps repeatedly so that Player B notices the item; (lower) Player B picks up the item and expresses his gratitude by crouching.

3.3 Provocation

Provocation (or "trolling") is an action that tries to frustrate the opponent when the player is in an advantageous situation; this gives some small impediment to the opponent with malice, or a player might put him/herself at disadvantage on purpose. This action often occurs when a player is able to keep superiority in the game continuously. Normally, human players do such actions in order to satisfy themselves. However, sometimes, the goal of provoking or trolling is to lure the opponent into a mistake and might be strongly related to the game's main objective. Reproducing such actions with Game-AIs might not increase human players' satisfaction, but these actions are important for human-likeness.

- Study case < 7 > (FPS: Call of Duty): Moving, jumping, and crouch-standing repeatedly around a defeated opponent character's (dead body) location to aggravate the defeated player (Fig. 3.).
- Study case < 8 > (Fighting game: Super Street Fighter II): In fighting games, after a round is finished, a player can punch or kick the dead body of the losing player to provoke the opponent.

Fig. 3. Provoking action: In an FPS game, moving, jumping, and crouch-standing repeatedly around a defeated opponent character to provoke the enemy.

3.4 Greeting

Greeting refers to an action where players communicate something like "Hello", "Nice to meet you", "Thank you", or "My bad" (this category often includes apologizing). Normally, greeting (or apologizing) is done via VOIP programs such as Skype or built-in chat systems in the game. However, in some cases when chat or VOIP are not available, actions in-game are used to express these sentiments. Greeting has a weak relationship with the game's main objective. In action games where a crouch action is available (normally for evasion from an attack), it is often used to perform greeting or apologizing.

- Study case < 9 > (Action fighting: Super Smash Bros): Players use crouch-standing repeatedly to express "Nice to meet you" when creating a team battle. The meaning of an action can change depending on when it is performed. After doing something considered as bad manners, a player can apologize to other players by crouch-standing repeatedly.

3.5 Expressing Empathy

Expressing empathy refers to actions that expect some response from an opponent or are used to provoke some action from an allied player; these express a "Let's have fun together" feeling. These actions are done without malice.

- Study case < 10 > (Fighting game: Super Street Fighter II): Some players enjoy using attack actions or jumping outside attack range for fun, expecting the opponent to do the same thing in response.
- Study case < 11 > (MMORPG: Final Fantasy XIV): Sometimes, mass numbers of players come together and try to use in-game actions called "emotes" to express some movement or dance at the same time.

3.6 Showing off

Showing off is an action based on appearances rather than performing to meet the game's objective. Sometimes, this action might be conducted in order to provoke an opponent, but many players try to perform this type of action seriously.

- Study Case < 12 > (3D Fighting: Soul Caliber, Fate/Stay night) In some fighting game, the combo (series of action) which difficult to perform, afford cost is higher than performance (damage), but the appearance is good, such combo is exist. Some player tries to perform such showoff combo.
- Study Case < 13 > (Street fighter III) Counter Attack or Blocking are existing in many fighting game. Using such attack allowed player to who encounter the attack avoid and strike back without taking any damages. However, blocking action has to be perform suddenly after opponent perform attack which is very difficult.

3.7   Self-satisfaction

Self-satisfaction actions include actions taken to pursue curiosity or to bind or constrain play. To bind play is to play the game with extra rules stated by the player him/herself, such as clearing the game at a low level, limiting item uses, or clearing a level or area without damage. Bind play is also performed for creating new styles of play.

Another type of action that players take to satisfy themselves is a creativity action. In games with a high degree of freedom such as Minecraft and Mario Maker, players can try to create innovative stages in their own style.

- Study case < 14 > (Action RPG: The Elder Scrolls V: Skyrim): Some players might enjoy exploring locations in the game that are normally hard to reach, such as the top of a mountain.
- Study case < 15 > (Action: Resident Evil): Some players implement extra rules such as "clear with limited equipment or weapons" or "stay alive at a low level of life or hit point throughout the game."

4   Appearance Conditions of Actions not Directly Related to the Game's Main Objective

In the previous chapter, we provided examples of study cases and classified them in seven categories. However, the conditions that cause this behavior to appear are very significant.

In-game behavior that is indirectly related to the main objective can be observed in many types of games. However, some of these actions require minimum knowledge of or skill at the game or the type of game in order to be interpreted correctly. For example, in study case < 7>, the action of moving around the dead body of a defeated player might not be understood by a beginner. However, along with the improvement of player skill, action comprehension becomes deeper. When reproducing such actions in a computer player's behavior, it is necessary to take into account the skill and knowledge of the human player.

Limiting the information that players have affects their comprehension of a behavior's intention. For example, in card games, we can help or impede an opponent by discarding a card, However, if the opponent only knows that a card has been discarded and not for what purpose it can be discarded, it may be difficult to distinguish the other player's intention. Thus, when information is limited, these actions rarely appear. On the other hand, in games with complete information such as fighting games (where health, time, and/or a special attack energy gauge are shown), the intention of actions is easier to understand.

However, in some kinds of games, even when information is limited, human players can estimate the situation by using action information. For example, in FPS games, if enemy attacks suddenly stop or weaken, then the player might assume that opponents have changed their strategy. In this situation, the player is able to fill in the missing information and estimate the intentions of actions.

Another factor is the amount of spare time a player has in game, which relates directly to the difficulty of the game and the situation in game. In a game in which chat is allowed and the player has spare time to use a chat, the game's main objective may become temporarily irrelevant while this action is performed. The degree of freedom of action regarding game tasks directly affects the appearance of this type of action. In games with busy tasks or games where every action in-game affects the score or victory such as Go or Tetris, this type of action will not be performed.

5   Emergence of Actions not Directly Related to the Main Objective

Most of the actions we introduced in this paper are unique to humans, though it is possible for some of them to emerge from systems without humans, as we mentioned in Sect. 4 and 5. Thus, we carried out two experiments to observe how actions not directly related to the game's main objective emerge from interactions between reinforcement learning agents.

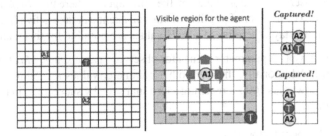

Fig. 4. Overview of the environment. Two agents try to catch a target. Each agent has a limited view. In this case, when both of the agents touch the target, the task is accounted a success.

5.1   Setting

The two experiments share a common setup. Two reinforcement learning agents with limited views try to catch a target while co-operating with each other, as illustrated in Fig. 4. We expected these (limited sight) agents to substitute their sequential movement actions for a signal that the target is located near the agent.

- Environment:
    - The field consists of 15 × 15 grid spaces in which agents can locate the target.
    - Two agents and one target are randomly arranged on the grid initially.
    - Each agent can move to an adjacent grid space in a compass direction each turn.
    - The field has a torus structure. Agents will appear in the right-most when they go left on the left-most space and appear on the top side when they go down on the bottom of the grid.
    - More than one character (agent or target) cannot be located in the same grid space at the same time.
    - The target does not move.

- In the case that both agents are located in grid spaces adjacent to the target before 100 turns passes from the initial state, the search and chase task is accounted a success. The task is accounted a failure otherwise. In both cases, the game state will be re-initialized.
- Agent: Each agent decides its action using a one-step Q-learning algorithm. The game state observed by each agent is a combination of feature values as below.
  - (F1) Coordinate of the target relative to the agent. The agent can find the target only when it is located inside the 7×7 grid area whose center coordinate is the agent; therefore, 49 values are possible for this feature.
  - (F2) Coordinate of the other agent relative to the agent. The limited eyesight of agents does not affect this information; thus, $224 \ (= 15 \times 15 - 1)$ values are possible for this future.
  - (F3) The number of turns during which the agent does not see the target. Once the agent finds the target, this value is set to zero. $\{MaxT + 1\}$ values are possible for this feature, where $MaxT$ is a parameter value of the agent (if the number of such turns becomes greater than $MaxT$, this feature value is set to $MaxT$).
  - (F4) The last $MaxH$ actions taken by the other agent, where the $MaxH$ is a parameter value. The number of possible actions an agent can take is five (go up, down, left, right, or stay), therefore, 5 $MaxH$ values are possible for this feature.

Our agents have two parameter values for observing game states, $MaxT$ and $MaxH$, as stated above. Additionally, there are other parameter values related to the learning algorithm. The reward is 100 for reaching a terminal state by succeeding in the catching task, 0 for failure.

Discount factor: 0.8.

$$\text{Learning late: } 0.1 \times \frac{1000000}{1000000 + \{Number of episodes trained\}}$$

The agent adopts the ϵ-greedy policy with ($\epsilon = 0.1$) as its behavior policy.

5.2 Experiment 1: Observing Emergence of Action Substitution

- Setting: We compared the movement patterns of agents under two parameter settings, that is $MaxT = 0$, $MaxH = 0$ and $MaxT = 0$, $MaxH = 2$. In the $MaxT = 0$, $MaxH = 0$ case, each agent must decide its action according only to the current positions of the other agent and the target (if it is located within eyesight). Therefore, agents cannot give their partner any clues to find out the target's location. On the other hand, in the $MaxT = 0$, $MaxH = 2$ case, each agent is able to pay attention to the movement patterns of its partner. Therefore, agents have a chance of telling their partner the location of the target by showing the partner some characteristic movement patterns.

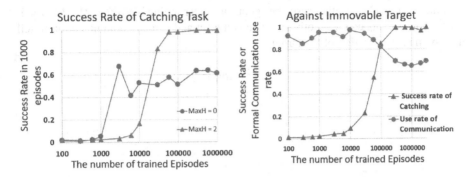

Fig. 5. (left) Success rate of the task. The success rate was enhanced by 40% when each agent memorized the last two moves of the other agent. (Right) Success rate and the increasing use rate of the communication function to signal the immovable target. Through the whole training process, agents came to rely on the function at a rate of 70% (i.e., any agent used the function in more than 700 episodes out of the last 1000 episodes on each plot).

- Result: We observed the movement patterns in both settings after 3,000,000 training episodes. In the case of *MaxH*:0, each agent moved chaotically until the target came into sight. After that, the agent rushed at the target. In the case of *MaxH*:2, each agent used regular zigzag movement patterns for exploring (e.g., goes {up, left, up, left, . . .}) until the target came into sight. Whenever an agent found the target, it changed its movement pattern, avoiding moving away from the target (e.g., goes {up, down, up, down,. . .}) to inspire its partner to approach. Figure 5. shows the performance of agents under these conditions. Introducing the information about the action history of the partner agent enhanced the success rate by 30% in the end, even though that information does not contain any direct clue for the target location. Therefore, we think the enhanced performance was caused by the emergence of an action substitution, that is, agents substituting their movement action to signal their partner.

5.3 Experiment 2: Encouraging Action Substitution

In the experiment described below, we aimed to show that even if there is a formal way to communicate with partners, agents prefer to communicate through action substitution if the situation is urgent and the formal method requires more time.

- Setting: We added two rule options for the system.
  - Escaping target: The target can also move in this rule. It moves away from agents once every four turns and in the case that any agent catches the target in its (limited) field of view.
  - Formal communication: Each agent can inform the other agent of the precise current location of the target at the cost of becoming immovable during the following four turns.

We compared the movement patterns of agents under two option settings: Escaping target: Off, Formal communication: On and Escaping target: On, Formal communication: On. In either case, the agent parameter setting is $MaxT = 21$, $MaxH = 2$. That means agents can use both action substitution and formal communication to tell their partner the location of the target.

Fig. 6. Success rate and use rate of the communication function while chasing the escaping target. Eventually, agents began to avoid using the communication function in all but 20% of episodes.

Compared with action substitution, formal communication requires a larger number of turns to communicate and inform the partner of the more precise location of the target. Thus, the formal method imitates text chat or Skype in actual multiplayer video game situations. In this experimental setting, we observed how the frequency of formal communication adopted by the agents varies.

- Result: The success rate of capturing the target and frequency of use for formal communication are shown in Fig. 5. (Left) and (Right). In the Escaping target: Off case, the rate of use for formal communication is around 70%. We think this is because the communication method is useful in capturing the target. Meanwhile, in the Escaping target: On case, agents adopt the communication method in only 20% of episodes. We think the reason why is that the "capturing escaping target task" does not allow agents enough time for formal communication. On the other hand, the success rate of tasks after training is similar in both settings. This means that agents use action substitution more frequently in the scenario with an escaping target than with an immovable target, but they are able to use this method with comparable effectiveness to capture the target. Otherwise, the success rate would have largely dropped off in Fig. 6.

5.4 Conclusion of Experiments

Experiment 1 showed the emergence of action substitution, in which movement actions are used as signals between agents. The agents obtained this method automatically through reinforcement leaning, without any specific if-then routines for action substitution emergence. Therefore, we insist that agents in a system without humans can automatically obtain a type of in-game action that does not directly achieve the main goal (or at least an action pattern that appears to fall in such a category).

Experiment 2 demonstrated how the degree of urgency affects the probability of action substitution emergence. A higher degree of urgency makes agents less likely to use a formal method of communication and encouraged them to use substituted actions for their communication.

6 Conclusion

In this research, we showed new aspects of human-like behavior that it is possible to categorize in two sets of categories and in four ways: inside or outside the game, related or not directly related to the game's main objective. We focused on actions without the intention to clear the main objective of the game, which we think are a significant behavior specific to humans and necessary to achieve human-like computer players. So far, 50 study cases of human actions were collected. These study cases were classified into seven types of behavior (i.e., warning, notification, provocation, greeting, expressing empathy, showing off, and self-satisfaction) and we discussed the occurrence conditions and possibility of reproduction by computer players. Furthermore, we conducted an experiment that shows the natural emergence of such behavior by learning between multiple Q-learning agents. This experiment successfully demonstrates the emergence of actions that are similar to the communication of humans.

References

1. Silver, D., et al.: Mastering the game of go with deep neural networks and tree search. Nature **529**, 484–489 (2016)
2. Mnih, V., et al.: Playing atari with deep reinforcement learning. In: NIPS Deep Learning Workshop 2013 (2013)
3. Mnih, V., et al.: Human-level control through deep reinforcement learning. Nature **518**, 529533 (2015)
4. Soni, B., et al.: Bots trained to play like a human are more fun. In: 2008 IEEE International Joint Conference on Neural Networks IJCNN 2008 (IEEE World Congress on Computational Intelligence), pp. 363–369 (2008)
5. Ikeda, K., Viennot, S.: Production of various strategies and position control for Monte-Carlo Go - entertaining human players. In: IEEE Conference on Computational Intelligence and Games (CIG2013), pp. 145–152 (2013)
6. Togelius, J., et al.: Assessing Believability Believable Bots: Can Computers Play Like People?, pp. 215–230 Springer, Heidelberg (2012)
7. Fujii, N., Sato, Y., Wakama, H., Kazai, K., Katayose, H.: Evaluating human-like behaviors of video-game agents autonomously acquired with biological constraints. In: Reidsma, D., Katayose, H., Nijholt, A. (eds.) ACE 2013. LNCS, vol. 8253, pp. 61–76. Springer, Cham (2013). doi:10.1007/978-3-319-03161-3_5
8. Shiratori, et al.: 感情表現生成を行う仮想ゲームプレイヤ. The Society for Art and Science, Vol. 7(2), pp. 65–74 (2008). (Japanese)
9. The 2 k bot prize. http://botprize.org/. Accessed 20 Apr 2017
10. http://www.marioai.org/turing-test-track

11. Shaker, N., et al.: The turing test track of the 2012 Mario AI championship: Entries and evaluation. In: 2013 IEEE Conference on Computational Intelligence in Games (CIG), pp. 1–8 (2013)
12. Taylor, T.L.: The Assemblage of Play. Game Cult. **4**(4), 331–339 (2009)
13. Turing, A.M.: Computing machinery and intelligence. Mind **59**(236), 433–460 (1950)

Designing a Creature Believability Scale for Videogames

Nuno Barreto[✉], Rui Craveirinha, and Licinio Roque

CISUC, Department of Informatics Engineering, University of Coimbra,
3004 516 Coimbra, Portugal
nbarreto@dei.uc.pt

Abstract. This paper describes the design, and early evaluation of a scale aimed at assessing the believability of creatures in videogames. These creatures include all zoomorphic entities that do not qualify as fundamentally human-like, whether or not they have characteristics identifiable as anthropomorphic. The work is based on principles drawn from biology, animation, illustration and artificial intelligence. After developing the scale's 46 original items, it was administrated as a Likert Scale questionnaire. The results were analyzed through Principal Component Analysis and they suggest that 26 items, out of the original 46, spread across 4 dimensions, could be used to evaluate creature believability.

Keywords: Believability scale · Game design · Experience evaluation · Videogames

1 Introduction

This paper reports on the process of creation of a scale to assess believability of a subset of videogame creatures. We limit this subset to zoomorphic entities, inspired by (contemporary or otherwise) living or fictional beings, that are not identifiable as human, nor fundamentally human-like, despite whatever anthropomorphic characteristics they might have. Creatures belonging to this subset will henceforth be referred to as creatures, for simplicity.

Defined, by Fogg and Tseng, as a synonym for credibility, believability is a construct measured by the perception users have of a given artifact [8]. This is because the authors consider artifacts as a source of information and their perceived veracity contributes to their believability. In multimedia, or at least in videogames, believability can be fundamental in inducing immersion [39], a form of Presence [18], more so when such artifacts deal with unrealistic themes (fantasy, sci-fi, mythology, etc.).

In particular, believability can be a crucial element of the game's world's actors, leading humans to accept they are "alive and thinking" [28]. This is the goal behind believable agents, an artificial intelligence field focused on simulating agents with credible behaviors. However, developing believable agents transcends

© IFIP International Federation for Information Processing 2017
Published by Springer International Publishing AG 2017. All Rights Reserved
N. Munekata et al. (Eds.): ICEC 2017, LNCS 10507, pp. 257–269, 2017.
DOI: 10.1007/978-3-319-66715-7_28

artificial intelligence as it is assumed to be one of the driving factors when crafting videogame experiences [39]. In fact, studies have shown such actors are perceived to be more engaging than non-believable ones [2,13,28,39].

Studies in believability mainly follow two directions: one studying how to create behavioral patterns which, when observed, incite believability. This is, as previously explained, the scope of the Believable Agents field study [13]. The other, has its roots in animation where artists were concerned with creating life-like beings, then known as believable characters. Here, anthropomorphism was key to make viewers relate to them [2]. Nonetheless, the literature behind both directions appears to focus extensively on simulating humans. On one hand, as either in-game characters, or players [36] and, on the other, as compelling and emotional characters, part of a narrative [2]. It is worth noting however, that believability is in no way a synonym for realism. In fact, some of the construct's earlier studies were conducted with cartoons [35]. This strengthens the idea that believability is achieved from the mental model constructed via an observer's interpretation of a given artifact.

While synthetic humans, and humanoids, are abundant in videogames, they are not the only type of existing virtual "living"-entities. The overwhelming focus on the first, despite the existence of the latter, helps set the ground for our research. Specifically, we aim to study believability in creatures, under the hypothesis that, similarly to how studies suggest virtual humans/humanoids are more engaging if considered believable, creatures are also more appealing if presented in a believable manner. This is particular important on games where they either play a central role, such as Life-Simulation games, or are an integral part in supporting the game's environment (this is most notably true in the fantasy open-world genre).

However, while there is already a well-defined set of expectations towards humans, [2] (which helps their believability assessment), there is, as far as could be assessed, none for creatures. Therefore, in order to verify our hypothesis, we must first answer "What makes a creature feel believable?". The scale proposed in this paper is a step towards that goal. Moreover, by creating such a tool, potential pitfalls in existing videogame creatures may be identified, and the design of future ones may be founded on a better understood basis. The contribution of this paper is then a methodological one [42]: an instrument to measure creature believability and aid the design process to maximize that perception.

This paper is structured as follows: Sect. 2 will describe the methodology behind the scale's construction including item generation and the setup behind administering the scale. This is followed by Sect. 3, Results and Scale Revision, where the data collected is used to validate and help revise the scale itself. Finally, Sect. 4, will conclude the paper.

2   Methodology

This research is being developed using a Design Science Research methodology [12] (focused on the creature believability scale as a model output), with this paper's work corresponding to an iteration cycle. Next we will present the following steps in the process: problem awareness, and its foundation on previous literature, construction of the creature believability scale proposal and a first evaluation and revision based on Principal Components Analysis.

2.1   Creature Believability Scale Construction

The main reason behind the creation of a scale, over another instrument, was due to the nature of believability. Because it is a construct originating from an observer's perception, we chose rating scales [32].

The scales's proposal construction underwent a three-step process, inspired by the method described by Spector [32]. Firstly, we defined what we would consider "creatures", establishing a division between humans (and humanoids) and the entities under our study. Based on the definition proposed by Whithlatch [41] (which went in the desired direction) we defined creatures as stated in the introduction: zoomorphic entities, inspired by (contemporary or otherwise) living or fictional beings, that are not identifiable as human, nor fundamentally human-like, despite whatever anthropomorphic characteristics they might, or might not, have.

The second step consisted in defining a list of underlying constraints of our scale:

1. Unlike humans, and humanoids, who have a distinct (limited) set of characteristics, our definition includes markedly heterogeneous beings, ranging from insectoid to mammal-like. With this in mind, our first concern was to create a sufficiently broad set of identifiable elements to evaluate the wide variety of creatures.
2. Instead of considering believability as a binary factor, we opted to work with a fuzzy set. This would allow us to better quantify the qualitative, and variable, nature of the believability a given creature may have, as well as better identify which elements contribute to that perception.
3. As believability is intrinsically perceptual [8], we considered limiting the evaluation of the creatures to perceivable (phenotypic) elements.
4. Whilst the creature definition given includes entities inspired by both living and fictional beings, the everyday experience of a human is with living beings. Therefore, the starting point for the evaluation elements was plausible characteristics.
5. Finally, since our objective is to validate and, subsequently, use this scale with gamers, which may or may not have a scientific background, the language was made accessible, deprived of technical terminology.

After analyzing the constraints, we constructed several candidate statements. This was done both through induction on examples and with the support of extant literature. For the latter we surveyed multiple study fields such as, but not limited to, believable agents, ethology, biology, human perception of living-beings, illustration and animation.

This work began with a survey of existing believable-agents literature to retrieve cognition-related items. One source, by Togelius, et al. [36], cited ConsScale [25] as a basis for their work. ConsScale is an evaluation tool designed to quantify the "level of consciousness" in artificial agents [25] by analyzing their architecture. The tool is composed of 13 levels where each contains a set of statements illustrating the cognitive skills an agent must have at that given level. These levels go from "Disembodied" (entities lacking defined boundaries or cognitive skills) to "Super-Conscious" (entities surpassing human-beings, capable of managing several consciouses simultaneously).

Similarly to Togelius, et al., we used ConsScale to derive some of our scale's items, albeit with some preprocessing. Firstly, we used only a subset of the scale, each of the scale's levels' biological phylogeny working as a heuristic to observe constraints 1 and 4. Thus, only level 2 (viruses) through 8 (primates) were used. Subsequently, we rewrote the levels' items to enumerate the phenotypic traits corresponding to the respective statements. The resulting items accounted for reaction to the environment, intention (underlined by the human need to attribute intention to the actions of living-beings [7]) and display of emotions and sociability (both supported by ethological studies [1,6,19]). We also added an item for personality, as it is a trait that has been identified in animals [11].

From a different perspective, Thomas and Johnston argue that cognitive processes can be illustrated through expressions [35]. They explain, in fact, that workers at Disney, throughout its early years, extensively studied animals, concluding they "communicate their feelings with their whole body attitude and movement" [35]. This was the origin of the 12 Principles of Animation, 9 of which were incorporated into our scale. Particularly, we did not consider those detailing how to make appealing characters, 2D animations and narratives as these were beyond the scope of our assessment.

In the case of biology, living beings are viewed as open systems [14]: they retrieve matter and energy from the environment and, in return, perform actions and produce waste material. From this perspective, a living entity is expected to, at the very least, grow in size and number of cells, and reproduce sexually or asexually to generate offspring.

Within the scope of illustration, Whitlatch identifies the importance of internal an external coherence [40,41]: the coherence between a creature's behavior and their body's design ("why a creature looks the way it does" [41]) and, likewise, between its body and its habitat ("the anatomical structure supports and makes possible the lifestyle" [41]).

The research developed up to this point resulted in a list of 46 statements (revised once for form simplification) depicted in Table 2.

2.2 Administering the Initial Creature Believability Questionnaire

To administer the initial iteration of the scale, we designed a questionnaire[1] where participants, after filling out demographic data, are shown 28, 20 to 30 seconds long, clips, obtained from various videogame sources. These clips all included at least one creature engaged in a specific activity. We used short clips because we meant to incite immediate responses rather than evaluating the participant's recollection of the clips (which could be contaminated by memory inaccuracy).

After viewing each clip, subjects were prompted to:

1. Describe how many creatures were present in the video. This was included as a fail-safe measure [15,20] to allow deployment to Mechanical Turk.
2. Score 6 statements, taken from our believability items, through a 5-point Likert Scale. These items were displayed in a randomized order. Moreover, to reduce confirmation bias, 3 of the 6 items refer to elements absent in the respective clip. There were two reasons behind showing only a subset of the scale. The first involves user fatigue as administering the complete questionnaire would account for 1288 items (46×28). While one could argue that increasing the video length would potentially reduce the number of clips and subsequently the items' total, it would force the users to recollect more information, something we previously stated we wanted to avoid. The other reason was due to the fact that, to our knowledge, not every game has creatures with the characteristics present in the scale's items. However, grouping creatures from different games together would, on one hand, cause the issue we previously discussed and, on the other, potentially introduce a bias due to the change of context between games.
3. Rate the clip's creatures' believability using a 10-point Differential Semantic Scale with a Non-Believable-Believable pair. This was meant to assess the presence of correlations between Likert items and the creature's believability.
4. Similarly rate the clip's setting's believability. This was to reveal whether or not (and to what extent) the setting's and the creature's perceived believability are correlated.

2.3 Choosing Content for Evaluation

The games, included in this experiment, were chosen, by taking into account the following factors: first, we selected ones where creatures had an extensive on-screen presence, as we assume that, in these games, creatures have an additional development effort that would not be justified otherwise. As such, most of the games we considered are ones with open-world elements and life-simulation games. Finally, we chose to consider games made in the last 15 years. The main reason behind this lies in our belief that such games incorporate recent technology. This way, we mean to reduce any bias which could arise from notorious technological limitations.

This selection process resulted in several creatures from 19 games:

---

[1] https://goo.gl/forms/XNe60psywQlILq302.

- Hyenas and cheetahs from Afrika [26]
- D-Horse and D-Dog from Metal Gear Solid V: The Phantom Pain [16]
- The EyePet from EyePet [29]
- The dog from Fable 2 [17]
- Dogmeat from Fallout 4 [4]
- A rhino from Far Cry 4 [37]
- An Adamantoise from Final Fantasy XIII [33]
- Chop from Grand Theft Auto V [27]
- A black panther and a Bengal tiger from Kinectimals [9]
- A Rathian and a Rathalos from Monster Hunter Freedom Unite [5]
- The Artic Fox from Never Alone [38]
- A dog from Nintendogs [24]
- Red Pikmins from Pikmin [23]
- Dogs and a cat from The Sims 2 [21]
- A sabertooth tiger from The Elder Scrolls V: Skyrim [3]
- Chaos from Sonic Adventure 2: Battle [30] and Sonic Adventure DX: Director's Cut [31]
- Creatures from Spore [22]
- Trico from The Last Guardian [10]

Before deploying to a larger population, the survey then underwent a pilot testing process with 5 test subjects, correcting typos and other errors.

3   Results and Scale Revision

The following subsections detail the process used in the revision of the believability scale.

3.1   Process and Population Profile

Our survey was deployed to Mechanical Turk, where 43 users participated (32 Males and 11 Females) with an average age of 31 ± 6. Regarding education, 19% of the participants had an Highschool degree, 70% had a Bachelor's degree whilst 12% had a Master's degree. Finally, 35% of these users had a weekly exposition to media (videogames, movies, tv) of up to 20 h, while others had 20 to 40 weekly hours (42%), 40 to 60 weekly hours (16%), or 60 to 80 weekly hours (7%).

The results' analysis was performed under a two-step method. Firstly, we analyzed the items on a per-clip basis. This allowed us to study how the believability scores could correlate with the clip's items and remove the ones who did not. This is explained in Subsect. 3.2. Secondly, we grouped the items together and performed a reliability and factor analysis, on the questionnaire as a whole, as depicted in Subsect. 3.3.

3.2   Analysis 1

Before analyzing the items on a per-clip basis, we first studied the reliability of the believability semantic differential scales, which will be henceforth named as believability ratings. Specifically, we grouped them together and then calculated their Cronbach Alpha coefficient. As expected, results show a value of 0.96. While this is considered redundant [34], it is as predicted since the group consisted in the same question across all clips.

Having an indication that the believability ratings were internally consistent, we ran a Principal Components Analysis (PCA) on each group of items (the 3 non-control items plus its corresponding believability rating). By fixing one factor, we considered to be Believability, we used the believability ratings as a control value: if the result loaded in factor as well as other items, they were assumed to measure the same construct and thus, were kept for the next analysis. Furthermore, we used cut-threshold loading value of 0.4. The resulting items are indicated in the column "Analysis 1" of Table 2.

As depicted in the table, most items were able to load alongside the believability ratings. In fact, only 6 items were left out because their loadings were inferior to 0.4. These were item 16 (The creatures have diverse priorities), item 21 (The creatures feel empathy towards other creatures), item 26 (The creatures work with other creatures for a common goal), item 32 (The creatures absorb substances/energy from the environment to survive), item 40 (The creatures have traits particular to their sex) and item 46 (The creatures play with others).

3.3   Analysis 2

Having now a filtered list of items, we grouped the remainder 40 items together and analyzed them as a whole questionnaire. First, we analyzed the group's internal consistency by calculating its Cronbach Alpha coefficient. With a value of 0.9, between the accepted values [34], we did not, at this point, remove any further item.

We then performed an exploratory factor analysis. The technique used was PCA with a Varimax Rotation, utilizing Eigenvalues $>= 1$ as a stopping criteria. This resulted in 11 components, illustrated in Table 1. However, the number as being too many for practical application of the scale. In order to find a more satisfactory solution, one with less factors, we established an additional criteria: a total variance explained minimum value of around %50. As expressed in Table 1, this accounts for retaining either 4 or 5 components.

Our next step involved choosing between 4 or 5 factors. To this extent, we ran two additional PCA, with the same rotation method as before, one by fixing 4 and the other 5 factors. However, this time, we used a cut threshold loading factor value of 0.4. From observing the resulting loaded items, we concluded that using 4 factors, over 5, grouped items with similar underlying semantics and thus, would facilitate the process of naming/categorizing those factors. The factor loadings, resulting from a PCA with 4 fixed factors, are described in Table 2.

Table 1. The extracted components using a PCA, with a Varimax Rotation and a stop criteria of Eigenvalue >= 1.

Component	Eigenvalue	% of Variance	Cumulative %
1	9.067	23.859	23.859
2	3.551	9.346	33.205
3	3.118	8.205	41.410
4	2.765	7.276	48.686
5	1.923	5.061	53.747
6	1.875	4.933	58.680
7	1.693	4.455	63.135
8	1.471	3.870	67.005
8	1.393	3.667	70.672
10	1.306	3.437	74.109
11	1.119	2.945	77.054

Next, three of the researchers analyzed independently the factors' loadings in order to find categories to represent each factor. This process underwent as follows:

1. Each of the three researchers individually studied the obtained factors and corresponding loadings and came up with naming proposals which would explain most, if not all, of the loaded items. This included deciding in which factors cross-loading variables would be kept.
2. We then gathered to discuss our proposals. During this step, we considered discarding items which deviated from our proposed semantics.
3. The process ended when we reached a consensus.

This processed originated the Relation with the Environment, Biological/Social Plausibility and Sociability, Adaptation and Expression concepts for explaining factors 1 through 4 respectively. From this process, besides removing items with factor loadings below 0.4, an additional 5 items were removed. This included item 6 (The creatures' actions involve more than one step) and 17 (The creatures alternate between tasks) because their underlying concept did not align with the other factor-adjacent items; items 19 (The creature show expressions to known stimuli) and 41 (the creatures' postures and expressions are coherent with their behavior) who appeared to be better suited for loading with the Expressions factor; and, finally, item 44 (the creatures' bodies and behaviors are consistent) which we considered to belong to the Biological/Social Plausibility factor. The final scale, and encompassing items, are then as follows:

1. **Relation with the Environment** - This category corresponds to the items related to environment interactions, ranging from reactions to environmental cues or directed behaviors to systemic exchanges. The originated items are then as follows:

Table 2. The Believability Scale Analysis. The first column depicts the original scale's items after their phrasal revision. The second column display which items were kept during the per-clip PCA with one fixed factor and a loading cut-threshold value of 0.4. The third column shows the loadings obtained after the second analysis performed using a PCA, with 4 fixed factors, Varimax Rotation and a loading cut-threshold value of 0.4. Values are omitted when their loading fails to meet the threshold. The items kept on the final iteration of the scale are depicted in bold.

	Item	Analysis 1 (Passed)	Analysis 2			
			1	2	3	4
1.	The creatures move by themselves	✓	0.442	**0.513**		
2.	The creatures' motions are fluid	✓			**0.516**	
3.	The creatures' motions reflect their weight/size	✓		**0.464**		
4.	The creatures' expressions anticipate their actions	✓				**0.539**
5.	The creatures make several simultaneous motions	✓		**0.714**		
6.	The creatures' actions involve more than one step	✓	0.622			
7.	Each of the creatures' body parts have inertia	✓				
8.	The creatures interact with the environment	✓	**0.617**			
9.	The creatures react to stimuli	✓		**0.735**		
10.	The creatures controls their body	✓	**0.587**			
11.	The creatures recognize themselves	✓				
12.	The creatures' behaviors differ from other creatures of the same species	✗				
13.	The creatures focus on stimuli	✓		**0.620**		
14.	The creatures direct their behaviors towards targets	✓	**0.763**			
15.	The creatures locate objects in the environment	✓	**0.514**	0.454		
16.	The creatures have diverse priorities	✗				
17.	The creatures alternate between tasks	✓			0.580	
18.	The creatures show positive (or negative) emotions towards objects, or events	✓				**0.593**
19.	The creatures show expressions to known stimuli	✓	0.416			**0.691**
20.	The creatures express moods through their body	✓				
21.	The creatures feel empathy towards other creatures	✗				
22.	The creatures' same-stimuli reactions change over time	✓			**0.668**	
23.	The creatures learn from past events	✓			**0.544**	
24.	The creatures learn through imitation	✓				**0.620**
25.	The creatures are able to apply old behaviors to new, similar, situations	✓			**0.444**	0.564
26.	The creatures use objects from the environment	✗				
27.	The creatures make tools	✓				
28.	The creatures work with other creatures for a common goal	✗				
29.	The creatures coordinate with other creatures	✓		**0.744**		
30.	The creatures communicate with other, same-species, creatures	✓		**0.723**		

(continued)

Table 2. (*continued*)

31.	The creatures communicate with other, different-species, creatures	✓				**0.519**	
32.	The creatures absorb substances/energy from the environment to survive	×					
33.	The creatures expel material	✓	**0.632**	0.449			
34.	The creatures have different life-stages	✓					
35.	The creatures change the way they look with age	✓				**0.682**	−0.425
36.	The creatures change the way they sound with age	✓				**0.583**	
37.	The creatures change the way they behave with age	✓				**0.724**	
38.	The creatures engage in reproductive acts	✓			**0.539**		
39.	There are signs of previous reproductive acts, such as eggs, cubs, pregnancy, etc	✓			**0.495**	0.433	
40.	The creatures have traits particular to their sex	×					
41.	The creatures' postures and expressions are coherent with their behavior	✓	0.621				
42.	The creatures' actions are appropriate to their context	✓	**0.654**				
43.	The creatures' body are adapted to their habitat	✓					**0.694**
44.	The creatures' bodies and behaviors are consistent	✓	0.702				
45.	The creatures play by themselves	✓					
46.	The creatures play with others	×					

- The creatures interact with the environment
- The creatures controls their body
- The creatures direct their behaviors towards targets
- The creatures locate objects in the environment
- The creatures expel material
- The creatures' actions are appropriate to their context

2. **Biological/Social Plausibility** - Corresponds to the creature's plausibility as a biological organism. This is demonstrated by showing autonomy and reactivity to its surroundings. Additionally, this category also encompasses the creature's ability to interact with other creatures. The items are as follows:
   - The creatures move by themselves
   - The creatures' motions reflect their weight/size
   - The creatures make several simultaneous motions

- The creatures react to stimuli
- The creatures focus on stimuli
- The creatures coordinate with other creatures
- The creatures communicate with other, same-species, creatures
- The creatures engage in reproductive acts
- There are signs of previous reproductive acts, such as eggs, cubs, pregnancy, etc.

3. **Adaptation** - This category involves learning behaviors and growing (which we considered to be an adaptation at the biological level). The originated items are as follows:
   - The creatures' same-stimuli reactions change over time
   - The creatures learn from past events
   - The creatures are able to apply old behaviors to new, similar, situations
   - The creatures change the way they look with age
   - The creatures change the way they sound with age
   - The creatures change the way they behave with age

4. **Expression** - Expression encompasses the elements wherein creatures use their body as a means to communicate, learn or survive. The items are as follows:
   - The creatures' expressions anticipate their actions
   - The creatures show positive (or negative) emotions towards objects, or events
   - The creatures show expressions to known stimuli
   - The creatures learn through imitation
   - The creatures' body are adapted to their habitat

Finally, we performed an additional reliability test on the remainder items as a confirmation. By calculating the Cronbach Alpha coefficient, it yielded 0.88 which is inside the acceptable range [34].

4 Conclusion

In sum, we presented the initial design and validation of a Believability Assessment scale, meant to be applied to videogame creatures. This included the process underlying the scale's items' generation as well as the validation of the scale as a whole.

We administered the scale as a questionnaire involving the visualization of videogame-related short clips. The answers were then analyzed using a two-step process. Firstly, the answers were analyzed on a per-clip basis, in order to study how the believability scores could correlate with the clip's items and filter them accordingly. Secondly, the remainder items were grouped together so reliability and factor analysis could be performed. Finally, these results were used to revise the scale. After revision, out of the original 46 devised items, 26 were kept, divided among 4 factors.

However, this scale still needs further research. While the exploratory factory analysis suggested how the scale could be divide among several dimensions, the resulting structure still needs validation. Thus, Confirmatory Factor Analysis is still required as future work. Once the structure has been validated, a spectrum can be constructed out of an ordered set of creatures, from several videogames, to be used as a case study.

The creation of such a scale provides an insight into creature design, as the existing literature on believability is either focused on humans, narratives, or follows two distinct directions: one centering on behaviors whilst the other revolving around expressions. With our scale, we attempt not only to provide a tool to assess believability on non-human creature, but also one which unifies several perspectives on how to convey believability.

Acknowledgements. This work was supported by the FCT Ph.D. Grant SFRH/BD/100080/2014.

References

1. Adkins-Regan, E.: Hormones and Animal Social Behavior. Princeton University Press, Princeton (2005)
2. Bates, J.: The role of emotion in believable agents. Commun. ACM **37**, 122–125 (1994)
3. Bethesda Game Studios: The Elder Scrolls V: Skyrim. [DVD-ROM] (2011)
4. Bethesda Game Studios: Fallout 4. [DVD-ROM] (2015)
5. Capcom: Monster Hunter Freedom Unite. [UMD] (2008)
6. Darwin, C.: The Expression of the Emotions in Man and Animals. John Murray, London (1889)
7. Dennett, D.: Intentional systems theory. In: The Oxford Handbook of Philosophy of Mind, pp. 1–22. Oxford University Press (2009)
8. Fogg, B., Tseng, H.: The elements of computer credibility. In: Proceedings of the SIGCHI conference on Human Factors in Computing Systems (1999)
9. Frontier Developments: Kinectimals. [DVD-ROM] (2010)
10. genDESIGN and SIE Japan Studio: The Last Guardian. [Blue-Ray] (2016)
11. Gosling, S.D.: Personality in non-human animals. Soc. Pers. Psychol. Compass **2**, 985–1001 (2008)
12. Hevner, A.R., March, S.T., Park, J., Ram, S.: Design science in information systems research. MIS Q. **28**, 75–105 (2004)
13. Hingston, P.: Believable Bots: Can Computers Play Like People?. Springer, Heidelberg (2011)
14. Kadhil, N.: Characteristics of living organisms. In: Biology, pp. 1–10. Cambridge University Press (2007)
15. Kittur, A., Chi, E.H., Suh, B.: Crowdsourcing user studies with mechanical turk. In: Proceedings of the SIGCHI Conference on Human Factors in Computing Systems, CHI 2008, pp. 453–456. ACM, New York (2008)
16. Kojima Productions: Metal Gear Solid V: The Phantom Pain. [Blu-Ray] (2015)
17. Lionhead Studios: Fable II. [DVD-ROM] (2008)
18. Lombard, M., Ditton, T.: At the heart of it all: The concept of presence. J. Comput. Mediated Commun. **3**(2), 0–39 (1997)
19. Lorenz, K.Z.: The Foundations of Ethology. Springer, New York (2010)
20. Mason, W., Suri, S.: Conducting behavioral research on amazon's mechanical turk. Behav. Res. Methods **44**(1), 1–23 (2012)

21. Maxis: The Sims 2. [DVD-ROM] (2005)
22. Maxis: Spore. [DVD-ROM] (2008)
23. Nintendo EAD: Pikmin. [Mini Disc] (2001)
24. Nintendo EAD: Nintendogs. [Flash Card] (2005)
25. Raúl, A., Ledezma, A., Sanchis, A.: ConsScale: A pragmatic scale for measuring the level of consciousness in artificial agents. J. Conscious. Stud. **17**, 131–164 (2010)
26. Rhino Studios: Afrika. [Blu-Ray] (2008)
27. Rockstar North: Grand Theft Auto V. [Blu-Ray] (2013)
28. Rosenkind, M., Winstanley, G., Blake, A.: Adapting bottom-up, emergent behaviour for character-based AI in games. In: Bramer, M., Petridis, M. (eds.) Research and Development in Intelligent Systems XXIX, pp. 333–346. Springer, Heidelberg (2012)
29. SCE London Studio and Playlogic Game Factory: Eye Pet. [Blu-Ray] (2009)
30. Sonic Team USA: Sonic Adventure 2: Battle. [Mini Disc] (2002)
31. Sonic Team USA: Sonic Adventure DX: Director's Cut. [Mini Disc] (2003)
32. Spector, P.E.: Summated Rating Scale Construction: An Introduction. Sage Publications, Thousand Oaks (1992)
33. Square Enix 1st Production Department: Final Fantasy XIII. [Blu-Ray] (2010)
34. Steiner, D.L.: Starting at the beginning: an introduction to coefficient alpha and internal consistency. J. Pers. Assess. **80**(1), 99–103 (2003)
35. Thomas, F., Johnston, O.: The Illusion of Life: Disney Animation. Hyperion (1997)
36. Togelius, J., Yannakakis, G.N., Karakovskiy, S.: Assessing believability. In: Believable Bots: Can Computers Play Like People?, pp. 215–230. Springer, Heidelberg (2011)
37. Ubisoft Montreal: Far Cry 4. [DVD-ROM] (2014)
38. Upper One Games: Never Alone. [Digital] (2014)
39. Warpefelt, H.: The Non-Player Character Exploring the believability of NPC presentation and behavior. Ph.D. thesis, Stockholm University, Faculty of Social Sciences, Department of Computer and Systems Sciences, Stockholm, Sweden (2016)
40. Whitlatch, T.: Principles of Creature Design: Creating Imaginary Animals. Design Studio Press, Culver City (2015)
41. Whitlatch, T.: Science of Creature Design: Understanding Animal Anatomy. Design Studio Press (2015)
42. Wobbrock, J.O., Kientz, J.A.: Research contributions in human-computer interaction. Mag. Interact. **23**(3), 38–44 (2016)

An Analysis of DOTA2 Using Game Refinement Measure

Long Zuo$^{(\boxtimes)}$, Shuo Xiong$^{(\boxtimes)}$, and Hiroyuki Iida$^{(\boxtimes)}$

School of Information Science, Japan Advanced Institute of Science and Technology,
1-1 Asahidai, Nomi, Ishikawa 923-1211, Japan
{zuolong,xiongshuo,iida}@jaist.ac.jp

Abstract. DotA is one of the most attractive and influential MOBA games, which has been popular in many countries for over 10 years. It was designed for fun at first, however, after the emerge of DOTA2 it soon became the highest prize e-sports game. This paper analyzes the evolutionary changes of the DOTA2. The game refinement measure is employed for the assessment of game sophistication of DOTA2 series. The analyzing results show that the rules of DOTA2 have regularly been changed in its history to maintain an appropriate range of game refinement. We clearly see two directions during the evolutionary changes which are the skillfulness and popularity. Thus, the analysis makes it possible to overview these evolutionary changes of DOTA2 and find some drawbacks to be improved.

Keywords: MOBA game · Game refinement theory · Evolutionary changes · DOTA2

1 Introduction

The rules of sports and mind sports have been elaborated in its long history to be more sophisticated and fascinating. It is interesting to know their characteristics and evolutionary changes using a measurement of game sophistication, which have recently been reported. For example, in the domain of sports, soccer and basketball [1], volleyball [2], table tennis and badminton [3], baseball [4] and boxing [5] have their own unique histories of the rules change to be more sophisticated. In the domain of mind sports, chess [6], Mah Jong [7] and shogi [8] have also a similar way. These reports indicate that the rules of sports and mind sports have been changed to be more sophisticated, but at the comfortable level. This may relate to the flow theory [9]. DOTA2 is a free-to-play MOBA video game developed and published by Valve Corporation. The game was released for Microsoft Windows, OS X, and Linux in July 2013, following a Windows-only public beta testing phase that began in 2011. DOTA2 is one of the most actively

---

DOTA2$^{\circledR}$ is a registered trademark. All intellectual property rights in and to the game are owned by Valve Corporation.

N. Munekata et al. (Eds.): ICEC 2017, LNCS 10507, pp. 270–276, 2017.
DOI: 10.1007/978-3-319-66715-7_29

played games on Steam, with maximum peaks of over a million concurrent players. The game follows the same paradigm of a similar game, which was inspired from the original DotA map. Both games follow the same idea of leveling of a character, gaining items and hunting down non-player controlled monsters and player-controlled heroes with the ultimate goal of destroying the opponent's base. A match ends when one side breaches the opponent's stronghold and destroys the Ancient therein. In this study we focus mainly on the domain of e-sports and have chosen DOTA2 as a benchmark. One of the big issues in our society is the online gaming addiction on youth since many teenagers spend more than 15 h a day online games [10]. However, little is known about the degree of game sophistication of e-sports. Therefore, we investigate the evolutionary changes of DOTA2 with the following two research questions:

- What is the degree of game sophistication of DOTA2 series?
- What is the most remarkable change in the history of DOTA2 series?

The structure of this paper is as follows. Section 2 presents our assessment methodology with a focus on game refinement theory. In Sect. 3 the game refinement theory is applied to DOTA2 for its assessment and the results are discussed. Finally, concluding remarks are given in Sect. 4.

2   Assessment Methodology

DOTA2 is a game with complex game information, so we need to consider the essential game progress for this game. During the in-game period, there are totally 3 game information progresses. One is the gold progress, another two are the experience progress and killing progress. Thus, we need to figure out an appropriate game progress model of DOTA2 to apply game refinement theory. Even though DOTA2 is not a score limited game, we can still clearly find a conspicuous scoring board of killing at the top of the interface. This is the only scoring information that two teams both know during the in-game period and they do not know the exact gold and experience the opponent achieved. The "game progress" is twofold [11]. One is game speed or scoring rate, while another one is game information progress with a focus on the game outcome. In sports such as soccer and basketball, the scoring rate is calculated by two factors: (1) the goal, i.e., total score and (2) time or steps to achieve the goal. Thus, the game speed is given by the average number of successful shoots divided by the average number of shoot attempts. On the other hand, "game information progress" presents how certain is the result of the game in a certain time or steps. Let K and T be the average number of successful killings and the average number of attempt per game, respectively. If one knows the game information progress, for example after the game, the game progress $x(t)$ will be given as a linear function of time t with $0 \leq t \leq T$ and $0 \leq x(t) \leq K$, as shown in Eq. (1).

$$x(t) = \frac{K}{T} t \tag{1}$$

However, the game information progress given by Eq. (1) is usually unknown during the in-game period. Hence, the game information progress is reasonably assumed to be exponential or so. This is because the game outcome is uncertain until the very end of game in many games. Hence, a realistic model of game information progress is given by Eq. (2).

$$x(t) = K(\frac{t}{T})^n \qquad (2)$$

Here n stands for a constant parameter which is given based on the perspective of an observer in the game under consideration. Thus, the acceleration of game information progress is obtained by deriving Eq. (2) twice. Solving it at the end of the game $(t = T)$, the equation becomes

$$x''(T) = \frac{Kn(n-1)}{T^n}t^{n-2} = \frac{K}{T^2}n(n-1)$$

It is assumed in the current model that the game information progress in any type of games is happening in our minds. We do not know yet about the physics in our minds, but it is likely that the acceleration of information progress is related to the force in mind. Hence, it is reasonably expected that the larger the value $\frac{K}{T^2}$ is is, the more the game becomes exciting due to the uncertainty of game outcome. Thus, we apply its root square $\frac{\sqrt{K}}{T}$, as a game refinement measure (say GR). We show, in Table 1, several sophisticated games including chess and Go from boardgames, basketball and soccer from sports and DotA from MOBA games [12]. We see that sophisticated games have a similar GR value which we recognize a zone value between 0.07 and 0.08. This indicates the same or similar degree of game sophistication where players may feel the same level of engagement or excitement regardless of different type of games.

Table 1. Measures of game refinement for various type of games

Game	G	T	GR
Chess [6]	35	80	0.074
Go [6]	250	208	0.076
Basketball [3]	36.38	82.01	0.073
Soccer [3]	2.64	22	0.073
Badminton [3]	46.34	79.34	0.086
Table Tennis [3]	54.86	96.47	0.077
DotA 6.80 [12]	68.6	106.2	0.078

3   Analysis and Discussion

This section presents the analyzing results of DOTA2 series using the game refinement measure and discusses its rule changes with a focus on prize in a championship.

3.1 Analyzing Results

To obtain the latest GR of DOTA2 series, we collect the data from the historical TI championships. For this purpose, we download all the replay of the final to calculate its GR values. We show, in Table 2, GR value of each TI championship, together with prize money compared [13]. Table 2 and Fig. 1 shows that from 2011 to 2014 GR value decreases. The rules of DOTA2 have been changed for that period to be more competitive as the prize became higher. However, such rule changes (decreasing of GR value) made DOTA2 boring for the viewers.[1] On the other hand, the designer of DOTA2 has attempted many rule changes with expectation that DOTA2 would have more uncertainty while adding new items and incorporating the unexpected factors which mean that a lower rating team would win against a higher rating team with higher probability than before. Thus, after 2014 until now, GR values are increasing.

Table 2. Measures of game refinement for DOTA2 series and prize at TI championship

Year	Championship	K	T	GR	Prize (US dollars)
2011	TI1	51.3	93.0	0.077	1,600,000
2012	TI2	32.5	76.3	0.075	1,600,000
2013	TI3	36.6	81.8	0.074	2,874,380
2014	TI4	30.0	77.3	0.071	10,925,709
2015	TI5	39.8	89.4	0.074	18,429,613
2016	TI6	54.0	94.3	0.078	20,746,930

3.2 Rule Changes in 2011–2013: Towards More Skillful

The TI championship series is the most significant and profitable annual event for DOTA2 since 2011 [14]. The game designer has attempted to modify the rules as described in Table 2. In 2011, Smoke was introduced for DOTA2 Ver. 6.70. The Smoke of Deceit is an item purchasable at the Main Shop, under Consumables. It turns the user and nearby ally heroes invisible, letting them slip by wards and creeps undetected. Upon activation, the user and all nearby allied player-controlled units gain invisibility and bonus movement speed for a brief time. Thus, many new tactics were explored after the emerge of Smoke items. Then the team behavior became conservative after the only three Smoke items were included during the in-game period. In 2012 the nerfed numerous heroes in Ver. 6.74 has established the foundation for the TI championship to enhance the game rigorism since DOTA2 has become a game to be played not only for fun but also for prize seriously. The appearance of the new captain mode in 2013 of Ver. 6.79 has contributed to maintain the fairness at the initial with the

---

[1] Actually many people complained about the conservative game progress.

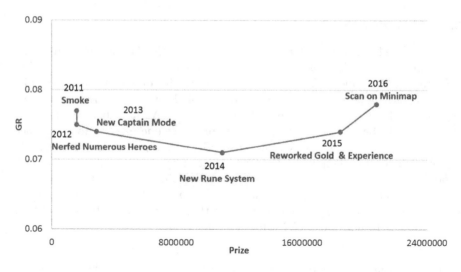

Fig. 1. GR values and prize pool of DOTA2 in 2011–2016

expectation that the rule of ban and pick system greatly would influence the game result. For both teams, it is no longer easy to choose an unbalanced hero and relatively hard to successfully kill the enemy as before. For the period 2011–2013, the average number of killing, denoted as K in the game progress model, has decreased year by year. This implies that GR value has become lower. As a result DOTA2 has become more skillful and competitive. Note that DOTA2 mainly focused on hero development and less gank or battle.

3.3   Rule Changes in 2014–2016: Towards More Popular

A highly skill-based game would not become popular since skill itself is unfriendly to the beginners. In 2014 the new rune system in Ver. 6.82 came out and added bounty rune. Runes are special boosters that spawn on the game map. Picking up a non-bounty rune grants the player a powerful effect for a short time. Runes spawn at two points in the river. The emerge of bounty rune makes the supporter or carry get money easier and the player can purchase the items earlier than before. This also accelerates the game progress. In 2015 the game designer reworked the gold and experience mechanism in Ver. 6.84. The new mechanism encouraged two teams to take part in more battle activities as they can get more gold and experience than before. The new rules focus more on gank and push issue instead of hero development. Another interesting mechanism of scan appeared in 2016 of Ver. 6.87 and we can comprehend this mechanism as a strategic skill for both teams. Players can use the Scan ability on top of the minimap UI to detect any enemy heroes in an area. This mechanism greatly made the game more exciting and added an extra level of uncertainty as the players do not know the exact number of enemies. To summarize all these new mechanisms accelerated the game progress and enhanced the uncertainty during the in-game period. The new mechanism offers more uncertainty for both teams to win or make mistake in the game. Then, the game has become more uncertain until the very end of the game. Thus, we see that GR value has increased after 2014 and it is supposed that DOTA2 will become more and more popular in the future. We see that the balance between skillfulness and popularity is so important for the survival of a game.

3.4 High Prize

As we have mentioned above, DOTA2 has over one million concurrent players while being the most profitable sports in the world. It seems that DotA was first designed only for fun, however, with the contributions of sponsors and game designer, DOTA2 has become a main trend of e-sports. The dynamic changes of each version and high prize made DOTA2 the most successful and profitable e-sports even in its short history. Now DOTA2 has lack of popularity as this game is still unfriendly to the novice players and has a relatively complex game information to learn, as there are totally over 110 heroes and 150 items. However, compared with other sports, we see that DOTA2 is now at the peak, as shown in Table 3 [15].

Table 3. Tournament prize in sports, mind sports and e-sports compared

Event	Sports	Prize (US dollars)	1st prize
Australia Open	Tennis	35,530,000	1,040,000
NBA	Basketball	14,000,000	4,100,000
FIFA Club World Cup	Soccer	28,000,000	5,490,000
Ing Cup	Go	650,000	400,000
S6	League of Legends	5,070,000	2,130,000
TI 6	DOTA2	20,746,930	9,140,000

4 Concluding Remarks

In this study we evaluated the DOTA2 series using the game refinement measurement. The results indicate that DOTA2 has a similar zone value with sophisticated sports and boardgames. In addition, DOTA2 championship of every year during 2011–2016 was analyzed. The results show that the game refinement value has stayed within 0.071-0.077, which is slightly lower than DotA. The prize of the championship has strongly influenced the development of DOTA2. Higher prize enforced the players to be more conservative and the game refinement value became lower which implies that DOTA2 became more skillful. However, such a direction of game evolution was not accepted in DOTA2 community due to the lack of entertainment. Later, the direction of DOTA2 evolution was shifted to be more popular while taking stochastic elements into consideration. Thus we see that a good balance between skillfulness and popularity is essential to survive.

References

1. Sutiono, A.P., Purwarianti, A., Iida, H.: A mathematical model of game refinement. In: Reidsma, D., Choi, I., Bargar, R. (eds.) INTETAIN 2014. LNICSSITE, vol. 136, pp. 148–151. Springer, Cham (2014). doi:10.1007/978-3-319-08189-2_22

2. Takeuchi, J., Ramadan, R., Iida, H.: Game refinement theory and its application to Volleyball. Research Report 2014-GI-31 (3), Information Processing Society of Japan, pp. 1–6 (2014)

3. Nossal, N., Iida, H.: Game refinement theory and its application to score limit games. In: 2014 IEEE Games Media Entertainment (GEM), pp. 1–3. IEEE, October 2014

4. Yuranana, K., Panumate, C., Iida, H., Tanaka, K.: Measuring Sophistication of Sports Games: The First Result from Baseball (2016)

5. Panumate, C., Iida, H.: An Approach to Quantifying Boxings Entertainment

6. Cincotti, A., Iida, H., Yoshimura, J.: Refinement and complexity in the evolution of chess. In: Proceedings of the 10th International Conference on COmputer Science and Informatics, pp. 650–654 (2007)

7. Iida, H., Takahara, K., Nagashima, J., Kajihara, Y., Hashimoto, T.: An application of game-refinement theory to mah jong. In: Rauterberg, M. (ed.) ICEC 2004. LNCS, vol. 3166, pp. 333–338. Springer, Heidelberg (2004). doi:10.1007/978-3-540-28643-1_41

8. Iida, H., Takeshita, N., Yoshimura, J.: A metric for entertainment of boardgames: its implication for evolution of chess variants. In: Nakatsu, R., Hoshino, J. (eds.) Entertainment Computing. ITIFIP, vol. 112, pp. 65–72. Springer, Boston, MA (2003). doi:10.1007/978-0-387-35660-0_8

9. Csikszentmihalyi, M.: Flow. The Psychology of Optimal Experience. HarperPerennial, New York (1990)

10. Perrin, A., Duggan, M.: Americans' Internet Access: 2000–2015: As Internet Use Nears Saturation for Some Groups, a Look at Patterns of Adoption (2015). (Pew Internet project data memo)

11. Májek, P., Iida, H.: Uncertainty of game outcome. In: 3rd International Conference on Global Research and Education in Intelligent Systems, pp. 171–180 (2004)

12. Xiong, S., Zuo, L., Iida, H.: Quantifying engagement of electronic sports game. Adv. Soc. Behav. Sci. **5**, 37–42 (2014)

13. e-Sports Earnings. Top Games of 2016 (2017). http://www.esportsearnings.com/history/2016/games

14. GAMEPEDIA. DOTA2Wiki (2017). http://DOTA2.gamepedia.com/DOTA2Wiki

15. List of prizes, medals and awards, 14 June 2017. https://en.wikipedia.org/wiki/Listofprizes,medalsandawards

A Method for Illustrating Shogi Postmortems Using Results of Statistical Analysis of Kifu Data

Nobutane Hanayama$^{(\boxtimes)}$ and Ryuichi Nogami

Shobi University, Kawagoe 350-1110, Japan
nob-hanayama@jcom.home.ne.jp

Abstract. Kifu, which is a Japanese term for a game record for a shogi games, is considered as a special type of multi-dimensional time series data, because it consists of items indicating who moved a piece and where it was moved on a grid diagram. Because of its complexity, however, it is not easy for amateur or non-players of shogi to grasp or understand overall shogi games from it. In this study we suggest averages, variances, skewness of row numbers where pawns are put, numbers of times gold and silver generals and nights are moved, which are easily calculated and understandable without comprehensive knowledge of shogi game, as features of position of shogi games. And the usability of those features is shown by a result of discriminant analysis for winner of game based on those features. Further, a software for illustrating shogi postmortems using discriminant scores obtained from discriminant analysis of Kifu data are shown.

Keywords: Discriminant analysis of winner of shogi game · Feature of position of shogi game · Statistical indicator of position of shogi game

1 Introduction

Kifu, which is a Japanese term for a game record for a shogi games, is considered as a special type of multi-dimensional time series data, because it consists of items indicating who moved a piece and where it was moved on a grid diagram. In Kifu each move of piece is noted like "the first move, (3, 6), pawn". Because of its complexity, however, it is not easy for amateur or non-players of shogi to grasp or understand overall shogi games from it. In this study we suggest to consider averages, variances and skewness of row numbers where pawns (FUs) are put, and times gold and silver generals (KIs and GIs) and nights (KEs) are moved as features of position of shogi games.

Shogi game has been mainly studied in the field of artificial intelligence (AI) as related to the chess game study. In this field, "evaluation functions" [1] are frequently used when AIs evaluate which player or which of human player or computer is superior and determine the next move at a certain position. However, evaluation functions require us comprehensive knowledge of shogi game when we make AIs calculate from "features", "material" or "mobility" for examples. On the other hand, average, variance and skewness of row numbers where pawns (FUs) are put are simple statistical indicators, which can be easily calculated. So in this study, we propose that average, variance and skewness of row numbers where pawns (FUs) are put, times gold and silver generals (KIs and GIs) and nights (KEs), which are all easily calculated and understandable without comprehensive knowledge of shogi game, as features of shogi games (Sect. 2). And we show the usability of proposed features by a result of discriminant analysis of winner/looser based on kifu data (Sect. 3).

So far, the aim of shogi game study concerning AI is to make computer software win against first-rate professional shogi players [2]. However, the strengthening promotion committee "Akara", which was a computer software developed by a project team organized by IPSJ (the information society of Japan) or "Ponanza" produced great results [3], which means that the shogi game study concerning AI has achieved most of its aims [4]. Hence, studies of methods concerned with entertainment, methods for conducting a post-mortem for an example, may become more important [5] recently. So in this study, we suggest a method for illustrating shogi postmortems using discriminant scores obtained from discriminant analysis of Kifu data, and show its usability by introducing a software incorporated with the suggested method (Sect. 3).

2   Average, Variance and Skewness of Row Numbers Where Pawns (FUs) Are Put

Let $J_i^{(k)}$ indicate number of pawns (FUs) at the i-th move ($i = 1, 2, \ldots$), where it is for the white player (the first move) if $k = 1$ and for the black player (the defensive move) if $k = 2$, and let $h_{i,j}^{(k)}$ indicate row number of the j-th pawn (FU) at the i-th move. Then average, variance and skewness of row numbers where pawns (FUs) are put at the i-th move, $\bar{h}_i^{(k)}$, $\tilde{h}_i^{(k)}$ and $\ddot{h}_i^{(k)}$ are calculated by

$$\bar{h}_i^{(k)} = \frac{1}{J_i^{(k)}} \sum_j^{J_i^{(k)}} h_{i,j}^{(k)}, \; \tilde{h}_i^{(k)} = \sum_j^{J_i^{(k)}} \frac{(h_{i,j}^{(k)} - \bar{h}_i^{(k)})^2}{J_i^{(k)} - 1}, \; \ddot{h}_i^{(k)} = \frac{1}{J_i^h} \sum_j^{J_i^h} (h_i^{(j)} - h_i^a)^2 / h_i^{v3/2}. \quad (1)$$

In the above, though averages $\bar{h}_i^{(k)}$. variances $\tilde{h}_i^{(k)}$ and skewnesses $\ddot{h}_i^{(k)}$ are indicators calculated for i, that is, every move, whole game are analyzed rather than every move in this study. Hence, let's consider every 10 moves as "phase". In addition, numbers of moves from the first move to the end/resigned move are different among games. So let's consider $\bar{h}_i^{(k)}$, $\tilde{h}_i^{(k)}$ and $\ddot{h}_i^{(k)}$ calculated for 40 moves from the first move to the end/resigned move as features of whole game, that is, moves from the first to the 10th as the first phase, moves from the 11th to the 20th as the second phase, moves from the 21th to the 30th as the third phase and moves from the 31th to the 40th as the fourth phase and

$$\bar{p}_l^{(k)} = \sum_{i=1+(l-1)\times 10}^{l \times 10} \frac{\bar{h}_i^{(k)}}{10}, \tilde{p}_l^{(k)} = \sum_{i=1+(l-1)\times 10}^{l \times 10} \frac{\bar{h}_i^{(k)}}{10} \ddot{p}_l^{(k)} = \sum_{i=1+(l-1)\times 10}^{l \times 10} \frac{\ddot{h}_i^{(k)}}{10} \quad (2)$$

for $l = 1, 2, 3, 4$, as features for whole games. In addition to the above, consider numbers of times gold and silver generals (KIs and GIs) and nights (KEs) are moved calculated by

$$g_l^{(k)} = count(< r_{1+(l-1)\times10}^{(k)}, r_{1+(l-1)\times10+1}^{(k)}, \cdots, r_{1+l\times10}^{(k)} >, \text{"gold"})$$

$$s_l^{(k)} = count(< r_{1+(l-1)\times10}^{(k)}, r_{1+(l-1)\times10+1}^{(k)}, \cdots, r_{1+l\times10}^{(k)} >, \text{"silver"}) \quad (3)$$

$$n_l^{(k)} = count(< r_{1+(l-1)\times10}^{(k)}, r_{1+(l-1)\times10+1}^{(k)}, \cdots, r_{1+l\times10}^{(k)} >, \text{"night"})$$

as features of position of shogi games, where $r_i^{(k)}$ indicates the i-th character and $<s_1, s_2, \ldots>$ is a concatenation of strings $s_1, s_2, \cdots$ and $count(<s_1, s_2, \cdots>,$ "string") indicates the number of characters in string "string".

3 Result of Discriminant Analysis of Winner/Looser Based on Kifu Data

Now let us consider a discriminant function:

$$z_m = \sum_{l=1}^{4} \sum_{k=1}^{2} (a_l^{(\bar{p})} \bar{p}_{l,m}^{(k)} + a_l^{(\tilde{p})} \tilde{p}_{l,m}^{(k)} + a_l^{(\ddot{p})} \ddot{p}_{l,m}^{(k)} + a_l^{(g)} g_{l,m}^{(k)} + a_l^{(s)} s_{l,m}^{(k)} + a_l^{(n)} n_{l,m}^{(k)}) + c. \quad (4)$$

where $a_{l,m}^{(\cdot)}$ are discriminant coefficients c is a constant and z_m are discriminant scores. In the discriminant analysis using the function (4), the white player (the first move) is discriminated as a winner when $z_m \geq 0$ and the black player (the defensive move) is discriminated as a winner when $z_m < 0$.

Table 1 indicates the accuracy of discriminant function (4) estimated based the kihu data for 50 shogi games ($M = 50$) form the 14th Young Lion Tournament is shown, Because the number of parameters to be estimated is $4 \times 6 \times 2 = 28$, which is around 3/5 of the number of games, discriminant coefficients are estimated with the forward selection method by $F = 2$. As indicated on the table, the estimated discriminant function is significant to some extent because the percentage of correct classifications is 84%, and it is found that the estimated discriminant function is significant to some extent.

Table 1. Accuracy of discriminant analysis with the forward selection method by $F = 2$

Percentage of correct classifications	84.00%
Percentage of incorrect classifications	16.74%
Mahalanobis square distance	372.03%
Correlation ratio	49.21%

Table 2 indicates the estimates of the discriminant coefficients estimated with the forward selection method by $F = 2$. Descriptions for selected variables on the table are corresponding to formulas (3) as follows:

times black moves silver in the 4th phase: $g_{4,m}^{(2)}$,

skewess of pawn (FU) for black in the 3rd phase: $\ddot{p}_{3,m}^{(2)}$,

times white moves nights (KEs) in the 2nd phase: $n_{2,m}^{(1)}$,

variance of pawns (FUs) for black in the 2nd phase: $\tilde{p}_{2,m}^{(2)}$,

variance of pawns (FUs) for white in the 2nd phase: $\tilde{p}_{2,m}^{(1)}$,

times white moves nights (KEs) in the 4th phase: $n_{4,m}^{(1)}$.

Table 2. Estimates of the discriminant coefficients estimated with with the forward selection method by $F = 2$

Selected variable	Discriminant coefficient	Standard discriminant coefficient	F-value	p-value	Judge
Times black moves silver in the 4th phase	0.96	0.04	15.60	0.00	[**]
Skewess of pawn for black in the 3rd phase	1.54	0.29	3.60	0.06	[]
Times white moves nights in the 2nd phase	−20.04	−4.78	10.43	0.00	[**]
Variance of pawns for black in the 2nd phase	6.11	1.77	9.64	0.00	[**]
Variance of pawns for white in the 2nd phase	4.71	0.49	4.70	0.04	[*]
Times white moves nights in the 4th phase	−0.54	−0.11	2.28	0.14	[]
Constant	−6.70				

The followings are found from the above results:

- the probability that white players (the first move) win games increases if numbers of times black players (the defensive move) move silver generals (KIs) from the 31th to the 40th moves, skewness of row numbers where pawns (FUs) are put for black players (the defensive move) from the 21th to the 30th moves, variances of row numbers where pawns (FUs) are put for black players (the defensive move) from the 11th to the 20th moves and variances of row numbers where pawns (FUs) are put for white players (the first move) from the 11th to the 20th moves increase,
- the probability that black players (the defensive move) win games increase if numbers of times white players (the first move) move nights (KEs) from the 11th to the 20th moves and numbers of times white players (the first move) move nights (KEs) from the 31th to the 40th moves increase.

4 A Method for Conducting Shogi Postmortems Using Discriminant Scores Obtained from Discriminant Analysis of Kifu Data

In this section, we suggest a method for conducting shogi postmortems using discriminant scores obtained from discriminant analysis of Kifu data, and show the usability of the proposed method by introducing a software incorporated with the suggested method. Discriminant scores are calculated for every game and not ones indicating which player is superior at a certain position. However, in our data used for discriminant analysis, explanatory valuables are given by phase ($l = 1, 2, 3, 4$). So, we calculate discriminant scores separately by phase $l = 1, 2, 3, 4$ and game $m = 1, \cdots, 50$ like

$$
\begin{aligned}
z_{l,m} = a_{l,m}^{(\bar{p})}\bar{p}_l^{(k)} + a_{l,m}^{(\tilde{p})}\tilde{p}_l^{(k)} + a_{l,m}^{(\ddot{p})}\ddot{p}_l^{(k)} + a_{l,m}^{(g)}g_l^{(k)} \\
+ a_{l,m}^{(s)}s_l^{(k)} + a_{l,m}^{(n)}n_l^{(k)} + cl/4,
\end{aligned}
\tag{5}
$$

and consider $z_{l,m}$ as scores indicating which player is superior, that is, white player (the first move) is superior if $z_{l,m} \geq 0$ or black player (the defensive move) is superior if $z_{l,m} < 0$ at phase $l = 1, 2, 3, 4$. Further, we divide $z_{l,m}$ into ones concerning movement of pawns (FUs):

$$
z_{l,m}^{(p)} = a_{l,m}^{(\bar{p})}\bar{p}_l^{(k)} + a_{l,m}^{(\tilde{p})}\tilde{p}_l^{(k)} + a_{l,m}^{(\ddot{p})}\ddot{p}_l^{(k)}
\tag{6}
$$

and one concerning movement of gold, silver generals (KIs, GIs) and nights (KEs):

$$
z_{l,m}^{(gsn)} = a_{l,m}^{(g)}g_l^{(k)} + a_{l,m}^{(s)}s_l^{(k)} + a_{l,m}^{(n)}n_l^{(k)},
\tag{7}
$$

and use $z_{l,m}$, $z_{l,m}^{(p)}$ and $z_{l,m}^{(gsn)}$ as indicators for illustrating shogi postmortems.

Figure 1 indicate the images of developed software for illustrating shogi postmortems using $z_{l,m}$, $z_{l,m}^{(p)}$ and $z_{l,m}^{(gsn)}$. In the figure, the final match between Satoshi Murayama vs. Manabu Senzaki at the 14th Young Lion Tournament on the 22nd in October, 1991 is illustrated. Figure 1 illustrates that the black player (the defensive move) was superior to the white player before his 20th move, and Fig. 1 is illustrating that the white player became superior after the 60th move because of his way of moving pawns, from which the significance of the suggested method for illustrating shogi postmortems may be shown.

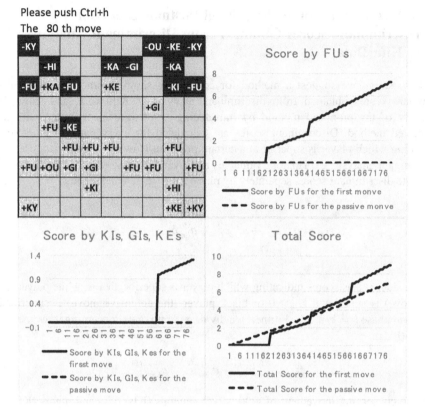

Fig. 1. Illustration of the final match between Satoshi Murayama vs. Manabu Senzaki at the 14th Young Lion Tournament on the 22nd in October, 1991 at the 80th move

5 Concluding Remarks

In this article, average, variance and skewness of row numbers where pawns (FUs) are put, in addition to times gold and silver generals (KIs and GIs) and nights (KEs) were proposed as features of shogi games and their significance as features was shown by the result of discriminant analysis of actual Kifu data base on the proposed features. In addition, a software developed for illustrating shogi postmortems was introduced and usability of proposed features was shown.

Sawa and Ito [6] showed what kinds of features determined people's impression for play style base on their result of statistical analysis of Kifu data. In their study they use the numbers of times players move gold and silver generals (KIs and GIs) and nights (KEs). In this their study has something to do with our study. However, our way of studying is different from theirs in the meaning that we consider the numbers of times players move gold and silver generals (KIs and GIs) and nights (KEs) as a time series by dividing games into phases consisting of 10 moves.

The aim of this study illustrate important point or move determining winners of shogi games, average, variance and skewness of row numbers where pawns (FUs) are put and times gold and silver generals (KIs and GIs) and nights (KEs) are moved may be too simple to determine winner of games [7]. So our next aim is to seek other features to determine winners of games and incorporate such features into our software for illustrating shogi postmortems.

References

1. Hoki, K., Kaneko, T.: Large-scale optimization for evaluation functions with minimax search. J. Artif. Intell. **49**, 527–568 (2014)
2. Matsubara, H.: A special issue for the way of winning since 2010. J. Inf. Process. **52**(2), 152–190 (2011). (in Japanese)
3. Takizawa, T.: Contemporary Computer Shogi. IPSJ SIG Technical reports, vol. 30, pp. 1–8 (May 2013). (in Japanse)
4. Kotani, Y.: Looking Back on the 3rd Shogi Dennou-sen: 3. An objective analysis on the strength of computer Shogi - did it reach to the human top player? IPSJ Mag. **55**(8), 851–852 (2014). (in Japanese)
5. Kajiwara, K., Miura, R., Tarumi, M.: Searching Positions from Shogi Game Recores unsing Jargous. In: The Proceeding of Enternaimnet Computing Symposeum 2016, 3–5 November, Osaka (2016). (in Japanese)
6. Sawa, N., Ito, T.: Statistical analysis of Elements of Play Style in SHOGI (Japanese Chess). Game Inf. **26**(3), 1–8 (2011). (in Japanese)
7. Sato, Y., Takahashi, D.: Learning weights of training data by large game results. In: The Proceeding of Game Programing Workshop, vol. 6, pp. 22–29 (2012). (in Japanese)

Predicting Human Computation Game Scores with Player Rating Systems

Michael Williams, Anurag Sarkar, and Seth Cooper$^{(\boxtimes)}$

College of Computer and Information Science, Northeastern University, Boston, USA
{williams.mi,sarkar.an}@husky.neu.edu, scooper@ccs.neu.edu

Abstract. Human computation games aim to apply human skill toward real-world problems through gameplay. Such games may suffer from poor retention, potentially due to the constraints that using pre-existing problems place on game design. Previous work has proposed using player rating systems and matchmaking to balance the difficulty of human computation games, and explored the use of rating systems to predict the outcomes of player attempts at levels. However, these predictions were win/loss, which required setting a score threshold to determine if a player won or lost. This may be undesirable in human computation games, where what scores are possible may be unknown. In this work, we examined the use of rating systems for predicting scores, rather than win/loss, of player attempts at levels. We found that, except in cases with a narrow range of scores and little prior information on player performance, Glicko-2 performs favorably to alternative methods.

Keywords: Human computation games · Player rating systems · Prediction · Elo · Glicko-2

1 Introduction and Background

Human computation games (HCGs) have been shown to provide a unique lens into solving problems that are computationally hard or ill-defined [12,13]. Some notable examples include *The ESP Game*, which asks users to complete relatively simple image recognition tasks [1], and *Foldit*, which involves relatively complex protein folding problems [4].

One potential upside to leveraging a gaming environment when utilizing human intelligence is the potential to harness the motivational power of games. However, even with exemplar cases such as *Foldit*, human computation games generally have issues engaging and retaining players. Engagement is widely considered a foundational element in a good game. Additionally, the level of engagement experienced by the player can influence how motivated they are to play. The prime factor of engagement is the construct of flow [5], which embodies a range of subjective experiences, but most notably "is the idea that there should be an optimal match between the skills an individual possesses and the challenges presented by an activity" [2, pp.2].

© IFIP International Federation for Information Processing 2017
Published by Springer International Publishing AG 2017. All Rights Reserved
N. Munekata et al. (Eds.): ICEC 2017, LNCS 10507, pp. 284–289, 2017.
DOI: 10.1007/978-3-319-66715-7_31

Furthermore, HCGs have several design constraints which limit the extent to which the core task of the game can be edited or modified. Knowing the difficulty of each task within the game beforehand may not be possible, as determining the difficulty of each task by hand circumvents the need to crowdsource the solution. It has been suggested in Cooper et al. [3] that dynamic difficulty adjustment through task ordering may be a logical solution, and that this could be accomplished through the use of player rating systems and matchmaking. They applied player rating systems to an HCG when examining the effect of the bipartiteness of the graph of matches on prediction accuracy of player attempts at levels. To accomplish this, they put in place a somewhat ad-hoc threshold as a "target score", where going beyond the target score counted as a win and failing to do so counted as a loss.

Player rating systems were designed with the intent to give players more fair matches. Several rating systems exist, but the most noteworthy examples include Elo, Glicko-2 and TrueSkill. Elo [7] is a system created by Arpad Elo to rate the relative skill of chess players. His system revolves around a few key assumptions. Mainly, that a player's performance in each match is a normally distributed random variable, and the outcome of a match is the result of a pairwise comparison. Glickman developed the Glicko [9] and Glicko-2 [8] systems, which built upon this model by incorporating additional parameters, notably, a rating deviation parameter and a volatility parameter, which capture the expected rating reliability and fluctuation of a given player. TrueSkill [10] is a rating system developed by Microsoft Research for the purposes of multi-player rating and matchmaking, encompassing both individuals and teams. This is important for their uses and an interesting development because it allows the use of virtually any match configuration (for example, team versus team or free for all).

In this work, we explore generalizing the use of player rating systems to predict outcomes of HCGs from win/loss to continuous scores. As a case study, we used player data from the HCG *Paradox*. Ultimately, when attempting to predict scores, we found that the Glicko-2 player rating system usually outperforms Elo and our baseline measure.

2 Methods

2.1 Data Collection

For this work, we collected data from the puzzle game *Paradox* [6], an HCG that draws on the maximum satisfiability problem (MAX-SAT) to create levels for the players to solve. The game, initially designed to crowdsource formal verification of software, provides various "brushes" for the player to use. These brushes are essentially player guided algorithms to help solve the problems. A player's score is represented as a percentage of satisfied clauses (0%–100%), and the player is given a target score within that range. If a player can complete a level, they have contributed a solution to the underlying MAX-SAT problem. A screenshot of the version of *Paradox* used is given in Fig. 1.

Players were recruited to play *Paradox* through Amazon Mechanical Turk (MTurk), where we posted a Human Intelligence Task (HIT). We recruited 50 players, who were paid $1.50 when they completed the HIT. Upon accepting the HIT, players were given brief instructions about the HIT and game. They then had to complete 9 short tutorial levels meant to introduce gameplay. Data from tutorial levels was not used in our analysis. Players then proceeded to the challenge levels. We selected 33 challenge levels, each of which was either derived from SATLIB Benchmark Problems[1] or randomly generated. These levels were served to the players in random order. Players would not see the same level a second time until they had seen each level at least once. For the challenge levels, players were given a target score of 100% (which is not always necessarily possible). Players were able to skip challenge levels without completing them, and upon skipping 3 levels they could then also exit to complete the HIT. We excluded data from one participant who merely skipped 67 matches without attempting any of them. This brought the participant count to 49 and the total number of matches played to 221.

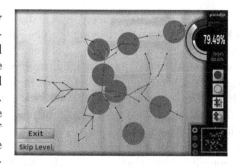

Fig. 1. A screenshot of the game *Paradox* used in this work.

2.2 Rating System Implementation

Our goal was to compare the error of different rating systems when predicting scores achieved by players attempting levels in *Paradox*. Since these systems are conventionally used for the player versus player style games, we have to treat both the players and levels as "players" in the rating system. A match is between a player and a level; players cannot play other players and levels cannot play other levels. The data extracted from the MTurk HIT was played back into the rating systems. We used our own implementation of Elo with a K factor of 24 and the pyglicko2 [11] implementation of Glicko-2. To predict score outcomes using the rating systems, we used expected score of a match based on the ratings of the player and level in the match. For a baseline comparison, we used a simple system that used the average score of all preceding matches to predict the outcome of a match.

To measure the prediction error of each approach, we set up the playback simulation to predict match outcomes *before* playing them back on matches where both the player and level had been in at least some minimum number of matches M. This allowed us to examine the impact the minimum number of matches played on the performance of the rating systems relative to the baseline. It also let us determine how many matches a player and level needs to play before

---

[1] http://www.cs.ubc.ca/~hoos/SATLIB/benchm.html.

the rating system starts to outperform the baseline. We used $M = 0$, 3 and 6. If $M = 0$, for example, we predicted the outcome of all matches, and if $M = 3$, we only predicted for matches where the player and level have been in at least 3 previous matches. The simulation is constructed this way because this is the desired use case for a rating system implemented into an HCG. The specific order of the matches played influences the early state of play for both players and levels.

3   Results

Paradox scores can range from 0%–100% but were scaled to a range of 0.0–1.0 for use within the player rating systems. We examined scaling with absolute score (linearly mapping 0% to 0.0 and 100% to 1.0, which is the score shown to the player in game) and relative score (linearly mapping each level's starting % to 0.0 and 100% to 1.0, capturing player improvement over the starting score). The minimum, mean, and maximum absolute scores observed were 0.52, 0.88, and 1.0, respectively, and the minimum, mean, and maximum relative scores were 0.0, 0.53, and 1.0, respectively. The error between observed and predicted values was computed using root mean squared difference (RMSD). Generally speaking, RMSD is a good measurement of accuracy, but specifically accuracy between models measuring the same variable as the scales need to be the same.

Results of our predictions are shown in Table 1. Glicko-2 performs the best in every case except for absolute score with $M = 0$, and improves error over our baseline predictions by up to 32%. As the absolute scores cover a smaller range of possible scores, it is unsurprising that for absolute score predictions the RMSDs are in general lower, and the baseline average score predictions are more accurate.

Table 1. RMSD error and percentage improvement over baseline. The lowest error in each row is shown in **bold**.

	Absolute Score				Relative Score		
M	Average	Elo	Glicko-2	M	Average	Elo	Glicko-2
0	**0.099**	0.362	0.203	0	0.430	0.408	**0.372**
		(−266%)	(−105%)			(−5%)	(14%)
3	0.126	0.239	**0.086**	3	0.508	0.434	**0.359**
		(-100%)	(32%)			(15%)	(29%)
6	0.093	0.184	**0.082**	6	0.491	0.469	**0.398**
		(-158%)	(12%)			(-4%)	(19%)

4   Conclusion

The fact that Glicko-2 outperforms our baseline measure as the system is fed more information about player performance (as M increases) suggests that utilizing a player rating system as a basis for dynamic difficulty adjustment tool could work for HCGs. This is due to the fact that both 3 and 6 minimum matches played seems like a reasonable requisite number of matches played for HCGs before beginning to make predictions. This is especially true if in the long run a system such as Glicko-2 improves player retention. In this sense, the system works to improve player retention but also does its job better the longer they are retained.

Although we found that player rating systems improved prediction error over baseline, it remains to be determined if the accuracy achieved is practically useful. Additionally, the impact of using a matchmaking system based on player rating system score predictions remains to be explored.

Utilizing continuous data as opposed to win/loss unlocks a lot of potential when serving levels to players in HCGs. The surface level improvement is that there is no longer a need to implement a fixed "target score" to allow the rating system to function. Additionally, the precision of predicting and utilizing the score allows for a better determination of what levels are appropriate for which players. For example, if previously the target score was set a threshold of 80%, we can now appropriately differentiate between players who barely beat that target score (i.e. 82%) and players who did far better than the target score (i.e. 98%). Additionally, this may allow for more fine-tuned matchmaking, where each potential player-level match combination has an individualized expected score, and the system recognizes a player who can potentially achieve a new record score on a given level—a very useful feature for HCGs seeking to find new solutions to problems.

Acknowledgements. This work was supported by a Northeastern University TIER 1 grant. This material is based upon work supported by the National Science Foundation under Grant No. 1652537. We would like to thank the University of Washington's Center for Game Science for initial *Paradox* development.

References

1. von Ahn, L., Dabbish, L.: Labeling images with a computer game. In: Proceedings of the SIGCHI Conference on Human Factors in Computing Systems, pp. 319–326 (2004)
2. Boyle, E.A., Connolly, T.M., Hainey, T., Boyle, J.M.: Engagement in digital entertainment games: A systematic review. Comput. Hum. Behav. **28**(3), 771–780 (2012)
3. Cooper, S., Deterding, S., Tsapakos, T.: Player rating systems for balancing human computation games: testing the effect of bipartiteness. In: Proceedings of the 1st International Joint Conference of DiGRA and FDG (2016)
4. Cooper, S., Khatib, F., Treuille, A., Barbero, J., Lee, J., Beenen, M., Leaver-Fay, A., Baker, D., Popović, Z.: Foldit players: Predicting protein structures with a multiplayer online game. Nature **466**(7307), 756–760 (2010)
5. Csikszentmihalyi, M.: Flow: The Psychology of Optimal Experience. Harper and Row, New York (1990)

6. Dean, D., Gaurino, S., Eusebi, L., Keplinger, A., Pavlik, T., Watro, R., Cammarata, A., Murray, J., McLaughlin, K., Cheng, J., Maddern, T.: Lessons learned in game development for crowdsourced software formal verification. In: Proceedings of the 2015 USENIX Summit on Gaming, Games, and Gamification in Security Education (2015)
7. Elo, A.E.: The Rating of Chessplayers, Past and Present. Arco, New York (1978)
8. Glickman, M.E.: Dynamic paired comparison models with stochastic variances. J. Appl. Stat. **28**(6), 673–689 (2001)
9. Glickman, M.E., Jones, A.C.: Rating the chess rating system. Chance **12**, 21–28 (1999)
10. Herbrich, R., Minka, T., Graepel, T.: TrueSkill(TM): a Bayesian skill rating system. Adv. Neural Inf. Process. Syst. **20**, 569–576 (2007)
11. Kirkman, R.: Pyglicko2: a Python Implementation of the Glicko-2 algorithm (2010). https://code.google.com/p/pyglicko2/
12. Law, E., Von Ahn, L.: Human Computation. Morgan & Claypool, San Rafael (2011)
13. Pe-Than, E.P.P., Goh, D.H.L., Lee, C.S.: A survey and typology of human computation games. In: Proceedings of the 9th International Conference on Information Technology: New Generations, pp. 720–725 (2012)

Playful-Consumption Experience in Digital Game Playing: A Scale Development

Amir Zaib Abbasi[1(✉)], Ding Hooi Ting[1], and Helmut Hlavacs[2]

[1] Department of Management and Humanities, Universiti Teknologi Petronas, Tronoh, Malaysia
amir_zaib_abbasi@yahoo.co.uk
[2] Research Group Entertainment Computing, University of Vienna, Vienna, Austria

Abstract. This paper intends to develop a scale to measure a videogame player's emotional, sensory, and imaginal experiences in digital gaming. We first define the construct of playful-consumption experience in videogame playing and accordingly, develop a scale for measuring playful experiences in videogames. We collected the data of 225 valid respondents which were further analyzed through exploratory factor analysis (EFA) and reliability analysis. The results of EFA and reliability analysis reported that the loaded items were emerged into a seven factor solution and all constructs have good reliability. This study is unique in the videogame literature as it uses the theoretical definition of playful-consumption experience to define and measure the player's experiences in videogame playing as playful-consumption experience of videogame play.

Keywords: Videogame · Playful-consumption experience · Imaginal experience · Emotional experience · Sensory experience · Scale development

1 Introduction

Since last decade, the priorities of the children and teenagers have significantly changed in how they spend their spare time [1]. Karsten [2] observed that adolescents are less likely to socialize with peers outside the home, as they are more likely to get involved in adult-regulated leisure activities and spend most of their time with indoor activities. Such a change in the characteristics of the young generation may indicate that the present group of people are less likely to engage in exploratory and health-risk activities with their friends outside the home [3]. Hence, the indoor leisure activities have become an important component in the lives of children and young people [1]. Kuntsche, et al. [4] have discussed that the current generation of teenagers are noticeably different from the previous generations with respect to their access to a virtual play area. Large numbers of adolescents now engage in digital game playing as a leisure activity [1, 5].

As a consequence, videogame playing has become the fastest growing form of recreational activity for the consumers [6]. Hence, it is now considered the most common activity to many individuals in their everyday lives [7]. Consumers play videogames on various platforms such as dedicated gaming consoles, smartphones, personal computers, handheld gaming consoles, etc. [8]. The popularity of videogame playing has

N. Munekata et al. (Eds.): ICEC 2017, LNCS 10507, pp. 290–296, 2017.
DOI: 10.1007/978-3-319-66715-7_32

significantly increased since the last decade, and it has also facilitated the gaming industry to become a booming and multi-Billion Dollar industry [8]. Newzoo [9] has revealed the list of top 100 countries by videogame revenues and consumer spending on videogame related products; China is on the top of the list with 24.2 Billion Dollars, US is ranked 2nd with $23.5 Billion Dollars [9], Japan is placed in 3rd position with 12 Billion Dollars, while Malaysia ranks 18th out of 100 with 539.5 Million Dollars as shown in [10, 11]. This prominent growth in the gaming industry has called researchers to study player experiences that arise from digital game-playing [12]. The experience of digital game playing is assumed as the subjective association between the player and the respective videogame beyond the real application of a game [13].

An extant literature review revealed that many studies have conducted their researches to define and measure the multidimensional nature of experience in game playing [8, 14–19]. This can be seen in the studies of [14–19], who used the concept of immersion to develop an immersion questionnaire, a game experience questionnaire and a game immersion questionnaire to measure a player's game-playing experience. Few other studies applied the theoretical model of flow to examine player engagement in digital gaming [20–22]. We also found some more studies by [23–26] who have employed the basic essences of fun theory to assess player media-related experiences. Many other researchers have frequently used the following theoretical definitions such as flow, cognitive-absorption, presence, and immersion to describe and evaluate player experiences in digital game playing [13, 15–17, 27]. However, we found that previous studies are still limited in their findings as they have only considered those theoretical constructs which are referred to the subjective mental state of the player and neglected to investigate other experiences such as emotional and sensory experiences in videogame playing. Hence, we realize the importance of other experiences and aim to apply the theoretical definition of a playful-consumption experience comprising imaginal, emotional, and sensory experiences to develop a scale to measure player experiences in videogame playing.

In this paper, we fill this research gap through developing a new scale to measure playful experiences in game playing. This study is unique in its investigation as it develops a scale for playful-consumption experience in videogame playing to measure imaginal, emotional, and sensory experiences.

2   Scale Development Steps

The present study applied the scale development procedure as recommended and applied by several studies [28, 29], and includes four core steps: (I) conceptualization, (II) questionnaire development, (III) data collection for study 1, and (IV) scale purification and validation. The present study initially took an initiative to conceptualize the construct of playful-consumption experience.

2.1   Conceptualization of Playful-Consumption Experience

Holbrook, et al. [30] argued that playful-consumption falls into the broad category of *intrinsically motivated consumer behavior* comprising hobbies, esthetic appreciation, creativity, sports, and games. Most recently, few studies by [6, 30, 31] have conceptualized the act of playing a videogame as playful-consumption experience and reported that the perspective of playful-consumption has become mainly important for the unique kinds of play, which is facilitated by computer-mediated settings such as videogames. On this basis, we can conclude that playful-consumption experience is defined as an intrinsically, motivating, active, and self-based videogame playing behavior that is executed for a player's own sake and pleasure, which in turn involves a player to get playful hedonic experiences (feelings, sensory and fantasy). On the basis of this definition, the construct of playful-consumption experience is specified as a multi-dimensional construct that consists of three main dimensions including imaginal, sensory, and emotional experiences [6, 30, 31]. Besides three main constructs, the imaginal experience is further defined by three main dimensions, namely escapism, role-projection, and fantasy [32–34], while emotional experience is classified by three factors such as arousal, emotional involvement, and enjoyment [33–38]. Through an extensive literature, we identified seven sub-dimensions (fantasy, role-projection, escapism, arousal, emotional involvement, enjoyment and sensory experience) that collectively explain the three focal playful-hedonic experiences (imaginal, sensory and emotional experience). Next, we developed the questionnaire for seven constructs.

2.2   Questionnaire Development

We applied various techniques *(literature review, previous theoretical and empirical studies on the main variable, deduction from the theoretical definition of the construct, suggestions from professionals of the field, and open-ended survey questionnaire)* suggested by [28, 29] to get a list of scale items for the identified factors that contribute to the overall construct of playful-consumption experience. Initially, we conducted a review of the existing literature to collate an inventory of scale items and managed to get a pool of items for the seven identified constructs. For instance, we adapted the items of fantasy and role-projection from these studies [32, 34, 39]. The scale items of escapism were adapted from these scholars [32, 34, 40–42]. We have obtained and adapted the items of emotional involvement from these studies [34, 42]. The items for the enjoyment scale were adapted from these sources [40, 43] and for the arousal scale, we adapted from these academics [30, 34]. While for sensory experience, the previous items were not reflecting to the context of game playing, so we generated six items for sensory experience through using the two other techniques of items generation *(deduction from the theoretical definition of the construct and open-ended survey questionnaire)* from eight experienced videogame users. Once items were developed, we submitted a pool of 38 items to the experts to evaluate the content validity. As a result, we deleted two items from emotional involvement, enjoyment, and escapism due to having semantic redundancy in the items and left with 32 items.

2.3 Sampling and Data Collection

Afterwards, we picked young student participants whose age was between 16–19 years, studying at Malaysian institutes. The primary reason for the selection of young students was that they are still seen as focal individuals for studying the videogame playing behavior [44]. A multistage sampling was utilized to collect study data. We first listed four main states *(Selangor, Perak, Johor, and Penang)* of Malaysia in terms of population and density then randomly chosen one state *(Perak)*. We then generated a list of institutions *(Schools, Colleges, and Universities)* and randomly selected three private universities, one public university, three colleges, and two schools in the Perak state. In each selected institution, we randomly selected few classes and within the class environment, we distributed 275 questionnaires in total and collected 225 valid data from teen gamers. We further used 225 valid responses for EFA and reliability analysis.

2.4 Scale Refinement and Validation

The results of EFA explicated that KMO was 0.861 that exceeded the critical value of 0.50, suggested by [45]. In addition, we checked Bartlett's test of sphericity and results reported that it was 3450.916, df = 351, and significant at p = 0.000, showing the suitability for factor analysis. During EFA, We loaded 32 items of the playful-consumption experience construct to explore its related factors and considered items for deletion, if items have a loading of (< 0.40) on a specific construct or have a cross-loading (> 0.40) on a particular item [46]. The results reported that five items were deleted due to poor loadings and cross-loadings. Thus 27 items were retained out of 32 items. These 27 items were further emerged into a seven factors solution that was extracted based on eigenvalues (> 1), as recommended by [47]. In addition, these seven factors *(escapism, fantasy, role projection, enjoyment, emotional involvement, arousal, and sensory experience)* had an eigenvalue of minimum 1.0 or greater. A reliability test was also conducted on the seven factors and we found that every factor has exceeded the critical value of 0.70 as recommended by [48].

3 Conclusion

This study indicates that playful-consumption experience is a multi-dimensional construct which consists of seven sub-dimensions and these dimensions also meet the critical value of reliability test. This scale brings new insights in the field of gaming as it has the potential to measure three main experiences such as imaginal, emotional, and sensory experience. This study only validated the playful-consumption experience scale through EFA and another study is required to further confirm the factors extracted in EFA stage. This scale can be applied in all videogame settings and it would be interesting to see how the results fit with other genres of videogames.

References

1. Brooks, F.M., Chester, K.L., Smeeton, N.C., Spencer, N.H.: Video gaming in adolescence: factors associated with leisure time use. J. Youth Stud. **19**, 36–54 (2016)
2. Karsten, L.: It all used to be better? Different generations on continuity and change in urban children's daily use of space. Child. Geographies **3**, 275–290 (2005)
3. Brooks, F., Magnusson, J., Klemera, E., Spencer, N., Morgan, A.: HBSC England National Report: Health behaviour in school-aged children (HBSC). World Health Organization collaborative cross national study (2011)
4. Kuntsche, E., Simons-Morton, B., Ter Bogt, T., Queija, I.S., Tinoco, V.M., de Matos, M.G., et al.: Electronic media communication with friends from 2002 to 2006 and links to face-to-face contacts in adolescence: an HBSC study in 31 European and North American countries and regions. Int. J. Public Health **54**, 243–250 (2009)
5. Olson, C.K., Kutner, L.A., Warner, D.E., Almerigi, J.B., Baer, L., Nicholi, A.M., et al.: Factors correlated with violent video game use by adolescent boys and girls. J. Adolesc. Health **41**, 77–83 (2007)
6. Mukherjee, S., Mukherjee, S., Lau-Gesk, L., Lau-Gesk, L.: Retrospective evaluations of playful experiences. J. Consum. Mark. **33**, 387–395 (2016)
7. Borderie, J., Michinov, N.: Identifying flow in video games: towards a new observation-based method. Int. J. Gaming Comput. Mediated Simul. (IJGCMS) **8**, 19–38 (2016)
8. Phan, M.H., Keebler, J.R., Chaparro, B.S.: The Development and Validation of the Game User Experience Satisfaction Scale (GUESS). Hum. Factors: J. Hum. Factors Ergon. Soc. 58(8), 1217–1247 (2016). doi:10.1177/0018720816669646
9. Newzoo: Top 100 countries by game revenues, 4 April 2017
10. Kuah, K.: MDEC and The Malaysian Gaming Industry (2016)
11. Newzoo: 2016 Global games market report: an overview of trends & insights (2016)
12. Seo, Y., Buchanan-Oliver, M., Fam, K.S.: Advancing research on computer game consumption: A future research agenda. J. Consum. Behav. **14**, 353–356 (2015)
13. Calvillo-Gámez, E.H., Cairns, P., Cox, A.L.: Assessing the core elements of the gaming experience. In: Bernhaupt, R. (ed.) Game User Experience Evaluation, pp. 37–62. Springer, Heidelberg (2015)
14. Brown, E., Cairns, P.: A grounded investigation of game immersion. In: CHI 2004 Extended Abstracts on Human Factors in Computing Systems, pp. 1297–1300 (2004)
15. Cheng, M.T., She, H.C., Annetta, L.A.: Game immersion experience: its hierarchical structure and impact on game-based science learning. J. Comput. Assist. Learn. **31**, 232–253 (2015)
16. Ermi, L., Mäyrä, F.: Fundamental components of the gameplay experience: Analysing immersion. In: Worlds in play: International perspectives on digital games research, vol. 37, p. 2 (2005)
17. Jennett, C., Cox, A.L., Cairns, P., Dhoparee, S., Epps, A., Tijs, T., et al.: Measuring and defining the experience of immersion in games. Int. J. Hum. Comput. Stud. **66**, 641–661 (2008)
18. Qin, H., Patrick Rau, P.-L., Salvendy, G.: Measuring player immersion in the computer game narrative. Int. J. Hum. Comput. Interact. **25**, 107–133 (2009)
19. IJsselsteijn, W., Van Den Hoogen, W., . Klimmt, W., De Kort, Y., Lindley, C., Mathiak, K., et al.: Measuring the experience of digital game enjoyment. In: Proceedings of Measuring Behavior, pp. 88–89 (2008)
20. Chen, J.: Flow in games (and everything else). Commun. ACM **50**, 31–34 (2007)
21. Fu, F.-L., Su, R.-C., Yu, S.-C.: EGameFlow: A scale to measure learners' enjoyment of e-learning games. Comput. Educ. **52**, 101–112 (2009)

22. Sweetser, P., Wyeth, P.: GameFlow: a model for evaluating player enjoyment in games. Comput. Entertain. (CIE) **3**(3), 3 (2005)
23. Koster, R.: A Theory of Fun in Game Design. Paraglyph Press, Scottsdale (2005)
24. Koster, R.: Theory of Fun for Game Design. O'Reilly Media Inc., Sebastopol (2013)
25. Poels, K., de Kort, Y., Ijsselsteijn, W.: It is always a lot of fun!: exploring dimensions of digital game experience using focus group methodology. In: Proceedings of the 2007 Conference on Future Play, pp. 83–89 (2007)
26. Poels, K., de Kort, Y., Ijsselsteijn, W.: FUGA-The fun of gaming: Measuring the human experience of media enjoyment. Deliverable D3. 3: Game Experience Questionnaire. FUGA project (2008)
27. De Kort, Y.A., IJsselsteijn, W.A., Poels, K.: Digital games as social presence technology: Development of the Social Presence in Gaming Questionnaire (SPGQ). In: Proceedings of Presence, vol. 195–203 (2007)
28. Churchill Jr., G.A.: A paradigm for developing better measures of marketing constructs. J. Mark. Res. **16**(1), 64–73 (1979)
29. MacKenzie, S.B., Podsakoff, P.M., Podsakoff, N.P.: Construct measurement and validation procedures in MIS and behavioral research: Integrating new and existing techniques. MIS Q. **35**, 293–334 (2011)
30. Holbrook, M.B., Chestnut, R.W., Oliva, T.A., Greenleaf, E.A.: Play as a consumption experience: The roles of emotions, performance, and personality in the enjoyment of games. J. Consum. Res. **11**(2), 728–739 (1984)
31. Buchanan-Oliver, M., Seo, Y.: Play as co-created narrative in computer game consumption: The hero's journey in Warcraft III. J. Consum. Behav. **11**, 423–431 (2012)
32. Hirschman, E.C.: Predictors of self-projection, fantasy fulfillment, and escapism. J. Soc. Psychol. **120**, 63–76 (1983)
33. Hirschman, E.C., Holbrook, M.B.: Hedonic consumption: emerging concepts, methods and propositions. J. Mark. **46**(3), 92–101 (1982)
34. Wu, J., Holsapple, C.: Imaginal and emotional experiences in pleasure-oriented IT usage: A hedonic consumption perspective. Inf. Manag. **51**, 80–92 (2014)
35. Mizerski, R., Pucely, M.J., Perrewe, P., Baldwin, L.: An experimental evaluation of music involvement measures and their relationship with consumer purchasing behavior. Popular Music Soc. **12**, 79–96 (1988)
36. Pucely, M.J., Mizerski, R., Perrewe, P.: A comparison of involvement measures for the purchase and consumption of pre-recorded music. NA-Adv. Consum. Res. **15**, 37–42 (1988)
37. Stewart, S.M.: Artist-fan engagement model: Implications for music consumption and the music industry. The University of Alabama TUSCALOOSA (2013)
38. Lee, O.-K.D., Xu, P., Kuilboer, J.-P., Ashrafi, N.: User acceptance of second life: An extended TAM including hedonic consumption behaviours (2009)
39. Lacher, K.T., Mizerski, R.: An exploratory study of the responses and relationships involved in the evaluation of, and in the intention to purchase new rock music. J. Consum. Res. **21**, 366–380 (1994)
40. Mathwick, C., Malhotra, N., Rigdon, E.: Experiential value: conceptualization, measurement and application in the catalog and Internet shopping environment☆. J. Retail. **77**, 39–56 (2001)
41. Overmars, S., Poels, K.: How product representation shapes virtual experiences and re-patronage intentions: the role of mental imagery processing and experiential value. Int. Rev. Retail Distrib. Consum. Res. **25**, 236–259 (2015)
42. Swanson, G.E.: Travels trough inner space: family structure and openness to absorbing experiences. American Journal of Sociology **83**(4), 890–919 (1978)

43. Agarwal, R., Karahanna, E.: Time flies when you're having fun: Cognitive absorption and beliefs about information technology usage. MIS Q. **24**(4), 665–694 (2000)
44. Lee, D., LaRose, R.: A socio-cognitive model of video game usage. J. Broadcast. Electron. Media **51**, 632–650 (2007)
45. Kaiser, H.F.: An index of factorial simplicity. Psychometrika **39**, 31–36 (1974)
46. Kim, J.-H., Ritchie, J.B., McCormick, B.: Development of a scale to measure memorable tourism experiences. J. Travel Res. **51**, 12–25 (2012)
47. Jolliffe, I.: Principal component analysis. Wiley Online Library (2002)
48. Hair Jr., J.F., Hult, G.T.M., Ringle, C., Sarstedt, M.: A primer on Partial Least Squares Structural Equation Modeling (PLS-SEM). Sage Publications, Thousand Oaks (2013)

Game Design

Generating the Expression of the Move of Go by Classifier Learning

Natsumi Mori[1] and Takehito Utsuro[2(✉)]

[1] Graduate School of Systems and Information Engineering,
University of Tsukuba, Tsukuba, Japan
[2] Faculty of Engineering, Information and Systems,
University of Tsukuba, Tsukuba, Japan
utsuro_@_iit.tsukuba.ac.jp

Abstract. The ancient Chinese board game, Go, with its simple rules yet highly complex strategies, requires players to encircle more territory than their opponent. However, owing to the rise in the capabilities of Go-playing software and a lack of Go instructors in Japan, there is a need for a software that actively assists human players in learning the high-level strategies required to win the game. This study focuses on generating a review for each consecutive player's move. This paper studies how to generate an expression for each move based on the distribution of the stones on the board. To this task of generating the expression for each move in a game of Go, we apply a classifier learning technique.

Keywords: Entertainment computing · Go · Classifier learning · Move · Expression

1 Introduction

With the recent, well-known success of the computer Go program AlphaGo [4] that beat a high-level professional without handicaps, computer-based Go programs now represent a serious challenge to professional human players. Therefore, from an entertainment and educational perspective, developing software particularly designed to teach human players high-level techniques is an important task. This is an especially pressing task because, at present, Japan has only a small number of professional Go players who are capable of teaching amateurs. Furthermore, there is a need to develop high-level software that can play so-called "customer" Go, where the software analyzes a human player's habits and predicts their next moves, allowing them to win on purpose while concealing the fact that they won with the aid of the software.

Based on those arguments, this paper aims at developing a software which assist human players to learn high level techniques on the move of Go. Within various functions of such a software of assisting human players to learn the techniques of the game of Go, this paper focuses on the task of generating a

© IFIP International Federation for Information Processing 2017
Published by Springer International Publishing AG 2017. All Rights Reserved
N. Munekata et al. (Eds.): ICEC 2017, LNCS 10507, pp. 299–309, 2017.
DOI: 10.1007/978-3-319-66715-7_33

review for each move in a game of Go[1] It is strongly required to develop such a software of generating a review for each move in a game of Go mainly because it can assist amateur human players to learn high level techniques on the move of Go. Then, according to such a requirement on developing a software of generating a review for each move in a game of Go, this paper more specifically proposes to generate the expression for each move in a game of Go from the pattern of the stones on the Go board. Furthermore, to this task of generating the expression for each move in a game of Go, we apply a classifier learning technique.

In related research, Ikeda et al. [2] propose generating expressions of the shape of a particular move based on the pattern of the stones on the board by applying a classifier-learning technique. Out of the overall types of expressions of a move, Ikeda et al. [2] concentrated on generating those based on the shape of a move but failed to analyze strategic moves. Thus, one of the major contributions of the present study compared to Ikeda et al.'s [2] research is that it investigates expressions based on the shapes of moves while also taking strategic moves into account. Furthermore, in terms of the features of the classifiers used to generate an expression for each move, in addition to lower-level features, most of which have been studied by Ikeda et al. [2] (see Sect. 3.1), the current study illustrates the effects of higher-level features (examined in detail in Sect. 3.2). Finally, in Sect. 4, we show the optimal combination of features for each expression required to achieve the best-possible performance in a game, an aspect that was overlooked by Ikeda et al. [2].

2   Expressions of Go Moves

2.1   Expressions Based on the Shape of the Move

Expressions based on the shape of a particular move are typically identified by considering the static local pattern of the stones on the board. As illustrated in Sect. 2.3, we focus on the 10 most frequent expressions for the shapes of moves listed in Table 2. For each of these 10 expressions, Fig. 1 shows a typical example of a move; the black stone with a white triangle within it represents the last move with the expression of its shape.

2.2   Expression for the Strategic Move

As we mentioned in the previous section, the expressions for the shape of a move are typically identified by considering the static local pattern of the stones on the board. On the other hand, expressions for strategic moves are typically identified by considering a much broader view of the patterns of the stones. Each of these expressions of strategic moves represents fairly characteristic situations encountered throughout the whole-state transition within a game. Moreover, from the perspective of the overall time-series state transition of the moves

---

[1] Yoshikawa et al. [5] studied the protocols of the game of Go with respect to the relations between the player's skill and the use of Go terms.

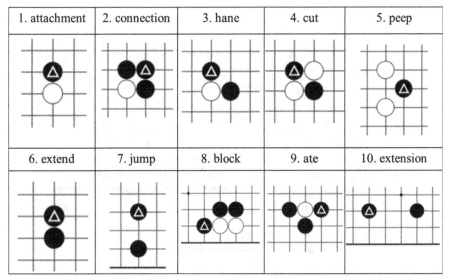

1. attachment	2. connection	3. hane	4. cut	5. peep

6. extend	7. jump	8. block	9. ate	10. extension

the last move with the
expression of its shape

Fig. 1. The most frequent 10 expressions for the shape of a move (expression for each last move)

within a game, a move's time-series sequences can be approximately segmented by strategic moves. Therefore, each strategic move is typically played separately from the previous moves.

As mentioned in Sect. 2.3, we focus on the three most frequent expressions for the strategic moves listed in Table 2. A detailed description of each of these three expressions is given below.

- *Protect*—represents that the move by the current player is intended to protect one's own stones from the opponent using various strategies.
- *Approach move*—represents that the move by the current player is intended to start approaching the opponent's stone.
- *Invasion*—represents that the move by the current player is intended to invade an area occupied by the opponent.

Figure 2 illustrates examples of two of these three expressions for strategic moves as well as typical situations in which ambiguities against those for the shape of the move are present. In short, a particular move and the pattern of the stones on the board can be interpreted as strategic when considering it more seriously and trying to react to it as much as possible; conversely, it can also be interpreted as simply representing the shape of a particular move when it is considered less seriously, for example, by ignoring the opponent's move and attempting not to react to it. However, in both of the cases shown in Fig. 2 considering the pattern of the stones on the board more seriously and interpreting these moves as strategic is the correct approach.

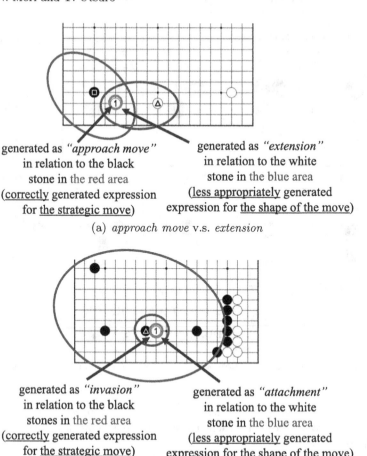

generated as *"approach move"*
in relation to the black
stone in the red area
(<u>correctly</u> generated expression
for <u>the strategic move</u>)

generated as *"extension"*
in relation to the white
stone in the blue area
(<u>less appropriately</u> generated
expression for <u>the shape of the move</u>)

(a) *approach move* v.s. *extension*

generated as *"invasion"*
in relation to the black
stones in the red area
(<u>correctly</u> generated expression
for <u>the strategic move</u>)

generated as *"attachment"*
in relation to the white
stone in the blue area
(<u>less appropriately</u> generated
expression for <u>the shape of the move</u>)

(b) *invasion* v.s. *attachment*

Fig. 2. Examples of the ambiguity of the expressions for *shape* and *strategic moves* (Color figure online)

2.3   The Dataset

The dataset used to evaluate the classifier for generating the expressions of the moves from the pattern of the stones was constructed from the SGF-move coordinates file as well as the game review text. We first collected these data from reviews of Go games available in newspaper articles over a period of 5 years. This included 60 game reviews played on a 19 × 19 size board and comprising 9,209 moves in total. Then, as shown in Table 1, from each SGF-move coordinate file and the game review text for each move, its order, coordinates (x, y), as well as expression were manually extracted. However, from the total number of moves, the expression for each move is available to a certain extent. This amounts to 1,207 moves out of a total of 9,209 moves. Of these 1,207 moves, 238 types of expressions were manually extracted and within this set, only 34 types were

Table 1. Generating the training/test dataset of the expression of the Go move from the SGF-move coordinates file and the game review text

Game review text (English translation)	Order of the move	Coordinate (x, y) of the move	Expression of the move
...	1	(16,4)	...
...	2	(4,4)	...
...	3	(16,17)	...
...	4	(4,16)	...
...	5	(6,17)	...
In the lower right, only with the single *approach move* of the 6th white stone,	6	(16,15)	Approach move
ϕ	7	(16,12)	ϕ
it is unusual to change into the *pincer* move of the 8th white stone	8	(8,17)	Pincer
Yamada's move of the 9th black stone is also a careful *one-space jump*.	9	(14,17)	One-space jump
...	...	...	...

observed more than or equal to 10 times. Then, these 34 types of expressions (with 667 moves in total) were employed as the overall resource for evaluating the classifier for generating the expression of particular moves.

These 34 expressions can be further classified into 21 expressions based on the shape of the move at 478 moves (71.7% of the 667 moves) and the remaining 13 expressions for strategic moves at 189 moves (28.3% of the 667 moves). Then, as shown in Table 2, the 10 most frequent expressions for the shape of the move as well as the 3 most frequent expressions for the strategic move were selected (422 in total) as the positive/negative samples of the training/test dataset.

3 Features

The features examined in this study comprise lower-level features aimed at identifying the shape of a particular move as well as higher-level features that seek to identify strategic moves specifically.

3.1 Lower Level Features of a Particular Move's Shape

Most of the lower-level features examined here have been studied in previous work [2] on generating expressions for the shape of a move.

FL_1: Coordinates of a Move

The x and y coordinates of a move are used as two features, which are denoted as FL_1.

FL_2: Number of Stones

Table 2. Numbers of positive samples in the dataset for each expression of the moves

Type of move and expression	ID	Expression	# of positive samples
Expression for the shape of the move	1	Attachment	60
	2	Connection	57
	3	Hane	42
	4	Cut	37
	5	Peep	30
	6	Extend	29
	7	Jump	25
	8	Block	25
	9	Ate	21
	10	Extension	19
Expression for a strategic move	11	Protect	29
	12	Approach move	25
	13	Invasion	23
Total			422

The number of stones on the board when a move is made is used as a feature that represents the order of the move from the beginning of the game. This feature is denoted as FL_2.

FL_3: Distance to the Closest Board Edge

As shown in Fig. 3, the distance from a stone used in a particular move to the closest board edge is used as a feature and is denoted as FL_3.

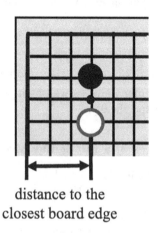

distance to the
closest board edge

Fig. 3. FL_3: distance to the closest board edge

FL_4/FL_5: Distance to the Closest Current Player's/Opponent's Stone

As shown in Fig. 4, the distance from the stone resulting from a move to the closest current player's or an opponent's stone is used as a feature and these are denoted as FL_4 or FL_5 respectively. In terms of the distance measurement used for these features, that used by previous research [1,2] is employed. Thus δx and δy denote the differences of the x and y coordinates of the two stones, respectively:

$$\text{distance}(\delta x, \delta y) = |\delta x| + |\delta y| + \max(|\delta x|, |\delta y|) \tag{1}$$

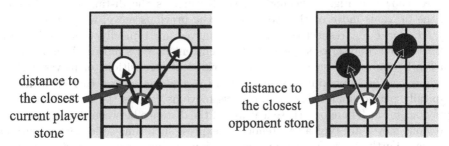

(a) FL_4: Distance to the Closest Current Player's Stone

(b) FL_5: Distance to the Closest Opponent's Stone

Fig. 4. FL_4/FL_5: distance to the closest current player's/opponent's stone

In our implementation of these features, feature values over six are ignored.

FL_6/FL_7: Distance From the Closest Current Player's/Opponent's Stone to the Board Edge

As shown in Fig. 5, the distance from the closest current player's or opponent's stone to the board edge is used as a feature. This denoted as FL_6 or FL_7, respectively.

distance from the closest current player stone to the board edge

distance from the closest opponent stone to the board edge

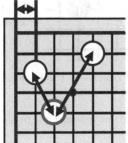

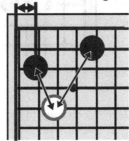

(a) FL_6: Distance from the Closest Current Player's Stone to the Board Edge

(b) FL_7: Distance from the Closest Opponent's Stone to the Board Edge

Fig. 5. FL_6/FL_7: distance from the closest current player's/opponent's stone to the board edge

3.2   Higher-Level Features for Strategic Move

In addition to employing the features of lower levels to identify the shape of a
particular move, this section presents features of higher levels that specifically
aim to identify strategic moves. This study uses the following type of higher-level
features.

FH_1/FH_2: Distance to the Stone from the Previous/Move Before the Previous Move

As shown in Fig. 6, the higher-level features is the distance to the stone
of the previous move or the move before the previous move, which is denoted
as FH_1 or FH_2, respectively. Strategic moves are typically characterized in
terms of the time-series sequences of the current player's moves. As illustrated
in Fig. 2, the overall sequence of time-series state transitions of moves within
a game can be approximately segmented by strategic moves, each of which is
typically played apart from the previous move as well as the move before the
previous move. Therefore, these features of the distance between the current and
previous moves are typically intended to express such time-series factors within
a game. Furthermore, in our implementation of these features, instead of the
distance measurement presented by Eq. (1) in the previous section, the following
definition of the distance is employed, where δx and δy denote the differences
between the x and y coordinates of the two stones, respectively:

$$\text{distance}(\delta x, \delta y) = |\delta x| + |\delta y| \qquad (2)$$

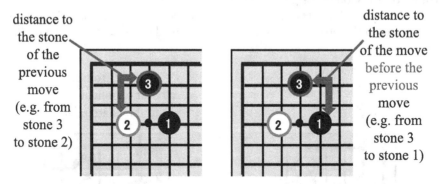

(a) FH_1: Distance to the Stone of the Pre-   (b) FH_2: Distance to the Stone of the Move
vious Move   before the Previous Move

Fig. 6. FH_1/FH_2: distance to the stone of the previous/move before the previous move

This is because these features are required to be sensitive to a much broader
area on the board compared to those of FL_4 and FL_5, aiming at identifying the
shape of a move, but not a strategic move.

4   Evaluation

4.1   The Procedure

In the evaluation of the classifier for generating the expression of a particular move from the pattern of stones on a Go board, for each of the 13 expressions listed in Table 1, we train a binary classifier with all of the samples of the expression (as listed in Table 2) as positive samples. An equal number of negative samples are randomly selected from the pool of negative samples that is constructed by removing all the positive samples from the 422 samples listed in Table 2. The classifier for each binary classification is implemented using the decision tree's[2] module of the scikit-learn toolkit [3]. The parameters of the lower bound of the number of training samples within each node of the decision tree (in the range from 1 to 7) as well as the upper bound of the depth of the decision tree (in the range from 2 to 8) are tuned through a preliminary round of a 10-fold cross-validation with a random split into the training and test sets. This is also implemented through a module of the scikit-learn toolkit. The final evaluation results are obtained through another round of 10-fold cross-validation with the two parameters optimally tuned as above.

4.2   Evaluation Results

Table 3 shows the optimal combination of features as well as the optimal performance achieved by the combination of these particular features for each expression. Overall, for most expressions, including both those of the shape of a move as well as the strategic moves, optimal combinations of features tend to include FL_4/FL_5 (the distance to the closest current player's/opponent's stone). FL_6 (the distance from the closest current player's stone to the board edge), and FH_1/FH_2 (the distance to the stone from the previous/before the previous move). These features typically represent the characteristics of the patterns of stones on a Go board. Other features such as FL_1 (the coordinates of a move), FL_2 (the number of stones on the board), and FL_3 (the distance to the closest board edge) typically contribute little to achieving the optimal performance. This is mainly because such features represent the physical layout of the stones on the board that are not critically sensitive to detecting the expression of a move.

Notably, the higher-level features are more effective in the identification of the shapes of moves rather than those of strategic moves. This is because even in the binary classification task of a single expression for the shape of the move and the others, negative samples comprise not only other expressions for the shape of a move but also all the expressions for a particular strategic move. These results provide important clues for devising new types of features in future work.

---

[2] In this study, we applied decision trees as the classifier for identifying and generating the expression of moves as it was employed successfully by Ikeda et al. [2].

Table 3. Evaluation results (%)

Type of the move and the expression	ID	Binary classification	Evaluation results	Optimal features
Expression for the shape of a move	1	Attachment/rest	95.0	FL_4, FL_6
	2	Connection/rest	86.1	FL_4, FL_5, FL_6, FH_2
	3	Hane/rest	89.5	FL_4
	4	Cut/rest	84.2	FL_2, FL_4, FL_6
	5	Peep/rest	81.7	$FL_2, FL_6, FH_1/FH_2$
	6	Extend/rest	95.0	FL_6, FL_7
	7	Jump/rest	91.7	FL_4
	8	Block/rest	82.5	FH_1
	9	Ate/rest	83.3	FL_7, FH_2
	10	Extension/rest	87.5	FL_6
	Average		87.6	—
Expression for a strategic move	11	Protect/rest	71.7	FL_1, FL_2
	12	Approach move/rest	95.8	FL_4
	13	Invasion/rest	94.2	FL_6
	Average		87.2	—
Average			87.5	—

5   Conclusion

This study aims to develop a software that assists human players in learning high-level Go strategies by focusing on generating a review for each individual move in a game of Go. In particular, this study proposes generating an expression for each move based on the pattern of stones on the board. Furthermore, to this task of generating the expression for each move in a game of Go, we applied a classifier learning technique. In terms of future work, we aim to scale up the dataset to allow more accurate evaluation of the results and evaluate other types of classifiers such as support vector machines.

References

1. Coulom, R.: Computing elo ratings of move patterns in the game of Go. In: Proceedings of Computer Games Workshop (2007)
2. Ikeda, K., Shishido, T., Viennot, S.: Machine-learning of shape names for the game of Go. In: Plaat, A., Herik, J., Kosters, W. (eds.) ACG 2015. LNCS, vol. 9525, pp. 247–259. Springer, Cham (2015). doi:10.1007/978-3-319-27992-3_22
3. Pedregosa, F., Varoquaux, G., Gramfort, A., Michel, V., Thirion, B., Grisel, O., Blondel, M., Prettenhofer, P., Weiss, R., Dubourg, V., Vanderplas, J., Passos, A., Cournapeau, D., Brucher, M., Perrot, M., Duchesnay, E.: Scikit-learn: machine learning in python. J. Mach. Learn. Res. **12**, 2825–2830 (2011)

4. Silver, D., Huang, A., Maddison, C.J., Guez, A., Sifre, L., van den Driessche, G., Schrittwieser, J., Antonoglou, I., Panneershelvam, V., Lanctot, M., Dieleman, S., Grewe, D., Nham, J., Kalchbrenner, N., Sutskever, I., Lillicrap, T., Leach, M., Kavukcuoglu, K., Graepel, T., Hassabis, D.: Mastering the game of Go with deep neural networks and tree search. Nature **529**, 484–503 (2006)
5. Yoshikawa, A., Kojima, T., Saito, Y.: Relations between skill and the use of terms. In: Herik, H.J., Iida, H. (eds.) CG 1998. LNCS, vol. 1558, pp. 282–299. Springer, Heidelberg (1999). doi:10.1007/3-540-48957-6_19

Eye Contact: Gaze as a Connector Between Spectators and Players in Online Games

Michael Lankes[1]([⊠]), Daniel Rammer[1], and Bernhard Maurer[2]

[1] Department of Digital Media, University of Applied Sciences Upper Austria,
Softwarepark 11, 4232 Hagenberg, Austria
{Michael.Lankes,Daniel.Rammer}@fh-hagenberg.at
[2] Center for Human-Computer Interaction, University of Salzburg,
Jakob-Haringer-Straße 8, Salzburg, Austria
Bernhard.Maurer@sbg.ac.at
https://www.fh-ooe.at
https://hci.sbg.ac.at

Abstract. This paper proposes an experimental setting that investigates shared gaze integrations (constant gaze and eye contact) in games and their effects on the social presence perceived by different roles (players and spectators) in a remote scenario. In order to get insights, we conducted a study that is made up of 4 different conditions (2 roles and 2 gaze integrations). Results show, depending on the type of the gaze integration and the role, positive effects of gaze towards an increased awareness and engagement among participants. Through the inclusion of shared gaze information, a new nonverbal communication channel for players and spectators is created that presents an interesting design resource for future approaches of digital play. Designers should receive information on how to design gaze-based interfaces that do not distract players during play, and also give spectators the possibility to experience a game via the player's eyes.

Keywords: Gaze-based interaction · Social presence · Shared gaze

1 Introduction

Games and playful interactions have the power to foster social connections and establish interpersonal bonds among players. On the one hand social behavior in this context may occur in co-located settings, where the physical presence of players is inherently part of the social interaction, and, on the other hand, remote online settings, where the information flow has to happen via different mediated channels. One of those channels can be seen in the human gaze that forms one of the key factors in interpersonal communication [6, p. 86] and information flow [5, p. 67]. Apart from communication tools such as chat features, human gaze may serve as an additional channel for players to get in contact with the audience and other players. In contrast to standard game controllers, such as a mouse

© IFIP International Federation for Information Processing 2017
Published by Springer International Publishing AG 2017. All Rights Reserved
N. Munekata et al. (Eds.): ICEC 2017, LNCS 10507, pp. 310–321, 2017.
DOI: 10.1007/978-3-319-66715-7_34

or a keyboard, no explicit input is required, as gaze, and more specifically eye contact, is part of the human repertoire to get in contact with other players. This aspect may also be relevant for audience integration in games as it might enrich the experience via participation. Although the inclusion of gaze may contribute to the social experience among players and spectators, social playful gaze can be rarely found in distributed and remote settings, such as online gaming. This can be explained by the fact that eye tracking technology in games is mainly employed as an input method for single player games with a focus on augmenting or replacing typical game controllers and game interfaces (e.g., using gaze interaction instead of a mouse to select game objects, increasing the opacity of interface elements by looking at them, etc.) [13].

Consequently, gaze-based input as a tool for interpersonal communication in multiplayer games is still an under-explored research area, which offers opportunities for both designers and researchers [14]. First attempts indicate that gaze can be harnessed for onlooker integration resulting in an increased social interaction among participants [10]. Other projects highlight the potential of social gaze in cooperative and competitive game settings (e.g., [7,11]).

Our contribution should shed some light on how social gaze can be integrated and visualized in remote settings. Typically, the current gaze position of a player is constantly shown to the other players (constant gaze integration). In this paper we want to explore alternative strategies by investigating if event-driven gaze-based interactions (in our case: eye contact between a player and a spectator) can be used as a linking element between spectators and players, and if this strategy leads to a higher social presence experience in remote settings than constant gaze implementations. Via an asymmetrical experimental game setup (player as an active part, spectator as a passive element), we want to research if there is preference for a specific social gaze integration (constant gaze VS eye contact) by spectators and players.

By doing so, readers should gain an understanding of how to use gaze as a way to reduce the gap between the participants in remote settings. Game and interface designers should receive information on how to design gaze-based interfaces that do not distract players during play (i.e., "calm" integration), and also give spectators the possibility to experience a game via the player's eyes. Furthermore, researchers should get insights on the eye contact integration strategies and its effects on the player experience.

2   Related Work

A range of previous studies (e.g., [9]) identified a relationship between non-verbal communication and the perceived social presence (i.e., a phenomenon when subjects successfully simulate other humans or non-human intelligences in computer-mediated environments [8]).

In that regard, Mansour et al. [9] point out that the complex nature of in-game conversation in multiplayer settings, e.g., clarifying mutual goals or discussing tactics, is based on both, verbal as well as nonverbal communication.

Shahid et al. [12] investigated a setting with mutual gaze regarding perceived social presence and game experience, and found out that mutual gaze has a strong effect on the quality of interpersonal interactions between players in a video-mediated gameplay setting. This inclusion of shared gaze-based interaction in both, competitive [7] as well as cooperative gameplay [11], has shown to positively influence social presence, but also drastically changes in how players perceive each other and how they communicate (e.g., via combinations of gaze and verbal communication or by unintended communication via gaze). In a similar direction, Maurer et al. [10] investigated a shared gaze approach as a way to integrate a spectator in a co-located gameplay setting into the gaming experience. In this asynchronous setting (player with controller-based input; spectator with gaze-based input), they explored different levels of onlooker integration and identified a positive impact of this integration on the overall gaming experience for both, spectator as well as player. Based on their results, the researchers propose gaze-based interaction in games as an embodied means to mirror the experience of another player, thus, fostering social couplings and behavioral engagement.

However, research addressing the interpersonal link between audience and spectator via gaze is still very limited. Especially social presence can be an important aspect in such gameplay settings [2]. Hudson & Cairns point out the importance of social relationships between players having an influence on how a game is experienced [4].

Social presence does not only play an important role in co-located play scenarios, but is also relevant in the online games domain. This fact, however, leads to several research challenges. In contrast to co-located play the communication between players in mediated settings is filtered by the media technology [3]. Players cannot make use of all the available cues that are typically employed in face to face communication (verbal, paraverbal, and nonverbal communication). De Kort et al. [3] further note that the level of social presence is influenced by the properties of the media technology and its interface. Via the interface players are enabled to communicate both verbally and non-verbally granting various levels of representations in terms of appearance and behavior.

3   Using Social Gaze as an Interpersonal Link

Until now, research efforts employed gaze interaction without addressing specific in-game events, thus, following an always-on approach (constant gaze), where the gaze of a person is constantly visualized without any triggering mechanic. Studies indicated that, although the integration of gaze was experienced positively, in some situations the constant visualization of the current gaze position distracted players, and also led to ambiguous information. Thus, we argue that design strategies for visualizing gaze in-game are required to address this issue. In this paper, these strategies are considered and explored under the light of spectators integration. Our related research question is: How should gaze be integrated within the game interface without distracting players and giving the spectators a way to participate in a meaningful way?

The aforementioned beneficial aspects of including gaze interaction in games are especially relevant for players and spectators scenarios in remote settings, where people take both active and passive roles. Therefore, we explore the notion of gaze as a motivator for players, as well as gaze input as a way for spectators to participate in the gaming experience. Therefore, we focus both on the player and on the spectator. In our experiment, we wanted to find out if gaze can serve as a connector between players and spectators and how it impacts the perceived social presence between those two sides. We followed the notion of eye contact to drive our design. As gaze doesn't relate to a required explicit input (in contrast to a mouse input device, a keyboard, a gamepad, etc.), it is part of the human repertoire to get in contact with others (specifically via eye contact). The gaze interaction we use in our experiment aims at creating an additional channel for players and spectators to get in contact with each other (apart from communication tools such as chat features).

The main contribution of this paper lies in researching strategies of integrating game spectators and players via gaze and creating an interpersonal nonverbal link between the player and the spectator. Via our approach we want to give the notion of being a spectator a meaning and function within the game by considering mutual gaze locations in the game as the event-based approach to trigger different gaze-visualization strategies. In doing so, we explore ways of how spectators can be integrated into the game experience, and create a bidirectional interaction.

3.1 Experiment Description

To investigate the impact of gaze-based nonverbal communication on players and spectators in remote settings, we created an experimental setting supported via eye tracking technology. It focuses on the examination regarding the effects of a shared gaze within a game in a remote setting on the perceived social presence among the participants. The main idea behind the experiment was to visualize the counterpart's gaze on the subject's screen and vice versa (player or spectator). The gaze information is employed in two different ways: one strategy was to constantly show the current counterpart's gaze position (abbreviated: ConstGaze), while in the second version the shared gaze information is shown when both, the player and the spectator, look at the same game entity (abbreviated: EyeCon). The experiment requires two subjects per session (a player and a spectator), and consists of four conditions along with two varying gaze-based communication modalities for the participants that are randomized in presentation order (i.e., randomized block factorial design): 1.a ConstGaze.Spectator, 2.a ConstGaze.Player, 1.b EyeCon.Spectator, and 2.b EyeCon.Player.

3.2 Conditions

In condition 1.a ConstGaze.Spectator and condition 2.a ConstGaze.Player, both participants, the player and the spectator, constantly see their partner's current gaze position (see Fig. 1) — the own gaze is never exposed. On both sides, the gaze is visualized via a circle Fig. 1. In contrast to the player (game control via gamepad), spectators, besides using the eye tracking device, do not have further input possibilities at their disposal.

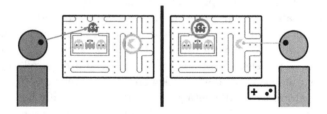

Fig. 1. ConstGaze condition 1.a and 1.b: the current gaze position is constantly shown to the spectator (left: blue color) and the spectator (right: yellow color).Only the gaze position of the counterpart is visible. A participant's own gaze is not displayed. (Color figure online)

In condition 1.b (EyeCon.Spectator) and 2.b (EyeCon.Player) we utilized a different strategy to set up a shared gaze experience (see Fig. 2). Any gaze visualization is triggered by an eye contact between the player and the spectator. Particularly when both subjects are gazing near the same entity, the entity then is marked with a circle (it has the same visual quality as in condition 1.a and 2.a) on the players' and the spectator's screen. Additionally, the exact gaze point of the counterpart is displayed as a small dot. As in condition 1.a and 2.a the own gaze spot, however is not exposed.

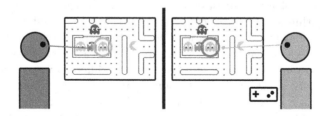

Fig. 2. EyeCon Condition 2.a and 2.b: a game entity is visually highlighted via a circle when both participants (left: spectator in blue color and right: player in yellow color) look at it. Also a subtle dot indicates the unfiltered counterpart's gaze information. (Color figure online)

3.3   Game

To minimize hurdles before entering and to allow the subjects to start playing without spending too much time in learning the game, we chose the very popular game Pac-Man for our experiment. Although the game is easy to learn, it offers several interesting game mechanics. Pac-Man is a single player game, where the player navigates the game character, a yellow puck, through a maze. To complete a level, the player has to collect dots. The player also has to avoid four enemies (ghosts), which are roaming around in the levels. Each time Pac-Man touches an enemy, he loses one of his three lives. The game ends when all lives are lost. Each level also provides four Power Pallets. After collecting one Power Pallet, Pac-Man temporarily is able to eat the enemies.

The overall goal of the game is to reach a high-score. The score can be increased by eating the different game entities. For our experiment we modified an open source version of the game[1] made with the Unity game engine[2].

3.4 Technical Setup

For the experiment two PCs, connected via ethernet, and two screens were set up in two separate rooms. Each PC was connected to an eye tracking device (Tobii EyeX[3]). While the game was installed on the first PC (player-PC) only, the second one (spectator-PC) exclusively served as a tracking data provider. Both screens were connected to the player-PC (see Fig. 3). The application installed on the spectator-PC connected to the player-PC and started sending eye tracking data. To minimize delays, caused by the network connections, the data was sent unreliable sequenced. This means that not the delivery, bu the order is guaranteed (only the newest packet is accepted).

The main application, the modified Pac-Man game, renders the game two times simultaneously. Each rendering includes one of the two gaze positions. Hereby, it is achieved to visualize only the desired gaze on the respective screen (e.g. player gaze on spectator screen). Thus, the processing of the tracking data

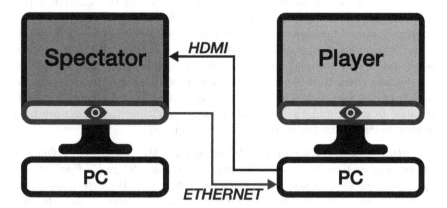

Fig. 3. An illustration of the technical setup consisting of 2 connected PCs and 2 eye trackers.

---

[1] https://github.com/vilbeyli/Pacman.

[2] https://unity3d.com/.

[3] http://www.tobii.com/xperience/.

exclusively takes place on the main application. To optimize the application and to set it up for the experiment, a few parameters can be changed. The strength of the filtering of the eye tracking data can be altered to avoid jitter artifacts of the gaze information. Also the radii of the different trigger areas, used for the EyeCon conditions (see Sect. 3.2), around the game entities can be changed.

3.5 Hypotheses

Based on the aforementioned considerations, we assume that the four conditions will arouse a different feeling of social presence. As our conditions are based on the very well-known and rather simple Pac-Man game design with a short interaction time in mind, we focused only on two aspects that are associated with social presence: co-presence and psycho-behavioral interaction (sub dimension: attentional engagement) introduced by [1]. The more complex aspects of social presence, subjective and intersubjective symmetry, were not examined in the study (see Sect. 3.7 for a more detailed description of the scales). The following two hypotheses were formulated:

H1 - co-presence: *Dependent on the player role (player VS spectator) and on the social gaze-based interaction (ConstGaze VS EyeCon) players will perceive co-presence differently. We expect an interaction effect of the social gaze-based interaction and the player role on co-presence: (a) Among spectators, ConstGaze will result in a higher co-presence as compared with EyeCon; (b) Among players ConstGaze will result in a lower co-presence as compared with EyeCon.*

H1 addresses the question how players and spectators experience co-presence if the social gaze-based interaction is either constantly shown or displayed when the participants' eyes meet. It is hypothesized that condition 1 (ConstGaze.Spectator) will have higher ratings in comparison to condition 3 (EyeCon.Spectators), as this way provides relevant information for spectators about the current players' behavior (strategies, goals, etc.). On the contrary, we deem that the continuous display of the spectators' gaze position will lead to low co-presence ratings by the players as it might distract them from game-relevant events leading them to a blend out the gaze visualization (gaze info perceived as background noise). Issues in the context of game-relevant events in Pac-Man may range from occluding enemies via gaze to confusing the animation of the gaze visualization with the movement of the enemies.

H2 - attentional engagement: *Dependent on the player role (player VS spectator) and on the social gaze-based interaction (ConstGaze VS EyeCon) players will perceive the attentional engagement differently. We expect an interaction effect of the social gaze-based interaction and player role on the attentional engagement: (a) Among spectators, ConstGaze will result in higher attentional engagement as compared with EyeCon; (b) Among players ConstGaze will result in lower attentional engagement as compared with EyeCon.*

Like in H1 we hypothesized that condition 1 (ConstGaze.Spectator) would have higher ratings in comparison to condition 3 (EyeCon.Spectators). Based on the aforementioned considerations, we thought that ConstGaze.Player (condition 2) would receive lower ratings than the EyeCon.Player condition (condition 4).

3.6   Participants and Procedure

The sample consisted of 20 participants, age 19 to 30 years (11 female, mean age = 22.15, SD = 2.65). All participants were either students or research staff of the University of Applied Sciences Upper Austria. Furthermore, subjects represented a variety of disciplines of education having a background in 3D animation, software engineering, or in game design. A majority of the participants (15 people) are keen in playing video games, as they indicated to play games at several times a week or daily.

Each evaluation session was made up of two subjects that either played (role: player) or watched (role: spectator) the game Pac-Man in two separate rooms. By choosing a within-subject design, all participants had to play each of the aforementioned conditions (play time limit for each condition: 3 min). If a subject lost the game earlier, the game was restarted. The time limit resulted in a maximum active testing time of twelve minutes.

The experiment was made up of the following procedure: as a first step, the experimenter welcomed the two participants and provided a short introduction that gave an overview of the overall procedure. After the eye tracking devices were calibrated, subjects were instructed about the game rules, goals and mechanics of the game. When subjects confirmed that every aspect was clear to them, the experiment began. When the interaction with one condition was completed, the experimenter instructed the participants to fill out a questionnaire (Networked Minds Social Presence Inventory by [1]). To minimize distractions caused by adjustments, subjects switched roles only once during the experiment. After participants were finished with the first condition, the remaining three were evaluated. Following, participants had the possibility to give comments on the conditions with a focus on social presence and their experience with the gaze interaction, via a interview carried out by the experimenter. The procedure itself took between 50 to 60 min.

3.7   Measures

All dependent measures were collected by using validated scales. To measure the co-presence and attentional engagement dimensions, the Networked Minds Social Presence Inventory by [1] was employed, which consists of three scales (co-presence, psycho-behavioral interaction, and subjective and inter-subjective symmetry). We only employed the first two scales, co-presence and psycho-behavioral interaction.

Co-presence (4 items) forms a core component of social presence and measures the degree to which the players feel as if they are together in the same space. It emerges when players have the impression that they automatically detect and classify a form as another, which is moderated by the degree to which the user and the agent appear to share an environment together. The second scale, psycho-behavioral interaction, measures the player's perception of attention, emotional contagion, and mutual understanding with participants. In our study we only made use of the sub-scale perceived attentional engagement (3 items), which measures the degree to which a subject reports attention to the other. Items of the perceived attentional engagement-scale include statements such as "I was easily distracted from the spectator when other things were going on". Furthermore, data on demographics as well as pre-experience with games was gathered.

3.8   Data Analysis

Data analysis for co-presence and attentional engagement ratings were analyzed using a repeated measures analysis of variance (ANOVA) with the two within-subject factors (CRF-22 design) comprising the player role (player VS spectator), and the type of social gaze interaction (ConstGaze VS EyeCon), as well as the social presence as the dependent variable (co-presence vs. attentional engagement). All statistic tests were carried out with SPSS 22. Significance was set at $\alpha = 0.05$.

4   Results

In the following section results of the study are presented (dimensions co-presence and attentional engagement). Insights are provided if the various conditions (with the different roles in the game) have an influence on the perceived social presence (dependent variable: co-presence and attentional engagement). Gender, age, and occupation were not significantly related to social presence ratings.

The results of the ANOVA indicate that co-presence was generally higher in the conditions where participants were in the role of the player than in the condition where participants were in the role of the spectator, $F(1, 19) = 25.60$, $p = 0$. The player role in combination with the type of social gaze interaction, $F(1, 19) = 21.25$, $p = 0$, indicate that, depending on the player role (spectator VS player), the perceived co-presence was either significantly higher (Const.Gaze Spectator: M = 5.26, SD = 1.4, EyeCon.Player: M = 6.03, SD=0.86) or lower (EyeCon.Spectator: M = 3.84, SD = 1.35, ConstGaze.Player: M = 5.36, SD = 1.08) (see Fig. 4). In general, it has to be noted that co-presence did not differ significantly between the conditions with ConstGaze and EyeCon, $F(1, 19) = 2.19$, $p = .15$.

The second dimension, attentional engagement, was rated by subjects in a similar fashion. As in the co-presence dimension the results of the ANOVA revealed a significant main effect of player role, $F(1, 19) = 44.19$, $p = 0$, and the combination of the player with the type of the social gaze interaction, $F(1, 19) = 26.86$, $p = 0$. Thus, in the case that participants were in the role of

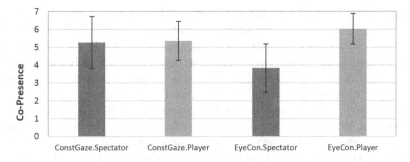

Fig. 4. Mean values and standard deviation bars for co-presence of all conditions (player roles, social gaze interaction) on a scale from 1 ("strongly disagree") to 7 ("strongly agree").

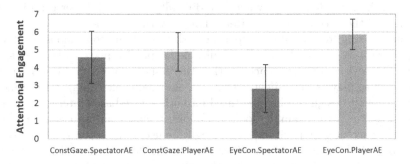

Fig. 5. Mean values and standard deviation bars for attentional engagement of all conditions (player roles, social gaze interaction) on a scale from 1 ("strongly disagree") to 7 ("strongly agree").

the player, social presence was higher with EyeCon (M = 5.85, SD = 0.92) than with ConstGaze (M = 4.89, SD = 1.08); if participants were in the role of the spectator, ConstGaze resulted in higher attentional engagement (M = 4.58, SD = 1.66) than EyeCon (M = 2.82, SD = 1.35) – see Fig. 5). As in co-presence, no significant could be found regarding the type of social gaze integration, $F(1, 19) = 1.07$, $p = .32$.

5   Discussion

In general, our study showed, dependent on the type of the gaze integration and the player role, the positive effects of a shared gaze towards an increased awareness and engagement among the players and the spectators. It presented a new way of nonverbal interaction for the audience and the players, which in turn, resulted in a range of gaze-based qualities emerging from this interaction channel. As anticipated, condition 1.a (ConstGaze.Spectator) received higher ratings by the audience in comparison to condition 1.b (EyeCon.Spectators) on both scales (co-presence and attentional engagement). Subjects indicated that it was interesting for them to see where the player was currently looking at, as it gave them information about their strategies to evade the ghosts, if the player was aroused, or when they would eat the next Power Pellet.

Additionally, it was revealed that the continuous display of the spectators' gaze position led to relatively low social ratings by the players. This can be explained by the fact that several players mentioned that they were annoyed and distracted by the current gaze position of the spectators. Although they were aware of the spectators presence in the beginning of the play session, they tended to ignore the visual cue after some time. In some cases the animation and position of the circle (that was driven by the gaze behavior of the spectator) made some players believe that the spectator, although not intended, wanted to give them tips to progress in the game. This effect could be frequently seen in level 1 of the *Pac-Man* game, where the difficulty was much lower than in level 2. In level 2 the spectators' was often ignored by the players.

Summarizing, results of the experiment show that the continuous display of the player's gaze information is more suitable for passive player roles (like spectators). The eye contact approach, on the other hand, is preferred by active game roles (such as players or audiences that can alter game elements). Furthermore, our eye contact design can be integrated into other gaze-based interactions, such as pointing via gaze (example: look at an game element and press a button to reveal the current gaze position). This might be useful in a coop-remote setting, where one of the players uses his/her gaze to highlight an useful item for the other player. Generally, we deem that the gaze point could be incorporated more deeply into the actual mechanics of the game towards deliberately designing for in-game communication mechanics as an integral part of the game design.

6   Conclusion

This paper reported on an experimental setting that investigated two different shared gaze integrations in games (ConstGaze and EyeCon) and their effects on the social presence (co-presence and attentional engagement) perceived by player roles (player VS spectator). Our study findings show a positive effect of the shared gaze integrations on social presence depending on active and passive player roles. In general, we argue that our approach supports social couplings and interpersonal communication in remote gaming and shows promising results to increase the connection between players and spectators. Our findings stress that the inclusion of social and shared gaze information can create a new non-verbal communication channel for players and spectators alike that presents an interesting design resource for future designs of digital play. For future work, we plan to further investigate other genres for their potential to incorporate gaze interaction as well as explore our approach in situations with multiple players and spectators.

Acknowledgments. We would like to thank all of our survey participants for their time and for the data they generously provided.

References

1. Biocca, F., Harms, C.: Networked minds social presence inventory: measures of co-presence, social presence, subjective symmetry, and intersubjective symmetry (2003). http://cogprints.org/6742/
2. Bowman, N.D., Weber, R., Tamborini, R., Sherry, J.: Facilitating game play: how others affect performance at and enjoyment of video games. Media Psychol. **16**(1), 39–64 (2013)
3. De Kort, Y.A., IJsselsteijn, W.A., Gajadhar, B.J.: People, places, and play: a research framework for digital game experience in a socio-spatial context. In: DiGRA 2007 Proceedings Situated Play, pp. 823–830 (2007)
4. Hudson, M., Cairns, P.: Interrogating social presence in games with experiential vignettes. Entertain. Comput. **5**(2), 101–114 (2014)
5. Kendon, A.: Some functions of gaze-direction in social interaction. Acta Psychol. **26**, 22–63 (1967)
6. Kleinke, C.L.: Gaze and eye contact: a research review. Psychol. Bull. **100**(1), 78 (1986)
7. Lankes, M., Maurer, B., Stiglbauer, B.: An eye for an eye: gaze input in competitive online games and its effects on social presence. In: Proceedings of the 13th International Conference on Advances in Computer Entertainment Technology, ACE 2016, pp. 17:1–17:9. ACM, New York (2016). doi:10.1145/3001773.3001774
8. Lee, K.M.: Presence, explicated. Commun. Theory **14**(1), 27–50 (2004). doi:10.1111/j.1468-2885.2004.tb00302.x
9. Mansour, S.S., El-Said, M.: Building a bi-directional bridge between social presence and interaction in online games. In: 2012 17th International Conference on Computer Games (CGAMES), pp. 202–207. IEEE (2012)
10. Maurer, B., Aslan, I., Wuchse, M., Neureiter, K., Tscheligi, M.: Gaze-based onlooker integration: exploring the in-between of active player and passive spectator in co-located gaming. In: Proceedings of the 2015 Annual Symposium on Computer-Human Interaction in Play, CHI PLAY 2015, pp. 163–173. ACM, New York (2015). doi:10.1145/2793107.2793126
11. Maurer, B., Lankes, M., Stiglbauer, B., Tscheligi, M.: EyeCo: effects of shared gaze on social presence in an online cooperative game. In: Wallner, G., Kriglstein, S., Hlavacs, H., Malaka, R., Lugmayr, A., Yang, H.-S. (eds.) ICEC 2016. LNCS, vol. 9926, pp. 102–114. Springer, Cham (2016). doi:10.1007/978-3-319-46100-7_9
12. Shahid, S., Krahmer, E., Swerts, M.: Video-mediated and co-present gameplay: effects of mutual gaze on game experience, expressiveness and perceived social presence. Interact. Comput. **24**(4), 292–305 (2012)
13. Velloso, E., Carter, M.: The emergence of eyeplay: a survey of eye interaction in games. In: Proceedings of the 2016 Annual Symposium on Computer-Human Interaction in Play, CHI PLAY 2016, pp. 171–185. ACM, New York (2016). doi:10.1145/2967934.2968084
14. Vidal, M., Bismuth, R., Bulling, A., Gellersen, H.: The royal corgi: exploring social gaze interaction for immersive gameplay. In: Proceedings of the 33rd Annual ACM Conference on Human Factors in Computing Systems, CHI 2015, pp. 115–124. ACM, New York (2015). doi:10.1145/2702123.2702163

Possible Interpretations for Game Refinement Measure

Shuo Xiong[(✉)], Long Zuo[(✉)], and Hiroyuki Iida[(✉)]

Japan Advanced Institute of Science and Technology,
1-1 Asahidai, Nomi, Ishikawa 923-1211, Japan
{xiongshuo,zuolong,iida}@jaist.ac.jp

Abstract. This paper explores possible interpretations for game refinement measure which has been successfully used to quantify the game sophistication of various types of games such as boardgames and sports. It presents a brief sketch of game refinement theory with a focus on its early works with boardgames, expansion into continuous movement games such as sports, and a bridge between sports and boardgames. It then highlights the bridging idea while considering possible interpretations for game refinement measure, and the meaning of game refinement measure is discussed with a focus on the skill and chance aspects in game playing. It enables to have a new perspective of game refinement theory. Moreover, an example of interpretation for game refinement measure from boardgames and continuous movement games such as MOBA game is shown. The interpretation is well fitting to our intuition as game players and spectators.

Keywords: Game refinement measure · Game progress model · Boardgame · Continuous movement game, sports, MOBA game

1 Introduction

Game theory is a discipline which stands from the game player's point of view with a focus on how to win a game. However, game designers would consider another important aspect: how to make a game more attractive. With such motivation, a new game theory from the game designer's point of view, called *game refinement theory* [2,3] was proposed in the early 2000s. von Neumann [4] was a pioneer who formed the foundation for the modern game theory, which has widely been applied in various fields. For example, Shannon [5] and Turing [6] proposed the basic framework for computer chess that is the minimax game-tree search, being inspired by the concept of minimax equilibrium [4], typical framework of computer chess called game-tree search was proposed by Shannon [5] and Turing [6], respectively.

One direction with game theory was to find the best move in a game or to ensure the possibility of winning the game based on the understanding of

© IFIP International Federation for Information Processing 2017
Published by Springer International Publishing AG 2017. All Rights Reserved
N. Munekata et al. (Eds.): ICEC 2017, LNCS 10507, pp. 322–334, 2017.
DOI: 10.1007/978-3-319-66715-7_35

current positions. Another direction with game refinement theory was to assess the attractiveness or sophistication of a game. In particular, game refinement theory gives a measure to quantify the sophistication of a game. This enables to obtain the deep insight into the current game and improve the quality of the game [7,8].

The measure of game refinement can also be used to obtain the deep insight into the history of games. For example, it is observed that the evolution of chess has two different directions: one is to increase the search-space complexity and another one is to shift to the comfortable degree of game refinement measure [9]. Hence, it gives a reasonable look on the evolution of specific game variants.

In another way, game refinement theory provides us with another viewpoint of games from the entertainment aspect while game theory helps us understand about the game's mechanism itself. From that viewpoint, we can extend the idea of game refinement into other domains in human life such as sports games, video games, education or business. The possibility of extension comes from the core idea of game refinement theory that is quantifying the engagement. In many activities of human, the engagement is usually used as one of the important standards to evaluate the effectiveness of those activities.

Game refinement theory has been widely applied to many different types of games with the promising results. However, the theory has just one decade history, which may not be established yet. This paper explores possible interpretations for game refinement measure. It highlights the bridging idea between boardgames and continuous movement games like sports. Thus the meaning of game refinement measure is discussed with a focus on the skill and chance aspects in game playing. It will enable to have a new perspective of game refinement theory. Moreover, an example of interpretation for game refinement measure from boardgames and continuous movement games such as MOBA game is shown.

2   An Overview of Game Refinement Theory

In this section an overview of game refinement theory is presented. The model of game refinement was first investigated in the domain of boardgames such as chess, later expanded into continuous movement games such as sports games and video games while considering the gap between boardgames and continuous movement games.

2.1   Original Model

We review the early work of game refinement theory from [2]. The decision space is the minimal search space without forecasting. It provides the common measures for almost all boardgames. The dynamics of decision options in the decision space has been investigated and it is observed that this dynamics is a key factor for game entertainment. Thus a measure of the refinement in games was proposed [3].

Later, the following works are sketched from [7,10] that expands the model of game refinement which was cultivated in the domain of boardgames into continuous movement games such as sports games and video games.

The game progress is twofold. One is game speed or scoring rate, while another one is game information progress with a focus on the game outcome. Game information progress presents the degree of certainty of a game's result in time or in steps. Having full information of the game progress, i.e. after its conclusion, game progress $x(t)$ will be given as a linear function of time t with $0 \leq t \leq t_k$ and $0 \leq x(t) \leq x(t_k)$, as shown in Eq. (1).

$$x(t) = \frac{x(t_k)}{t_k} t \tag{1}$$

However, the game information progress given by Eq. (1) is unknown during the in-game period. The presence of uncertainty during the game, often until the final moments of a game, reasonably renders game progress as exponential. Hence, a realistic model of game information progress is given by Eq. (2).

$$x(t) = x(t_k)(\frac{t}{t_k})^n \tag{2}$$

Here n stands for a constant parameter which is given based on the perspective of an observer of the game considered. Only a very boring game would progress in a linear function, however, and most of course do not. Therefore, it is reasonable to assume a parameter n, based on the perception of game progress prior to completion. If the information of the game is completely known (i.e., after the end of the game) and the value of n is 1, the game progress curve appears as a straight line. In most games, especially in competitive ones, much of the information is incomplete, the value of n cannot be assumed, and therefore game progress is a steep curve until its completion, along with $x(t_k)$, t_k, $x(t)$ and t, just prior to game's end.

Then acceleration of game information progress is obtained by deriving Eq. (2) twice. Solving it at $t = t_k$, we have Eq. (3).

$$x''(t_k) = \frac{x(t_k)}{(t_k)^n}(t_k)^{n-2} n(n-1) = \frac{x(t_k)}{(t_k)^2} n(n-1) \tag{3}$$

It is assumed in the current model that game information progress in any type of game is encoded and transported in our brains. We do not yet know about the physics of information in the brain, but it is likely that the acceleration of information progress is subject to the forces and laws of physics. Too little game information acceleration may be easy for human observers and players to compute, and becomes boring. In contrast, too much game information acceleration surpasses the entertaining range and will be frustration, and at some points beyond that could become overwhelming and incomprehensible.

Therefore, we expect that the larger the value $\frac{x(t_k)}{(t_k)^2}$ is, the more the game becomes exciting, due in part to the uncertainty of game outcome. Thus, we use its root square, $\frac{\sqrt{x(t_k)}}{t_k}$, as a game refinement measure for the game under consideration. We call it R value for short as shown in Eq. (4).

$$R = \frac{\sqrt{x(t_k)}}{t_k}\sqrt{n(n-1)} = C\frac{\sqrt{x(t_k)}}{t_k} \qquad (4)$$

2.2   A Bridge Between Sports and Boardgames

Here we consider the gap of game refinement model between boardgames and sports games. We review the observation from [10]. One round in boardgames can be illustrated as decision tree. At each depth of the game tree, one will choose a move and the game will progress. Figure 1 illustrates one level of game tree. The distance d, which has been shown in Fig. 1, can be found by using simple Pythagoras theorem, thus resulting in $d = \sqrt{\Delta l^2 + 1}$.

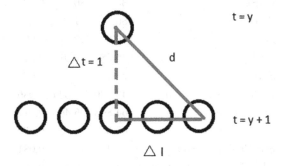

Fig. 1. Illustration of one level of game tree [10]

Assuming that the approximate value of horizontal difference between nodes is $\frac{B}{2}$, then we can make a substitution and get $d = \sqrt{(\frac{B}{2})^2 + 1}$. Here B stands for the average branching factor of a game tree. The game progress for one game is the total level of game tree times d. For the meantime, we do not consider Δt^2 because the value ($\Delta t^2 = 1$) is assumed to be much smaller compared to B. The game length will be normalized by the average game length D, then the game progress $x(t)$ is given by $x(t) = \frac{t}{D} \cdot d = \frac{t}{D}\sqrt{(\frac{B}{2})^2} = \frac{Bt}{2D}$. Then, in general we have Eq. (5).

$$x(t) = c\frac{B}{D}t \qquad (5)$$

where c is a different constant which depends on the game considered. However, we manage to explain how to obtain the game information progress value itself. The game progress in the domain of boardgames forms a linear graph with the maximum value $x(t)$ of B. Assuming[1] $c = 1$, then we have a realistic game progress model for boardgames, which is given by

---

[1] In this study we concern about this assumption.

$$x(t) = B(\frac{t}{D})^n. \tag{6}$$

We show, in Table 1, measures of game refinement for various games [11–13]. From the results, we conjecture the relation between the measure of game refinement and game sophistication, as stated in Remark 1.

Remark 1. Sophisticated games have a common factor (i.e., same degree of informatical acceleration value, say 0.07–0.08) to feel engaged or excited regardless of different type of games.

Table 1. Measures of game refinement for various types of games

Game	$x(t_k)$	t_k	R
Chess	35	80	0.074
Shogi	80	115	0.078
Go	250	208	0.076
Basketball	36.38	82.01	0.073
Soccer	2.64	22	0.073
Badminton	46.336	79.344	0.086
Table tennis	54.863	96.465	0.077
DotA ver 6.80	68.6	106.2	0.078
StarCraft II Terran	1.64	16	0.081
The king of the fighters 98	14.6	36.7	0.104

3   Game Refinement Measure Revisited

It seems that the bridge between boardgame and continuous movement game was successfully built. However, we claim that it is not yet completed. For this purpose we detail the problem while considering the meaning of parameter c in Eq. (5).

3.1   Possible Interpretations for Game Refinement Measure

For the sports games such as soccer, all the attempted shots or successful shots (goals) are parts of the strategy to win the match, so they are an integral part of the game. In the domain of video games such as StarCraft II, the branching factor was calculated only by reasonable strategies to be considered as part of the winning [12]. This suggests that parameter c in Eq. (5) is a key factor when considering the gap between boardgames and continuous movement games. It also indicates that the parameter c can be replaced with $\sqrt{n(n-1)}$ in Eq. (4).

From Eq. (5) we obtain the measure of game refinement for boardgame as shown in Eq. (7).

$$R = \frac{\sqrt{cB}}{D} \qquad (\frac{1}{B} \leq c \leq 1) \qquad (7)$$

Where we have $cB = B$ when $c = 1$, and $cB = 1$ when $c = \frac{1}{B}$. Hence, the assumption $c = 1$ means that we focus on a specific level of players or a certain property of the game under consideration. When we focus on a certain level of players like masters in boardgames, the crucial factor is the game property. If a game is skillful, the parameter c will decrease, whereas if the game is stochastic, c will increase. This is because it is usually hard in such a stochastic game to distinguish only fewer good candidates among all possible moves. On the other hands, it would be possible in boardgames like chess for masters to identify a few plausible moves. Note that continuous movement games such as sports games are basically stochastic when compared with boardgames.

Remark 2. The parameter $c = 1$ in Eq. (5) means that the game under consideration is assumed to be insufficiently deterministic to identify plausible candidates.

We show from [14], in Fig. 2, a model of move candidate selection based on skill and chance. This illustration shows that skillful players would consider a set (say b) of fewer plausible candidates among all possible moves (say B) to find a move to play. For example, in chess where $B = 35$ and $D = 80$, when assuming $c = 1$, then $R = 0.074$. On the other hands, as suggested in [14,15], masters in sophisticated boardgames would consider a very few moves on average in their look-ahead thinking framework. An estimation of the number of plausible candidates as a function of the strength of players (say s) may be given by Eq. (8) [3].

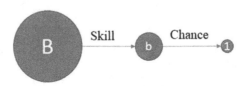

Fig. 2. A model of candidate move selection based on skill and chance [14]

$$b = B^{\frac{1}{s}} \qquad (1 \leq s \in \mathbb{N}) \qquad (8)$$

Let us consider the sports case with consideration on such a parameter. Like the boardgame case, we may have a parameter (say C_s), as shown in Eq. (9).

$$R = C_s \frac{\sqrt{G}}{T} \qquad (9)$$

Here we suspect that C_s may depend on the skill of teams. For the analysis, many data from soccer leagues with different ranking were collected. We show, in Table 2, measures of game refinement for each soccer league together with the average number of goals (G) and shots attempts (T) per game. Two typical groups are compared. The first group is clearly stronger than the second groups. England Premier League (EPL), Primera division de Liga (LIGA) and Serie A in the first group are the higher ranking leagues, whereas Chinese Football Association Super League (CSL) in the second group is the lower ranking league [16]. We notice from the results in Table 2 that when two similar-level teams play each other in their leagues R value is quite similar. Thus, we assume $C_s = 1$ in this study.

Table 2. Measures of game refinement for each league football match

	G	T	R
EPL (2016)	2.84	25.6	0.066
LIGA (2016)	2.75	23.6	0.070
Serie A (2016)	2.77	25.4	0.065
CSL (2014)	2.75	24.6	0.067
CSL (2015)	2.80	24.6	0.068
CSL (2016)	2.67	24.6	0.066

We show, in Fig. 3, the relationship between the parameter c and chance-and-skill aspect. Note that we assume the estimation of the plausible candidates as described in Eq. (8). From Fig. 3 we conjecture that the parameter c relates to the strength of players or the difficulty of a game, as stated in Remark 3.

Fig. 3. The parameter c and chance-and-skill aspect of games

Remark 3. The value of parameter c should be lower in the case where the game under consideration is simple to identify fewer plausible candidates or the case where players are very skillful like grandmasters.

Using the estimation of plausible candidates as shown in Eq. (8), we obtain game refinement measures as described in Table 3.

Table 3. Measures of game refinement for boardgames with different parameters

	R $(c = 1)$	R $(cB = b, s = 2)$
Chess	0.074	0.030
Shogi	0.078	0.026
Go	0.076	0.019

We here summarize the meaning of game refinement measure.

- In a game where its game refinement measure is higher than the zone value (0.07–0.08), people may feel more entertaining. This is because the game is too stochastic or players are too weak to identify fewer plausible candidates.
- The game with a zone value of game refinement measure has a good balance between chance and skill, in which people may feel comfortable and then the game is sophisticated or fascinating.
- In a game where its game refinement measure is smaller than the zone value, people may feel less entertaining. This is because the game is too simple or players are too strong to experience harmonic uncertainty during the game playing. In this situation the game tends to be competitive [17].

3.2 Relative Game Refinement Measure

The game refinement theory is basically used to evaluate the property (sophistication) of games with a focus on the game outcome uncertainty. Let us consider the individual match analysis using game refinement measure [18,19]. Since each match has an independent game process, game refinement measure can be applied.

We demonstrate an analysis of two extreme conditions and special cases. The first example is The 2014 World Cup semi-final [20]: Germany vs. Brazil, where the number of goals $G = 8$ and the number of shot attempts $T = 31$. When focusing on this match, R value is given by Eq. (10).

$$R = \frac{\sqrt{G}}{T} = \frac{\sqrt{8}}{31} = 0.091 \tag{10}$$

In fact, this match was not a well balanced. Brazil had 1 goal, whereas Germany had 7 goals. Individually, game refinement measure for Brazil (say R_B) and Brazil (say R_G) is given in Eqs. (11) and (12), respectively.

$$R_B = \frac{\sqrt{1}}{31} = 0.032 \tag{11}$$

$$R_G = \frac{\sqrt{7}}{31} = 0.085 \tag{12}$$

Apparently, the R value of Germany is higher than Brazil, which means that Germany had better playing skill. Even more we need to know the psychological meaning of game refinement value for each team's perception. Then the relative game refinement measure for Brazil (say R_r) is given by Eq. (13).

$$R_r = R \times \frac{R_B}{R_G} = 0.091 \times \frac{0.032}{0.085} = 0.034 \tag{13}$$

Similarly, the relative game refinement measure for Germany is given by Eq. (14).

$$R_r = R \times \frac{R_G}{R_B} = 0.091 \times \frac{0.085}{0.032} = 0.242 \tag{14}$$

From Eqs. (13) and (14) we see that from Germany's perspective, people can enjoy the game for fun. Meanwhile from Brazil's perspective, people may feel very tough and they must seriously face the game progress. Larger R value means higher fun, whereas smaller R value means more serious or competitiveness. Illustration in Fig. 4 shows the relation between R value and balance between skill and chance in boardgames as well as continuous movement games.

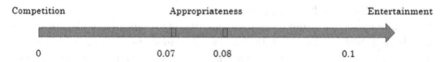

Fig. 4. An illustration of the meaning of game refinement measure

3.3 Analysis of MOBA Games

Multi-player On-line Battle Arena (MOBA) [21] is the most popular game type, in which a player controls a single character at one of two teams. MOBA game is a typical continuous movement game. The objective is to destroy the opponent team's main structure with the assistance of periodically spawned computer controlled units. Player characters typically have various abilities and advantages that improve over the course of a game and that contribute to a team's overall strategy. Mainly in the world market, it was followed by three spiritual successors: "League of Legends" (LOL), "Defense of the Ancients" (DotA) and "Heroes of the Storm" (HotS) [22].

The game progress model of MOBA is given by the average number of successful killing heroes and destroying fortress (say K) over the average number of attempts per game (say A) [13]. Hence, the game refinement measure of MOBA is given by Eq. (15).

$$R = \frac{\sqrt{K}}{A} \tag{15}$$

The measures of game refinement for various MOBA games are shown in Table 4. Because of the game battle system and macro mechanism, in DotA and LOL one tower equals to 1 kill, and in HotS one castle equals to 4 kills [22]. For killing tendency A, any tower or castle as 1 attempt is calculated. It is found that R-value of sophisticated games is located somewhere between 0.07 to 0.08 [2,10]. Distinctly, we notice that the game refinement value in LOL battle is so high. It means that LOL will be too excited with high entertainment and low competitiveness.

Table 4. Measures of game refinement for three MOBA games

	Map or version	K	A	R
HotS	Blackheart's bay	70.90	80.10	0.105
	Sky temple	77.68	79.90	0.110
	Dragon Shire	63.90	88.80	0.090
	Tomb of the SQ	75.00	98.00	0.088
	Infernal shrines	63.08	93.00	0.085
	Cursed hollow	69.55	100.70	0.083
	Battlefield of eternity	99.30	168.8	0.082
	Garden of terror	68.83	88.90	0.093
	Haunted mines	55.68	78.10	0.096
DotA	Version 6.48	69.2	110.8	0.075
	Version 6.51	68.4	110.2	0.074
	Version 6.59	69.8	110.0	0.076
	Version 6.61	70.0	111.6	0.075
	Version 6.64	68.4	110.4	0.075
	Version 6.69	67.8	108.4	0.076
	Version 6.74	62.4	102.6	0.077
	Version 6.77	62.8	102.8	0.077
	Version 6.80	68.6	106.2	0.078
LOL	Version 6.6	37.65	44.26	0.138

Below we summarize the entertaining and competitiveness aspect of MOBA games based on the game refinement values.

DotA: DotA is a very stable game, also it is a typical "G-T Model" (continuous movement games), for each version R-values are all seated between 0.07 to 0.08. Therefore, DotA is a well designed game with a good balance between entertainment and competitiveness, which is suited for competitions. For the activity population, DotA2 has 7.9 million per month all over the world [23]. The measure of game refinement indicates that DotA is the most successful and well balanced MOBA game in the world.

LOL: Generally, *R*-value in LOL is too high, whereas DotA is almost in the window value. It means that DotA fits for setting as e-sports competition, but LOL is suited to enjoy for entertainment. DotA has powerful skill and more visual impact for each hero, which cares more about management and running. Players need to make a stable and safe environment to carry and develop. Gank usually happens during the whole game. Generally, a DotA game may spend about 50 min but LOL usually takes around 30 min. LOL provides players with a new style of MOBA game that spends less time for each game and forms a fast rhythm. For the activity population, LOL has 67 million per month all over the world [23]. The rhythm of LOL is faster and its game refinement is higher than others. This implies that LOL is able to attract more children, female or beginners who prefer to play it because of the higher entertainment property [1].

HotS: For HotS, the most important point is large-scale team combat and the game rhythm is much higher than DotA or LOL. As a new game, HotS still has some insufficient aspects. According to Table 4, the most interesting and exciting map is 'Sky temple'. 'Battlefield of eternity' and 'Cursed hollow' have the highest level competitiveness. However, the game refinement measures of HotS are higher than 0.08, which means that compared with DotA, HotS is not so suitable for e-sports competition. Also some serious mechanism issue existed in HotS, DotA focuses on the ana-phase period during the game, but the core mechanism in HotS is wild monster. For this reason, the game depth of HotS is less than DotA and gets a larger R-value. Therefore, HotS cares more about teamwork than personal operation and game awareness, then we can only find valid data about the population of HotS in US server is 0.13 million, the expected number all over the world will not be larger than DotA2. Nevertheless, the fun of HotS is not derived only from the battle. The various heroes and their talents can provide a lot of enjoyment for Blizzard fans. In addition, they can design maps which become more interesting and well balanced. Also the design group of HotS needs to revise the game mechanism.

All property of these three MOBA games can be shown as Fig. 5.

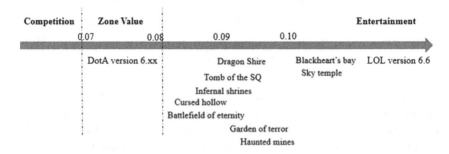

Fig. 5. Entertainment and competition property of three MOBA games

4   Concluding Remarks

The notion of game progress and game information progress model for continuous movement games was introduced in the development of game refinement measure. It seemed to be a successful bridge between continuous movement games like sports and boardgames. However, this paper claimed with a focus on the parameter c in the game progress model for boardgames.

The parameter c relates to the game balance. The condition $c = 1$ corresponds to the case where the game is more chance-based one. If the parameter c becomes lower, the game will be more skill-based one. Moreover, a new perspective of game refinement measure was obtained. Higher (lower) R value means more entertaining (competitive), whereas 0.07–0.08 should be a comfortable zone due to its good balance between skill and chance in game playing. The analysis of popular MOBA games using game refinement measure supports the observation. The concept of relative game refinement measure was proposed to focus on individual team performance in two team sports such as soccer. The game refinement measure has been used to quantify the game sophistication for the game under consideration. However, we considered the possibility of quantifying the game sophistication from the viewpoint of individual team.

Acknowledgements. This research is funded by a grant from the Japan Society for the Promotion of Science (JSPS), within the framework of the Grant-in-Aid for Challenging Exploratory Research (grant number 26540189) and Grant-in-Aid for JSPS Fellow.

References

1. Gaudiosi, J.: Riot games' league of legends officially becomes most played PC game in the world. Forbes (2012)
2. Iida, H., Takahara, K., Nagashima, J., Kajihara, Y., Hashimoto, T.: An application of game-refinement theory to Mah Jong. In: Rauterberg, M. (ed.) ICEC 2004. LNCS, vol. 3166, pp. 333–338. Springer, Heidelberg (2004). doi:10.1007/978-3-540-28643-1_41
3. Iida, H., Takeshita, N., Yoshimura, J.: A metric for entertainment of boardgames: its implication for evolution of chess variants. In: Nakatsu, R., Hoshino, J. (eds.) Entertainment Computing. ITIFIP, vol. 112, pp. 65–72. Springer, Boston, MA (2003). doi:10.1007/978-0-387-35660-0_8
4. Neumann, J.: Zur theorie der gesellschaftsspiele. Math. Ann. **100**(1), 295–320 (1928)
5. Shannon, C.E.: Programming a computer for playing chess. In: Levy, D. (ed.) Computer Chess Compendium, pp. 2–13. Springer, New York (1988). doi:10.1007/978-1-4757-1968-0_1
6. Turing, A.: Chess. Part of the collection Digital Computers Applied to Games. In: Bowden, B.V. (ed.) Faster Than Thought, a Symposium on Digital Computing Machines (1953)
7. Panumate, C., Xiong, S., Iida, H.: An approach to quantifying Pokemon's entertainment impact with focus on battle. In: 3rd International Conference on Applied

Computing and Information Technology/2nd International Conference on Computational Science and Intelligence, Okayama, pp. 60–66 (2015)

8. Punyawee, A., Panumate, C., Iida, H.: Finding comfortable settings of snake game using game refinement measurement. In: Park, J.J.J.H., Pan, Y., Yi, G., Loia, V. (eds.) CSA/CUTE/UCAWSN -2016. LNEE, vol. 421, pp. 66–73. Springer, Singapore (2017). doi:10.1007/978-981-10-3023-9_11

9. Cincotti, A., Iida, H., Yoshimura, J.: Refinement and complexity in the evolution of chess. In: Proceedings of the 10th International Conference on Computer Science and Informatics, pp. 650–654 (2007)

10. Sutiono, A.P., Purwarianti, A., Iida, H.: A mathematical model of game refinement. In: Reidsma, D., Choi, I., Bargar, R. (eds.) INTETAIN 2014. LNICSSITE, vol. 136, pp. 148–151. Springer, Cham (2014). doi:10.1007/978-3-319-08189-2_22

11. Nossal, N.: Expansion of game refinement theory into continuous movement games with consideration on functional brain measurement. Ph.D. Thesis, Japan Advanced Institution of Science and Technology (2015)

12. Xiong, S., Iida, H.: Attractiveness of real time strategy games. In: 2nd International Conference on Systems and Informatics (ICSAI), pp. 271–276. IEEE (2014)

13. Xiong, S., Zuo, L., Chiewvanichakorn, R., Iida, H.: Quantifying engagement of various games. In: The 19th Game Programming Workshop, pp. 101–106. Information Processing Society of Japan (2014)

14. Iida, H.: Fairness, judges and thrill in games. In: IPSJ-SIG-GI Technical Report, vol. 28, pp. 61–68 (2008)

15. De Groot, A.D.: Thought and Choice in Chess. Mouton Publishers, The Hague (1965)

16. Ranking data of soccer league. http://goal.sports.163.com. Accessed 2017

17. Xiong, S., Tiwary, P.P., Iida, H.: Solving the sophistication-population paradox of game refinement theory. In: Wallner, G., Kriglstein, S., Hlavacs, H., Malaka, R., Lugmayr, A., Yang, H.-S. (eds.) ICEC 2016. LNCS, vol. 9926, pp. 266–271. Springer, Cham (2016). doi:10.1007/978-3-319-46100-7_28

18. Prasertsakul, P., Iida, H., Kondo, T.: Boring game identification: case study using popular sports games. In: SICE Annual Conference, Society of Instrument and Control Engineers (2016)

19. Panumate, C., Iida, H.: Quantifying enjoyment of individual match in games. In: The Annual Conference on Engineering and Applied Science, Higher Education Forum (2016)

20. Groll, A., Schauberger, G., Tutz, G.: Brazil or Germany-who will win the trophy? Prediction of the FIFA World Cup. 2014 based on team-specific regularized Poisson regression (2014)

21. Johnson, D., Nacke, L.E., Wyeth, P.: All about that base: differing player experiences in video game genres and the unique case of moba games. In: Proceedings of the 33rd Annual ACM Conference on Human Factors in Computing Systems, pp. 2265–2274 (2015)

22. Xiong, S., Zahi, H., Zuo, L., Wu, M., Iida, H.: Analysis of the "Heroes of the Storm". Int. J. Adv. Comput. Sci. 4(6), 79–82 (2015)

23. Minotti, M.: League of Legends vs. DOTA2 vs. Smite vs. Heroes of the Storm. http://venturebeat.com/2015/07/15/comparing-mobas-league-of-legends-vs-dota-2-vs-smite-vs-heroes-of-the-storm/

A Framework to Determine the Suitability of Software Development Methodologies for the Development of Location-Based Games

Jacques Barnard, Günther Drevin[✉], and Magda Huisman

School of Computer, Statistical and Mathematical Sciences, North-West University, Potchefstroom Campus, Potchefstroom, South Africa
{gunther.drevin,magda.huisman}@nwu.ac.za

Abstract. To determine the suitability of an SDM (software development methodology) for the development of location-based games, it has to be determined to what degree SDMs address aspects that need to be addressed in the process of developing location-based games. These aspects have been identified from information gathered from the literature and were then validated using a survey. Their importance in the development process was also measured using the survey.

A framework that uses these aspects to determine the suitability of SDMs for the development of location-based games was then developed. Applying this framework to a number of existing SDMs it was found, among other, that in general SDMs are well suited for the development of location-based games as far as value to the player is concerned but that they are very lacking when it comes to security and privacy.

Keywords: Software development methodology · Mobile games

1 Introduction

The gaming industry is expanding rapidly with mobile games becoming an increasingly larger part of the industry. In the 2015 annual report of the Entertainment Software Association (ESA) [10] it was reported that 34% of commuters with a round-trip of more than 3 h play video games while commuting, with smart phones being used the most (80%) followed by tablets (43%). In 2016 the ESA reported that smart phones were used by 36% of gamers, with PCs being used by 56% of gamers and dedicated game consoles by 53% [11].

At the same time the complexity of developing games has increased exponentially [20] with one of the elements that contribute to this complexity being the multidisciplinary development process [8]. The interaction of different specialist areas, such as art, gameplay, sound, control systems, and human factors, with traditional software development, indicates that a specialised software engineering methodology is needed for this domain [8]. Elements that lead to the

N. Munekata et al. (Eds.): ICEC 2017, LNCS 10507, pp. 335–342, 2017.
DOI: 10.1007/978-3-319-66715-7_36

complexity of game development are the technical challenges for the developers as well as tools, project size, workflow and other technical aspects [6].

This paper focuses on location-based games, which can be defined both as a type of ubigame as well as a type of mobile game. Location-based games make use of the player's location and incorporates it in the game play thereby immersing the player even more into the game world [7].

In a previous study unique aspects that need to be addressed during the development of location-based games were identified from the literature and were then validated using a survey. The survey was also used to determine the importance of each of the identified aspects [3, 4].

In this paper these identified aspects are incorporated into a framework that can be used to determine the suitability of an SDM for the development of location-based games. A number of SDMs are then evaluated using the framework.

2 Identified Aspects

A list of 15 aspects was identified from literature that focuses on the development process of games, mobile applications and mobile games. These aspects, as well as their importance (column w), are given in Table 1 [3, 4]. The aspects are listed in decreasing order of importance.

The security and privacy aspect scored an average of 7.11, which is lower than the average of 7.33 for all the aspects. From this it would seem that although security and privacy is important to the developers it is not as important as one would expect in the light of security concerns regarding online activity [15, 24]. To ensure the development of secure location-based games, there should be more emphasis on security and privacy in the development process.

3 Software Development Methodologies

It is important to understand what SDMs are and how they work in order to develop a framework that can be used to evaluate the suitability of an SDM. An SDM can be defined as the totality of a systems development approach in that it is a set of recommended rules, processes and/or steps that need to be followed [2]. Each of these forms part of the total development process that is usually governed by an underlying philosophy that supports, justifies and incorporates coherent context for a specific development project. Furthermore, an SDM identifies the best procedures, phases, tools, techniques, rules, guidelines, documentation and tasks that are to be used, as well as the best manner to execute each of these.

An SDM in itself consists of four main components, namely a philosophical approach, method, process model and tools and techniques that work together to achieve an integrated process with the objective of improving the development of systems [2, 13]. These components make it possible to evaluate, analyse, compare and develop SDMs. The philosophical approach defines the perspective through which the system is developed [2, 20]. The next part of an SDM is the development method and consists of the steps that must be followed during the development process. These steps are executed as specified by the process model. This model therefore dictates the strictness of execution, dependencies and iterations of the steps. Finally, the tools and techniques facilitate the development process [2, 13].

A number of SDMs were evaluated using the framework developed in this study. The SDMs that were chosen for the study are usually associated with game development, mobile development or mobile game development [1, 2, 5, 14, 16, 18]. Furthermore, each SDM has a different combination of philosophical approach, method, process and set of tools and techniques to better represent SDMs that are used for these types of development. The SDMs used in this study are:

- Traditional Systems Development Life Cycle [2, 21]:
  The Traditional Systems Development Life Cycle (SDLC), or Waterfall model, was one of the first SDMs used to develop information systems and was later adapted and used to develop games.
- Scrum [17]:
  The Scrum framework is part of the agile development methodology family along with Extreme Programming and Feature Driven Development.
- MASAM [16]:
  Mobile Application Software Based on Agile Methodology (MASAM) is an agile methodology that focuses on rapid application development. The key goal of this methodology is simple development and fast deployment of new mobile applications.
- Mobile-D [1]:
  Mobile-D is based on Extreme Programming, Crystal Methodologies and Rational Unified Process and is considered to be an agile development approach. This methodology focuses on developing a mobile application in the shortest possible time.
- RAD with DSDM Atern [5, 9]:
  Rapid Application Development (RAD) focuses on developing and delivering high quality systems in the shortest possible time and at the lowest cost. RAD has been implemented as a new methodology, RAD Dynamic Systems Development Method (DSDM).
- MDA Framework [14]:
  Mechanics, Dynamics and Aesthetics framework (MDA) focuses on designing games by breaking the game down into its distinct components; that is rules that lead to the system and in turn lead to fun. After the components have been identified their counterparts for designing the game are identified, namely mechanics that lead to dynamics and in turn lead to aesthetics. The fundamental idea of MDA is that games are more like artifacts than media.
- Playability and Re-playability [18]:
  This methodology is based on the design process of the two key factors that contribute to the success of a game, viz. playability and re-playability. Playability and re-playability can be described in terms of six aspects: social reasons, challenge, experience, mastery, impact, and completion. These six

aspects of playability and re-playability are used to weigh game features and adjust the design phase of the methodology.

- Player-Centred game design [23]:

The basis for this method is that games differ from business applications in that a business application is developed to satisfy the requirements for which the client asked, whereas games are not developed to satisfy the requirements of a client. This complicates the development process, as the game should satisfy different types of game requirements without having been specifically developed for a specific group of direct clients. This is why this method of game design focuses on the players of the game.

4   Evaluation of SDMs

Each of the SDMs chosen for this study was analysed and measured against the aspects identified earlier. Each SDM was awarded a score, which was based on the extent to which the SDM supports all of the the aspects. The results of the evaluation are presented in Table 1. It should be noted that the first author, as well as three independent mobile games developers did the evaluation of the SDMs. The developers were given a blank copy of Table 1 and were asked to score, as a percentage, the extent to which each of the SDMs support each of the aspects in the development process.

4.1   Inter-Coder Reliability

To determine to what extent the four evaluators scored the aspects for each SDM the same, Krippendorff's alpha was used. The norm for a very good reliability is $\alpha >= 0.8$, while $0.8 > \alpha >= 0.67$ indicates a good reliability and $\alpha < 0.67$ should be rejected [12].

The Krippendorff's alphas that were obtained are given in the last line of Table 1. Each of the Krippendorff's alphas in the table represents the reliability of the evaluators' scores with regard to all of the aspects for each of the SDMs. The Krippendorff's alphas are between 0.706 and 0.828 with an average of 0.734. This confirms good inter-coder reliability for the scoring of the aspects and SDMs.

5   Results of Evaluating the SDMs

The summarised results of the evaluation of the SDMs across the aspects are given in Table 1. The weight (w) for each aspect is the importance that the aspect received in the survey. In the first row of each aspect the average scores given by the evaluators for each of the SDMs are given as percentages. The second row of each aspect gives the weighted scores of each of the SDMs for that aspect. The calculations for the framework are discussed below.

Using the weight (w) assigned to an aspect and the average score for an SDM, the framework can be used to score the suitability of each SDM for each aspect.

Table 1. Suitability analysis results

	w	SDLC	Scrum	MASAM	Mobile-D	RAD	MDA	Playability& Re-playability	Player centered	Aspect suitability
Playability	8.81	8.75	20	12.5	12.5	16.25	41.25	93.75	58.75	33%
		77.1	176.2	110.1	110.1	143.2	363.4	825.9	517.6	
Player Experience	8.70	67.5	55	83.75	87.5	84.5	86.25	95.75	95	82%
		587.3	478.5	728.6	761.35	735.2	750.4	833.0	826.5	
Usability	7.93	75.25	66.25	75	22.5	84.25	84.5	90	88.75	73%
		596.7	525.4	594.8	178.4	668.1	670.1	713.7	703.8	
Value to Player	7.67	78.75	82.5	88.75	90	87.5	88.75	93.75	93.75	88%
		604.0	632.8	680.7	690.3	671.1	680.7	719.1	719.1	
UI Design	7.47	17.5	55	81.25	20	78.75	86.25	73.75	77.5	61%
		130.7	410.9	606.9	149.4	588.3	644.3	550.9	578.9	
Development Team	7.37	11.25	87.5	52.5	86.25	88.75	13.75	56.25	86.25	60%
		82.9	644.9	386.9	635.7	654.1	101.3	414.6	635.7	
Re-Playability	7.34	7.5	23.75	10	5	12.5	56.25	95	73.75	35%
		55.1	174.3	73.4	36.7	91.8	412.9	697.3	541.3	
Learnability	7.15	7.5	15	47.5	7.5	41.25	50	57.5	55	35%
		53.6	107.3	339.7	53.6	295.0	357.5	411.1	393.3	
Efficiency	7.11	81.25	7.5	5	6.25	47.5	10	7.5	7.5	22%
		580.1	53.6	35.7	44.6	339.2	71.4	53.6	53.6	
Security & Privacy	7.11	77.5	8.75	5	7.5	43.75	5	5	11.25	20%
		551.0	62.2	35.6	53.3	311.1	35.6	35.6	80.0	
Availability & Accessibility	7.07	10	5	70	2.5	87.5	2.5	7.5	7.5	24%
		70.7	35.4	494.9	17.7	618.7	17.7	53.0	53.0	
Cognitive Support	6.90	68.75	10	56.25	5	42.5	77.5	87.5	86.25	54%
		474.4	69.0	388.1	34.5	293.3	534.8	603.8	595.1	
Compatibility	6.62	81.25	7.5	6.25	55	18.75	26.25	25	10	29%
		537.9	49.7	41.4	364.1	124.1	173.8	165.5	66.2	
Adaptability	6.40	71.25	20	51.25	5	13.75	81.25	82.5	82.5	51%
		456.0	128.0	328.0	32.0	88.0	520.0	528.0	528.0	
Organisational Structure	6.23	50	78.75	50	50	78.75	18.75	53.75	81.25	58%
		311.5	490.6	311.5	311.5	490.6	116.8	334.9	506.2	
Suitability of SDM		47%	37%	47%	32%	56%	50%	63%	62%	
α		0.726	0.743	0.709	0.706	0.828	0.763	0.738	0.733	

This suitability is in the form of a weighted score and is obtained by multiplying the weight (w) for an aspect by the average score that each SDM received for that aspect. For example: the suitability of SDLC for Playability is the weight $w = 8.81$ multiplied by the average score of 8.75 giving the weighted score of 77.1 as shown in Table 1 .

Table 1 also indicates the suitability that an SDM has for all the aspects, as well as the suitability all the SDMs have for a single aspect. Both these suitabilities are given as percentages. The suitability of an SDM for the development of a location-based game is the sum of the weighted scores that the SDM received for each of the aspects. These suitability scores are shown as percentages in Table 1. As can be seen in Table 1, the SDM that was most suitable, with a score of 63%, was Playability and Re-playability, with Mobile-D the least suitable with a score of 32%.

Also given in Table 1 is the degree, on average, to which the SDMs address the different aspects. This value is given in the last column of the table and is the average of the scores assigned by the evaluators. As can be seen in Table 1 the aspect, value to the player, received the highest score (88%), while the aspect, security and privacy, scored the lowest (20%). It is critical that the SDM ensures that the games developers incorporate security and privacy in the development of location-based games.

By evaluating the results of the framework, it is clear that there are a number of inadequacies in the available SDMs. The framework shows this by indicating that the highest suitability percentage for any of the SDMs was 64%. Although the highest scoring aspect across all the SDMs in this framework scored 88%, there are still a number of inadequacies that need to be addressed in the development of location-based games.

6   Conclusions and Future Work

Aspects that need to be addressed during the development of location-based games were identified from the literature and were then validated using an online survey to gather information from the gaming industry to determine the importance of each aspect. These aspects were then incorporated into a framework, which was used to evaluate a number of SDMs.

It was also noted that security and privacy was not regarded as an important aspect in the development process of location-bases games. An example of where more attention to security could have prevented players from getting into harm's way is the recently released Pokémon GO game [19, 22]. The issue of online safety of children has also been raised by the ESA [10].

The result of this study is a framework that can be used to determine the shortcomings of current SDMs for the development of location-based games and can therefore be used as a guide in the development of an SDM that is more suited for the development of location-based games.

References

1. Abrahamsson, P., Hanhineva, A., Hulkko, H., Ihme, T., Jäälinoja, J., Korkala, M., Koskela, J., Kyllönen, P., Salo, O.: Mobile-D: An agile approach for mobile application development. In: Companion to the 19th Annual ACM SIGPLAN Conference on Object-oriented Programming Systems, Languages, and Applications, OOPSLA 2004, NY, USA, pp. 174–175 (2004). http://doi.acm.org/10.1145/1028664.1028736
2. Avison, D., Fitzgerald, G.: Information Systems Development: Methodologies, Techniques and Tools, 3rd edn. McGraw Hill, London (2003)

3. Barnard, J.: A systems development methodology for developing location based games. Ph.D. thesis, Potchefstroom Campus of the North-West University (2017)
4. Barnard, J., Drevin, G., Huisman, M.: Aspects that need to be addressed during the development of location-based games. Technical Report FABWI-N-RKW-2017-525, School of Computer, Statistical and Mathematical Sciences, Potchefstroom Campus, North-West University (2017)
5. Beynon-Davies, P., Holmes, S.: Design breakdowns, scenarios and rapid application development. Inf. Softw. Technol. **44**(10), 579–592 (2002)
6. Blow, J.: Game development: Harder than you think. Queue **1**(10), 28–37 (2004). doi:10.1145/971564.971590
7. Buzeto, F.N., e Silva, T.B.P., Castanho, C.D., Jacobi, R.P.: Reconfigurable games: Games that change with the environment. In: 2014 Brazilian Symposium on Computer Games and Digital Entertainment, pp. 61–70, November 2014
8. Callele, D., Neufeld, E., Schneider, K.: Requirements engineering and the creative process in the video game industry. In: Proceedings of the 13th IEEE International Conference on Requirements Engineering, RE 2005, pp. 240–252 (2005). IEEE Computer Society, Washington, DC. http://dx.doi.org/10.1109/RE.2005.58
9. DSDM-Consortium: DSDM Atern: the Handbook (2008). https://www.dsdm.org/resources/dsdm-handbooks/the-dsdm-agile-project-framework-2014-onwards
10. Entertainment Software Association: Annual report. A year of innovation and achievement (2015). http://www.theesa.com/wp-content/uploads/2016/04/ESA-Annual-Report-2015-1.pdf
11. Entertainment Software Association: Sales, demographic and usage data. Essential facts about the computer and video game industry (2016). http://essentialfacts.theesa.com/Essential-Facts-2016.pdf
12. Hayes, A.F., Krippendorff, K.: Answering the call for a standard reliability measure for coding data. Commun. Methods Meas. **1**(1), 77–89 (2007)
13. Huisman, M., Iivari, J.: Deployment of systems development methodologies: Perceptual congruence between is managers and systems developers. Inf. Manage. **43**(1), 29–49 (2006). doi:10.1016/j.im.2005.01.005
14. Hunicke, R., Leblanc, M., Zubek, R.: MDA: A formal approach to game design and game research. In: Proceedings of the Challenges in Games AI Workshop, Nineteenth National Conference of Artificial Intelligence, pp. 1–5 (2004)
15. Jain, A.K., Shanbhag, D.: Addressing security and privacy risks in mobile applications. IT Prof. **14**, 28–33 (2012)
16. Jeong, Y.J., Lee, J.H., Shin, G.S.: Development process of mobile application SW based on agile methodology. In: 2008 10th International Conference on Advanced Communication Technology, ICACT 2008, vol. 1, pp. 362–366. IEEE (2008)
17. Keith, C.: Agile Game Development with Scrum. Pearson Education, Boston (2010)
18. Krall, J., Menzies, T.: Aspects of replayability and software engineering: Towards a methodology of developing games (2012)
19. Reuters: Pokémon GO: US senator probes maker over data privacy concerns, July 2016. http://gadgets.ndtv.com/apps/news/pokemon-go-us-senator-probes-maker-over-data-privacy-concerns-860167
20. Reyno, E.M., Cubel, J.A.C.: Model-driven game development: 2D platform game prototyping. In: Proceedings of the 13th IEEE International Conference on Requirements Engineering, GAMEON 2008, EUROSIS, Ostend, Belgium, pp. 5–7 (2008)
21. Royce, W.W., et al.: Managing the development of large software systems. In: Proceedings of IEEE WESCON, Los Angeles, vol. 26, pp. 1–9 (1970)

22. Summers, N.: UK children's charity says 'Pokémon GO' needs more safety features. https://www.engadget.com/2016/07/13/nspcc-letter-niantic-pokemon-go/
23. Sykes, J., Federoff, M.: Player-centred game design. In: CHI 2006 Extended Abstracts on Human Factors in Computing Systems, pp. 1731–1734. ACM (2006)
24. Zhu, H., Xiong, H., Ge, Y., Chen, E.: Mobile app recommendations with security and privacy awareness. In: Proceedings of the 20th ACM SIGKDD International Conference on Knowledge Discovery and Data Mining, KDD 2014, pp. 951–960. ACM, New York (2014). http://doi.acm.org/10.1145/2623330.2623705

Vetrina Attori: Scene Seek Support System Focusing on Characters in a Video

Masahiro Narahara[1(✉)], Kohei Matsumura[2],
Roberto Lopez-Gulliver[2], and Haruo Noma[2]

[1] Graduate School of Information Science and Engineering,
Ritsumeikan University, Kusatsu, Shiga 525-8577, Japan
mnarahara@mxdlab.net
[2] College of Information Science and Engineering,
Ritsumeikan University, Kusatsu, Shiga 525-8577, Japan

Abstract. In most video services, users watch only the scenes they are interested in, and look back on the scenes they have watched in the past. In these situations, users typically use a seek bar for seeking scenes of the video. They often have to operate the seek bar many times to get to the desired playback position. In this paper, we aim to support the seeking of specific scenes from video contents. In our preliminary study, we found that users seek scenes depending on when each character appears in the video. Therefore, we designed a system to support seeking scenes using the information of characters. We evaluated the usefulness of our proposed system by comparing it with an existing system. According to our qualitative evaluation, we confirm that our proposed system could ease scene seeking.

Keywords: Scene seeking · Video browsing · Character

1 Introduction

Most Internet users use video services. Video services include video sharing services like YouTube[1] and Niconico[2], and video on-demand services like Netflix[3] and Hulu[4]. The utilization rate of video sharing service reaches 60% to 70% among users [1].

Unlike traditional television broadcasting, the video services have on-demand and interactivity capabilities. On-demand and interactivity allow users to watch video contents at any time and to playback a video from any point of timeline.

Thanks to the on-demand and interactivity capabilities, users enjoy video content in various ways. For example, users watch the same scenes by repeatedly stopping and playing back the video. Some users watch scenes in which a specific character appears in a drama or a movie, or look back on a scene in sports such as baseball. While seeking

---

[1] https://www.youtube.com/.

[2] http://www.nicovideo.jp/.

[3] https://www.netflix.com/.

[4] http://www.hulu.jp/.

© IFIP International Federation for Information Processing 2017
Published by Springer International Publishing AG 2017. All Rights Reserved
N. Munekata et al. (Eds.): ICEC 2017, LNCS 10507, pp. 343–349, 2017.
DOI: 10.1007/978-3-319-66715-7_37

a specific scene in a video, users usually use a seek bar. The seek bar consists of a slider and a thumbnail. The user can change the playback position of a video with the slider and preview the contents of the playback position with the thumbnail. However, with a seek bar and a thumbnail, it is difficult to set the playback position accurately for a specific scene. The user is required to operate the seek bar many times to adjust the appropriate playback position with the thumbnail. Therefore, we aim to ease scene seeking for video contents by enhancing a traditional seek bar.

There are several methods to support scene seeking in videos. Karrer et al. have conducted studies on Direct Manipulation Video Navigation [2, 3]. In the service Pa-League TV, users watch their own interested play scenes of baseball game [4]. Masuda et al. developed a system that can seek scenes by using annotated tags [5, 6]. However, in these methods, they target specific videos, or they require time and effort from users to annotate them using tags. In this paper, we aim to ease seeking scenes regardless of the video structure or video genres and without requiring extra effort from users.

We firstly conducted a preliminary study and found that participants mainly use the information of characters in scenes while seeking scenes. Based on these findings, we then designed a system that uses the information of characters. Our proposed system generates timelines for each character under an existing seek bar. Figure 1 shows the interface of our proposed system. Users seek scenes by using these timelines as clues.

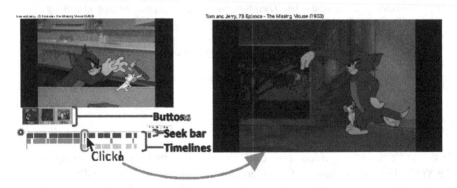

Fig. 1. Interface of our proposed system: Jumping directly to the scene with three characters

Finally, we evaluate and verify the usefulness of our proposed system from quantitative and qualitative perspectives. Participants use both the existing system and our proposed system. Results from the quantitative evaluation show that users took more time to seek scenes by using our proposed system. However, results from the qualitative evaluation show that users felt seeking scenes is easier by using our proposed system.

2   Proposed System Design and Implementation

2.1   Design

We conducted a preliminary study to investigate what kind of information users use as a clue for seeking scenes in video contents. We gave participants a task that seeking scenes in a video. As the result, we found that users seek scenes using characters as a main clue. Therefore, we use the information of characters to support scene seeking in video contents in our proposed system.

Figure 1 shows our proposed system. Our proposed system generates timelines, for each character in the video, under a traditional seek bar. Each of the timelines shows the characters' appearance time. By selecting a button with the face and the name of each character, users can switch on or off the display of that character's timeline. The colored part of the timeline shows the time slots that the character appears in the video. When the user selects multiple buttons, timelines of each character are displayed in rows below. As an example of usage (see Fig. 1): The video "Tom and Jerry, 73 Episode - The Missing Mouse (1953)[5]" has three characters. If the user wants to watch a scene where all the three characters appear at the same time in the video, the user can find the scene by clicking any place where the three timelines overlap. The background color of each button corresponds to the color of each timeline, and the color is different for each character.

2.2   Implementation

Our proposed system is implemented as follows:

1. The system detects and crops the face area of any character as a face image.
2. The system creates a database that associates face images of the characters with their appearance time in the video.

In our current prototype, we manually cut out the face area of the character as cropped face image and associate the characters with their appearance time. We use these to implement and build the timelines.

First, for each image frame of the video the face area is detected from the face feature points of a person in the image, the face area is cropped from the image frame and saved. We plan to methods for face detection from a video. One is a method using Haar-Like features [7]. The Haar-Like feature characterizes an image by the difference in brightness of the image. Masuda et al. proposed a different method based on Takayama's skin color region extraction [8] to detect the face region of animated characters from videos [9].

Second, we classify the extracted face images for each character, and create a database in which the character and its appearance time are associated with each other using the character information and frame number. This enables us to relate the character and its appearance time.

---

[5]   https://www.youtube.com/watch?v=YqGuxOH4Sg4.

3   Evaluation

We conducted a series of experiments to evaluate scene seeking time and ease of use of the system. 30 students (20 males, 10 females) aged 21 to 25 participated in the experiment. They regularly use video services such as YouTube and Netflix. In the experiment, we used six genres videos (movie, animation, music, sports, let's play and animal) that are widely shared and distributed in video services.

In the experiment, we asked participants to use the prototype of our proposed system (Fig. 2 left) and the existing system (Fig. 2 right). We replicated the interface of YouTube to reproduce the existing system. Specifically, it has a seek bar to manipulate the playback position of a video and it displays a thumbnail when the pointer is placed on the seek bar.

Fig. 2. Systems used in the evaluation (Left is the prototype of our proposed system. Right is the existing system.)

3.1   Procedure

We explain participants how to use our proposed system and ask them to actually use our proposed system on a test video. After that, we give the participants a task. The task consists of: given a still image from the video as target, seek a scene matching that target image. Participants use our proposed system in three videos chosen randomly and use the existing system in the remaining three videos. Order of videos is randomized and we chose the still image at random. Participants use a laptop computer to watch videos and to seek scenes. We display the still images on the tablet device. The still images are the scenes that another participants chose as interesting scenes in our preliminary study. There are three still images per video. We observe and video record participants during tasks. We ask participants to speak out what they think during the task (think aloud method). After the task, we interview participants.

We evaluate the usefulness of our proposed system from both quantitative and qualitative perspectives. For the quantitative analysis, we compare the difference of seeking time between our proposed system and the existing system. For the qualitative analysis, we conduct a semi-structured interview to participants.

3.2 Results

3.2.1 Quantitative Evaluation

Figure 3 shows the average scene seeking time using the existing system and our proposed system. In the existing system, the overall average time is 75.0 s and the standard deviation is 63.5. In our proposed system, the overall average time is 98.5 s and the standard deviation is 96.9. A two-tailed t-test ($\alpha = 0.05$) shows a significant difference in the overall average scene seeking time using the existing system and our proposed system ($p = 0.033 < 0.05$). There is no significant difference in genres other than sports ($p = 0.012 < 0.05$). We think that the reason why the standard deviations are quite large is due to the difficulty of tasks is different depending on still images. Some still images were easy to find and some were difficult to find. From these results, we see that users take more time to seek scenes by using our proposed system.

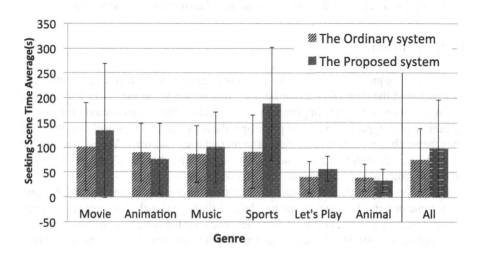

Fig. 3. Results of quantitative evaluation

3.2.2 Qualitative Evaluation

Most (26 out of 30) participants reported that seeking scenes feels faster while using our proposed system than the existing one. We found that users felt seeking scenes is faster because our proposed system can reduce the timeline range that they need to seek, as indicated by comments such as "*I could seek a scene easily because the system narrows down the seeking range for me*", "*It is useful because I can find when characters appear and I don't need to seek too many scenes*" and "*I think it is an advantage that I need to seek only the highlighted timeline range.*"

Users would prefer using our proposed system when they want to watch scenes that they are interested in, as indicated by comments such as "*I can find scenes easily if characters appear only in specific scenes in a video*", and "*When I want to watch only scenes where my favorite character appears, it is useful.*"

Users would not want to use our proposed system when they watch videos having many similar scenes or when they want to seek scenes with other information, as indicated by comments such as *"If the same characters appear often, there are many similar scenes and it is hard to find the scenes in the timelines"*, *"If the same character is appearing from the beginning to the end, eventually I need to watch everything from the beginning"* and *"When I want to seek scenes by using the information of serifs, I can not use this system."*

In our proposed system, there are still some usage difficulties on the interface and improvement points remain, as indicated by comments such as *"If the same character appears in video from the beginning to the end, I want to seek scenes by using the information of the background rather than characters"*, *"Because the face of all characters can be seen as face buttons from the beginning, it spoils users who have not be seen the video before"*, *"I wish I could zoom in a specific location of the timeline a bit more finely"* and *"The timelines are so small that I cannot specify the location."*

4 Conclusion

In this paper, we proposed a system for supporting scene seeking in video contents using information of the characters. From our experiment, we found that users felt faster in seeking scenes while using our proposed system and we also found several problems in our current prototype. In the current prototype, the interface becomes hard to understand when the number of characters is large or the character appears often. We plan to improve the method by changing the way the system displays the characters' buttons or to add the functionality to expand the relevant parts of the timeline.

Our proposed system can visualize the structure of video as timelines. Figure 4 shows an example in a music video. In the first half of the video, each character appears one by one. After passing the climax, all character appears at the same time in most of scenes. Our proposed system allows users to understand the structure such as verse and climax

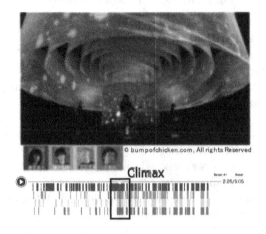

Fig. 4. Example of visualizing the structure of a video

while playing a music video. There is a possibility that our proposed system can also visualize the structure of other videos as a novel video player.

References

1. Ministry of Internal Affairs and Communications. http://www.soumu.go.jp/johotsusintokei/linkdata/h28_02_houkoku.pdf. Accessed 10 Apr 2017
2. Karrer, T., Weiss, M., Lee, E., Borchers, J.: DRAGON: a direct manipulation interface for frame-accurate in-scene video navigation. In: Proceedings of the SIGCHI Conference on Human Factors in Computing Systems, pp. 247–250. ACM (2008)
3. Karrer, T., Wittenhagen, M., Borchers, J.: DragLocks: handling temporal ambiguities in direct manipulation video navigation. In: Proceedings of the SIGCHI Conference on Human Factors in Computing Systems, pp. 623–626. ACM (2012)
4. Pacific-league TV. http://tv.pacificleague.jp/. Accessed 10 Apr 2017
5. Yamamoto, D., Ohira, S., Nagao, K.: Weblog-style video annotation and syndication. In: 2005 First International Conference on Automated Production of Cross Media Content for Multi-Channel Distribution, AXMEDIS 2005, p. 4. IEEE (2005)
6. Masuda, T., Yamamoto, D., Ohira, S., Nagao, K.: Video scene retrieval using online video annotation. In: Satoh, K., Inokuchi, A., Nagao, K., Kawamura, T. (eds.) JSAI 2007. LNCS, vol. 4914, pp. 54–62. Springer, Heidelberg (2008). doi:10.1007/978-3-540-78197-4_7
7. Papageorgiou, C.P., Oren, M., Poggio, T.: A general framework for object detection. In: 1998 Sixth International Conference on Computer Vision, pp. 555–562. IEEE (1998)
8. Takayama, K., Johan, H., Nishita, T.: Face detection and face recognition of cartoon characters using feature extraction. In: Image, Electronics and Visual Computing Workshop, p. 48 (2012)
9. Masuda, T., Hirai, T., Ohya, H., Morishima, S.: Recommending scenes of 2D characters based on image similarity in region of interest. In: Information Processing Society of Japan, pp. 601–602 (2013)

Poster and Interactive Session

Mining Preferences on Identifying Werewolf Players from Werewolf Game Logs

Yuki Hatori, Shuang Wu, Youchao Lin, and Takehito Utsuro[✉]

Graduate School of Systems and Information Engineering, University of Tsukuba,
Tsukuba, Japan
utsuro_@_iit.tsukuba.ac.jp

Abstract. The deception party game *"Are You a Werewolf?"* requires
players to guess other's roles through discussions that are based on one's
own role and other players' crucial utterances. This paper proposes a
method to mine the empirical preference data used to identify *werewolves*
from game logs. This involves obtaining an empirical preference related
to the practice of divination. In this method, if one of the three players
revealing oneself as a *seer* divines a player as a *human*, while the other
two players divine the player as a *werewolf*, then it can be judged that
the divined player's role is a *werewolf*.

Keywords: The werewolf game · *"Are You a Werewolf?"* · Game logs ·
Mining

1   Introduction

"Are you a werewolf?" is a party game that was created by the USSR in 1986. It
models a conflict between an informed minority, the werewolf, and an uninformed
majority, the villagers. The werewolf game has been popular in many countries
including Japan where it has inspired several other activities. Some of these
related activities include *Werewolf* TLPT (Werewolf: The live playing theater),
a live improvisation where the actors and actresses play the werewolf game, and
a TV variety show where comedians, actors, and actresses play the werewolf
game.

In the research community of artificial intelligence (AI), the werewolf game
is well known as one with imperfect information where certain information is
hidden from some players. This is contrary to games that provide players with
complete information such as chess, shogi, and go, where computer programs
won against a human champion. Within the Japanese research community, the
werewolf game has been employed to evaluate the performance of AI systems
since 2014 [2] which has inspired researchers to develop computer-agent programs
that actively participate in the werewolf game. The first Artificial Intelligence-
Based Werewolf (AIWolf) competition was held in August 2015.

© IFIP International Federation for Information Processing 2017
Published by Springer International Publishing AG 2017. All Rights Reserved
N. Munekata et al. (Eds.): ICEC 2017, LNCS 10507, pp. 353–356, 2017.
DOI: 10.1007/978-3-319-66715-7_38

However, in previous studies aiming at developing a computer-agent program that participates in the werewolf game tended to overlook research issues that are closely related to natural language processing and knowledge processing. These higher-level research issues include (i) understanding natural language conversations among the participants, (ii) inferring each player's roles on the basis of their utterances in game-related conversations, and (iii) deciding which player is the werewolf based on high-level inference.

The goal of this paper is to construct an agent that is able to analyze players' utterances and take an active role in the werewolf game. Firstly, we propose a method to mine empirical preferences used to identify *werewolf* players using game logs[1]. We obtain an empirical preference related to the practice of divination where, if one of the three players reveals himself as a seer divines a player as a *human*, while the other two players divine the player as a *werewolf*, then it can be judged that the divined player's role is the *werewolf*.

2   Mining a Preference Based on Conflict of Divination

Among these preferences related to correctly identifying a *werewolf*, our method employs the act of divination. We especially focus on the case where more than one player reveals themselves as *seers* yet their divination encounters a conflict. More specifically, we concentrate on the case shown in Fig. 1, where three players reveal themselves as *seers*, among whom one player divines a player as a *human*, while the other two players divine the player as a *werewolf*. Then, as a result of mining a preference to correctly identify a *werewolf*, in this case, we can judge that the divined player's role is actually a *werewolf*.

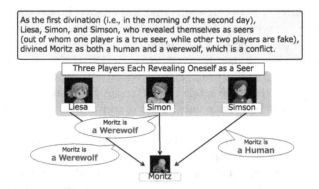

Fig. 1. An example of a conflict of divination

---

[1] We use WolfBBS (http://ninjin002.x0.com/wolff/ (in Japanese)) werewolf game log data. This is a werewolf game site on the Internet, where the players communicate with each other via a character-based text input communication channel. This werewolf game site keeps a record of the text data of the previous werewolf game logs and makes them publicly available.

Table 1. Distribution of the variation of divination when one or more players reveal themselves as seers

(a) Distribution of the variation of a human and a werewolf in divination

Variation of divination	# of games (%)
Only a *human*	37 (56.9)
Only a *werewolf*	0 (0)
Mixture of a *human* and a *werewolf*	28 (43.1)
Total	65 (100)

(b) Rate of games where the true role of the divined player being a werewolf when the variation of divination is the mixture of a human and a werewolf

Variation of divination	# of games (%)	# of games where the true role of the divined player being a werewolf (%)
A *human* and a *werewolf*	9 (32.1)	4 (44.4)
A *human*, a *human*, and a *werewolf*	12 (42.9)	4 (33.3)
A *human*, a *werewolf*, and a *werewolf*	7 (25.0)	7 (100)
Total	28 (100)	15 (53.6)

Before we mined the preference introduced above, we first randomly selected 65 game logs from the WolfBBS site. In every game, the *seers* are assumed to reveal themselves. Thus, in every game, one or more players will reveal themselves as *seers*. Considering this, in each of the randomly selected 65 games, we examine the result of the first divination (i.e., on the morning of the second day) by the player(s) who reveal themselves as *seer(s)*. Here, the variation of the divination by one or more player(s) who reveal themselves as *seer(s)* are among the following three: i.e., only a *human*, only a *werewolf*, and the mixture of a *human* and a *werewolf*. Table 1(a) shows the distribution of those three variations within the 65 games, where it is quite interesting to note that there is no observation of the divination variation as only a *werewolf*[2].

We further concentrate on those 28 games where the variation of the divination is the mixture of a *human* and a *werewolf*. Table 1(b) shows the distribution of the detailed variation of the divination, i.e., divination by two players as a *human* and a *werewolf*, divination by three players as:

- a *human*, a *human*, and a *werewolf*,
- and a *human*, a *werewolf*, and a *werewolf*.

For each of those three variations, Table 1(b) also shows the rate of the divined player's true role being a *werewolf*. This result clearly shows that the divined player is always a *werewolf* when the variation of the divination is a *human*, a *werewolf*, and a *werewolf*. Thus, we successfully mine a 100% correct preference in identifying a *werewolf* player that is based on the conflict in the divination process.

---

[2] This is simply because the werewolves' side usually do not abandon a true werewolf player by divining him/her as a werewolf.

Table 2. Variations of the roles of the three players who reveal themselves as seers and divine (when the three players revealing themselves as seers each divine a player as a *human*, a *werewolf*, and a *werewolf*)

Variation of divination	# of games (%)
(a) the seer divines the player as a *human*, the *werewolf* and *possessed* divine the player as a *werewolf*	0 (0)
(b) the *werewolf* divines the player as a *human*, the *seer* and possessed divine the player as a *werewolf*	0 (0)
(c) the possessed divines the player as a *human*, the *seer* and *werewolf* divine the player as a *werewolf*	7 (100)
Total	7 (100)

For the seven cases of the variation of the divination being a *human*, a *were-wolf*, and a *werewolf*, Table 2 further examines the variation of the true roles of the three players who reveal themselves as *seers*. Again, it is quite interesting to note that in all of those seven cases, the *possessed* divine the player as a *human*, while the *seer* and the *werewolf* divine him/her as a *werewolf* (i.e., case (c)). The reason why the *werewolf* tends to take this strategy of following the *seer's* divination but abandoning the divined true *werewolf* player is to simply avoid being executed even after the divined true *werewolf* player is executed and is exposed as a *werewolf*. Also, a *werewolf* does not tend to take the strategies in cases (a) and (b) in Table 2 simply because they avoid taking the risk of being exposed as a werewolf but take on the strategy of abandoning the divined true *werewolf* player (case (b)), or not taking the strategy of divining a *human* player as a *werewolf* (case (a)).

3   Conclusion

This paper proposed a method of mining empirical preferences of identifying werewolf players from game logs. In terms of the related work on developing a computer-agent program that participates in the werewolf game, most studies have examined face-to-face werewolf games and analyzed the non-verbal audio cues, physical gestures, and conversational features such as speaker turns (e.g., Chittaranjan and Hung [1]).

References

1. Chittaranjan, G., Hung, H.: Are you a werewolf? detecting deceptive roles and outcomes in a conversational role-playing game. In: Proceedings ICASSP, pp. 5334–5337 (2010)
2. Shinoda, T., et al.: "Are you a Werewolf?" becomes a standard problem for general artificial intelligence. In: Proceedings 28th Annual Conference JSAI (2014). (in Japanese)

Identifying Rush Strategies Employed in StarCraft II Using Support Vector Machines

Teguh Budianto[1], Hyunwoo Oh[2], Yi Ding[1], Zi Long[1], and Takehito Utsuro[1(✉)]

[1] Graduate School of Systems and Information Engineering,
University of Tsukuba, Tsukuba, Japan
utsuro_@iit.tsukuba.ac.jp
[2] Graduate School of Interdisciplinary Information Studies,
The University of Tokyo, Tokyo, Japan

Abstract. This paper studies the strategies used in StarCraft II, a real-time strategy game (RTS) wherein two sides fight against each other in a battlefield context. We propose an approach which automatically classifies StarCraft II game-log collections into rush and non-rush strategies using a support vector machine (SVM). To achieve this, three types of features are evaluated: (i) the upper bound of variance in time series for the numbers of workers, (ii) the upper bound of the numbers of workers at a specific time, and (iii) the lower bound of the start time for building the second base. Thus, by evaluating these features, we obtain the optimal parameters combinations.

Keywords: Real-time strategy game · StarCraft II · Rush strategy

1 Introduction

Real-time strategy (RTS) games make up a popular on line computer game genre wherein two sides fight against each other in a battlefield context. The players are required to gather specific resources to develop their combat strengths in the form of advanced buildings, technologies, and armies. Unlike other strategy games such as Go and Chess wherein complete information on the state of play is provided to both players, information in RTS games is limited and rapidly changes as the player's resources respond to various factors. Moreover, RTS game environments are formed from complex and dynamic sets of information depending on the actions taken by the players. These characteristics contribute to the game's difficulty level and prevent the improvement of RTS-based AI technologies. In this paper, the strategies employed in StarCraft II, a well-known RTS game, are analyzed. These strategies form the most important aspect of competing with opponent's playing styles in order to ultimately win the game. Liu et al. [2] investigated the player's styles to predict their future actions. This type

© IFIP International Federation for Information Processing 2017
Published by Springer International Publishing AG 2017. All Rights Reserved
N. Munekata et al. (Eds.): ICEC 2017, LNCS 10507, pp. 357–361, 2017.
DOI: 10.1007/978-3-319-66715-7_39

of analysis can aid human players to judge opponent's strategies and accordingly decide a defense strategy. An incorrect strategy judgment about an opponent's game plan and the resultant poor choice of action in StarCraft II leads to the selection of an inappropriate defense strategy which harms the player's strength. Thus, strategy identification in RTS games has become a prominent research area, including strategy prediction and strategy modeling. Studies focusing on strategy prediction also employ data mining techniques [3] and machine-learning approaches [1]. Improvements in strategy identification contribute to the advancement of RTS-game-based AI in order to discover the most effective strategies that human players can employ depending on their opponent's plan of action.

Considering these factors, this paper examines the strategies used in StarCraft II by classifying them into two main categories: rush and non-rush strategies. A rush strategy involves players that perform sudden attacks on an opponent's base as early as possible in the game. This strategy aims to interfere with the opponent's movements at the early stages of the game. Conversely, in a non-rush strategy, the players mainly focus on development (i.e., producing more workers and upgrading technologies) rather than attacking the opponent base. Therefore, to examine the strategies of the players, we designed a support vector machine (SVM)-based model that automatically classifies StarCraft II game logs into rush and non-rush strategies.

2   Game-Log Features and the Evaluation Procedure

We collected 5,150 one-vs.-one game replays of StarCraft II from http://www.spawningtool.com. All replay files were extracted into human-readable logs using a Python library: sc2reader[1]. Our study only focuses on the games between high-level players. This produced 753 game logs wherein each sample comprises a single player's game log, as summarized in Table 1.

Table 1. Data set for evaluation

Logs	Number of game logs
Rush strategy	137
Non-rush strategy	616
Total logs	753

We propose several types of features that are closely related to the number of workers each player has in a rush game. In particular, a major difference tends to exist between the number of workers on both sides. Generally, a player not employing rush strategy continues producing a much higher number of workers

---

[1] https://github.com/GraylinKim/sc2reader.

since the beginning of the game, while a player adopting a rush strategy produces only a moderate number of workers and stops production at a particular time. Thus, by considering these phenomena, we designed features based on the variance between the time-series number of workers and the number of workers at a specific time. We use the information about the number of workers a player has produced up until a certain time. The reason for this is because players cannot have a complete control over the number of workers each player possess at a certain time. In addition, we examine time required for constructing the second base (a building for collecting resources) in order to further design our features. We observe the differences in the timing of construction of the second bases of both players. Players employing a rush strategy do not necessarily build their second base as early as possible; however, it is expected that these players build their second base before a certain time. Based on the above observation, we propose three types of features: f_{vw}, f_{nw}, and f_b (Table 2).

Table 2. Features of a game log x

Features		Variables of x	
Upper bound of the variance of time-series number of workers $f_{vw}(x; u_0, d_0, e_0) = (x.f_{vw}^v \leq u_0) \wedge (x.f_{vw}^d = d_0) \wedge (x.f_{vw}^e = e_0)$	$x.f_{vw}^v$	Variance of x	
	$x.f_{vw}^d$	Time for calculating variance [s]	
	$x.f_{vw}^e$	End time of calculating variance [s]	
Upper bound of number of workers at a specific time $f_{nw}(x; t_0, n_0) = (x.f_{nw}^t = t_0) \wedge (x.f_{nw}^n \leq n_0)$	$x.f_{nw}^t$	Specific time [s]	
	$x.f_{nw}^n$	Number of workers	
Lower bound of the start time of second base construction $f_b(x; t_0) = (x.f_b^t \geq t_0)$	$x.f_b^t$	Start time of second base construction [s]	

In our proposed feature-based design, the parameter combinations of the three feature functions were examined to determine the optimal parameter combinations. For f_{vw}, the parameter combinations were examined by changing v_0 from 0 to 2, d_0 from 60 to 300, and e_0 from 240 to 360. For f_{nw}, the parameter combinations were examined by changing t_0 from 300 to 600 and n_0 from 25 to 40. Finally, for f_b, the parameter combination was examined by changing t_0 from 60 to 360. We first divided our data set into 10 subsets of equal size to perform 10-fold cross validation. From the training data of each fold, the optimal parameters combinations of each three feature functions f_{vw}, f_{nw}, and f_b were identified from the combinations possessing maximum recall, precision, and f-measure. Based on this procedure, each feature function generated three optimal parameter combinations in total resulting in nine optimal parameter combinations for each fold. Next, we created and implemented a feature vector constructed from these nine features. Each features represents a parameter of a set of optimal parameter combinations. Our design eventually resulted in 10 different sets of optimal parameter combinations, which we used to train the SVM classifier.

3   Evaluation of Results

We used the confidence in SVM to calculate the performance of each fold of our approach using recall and precision. Further, we generated the average performance curve of our approach, as shown in Fig. 1. The curves use 11 points plotted from 0 to 100 in order to display the average performance. We generalized the recall value of each fold to the closest position among these 11 points. Each of the three baseline curves was produced by removing each set of optimal parameter combinations of the three feature functions from the evaluation. Removing f_{nw} from the evaluation degraded its baseline performance. Probably, this occurred because the differences between the number of workers at a specific time has a significant impact on a rush game. Considering the overall performance, the F-score of the proposed design shows the highest value among all three baselines. Thus, considering the above, we found that there is a significant correlation between the optimal parameter combinations of the three features functions. This indicates that the proposed design incorporating all the combinations worked better than the design considering each combination separately. Therefore, the proposed design could possibly be effective in identifying the use of rush strategies in RTS game-logs-collections.

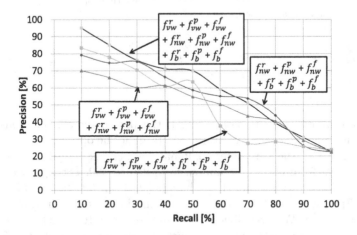

Fig. 1. Recall and precision curve of the overall design

4 Conclusions

This study proposed a method to identify the rush and non-rush strategies employed by players from RTS game logs. We examined nine optimal parameter combinations of the three feature functions f_{vw}, f_{nw}, and f_b. These combinations along with an SVM were used as the basis for constructing the features that could accurately identify a player's use of a rush strategy.

References

1. Park, H., et al.: Prediction of early stage opponents strategy for StarCraft AI using scouting and machine learning. In: Proceedings of the WASA, pp. 7–12 (2012)
2. Liu, S., et al.: Player identification from RTS game replays. In: Proceedings of the 28th CATA, pp. 313–317 (2013)
3. Weber, B.G., Mateas, M.: A data mining approach to strategy prediction. In: Proceedings of the 5th CIG, pp. 140–147 (2009)

Distorted Cartogram Visualization for Travelers

Jong-Chul Yoon, Jong-Sung Hong, and In Seob Yoon[✉]

Department of Broadcasting Technology, Kangwon National University,
Chuncheon, South Korea
{media19,jshong,isyoon}@kangwon.ac.kr

Abstract. Most maps are generated based on measures of distance. However, the time required to reach a points of interest can be more important than the distance for a tourist because it directly indicates availability. We propose a novel geographical visualization technique that represents cartography in terms of the time required to travel between the points of interest rather than the distance. Congestion makes areas of the map expand, whereas ideal traffic conditions make the map shrink in comparison to the actual distance scale of a traditional map. The proposed map visualization application enables a more intuitive scheduling for travelers.

Keywords: Cartogram · Geographic visualization · Web application

1 Introduction

Maps provide a simple, yet powerful visualization of geospatial information. Many maps are constructed to representationally reflect geospatial dimensions. Because maps faithfully reflect real-world geography (or try to reflect the three-dimensional Earth as a two dimensional construct as effectively as possible), individuals can intuitively estimate the distance between two points on a map by measuring the distance between them and multiplying this distance by some scale to determine a "real-world" equivalent. The concept of some distance between two points is quite naturally related to the cognitive notion of spatial availability. The proximity of two places is strongly related to how accessible they are from each other; therefore, the construction of a two-dimensional map based on spatial references effectively relates accessibility between places to the user. Unfortunately, proximity may not always predicate the most efficient accessibility. For representing spatial availability, a more direct metric than distance is time.

In this paper, we introduce a time-based distorted map visualization application for travelers. Travelers need scheduling to see many points of interest (POI) in limited time. As shown in Fig. 1(a), existing maps can be expressed as close to absolute distance without considering of roads or traffic volumes. This type of erroneous distance measurement can lead to a wrong schedule for a traveler (see Fig. 1(b)), and it would likely lead to a waste of time. However, our proposed map can realize more stable scheduling is possible because it is stretched based on the actual arrival time as shown in Fig. 1(c). For time-based map visualization, we use a classical dimension reduction technique to

N. Munekata et al. (Eds.): ICEC 2017, LNCS 10507, pp. 362–365, 2017.
DOI: 10.1007/978-3-319-66715-7_40

adjust the position between POIs and we propose a distortion method that maintains the shape of the entire map as much as possible based on the POI positions.

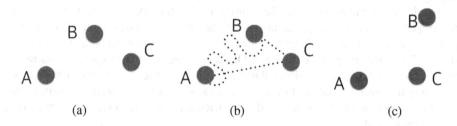

Fig. 1. Concept of time-based distorted map: (a) three POI at the absolute distance based map; (b) road connection information between POI; (c) POI coordinates changed based on arrival time.

With the growing interest in travel time, many researchers have tried to anticipate traffic situations by using various techniques. As a result, many interesting services have been made available to the public. For example, walk score marks a score for every location based on the travel time to surrounding amenities [1]. Traffigram [2] visualizes isochronous contours from a single position to represent arrival times. However, this study considers only the relation between the starting point and the sample points, and the relation between POIs is difficult to apply. We propose a new visualization technique that overcomes these limitations.

2   Time-Based Distortion Map Generation

2.1   POI Position Calculation Based on the Arrival Time

This study proposes a map distortion method based on each arrival time for a limited number of POIs. We tested this method in the Seattle area. To select POIs, 10 major sightseeing spots provided by TripAdvisor [3] were extracted (Chihuly Garden and Glass, The Museum of Flight, Washington State Ferries, Pike Place Market, Safeco Field, Kerry Park, Sky View Observatory, Space Needle, Benaroya Hall and Hiram M. Chittenden Locks). The travel time between the selected POIs was measured using the Google Maps API. Let the extracted arrival time be $T(x_i, x_j)$ which has a symmetric matrix form (where x is the POI position). We use the classical dimension reduction technique to change the POI position based on the reaching time. Multi-dimensional scaling (MDS) [4] is a traditional dimensional reduction method that has been used in various fields to analyze or visualize nonlinear data sets. MDS is based on the conservation of Euclidian distance in embedded data. If x_i is the original position of the POI and y_i is the embedded position of the POI based on the arrival time $T(x,y)$, then the objective function for MDS can be descried as follows:

$$F = \sum_{i}^{n} \left| T(x_i, x_j) - d(y_i, y_j) \right|^2, \tag{1}$$

where, $d(y_i,y_j)$ r represents the Euclidean distance between the calculated POI positions. By minimizing the change between the arrival time and the Euclidean distance, MDS largely conserves the relationships among the POI positions based on the arrival time. The limitation of the MDS is that the position y_i, which is changes position according to the metric T, may deviate from the original data range and orientation. To solve this problem, we used indiscal [5] as extended dimension reduction technique that solves the MDS problem by placing the four POIs at the outermost points as the constraint. Indiscal is a sequential dimension reduction method that uses weight type constraints. We apply the inverse number of the difference value between the original position and the changed position as the weight of the extracted four extracted POIs to minimize the overall movement.

2.2 Distorted Map Visualization

By using the calculated positions y_i, we warp the traditional map to the generate a geotemporal cartogram. For this distortion, we use thin-plate spline-based warping (TPS). TPS is a well-known algorithm for various warping applications owing to its low computational cost [6], and it has been widely used as a non-rigid transformation model for image alignment and shape matching. Furthermore, it provides closed-form solutions for interactive-timed warping and it can generate smooth maps while well preserving source images. For implementing this algorithm, we use the Google Maps Javascript API. Furthermore because the existing google map is too complex to represent POI effectively, we design a simple map that expresses representative roads and POI. In addition, in order to make it easier to compare the deformations of existing maps and distorted maps, we visualize the results of TPS warping in grid form, thereby enabling the user to easily grasp the degree of transformation.

3   Experimental Results and Conclusions

Figure 2 shows a demo of our proposed system. Figure 2(a) shows the result of visualization the original POI position on the abstracted map. Figure 2(b) shows the result of the distorted map based on the arrival time. For a POI located in the city, the results are relatively different owing to the increase in traffic volume and road complexity. POIs on the outskirts of the city tend to have poorer road accessibility. By using these visualization results, the traveler can determine a more efficient order for visiting various destinations. In addition, when a POI is added at the traveler's accommodation location, the arrival time at the starting point can be recognized easily.

Our proposed system uses a distorted map visualization technique based on the time of arrival for multiple POIs. This technique can be used for road planning beyond the purpose of travelers. One limitation of this system is that it cannot check the real-time road traffic volume; instead, it uses the traffic volume from the sampled time. We are currently developing a system that is distorted in real time by using an additional function of Google Maps. In addition, various experiments on the design method for map visualization are required, and a verification through a user test will be conducted.

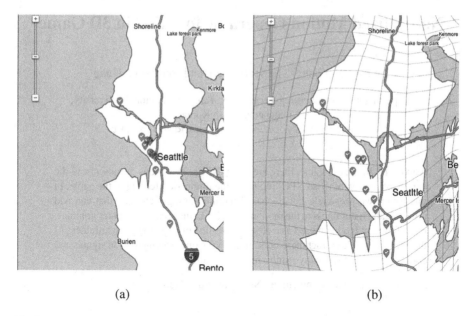

(a)   (b)

Fig. 2. Time-based distorted map for traveler: (a) abstraction map with ten POI which constructed by original map position; (b) distorted map by TPS warping by using the arrival time between ten POI.

Acknowledgements. This research was supported by 2014 Research Grant from Kangwon National University(No. 220140146) and Basic Science Research Program through the National Research Foundation of Korea(NRF) funded by the Ministry of Education, Science and Technology (NRF-2017R1D1A3B03033656).

References

1. Lightfoot, C., Steinberg, T.: Travel-time Maps and their Uses (2006). http://www.mysociety.org/2006/travel-time-maps
2. Hong, S.R., Kim, Y.-S., Yoon, J.-C., Aragon, C.R.: Traffigram: distortion for clarification via isochronal cartography. In: Proceedings of the SIGCHI Conference on Human Factors in Computing Systems (2014)
3. https://www.tripadvisor.com (2017)
4. Jain, A.K., Dubes, R.C.: Algorithms for Clustering Data. Prentice Hall, Upper Saddle River (1988)
5. Barra, J.R., Brodeau, F., Romier, G., van Cutsem, B.: Recent Developments in Statistics. American Statistical Association (1978)
6. Wahba, G.: Spline Models for Observational Data. Society for Industrial and Applied Mathematics, Philadelphia (1990)

Naturalized Motion Generator for NPC in 3D Game

Jong-Chul Yoon[✉], In Seob Yoon, and Jong-Sung Hong

Department of Broadcasting Technology, Kangwon National University,
Chuncheon, South Korea
{media19,isyoon,jshong}@kangwon.ac.kr

Abstract. In the 3D game, there are many NPCs for various purposes, and the variety of motion of these NPCs increases the immersion feeling of the game. In this paper, we propose a noise - based motion editing technique that can add diversity and naturalness to the motion of NPCs. In the area of computer graphics, noise function has been used as a classical method of applying the naturalness of the animation. We extract these noise functions from existing motion signals and control them to make many similar motions naturally.

Keywords: Character animation · Noise function · Noise fitting

1 Introduction

The NPC in the game is widely used as a hint to help the game progress or as an element to increase the fun factor. Most of these NPCs take only simplified motions because of the limitation of production, and these limited motions act as an obstacle to the immersion feeling of the game. To solve this simplicity, we propose a technique for applying styles to npc movements. In order to generate stable motion without special attention of the game maker, we propose a technique to change the motion richly using the noise function which is a classical computer graphics element.

Since Perlin [1] introduced the noise function, it has been used in various computer graphics applications for adding random patterns to naive animations or to produce procedural textures. Using noise function, we extract motion pattern from existing motions as non-uniform hierarchical functions, which we can then apply to synthesize new motions with similar characteristics. Users can control the randomness at specified frequencies by varying the parameters of the noise function, while preserving the features of the motion pattern. The advantage of Perlin's classical noise function compared to the various noise functions for the recently introduced anti-aliasing enhanced rendering [2, 3] is that Perlin noise is generated for a given random table. Since the motion of a each joint forms of a one-dimensional signal. it can be extracted as a sum of noise function and it is possible to generate a new motion with similar but diversity when the transformation is applied to the random table. Our system proposes a method to easily generate multiple similar motions using this noise function.

N. Munekata et al. (Eds.): ICEC 2017, LNCS 10507, pp. 366–369, 2017.
DOI: 10.1007/978-3-319-66715-7_41

2   Motion Analysis Based on the Noise Function

To construct a noise function that represents the motion signal, we need to find the representative frequency of motion signal. We use the discrete Fourier transform (DFT) to derive the representative frequency. Because general motion signal has a various frequencies, we use method of statistical stability to extract representative frequency which was introduced by Dischler and Ghazanfarpour [4]. Let fr be a representative frequency of given motion signal, then we can design the Perlin noise function as follows:

$$N(t) = Noise(f_r \cdot t), \tag{1}$$

where, t represent time parameter. Since our purpose is to represent the motion signal as a noise function, we need to fit a normalized motion signal is $S(t)$ to a noise function. We design the objective function which changes the random number table of the noise function newly and it to be as similar as possible to the given motion signal as follows:

$$\text{minimize} \sum_{i=1}^{n} (S(t) - N(t))^2 \tag{2}$$

The above optimization problem minimizes the squared difference between the noise value and the motion signal. We used the sequential equality constrained quadratic programming method [5] with the active-set technique [6] to solve the optimization problem.

As mentioned above, since the motion signal contains various frequencies, it is difficult to fit the entire motion signal with a noise function of a single frequency. So we have designed an iterative noise extraction algorithm which generates a function of pyramidal form. If we extract noise of a single frequency from motion signal that possibly includes frequencies outside that range, then fitting that single frequency noise may not match real motion signal particularly well. Nevertheless, a noise function

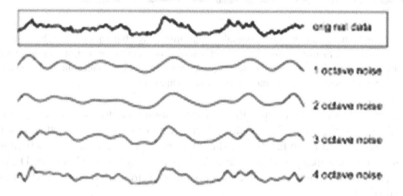

Fig. 1. Motion signal fitting by multiple noise function: refining the extracted noise using a hierarchical noise function.

obtained in this way will still approximate the input date to some extent, so the resulting error value have lower amplitude than the original motion signal. Therefore we find representative frequency of error signal and than fit the noise interactively until the error is smaller than a given threshold; the result is in the form of a fractal sum. Using this mechanism, which we call the noise pyramid, we can extract motion signal for various frequencies (see Fig. 1). The more octaves we use, the better the approximation that can be achieved.

3   Similar Motion Generation for NPC

To test our noise-based system, we selected a simple walking motion and a drunken motion and extracted the difference between the two motion as a noise pyramid. Since the noise function can generate random signals at infinite time, we can generate various similar motions with different time parameters. In an extended tome domain, the noise function repeatedly computes the similar patterns. This is because we preserve the statistical characteristics of the extracted pattern by retaining the distribution of random number table of noise function. Using this property, we simulate a crowd NPC motion by varying different frequencies. As shown Fig. 2, each of the resulting images shows the four different variations of a single motion simultaneously that from a crowd.

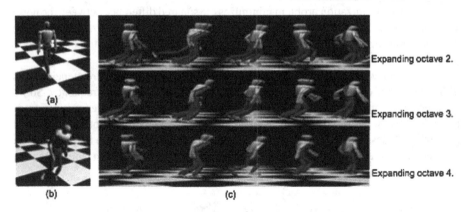

Fig. 2. Crowd simulation using time domain expansion: (a) is a base motion and (b) is the target motion for noise extraction. Using the hierarchical time domain expansion, we simulate a NPC crowd by controlling desired frequency terms (c). Each of these three images shows a crowd made by four different variations on the motion of a single character.

Figure 3 shows another application called motion analogy; in which a motion is adapted to a specific style. The analogy factor, drunken style, is extracted as a non-uniform hierarchical noise function as the difference between a pair of inputs (normal walking, drunken walking) and then the style is applied to a 'dancing' motion. The result is a 'drunken dance' and it is possible to apply this style to various types of NPC motion generation.

Fig. 3. Motion analogy: using the drunken motion pattern from Fig. 2, we create a the drunken dance (the blue figure is performing the original motion and the red figure performs the adapted motion). (Color figure online)

4   Conclusions

We have introduced a system that extracts signal pattern from given motion signal and uses it to create various similar motion pattern using noise function. Our method allows the user to control the randomness of particular frequencies within the pattern, while preserving its appearance, and this cab generate the various but similar motion for NPC. Because noise function does not require complex calculation, our method has advantages of lower complexity and it can be used real-time application like 3D game. The limitation of this paper is that it is difficult for the user to control motion detail because the noise depends on the randomness. We will develop a user-friendly interface to compensate for this.

Acknowledgements. This research was supported by Basic Science Research Program through the National Research Foundation of Korea(NRF) funded by the Ministry of Education, Science and Technology (NRF-2017R1D1A3B03033656).

References

1. Perlin, K.: Realtime responsive animation with personality. IEEE Trans. Vis. Compu. Graph. **1**(1), 5–15 (1995)
2. Cook, R.L., Derose, T.: Wavelet noise. ACM Trans. Graph. **24**(3), 803–811 (2005)
3. Goldberg, A., Zwicker, M., Durand, F.: Anisotropic noise. ACM Trans. Graph. **27**(3), 54:1–54:8 (2008)
4. Dischler, J.M., Ghazanfarpour, D.: A procedural description of geometric textures by spectral and spatial analysis of profiles. In: Proceedings of EURO- GRAPHICS 1997, pp. 129–139 (1997)
5. Spellucci, P.: An SQP method for general non- linear programs using only equality constrained subproblems. Math. Program. **82**, 413–448 (1998)
6. Fletcher, R.: Practical Methods of Optimization. Wiley, John (1987)

Reorientation Method to Suppress Simulator Sickness in Home Video Game Using HMD

Yuki Ueda[✉] and Junichi Hoshino

Graduate School of Systems and Information Engineering, University of Tsukuba,
1-1-1, Tennodai, Tsukuba-shi, Ibaraki, Japan
ueda.yuki@entcomp.esys.tsukuba.ac.jp,
jhoshino@esys.tsukuba.ac.jp

Abstract. While home-use HMD including Oculus Rift has been widely spread in the market today, simulator sickness mainly caused by difference between visual information and body sensation has taken up as a problem. Even though it has been proved that simulator sickness is reduced by reflecting actual physical movement to a VR space, many of approaches ever proposed had various restrictions and mechanisms easy to cause simulator sickness. In the current study, such an approach for moving within a VR space is proposed for home-use HMD that is less likely to cause simulator sickness.

Keywords: Virtual reality walking · Redirection · Simulator sickness

1 Introduction

With an expectation that home-use HMD including Oculus Rift is to be widely distributed in the market today, VR experience via home-use game machine and the like has become familiar to us. Image experience with a sense of immersion such as VR, however, is known to cause simulator sickness associated with symptoms including tiredness, headache, eyestrain, dizziness and nausea. Since discomfort caused by simulator sickness may turn user's long hours of VR experience into something associated with distress, it is an unavoidable bottleneck for content developers to cope with. While cause of simulator sickness is still in debate, it is believed, in particular, that difference in body sensation between reality and VR space is a major cause [1]. Approaches to make a body move within a VR space by actually moving the body were often proposed but many of them were not applied to VR experience at home because they required large experience space and extensive equipment as well. Further, in such approaches as walking back and forth within a small walking area such as Redirected Walking [2] and Reorientation Technique [3], there was a problem that the mechanism to correct direction when reached at the end of the walking area caused some restrictions to contents. In the current study, a sequential move approach within VR space is proposed which is less likely to cause simulator sickness without restricting experience environment and contents.

© IFIP International Federation for Information Processing 2017
Published by Springer International Publishing AG 2017. All Rights Reserved
N. Munekata et al. (Eds.): ICEC 2017, LNCS 10507, pp. 370–374, 2017.
DOI: 10.1007/978-3-319-66715-7_42

2   System Overview

With a purpose to achieve visually sequential horizontal movement without any restriction for experience environment and contents while inhibiting simulator sickness, the system has defined the requirements as follows:

① Not to require extensive equipment;
② To be able to realize within a small experience space;
③ Not to restrict contents;
④ To make users actually walk within the VR space to transfer; and
⑤ Not to generate difference in rotation angle during direction correction.

In order to meet the requirements above, we have determined to take an approach to give a sensation of continuous walk in a large VR space by walking back and force in a small walking area. Even though restrictions for routes and visual presentation of rotation angle different from reality has been adopted in order to prevent users from recognizing direction correction in previous studies on Redirected Walking [2] and Reorientation Technique [3], reduction of simulator sickness is tried in the system by intentionally make users notice that they are correcting direction.

By the system consisting of a PC for VR environment drawing, HTC vive as a home-use HMD capable of position estimation, base station and controller for exclusive use of HTC vive and a flat floor for walking, users are able to arbitrarily shift between the following two conditions by operating the controller:

[Movement phase]
Users are able to freely walk within the walking area. Since it is impossible to take a step further when reaching the end of the walking area, it is required to correct the direction by shifting to rotation phase. Besides, the walking area ground was colored by different color from that of surrounding ground in order for users to be able to recognize the walking area (Fig. 1).

[Rotation phase]
Users rotate on the spot. As foreground is rotated in synchronization with user rotation, the foreground of the users remains fixed in their eyesight. In this case, it is possible to present an eyesight without any difference in rotation angle to users by displaying independent visual background [4] fixed at global coordinate system making it further possible to give users a sensation that the foreground is rotating along with the body's rotation. Recommended rotating direction and angle guide is displayed for users as shown in Fig. 2.

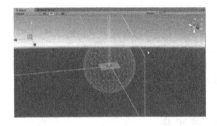

Fig. 1. Independent visual background

Fig. 2. Rotating direction recommendation guide

3 Experiments

In the current experiment cooperated by 8 persons in their 20's (male: 7, female: 1), a task was imposed to them in which they walk around through five check points set up in the VR space to move a route equivalent of about 45 m of distance both by a proposed approach preparing a walking area with a size of 2.0 m × 1.5 m and a movement approach based on a home-use game operation using a normal keyboard/mouse. Overview of VR environment and position of each check point is shown in Figs. 3 and 4, respectively. The two types of movement approaches were compared by time required for subjects to walk through all of the check points as well as evaluation value of SSQ [5] performed immediately after experiment completion and contents of hearing.

Fig. 3. Overview of VR environment

Fig. 4. Positions of check points

Table 1 below shows mean time required for subject to have completed the task and standard deviation. It has been proved that the proposed system requires much longer time compared with a movement approach by keyboard/mouse.

Table 1. Comparison of required time

	Keyboard/Mouse		The proposed system	
	Mean	SD	Mean	SD
Time	46 s	8 s	208 s	54 s

In addition, evaluation values were obtained by SSQ for SSQ (Total Score) as a comprehensive index for motion sickness, SSQ-N (Nausea), SSQ-O (Oculomotor) and SSQ-D (Disorientation). The result is shown in Table 2. The tougher is the symptom, the higher is the evaluation value. As a result of Mann-Whitney U test for each evaluation value, it has been proved that the proposed system shows significant difference in evaluation values of SSQ-TS ($Z = 2.013$, $p < 0.05$) and SSQ-O ($Z = 2.016$, $p < 0.05$) compared with those of the movement approach based on keyboard/mouse.

Table 2. Comparison of SSQ results

	Keyboard/Mouse		The proposed system	
	Mean	SD	Mean	SD
SSQ-TS*	38.80	23.28	20.57	15.19
SSQ-N	27.42	19.34	10.73	12.10
SSQ-O*	50.22	28.35	23.69	17.13
SSQ-D	59.16	53.35	36.54	40.55

4 Conclusion

It has been also revealed from the experiment that the proposed system is superior to the movement approach based on keyboard/mouse in degree of comprehensive motion sickness as expressed by SSQ-TS and degree of eye fatigue as expressed by SSQ-O in case of moving the same route. In the hearing after the experiment, such opinions were obtained that it was impossible for them to follow the movement on the screen by the movement approach based on keyboard/mouse even if operating on their own or that they got tired due to unintended movement. In contrast, there was an opinion for the proposed system that the system is intuitive causing less fatigue because images always moved in synchronization with their own movement. From the experiment results and opinions for it, it is believed that simulator sickness has been relieved in the proposed system by reducing difference in body sensation between the reality and VR space. For the proposed system, however, there was a complaint of feeling sick due to frequent correction of direction. It is understood as caused by the fact that many times of direction correction is required in order to move long distance because of the small walking area in reality. In addition, it is also believed that required time was greatly prolonged for the proposed system due to the frequent direction correction compared with movement approach based on keyboard/mouse. Resolution for the problem may include increase of moving speed within a range that users do not feel difference in the body sensation in addition to expansion of walking area in reality.

Since it took much more time by the system compared with the movement approach based on keyboard/mouse in the current experiment conducted in such a way to move along the same route, we thought it necessary to conduct also such experiments by the same movement speed and experiencing time as well. It is believed because the faster is the movement speed within a VR space the larger is the difference in the body sensation from the reality causing intense simulator sickness and longer time of experience may cause deterioration of simulator sickness. As we also felt a necessity to improve usability aiming at shortening a period of time until getting familiar with the system as well as method of displaying rotating direction not to cause cables to wind around the body in addition to opinions obtained, we would like to work on these challenges in the future.

References

1. LaViola Jr., J.: A discussion of cybersickness in virtual environments. ACM SIGCHI Bull. **32**(1), 47–56 (2000)
2. Razzaque, S., Kohn, Z., Whitton, M.: Redirected walking. In: EuroGraphics 2001 (2001)
3. Peck, T., Whitton, M., Fuchs, H.: Evaluation of reorientation techniques for walking in large virtual environments. In: Virtual Reality Conference, VR 2008. IEEE (2008)
4. Prothero, J.D., Draper, M.H., Furness, T.A., Parker, D.E., Wells, M.J.: The use of an independent visual background to reduce simulator side-effects. Aviat. Space Environ. Med. **70**(3), 135–187 (1999)
5. Kennedy, R.S., Lane, N.E., Lilienthal, M.G.: Simulator sickness questionnaire: an enhanced method for quantifying simulator sickness. Int. J. Aviat. Psychol. **3**(3), 203–220 (1993)

Augmented Reality Media for Cultural Experience in Shrines

Kei Kobayashi[✉] and Junichi Hoshino

Graduate School of Systems and Information Engineering,
University of Tsukuba, 1-1-1, Tennodai, Tsukuba-shi, Ibaraki, Japan
kobayashi.kei@entcomp.esys.tsukuba.ac.jp,
jhoshino@esys.tsukuba.ac.jp

Abstract. While intangible culture still remains as a custom, it is gradually losing the substance making it difficult for people to understand the value by their sensibility. Sensibility is important for conservation and dissemination of culture as well as cultural industry, and the augmented reality media convey meaning of shrine rituals, style of ritual manners and meaning as well as information about enshrined deities while appealing to people's sensibility. Media for the purpose consist of five works mixed with attractiveness of materials and system development. Users are supposed to experience the works sequentially by holding a scroll painting. The scroll painting is a centerpiece to be used, for example, as a screen for projecting works guide and images.

Keywords: Culture · Interaction · Media art · Texture · Augmented reality

1 Introduction

Japanese culture is expected to be disseminated to the world as a cultural industry's strategy by reaffirming and evaluating its own attractiveness. In this paper, we propose augmented reality media for shrines to convey intangible culture. As a part of traditionally continuous Japanese culture, shrines have taken roots in customs including New Year's visit and tourism even in modern times. However, less people know how to offer prayers correctly and what is enshrined. With a scroll drawing in their hands, users are able to obtain information easier in a step-by-step manner by sequentially experiencing spatial media consisting of multiple works based on images and graphic design as well as to learn subjects, styles and meaning of manners in shrines with their sensibility by experiencing prayer.

2 System Overview

Media to be proposed is centered by scroll drawing Fig. 1. Space consists of five elements; i.e. Origami paper of pigeon as shinshi (Divine servant) of subject shrine with the meaning of rituals described thereon, flag to show information of enshrined deity,

© IFIP International Federation for Information Processing 2017
Published by Springer International Publishing AG 2017. All Rights Reserved
N. Munekata et al. (Eds.): ICEC 2017, LNCS 10507, pp. 375–378, 2017.
DOI: 10.1007/978-3-319-66715-7_43

image operated by projecting detail of the enshrined deity and laying on of hands, animation of manner at Chozusha (purification trough) similarly projected on the scroll drawing, and animation of manner at a hall for worship projected on an acryl plate in order.

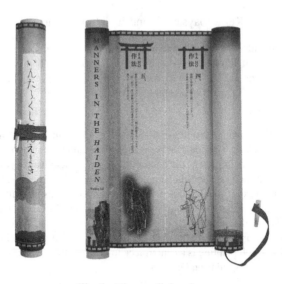

Fig. 1. The scroll drawing

In work Fig. 2 operated by projecting images on the scroll drawing for constructing a system, a framework was detected by RGB-D camera. With a coordinate designated for an icon projected on the scroll drawing by a projector, it was set up to replay a special effect by switching projected image when right or left hand entered into a range of the coordinate. With an idea that visual presentation is better to convey behaviors than a text, manners at Chozusha were expressed by animation and position at starting animation was changed by coordinates evenly divided for seek bar operation. In addition, such a function to temporary stop by grabbing a hand and to replay by unclenching the fist was equipped with in addition to the seek bar.

Fig. 2. Works using a system

For instruct manners at a hall for worship, a method to project images on a rear permeable film put on a transparent acryl plate was adopted. The screen is capable of making users feel uncanny aura of mystery without rupturing space while making matters appear to be floating visually compared with ordinary screen Fig. 3.

Fig. 3. Manners at a hall for worship

3 Experiments

Data was gathered from 12 persons who actually experienced a work by questionnaire about before and after they experienced the work Fig. 4. In order to confirm their degree of understanding of shrines before they view the work, we asked them to select from among four grades, i.e. "1. I know," "2. If anything, I know," "3. If anything, I don't know," and "4. I don't know," for questions on style and meaning of manners and what is enshrined as deity, respectively. As a result, about half of them responded as "If anything, I know" about style of the manners and what is enshrined but majority of them responded as "I don't know" about meaning of the manners Fig. 5.

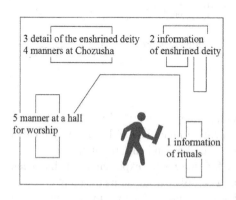

Fig. 4. Experiment environment

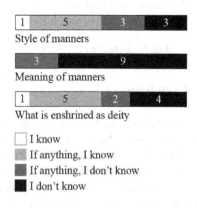

Fig. 5. Data before the works

After they viewed the work, we asked them to evaluate by four grades, i.e. "1. I understood," "2. I understood to some extent," "3. I didn't understand well," and "4. I didn't understand," and to describe the reasons in order to confirm their degree of understanding about style and meaning of the manners. The result was that all responses were made up by "1. I understood," and "2. I understood to some extent" Fig. 6. As the reason why they could understand, many of them described effect of animation. Some of them responded that they obtained information, which they might have not read by a text alone, with an interest due to the interactive method.

In order to recognize importance of manners relatively, we asked them to evaluate seven items in total, i.e. "Omikuji (paper fortune)", "Items including Omamori (charm) and Ema (votive horse tablets)", "Money offerings", "wish", "manners", "Timing for visiting" and "Existence as a specific shrine" on a 5-point scale Fig. 7. The result was compared by average values. Before viewing work, "wish" was the highest by a score of 4 and "manners" was the fifth position by 2.66. In the same question after viewing the work, "manners" increased to 3.66. "Existence as a specific shrine" showed large difference next to manners before and after viewing the work. It is considered that it had an effect to make them conscious about characteristics of the shrines such as enshrined deity because the work took up a specific shrine as the theme.

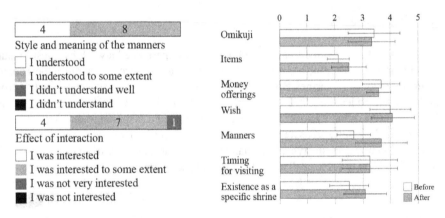

Fig. 6. Data after the works   **Fig. 7.** Comparison of importance

4 Conclusion

In the current study, we have created sequentially augmented reality media taking up shrines as a theme based on a notion that something intangible and sensitivity for it is important for conservation and dissemination of culture and cultural industry.

From a questionnaire survey conducted for those who experienced, it has been proved that shrines are a culture remaining as a part of custom but its meaning is fading while losing the substance in reality. In addition, it is interactive to convey manners and their meanings through targeted works and it has been achieved sufficiently by dynamic visual manner resulting in its increased importance.

WAR Bots: Combining Virtual and Augmented Realities for an Immersive and Enjoyable Gaming Experience

Jaryd Urbani[✉], Mohammed Al-Sada, Shubhankar Ranade,
Mingshu Zhang, and Tatsuo Nakajima

Department of Computer Science and Engineering, Waseda University, Tokyo, Japan
{Jaryd,Alsada,Shubi,Momochi,Tatsuo}@dcl.cs.waseda.ac.jp

Abstract. Despite the popularity of Augmented and Virtual Reality within gaming, the full potential of such technologies is yet to be fully taken advantage of. Thus, we introduce WAR Bots, a cyber-physical game which intends to investigate the use of both Augmented and Virtual Reality within a coherent gaming experience. We present the underlying architecture to realize our approach, and accordingly, implemented our proposed method in a multiplayer game. Finally, we present the future direction of our approach.

Keywords: Mixed reality · Augmented reality · Virtual Reality

1 Introduction

Nowadays, Virtual and Augmented Reality Head Mounted Displays (VR/AR HMDs) are more popular than ever due to their relative high quality and affordability. However, despite the wide availability of such technology, it is still in its infancy when it comes to gaming. For instance, most VR/AR games attempt to focus on a singular experience, such as the sole use of VR or AR, with limited interaction methods. While AR enables adding of digital contents to a real world's visual view, VR enables immersive virtual environments and experiences that engage multiple senses. Taking advantage of both VR and AR within a gaming context has high potential to deliver a gaming experience that leverages the advances of both interaction mediums. Thus, we take the first steps to investigate a gaming experience that attempts to combine elements from both VR and AR.

We introduce WAR Bots, a mutiplayer battle game where users pilot a physical robot vehicle from within a virtual cockpit in first person. We discuss various design elements and explain how such experience is delivered to players. Finally, we present our future direction of this project.

2 Related Work

Previous work and projects have investigated the use of either AR or VR seperately to enhance the gaming experience. "AR Drone" [2] and "AR Quake" [3, 4], have

N. Munekata et al. (Eds.): ICEC 2017, LNCS 10507, pp. 379–382, 2017.
DOI: 10.1007/978-3-319-66715-7_44

introduced AR based gaming elements to piloting drones. Players can engage in a drone fight using the drones equipped cameras and sensors. The drone's camera feed, viewed from a smartphone, is used to visualize missiles and opponents as well as other match related contents.

3 Approach

Improving on previous works, W*AR* Bots emphasizes the engagement of both VR and AR within a gaming experience for controlling robots. We extend each medium in the following method:

VR is utilized to immerse the player within the game's vehicle cockpit (see Figs. 1 and 2). Here users are able to naturally view the vehicle cockpit, within which we are able to introduce interaction methods to enhance the player's immersiveness and fun. Accordingly, this method enables flexible implementation of various interaction techniques and play mechanics that would suit various game types.

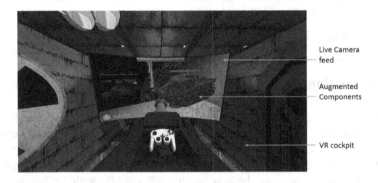

Fig. 1. Player's view in cockpit, with live camera feed and AR contents in the middle.

Fig. 2. Left and Right views of the cockpit as seen through the HMD.

AR is used to extend the robot's live camera feed of the real world by adding various 3D models, effects and other gaming elements. First, AR is used to enhance the opponents' robot, by augmenting it's physical appearance with a 3D model and energy shield (see Fig. 1). Elements such as player's Heads-Up Display (HUD), and damage and weapon effects are also shown as part of the AR environment, enabling players to view weapon trajectories, executions and outcomes.

As a result, we believe that VR can be utilized to enhance immersiveness and introduce increasingly interesting interaction mechanisms to enhance the gaming experience. Likewise, AR enhances the physical camera view by enhancing real-world game elements whilst also introducing additional game related information.

4 Implementation

The game is implemented in a client-server design structure, each host maintaining it's own connection to a single dedicated robot with all communications happening over wireless network (see Fig. 3). Game components such as hit points, shield points, ammunition, etc. are all held locally and are transmitted between corresponding clients, via the server, on such events as Shot Hit.

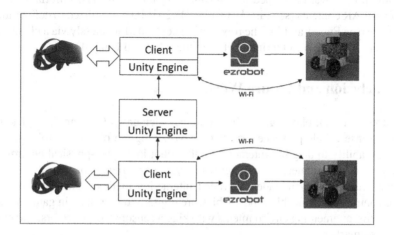

Fig. 3. W*AR* Bots system architecture.

4.1 Hardware

The game will successfully run on any VR capable PC, such were those used in design and implementation. The HMD used during testing and implementation was the Oculus DK2 coupled an Xbox 360 controller which was mimiced in the cockpit design for added immersion (see Fig. 1). Two EZ-Robot Adventure Bots [1], strapped with HD webcams, used as the robot battle vehicles. Each of the robots was also fitted with an AR-marker shell (see Fig. 4 Left).

Fig. 4. Robot fitted with AR-marker shell and webcam (left) and overlayed AR model (right).

4.2 Software

The entire project was developed within Unity3D game engine [7]. Vuforia [8] was the basis for all AR contents (see Fig. 4). Oculus DK2 HMD was utilized to deliver the VR experience (see Figs. 1 and 2). The robots were controlled wirelessly via a client-server architecture software script written between the robot and Unity3D.

5   Conclusion and Future Work

W*AR* Bots is a multiplayer game that combines elements of AR and VR. The game creates a sense of tele-presence for the user by having the player control a surrogate robot. The ability to tangibly interact with the robot in a cyber-physical environment, allows for a deeply immersive and highly enjoyable experience for all.

Future functionality includes upgraded interaction methods, such as motion and gesture control, customizable robots which are digitally represented in game including type benefits, augmenting environments with kinect sensors and projectors, and embedding nested markers.

References

1. Adventure Bot – Products – EZ-Robot. https://www.ez-robot.com/Shop/AccessoriesDetails.aspx? productNumber=34. Accessed 04 Apr 2017
2. ARDrone 2.0 Elite Edition. https://www.parrot.com/us/drones/parrot-ardrone-20-elite-%C3%A9dition. Accessed 04 Apr 2017
3. Thomas, B., Close, B., Donoghue, J., Squires, J., De Bondi, P., Morris, M., Piekarski, W.: ARQuake: an outdoor/indoor augmented reality first person application. In: 4th IEEE International Symposium on Wearable Computers, p. 139 (2000)
4. Piekarski, W., Thomas, B.: ARQuake: the outdoor augmented reality gaming system. Commun. ACM **45**(1), 36–38 (2002)
5. Aukstakalnis, S., Blatner, D.: Silicon Mirage: The Art and Science of Virtual Reality. Peachpit Press, Berkeley (1992)
6. Tachi, S.: Tele-Existence. Research Center for Advanced Science and Technology, University of Tokyo (1992)
7. Unity – Game Engine. https://unity3d.com. Accessed 04 Apr 2017
8. Vuforia SDK. https://www.vuforia.com. Accessed 04 Apr 2017

Japanese Anime Production Support System
with Digital Storyboards

Taisei Kurihara[✉], Luo Li, Masanori Ishida, and Junichi Hoshino

Graduate School of Systems and Information Engineering, University of Tsukuba,
1-1-1, Tennodai, Tsukuba-shi, Ibaraki, Japan
{ishikawa.yu,furudate.yuko}@entcomp.esys.tsukuba.ac.jp,
jhoshino@esys.tsukuba.ac.jp

Abstract. Storyboards are used in the beginning stages of making animation to explain the story or screenplay. This paper proposes a system which assists with storyboard writing and the production process. This system is used with a tablet that allows for input with a pen. It automatically calculates the number of cuts and time required for each scene and can automatically produce a schedule from storyboards. This system makes management for overall animation easy.

Keywords: Animation production · Storyboards · Schedule

1 Introduction

The number of animation titles on TV in Japan is increasing in recent years. In 2015, 233 new animation titles were produced throughout the year, while there were 108 continuing titles, making this the largest since 1963 [1].

Animation is produced by around 100 staff members working in directing, screenplay, character design, art direction, original drawings, video, art, mastering, shooting, and voice acting. A portion of this is also often outsourced [2]. It is therefore important to convey the director's designs to all staff through the production process in order to avoid delays and decrease the number of accidents during production. It is especially important in production management to ensure that the director's storyboards and the calculated length of each cut on the production process table match since the total length of an anime show is precisely decided. However, since animation production in Japan calculates time by combining the number of seconds and the number of frames, mistakes are prone to occur which causes a huge mental burden to the director and staff. Since calculating the wrong length causes mistakes in the total downstream process such as original art and video, this can result in the issue of materials being needlessly made and increased communication due to constant reorganization of the production process, putting pressure on the production industry.

This study proposes an animation production support system that makes production of the director's storyboards and management of the production process consistent.

Published by Springer International Publishing AG 2017. All Rights Reserved
N. Munekata et al. (Eds.): ICEC 2017, LNCS 10507, pp. 383–386, 2017.
DOI: 10.1007/978-3-319-66715-7_45

2   System Design

A storyboard app is created that uses a tablet PC as a pen tablet allowing one to make drawings similar to that of storyboards using conventional paper, and also makes it easy to calculate lengths with a combined number of seconds and number of frames. We will learn about the storyboarding management and drawing features of a tablet necessary for creating storyboards, design a UI, and develop a prototype focusing on ease of use for directors.

Automatically producing a process management table from the layered structure of scenes and cuts created by the director and from the time lengths reduces workload and mistakes when starting work. It also makes staff assignments for each cut, assists in making verifying and updating work status simple, and achieves the ability to individually edit areas that need more detailed scheduling.

In addition, it assists in managing the viewing of storyboards for staff involved in animation production. Figure 1 shows the system interface.

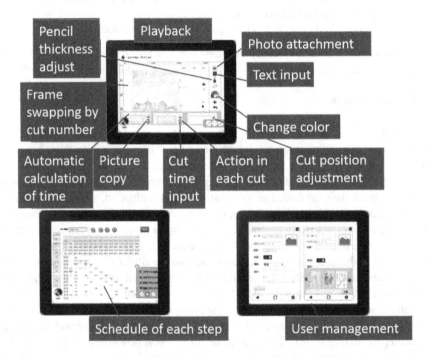

Fig. 1. (Up) Storyboards Drawing tool (Left) Scheduling tool (Right) User management tool

3   Implementation

Figure 2 shows the system structure (system transition diagram). A homepage displays when a user logs in. From there, they can jump to the following three main features.

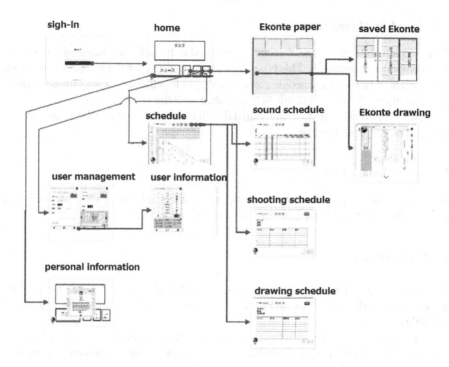

Fig. 2. Transition diagram

3.1 Storyboard Drawing

The storyboard drawing feature allows for drawing on the spot with a pen input on a one page, five column drawing screen (the same as a storyboard paper used in Japan). Colored handwriting, text, and straight lines can be entered here. Text can be inserted from the keyboard using the text box. Photos and existing illustrations can be called from an image file and pasted in the drawing area.

Columns are automatically filled when a cut that is no longer needed is deleted when drawing. Conversely, columns are automatically carried over when adding a new cut in between columns.

Here, lengths can also be automatically calculated. The number of seconds for each column arbitrarily set by the user is automatically added up, allowing them to know the total length. It also can calculate the length in frames from the number of frames per second. Since a calculator is taking care of the parts which conventionally were calculated manually, this saves time and also avoids any incorrect calculations.

The user can also playback a storyboard by displaying the columns in order according to the number of seconds for each column that they have set.

Previously drawn storyboards can also be displayed in a list and be referenced. Storyboards are stored in this area when saving them.

3.2 Schedule Management

A sample schedule can be automatically generated in the schedule management screen from completed storyboards. This is generated by counting back the amount of cuts from the deadline. Afterward a schedule can be easily put together as the user finds suitable. This also allows for modifications in accordance with the production process.

Besides an overall schedule, individual detailed schedules can also be assembled for sound, shooting, and drawing.

3.3 User Management

Staff data can be browsed by registering the production and drawing staff involved with a work, and browsing restrictions for storyboards can also be managed.

4 Conclusion

A storyboard system was proposed which assists with reducing mistakes in the production of animation by controlling storyboards on a tablet PC and automatically generating schedules.

Verification tests will be conducted in the future while furthering implementation of the system in order to verify the usefulness of the support methods and system proposed by this study. Tests in the animation contents industry are planned. Actual animation directors will be asked to use the system and their physical and mental reduction for production management will be studied using a survey to measure how much production time was shortened and identify how much easier storyboard quality and creation became. Overall judgment will be done through a survey using a five-step assessment and filling out comments.

References

1. The Association of Japanese Animations, Anime industrial report, p. 5 (2016)
2. Masumoto, K.: Japanese Anime Production Management. Kodansha, ISBN-10: 4061385496 (2014). (in Japanese)

Deep Photo Rally: Let's Gather Conversational Pictures

Kazuki Ookawara[1(✉)], Hayaki Kawata[1], Masahumi Muta[2], Soh Masuko[2],
Takehito Utsuro[1], and Jun'ichi Hoshino[1]

[1] Graduate School of Systems and Information Engineering,
University of Tsukuba, 1-1-1, Tennodai, Tsukuba-shi, Ibaraki, Japan
{okawara.kazuki,kawata.hayaki}@entcomp.esys.tsukuba.ac.jp,
utsuro@iit.tsukuba.ac.jp, jhoshino@esys.tsukuba.ac.jp
[2] Rakuten, Inc., Rakuten Institute of Technology, Rakuten Crimson House,
1-14-1, Tamagawa, Setagaya-ku, Tokyo, Japan
{masafumi.muta,so.masuko}@rakuten.com

Abstract. In this paper, we propose an anthropomorphic approach to generate speech sentences of a specific object according to surrounding circumstances using the recent Deep Neural Networks technology. In the proposal approach, the user can have pseudo communication with the object by photographing the object with a mobile terminal. We introduce some examples of application of the proposal approach to entertainment products, and show that this is an anthropomorphic approach capable of interacting with the environment.

Keywords: Augmented reality · Anthropomorphic · Deep Neural Networks

1 Introduction

Humans can feel familiarity and connection to personified objects [1]. In order for humans to personify something, expressions interacting with the environment (effectance motivation) are considered important [2]. In recent years, the Deep Neural Networks technology makes it possible to handle complex information such as the state of an object and its surrounding environment.

In this paper, we propose an approach to anthropomorphize a specific object using the state-of-the-art technology of Deep Neural Networks. The anthropomorphization of an object in the proposal approach can be realized by speech expressions suitable for the state of the object and environment. A user can communicate with an anthropomorphized object by photographing the specific object with a mobile terminal. Finally, we introduce examples of application of the proposal approach to entertainment products, and show that it is feasible to realize an anthropomorphization approach capable of interacting with the environment.

N. Munekata et al. (Eds.): ICEC 2017, LNCS 10507, pp. 387–391, 2017.
DOI: 10.1007/978-3-319-66715-7_46

2   User Interaction

Figure 1 shows the relatedness between a user and an object through the proposal approach. In the proposal approach, it is possible to anthropomorphize a specific object the user photographed with a mobile terminal. The object generates speech sentences based on the state of the object and the surrounding environment. The user receives organically changing speech sentences based on the environment. Then the object is anthropomorphized, and the user can feel familiarity with the object.

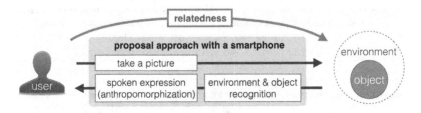

Fig. 1. The relatedness between a user and an object.

3   Anthropomorphization Based on Environment Recognition

3.1   Recognition of Environment and Object State

The object recognition technology in the proposal approach adopts YOLO 9000 [3] which is the state-of-the-art technology capable of detecting an object at high speed.

Figure 2 shows the network configuration of the actually adopted YOLO 9000. YOLO 9000 realizes extraction of input image features, detection of object regions, and estimation of object labels with a single Neural Network. Image features (information on the state of the object and environment) are extracted through multiple network layers. The image features are also used for speech generation described in Sect. 3.2. Object region coordinates and object label candidates are stored in the output layer. Multiple objects can be detected simultaneously by calculating the probability of the object candidates. For details of the model, see the document [3].

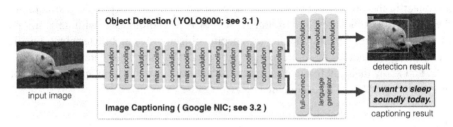

Fig. 2. The proposal approach for anthropomorphization.

3.2   Speech Generation for Anthropomorphization

The technology of Neural Network (i.e. Google NIC [4]) which automatically generates syntax from images has been proposed recently. In this paper, we adopt Google NIC as a speech generation technology for an object based on environment recognition.

Figure 2 shows a simplified network configuration of Google NIC. This network is constructed very simply: it is realized by network layers having such roles as image feature extraction, feature conversion, and syntax generation. The proposal approach aims to make a speech generation process more efficient by diverting the image features extracted by YOLO9000. By calculating the probability of the estimated word string, it becomes possible to generate a speech sentence reflecting the state of the object and environment. For details of the model, see the document [4].

3.3   Building a Network Model

To build a network model in the proposal approach, you need to prepare an image containing an object to be recognized and a speech sentence of the object. You also need to prepare a set of object labels and area coordinates.

The proposal approach begins with learning of the object detection model (YOLO 9000) to establish a network that extracts image features at the beginning. After that, it performs learning of the speech generation model (Google NIC) by diverting the image features extracted by the object detection model.

The application example of the proposal approach introduced in this paper uses a large scale image data set called Microsoft COCO (MSCOCO) [5] as learning data. MSCOCO is a data set with arbitrary object labels and captions provided for the image. This time, we have changed the captions to speech sentences of the image with arbitrary label combinations, and made it learn them.

4   Application Example

4.1   Photo Rally at the Zoo

The Photo Rally System is shown as an entertainment product example in which the proposal approach has been augmented for a zoo Fig. 3. In this system, you can photograph animals speaking based on the state of their own (i.e. eating, running) as well as their surrounding environment (i.e. people are gathered, staying near the water). You can also incorporate gamification factors such as creating your original animal encyclopedia, by using the object detection function.

Fig. 3. The photo rally system with anthropomorphization.

4.2 Play House with Plush Doll

You can enjoy the augmented play house by anthropomorphizing the plush doll with the proposal approach. Figure 4 shows the Play House System to which the proposal approach applies. Figure 4 shows how the teddy bear is speaking according to the surrounding environment. When a user changes the surrounding environment, the teddy bear's speech also changes according to the environment. This system enables a user to have pseudo communication with a plush doll by operating the doll and its surrounding environment.

Fig. 4. The play house system with anthropomorphization.

5   Conclusion

In this paper, we have proposed an approach to anthropomorphize a specific object using the state-of-the-art technology of Deep Neural Networks. The anthropomorphization of an object in the proposal approach can be realized by speech expressions suitable for the state of the object and environment. A user can communicate with an anthropomorphized object by photographing the specific object with a mobile terminal.

The proposal approach adopts the Deep Neural Network technology, including object detection and image captioning. We can apply this technology to various products by utilizing the results. This paper could confirm the operation of Photo Rally at the zoo and Play House with plush doll as concrete examples. Photo Rally System is capable of creating an original animal encyclopedia by utilizing the object detection results. Play House System is capable of ensuring pseudo communication between a user and a plush doll by recognizing the environment of the doll. From here, we would like to examine the "effect of playing" in the example already described in this paper.

References

1. Waytz, A.: Social connection and seeing human. In: The Oxford Handbook of Social Exclusion, pp. 251–256 (2013)
2. Epley, N., Waytz, A., Cacioppo, J.T.: On seeing human: a three-factor theory of anthropomorphism. Psychol. Rev. **114**(4), 864–886 (2007)
3. Redmon, J., Farhadi, A.: YOLO9000: Better, Faster, Stronger. arXiv preprint arXiv: 1612.08242 (2016)
4. Vinyals, O., et al.: Show and tell: A neural image caption generator. In: Proceedings of the IEEE Conference on Computer Vision and Pattern Recognition, pp. 3156–3164 (2015)
5. Chen, X., et al.: Microsoft COCO captions: Data collection and evaluation server (2015). arXiv preprint arXiv:1504.00325

The Little Doormaid: An Initial Literature Review Toward a Video Game About Mentoring, Social Innovation and Technology

Letizia Jaccheri[✉]

Department of Computer Science, Norwegian University of Science and Technology (NTNU), Trondheim, Norway
`letizia.jaccheri@ntnu.no`

Abstract. The Little Doormaid is a fairy tale about mentoring, social innovation and technology. In order to shed light on the research questions of how to develop the fairy tale into a video game and how to evaluate the effect of the game experience for its audience, we run a preliminary literature review. This paper reviews related efforts that will guide the development and evaluation of the Little Doormaid game prototype. We report about an initial set of relevant papers and an initial organization of the literature according to trends, such as interactive fairy tale development, Video game design and play as a space of resistance, creativity and sociability; Crowdfunding for production; The learner/player experience; Designing for diversity by evaluating for diversity.

Keywords: Video games · Mentoring · Social innovation · Technology · Gender · Women in videogames · Crowdfunding · Literature review

1 Introduction

The Little Doormaid is a story about technology, social innovation, and mentoring. This story, a modern fairy tale, has been presented in three workshops held with different demographics (one held with children age ten; one with immigrants recently arrived to Norway; and one with women) [8]. The purpose of this paper is to provide a preliminary literature review as part of the larger project of developing The Little Doormaid from a written story into a video game. The goal of this literature review is to identify research papers that may be used to answer either of the two research questions: 1. How could we develop this fairy tale into a video game? 2. How could we evaluate this video game?

2 Literature Review

The process started by searching Google Scholar using the following keywords: 'gender video games education' 'video games fairy tales' 'designing "inclusive video game" gender'. Searches were initially confined to results from 2012 or after, and were then repeated without that restriction. After establishing a narrower scope for the paper,

N. Munekata et al. (Eds.): ICEC 2017, LNCS 10507, pp. 392–395, 2017.
DOI: 10.1007/978-3-319-66715-7_47

further search terms were used: 'video games, technology, mentoring and social inno-vation.' This search was used to curate a bibliography of recommended resources for the next phase of research and development for this project. The following trends emerge from an initial revision of the literature (Fig. 1).

Fig. 1. Doory Mentor, Iva Aggressi, Sissi, and The Little Doormaid (Tappetina).

[14] reports about NeuroWander, an example of **interactive fairy tale** (Hansel and Gretel) development. NeuroWander utilizes a BCI interface with the objective to realize the principle: "think and make it happen without any physical touch". The interactive story implemented in [5] corresponds to a short story in the genre of swords and dragons.

Fisher and Jenson [6] posit digital game creation as a way in which **participants (girls) can be active in the construction** of their own subjectivities, leveraging different aspects of their identity and/or exercising an institutionally sanctioned (albeit temporary) autonomy to resist discursive positioning.' [3] explores the relation between gender and computer games. Christou et al. [4] proposes a framework for video game design and evaluation aimed at enhancing knowledge about the **creativity and sociability struc-tures** they place into their online games

One new tool or space for resisting the gendered nature of digital gaming – both in the production of video games and in the games themselves – may be **crowdfunding**. Marom et al. [11] investigated crowdfunding, as a new form of venture finance, that can reduce the barriers of female entrepreneurs to raise capital. [11] shows that both the gendered nature of technology development and the persistent (and false) perception of gamers as male contribute to a continuing lack of games designed for inclusion. Crowd-funding may then provide a significant alternative route for people seeking more diverse gaming experiences – both consumers-as-funders and game leads – to fund and produce games designed for inclusion.

Young et al. [15] found that evidence supporting the positive impact of **the learner/ player game experience** on student academic achievement was consistent. This finding was based on a thorough review of more than 300 articles and studies related to inter-actions between video games and academic achievement. De Lima et al. [5] describe the creation and evaluation of an innovative system for creating interactive narrative storytelling, arguably a type of video game. The authors note that motivation for the project was partly based on the observed enrichment leant to online games by the mid- and post-game discussions held among players, discussions which 'gamers love' and which 'contribute to the culture of the game.' This study focuses on how integrating social media into a video games user interface can change the experience of the game for its players. This study sets a useful precedent for novel ways of involving learner/players in in-game storytelling. In the experimental game created by De Lima et al., the nature and appearance of the world were essentially fixed, but the story as a "text" was uniquely open to interpretation and elaboration. The world and stock narratives created by De Lima et al. were founded on "swords and sorcery" story-telling building blocks. The use of social media integration by De Lima et al. was a deliberate attempt at accessing players' expectations and ease of discussing the game and collaborating socially.

Lacasa et al. [10] investigate video games primarily in relation to how they contribute to the development of narrative thought. Their study employs gender as a context, but questions more deeply how mass media messages – specifically video games – 'create an environment that can teach people about the rules, attitudes, values and norms of society.' The main results of the study show that 'children's reconstructions of video-games stories are dependent on specific contexts; for example, whether they are re-elaborating the content of the game while they are playing it, writing a script some days later, or developing a web page.' This study's conclusions provide a useful answer to research question one: designing a game with interactive narrative elements that require or invite the player to contribute elaborations could make that game more engaging for a diverse audience and/or facilitate stronger positive outcomes for the game as a learning tool. Admiraal et al. [1] hypothesized that although [digital] 'game-based learning is more acceptable to boys than to girls… game-based learning might improve the perform-ance of both boys and girls, depending upon the instructional design.' On completion of the authors' experimental study, they found that, 'Analysis of covariance revealed that both boys and girls of the game intervention group showed a higher test perform-ance, compared to students of the control group.'

Mora et al. [12] proposes a framework for developing interactive board games based on barcodes and RFID technology. To develop a game for learning starting from a game concept, one has to define the logic and rules, the interactions of the players with the game tokens, and the interaction among them as well as customization of the software libraries, production of objects that are not computerized, like the board and cases to tailor the appearance of tokens, e.g. using 3D-printing.

Prior research has established video games as effective pedagogical tools for Second Language Acquisition [1]. However, Rankin et al. [13] found that 'few game studies evaluate the gameplay experience from foreign language students' perspective,' and 'even fewer game studies specifically examine women's perceptions of language learning video games.' To foster better understanding of how to **design for diversity by evaluating for diversity**, it is important that future educational games developers pay attention to learning outcomes and reception of the game environment among a diverse group of participants. Beltrán et al. [2] report about a social innovation project, called "No One Left Behind" that evaluates how the software Pocket Code can become as attractive as possible to different female teenager user groups. Becoming creators of their own programs will transform them from mere consumers to active creators.

There is clearly a need to go a step further and run a systematic literature review (SLR) shaped by our revised research questions and position our SLR with respect to other reviews, like [7, 9, 15].

References

1. Admiraal, W., et al.: Gender-inclusive game-based learning in secondary education. Int. J. Inclusive Educ. **18**(11), 1208–1218 (2014)
2. Beltrán, M.E., Ursa, Y., Petri, A., Schindler, C., Slany, W., Spieler, B., los Rios, S., Cabrera-Umpierrez, M.F., Arredondo, M.T.: Inclusive gaming creation by design in formal learning environments: "girly-girls" user group in no one left behind. In: Marcus, A. (ed.) DUXU 2015. LNCS, vol. 9187, pp. 153–161. Springer, Cham (2015). doi:10.1007/978-3-319-20898-5_15
3. Bryce, J.O., Rutter, J.: Gender dynamics and the social and spatial organization of computer gaming. Leisure Stud. **22**(1), 1–15 (2003). Routledge, London
4. Christou, G., Law, E., Geerts, D., Nacke, L., Zaphiris, P.: Designing and evaluating sociability in online video games. In: CHI 2013 Extended Abstracts on Human Factors in Computing Systems, pp. 3239–3242. ACM (2013)
5. Lima, E.S., Feijó, B., Pozzer, Cesar T., Ciarlini, Angelo E.M., Barbosa, Simone D.J., Furtado, Antonio L., Silva, Fabio A.Guilherme: Social interaction for interactive storytelling. In: Herrlich, M., Malaka, R., Masuch, M. (eds.) ICEC 2012. LNCS, vol. 7522, pp. 1–15. Springer, Heidelberg (2012). doi:10.1007/978-3-642-33542-6_1
6. Fisher, S., Jenson, J.: Producing alternative gender orders: a critical look at girls and gaming. Learn. Media Technol. **42**(1), 87–99 (2017)
7. Gorriz, C.M., Medina, C.: Engaging girls with computers through software games. Commun. ACM **43**(1), 42–49 (2000)
8. Jaccheri, L.: The Little Doormaid. https://letiziajaccheri.org/the-little-doormaid
9. Kafai, Y.B., Richard, G.T., Brendesha, M. (eds.): Diversifying Barbie and Mortal Kombat, Intersectional Perspectives and Inclusive Designs in Gaming. ETC Press (2016)
10. Lacasa, P., Martínez, R., Méndez, L.: Developing new literacies using commercial videogames as educational tools. Linguist. Educ. **19**(2), 85–106 (2008)
11. Marom, D., Robb, A., Sade, O.: Gender dynamics in Crowdfunding (Kickstarter): Evidence on Entrepreneurs, Investors, Deals and Taste-based Discrimination (2016)
12. Mora, S., Fagerbekk, T., Monnier, M., Schroeder, E., Divitini, M.: Anyboard: a platform for hybrid board games. In: Wallner, G., Kriglstein, S., Hlavacs, H., Malaka, R., Lugmayr, A., Yang, H.-S. (eds.) ICEC 2016. LNCS, vol. 9926, pp. 161–172. Springer, Cham (2016). doi: 10.1007/978-3-319-46100-7_14
13. Rankin, Y.A.: diversity by design: female students' perception of a spanish language learning game. In: CHI Conference Extended Abstracts on Human Factors in Computing Systems, pp. 670–679. ACM (2016)
14. Yoh, M.S., Kwon, J., Kim, S.: NeuroWander: a bci game in the form of interactive fairy tale. In: 12th International Conference Ubiquitous Computing, pp. 389–390. ACM (2010)
15. Young, M.F., et al.: Our princess is in another castle a review of trends in serious gaming for education. Rev. Educ. Res. **82**(1), 61–89 (2012)

Lifestyle Agent: The Chat-Oriented Dialogue System for Lifestyle Management

Hayaki Kawata[1(✉)], Kazuki Ookawara[1], Masahumi Muta[2] ⓘ, Soh Masuko[2] ⓘ, and Jun'ichi Hoshino[1]

[1] Graduate School of Systems and Information Engineering, University of Tsukuba, 1-1-1, Tennodai, Tsukuba-shi, Ibaraki, Japan
{kawata.hayaki,okawara.kazuki}@entcomp.esys.tsukuba.ac.jp, jhoshino@esys.tsukuba.ac.jp
[2] Rakuten, Inc., Rakuten Institute of Technology, Rakuten Crimson House, 1-14-1, Tamagawa, Setagaya-ku, Tokyo, Japan
{masafumi.muta,so.masuko}@rakuten.com

Abstract. In this paper, we propose Lifestyle Agent, which manages user's lifestyle in a chat format. Lifestyle agent counsels users through chat and encourages the formation of motivation with the aim of improving users' lifestyle habits. In an evaluation experiment, we had users experience chat examples with Lifestyle Agent and gained knowledge on dialogue planning to promote improvement of lifestyle habits.

Keywords: Lifestyle improvement · Chat communication · Rule-based dialogue management

1 Introduction

Because lifestyle diseases account for the majority of domestic medical expenses in Japan, the Japanese government has promoted the prevention of lifestyle diseases of citizens [1]. Lifestyle-related diseases can be prevented by improving unfavorable daily lifestyle habits. However, because the daily internal changes due to lifestyle habits are extremely small, It is difficult to manage lifestyle habits with awareness of risks that lie a few years ahead. For lifestyle-related diseases caused by social stress, mental health care such as counseling is important.

In this paper, we propose a Lifestyle Agent that can is designed to improve lifestyle while enjoying communication. Lifestyle Agent performs user counseling through chat: the system asks questions about the user's lifestyle and health consciousness, gives advice appropriate to the user's lifestyle, provides support for improving lifestyle habits, etc. Users can improve their lifestyle habits while enjoying communication by counseling that is based on their own lifestyle habits. In evaluation experiments, we had users experience chat examples with the Lifestyle Agent, and gained insight on dialogue planning to make lifestyle habit improvement more effective and enhance the chat sustainability of users.

© IFIP International Federation for Information Processing 2017
Published by Springer International Publishing AG 2017. All Rights Reserved
N. Munekata et al. (Eds.): ICEC 2017, LNCS 10507, pp. 396–399, 2017.
DOI: 10.1007/978-3-319-66715-7_48

Chat systems are recently attracting attention in the dialogue field [2, 3]. The chat dialogue is treated as a non-target task: it is important to let the dialogue with the user continue longer. This seems to include the element of enjoying the dialogue itself. In this paper, we consider the dialogue system as a representation of entertainment products.

2 System Overview

This system is a chat-style dialogue system that is aimed at improving the lifestyle habits of users along with the agents. Figure 1 shows the operation of the system. The knowledge database of this system is cited from the policies of the Japanese government posted online to prevent lifestyle-related diseases. Of these, "diet," "sleep," "alcohol consumption," "smoking," etc. are mentioned regarding measures for prevention of lifestyle diseases, and information on these four items is used in the dialogue.

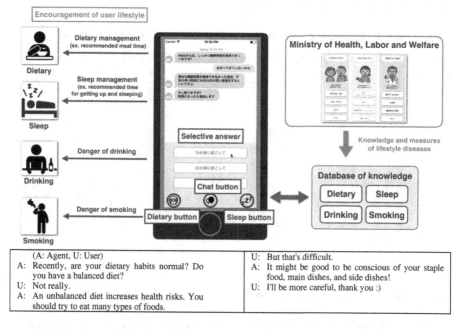

(A: Agent, U: User)	U: But that's difficult.
A: Recently, are your dietary habits normal? Do you have a balanced diet?	A: It might be good to be conscious of your staple food, main dishes, and side dishes!
U: Not really.	U: I'll be more careful, thank you :)
A: An unbalanced diet increases health risks. You should try to eat many types of foods.	

Fig. 1. Example of chat usage and system configuration in the proposed system.

Using the buttons at the bottom of the screen, users can talk to the system to encourage communication and record diet and sleep. Based on the user profile and the action history of the user, a common basis for dialogue is constructed, and the system provides knowledge suitable for each user and feedback based on it. The user can live a physically and mentally healthy life by acquiring correct knowledge and lifestyle habits.

3 Experiments

In constructing such a system, we examined what effect contents related to the user and contents not related to the user have on the user's interest/consciousness. As an impression evaluation experiment, we conducted an investigation of the impressions of persons who experienced the dialogue. A total of 12 subjects (11 men and 1 woman; subjects were in their 20s) experienced chat examples through the application, and we investigated changes in impression and consciousness in subjects.

Based on the results of the preliminary questionnaire, we classified subjects in Table 1 by the categories of eating habits, sleeping habits, alcohol consumption, and smoking. Here, the number represents the number of persons. Results of totaling the questionnaire results under this category are shown in Figs. 2 and 3. Figure 2 shows the degree of interest in lifestyle diseases before and after the experiment and the change in sense of crisis; Fig. 3 shows the feeling of crisis felt by persons in each category in response to the dialogue of each category.

Table 1. Criteria of classification of subjects and number of persons in each

Dietary consciousness		Sleeping consciousness		Drinking frequency		Smoking habits	
Yes	No	Yes	No	High	Low	Yes	No
5	7	5	7	6	6	6	6

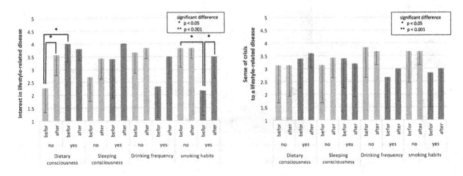

Fig. 2. Changes in interest level (left) and sense of crisis (right) before and after experiment

In Fig. 2, in the group without dietary consciousness and the group with smoking habits, there was a significant difference in the improvement of the degree of interest after the experiment. Moreover, in Fig. 3, differences were noted not only concerning categories related to the groups, but also concerning the feeling of sense of crisis for other categories.

These results revealed that it is effective to divide the user type by diet, alcohol consumption, and smoking habits. By constructing dialogue planning based on these user types, it will be possible to increase the value of the user experience in the proposed system.

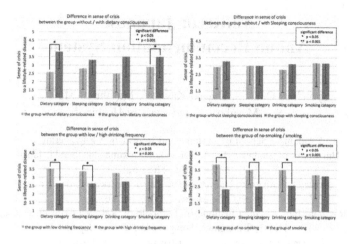

Fig. 3. Sense of crisis felt for each category of dialogue as seen by classification of lifestyle consciousness

4 Conclusion

In this paper, we propose a Lifestyle Agent that manages lifestyle habits of users through chat-style communication. The proposed system understands the user's lifestyle and conducts guidance for improvement based on dialogue. The user can review (be conscious of) his or her own lifestyle habits while enjoying communication through dialogue with the Agent, who tries to connect to his or her life.

The results of the evaluation experiment revealed that it is important to differentiate the user type using three criteria (diet, alcohol consumption, smoking) in order to make the user conscious of his or her own lifestyle. In the proposed system, it is possible to increase the value of the user experience by changing the dialogue contents for each of these user types.

Lifestyle Agent is a dialogue system that can walk the same time as the user. In the future, we would like to make products with more entertainment elements by using various information from the users' daily lives.

References

1. Welcome to Ministry of Health, Labour and Welfare. http://www.mhlw.go.jp/english/index.html. Accessed 30 Mar 2017
2. Banchs, R.E., Li, H.: IRIS: a chat-oriented dialogue system based on the vector space model. In: Proceedings of the ACL 2012 System Demonstrations. Association for Computational Linguistics (2012)
3. Lasguido, N., et al.: Utilizing human-to-human conversation examples for a multi domain chat-oriented dialog system. IEICE Trans. Inf. Syst. **97**(6), 1497–1505 (2014)

AniReco: Japanese
Anime Recommendation System

Syoichiro Ota[1](✉), Hayaki Kawata[1], Masahumi Muta[2] [iD],
Soh Masuko[2] [iD], and Jun'ichi Hoshino[1]

[1] Graduate School of Systems and Information Engineering,
University of Tsukuba, 1-1-1, Tennodai, Tsukuba-shi, Ibaraki, Japan
{ota.shoichiro,
kawata.hayaki}@entcomp.esys.tsukuba.ac.jp,
jhoshino@esys.tsukuba.ac.jp
[2] Rakuten, Inc., Rakuten Institute of Technology, Rakuten Crimson House,
1-14-1, Tamagawa, Setagaya-ku, Tokyo, Japan
{masafumi.muta, so.masuko}@rakuten.com

Abstract. Along with development of animation works and their market, it has become more difficult for users to find out works corresponding to their own preference from among huge number of animation works as well as to recognize the whole picture of contents related to them. Therefore, "AniReco" is proposed in this paper which is an animation work recommendation system capable of recommending animation works and their related contents in a cross-sectional fashion while reflecting users' potential preference. As a result of evaluation experiment performed aiming at verifying the system usability and contents of recommendation; it has been proved that the recommendation system is capable of recommending animation works which reflect users' preference.

Keywords: Recommendation system · Interface design · Anime

1 Introduction

With more than 200 pieces of animation works broadcast annually in Japan in recent years, animation market scale in a broad sense including contents such as related goods has reached approximately 1.8 trillion yen [1]. In addition, places where animation work and manga titled as "Pilgrimage" was set and locations related to it have been frequently taken up as a topic these days because of many people visiting there, having impacts on regional industries including local governments which develops goods and services in collaboration with animation works. Moreover, about 30% of the animation industry market as mentioned above is shared by overseas sales and animation makes up the largest share in export value of Japanese broadcast contents [2]. In consideration of the situations above, animation is believed to be one of important industrial markets.

Animation is content with various elements including genre, scenario, drawing, music and voice actor, however, the related contents such as goods and sacred places may expand along with the development of works. Therefore, it has become not easy

© IFIP International Federation for Information Processing 2017
Published by Springer International Publishing AG 2017. All Rights Reserved
N. Munekata et al. (Eds.): ICEC 2017, LNCS 10507, pp. 400–403, 2017.
DOI: 10.1007/978-3-319-66715-7_49

for audiences to find out works corresponding to their own preference and recognize related contents in a cross-sectional manner from among increasing works.

In order to resolve these problems, it is believed that such system is necessary for users capable of finding out animations corresponding to their preference easily, to recognize what kind of constituent elements of animation they prefer, and to enhance their interest in related contents. In this paper, "AniReco" is proposed which is an animation work recommendation system capable of recommending animation works and their related contents in a cross sectional fashion while reflecting users' potential preference.

2 System Overview

AniReco is a recommendation system via visualization using a network diagram based on calculation of user's preference from history of watching works and evaluation for them by using information regarding constituent elements of animation works. General outline of the system is shown in Fig. 1. (A) is a screen to display recommended works. User is represented by the center of the network spread in a radial fashion, and the closer to the center is a work located the higher is the rank of recommendation of the work. (B) is a screen to display information of works and related contents as well as to enter evaluation. User profile is updated and contents of recommendation vary when users watch animation works and evaluate them.

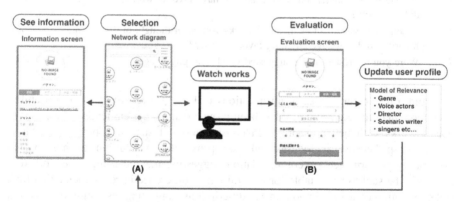

Fig. 1. System view and system configuration

With a recommendation approach by content-based filtering adopted, the system has defined similarity and association between animations using a vector space model expressing metadata of each animation by n-hot vector in reference to [3]. Users are able to recognize recommendation rank of each work visually and intuitively by suggestion of recommendation using a network diagram as described above. In addition, low diversity of content-based filtering recommendation has been resolved because even works with low recommendation rank are available as selection candidates.

3 Experiments

An evaluation experiment was performed to examine usability and recommendation accuracy of AniReco. The experiment was performed for 13 subjects aged from 22 to 28 (male: 11, female: 2) for two weeks (14days). Contents of the questionnaire and the results are shown in Table 1 and Fig. 2, respectively. Evaluation method of the questionnaire was five-level Likert scale.

Table 1. Questionnaire

Questionnaire		Mean	sd
About the system usability			
Q1	Was AniReco easy to use?	3.54	0.66
Q2	Was the network diagram easier to find the work?	3.54	0.88
Q3	Compared to searching on the internet, is it easy to find favorite works?	4.15	0.90
Q4	Do you want to continue using this system in the future?	4.23	0.83
About the content of recommendation			
Q5	Among the recommended works, did you have favorite works you have watched?	3.77	0.83
Q6	Among the recommended works, did you have works you did not know?	4.46	0.52
Q7	Among the recommended works, did you have favorite works you did not know?	3.77	0.60
Q8	Among the constituent elements of works you never thought of it as favorites, did you have anything favorite newly?	3.39	1.56
Q9	Were you interested in the suggested goods and pilgrimages?	1.85	1.14

From a result that scores in all questions (Q1 ∼ Q4) regarding system usability were more than middle score 3, it has been proved that the system tends to be easier to search works with better usability. In consideration of such an opinion that "it is easy-to-grasp because it focuses only on proximity in addition to high visual exploratory performance", recommendation suggesting method using a network diagram may be said to be suitable for recognition of difference in recommendation rank and exploration of works. In addition to descriptions suggesting resolution of selection from large number of animation works which is a background of the study such as "it's useful because it was difficult to determine which animation was interesting due to large number of animations", an effect to enhance animation watching were also suggested by opinions such as "recommendation provides an opportunity to watch animations," and "it is possible to encounter unknown works."

Q5 ∼ Q8 are questions regarding content of recommendation. From a result of Q5 and Q7, it is understood that no recommendation of works has been made which is greatly departed from user's preference. such a trend is recognized from Q7 and Q8 that recommendation with novelty and serendipity has been made reflecting potential preference of users. In addition, it is understood from Fig. 3 that some of works with

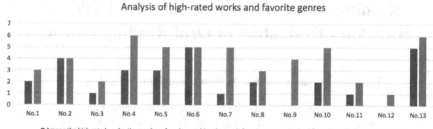

Fig. 2. Analysis of high-rated works and favorite genres. No. is subjects' number.

high evaluation obtained from many subjects include animations in genres which have not been recognized by them to be preferable in advance. From those mentioned above, it has been suggested that the system is capable of recommending both preferences which users have and have not recognized in both subjective and objective evaluations.

Result of Q9 with a score greatly lower than middle score 3 indicates that the system has less effect to enhance interest in related contents of works such as goods and sacred places. The reason why is believed that presentation of related contents information just with animation works information had less effect to draw attention to related contents.

4   Conclusion

With a problem presentation that it has become difficult to find out animation works corresponding to individual preference from among tremendously increased works as well as to recognize expanding related contents in a cross-sectional manner in recent years, an animation work recommendation system "AniReco"has been proposed which reflects users' potential preference. Consequently, recommendation presenting method using a network diagram has obtained a high evaluation in system usability clarifying that the system has an effect to reduce burden for animation works exploration and leads to new discovery of works as well. In addition, it has been proved that the system is possibly capable of making recommendation of animation works reflecting not only users' known preference but also potential one by preference extraction using frequency of watching of works and evaluation for the works.

References

1. Anime industry report (2016). http://aja.gr.jp/jigyou/chousa/sangyo_toukei. Accessed 30 Mar 2017
2. Analysis on overseas deployment of breadcast contents (2014). http://www.soumu.go.jp/menu_news/s-news/01iicp01_02000045.html. Accessed 30 Mar 2017
3. Fleischman, M., Hovy, E.: Recommendations without user preferences: a natural language processing approach. In: Proceedings of the 8th International Conference on Intelligent User Interfaces. ACM (2003)

Reading Aloud Training Game for Children with Auto Evaluation of Oral Reading Fluency

Toshiaki Takita, Kazuhisa Akimoto, and Junichi Hoshino[✉]

Graduate School of Systems and Information Engineering,
University of Tsukuba, 1-1-1, Tennodai, Tsukuba-shi, Ibaraki, Japan
jhoshino@esys.tsukuba.ac.jp

Abstract. Reading aloud is an important study method of acquiring information and building knowledge from text. This article proposes an objective and automatable method that evaluates fluency of children's reading by reflecting the evaluation by those who are experienced in book reading (to children), and presents the outcomes of building an automatic evaluation system on the fluency of reading with that method.

Keywords: Read aloud training · Gamification · Evaluation of oral reading fluency

1 Introduction

Upon obtaining information and building knowledge, reading aloud is a basic and important learning method. It has been indicated that there is a correlation between children's fluency in reading aloud and their reading comprehension [1]. It has been also indicated that, by enhancing children's fluency of reading aloud, their reading comprehension can be also enhanced [2]. Therefore, it can be said that it is important to enhance children's fluency in reading aloud.

In this article, by reflecting the evaluation of reading fluency by those who are experienced in book reading, an objective and automatable evaluation method on children's reading fluency was proposed, and using that method, an automatic reading fluency evaluation system was built. Upon building the system, it was designed to be capable of enhancing children's reading fluency in their reading practices with the automated evaluation system without having a teacher with them. In the evaluation experiment of the proposed system, the actual system was used by children, and a questionnaire survey was conducted on both children and their parents. As a result, it was revealed that the proposed system was easy to use, and it enhanced children's motivation for reading aloud, resulting in the enhanced reading fluency, not only in the material they practiced on, but also in other materials as well.

2 Game Design

The proposed system aimed to be a system that could motivate children to practice reading, and to help enhance their reading fluency. By implementing the proposed system in a terminal, it would allow children to practice their reading aloud and have it

© IFIP International Federation for Information Processing 2017
Published by Springer International Publishing AG 2017. All Rights Reserved
N. Munekata et al. (Eds.): ICEC 2017, LNCS 10507, pp. 404–408, 2017.
DOI: 10.1007/978-3-319-66715-7_50

evaluated anytime without having a teacher or parents around. In order to realize such system, three requirements were set: (1) being capable of enhancing children's reading fluency, (2) being capable of motivating them to practice reading aloud, and (3) being easy to use.

The reading-aloud game consists of three functions: the reading-aloud practice function, practice recording function and the raising game function. The screenshot of the reading-aloud practice function is sown in Fig. 1. A line of the text is displayed in the screen each time, and children read it aloud one by one. Once they have completed reading the whole text, it will display their scores of reading aloud as shown in Fig. 2, using the automated fluency evaluation system that would be described later in this article. The evaluation uses three patterns of (1) 'not fluent', (2) 'neither' and (3) 'fluent'. These marks are shown in a, b and c in Fig. 2.

The reading-aloud practice recording function keeps record of reading-aloud practices. This function consists of switchable two different screens: visualized display of the number of practices and the evaluations as shown in Fig. 3, and text-written displays of the dates and evaluations as shown in Fig. 4.

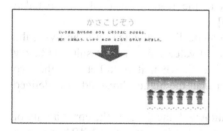

Fig. 1. Record of oral reading practice1

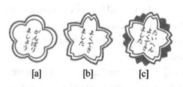

Fig. 2. Record of oral reading practice2

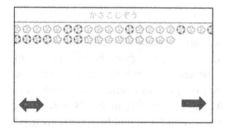

Fig. 3. Record of oral reading practice3

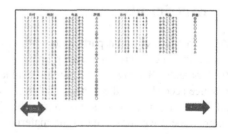

Fig. 4. Record of oral reading practice4

The raising game function is created for the purpose of motivating children to practice reading aloud. They can raise a 'character' with their scores and the number of times they are evaluated. They can play with this character, going on adventures in response to the number of times they practiced.

3   Automatic Evaluation of Oral Read Fluency

As the evaluation of reading fluency, S'IPA proposed in [3] was used. S'IPA averages the time duration of each phoneme recorded in advance in children's readings, and took the difference from what was recorded during the automatic evaluation. This is defined in the following formula.

$$s_{\text{IPA}} = \sum_{i=1}^{L} \left| \overline{IPA_i} - IPA_i \right|$$

$$\overline{IPA_i} = \frac{1}{N} \sum_{x=1}^{N} IPA_{i,x}$$

'IPA' is the time it takes to read the i-th phoneme, comma or period, and 'IPAi, x' is the time the reader 'x' took to read the i-th phoneme, comma or period. 'L' indicates the numbers of phonemes, commas and periods in the reading material. The detailed explanations on 'S'IPA' will be referred in [3].

The evaluation of reading fluency was automatically conducted by quantifying the reading fluency using S'IPA, setting the threshold values. When the result was below the lower threshold value, it is defined as 'fluent', when it is in-between the two thresholds, it is 'neither', and when it is higher than the higher threshold, it is defined 'not fluent'.

In [3], taking into account the close correlation with the fluency, the applicability of the reading fluency evaluation index was verified that indicated that S'IPA was best applicable. In addition, it suggested that CIPA and C'IPA that used average time length of each phoneme in model reading materials are the index adequately applicable to evaluate the reading fluency.

4   Experiments

After having 8 children participate in the reading-aloud practice for a week, an evaluation experiment was conducted by having a questionnaire survey on both children and their parents. By having the parents evaluate children's reading before and after the practice according to the items of Table 3, the improvement of fluency was observed in all the reading materials as shown in Table 2. Among the reading materials, significant improvement was observed in the material A and C, and those children who practiced reading with the proposed system not only improved in fluency of reading in the practiced material, but also in other materials as well. From this result, it was suggested that the proposed system was capable of enhancing children's general fluency of reading.

Moreover, the usability of the system was asked to the children. The content of the questions and the obtained answers were shown in Table 1. All the question items received favorable answers as shown in Table 1, and it was revealed that they found the proposed system easy to use, and were motivated to practice reading.

Table 1. Questionnaire and choices

Question	Did the child read it fluently?	
Choices	12	Yes. VERY Fluent.
	11	Yes. Very Fluent.
	10	Yes. Fluent.
	9	Yes. A little fluency.
	8	Neither. Become fluent a little more.
	7	Neither. If I had to choose one, fluent.
	6	Neither. If I had to choose one, non-fluent.
	5	Neither. Become non-fluent a little more.
	4	No. A Little non-fluent.
	3	No. Non-fluent.
	2	No. Very non-fluent.
	1	No. VERY non-fluent.

Table 2. Questionnaires about oral reading practice and the proposed system

	Question	Anser
1	Was it fun to practice reading reading?	5.0
2	Did you practice reading well?	4.0
3	Did you do your best and practice?	4.4
4	Did you feel bad when you were practicing?	1.4
5	Was it easy to use?	4.9
6	Was the scoring result help-ful?	4.5
7	Did you help in practicing reading aloud?	5.0
8	Can you keep using it all the time?	4.6
9	Do you want to USE it again?	4.8

Table 3. Result of oral reading fluency evaluation

	Before	After
Book 1	8.3	9.1
Book 2	8.5	8.8
Book 3	6.8	7.8

Furthermore, as a questionnaire survey was conducted on the parents, it was reported that there were children who practiced reading-aloud proactively everyday, or who raised hands to speak during Japanese class, as well as those who became better in reading aloud in short time. However, since the system offered only one reading material this time, it was reported that some children got bored after a while.

5 Conclusion

In this article, an automatic evaluating system on the fluency of reading aloud was developed, using the evaluation index that reflected the evaluation by experienced book readers (to children). In the children's fluency evaluation, the feature amount S'IPA that compared the time duration of each phoneme read by a child with the average time duration of the preliminarily recorded reading. The evaluation experiment of the proposed system revealed that it was capable of enhancing the fluency of children's reading. Moreover, children were able to use the proposed system easily, and became motivated to engage in reading aloud proactively. On the other hand, as the system offered only one reading material, it would be necessary to have multiple materials to keep children interested.

References

1. Reutzel, D.R., Hollingsworth, P.M.: Effects of fluency training on second grader's reading comprehension. J. Educ. Res. **86**(6), 325–331 (1993)
2. Stayter, F.Z., Allington, R.L.: Fluency and the understanding of texts. Theor. Into Pract. **30**(3), 143–148 (1991)
3. Takita, T., Nakadai, H., Hoshino, J.: Fluency of reading reading by children automatic evaluation index. Inf. Process. Soc. Jpn **57**(3) (2016)

AirMeet: Communication Support System by Temporarily Sharing Personal Information for Social Gathering

Rina Kotake[✉], Kazuma Kimura, Akiko Kawabata, Go Sato, Momoka Shiohara, and Junichi Hoshino

Entertainment Computing Laboratory, University of Tsukuba,
1-1-1, Tennodai, Tsukuba-shi, Ibaraki, Japan
kotake.rina@entcomp.esys.tsukuba.ac.jp,
jhoshino@esys.tsukuba.ac.jp

Abstract. In this paper, we propose a system "AirMeet" that supports temporary communication within the venue of the social gathering by limiting personal information to be shared at the time of the social gathering according to its purposes. As a result of carrying out the experiment at the social gatherings, we confirmed that we can promote sharing within the boundary of meeting venue by limiting the personal information participants had not disclosed on the Web. In addition, it confirmed that communication is supported by sharing personal information according to the purpose of the social gathering and using the application in the venue, and it showed the usefulness of the application.

Keywords: Social gathering · Communication support · Personal information

1 Introduction

A "social gathering" is regarded important that supports new connections by collecting many people who are first meeting. However, in the real world, it is difficult to find a chance to start conversation with the other person as personal information is invisible. Here, it sometimes helps solve problems by distributing nameplates containing personal information and hanging them from necks of the individuals. In order to make a chance of conversation at academic meetings or exhibitions for example, personal information according to the purpose of a social gathering such as "contents of presentation" that may be a trigger of conversation is written in many cases on the nameplate. In addition, the nameplate can be viewed only by people inside the social gathering, realizing privacy protection in places where many and unspecified people gather.

However, there are problems in the limited amount of information that can be written, or problems that the written information is visible only from close distance. Therefore, in this paper we propose a system "AirMeet" that supports communication by temporarily sharing personal information that should be shared at that time according to the purpose of the social gathering only to people in the social gathering venue. As of April 2017, iOS application "AirMeet" which used part of the result of this paper is open to the public (http://airmeet.tk/).

© IFIP International Federation for Information Processing 2017
Published by Springer International Publishing AG 2017. All Rights Reserved
N. Munekata et al. (Eds.): ICEC 2017, LNCS 10507, pp. 409–413, 2017.
DOI: 10.1007/978-3-319-66715-7_51

2 System Overview

AirMeet is a smartphone application with low introduction cost which expands the function of the nameplate distributed at the social gathering. An outline of the system is shown in Fig. 1.

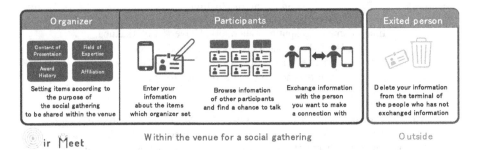

Fig. 1. Outline of system

The organizer of the social gathering has a role of establishing items of personal information to be shared at the place and at the time according to the purpose of the social gathering and a role of judging whether participants are inside the meeting venue.

At the social gathering, after participants enter the profile information to be shared within the meeting place, they see the profile information of other participants on the screen shown in Fig. 2 and discover a person whom he/she wishes to communicate with and triggers a conversation. This is supposed be how it works. Also, in order to support creating connections, there is a "MEET function" that exchanges profile information with the person who communicated.

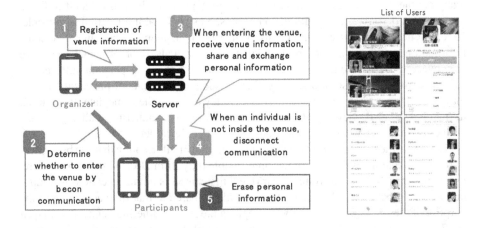

Fig. 2. System configuration and system screen

When a participant exit from the venue, information shared with other smartphone terminals and servers is automatically deleted, and information on other participants is deleted also from the smartphone terminal of the participant exited. At that time in case "MEET function" had been used for exchanges of profile information with the person, the information on the smartphone terminal of the person with whom he/she had been communicating will not be deleted. The configuration of the installed system is shown in Fig. 2, and the explanation below is added.

[1] Register the venue information from the terminal possessed by the organizer through HTTP communication.
[2] The organizer's terminal is responsible for determining whether participants are in the venue by use of beacon communication.
[3] When it is determined that the participant is in the venue, HTTP communicates reception of venue information, sharing and exchange of personal information.
[4] When it is judged the person is not in the venue, it will disconnect communication and erase personal information from the database on the server side.
[5] Information exchanged is stored in the client database.

3 Experiments

We conducted an operational experiment at two social gatherings held on the night of the first and second days of the 2 nights/3 days overnight workshop conducted by the Japan Software Society Interactive System and Software (ISS) Study Group. The results are described below.

Profile information shared within the venue is judged and set by the author to activate discussion and communication that would serve the purpose of the social gathering held during the workshop, namely "company/school", "job title/grade", "research field", "presentation title", "trademark gag", "favorite programming language". Regarding the usage of the application, 72 of the 162 participants in the workshop owned the iOS terminal and agreed to cooperate launched the application. There were 44 participants on the first day and 29 on the second day and 19 participated on both days, totaling 54 who offered cooperation in the event to enter the profile information. 38 people used the MEET function.

Described results of questionnaire after using/application for cooperators who participated in the event. The evaluator was 9 people (3 males and 6 females) with ages 22 to 43 (average age 27.8, standard deviation ± 11.3). In order to verify whether participants can promote sharing of personal information in the confined venue, we have set questions on each item about the scope of disclosure of profile information on the Web, and summarized the input situation to applications as shown in Fig. 3[A]. In all the items, there were evaluators who entered profile information to the application, which they make limitedly public or undisclosed on the Web.

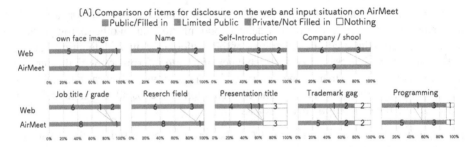

Fig. 3. Survey results: Can promote the sharing of personal information through information sharing was limited at the social gathering?

As "information is shared only among the people who are at the place and not remaining on the Web" etc., sense of security is obtained by allowing share of information in a controlled manner at limited place and time in a natural way. Comments were given indicating the usefulness of information sharing limited in a venue for a temporary time.

In order to verify whether it will be supporting communication by sharing personal information according to the purpose of the social gathering, [B] Whether there was someone who wanted to talk to looking at the information available on the application and was able to talk actually, [C] Whether it has been possible to establish a connection; Result of these questions are summarized in Fig. 4.

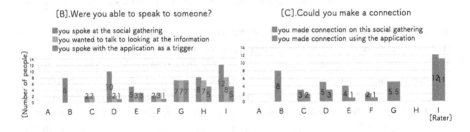

Fig. 4. Survey results: Can support communication by sharing personal information according to the purpose of the social gathering?

[B] There were 7 evaluators out of 9 who saw the information on the application and wanted to talk to them, and among them 6 evaluators who were able to speak to them actually. In the free description of the evaluator who had someone whom he/she wanted to speak to, it was noted that he/she wanted to talk to looking at profile items such as "face photograph", "job title/grade", "research field" and "presentation content", and it was confirmed that sharing the characteristic personal information according to the purpose of the social gathering will be helpful in communication support at the social gathering. In addition, there was a dialogue asking/being asked "if you are using AirMeet?" indicating that use of an application became a trigger of conversation.

[C] Seven of the nine evaluators were able to make a connection at least once at this social gathering, and six of the evaluators used the application. In order to make a connection with Facebook communication in the real world, it is necessary to search the name with an accurate notation and search for the other party. In this application, there were many advantages as being able to easily make connections using the MEET function on condition that they are inside the venue.

4 Conclusion

We proposed AirMeet which temporarily shares personal information according to the purpose of the social gathering only to the people inside the social gathering venue. By conducting the experiment at the social gathering and limiting the Web restricted profile information to stay only within the venue to be shared by the participants, it has been confirmed that the sharing can be promoted by participants.

In addition, we have clarified that it will support communication by sharing participants' profile information according to the purpose of the social gathering and using the application within the venue.

Reference

1. Kotake, R., Hoshino, J.: AirMeet: communication support system for social gathering. HCI, IPSJ, vol. 172, no. 11 (2017). (in Japanese)

Make-up Support System Based on the Colors of Favorite Image

Rina Kotake and Junichi Hoshino[✉]

Entertainment Computing Lab, University of Tsukuba, 1-1-1, Tennodai,
Tsukuba-Shi, Ibaraki, Japan
kotake.rina@entcomp.esys.tsukuba.ac.jp,
jhoshino@esys.tsukuba.ac.jp

Abstract. It is difficult to choose the right combination of make-up to reflect each individual taste since there are many products for each part of your face such as your cheek and mouth. Here we propose a make-up support system based on your choice of facial color. This system will present a make-up simulation image based on your favorite facial image and a list of make-up products to make that happen from the user's favorite facial image and the user's own facial image. From the user's evaluation, this system will suggest a color simulation image and make-up products that will bring you closer to your choice of facial image color and we have confirmed that this will help you choose the right combination of make-up products that will reflect your taste.

Keywords: Make-up · Face image processing · Reflecting preferences

1 Introduction

Since your face is an important part of your body that leads to your overall attractiveness [1], women mainly use make-up as a method of changing the impression of their face [2]. However, with make-up, there are many products for each part of your face such as your cheek and mouth, therefore it is difficult to choose which products to buy and how to combine them.

To resolve this issue, you can get advice from a make-up advisor to suit your skin color and facial contour but your desire may fade due to the difference between the advice offered and your own preference. As a method of reflecting the preference of an individual such as when deciding on a hairstyle at a hair salon, you designate a particular style from a magazine or a catalogue. With make-up, as well, if you can choose a facial picture that you want to be from a facial image with make-up done and decide on the make-up, we believe each individual's taste can be reflected to the fullest. However, it is not simple to determine a specific make-up method and products to bring you close to the facial picture chosen.

Therefore, in this paper, we propose a make-up support system based on the facial image chosen by an individual to help you do make-up that reflects your taste. The outline of the system is shown in Fig. 1. If you input the facial image chosen by the user

N. Munekata et al. (Eds.): ICEC 2017, LNCS 10507, pp. 414–418, 2017.
DOI: 10.1007/978-3-319-66715-7_52

and the user's own facial image into the system, the system will show a make-up simulation image that will bring the user close to her favorite facial image and a list of make-up products to realize the simulation. We believe, by using this system, user's will have an image of their own face with make-up done reflecting their taste and will make it easier for the user to choose the right combination of make-up products to realize that. As of April 2017, iOS application "YUMEKA" which uses part of the result of this paper is open to the public (http://yumeka.tokyo/).

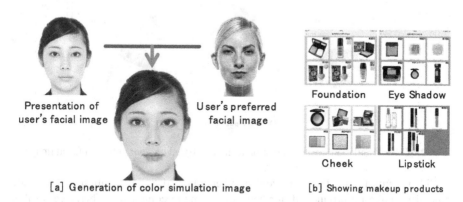

[a] Generation of color simulation image   [b] Showing makeup products

Fig. 1. Outline of system

2 System Overview

This system, to assist make-up reflecting the user's taste, is made up of [a] color simulation image generating function based on facial image of the user's choice and [b] make-up product presentation function to realize the color simulation image. With make-up there are many components including quality such as color, laminate and matt and materials but as we expect the resolution of the inputted image to be not always high, we concentrated on especially important colors that change the image of the face [3] and therefore decided on the four varieties of foundation, eye shadow, cheek and lipstick which are techniques used to change the impression by layering color on the face.

With regards to [a], it is shown in Fig. 2 and further explanations are given below.

(1) Facial image of the user and characteristics of the user's favorite facial image is outputted and the user manually adjusts the points and saves the result
(2) From the characteristics saved each part of the face where color is to be extracted is identified
(3) The specific color of each facial region that has been identified is extracted
(4) From the specific color of each area of the two facial images, the color to be superimposed to the user's facial image is calculated
(5) Simulation area to be superimposed to the user's facial image is determined from the characteristics and a mask is generated
(6) The mask is superimposed to the user's facial image

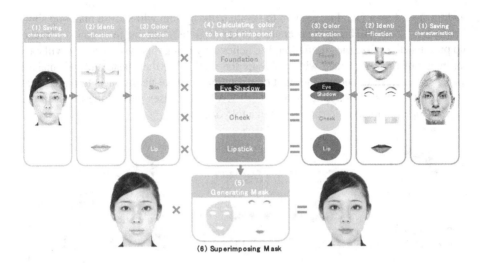

Fig. 2. Color simulation image generation technique based on your preferred facial image

With regards to [b], the name and number attached as information of the color included in make-up products differ between cosmetic companies. Therefore, in this paper, we propose a technique of obtaining make-up product images from an internet mail order site and analyzing the product color by image processing and presenting products which match the make-up color extracted from the favorite facial image.

3 Experiments

The result and study of subjective evaluation by the user will be noted. The assessors are 18 women aged between 18 to 27 years of age (average age 22.2 years old, SD ± 1.9) and the assessors used an iOS application running on iPad Air2 and answered questions in the questionnaire. Each question was given a score of 1 to 5 ((a)(b): 1. Do not think so 2. Probably not 3. Neither 4. Probably so 5. Think so, (c): 1. I don't know 2. Hard to tell 3. Neither 4. Probably understand 5. Understand) and evaluated in 9 grades of 0.5 intervals.

(a) Do you think color simulation close to your favorite facial image is presented?
(b) Do you think make-up products which will bring you close to your favorite facial image is presented?
(c) Do you understand the combination of make-up reflecting your own taste?

With regards to (a), whether you think color simulation close to your favorite facial image is presented, each make-up's average score excluding the cheek was above 4.0. With regards to (b), whether you think make-up products which will bring you close to your favorite facial image is presented, average score was more than 4.0 with each make-up. The comments received regarding (a) was that it was easy to imagine the actual make-up by viewing the simulation image and that it would lead to the desire to purchase the product such as "it was easy to imagine what it would be like when the same make-up as that of the favorite facial image was done to my face and I thought it would make me want to buy that product" and hence we were able to confirm that this system was very useful in presenting a simulation image. Comment received regarding (b) was "I was able to understand what cosmetics to use and which colors to combine to bring me closer to my favorite facial image" and hence we were able to confirm that the system was very useful in presenting make-up products (Fig. 3).

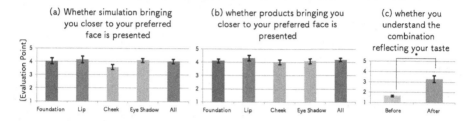

Fig. 3. Average and SD of questionnaire evaluation result(*: $p < 0.001$)

With regards to (c), whether you understand the make-up combination reflecting your taste, the paired t-test result for both before and after the system use showed significant difference of 0.1% ($p < 0.001$), and before use < after use. Significant difference was seen in the increased level of understanding, therefore there is a high likelihood that this system of presenting a simulation image and make-up products bringing the user closer to their favorite facial image will help find make-up reflecting the taste of the assessor. However, since the increase in the level of understanding did not go above 3.5 points there is a possibility that the information provided by the system is not sufficient to do make-up that will bring the user close to their actual preferred facial image. From comments like "I could find out the right combination but I could not understand how to do the make-up", technical advice of presenting how to use make-up products was seen to be necessary to improve the level of understanding.

Among others there was a comment of "I did not know the color of the cheek that I was after but after using this system it was good to find out that it was not pink as I thought but an orange type of color", hence it led to the discovery of the preference of the assessor who did not understand her own preference. Therefore, we were able to confirm the usefulness of doing make-up that will bring you closer to your preferred face which reflects your taste.

4   Conclusion

We proposed an assistance system that presents simulation and products that will bring the user closer to the color of the facial image desired by the user. The result of the subjective user evaluation confirmed that the proposed system presented color simulation image and make-up products bringing the user closer to the favored facial image color and this assisted in combining make-up reflecting the user's preference.

References

1. Langlois, J.H., Kalakanis, L., Rubenstein, A.J., Larson, A., Hallam, M., Smoot, M.: Maxims or myths of beauty? A meta-analytic and theoretical review. Psychol. Bull. **126**, 390–423 (2000)
2. Graham, J.A., Jouhar, A.J.: The effects of cosmetics on person perception. Int. J. Cosmet. Sci. **3**, 199–210 (1981)
3. Kiritani, K., Ushikubo, A., Takano, R.: Relationship between impression evaluation of cosmetic color scheme and expressive medium. Soc. Kansei Eng. **5**(1), 27–32 (2004)

Tourist Spot Recommendation System with Image Selection Interface

Motoi Okuzono[1]([✉]), Masahumi Muta[2], Soh Masuko[2],
Hayaki Kawata[1], and Junichi Hoshino[1]

[1] Graduate School of Systems and Information Engineering,
University of Tsukuba, 1-1-1, Tennodai, Tsukuba-shi, Ibaraki, Japan
{motoi,kawata.hayaki}@entcomp.esys.tsukuba.ac.jp,
jhoshino@esys.tsukuba.ac.jp
[2] Rakuten, Inc., Rakuten Institute of Technology, Rakuten Crimson House,
1-14-1, Tamagawa, Setagaya-ku, Tokyo, Japan
{masafumi.muta,so.masuko}@rakuten.com

Abstract. Nowadays, we often plan our travels by using tourism-related information abundantly available on the web. However, it is not simple to find useful information for your travel plans from enormous amount of information. This study, therefore, proposes a system that can make recommendations to you based on your preferences without you having to search information. Extracting the preferences of the users will be done simply by having images of their preferences selected by the users from the touristic images. The performance evaluation test on the system was also conducted.

Keywords: Recommendation system · User interface · Decision support

1 Introduction

Along with the explosive diffusion of the Internet, enormous amout of touristic information has become available on the web, and we now often use the web information to plan our travels. However, such touristic information is provided randomly in various forms, sometiems created by municipalities, or in toursims information sites, blogs of individual persons as well as in reviews sites, and it is difficult for users to find useful information for their travel plans from the flood of touristic information.

In this article, we, therefore, propose a system that can recommend destinations of users' preferences to them that only requires a simple operation. Supposing that the travel dates are already set, and users are trying to make plans and itineraries, this system would help and simplifies the travel planning. In order to realize the simple operation, the interface was set as users only need to select tourism-related photos of their preferences repeatedly with their intuition. Also, in order to examine the preference-analysis method of this system, an evaluation test on the recommendation performance was conducted.

© IFIP International Federation for Information Processing 2017
Published by Springer International Publishing AG 2017. All Rights Reserved
N. Munekata et al. (Eds.): ICEC 2017, LNCS 10507, pp. 419–422, 2017.
DOI: 10.1007/978-3-319-66715-7_53

2   System Architecture

2.1   System Overview

In this system, 16 image photos of different sightseeing destinations are displayed in the 4 × 4 boxes, and a user is to select 4 of them (Fig. 1). This process is to be repeated 10 times with different sets of image photos. This interface realizes the simplicity of extracting the users' preferences. The photos displayed corresponds the node of the preference model mentioned in the next section, and as images are selected, the parameters of the node increase. Moreover, as the image photos are displayed in the manner that it covers the entire categories the system deals, it can be expected that the users would discover their new preferences they were not aware of themselves. The kinds of photos to be displayed will be mentioned in the section of the database.

Fig. 1.   User interaction on the proposal system.

2.2   User Preference Model

A preference model was created by defining user preferences in travels as:

- Categories of sightseeing spots they would like to visit
- Activities they would like to do at the destinations

The categories of sightseeing spots are set in a hierarchical structure such as "seeing-natural landscape-canyons", and the preference model was set in the same hierarchical structure as well. And by input, parameters that indicate how much they value each item are added to the model. An example of the actual preference model is shown in Fig. 2.

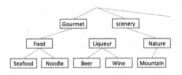

Fig. 2.   User preference Model.

When the evaluation value of a node N s $|N|$, and the node group that belongs to the node is $Nx(x = 1, 2, \ldots, n)$, it would be:

$$|N| = \sum_{i=0}^{n} N_i \tag{1}$$

and, the evaluation value of the parent node directly affect the child node.

The characterization of the recommended tourist destinations would be determined by the categories and numbers of sightseeing spots of that destination. The number of the sightseeing spots is added with parameters to make it into the same model as the preference model, which would be normalized and expressed as the vector. The sightseeing spots and their categories, as well as the area they belong to were determined by referencing "Rakuten Travel Note" operated by Rakuten, Inc. As a result, the number of the sightseeing spots was 17,138, the number of the categories was 125 and the number of recommendation candidate areas was 209. The photos displayed in the input interface were those of the sightseeing spots obtained, and the categories of the photos correspond those of the sightseeing spots.

3   Evaluation Testing

3.1   Definition of Performance Index

They are known for their accuracy as an index for information search system, and often used for the evaluation index for recommendation systems [2]. These are defined as follows:

$$Precision = \frac{|T_i^x \cap imL_i^x|}{imL_i^x} \tag{2}$$

T_i^x is the group of items thde user preferred in recommendation candidates, and $|T_i^x|$ is the number of the item, imL_i^x is the map of L_i^x mapping that indicates all the items in the map of L_i^x mapping that indicates all the items in the recommendation list. The accuracy is defined as the percentage of the preferred items $b \in T_i^x$ in T_i^x against the size of the recommendation list.

3.2   Content of the Evaluation

Following test was conducted, using the above-mentioned index:

1. To men and women from 22–26 years of age, all of the 209 areas that were candidates of recommendation areas were displayed randomly along with the sightseeing spots of their preferences, and had them answer how attractive they found them in Likert scale from 1 to 5 (1: "not attractive at all" – 5: "very attractive").
2. The areas they answered as 4 and 5 in 1 are defined as their preferred items.

3. Using the system, the top three recommendation outcomes were created, and it was assessed how many places of their preferences are actually recommended.

3.3 Result of the Test

Table 1 is the average of each user's knowledge and evaluation value of the 209 candidates for recommendation areas.

Table 1. The average of user's knowledge.

Unlike	Like
113.5	95.5

Table 2 shows the results of the accuracy calculations.

Table 2. The system performance.

Precision
0.556

While among the candidates sites, the preferred sites were slightly less than half, the accuracy of the recommendation outcomes turned out to be slightly more than half. Although it can be considered effective in certain degree, in terms of the accuracy, there is plenty of room for improvement.

References

1. Rakuten, Inc., Rakuten Travel - Get the best deals on Japanese Hotels and Ryokans. http://travel.rakuten.com. Accessed 10 Dec 2016
2. Zhang, F.: Improving recommendation lists through neighbor diversification. In: IEEE International Conference on Intelligent Computing and Intelligent Systems, ICIS 2009, vol. 3, pp. 222–225 (2009)

Partner Character Attracting Consumers to a Real Store

Motoi Okuzono[1]([⊠]), Masahumi Muta[2], Soh Masuko[2], Hayaki Kawata[1],
and Junichi Hoshino[1]

[1] Graduate School of Systems and Information Engineering, University of Tsukuba, 1-1-1,
Tennodai, Tsukuba-shi, Ibaraki, Japan
{motoi,kawata.hayaki}@entcomp.esys.tsukuba.ac.jp,
jhoshino@esys.tsukuba.ac.jp
[2] Rakuten, Inc., Rakuten Institute of Technology, Rakuten Crimson House, 1-14-1, Tamagawa,
Setagaya-ku, Tokyo, Japan
{masafumi.muta,so.masuko}@rakuten.com

Abstract. The diversification of personal tastes and the rapid increase in choices makes it difficult to select things that suits them. For service providers it is fixedly segmented like a conventional mass media It is becoming more difficult to provide advertisements and services to individuals. Because of these circumstances, it is requested that we can accurately acquire personal preferences and analyze them. On the other hand, attention is focused on O2O, which connects online actions to offline online shopping in real stores. We also use gaming which makes various elements of everyday life into a game, Measures have also been taken to immerse and positively tackle purchasing behavior. In the marketing field, it is said that narrative is important for inducing user's behavior. Therefore, in this research, we construct a partner character system based on scenario game and verify whether we can increase purchasing behavior in a real shop by making users engage in the system using scenarios and characters that can be friends with users.

Keywords: Pertner character · O2O · Gamification

1 Introduction

Interests in O2O are increasing. So far, they are used for promoting visits and purchasing activities at physical retail stores with email marketing and online campaigns; there are also initiatives to lead online members and internet visitors to stores and actual off-line purchasing behaviors. There are also measures being carried out to utilize gamification which turns various factors in everyday life into a form of game to draw in users and get them to proactively undertake purchasing behaviors. Moreover, in the field of marketing, having narrativity is considered important for inducing user actions [1]. Therefore in this study, a partner character system is constructed using a scenario based game, to verify whether purchasing behaviors at physical retail stores can be increased by heightening engagement of users with the system, utilizing a scenario and a character

© IFIP International Federation for Information Processing 2017
Published by Springer International Publishing AG 2017. All Rights Reserved
N. Munekata et al. (Eds.): ICEC 2017, LNCS 10507, pp. 423–426, 2017.
DOI: 10.1007/978-3-319-66715-7_54

that can befriend users. In this system, preferences of users are checked using conversation based on scenarios, and scenarios are changed depending on actions or location information of users. For this study, bakery was chosen as target purchasing category.

2 System Overview

This system uses a character for its interface.

- This character uses expressions of emotional feelings (delight, anger, sorrow and pleasure) as shown on Fig. 1

Fig. 1. Example of character expression

- Backgrounds change depending on the scenario scene
- Texts are displayed at lower part of the screen, to make it feel as if the character is talking to users
- Users have pseudo-conversations with the character by selecting choices that are presented

The responsibilities of this front end character are;

- Controlling the story
- Estimation of user model from interactions with users

By using this front end character, the system renders a story and carries out dialogues with users. Three levels are set for the front end character depending on how engrossed a user becomes, and new stories develop as levels go up. Moreover, a character that resides on smartphones of users is used to accumulate knowledge about users, by continuously having dialogues with users. Users would convey their preferences through dialogues with the partner, as well as evaluating proposals from the character.

This system tries to lead to purchases at physical retail stores, by proposing buns that users would like. To that end, a questionnaire allowing multiple answers is carried out to 32 men and women, where favorite buns are selected out of 73 types of buns quoted from a corporate website [2] of a company that holds cooking classes on baking buns; and the results from this questionnaire are used to enable recommendation with a collaboration filter. When using this system for the first time, questions in Table 1 are asked by the front end character. The results from this and right or wrong of answers on quiz regarding buns that the front end character posed to users are utilized to specify buns that users would like, and based on data obtained from the aforementioned preliminary survey, collaboration filtering is carried out.

Table 1. Initial questionnaire

Questionnaire
Do you often eat breads?
Which do you like pastries or deli breads?
Do you like sweet breads?
Do you like breads for staple food?

As an engagement parameter of users to the system, a degree of closeness is implemented in this system. There are four levels in the degree of closeness including the initial stage, with several criteria for going up in the level. Criteria are;

- Visit a bakery
- Listen to trivia on buns
- Provide correct answer on quiz relating to buns
- Experience bakeries or buns that the system recommended
- Give a high evaluation to the bakery or buns that the user experienced

By going up in the level, events would proceed and the character will become friendlier in its manner of speaking to users, showing more expressions.

3   Evaluation Testing

Test subjects are 16 male students between the ages of 20 to 25 who are studying at University of Tsukuba. They are asked to spend a week using the system. Furthermore, while there are no rules set forth to enforce use of the system, allowing the system to use location information and to use push notification at 12:00 every day were mandatory.

Test subjects were classified based on their degree of closeness with the character, and their average number of visits to physical retail stores was summarized in Fig. 2. The results showed that higher the degree of closeness, the more they tended to visit stores. Therefore this showed that the more users become closer with a character in a system with narrativity, the more they visit physical retail stores, which means leading to purchasing behaviors.

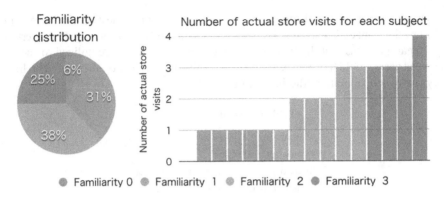

Fig. 2. Familiarity distribution and number of actual store visits for each subject

4 Conclusion

While it showed that higher degree of closeness resulted in attracting more customers to physical retail stores, a third of test subjects were at the initial state of closeness; therefore more contrivance is needed to heighten engagement with the system. Moreover, since the scope was limited to buns as subjects in this study, algorithm for the system to recommend buns to users had remained a simple collaborative filtering as well. In future, it would be good to collaborate with commercial facilities and such to create partner characters that span across several fields such as apparels, books and films. And as volume of contents being handled increases, creation of contents and store database that are currently being prepared manually will likely need to be automated, by collaborating with EC (electronic commerce) websites.

References

1. Shankar, A., Elliott, R., Goulding, C.: Understanding consumption: contributions from a narrative perspective. J. Mark. Manag. **17**(3-4), 429–453 (2001)
2. Book of kind of breads I COOKTWON. https://papatto-cooktown.jp/contents/kind_of_bread. 10 Apr 2017

TamaPeeler: An Interactive Cooking Tool for Children's Dietary Education

Yu Ishikawa[✉], Yuko Furudate, and Junichi Hoshino

Graduate School of Systems and Information Engineering, University of Tsukuba, 1-1-1, Tennodai, Tsukuba, Ibaraki, Japan
{ishikawa.yu,furudate.yuko}@entcomp.esys.tsukuba.ac.jp,
jhoshino@esys.tsukuba.ac.jp

Abstract. With the change in our diet, importance was placed on dietary education, and various systems for dietary education have been proposed. However, there has been no system that deals cooking tools. This article, therefore, proposes a peeler-type device, 'TamaPeeler', in the hypothesis that touching the food directly and being involved in cooking would raise their interest in food. TamaPeeler detects motions of peeling vegetables, and simultaneously makes various peeling sounds from the wirelessly connected smart phone. As we observed children during its exhibit, we have observed them proactively peeling vegetables, or showing interests in peeling other vegetables, and it was suggested that using an interactive cooking tool can raise the interests of children in food and diet.

Keywords: Dietary education · Children · Cooking tool

1 Introduction

As our diet keeps changing, dietary education was considered important in Japan, and in 2005, Basic Act on Food Education that stipulated the basic concepts and items of the measures for food education was established. Its foreword defined food education as an effort to "cultivate knowledge on food and abilities to select them through various experiences, and foster individuals who can practice healthy diet", and importance was placed on the dietary education of children particularly.

Although some systems have been proposed related to food and diet such as a fork-type device [1] that makes sounds while eating, and as a system for food education, a fork-type device [2] linked with an application, and a tray-type device [3], as well as projection system [4] have been proposed, but all of these are systems that can be used after food is laid out on the table.

This article proposes "TamaPeeler" – a cooking tool that would motivate children to help in cooking voluntarily (Fig. 1) – in the hypothesis that touching the food directly and being involved in cooking would raise their interest in food. TamaPeeler is a peeler-type device that detects motions of peeling vegetables, and coupled with the wirelessly linked smart phone, it makes various sounds.

© IFIP International Federation for Information Processing 2017
Published by Springer International Publishing AG 2017. All Rights Reserved
N. Munekata et al. (Eds.): ICEC 2017, LNCS 10507, pp. 427–430, 2017.
DOI: 10.1007/978-3-319-66715-7_55

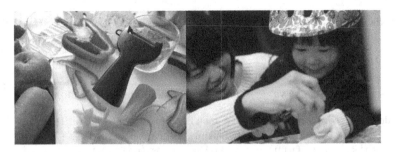

Fig. 1. Overview of TamaPeeler: (Left) TamaPeeler, (Right) Appearance in experience

2   System Design

TamaPeeler is a peeler that has an eye-catching aesthetics for children, and system that makes various sounds in response to the motions of peeling as an entertainment factor so it raises children's interests in cooking itself. It detects: (1) when the peeler touches the vegetable, and (2) the motions of peeling, both of which are called 'sound-creating conditions', and when both conditions were fulfilled simultaneously; the sound will be played on the smart phone.

For judgement of the sound creating conditions, a touch sensor and an acceleration sensor are used in consideration of children's safety. An acceleration sensor alone can be adequate to detect the motions of peeling, but by coupling with a touch sensor, it can prevent from making sounds when children swing the device around with a playful manner.

The peeler also has a function to change some of the sound effects according to the number of times of peeling motions. It counts the number of times that fulfilled sound-creating conditions and after 3n-th time (n = 1, 2, 3...), it will make another kind of sound. As the sound changes after certain times of peeling motions, children could be motivated to keep peeling to hear different sounds.

3   Implementation

System configuration is shown in Fig. 2. To simplify the implementation, the prototype has a rotary DIP switch on the peeler to select kinds of sound, and the sound is played on the wirelessly connected smart phone.

3.1   Detection of Contact Between the Blade and a Vegetable

Electrodes are attached to the both ends of the blade of the peeler, and they work as a touch sensor mounted. Then, it detects the blade contacts with a vegetable by the change of the electric voltage. As there normally is an allowance for the angle of the blade of a peeler, the terminal of the touch sensor was aligned so it connects at the proper angle when the blade touches the vegetable.

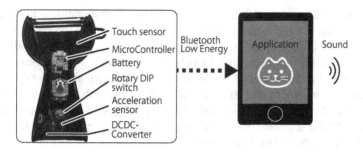

Fig. 2. System configuration

3.2 Detection of Peeling Motions

An acceleration sensor is used to detect the peeling motions. In the prototype, based on the most basic peeling motion, the shift of an axis by time are measured and processed with threshold value. The threshold value are tested and set at the value so that it did not make sound when adults swing the peeler around in the air.

3.3 Playing the Sound

The sound is played via the specific application on the smart phone's speakers. It has 14 different kinds of sound and part of them is shown in the Table 1. The electric circuit of the peeler and the smart phone are connected wirelessly by an energy-saving close range transmitter, 'Bluetooth Low Energy. The variations of the sounds according to the times of peeling motions are such as, when it is set to play the meows of a cat as in Table 1, No. 1, after $3n$-th time, it switches to bow-wows of a dog.

Table 1. Some sound examples

No.	Name	Onomatopoeia
1	Cat	meow
2	Dog	bowwow
3	Jack-in-the-Box	boing

4 Evaluation

To verify the applicability of the prototype, we exhibited it, and observed children peeling vegetables with it. The exhibit and the observation were conducted at the Hardware Contest, GUGEN, held in December 2015 in Akihabara.

5-year old girl was observed to be absorbed in peeling vegetables for long time. When the sound effect is played, she smiled, and looked amused, and she was willing to continue peeling vegetables until the sound changed to a new one. This girl finished her 'peeling' and went off to see other exhibits, but came back afterwards and wanted to do it again. She was once again absorbed in peeling until her father finally suggested that they should go home. Also, a boy was observed to keep peeling until he could hear all the different kinds of sound. Moreover, it was observed that multiple children wanted to peel other kinds of vegetables voluntarily for the sounds from the smart phone.

The fact that children kept peeling vegetables, and wanted to hear other sounds suggests a possibility that, being able to make sounds by their own motions raised their interests in cooking and positively influenced their voluntary actions. And from their remarks that they wanted to peel other vegetables, it is thought that it raised their interests in other vegetables as well. This suggests that the peeling work they were motivated to try by TamaPeeler triggered their interests, not only in the vegetable they actually touched, but also other related food as well.

5   Conclusion

We experimentally created a peeler-type device, TamaPeeler, to promote voluntary participations of children in cooking, and to help food education at home. And at the exhibit of the device, it was observed that, from their motivation to play sounds, children repeatedly peeled the vegetables, and wished to peel other vegetables, wanting to touch many vegetables proactively. From this, it was suggested possible that TamaPeeler can raise children's interests in food through the cooking activities at a kitchen.

In the future, it is our hope that we can compare, by conducting a mid-to-long term experiment, the difference in their interests with or without this device, and study the effects of the sounds as well as the modification of the system and application to other cooking tools besides a peeler.

References

1. Kadomura, A., Nakamori, R., Tsukada, K., Siio, I.: EaTheremin. In: SIGGRAPH Asia 2011 Emerging Technologies, p. 7. ACM (2011)
2. Kadomura, A., Li, C.Y., Tsukada, K., Chu, H.H., Siio, I.: Persuasive technology to improve eating behavior using a sensor-embedded fork. In: Proceedings of the 2014 ACM International Joint Conference on Pervasive and Ubiquitous Computing, pp. 319–329. ACM (2014)
3. Lo, J.-L., Lin, T., Chu, H., Chou, H.-C., Chen, J., Hsu, J.Y., Huang, P.: Playful tray: adopting ubicomp and persuasive techniques into play-based occupational therapy for reducing poor eating behavior in young children. In: Krumm, J., Abowd, Gregory D., Seneviratne, A., Strang, T. (eds.) UbiComp 2007. LNCS, vol. 4717, pp. 38–55. Springer, Heidelberg (2007). doi: 10.1007/978-3-540-74853-3_3
4. Mori, M., Kurihara, K., Tsukada, K., Siio, I.: Dining presenter: Augmented reality system for a dining tabletop. In: Proceedings of the 2009 ACM Conference on Ubiquitous Computing Supplemental Publication, UbiComp 2009 Supplemental, pp. 168–169. ACM (2009)

Karaoke Entertainment Character Based on User Behavior Recognition

Minkyu Choi[1] and Junichi Hoshino[2(✉)]

[1] Graduate School of Systems and Information Engineering,
University of Tsukuba, 1-1-1 Tennodai, Tsukuba, Ibaraki 305-8577, Japan
Choi.minkyu@entcomp.esys.tsukuba.ac.jp
[2] Systems and Information Engineering, University of Tsukuba, 1-1-1 Tennodai,
Tsukuba, Ibaraki 305-8573, Japan
jhoshino@esys.tsukuba.ac.jp

Abstract. In recent years, research on CG technology has advanced. However, the current CG character can only perform deterministic behavior; there is a problem that interaction cannot be real. Therefore, it is necessary to change the facial expression and gaze in real time to the user by the CG character to select a specific user in the space where there are multiple users, and to do real interaction with the user by using the episode control system and user recognition. In this paper, Kinect V2 recognizes the behavior of a specific user from multiple users, generates a complex gesture of CG characters, gaze representation etc., and proposes a system that CG character supports the provision of services. In this paper, we verify behavior recognition when there is one user and verify behavior recognition by priority when there are multiple users. Because there were many misrecognition of the skeleton, there were many times when the behavior was not recognized. In the evaluation experiments, we will realize even CG character's behavior generation in relation to episode control technology.

Keywords: Multi-user recognition · Behavior generation · CG character

1 Introduction

Karaoke is an entertainment that only the musical accompaniment of each song is recorded, and users sing along with the accompaniment when it's played. In Japan, 'karaoke boxes' that provide karaoke became popular in 1980's, and ever since, they have been widely used for friends' gatherings, social occasions, and 'after-drink parties' as well as stress release purposes. In 2015, there are over 150,000 karaoke places and the market size of the karaoke boxes is said to be about 400 million yen. Karaoke is also widely popular in Asia, America, and in Europe, and there is the World Grand Prix of karaoke held as well. It is also impacting the music industry as popularities of songs in Karaoke influences the sales of CDs and downloads as well.

A typical karaoke room in Japan normally has a large monitor that displays promotion videos or image videos of songs and devices to select songs. As users input songs they would like to sing, it will play them in turn. Sometimes, it has scoring system to judge how good they sang their songs, or video recording system that records

© IFIP International Federation for Information Processing 2017
Published by Springer International Publishing AG 2017. All Rights Reserved
N. Munekata et al. (Eds.): ICEC 2017, LNCS 10507, pp. 431–434, 2017.
DOI: 10.1007/978-3-319-66715-7_56

them singing and post it on SNS. However, there is a room for improvement, in terms of some gismos to entertain the user, or pick up his/her preferences and make recommendations of songs and services.

This article proposes an entertainment character that, when multiple users are using at a karaoke room, recognizes the behaviors of the users to entertain them accordingly, and promote songs and food & drink services to them.

2   Entertainment Character for Karaoke Room

Figure 1 shows a scene in a karaoke room. A CG character as a companion is displayed on the large monitor. Also, on the table is a small monitor for selecting songs. The character talks with voice to the users, and the users are to select answers displayed on the monitor. During the conversations, the character picks up your preferences, promotes songs and also recommends some foods and drinks as well as other services.

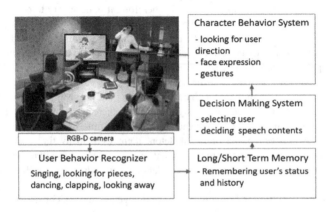

Fig. 1.   Scene in a karaoke room and system architecture

In this system, the character recognizes users' behaviors such as singing, dancing and selecting songs, and it would sing along together, help you select songs and such. In this way, the character can avoid doing improper things such as talking to users when they are singing, and it can talk to you in appropriate timing. The judging of the character is done according to the priority degree shown in Table 1, using the results of state recognition on users, by selecting action module, in which some behavior or contents of talks are recorded. When someone is looking sideways, and is not paying attention to the singer, the character talks to motivate him/her to participate. Or, when users are enjoying karaoke, the character would also join them and take behaviors to entertain them such as singing, or clapping its hands. When no one is singing and they are selecting songs, it would recommend some songs, talk about itself, chat about random things based on the news of the day or it would recommend other services.

As a method to recognize users's behaviors, as there are many irregular lights such varying lighting and light from monitors, it uses RGB-D camera that can obtain images

Table 1. User behavior and priority

User's state	Acting expression	Priority
(a) Not paying attention to the singer	Focusing one's attention	1
(b) Singing	Livening up the mood, Dancing together	2
(c) Dancing	Dancing together	3
(d) Clapping one's hands	Clapping together	4
(e) Choosing a song	Recommending a song	5

of certain distances to record users, and obtain their framework information such as bodies and limbs (Fig. 2). For extraction of framework information, the kinect library was used. By matching with preliminarily recorded postures and behavior patterns of users, it recognizes users' behaviors. Figure 2 shows an example of extracting framework information. As shown here, it is capable of detecting basic postures of users in karaoke scenes.

Fig. 2. RGB-D image

3 Preliminary Evaluation

In this chapter, how the system recognizes users' behaviors and how the judgment of the character is made that were mentioned in chapter 2 were verified by an experiment.

(1) Recognition of single user's behavior and the behavior generation by the character
It was verified, when a behavior of a user is recognized, whether the character was able to generate an anticipated behavior. Table 2 shows the rate of correct recognition when one behavior was showed 10 times. It was able to recognize behaviors from (A) to (D) mostly. However, the recognition rate was down for (E) choosing a song, as the monitor for selecting songs blocked the user's lower body, making it difficult to judge whether the user was sitting or standing.

(2) Recognition of two users' behaviors and behavior generation by the character
It was verified whether the character could choose appropriate behavior according to the priority degree of the behavior when there are two users. For instance, each of the two users took behaviors of (A) and (B), (A) is to be selected as its priority is higher. Table 3 shows, when one pattern of behavior was showed 10 times, the

Table 2. Accuracy of user recognition

User's state	Accuracy of recognition
(a) Not paying attention to the singer	100%
(b) Singing	80%
(c) Dancing	70%
(d) Clapping one's hands	80%
(e) Choosing a song	40%

Table 3. Recognition result of behavior by priority

User 1	User 2	Expected result	Accuracy of recognition
A	B	A	25%
A	C	A	100%
A	D	A	100%
A	E	A	100%
B	C	B	100%
B	D	B	50%
B	E	B	100%
C	D	C	50%
C	E	C	100%
D	E	D	75%

anticipated behaviors of the character and actual behaviors it generated. In many cases, anticipated behavior was generated, but when two users overwrapped each other and part of their bodies were blocked, recognition errors tended to occur. For instance, when a user was not paying attention to the singer as in (A), if part of her body was not visible, it was recognized that the user was merely stand-by state.

As explained, the recognition capability of RGB-D camera was mostly stable, but recognition errors tended to occur when part of users' bodies were blocked by an object or other users. In such cases, the character would generate unexpected behaviors, and this should be examined in actual karaoke scenes, how disturbing they would be.

4 Conclusion

This article proposed an entertainment character that, in a karaoke room where one or multiple users are singing, recognizes users' behaviors and entertains them in karaoke. For the future projects, the recognition ability and contents of its conversations of the character should be improved by creating a mock karaoke room where users are actually engaged in karaoke to observe whether the reactions of the character are appropriate, and whether it can entertain the users.

References

1. Hase, M., Mori, H., Shiratori, K., Hoshino, J.: Action control of shop character based on customer state, IPSJ SIG Technical report (EC)2008(129(2008-EC-011)), pp. 37–40 (2008)
2. Nakano, A., Koumura, J., Miura, E., Hoshino, J.: Spilant world: interactive emergent story game using episode tree. J. Soc. Art Sci. 6(3), 145–153 (2007)

Watching Support System by Annotation Displaying According to Fighting Game Situations

Tomoki Kajinami[✉] and Kazuya Hasegawa

Okayama University of Science, 1-1 Ridai-cho, Okayama, Japan
kajinami@mis.ous.ac.jp

Abstract. This study proposes a watching support system for a beginner watcher of fighting games. The fighting games is a type of e-Sports genre similar to Karate and boxing. Two game characters (e.g., a grappler) fight each other in the game. As with actual fighting sports, positioning on the game field of the game character in this game is important in winning the match. A concept of displaying annotation according to situations based on the characters' positioning for a beginner watcher of the fighting games is proposed from a previous study. The present paper defines three typical situations and proposes keyword and graphic annotations to encourage understanding of the match and emphasize amusement for the beginner watcher of fighting games. This study also develops a prototype system, and their annotations are superimposed on the match video. As a result, the proposed system can support beginner watchers through subjective experiments.

Keywords: e-Sports · Fighting game · Watcher support

1 Introduction

This study proposes a watching support system for a beginner watcher of fighting games, a type of e-Sports genre similar to Karate and boxing. Two game characters (e.g., a grappler) fight each other in the game. A vast amount of e-Sports competitions have recently been held worldwide [1]. Accordingly, the analysis of the competitive game players' community has been studied [3]. As with actual fighting sports, the players must consider the positioning of the game characters on the game field to win a fighting game match. A concept of displaying annotation according to situations based on the characters' positioning for a beginner watcher of the fighting games is proposed herein from a previous study [2]. The present paper defines three typical situations, namely long-distance, short-distance, and corner situations, and proposes keyword and graphic annotations to encourage understanding of the point of the match and emphasize amusement for a beginner watcher of the fighting games. The game characters' positions are extracted from the match video by template matching. Furthermore, this study develops a prototype system, and their annotations are superimposed on the match video. This study shows that the proposed system can support beginner watchers through subjective experiments.

© IFIP International Federation for Information Processing 2017
Published by Springer International Publishing AG 2017. All Rights Reserved
N. Munekata et al. (Eds.): ICEC 2017, LNCS 10507, pp. 435–438, 2017.
DOI: 10.1007/978-3-319-66715-7_57

2   Displaying Annotation According to Three Typical Situations

Long-distance, short-distance, and corner situations are defined herein. The game screen width is assumed to be 1280 pixels. The x coordinate of the game character on the left is x_l, while that on the right is x_r. Figure 1(a) shows the long-distance situation defined by $x_r - x_l \geq 300$ pixels. Figure 1(b) presents the short-distance situation defined by $x_r - x_l < 300$ pixels. Meanwhile, Fig. 1(c) illustrates the corner situation defined by $(x_l < 200 \wedge 200 \leq x_r \leq 1080) \vee (200 \leq x_l \leq 1080 \wedge 1080 < x_r)$.

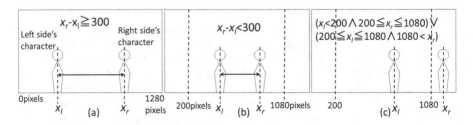

Fig. 1. Three typical situations in fighting games.

In this study, keyword and graphic annotations are proposed depending on the three typical situations. Table 1 summarizes the correspondence relationship between their situations and displayed annotations. The keyword annotations vividly show the contents of situations. The graphic annotations indicate the places, where a high possibility of a battle occurrence on the screen exists. The game players in the long-distance situation tend to wait and see the play of the opponent, and too much intense battle is not done. "Wait and see" is displayed, and a large blue rectangle is displayed between the characters. Meanwhile, the game players in the short-distance situation tend to actively attack opponents. Intense battle is done, and the victory or defeat tends to be decided at a stretch. "! Explosive !" is displayed, and a small rectangle is displayed around the characters. In the corner situation, the other character is advantageous, while the other chasing a corner is not. The character on the advantage side tends to move to close off the escape path of the disadvantage-side character. An important battle in the game tends to be done in the sky space rather than in front of both characters. "Chance" and "!" are displayed according to the advantage or disadvantage side. A rectangle is displayed in the sky between the two characters. Section 3 presents the displaying examples of the annotations.

Table 1. Displaying annotations according to the three situations.

Situations	Keyword annotation	Graphic annotation
Long-distance	Wait and see	Large blue rectangle
Short-distance	! Explosive !	Small green rectangle
Corner	Chance (Advantage side) ! (Disadvantage side)	Red rectangle

3 Prototype System

The character positions herein are extracted from a game movie by template matching using OpenCV. The template image is an image of a part of the character image of 40 × 40 pixels. The prototype system is developed for a specific game title "Street Fighter V."

Figure 2 shows an execution example of the proposed system. Figure 2(a) presents an example, in which an annotation is displayed in the long-distance situation. "Wait and see" is displayed, and a blue rectangle is shown to cover a large area between the two characters. Figure 2(b) depicts an example, in which the annotation is presented in the short-distance situation. "Explosive" and a green rectangle are displayed around both characters. Figure 2(c) shows an example, in which the annotation is presented in the corner situation. "Chance" is displayed around the advantage-side character, while "!" is displayed around the disadvantage side character. A red rectangle is displayed on the sky between the two characters.

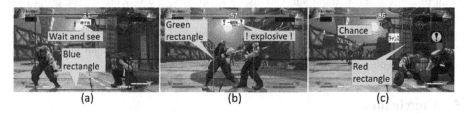

Fig. 2. Execution example of the prototype system. (Color figure online)

4 Experiment

The experiment aimed to evaluate whether the point of the match becomes easy to understand and emphasize amusement by the proposed system. We prepared the match videos with annotations using the proposed system and without annotations. The subjects were beginner watchers, who were not competitive players. Each subject watched the match videos with proposed annotations and without annotations. The order of video watching was different for each subject. A total of 10 subjects (A–J) participated in the experiment.

Table 2 summarizes the experimental result on the amusement by easiness of point of the match (7: Good, 1: Bad). We asked the subjects to evaluate whether the point of the match became easy to understand with the proposed annotation. Table 2 shows that the average evaluation value was higher in the proposed system. Eight out of 10 subjects highly evaluated the proposed annotations. In other words, there is a tendency that the proposed annotations can emphasize amusement by the easiness of the match highlight. We then focused on the comments obtained by the subjects, and performed a qualitative evaluation of the proposed system.

The typical positive comments obtained by the subjects were as follows. "I could get prediction of the battle (I could understand the point of the battle). (A and I);" "It is interesting by displayed annotations. (E, F, and G);" "Even in an unknown game, I could

Table 2. Evaluation scores by the subjects.

	A	B	C	D	E	F	G	H	I	J	Average
Video with annotations	7	3	5	5	4	7	3	7	7	6	5.4
Video without annotations	3	5	2	4	3	3	3	3	6	4	3.6

know where to focus on. (H);" and "It become easy to follow changing in battle. (J)." These comments, especially those from subject H, implied that the point of the match became easy to understand with the proposed system. The proposed system can support a beginner watcher with poor prior knowledge of the game title.

The typical negative comments obtained by the subjects were as follows. "The screen was complicated, and the screen was sometimes difficult to see. (D, E, G, and J)" and "When the keyword and graphic annotations are viewed at the same time, the game characters are difficult to see. (F and G)." These comments expressed the need for improvements in visibility as the future works. Moreover, subject B said "I can note point of battle when without annotations," and obtained a low score for the proposed system. He was a beginner of the fighting game, but had experience of a similar action game. Therefore, his watching level can be considered higher than that of the other beginner watchers. His comment imposed a consideration of the annotation displaying methods according to the watchers' watching levels as a future work.

5 Conclusion

This study proposed a watching support system for a fighting game's beginner watchers. Three typical situations were defined herein based on the game characters' positions in the game field. The proposed system displayed keyword and graphic annotations depending on the situations to support understanding of the watching point of the match. The effectiveness of the proposed system was examined through subjective experiments. The result showed that the proposed system can support understanding of the point of battle and emphasize amusement as regards watching the fighting game matches. The future work will focus on improving visibility and examining the annotation presentation methods according to the watchers' watching levels.

References

1. Adamus, T.: Playing computer games as electronic sport: in search of a theoretical framework for new research field. In: Fromme, J., Unger, A. (eds.) Computer Games and New Media Cultures: A Handbook of Digital Game Studies, pp. 477–490. Springer, Dordrecht (2012). doi: 10.1007/978-94-007-2777-9_30
2. Kajinami, T.: Supporting method for watching e-Sports considering relationship between player's conception and game field. In: Replaying Japan Again: 2nd International Japan Game Studies Conference 2014, pp. 50–51 (2014)
3. Taylor, T.L.: Raising the Stakes: E-Sports and the Professionalization of Computer Games. The MIT Press, Cambridge (2012)

Real-Time Expression Control
System for Wearable Animatronics

Hisanao Nakadai[1(✉)], Takuya Hirano[2], and Jun'ichi Hoshino[3]

[1] Art and Design, University of Tsukuba, 1-1-1 Tennodai, Tsukuba, Ibaraki 305-8577, Japan
hnaka@geijutsu.tsukuba.ac.jp
[2] Graduate School of Systems and Information Engineering, University of Tsukuba,
1-1-1 Tennodai, Tsukuba, Ibaraki 305-8573, Japan
hirano.takuya@entcomp.esys.tsukuba.ac.jp
[3] Systems and Information Engineering, University of Tsukuba, 1-1-1 Tennodai,
Tsukuba, Ibaraki 305-8573, Japan
jhoshino@esys.tsukuba.ac.jp

Abstract. The animatoronics is used for the expression of the character with many picture works which includes movies. As for the animatronics mask that the person wears of the lively character, the expression of lively character is truly possible because the actor's performance is reflected directly. In this research, I suggest using an animatronics mask in order to reflect the character's feelings and expressions real time by the actor wearing the mask. Conventionally, it is necessary for the actor to look good with the movements and facial expressions beforehand in order to determine if the actor can intuitively play the character but thinks that an actor can play a character intuitively by using this system.

Keywords: Animatoronics · EOG · Facial expression

1 Introduction

Various characters that we enjoy appear in visual works such as films. One method for presenting those characters is animatronics. This is the combined technology of special effect modeling and mechatronics and is used in various areas such as for the president of Disney World or the creatures in Star Wars. In recent years they are also used in live spectacles combined with projection mapping and provide spectators with a life-like experience. One way of using animatronics is a performer gets into a suit and controls it themselves. This method reflects the body movements of the performer and allows direct interaction with other actors and guests, giving a true sense of presence without using any CGI. But animatronics using suits often involve multiple controlling staff moving parts of the lead character with a remote control in accordance with the performer's movements and it is difficult to match movement with that of the performer playing the character. Detailed acting such as character facial expressions also largely depends on the experience and senses of the controlling staff.

© IFIP International Federation for Information Processing 2017
Published by Springer International Publishing AG 2017. All Rights Reserved
N. Munekata et al. (Eds.): ICEC 2017, LNCS 10507, pp. 439–442, 2017.
DOI: 10.1007/978-3-319-66715-7_58

This study proposes a combined system that allows for the facial expressions of the performer to be expressed on the character in real-time. This system uses multiple photo reflectors and EOG and verifies expression and gaze. With this it is possible to operate in small spaces and use within animatronics without the need of a camera. This system can sync the body movements and expressions of the performer and allows the performer to intuitively act out a character, making it possible for other actors and guests to achieve a high level of interaction with the character.

2   System Overview

This study aims to develop a new space-saving and light weight sensor unit that can be used within an animatronic suit and recognize and express the facial expressions of a performer in real-time. This study will develop a sensor unit that recognizes facial expressions and develop an animatronic which expresses the recognized facial expression information.

2.1   Development of Sensor Unit that Recognized Expressions

A person's face has 22 types of facial muscles which create the various facial expressions of a person when moved in complex ways. The shape of the face's skin surface also changes with change in facial expression.

This study recognizes these changes using multiple photo reflectors and estimates the facial expressions of the interior performer. This system also aims to recognize blinking and gaze by combining these with the obtained EOG. Figure 1 to obtain the EOG, biological signals obtained from an off-the-shelf myoelectric sensor were

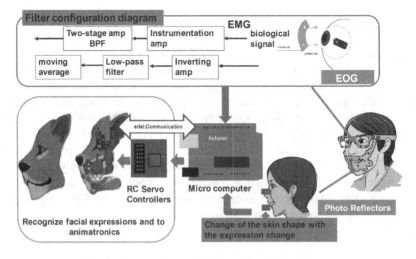

Fig. 1. System chart and filter configuration diagram.

processed through a filter Fig. 1, the moving average was multiplied with a micro-computer (Arduino Mega2560) and treated as the input signal. The myoelectric sensor used was a Grove-EMG Detector from Groove.

2.2 Development of Animatronic that Shows Expressions

An animatronic is developed which actually outputs the facial expression changes of the performer recognized by the sensor unit as facial expressions. Small arms corresponding to each area of the face which create all facial expressions are controlled with the variation amounts estimated by the sensor units as target values. The skin of the animatronic uses silicon (Gel-10) which is used in prosthetic makeup. Gel-10 is an extremely flexible material which allows for rich expression.

3 Experiments

Figure 2 shows the experimental results of this proposed method. The facial expression changes are recognized in real-time and reflected in a CG adapter acting as an animatronic. At present, the range of line of sight movement is recognized by being split into three steps. The five expressions of "Joy", "Anger", "Sadness", "Surprise", and "Normal" are recognized. However, complicated movement such as sudden eye movement, diagonal movement, or circular movement is not supported. Although change in five large expressions is recognized, incorrect recognition is prone to occur in between all expressions. There is noise contained in the EOG obtained using the myoelectric sensor primary due to difficulty in obtaining quick and complicated eye movements.

(a) Gaze recognition.

(b) Facial expression recognition.

Fig. 2. Experimental results.

While multiple filters and amps are used for noise processing and amplification, the EOG is a biological signal and touch sensor, so it is prone to various types of interference such as being affected by open air or the state of a subject's skin. Thus, it is difficult to process noise with just a LPF or HPF. In addition, an EOG characteristic phenomenon occurs when electrodes have been connected for a long period of time where the drift voltage gradually rises [1]. It is therefore considered that the regular voltage value in this experiment could possibly have changed due to drift. In the future it will be necessary to revise the noise processing method, implement machine learning, and aim to design a system that is not prone to noise influence. Furthermore, the primary reason for incorrect recognition of facial expressions with this system was that although four photo reflectors were used to recognize five large expression changes, including how someone is regularly, partial changes from "Sadness" to "Anger" and "Sadness" to "Joy" were incorrectly recognized. It is thought that the current sensor is badly positioned and unable to correctly obtain changes in skin shape for facial expressions. In the future we will review the sensor position, increase the number of sensors, and aim to recognize changes in detailed facial expressions that occur in-between expressions.

4   Conclusion

This paper developed a space-saving and light weight sensor unit that can be used within animatronic suits, aimed to recognize and express the facial expressions of a performer in real-time, and conducted experiments. By using multiple photo reflectors and EOG signals, we were able to recognize simple eye movements (one-dimensional movements) and five large facial expression changes.

In the future we plan to improve the accuracy of recognizing facial expressions and eye movements with sensors and to actually proceed with the production of an animatronic mask which reflects facial expressions Fig. 3.

 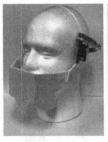 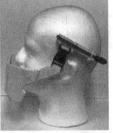

Fig. 3. Experimental animatoronics mask and sensor unit.

Reference

1. Kuno, Y.: Development of eye - gaze input interface using EOG. IPSJ 39(5), 1455–1462 (1998)

Delivering Active Fashion Advertisement to Potential Viewers

Mitsuru Nakazawa$^{(\boxtimes)}$, Jiu Xu, and Soh Masuko

Rakuten Institute of Technology, Rakuten, Inc., Rakuten Crimson House,
1-14-1 Tamagawa, Setagaya-ku, Tokyo, Japan
{mitsuru.nakazawa,jiu.xu,so.masuko}@rakuten.com

Abstract. Nowadays, more and more fashion stores have started to introduce digital signage displays for dynamically switching advertisement contents of their products. To attract people's attention and interest towards a display, some signage systems distribute suitable contents for each individual based on personal attributes, acquired through a camera. However, if there are people who are not interested in the digital signage around the display, suitable contents are not necessarily distributed to those who really intend to view it. Therefore, in this paper we propose a digital signage that can take into account people who have higher potential of viewing the display. First, we acquire human behavior and personal attributes of each person. Then, the potential degree of viewing the display is calculated for each person. Next, our system searches content candidates for each person based on their personal attributes. Finally, the distributed contents are determined by selecting more candidates for people with a higher viewing potential.

Keywords: Digital signage · Fashion advertisement · Viewing potential

1 Introduction

Generally, in fashion stores, advertisements come in the form of actual products or their posters. Recently, more and more stores have begun introducing digital signage displays as the advertisement contents can be easily updated. At the end of 2016, over 37 million digital screens were in use all over the world [1].

To change the advertisement contents of a digital signage, one of the simplest ways is to loop them on repeat. To make people more attracted, some signages can change contents by the time of day and using weather information [8], or based on social media [3], or a specific human action as the trigger such as approaching the display [2]. Moreover, to provide suitable contents for a certain person, that is, "for content personalization", [5] can change contents based on gender and age as personal attributes, which are acquired using a camera mounted on the display. However, if there are people who are not interested in the digital signage around the display, suitable contents are not necessarily distributed to those who really intend to view it.

© IFIP International Federation for Information Processing 2017
Published by Springer International Publishing AG 2017. All Rights Reserved
N. Munekata et al. (Eds.): ICEC 2017, LNCS 10507, pp. 443–446, 2017.
DOI: 10.1007/978-3-319-66715-7_59

To solve the aforementioned issue, in this paper we propose a digital signage system that can take people who have higher potential of viewing the display into account, as shown in Fig. 1. In our system we first use an RBG-D sensor to acquire human behavior, including walking speed and face orientation, together with personal attributes such as gender, and the representative colors of the upper and the lower body. Then, based on their behavior, the potential degree of viewing the display is calculated for each person. Next, our system searches content candidates for each person based on their personal attributes. Finally, the distributed contents are determined by selecting more candidates for people with a higher viewing potential.

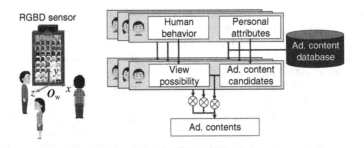

Fig. 1. System overview

2   Proposed System

Our proposed system assumes that people are passing in front of the system as shown in Fig. 1. To acquire human behavior and personal attributes, a sensor is mounted on the top of the system; we chose to adopt an RGB-D sensor as it can easily detect people and obtain point cloud data of each person in the metric scale. The angle of the sensor is set downwards so that it can observe people from a bird's-eye view. The following subsections describe the details of our proposed system, which observes time-series point cloud data from the RGB-D sensor as source data.

2.1   Acquiring Human Behavior and Personal Attributes

As preparation for the acquisition, we extract time-series point cloud data of each person from the source data. First, the coordinate system is converted from the camera coordinates to world coordinates, where the xy and the xz plane are aligned to the display and the floor plane respectively and the origin O_w is located at the bottom center of our system as shown in Fig. 1. Then, the 3D region of each person is detected at each frame by Munaro et al.'s method [4] focusing on the shape of a human head. Finally, person tracking is performed by matching detected persons between the current and the previous frame. In our system, a greedy algorithm is used to find matching correspondences that minimize the Euclidean distance between the center position of a person at the current frame and the estimated position from a person's walking trajectory.

From the time-series point cloud data of each person, we obtain their behavioral and personal attributes. In terms of behavioral attributes, we acquire the position x_i, the vector of walking speed v_i and horizontal face orientation θ_i of the i-th person. In this paper, θ_i is set as 1 if Viola and Jones' detector [7] detects a frontal face from the color image of his or her head region; otherwise 0. As personal attributes, we acquire the representative colors of the upper and lower body, and the gender of each person. Additionally, a compatible color with the two representative body colors is chosen based on the accent color and separation color of fashion color theory [6].

2.2 Calculating Potential Degree of Viewing the Display

The potential degree of viewing the display of the i-th person p_i is calculated from his or her personal behavior. In the calculation, we consider "from where, how frequently, and how they are walking whilst viewing" as the state of viewing behavior.

$$p_i\left(x_i,\ \theta_i,\ v_i\right) = f\left(x_i\right) g\left(\theta_i\right) h\left(v_i\right), \tag{1}$$

where θ_i is the vector of face orientation in the past N frames; f is a negative piecewise linear activation function of the distance between the person and the display plane, which returns higher values for people closer to the display; g is a monotone increasing function of the frequency of detected frontal faces in the N frames, which returns higher values for people viewing the display more frequently; and h is a step function of the walking speed that returns 0 for a person walking more quickly than a threshold speed, otherwise 1.

2.3 Distributing Suitable Advertisement Contents

In preparation for the content distribution, a database is constructed beforehand so that suitable advertisement contents can be searched by personal attributes. Our database consists of the image, gender information (i.e. men's, ladies' and unisex), the representative color and the type of clothes (e.g. tops and bottoms) of each fashion item.

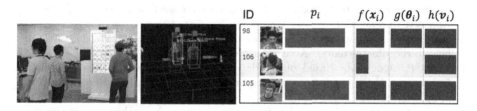

Fig. 2. Developed system (Left: scene image, middle: analyzed point cloud data, right: potential degree p_i and its component parameters)

To distribute suitable advertisement contents, first our system searches content candidates for each person from the database by their gender and compatible color. Then, the distributed contents are selected from the content candidates of each person so that the ratio of the number selected contents for each person is the same as the normalized potential degree $p'_i = p_i / \sum_i p_i$. The above procedure is repeated to update advertisement contents at a certain interval.

3   Conclusion

In this paper, we proposed a digital signage system that can take people who have higher potential of viewing the display into account. First, we acquired the human behavior and the personal attributes from time-series point cloud data observed from a RGB-D sensor. Next, the potential degree was calculated from the human behavior with consideration of their state of viewing behavior. Then, content candidates that are suitable for each person are searched from the database by using the personal attributes. Finally, distributed contents are selected from the candidates so that the ratio of selected content candidates for each person matches their normalized potential viewing degree.

As shown in Fig. 2, we have finished developing the proposed system, which will be demonstrated in the interactive session of ICEC2017. As future work, for better personalization of advertisement contents, we will try to acquire new personal attributes including age or the fashion style of pedestrians from the RGB-D sensor.

References

1. Digital Signage M2M and IoT Applications - 2nd Edition. Research and Markets (2017)
2. ImpactTV: Pista (in Japanese). http://impacttv.co.jp/product/. Accessed 10 May 2017
3. Mevato: Social marketing display for any screen. http://www.mevato.com/display. Accessed 10 May 2017
4. Munaro, M., Basso, F., Menegatti, E.: Tracking people within groups with RGB-D data. In: IEEE/RSJ International Conference on Intelligent Robots and Systems (2012)
5. Anewtech Systems: Intelli-signage: age and gender recognition system. http://intelli-signage.com/technologies/age-and-gender-recognition-system-agrs/. Accessed 10 May 2017
6. Tsurumaki, A.: How to coordinate fashion colors (in Japanese). https://tokila.jp/how-to-coordinate-colors/. Accessed 10 May 2017
7. Viola, P., Jones, M.: Rapid object detection using a boosted cascade of simple features. In: IEEE Conference on Computer Vision and Pattern Recognition, vol. 1, pp. I-511–I-518 (2001)
8. Ads of the world: Mcdonald's McMuffin sunrise. http://adsoftheworld.com/media/outdoor/mcdonalds_mcmuffin_sunrise. Accessed 10 May 2017

Zapzap: A Table-Top Device that Presents the Rough Contents of a Book to Support Book Browsing in Bookstore

Masahumi Muta(✉) and Soh Masuko(✉)

Rakuten Institute of Technology, Rakuten, Inc., Rakuten Crimson House,
1–14–1 Tamagawa, Setagaya-ku, Tokyo, Japan
{masafumi.muta,so.masuko}@rakuten.com

Abstract. In this paper, we present the concept, prototype design and implementation of Zapzap, a table-top device that shows the rough contents of a book placed on it. Zapzap is expected to be deployed in bookstores to support customers browsing books. When the user places a book on the display, the system shows keywords, i.e., words often included in the book. When the user taps one of the displayed words, a sentence that includes the selected word is shown. Zapzap aims to present the atmosphere of a book without spoiling its story.

Keywords: Table-top · Book · E-book · Shopping · Entertainment computing

1 Introduction

With the rise of electronic books (e-books) and the Internet bookstore such as Amazon, the number of brick and mortar bookstores is decreasing [4]. The merit of using an Internet bookstore is that we can easily order books that we have already decided to buy. However, physical bookstores provide us with the possibility of discovering new books. Therefore, we believe that Internet bookstores and traditional bookstores should coexist. In this paper, we propose Zapzap, which supports a user in discovering new books in a bookstore, by presenting the rough contents of a book, thereby enticing the user into buying the book.

© IFIP International Federation for Information Processing 2017
Published by Springer International Publishing AG 2017. All Rights Reserved
N. Munekata et al. (Eds.): ICEC 2017, LNCS 10507, pp. 447–451, 2017.
DOI: 10.1007/978-3-319-66715-7_60

Fig. 1. A user using Zapzap.

2 System Overview

Zapzap is a table-top device and comprises a RGB-D sensor and two displays, called the top display and the side display. The top display includes a touch sensor. We used ELO 3230L touchable monitor for the top display, a Philips BDM3201FC/11 monitor for the side display, and Intel Realsense F200 camera for the RGB-D sensor. Figure 2 shows a schematic of the device.

Once the user places a book on the top display, the system recognizes the book via the RGB-D sensor and then displays keywords, i.e., words often included in the story, around the book. Simultaneously, the side display shows the blurred cover of the book so that users know that the book has been recognized by the system. The user can tap any of the words shown on the top display. On tapping, the system shows a random sentence that contains the keyword.

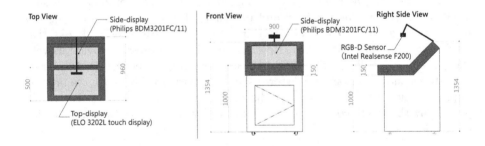

Fig. 2. Schematic of Zapzap.

2.1 Book Recognition and Keyword Positioning

To display the keywords of the placed book, we need to identify which book is on the table. It is also important to track its location to layout the keywords around the book. We used AlexNet [2] to identify the book cover. To prevent flickering due to temporal misrecognition, we designed the system to accept the output from AlexNet only when it has recognized the same book for three consecutive frames.

For book tracking, we used the depth image obtained from the RGB-D sensor. As the sensor is placed on the display, the surface of the book is closer to the sensor compared with the display surface; therefore, we can assume the centroid of the closer pixels as the center of the book. We only extract pixels that are closer to the sensor but limit extraction within 3 cm of the top display so that the user's hand can be maintained over the display without affecting tracking.

2.2 Extracting Keywords

We extract the keywords from the full text of the electronic version of the book. We morphologically analyze the full text and then pick the top ten common and proper nouns. We show an example of the extracted words as follows. The words with (n) are character names, (l) indicates a location, and (b) indicates a brand. This method tended to preferentially extract character names.

Ikebukuro West Gate Park[1]

Kana (n), Ikebukuro (l), Makoto (n), Takashi (n), Shun (n), Kyoichi (n), Isogai (n), Yamai (n), Kazunori (n), Kenji (n)

Mr. Mercedes (part 1)[2]

Brady (n), Mercedes (n/b), Pete (n), Paula (n), Handley (n), Barbara (n), Frankie (n), America (l), Toyota (b)

2.3 Placing Keywords

When displaying the keywords, we decided their placement by applying a force directed graph [1]. We considered a graph with all the words and a virtual middle point, which represents the position of the book, as its nodes. Then, we set the links between all the nodes. We set the strength of the links to $K_{ww} > K_{ww} > K_{wc}$, where K_{ww} is the strength of the links between each word and K_{wc} is for the links between each word and the virtual middle point. This causes the words to be arranged such that they spread around the middle point. In addition, we added gravity, which forces the words to gather around the center of the display so that the words is not placed outside the display even when the book is placed on the corner. Note that we indicate the virtual middle point to be where the book is placed to help with understanding, even though the book is not actually visible.

---

[1] Written by Ira Ishida, Bungeishunju Ltd.

[2] Written by Stephen King, Translated by Rou Shiraishi, Bungeishunju ltd.

(a) When the book is placed at the center.   (b) When the book is placed at the corner.

Fig. 3. Examples of keyword layouts.

Figure 3 shows an example of the layouts. Figure 3a shows the layout when the user places the book to the center of the display, while Fig. 3b shows the layout when they place it at a corner of the display.

3   Related Work

Murai and Ushiama proposed an interface to support the effective browsing of e-books by users [3]. Their system displays an attractiveness map, which visualizes the estimated transition of a user's interest through the story of the book, thereby allowing users to know where to first look in the book. While their interface aims to be used in a computer display to browse e-books, our interface aims to be used in physical book stores to browse actual books.

4   Conclusion and Future Work

We presented the concept, prototype design and implementation of Zapzap, a table-top device that shows the rough contents of a book to support a user browsing books in a physical bookstore. The system recognizes the book and then presents the content as keywords and sentences to avoid ruining the entire story. In a future study, we plan to extract more attractive keywords compared to the current method, i.e., the most frequent words. To achieve this, the attractiveness map proposed in Ref. [3] may be applicable. Moreover we plan to show additional information gathered outside the book such as the author information or online reviews.

After making these improvements, we will conduct an experiment to determine how informative the system is for the user and whether it motivates the user to read or purchase the books.

References

1. Dwyer, T.: Scalable, versatile and simple constrained graph layout. In: Proceedings of the 11th Eurographics/IEEE - VGTC Conference on Visualization, pp. 991–1006 (2009)
2. Krizhevsky, A., Sutskever, I., Hinton, G.E.: Imagenet classification with deep convolutional neural networks. In: Advances in Neural Information Processing Systems, vol. 25, pp. 1097–1105 (2012)
3. Murai, S., Ushiama, T.: Review-based recommendation of attractive sentences in a novel for effective browsing. Int. J. Knowl. Web Intell. **3**(1), 58–69 (2012)
4. Statista: Number of bookstores in the U.S. (2017). https://www.jpoksmaster.jp/Info/documents/top_transition.pdf

MR-Shoppingu: Physical Interaction with Augmented Retail Products Using Continuous Context Awareness

Kelvin Cheng(✉) ⓘ, Mitsuru Nakazawa ⓘ, and Soh Masuko ⓘ

Rakuten Institute of Technology, Rakuten, Inc., 1-14-1 Tamagawa, Tokyo, Setagaya, Japan
{kelvin.cheng,mitsuru.nakazawa,so.masuko}@rakuten.com

Abstract. In-store physical shopping experiences are often complemented with searches for product related information on mobile devices. However, there is a distinct gap between the physical reality at the shop and the digital content on mobile devices. At the same time, in the not-too-distant future, we envision a world where mixed-reality technologies become ubiquitous, in much the same way as mobile devices have become today. In this context, we proposed *MR-Shoppingu*, a novel interactive retail shopping experience by using a combination of continuous context awareness, natural user actions, and augmented physical products with online content. Users can interact with products physically and naturally, and are provided with relevant content and recommendations virtually in mixed-reality. This may help consumers in the purchasing process by increasing efficiency and certainty of purchase, and enabling a more personalized and entertaining shopping experience.

Keywords: Context awareness · Interactive retail shopping · Mixed Reality

1 Introduction

The ubiquity of personal mobile devices enables consumers access to a wealth of online product and shopping information at their fingertips. Even while holding a product within a retail shop, consumers can browse detailed product information, lookup reviews, and compare prices online through their devices. However, there is a distinct gap between what users see and touch physically at the shop, and the digital content that they are reading on their mobile devices, in terms of the interaction experience. One approach to reducing this division of physical and digital information spaces is to combine the two spaces, to make digital content accessible directly on physical objects.

Augmented Reality (AR) or Mixed Reality (MR) is an interactive technology that combines real and virtual content, and which are registered in 3D [1]. Currently, mobile AR is one of the most common form as it is easily accessible by anyone with a mobile phone, and has been used extensively to increase various retail experiences [2]. However, the main drawbacks are that users need to hold their device with their hand, and they have to switch their device "on" to use it, creating an extra barrier to activation.

Mixed Reality that uses head-mounted displays (HMD) has the potential to overcome these challenges. It allows for a more immersive experience, and removes the need to

N. Munekata et al. (Eds.): ICEC 2017, LNCS 10507, pp. 452–455, 2017.
DOI: 10.1007/978-3-319-66715-7_61

hold any devices in the hand. Hardware technologies, such as Microsoft HoloLens, have become increasingly popular recently as they become more portable and untethered, enabling users more freedom while using them. In the near future, when hardware devices become even more compact and less cumbersome, e.g. in the form of a normal pair of glasses, MR will be ubiquitous. It is this future vision where we are aiming this work towards.

In this paper, we propose the use of continuous context awareness, natural user actions, and augmented physical products, in order to provide users with relevant digital content at their context of use. This combination enables a novel, entertaining, and personalized interactive retail shopping experience for consumers. We contribute to the research community by presenting our *MR-Shoppingu* concept and design guidelines.

2   Related Work

Context is defined as "any information that can be used to characterize the situation of an entity" [3]. Based on contextual information such as location, activities or user actions, more relevant content specific to the situation can be presented to the user.

Valkkynen et al. presented a mobile handheld AR system that takes into account the location context [5]. Depending on whether the user is at home or at the store, different content is overlaid on top of product packaging. In ShelfTorchlight [4], while moving a mobile camera projector over a product shelf, coloured circles are projected onto the products, green for products that suit the user, red for ones that do not.

An advantage of using HMD is that it is always "on" and can potentially capture, or be aware of, not only the activity or location of the user, but also the activity and location of the products themselves. We also aim to enable users to just walk-up and use, without the need for prior-knowledge of how the system is to be used.

3   System Design and Implementation

In this section, we describe the design and implementation of our proof-of-concept prototype, *MR-Shoppingu*. In order to create an interactive in-store shopping experience that enhances physical products with augmented online content, we envision that users would interact with physical products naturally, without the need for any special input; the system would be able to continuously detect these user actions, and react by augmenting the physical products with relevant information. In order to achieve this, our system is guided by these design requirements:

(1) *Continuous Context Awareness* - the system is continuously aware of the context surrounding its users and the products that they are interacting with;
(2) *Natural User Actions* - Users only need to use their natural gestures and physical actions, without the need to learn a new interface, or interaction method. The system should be able to react to user's everyday activities and actions;
(3) *Incorporate online capabilities & content* – make use of digital capabilities, such as those information and functionalities that are currently only available online (e.g.

virtual bookmarks and reviews), and combine them with the physical shopping experience, bridging the gap between physical and digital worlds.

Using these design requirements, we aim to provide relevant information and recommendation to the user at the appropriate time.

MR-Shoppingu, is an application for Microsoft HoloLens and was built with Unity, Microsoft Visual Studio, HoloToolkit, and Vuforia SDK. The design requirements are realized in our system in the form of four main components:

- Context detection – The context can be detected via activities between the user, objects, and the situation in the scene. We have divided possible context into 6 predefined states: *idle, approach, gaze, grab, reverse, return* (Fig. 1). Predominately, the distance between the user and the object is used to distinguish the states in the current context, e.g. the distance at *idle* is the largest, while *grab* and *reverse*, are the smallest. Sequence information from the different states are also used to identify the context, e.g. *grab* must happen before *reverse*.

Fig. 1. (a) A user using our system. (b–f) Screenshots taken from user's view. The 6 states of our *MR-Shoppingu* system: *idle*, (b) *approach*, (c) *gaze*, (d) *grab*, (e) *reverse*, (f) *return*

- Gaze detection - The gaze direction provided by HoloToolkit is used in conjunction with Vuforia to determine when products are being gazed at.
- Product recognition and tracking - An image of each side of the product are first scanned manually and registered as a cuboid, Vuforia will then return the object location in 3D space. The side of the object that is facing the user can then be calculated, and used to determine if the object is in *reverse*.
- Visualisation - Texts and basic geometries are used in our current system, while videos, text descriptions and text reviews are pre-defined for each state, and for each product.

4   User Scenario

In order to demonstrate the use case of our proof-of-concept system, we showcase one specific user scenario that it is designed to support:

(a) In a café, a shelf with a variety of coffee beans are being displayed (*idle*).
(b) As the user walks closer to the shelf, the Peru bag is recommended to the user, shown as a message displayed next to the product. The Peru bag is recommended as the system knows the cup of coffee that the user has just purchased in the café (*approach*).
(c) As the user gazes at the various products, each product "highlights" by showing a bounding box, as well as its price and rating information (*gaze*).
(d) As the user picks up the Peru bag, further description of the product as well as the top user review is shown to the user (*grab*).
(e) The user turns the product around for further information at the back. The system plays a video showing provenance information about the coffee plantation in Peru and how coffee beans are processed (*reverse*).
(f) As the user places the bag down, the system detects that he may not be interested in the bag anymore, it then recommends another bag nearby (*return*).

5   Conclusion and Future Work

In this paper, we proposed *MR-Shoppingu*, a novel mixed-reality interactive in-store shopping experience that enhances physical products by combining continuous context awareness, natural user actions, and augmented online content that is relevant to the user and their context of use at the particular time. This combination may help to increase efficiency and certainty of purchase, and enables a more personalized and entertaining experience for consumers.

As our next step, we aim to conduct a user study to investigate how much users prefer using *MR-Shoppingu* to purchase, and how effective it is in helping consumers shop in physical retail shops. In the long term, we hope to be able to make the system more flexible and robust, by automatically detecting objects, and recognizing products by searching in online product databases in real-time.

References

1. Azuma, R.T.: A survey of augmented reality. Presence **6**(4), 355–385 (1997)
2. Dacko, S.G.: Enabling smart retail setting via mobile augmented reality shopping apps. Technol. Forecast. Soc. Chang., 1–14 (2016)
3. Dey, A.K.: Understanding and using context. Pers. Ubiquit. Comput. **5**, 4–7 (2001)
4. Löchtefeld, M., et al.: ShelfTorchlight: Augmenting a shelf using a camera projector unit. In: Adjunct Proceedings of the 8th International Conference on Pervasive Computing (2010)
5. Välkkynen, P., Boyer, A., Urhemaa, T., Nieminen, R.: Mobile augmented reality for retail environments. In: Proceedings of Workshop on Mobile Interaction in Retail Environments in Conjunction with MobileHCI (2011)

Creating a Regional and Historical Streetscape Simulation System

Yasuo Kawai[✉]

Bunkyo University, 1100 Namegaya, Chigasaki, Kanagawa 253-8550, Japan
kawai@shonan.bunkyo.ac.jp

Abstract. The purpose of this study is to create a streetscape simulation system to support local cultural succession by conveying—in a clear and simple way— local history and culture to interested members of the public. We developed an interactive system, based on a game engine, for the streetscape of Fujisawa-juku, which is a post-station town on the former Tokaido Road of the late Edo period. We designed 3D models for former architecture and urban facilities, using Ukiyo-e and old documents provided by the Fujisawa city archive as references. In addition, regarding dynamic spatial elemental components that encourage users to visually survey the area, we prepared non-player characters that walk in a specified range and communicate a fixed set of remarks. Furthermore, we created soundscapes, which correspond to particular locations, using sound effects in the 3D models by incorporating natural sounds. The developed streetscape simulation system is on permanent exhibition at the Fujisawa-juku Intersection Hall and is widely accessible to the public.

Keywords: Streetscape simulation · Game engine · Post-station town

1 Introduction

In this study, we developed a simulation system that reproduces the historical and cultural landscape in order to transmit information and knowledge regarding a district's history and culture in a clear and simple way. Due to a variety of societal changes, such as urbanization, depopulation, declining fertility, and population aging, it is difficult to pass on regional history and culture in Japan. In 2007, the Agency for Cultural Affairs of Japan proposed the Basic Scheme for Historic and Cultural Properties to capture districts' cultural assets, regardless of designation or specification, in a comprehensive effort to preserve and use these assets as well as their surrounding environments.

Through our study of the development of an urban space simulation system using a game engine, we were able to modify the spatial component such that we could remove objects influencing the landscape and evaluate the remaining landscape image. Thus, in this study, we applied knowledge of this urban space simulation system to develop a simulation system that reproduces the historical cultural landscape in virtual space.

Previous studies have incorporated virtual reality technology in landscape simulation systems [1]. These systems, however, were typically developed for a dedicated

© IFIP International Federation for Information Processing 2017
Published by Springer International Publishing AG 2017. All Rights Reserved
N. Munekata et al. (Eds.): ICEC 2017, LNCS 10507, pp. 456–459, 2017.
DOI: 10.1007/978-3-319-66715-7_62

application and, consequently, lack the versatility necessary for use in alternate locations. However, there are studies more relevant to our objective that focus on landscape simulation using game engines. Within these studies, several successfully developed simulation systems for historical sites [2, 3]. In fact, some systems were able to reproduce historical architecture; however, only a few studies developed their simulation systems to work on a town scale.

2   Methods

2.1   Study Area

The study area of this system was Fujisawa-juku (currently Fujisawa city, Kanagawa Prefecture), which is the sixth post-station town on the former Tokaido Road. Fujisawa-juku flourished as the temple town of Shojoko-ji (Yugyo-ji) Temple, which is the grand head temple of the Ji-Shu sect, and was designated as one of the first post-station towns in 1601. In 1843, Fujisawa-juku contained one *honjin* (inn designated as an official lodging for a *daimyo* (great lord)), one *waki honjin* (subsidiary inn used by *daimyo* attendants), and 45 inns.

Based on *Ukiyo-e* (color prints of everyday life during the Edo period) and old documents, this study developed a schematic of Fujisawa-juku during the late Edo period. In this system, we reproduced the area around the Daigiri Bridge over the Sakai River from Shojoko-ji Temple in the northeastern part to *Maita honjin* in the west (Fig. 1).

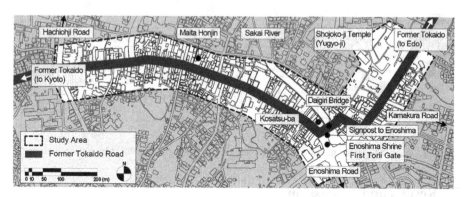

Fig. 1. Fujisawa-juku that was the post-station town on Former Tokaido Road

2.2   Development

To develop our simulation system, we used a game engine called Unreal Engine. We decided to create a model of individual spatial components in the three-dimensional computer graphics production environment and to incorporate texture map and normal map in image format into the game engine. We designed 3D models for architectural structures, such as the temple, *honjin*, *waki-honjin*, inns, merchant houses, and urban facilities, such as *torii* (gateway entrance to an Enoshima shrine), *kosatsu-ba* (street bulletin board), bridges, trees, plants, and so on.

In addition, regarding dynamic spatial elemental components that encourage users to visually survey the area, we prepared non-player characters (NPC) that walk in a specified range and communicate a fixed set of remarks to coincide. To reproduce the streetscape with friendly feeling, we arranged NPC models based on the behaviors of the people who lived in Fujisawa-juku, such as tradesmen, Buddhist monks, *meshi-mori-onna* (maid at an inn), as well as the visitors to the post-station town, such as *samurai* and travelers. Furthermore, we created soundscapes, which correspond to particular locations, using sound effects in the 3D models by incorporating natural sounds, such as the river flowing, birds singing, and insects chirping.

2.3 Interface

We designed the system to be interactive so that we could freely move in the post-station town. The operational method of the first-person perspective is to move the point of view using the keyboard and to rotate the line of sight using the mouse. When it is released to the public, it will be easy to operate using a gamepad. In this operational method, movement by the left analog pad and rotation by the right analog pad are set as the basic operating methods. Furthermore, various activities, such as jumping, respawning (moving to preset position), horse riding, and *saisen* (offering of money to temples), are offered, and several keys and buttons were assigned to these activities in each interface. For the gamepad, we decided to match activities to conditions (Fig. 2).

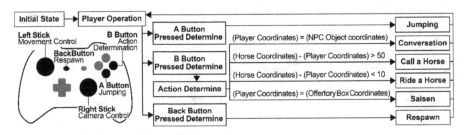

Fig. 2. Basic operation method of game pad and processing of activities by button actions.

3 Results and Discussion

The developed streetscape simulation system is on permanent display at the Fujisawa-juku Intersection Hall and is widely accessible to the public (Fig. 3). The public exhibition is displayed on a 40-inch monitor connected to a PC controlled with a gamepad. This is an independent system not connected to a network, and, by automatically launching the executable file when the computer is booted up, it is set so that even curators unfamiliar with the system could operate it with ease. There are no major problems in its current operation and it functions stably. After opening the public exhibition, we received some user suggestions with which we could improve the system. For example, certain spatial elements visually expressed in *Ukiyo-e* were deformed, and a few elements, such as the Enoshima signpost, allegedly differed from the actual shapes of the past. Therefore, to assess these matters, we referenced old documents provided by the Fujisawa city archive. In the future, we will increase the accuracy of this system through comparisons with a variety of literature and user evaluations.

Fig. 3. Operation screen of proposed system, the left side shows the Former Tokaido Road, while the right side shows the precincts of the Shojoko-ji (Yugyo-ji) Temple.

4 Conclusions

The purpose of this study was to develop a system to support local cultural succession by conveying—in a clear and simple way—the Fujisawa-juku of the late Edo period to members of the public interested in the local history and culture. Currently, the system comprises the Yugyo-ji Temple across the Daigiri Bridge to the area leading to *Maita honjin*. In the future, we plan to update the contents, which will expand the system to cover the entire town of Fujisawa-juku, address the feedback obtained from the public exhibition, and improve the system to be a post-station town streetscape simulation system that is as realistic as possible. Furthermore, based on the findings obtained with this system, we plan to convert it to general application and develop a platform for a historical cultural landscape simulation system that can be used in other areas.

Acknowledgment. This work was supported by JSPS KAKENHI Grant Number JP16K00718.

References

1. Santosa, H., Ikaruga, S., Kobayashi, T.: Development of landscape planning support system using interactive 3D visualization: a case study in Malang, Indonesia. J. Archit. Plan. **79**(706), 2699–2709 (2014)
2. Fukuda, T., Ban, H., Yagi, K., Nishiie, J.: Development of high-definition virtual reality for historical architectural and urban digital reconstruction: a case study of Azuchi castle and old castle town in 1581. In: Celani, G., Sperling, D.M., Franco, J.M.S. (eds.) CAAD Futures 2015. CCIS, vol. 527, pp. 75–89. Springer, Heidelberg (2015). doi:10.1007/978-3-662-47386-3_5
3. Sheng, W., Ishikawa, K., Tanaka, H.T., Tsukamoto, A., Tanaka, S.: Photorealistic VR space reproductions of historical kyoto sites based on a next-generation 3D game engine. J. Advan. Simul. Sci. Eng. **1**(1), 188–204 (2015)

Virtual Co-Eating: Making Solitary Eating Experience More Enjoyable

Monami Takahashi[✉], Hiroki Tanaka, Hayato Yamana, and Tatsuo Nakajima

Department of Computer Science and Engineering, Waseda University, Tokyo, Japan
{m.takahashi,tatsuo}@dcl.cs.waseda.ac.jp,
{mizurin,yamana}@yama.info.waseda.ac.jp

Abstract. Recently, a research on eating habits of Japanese college students revealed that they have a highly desire to communicate with others through co-eating. Even though better eating experience through co-eating is important, they often tend to be alone even more because of some reasons like small households, living alone, and having no time to find others for co-eating. Therefore, we believe that it may improve eating experience by incorporating a fictional character into the real space as a partner to eat together. For validating the idea, we have developed a *virtual co-eating* system for solving issues caused from solitary eating, and show some insights from its user study.

Keywords: Co-eating solitary · Eating · Augmented reality

1 Introduction

Recently, Japanese college students tend to eat alone even more because of some reasons like small households, living alone and having no time to find others for co-eating. However, they have a highly desire to communicate with others thorough co-eating [1]. Co-eating gives them better eating experience that cannot gain from solitary eating, and recent researches showed that good eating experience through co-eating closely related to positive emotion such as 'enjoyable', 'family', 'talking', 'together', 'friend', and 'smile' [1]. Especially, 'family' and 'talking' are strongly related to good experience [2]. Therefore, we believe that a partner to eat together is essential as a factor for improving solitary eating experience.

Typically, good eating experience is comprehensively obtained by combining not only the taste of food but also the environment, memory and experience such as a condition, feelings and atmosphere while eating. Therefore, there are several investigations on whether it is possible to improve eating experience by changing a variety of information other than the taste of food. For example, in a past study to report a system that enhances eating experience, a feeling of a full stomach is maintained due to changing the meal amount, if its appearance size is not changed by an augmented reality technology [3].

© IFIP International Federation for Information Processing 2017
Published by Springer International Publishing AG 2017. All Rights Reserved
N. Munekata et al. (Eds.): ICEC 2017, LNCS 10507, pp. 460–464, 2017.
DOI: 10.1007/978-3-319-66715-7_63

In this study, we introduce an alternative approach named *virtual co-eating* to improve eating experience by allowing a user to talk with a virtual partner and dissolving his/her dull eating experience for college students who frequently eat food alone.

2 Virtual Co-Eating System

In order to improve eating experience, the virtual co-eating system is designed by focusing on the two factors: "*a preferable eating partner*" and "*enjoyable conversation*". For considering the first factor; we adopted a 3D virtual character named Kurei Kei (Pro-Nama-Chan, https://github.com/kureikei), who is typically preferable from the main target users of the virtual co-eating system who are Japanese computer science course students as a virtual partner because the character is very popular in young Japanese information technology communities. This character can easily guide to an enjoyable conversation with various common topics with the main target users. Also, in order to increase a feeling of the reality on the character, we decided to use the mirroring effect, which is the effect of having favor with others who do the same actions as a user. As shown in Fig. 1(a), for example, in the virtual co-eating system, the user's smile is detected while talking with the virtual partner, and the partner also smiles as a feedback.

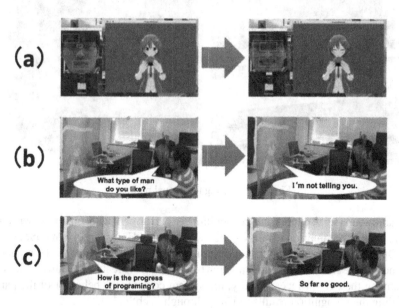

Fig. 1. An overview of virtual co-eating system.

For considering the second factor: enjoyable conversation, the virtual partner answers appropriate responses when a user speaks to her as shown in Fig. 1(b) and (c). On the other hand, when the user is silent, the partner asks the user a question. The partner talks three topics; common topics with users, topics related to the meal, and typical daily conversation. Also, in order to direct the atmosphere to a pleasant dining table and to guide a user to an enjoyable conversation experience, the system offers a background music taken from a video game for making eating atmosphere calm.

In the virtual co-eating system, the partner's behavior is generated in software that can create 3D character's motions called MMD. In addition, the voice of the partner is generated by a voice synthesizing software using 500 kinds of voice materials from actual voice actors. The character's 3D model, motion materials and voice materials are loaded into Unity, which is a game development platform. We wrote C# scripts and to control the playback timing of the partner's motion, expressions and voice.

If the system requires to wear a wearable device such as a head-mounted display, it makes a user hard to eat and to see, then it makes difficult to improve eating experience. Therefore, the system uses a projection technique to present the virtual partner in the real space. The screen of the mesh fabric is adopted for the projection to make the partner to be more three-dimensional in the real space as shown in Fig. 2.

Fig. 2. Projecting the virtual partner

In addition, facial expression recognition is performed with OpenCV written in Python, and the recognition results can be transmitted to Unity through WebSocket. By using OpenCV's haar-like feature classifier in two stages, we cut out the face, then we implemented the smile recognition function by detecting the feature quantity of the smile from among the cut out faces. Finally, the system controls the behavior of the partner by sending the recognition results to Unity through WebSocket.

3 Preliminary User Study

We conducted an experiment to investigate whether it is possible to improve eating experience by changing solitary eating experience to co-eating experience through the dialogue between participants who join to the experiment and the virtual partner. The main purpose of the user study is to find potential pitfalls of the current design not to validate the effectiveness of the design. This experiment was carried out by five participants; 20's male Japanese computer science course students who like animation and game content characters and who are usually eating alone. In the experiment, each participant first silently eats white rice balls with no good taste alone. Then, he uses this system to have the conversation with the virtual partner and eats the same rice balls. Finally, we analyzed the evaluation of each factors designed in the system through the questionnaires and the interview with him.

From the results of the questionnaires, when comparing with the eating experience to eat food alone and with the virtual partner, 4 out of 5 participants answered that their eating experience was improved. From the interviews, three participants said *"I felt it was more delicious than when I was eating alone."* In addition, a participant claimed *"It were not tasty because I were hungry at the time when eating alone."*, and also commented *"I did not matter for me."* when eating with the system. On the other hand, some participants who did not change eating experience with the system answered *"Because I were talking with the partner, I did not pay an attention to meal."* Thus, it is essential how the system supports the conversation with the partner.

More than half participants answered *"Whichever"* for the background music and talking common topics in the conversation with the virtual partner. Regarding common topics, in particular, three participants commented *"It is better to have a daily conversation than to talk about programming as common topics during eating."* In addition, one participant commented *"I want to share feelings of delicious food through conversation."*

Regarding a background music, one participant answered *"There is no background music in my actual daily life."*, and two participants answered *"I did not feel loneliness when there is a background music."* On the other hand, two participants answered, *"It would be better to use environmental sounds such as talking sounds and tableware sounds, not a background music from a video game."*

Regarding a smile feedback, four participants answered *"I felt that my partner was smiling if I laughed, then I became more smiling."* Thus, this approach seems that participants were able to make the virtual partner feel more preferable. On the other hand, one participant commented *"It looked she was always laughing."*

4   Conclusion

In this study, we developed a virtual co-eating system to improve eating experience. The system provides better eating experience through a conversation with an empathetic virtual partner. The current system focuses on improving eating experience of 20's Japanese computer science course students. We conducted an experiment to extract pitfalls of the current design, and extracted some insights for future improvement of the current prototype system.

References

1. Nakagawa, M., Nagatsuka, M.: The function and the possibility of "Kyoshoku" (eating together). J. HortResearch **64**, 55–65 (2010)
2. Iitsuka, Y.: Analysis of the Psychological and Behavioural Pattern in Eating with Others and Eating Alone I, Shimane University (2014)
3. Narumi, T., Ban, Y., Kajinami, T., Tanikawa, T., Hirose, M.: Augmented perception of satiety: controlling food consumption by changing apparent size of food with augmented reality. In: Proceedings of the SIGCHI Conference on Human Factors in Computing Systems, pp. 109–118 (2012)

Rapid Finger Motion Tracking on Low-Power Mobile Environments for Large Screen Interaction

Yeongnam Chae$^{(\boxtimes)}$ and Daniel Crane

Rakuten Institute of Technology, Rakuten, Inc., Rakuten Crimson House,
1-14-1 Tamagawa, Setagaya-ku, Tokyo, Japan
{yeongnam.chae,daniel.crane}@rakuten.com

Abstract. Motion and gesture are garnering significant interest as the sizes of screens are getting larger. To provide lightweight finger motion tracking on low-power mobile environments, we propose an approach that breaks down the stereotypes of camera view points. By directing the camera view angle towards the ceiling, the proposed approach can reduce the problem complexity incurred by complicated background environments. Though this change incurs poor lighting conditions for image processing, by clustering and tracking the fragmented motion blobs from the motion image of the saturation channel, rapid finger motion can be tracked efficiently with low computational load. We successfully implemented and tested the proposed approach on a low-power mobile device with a 1.5 GHz mobile processor and a low specification camera with a capture rate of under 15 fps.

Keywords: Motion tracking · Mobile environment · Remote interface

1 Introduction

As screens are getting larger, multi-modal interaction including gesture and voice is becoming a significant research topic due to their intuitiveness and convenience in order to handle more information. Since the introduction of the RGB-D sensor, hand gesture and motion tracking have become rapidly studied fields [3,6,7] among multi-modal interfaces.

However, the approaches adopting RGB-D sensors belong to an area that is struggling to secure popularity due to the requirement of specialized depth sensors for the motion interface. On the other hand, with the growth of the computer vision technology, recognizing hand posture using RGB sensors is also seeing enhanced accuracy [2,4,5]; although this approach still has problems dealing with complex backgrounds, and working in low-power environments. In addition, both RGB and RGB-D based approaches have restrictions on the distance between the human and the sensor if the sensor is installed on a screen.

© IFIP International Federation for Information Processing 2017
Published by Springer International Publishing AG 2017. All Rights Reserved
N. Munekata et al. (Eds.): ICEC 2017, LNCS 10507, pp. 465–468, 2017.
DOI: 10.1007/978-3-319-66715-7_64

Fig. 1. Overview: remote finger motion interface for large screens

In order to overcome such limitations, in this paper we propose an approach that tracks rapid finger motion in low-power mobile environments. By breaking down the stereotypes of camera view points, we successfully show the potential of using low-power mobile devices as remote motion capturing devices. In addition, by focusing on finger motion rather than gesture we can successfully implement the tracking system on low-power mobile devices, and configure it as a remote interface for large screen interaction, even in the case of blurry images.

2   Proposed Approach

Compared to traditional motion capturing systems on large screens, we separate the capturing sensor from the screen and hand its functionality to remote mobile devices that are more broadly distributed than specialized sensors like RGB-D. By directing the camera view angle towards the ceiling from around 20 cm under the hand we can expect a relatively simple and static background compared to camera perspectives used in traditional motion capture systems. Challenging problems in the proposed system include minimizing lighting effects and detecting fast hand movement within a short distance between the hand and the mobile camera. In this paper we focus on the motion of two fingers to extract more robust finger position than using a single finger, and to open the possibility of extending the method to include recognition of gestures such as finger picking in the future. The overview of the proposed approach is illustrated in Fig. 1. We will describe each of the issues and how we resolved them in the following sub-sections.

2.1   Acquiring Image and Noise Removal

The reasons for most traditional motion capture systems used for large screens being directed towards the human body (along with potentially complex background information) include the camera's mount position, and the spatial relationship between the user and the camera. In the proposed system, by separating the capture function from the screen body to a remote mobile device, we can configure the spatial relationship between the user and the camera more flexibly. However, by directing the camera to the ceiling, the proposed system can not

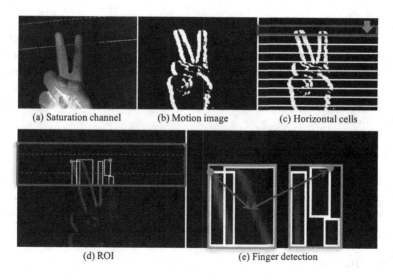

Fig. 2. Rapid finger motion detection (Color figure online)

avoid the effect of lighting which is one of the most challenging problems in the field of computer vision. In order to minimize the effects of lighting, we capture an HSV (Hue, Saturation, Value) image rather than RGB image, and use only the saturation channel, which is known to be robust to changes in lighting. Figure 2(a) shows the captured saturation channel. From the saturation channel, we calculate the motion difference after the noise removal using a morphological operation.

2.2 Rapid Finger Motion Detection and Tracking

Though saturation is relatively robust to changes in lighting compared to RGB, it is not invariant; as such, there can occur fragments of motion blobs in the differential image. Many motion detection approaches adopted Motion History Image (MHI)[1] which accumulates image differentials over time to acquire robust motion blobs. However, in the case of low-power environments it is hard to use MHI because the frame rate of the device is too low to capture rapid finger motion. In the proposed approach, we emphasize differential image by horizontal morphological operation accepting fragmented blobs, as shown in Fig. 2(b). In order to find the fingers in the fragmented motion image, we divide the entire image horizontally and compress each horizontal cell with the column-wise OR operation; Fig. 2(c) shows these horizontal cells. By checking the number of black and white transitions from the top compressed cell to the bottom, we can find the first cell that includes the fingers. Based on the detected horizontal cell, we set up wider ROI (Region Of Interest) and extract the image blobs of each fragmented finger motion, as seen in Fig. 2(d). In order to classify the motion blobs as left finger or right finger, we first find the upper-left and upper-right corners of the region spanned by the motion blobs (indicated by the light-blue dots in

Fig. 2(d)) by comparing the distance of the corners of each bounding box with upper-left and upper-right points of the ROI (indicated by red dots). Using the upper-left and upper-right corners of the region of motion, we can then classify each blob by the corner to which its center is nearest; illustrated in Fig. 2(e). In order to track the motion robustly, we track each finger's motion over time and verify it by comparing size, aspect ratio and overlapping region with the previous frame.

3   Performance

We implemented the proposed approach in a low-power mobile environment with a 1.5 GHz mobile processor and a low specification camera with a capture rate of under 15 fps. Under these conditions, our method successfully detected and tracked rapid finger motion at 21 ms/frame in 320 × 240 resolution.

4   Conclusion

In this paper, we proposed a rapid finger motion tracking methodology on low-power mobile environments for large screen interaction. In order to reduce the complexity of the problem caused by complicated and dynamic background conditions, we separated the capture function from the screen to a remote mobile device and changed the camera view, accepting fragmented motion caused by rapid finger motion and poor lighting conditions. By detecting finger motion efficiently from the fragmented motion blobs, we have successfully tracked rapid finger motion in a low-power environment. We implemented and verified the proposed approach on a low-power mobile device, which demonstrated real-time performance. In our future work, we will extend this approach to recognize finger motion gestures to provide more flexible interaction.

References

1. Bobick, A.F., Davis, J.W.: The recognition of human movement using temporal templates. In: TPAMI (2001)
2. de La Gorce, M., Fleet, D.J., Paragios, N.: Model-based 3D hand pose estimation from monocular video. In: TPAMI (2011)
3. Sharp, T., Keskin, C., Robertson, D., Taylor, J., Shotton, J.: Accurate, robust, and flexible real-time hand tracking. In: CHI (2015)
4. Simon, T., Joo, H., Matthews, I., Sheikh, Y.: Hand keypoint detection in single images using multiview bootstrapping. In: CVPR (2017)
5. Stenger, B., Thayananthan, A., Torr, P.H., Cipolla, R.: Model-based hand tracking using a hierarchical Bayesian filter. In: TPAMI (2006)
6. Wan, C., Yao, A., Gool, L.: Hand pose estimation from local surface normals. In: Leibe, B., Matas, J., Sebe, N., Welling, M. (eds.) ECCV 2016. LNCS, vol. 9907, pp. 554–569. Springer, Cham (2016). doi:10.1007/978-3-319-46487-9_34
7. Ye, Q., Yuan, S., Kim, T.-K.: Spatial attention deep net with partial PSO for hierarchical hybrid hand pose estimation. In: Leibe, B., Matas, J., Sebe, N., Welling, M. (eds.) ECCV 2016. LNCS, vol. 9912, pp. 346–361. Springer, Cham (2016). doi:10.1007/978-3-319-46484-8_21

Analyzing Video Game Completion Achievements Implications for Game Project Scope

Eric Nelson Bailey(✉) and Kazunori Miyata

Japan Advanced Institute of Science and Technology, Nomi, Japan
bailey@jaist.ac.jp

Abstract. Game development project managers and product owners, such as directors, producers, and studio heads, rely on experience-based tacit knowledge to decide how much content to create for players. However, they could be operating on a misunderstanding of the way their players consume game content and how much game content is even desirable to players.

This paper presents the initial findings of our efforts to mine video game achievement data to discover trends in game completion rates and correlations to factors outside of the length of the game itself. Through tagging a sample of game achievements that signal a player has "finished" the primary single-player content, we discover that, for most games, few players will consume all of the provided content. With a better understanding of how players consume game content, project managers and product owners can make more informed decisions on project scope, which could reduce game budgets, make schedules easier to meet, and improve overall production efficiency.

Keywords: Game development · Project scope · Player retention · Completion rates · Achievements · Overdesign · Project management

1 Introduction

The video game industry generated over $100 billion in revenues in 2016 and is projected to continue growing in the coming years [1]. However, pressures from free-to-play, mobile, and independent games as well as competing entertainment products are forcing video game publishers and studios into difficult positions. The market, despite its size, is growing more difficult to profitably compete in, and video game budgets are growing to the point where many existing companies are one miscalculated project away from bankruptcy. With so much money at stake, publishers and studios in the video game industry need methods for determining the value of production tasks for their consumers and for deciding a scope for their projects that will generate the best return on investment.

© IFIP International Federation for Information Processing 2017
Published by Springer International Publishing AG 2017. All Rights Reserved
N. Munekata et al. (Eds.): ICEC 2017, LNCS 10507, pp. 469–472, 2017.
DOI: 10.1007/978-3-319-66715-7_65

2 Background

2.1 Video Game Project Scope Issues

Project scope is important because it is tied to schedules and development budgets. However, optimum scope is difficult to determine for any software development project, let alone for video game development projects, in which value can be much more difficult to define.

The video game industry suffers from poor project management practices, so improvements could not only improve the quality of life for game developers, but could also improve the quality of games and raise profits [2]. Of development issues, project scope is a critical problem for video game developers [3].

Game development might differ in some ways from other forms of software development, but software engineering principles can still be applied [4, 5], and a well-defined scope can remain flexible, while avoiding overdesign, feature creep and other risks [3].

The reality that players are not finishing their games and the development waste this might entail has come to some attention [6–8]. With regards to playtimes, prior research into player engagement discovered that player interest tends to fall according to a Weibull distribution [9], regardless of the properties of the game itself [10].

2.2 Achievement Data

Video game achievements reward players with digital badges for triggering events linked to game tasks such as single-player story progression, skill tests, or multiplayer-based challenges. Microsoft, Valve, Sony, Apple, Google, and some other platform holders have all implemented some form of achievement system for their games.

Valve makes much of their Steam service's game data available to the public through an API, which has inspired people such as Kyle Orland, at Ars Technica, Sergey Galyonkin, creator of Steam Spy, and "xPaw" and "Marlamin", creators of SteamDB, to scrape the available data to discover various trends in sales and usage patterns. Through this data, it has been discovered that over a quarter of games (26.1%) have never been played, and, including the unplayed games, almost half (45%) have been played less than an hour, with just over a quarter of games (27.4%) having been played for more than 10 h [11].

Of the data Valve provides, achievement data provides a rich source of information about the way players engage with their games that could be analyzed to help improve project scope decisions.

3 Methodology

Valve's Steam service keeps publicly visible information regarding achievement rarities. Using publicly available data from Steam, a list of 31,962 store entries, 5,489 of which had both single-player mode and achievements, was obtained. The achievement statistics data for each of these games was downloaded via Steam's API. Subsequent data analysis focused on progression-based achievements that indicated the primary, or "main path," single-player content was completed by the player, excluding achievements that relied on game difficulty settings or branching endings.

In some cases, the achievement descriptions were enough to determine the appropriate game completion achievement, but often the entries needed to be checked against other sources, such as game walkthroughs or achievement guides, to determine what, if any, achievement marked completing the single-player content and whether any conditions existed. If the completion achievement was unclear, or the overall achievement rarity pattern indicated broken or post-release achievement implementation, the entry was pruned from further statistic calculations.

4   Results

Currently, we have checked 15% of the 5,489 candidate samples obtained from Steam. Of the 825 entries checked, 412 samples were identified as having completion achievements that did not rely on any special conditions other than clearing the game. Completion rates ranged from 0% to 56% completion with a mean of 14% (95% confidence interval of 13–16% with a margin of error of 1%), a median of 10%, and a standard deviation of 13%.

The distribution frequency in Fig. 1 shows that, for nearly half of the games measured (202), 10% or fewer players finish the main game. Only about a quarter of games (106) had more than 20% of their players finishing the game, and only about 2% of games (9) had more than half seeing the game through to the end.

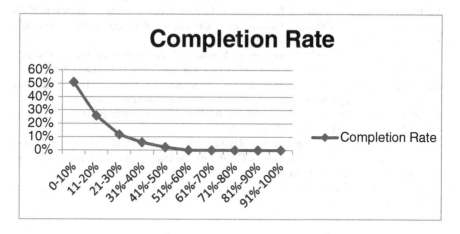

Fig. 1. Distribution of video game completion ratings based on achievements.

5   Conclusions and Future Work

Player retention falls over time, and few games, even short ones, have most of their players reaching the end of their single-player content. With an understanding of how players consume their game content, developers can take steps to examine their games against the backdrop of the market and decide whether the project scopes they have are appropriate to the value they wish to offer their players. By better tailoring project scope to the needs of their market, developers have the potential to avoid resource waste and schedule overruns.

In addition to analyzing more samples, we will continue our preliminary work testing correlations between completion rates and other data factors.

References

1. McDonald, E.: The global games market will reach $108.9 billion in 2017 with mobile taking 42%. Newzoo. https://newzoo.com/insights/articles/the-global-games-market-will-reach-108-9-billion-in-2017-with-mobile-taking-42/. Accessed 24 May 2017
2. Della Rocca, J.: Friction costs: how immature production practices and poor quality of life are bankrupting the game industry. Escapist Mag. http://www.escapistmagazine.com/articles/view/video-games/issues/issue_40/243-Friction-Costs. Accessed 24 May 2017
3. Petrillo, F., Pimenta, M., Trindade, F., Dietrich, C.: What went wrong? a survey of problems in game development. Comput. Entertain. (CIE) 7(1), 13 (2009). doi:10.1145/1486508.1486521
4. Kanode, C.M., Haddad, H.M.: Software engineering challenges in game development. In: Proceedings of the 2009 Sixth International Conference on Information Technology: New Generations, pp. 260–265. IEEE (2009). doi:10.1109/ITNG.2009.74
5. Musil, J., Schweda, A., Winkler, D., Biffl, S.: A survey on the state of the practice in video game software development. Technical report, QSE-IFS-10/04, TU Wien (2010)
6. Phillips, B.: Peering into the black box of player behavior: the player experience panel at Microsoft game studios. In: Games Developers Conference (GDC 2010) (2010)
7. Hullett, K., Nagappan, N., Schuh, E., Hopson, J.: Data analytics for game development: NIER track. In: Proceedings of the 33rd International Conference on Software Engineering (ICSE), pp. 940–943. IEEE (2011). doi:10.1145/1985793.1985952
8. Zimmermann, T., Phillips, B., Nagappan, N., Harrison, C.: Data-driven games user research. In: CHI Workshop on Game User Research (CHI-GUR 2012), pp. 1–4. ACM (2012)
9. Bauckhage, C., Kersting, K., Sifa, R., Thurau, C., Drachen, A., Canossa, A.: How players lose interest in playing a game: an empirical study based on distributions of total playing times. In: 2012 IEEE Conference on Computational Intelligence and Games (CIG), pp. 139–146. IEEE (2012). doi:10.1109/CIG.2012.6374148
10. Sifa, R., Bauckhage, C., Drachen, A. The playtime principle: large-scale cross-games interest modeling. In: 2014 IEEE Conference on Computational Intelligence and Games (CIG), pp. 1–8. IEEE (2014). doi:10.1109/CIG.2014.6932906
11. Orland, K.: Steam Gauge Ars Series. https://arstechnica.com/series/steam-gauge/. Accessed 24 May 2017

DanceDanceThumb: Tablet App for Rehabilitation for Carpal Tunnel Syndrome

Takuro Watanabe[1(✉)], Yuta Sugiura[1], Natsuki Miyata[2], Koji Fujita[3],
Akimoto Nimura[3], and Maki Sugimoto[1]

[1] Keio University, 3-14-1 Hiyoshi, Kohoku, Yokohama, Kanagawa 223-8522, Japan
{t.tawatana,sugiura,sugimoto}@imlab.ics.keio.ac.jp
[2] National Institute of Advanced Industrial Science and Technology, 2-3-26 Aomi,
Koto, Tokyo 135-0064, Japan
n.miyata@aist.go.jp
[3] Tokyo Medical and Dental University, 1-5-45 Yushima, Bunkyo, Tokyo 113-8510, Japan
{fujiorth,nimura.orj}@tmd.ac.jp

Abstract. We propose a tablet app that aids in rehabilitation for carpal tunnel
syndrome. Patients play a game on a tablet PC in which they catch animal characters displayed on the screen with their thumb. In addition, we developed a
system that records patient rehabilitation logs from the tablet and sends them to
the cloud, where doctors can observe a patient's condition remotely.

Keywords: Rehabilitation · Carpal tunnel syndrome · Gamification

1 Introduction

Thumbs make it possible to grasp and pick stuff up, such as pens, with other fingers are
very important. However, the aging process and applying too much daily stress on the
fingers lead to convulsions in the carpal tunnel, causing paralysis of the thumbs that
makes it difficult to move them. This condition is called "carpal tunnel syndrome" (CTS).

For CTS patients, doctors recommend using the thumbs daily for rehabilitation.
However, because rehabilitation programs are often boring, it is difficult for patients to
remain motivated. As a result, problems occur, such as the thumbs having a limited range
of motion because there has not been enough exercise.

In this paper, we propose a tablet application that supports CTS rehabilitation. CTS
patients play a game in which they catch animal characters displayed on the screen with
their thumb. We also develop a system that records patient rehabilitation logs on a cloud
system, so doctors can observe a patient's condition remotely.

2 Related Work

Ploderer et al. developed a system that visualizes body movement during rehabilitation
and analyzes performance by using a heat map display used with wearable sensors

© IFIP International Federation for Information Processing 2017
Published by Springer International Publishing AG 2017. All Rights Reserved
N. Munekata et al. (Eds.): ICEC 2017, LNCS 10507, pp. 473–476, 2017.
DOI: 10.1007/978-3-319-66715-7_66

attached to multiple parts of the human body [1]. While the system can accurately measure a user's performance, there is the possibility that troublesome preparation will be required to use it, and body movement could be impeded. Kadomura et al. proposed a system that improves the motivation to exercise by measuring body movement with Microsoft Kinect and sharing it with people in remote places [2]. Kinect does not impede body movement or require attaching sensors to the body, which can be troublesome. However, there is the possibility that objects such as furniture may become an occlusion between Kinect and users. Also, these applications target whole body exercise, there is no rehabilitation specialized in finger movement.

There is a smartphone app that collects patient's use logs and analyzes neurological disorders [3]. However, this is specialized for estimating diseases and does not aim to aid in rehabilitating patients suffering from them.

3   DanceDanceThumb

3.1   Overview of System

In this paper, we propose DanceDanceThumb, a tablet app that supports the rehabilitation process for CTS patients. We developed a game in which players collect animal characters by using a simple user interface because most patients with CTS are elderly. We aim for patients to maintain the rehabilitation process with this app. In addition, the app can measure the range of motion of the thumb. Patients can see how much of the ability of their thumb has been recovered by looking at the range of motion of the thumb recorded on the tablet.

3.2   Flow of Experience

First, the patient inserts and fixes their other fingers into a finger guide. Next, the patient measures the extent of thumb movement by drawing a "circle" with the thumb. The circle is recorded in the cloud as two-dimensional coordinates. In addition, the app uses this circle data to set the difficulty of the game. The patient touches any point on the screen with the thumb.

When the patient touches the screen with the thumb, a small green circle is displayed around the position of the thumb (Fig. 1, left). The size of this green circle is approximated to the registered circle at the beginning. At the same time, an illustration of the thumb appears in a large green circle. Thumb movements made in the small green circle are amplified and displayed on the large circle. This makes it easier for patients to understand their own movement because the range of thumb motion after surgery is extremely small. The movement of the thumb is expanded three times and reflected in the illustration of the thumb in the large circle. By controlling the illustration, the patient collects animal characters that appear until they reach a set number. When the patient plays again, the range of thumb motion is re-measured.

3.3 Implementation

We created a finger guide that is attached to the upper part of a tablet in order to fix fingers except the thumb (Fig. 1 left). The guide was designed so that the distance between each finger was 2 cm, and it is printed by using a 3D printer.

We developed the app with Unity software (Fig. 1 right). The touch position of thumb on the touch screen is recorded to a database as 2-dimensional coordinates. The app displays the results of daily rehabilitation with a monthly calendar. The calendar shows the total rehabilitation time for each day with numbers and color gradations. The database was developed by using an existing cloud service, NIFTY Cloud. Recorded data are stored in this database.

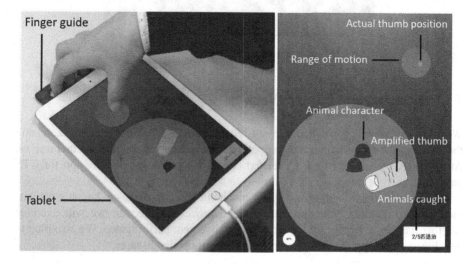

Fig. 1. Game screen of DanceDanceThumb

4 User Trial

We are currently conducting a user trial with actual patients with CTS. All subjects provided full informed consent, and the study was approved by the Tokyo Medical and Dental University Review Board. They have been able to use the system well so far. Hereafter, we are going to collect data from them for 2 months. Figure 2 shows a patient using the app.

Fig. 2. Actual patient using app

5   Conclusion and Future Work

We developed a tablet app that aids in self-rehabilitation for CTS patients. By exercising the thumb on the screen to play a game, patients can become rehabilitated by themselves. At this time, we focused on CTS related conditions and developed the app for CTS patients.

As future work, we will observe how much our app contributes to keeping patients motivated to continue with the rehabilitation process. Moreover, we will examine whether the app is significant for recovering movement performance. We also plan to develop apps to support rehabilitation for other orthopedic diseases.

Acknowledgements. This work was supported by JSPS KAKENHI Grant Numbers JP2670 0017 and JP16H01741.

References

1. Ploderer, B., Fong, J., Withana, A., Klaic, M., Nair, S., Crocher, V., Vetere, F., Nanayakkara, S.: ArmSleeve: A patient monitoring system to support occupational therapists in stroke rehabilitation. In: Proceedings of the DIS 2016, pp. 700–711. ACM (2016)
2. Kadomura, A., Matsuda, A., Rekimoto, J.: CASPER: A Haptic Enhanced Telepresence Exercise System for Elderly People. In Proceedings of the AH 2016. ACM, Article 2, 8 pages. Conference 2016. LNCS, vol. 9999, pp. 1–13. Springer, Heidelberg (2016)
3. Montfort Your Personal Checkup. http://www.mon4t.com/

Novest: Position Estimation of Finger on Back of Hand with a Small Ranging Sensor Array

Yu Ishikawa[✉] and Junichi Hoshino

Graduate School of Systems and Information Engineering, University of Tsukuba, 1-1-1, Tennodai, Tsukuba-shi, Ibaraki, Japan
ishikawa.yu@entcomp.esys.tsukuba.ac.jp,
jhoshino@esys.tsukuba.ac.jp

Abstract. This article suggests a technique to make back of the hand (BOH) a track pad by attaching a distance ranging sensor on the side of a smart watch. It does not only estimate the position of a finger on BoH but also distinguishes the presence or absence of distance between the operating finger and BoH, which functions as an operating surface. Distance data and signal strength data are obtained by distance ranging sensor array, and the presence of distance is distinguished by machine learning. Our performance evaluation shows the accuracy of finger position estimation is 4.2 mm (SD = 1.2 mm).

Keywords: Smartwatch · Position estimation · Ranging sensor array

1 Introduction

The input method of smartwatches depends on a touch panel and buttons. The size of their interface gets smaller in proportion to the size of the devise; therefore, an operating finger becomes relatively large and hides information on screen, which leads to a problem of lowered operating efficiency.

For this problem, a technique to use the fringe area of the device as an input interface is being suggested, and there are types that use permanent magnet [1], interchange signal [2], and supersonic wave [3].

This article proposes a technique to use BoH like a trackpad with a small ranging sensor array. The two-dimensional position of a finger and distance between the finger and BoH is distinguished by obtaining distance data and signal strength data with a sensor attached to the side of a smart watch. Using BoH as a trackpad allows operation without hiding any information on display. Also, it solves the problem of having a difference between an operating object and an input area on screen, by estimating the two-dimensional position of the finger while distinguishing the presence or absence of distance between the finger and BoH.

Published by Springer International Publishing AG 2017. All Rights Reserved
N. Munekata et al. (Eds.): ICEC 2017, LNCS 10507, pp. 477–480, 2017.
DOI: 10.1007/978-3-319-66715-7_67

2 Concept

This study estimates the position of a finger on BoH, and distinguishes the presence or absence of distance between the operating finger and BoH by attaching a small sensor on the side of a smart watch.

Figure 1 (Left) shows the overview of Novest, and 3 states (out of range, hovering, touching) are differentiated while distinguishing the presence or absence of a distance. Out of range is a state where the sensor does not detect the finger, hovering is a state in which there is a certain level of distance between the finger and BoH, and touching is a state in which there is a small amount of distance between the finger and BoH or they are in contact.

To distinguish the distance between a finger and BoH, ranging sensors are arranged vertically on BoH.

The gap between the operating object on display and the input area on BoH is solved by treating them like the relation between a mouse and a mouse pointer, setting up the touching state. Touching is equivalent to clicking on a mouse.

This article only refers to the case of operating with one finger (index finger on right hand) Fig. 1: (Left).

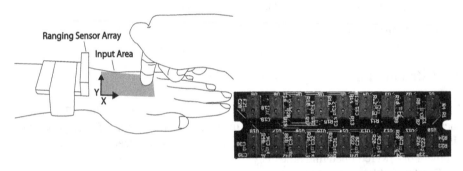

Fig. 1. Overview of Novest: (Left) Usage of Novest, (Right) Ranging sensor array of Novest

3 Implementation

The implemented ranging sensor array is shown in Fig. 1 (Right). The size of the sensor board is 15 mm in length, 50 mm in width and 8 mm in thickness. The width is determined in reference to the side of SONY Smart Watch 3 [4] (10 mm height, 51 mm width). As ranging sensor, 18 (2 × 9) of Time of Flight system STMicroelectronic VL6180Xs are arranged. This arrangement is made during the preliminary experiment to make sure that a finger 20 mm away from the sensor is in the view area of at least one sensor. The minimal vertical intervals implementable are set, and the intervals in the luminescent part are approximately 8 mm. This sensor board is connected to NXP Semiconductors prototyping board mbed LPC1768 with a flat cable, controlled by I2C communication.

Additionally, the noise of distance data and signal strength data obtained by sensor array is suppressed using a low-path filter.

3.1 Finger Position Estimation

Coordinate system is set as Fig. 1 (Left). Strength data of 9 signals of a top column on the ranging sensor is used for Y coordinate derivation. Since this time one finger is assumed to operate, strength data of 9 signals is processed with spline interpolation, determines the position with the strongest signal as Y coordinate.

After that, the sensor distance data closest to the derived Y coordinate is used as X coordinate.

3.2 Finger State Classification

Support Vector Machine is used to classify the distance between the operating finger and BoH. 44 features are used, and they consist of the signal strength ratio of lower column to upper column (9) and its average value, total value, standard deviation, maximum value, minimum value, range, signal strength difference with the adjacent sensor (16), signal strength difference between the lower column and upper column (9), its average value, standard deviation, total value, and the ratio of total signal strength in lower column to total signal strength in upper column. These are scaled from −1 to 1 for use.

4 Evaluation

To evaluate the performance of this technique, experiments under 4 situations were carried out, with a finger and a round stick grasped by a robot arm as a direction method, and a flat surface and BoH as a directed surface. Subjects were 9 university and graduate school students (1 female, 8 males, 23.8 years old (SD = 3.7 years)). The purpose is to confirm the finger and BoH effect on this technique by comparing the position estimate accuracy and the distance distinguishing accuracy under 4 experimental situations.

In this evaluation experiment, pointing task which is to point a marker on BoH or a surface with one's index finger on right hand was implemented, and 20 markers were set up for a random indication.

The task was implemented under the environments of (1) finger and BoH, (2) finger and flat surface, (3) round stick and BoH. The above 3 environments were of evaluation in touching, and after they were completed, same tasks were implemented with hovering in the environment of finger and BoH. With hovering, it was instructed to keep 10–15 mm distance between a finger and BoH.

As a result, the position estimation accuracy of touching was 4.2 mm (SD = 1.2 mm), and the estimate accuracy of hovering was 5.5 mm (SD = 2.8 mm). Additionally, the distance distinguishing accuracy was 91.8% (SD = 8.3%) with per-user classifier.

5 Conclusion

We proposed Novest which is a technique to make BoH a trackpad by setting up a small ranging sensor array on the side of a smart watch. Novest did not only distinguish the two-dimensional position of a finger, but also the presence or absence of a distance from BoH. Then, accuracies of the position estimate and distinguishing distance between touching and hovering were confirmed by implementing pointing tasks under 4 kinds of environments for experiments. As for the position estimate accuracy, a highly accurate estimate of 4.2 mm (SD = 1.2 mm) was possible with touching. Finally, this technique can be expected to be applied to small devices other than a smart watch such as Smart-glasses, because it distinguishes the two-dimensional position of a finger and the presence or absence of distance without attaching a sensor directly on skin.

References

1. Harrison, C., Hudson, S.E.: Abracadabra: wireless, high-precision, and unpowered finger input for very small mobile devices. In: Proceedings of the 22nd Annual ACM Symposium on User Interface Software and Technology, pp. 121–124. ACM (2009)
2. Zhang, Y., Zhou, J., Laput, G., et al.: SkinTrack: using the body as an electrical waveguide for continuous finger tracking on the skin. In: Proceedings of the 2016 CHI Conference on Human Factors in Computing Systems, pp. 1491–1503. ACM (2016)
3. Nandakumar, R., Iyer, V., Tan, D., et al.: FingerIO: using active sonar for fine-grained finger tracking. In: Proceedings of the 2016 CHI Conference on Human Factors in Computing Systems, pp. 1515–1525. ACM (2016)
4. Sony Mobile Communications Inc.: Sony Smart Watch 3 SWR50, Sony Mobile Communications Inc. https://www.sonymobile.com/global-en/products/smart-products/smartwatch-3-swr50/. Accessed 7 June 2017

DecoTouch: Turning the Forehead as Input Surface for Head Mounted Display

Koki Yamashita[✉], Yuta Sugiura, Takashi Kikuchi, and Maki Sugimoto

Keio University, Yokohama-shi, Kanagawa, Japan
zenki@imlab.ics.keio.ac.jp

Abstract. In this paper, we propose a new interaction technique for controlling applications by touching the forehead that the skin deformation is detected by an enhanced Head-Mounted Display (HMD). This technique envisions supporting commands and controls for applications as map applications and photo viewers without carrying additional controlling device which removes the user's eye from the display. In this technique, the skin deformation is measured by attaching light sensors to the HMD. The deformation of the skin is caused by the user touching the forehead with the finger. In this paper, we support the recognition of multiple gestures with a Support Vector Machine (SVM).

Keywords: HMD · Gesture · Recognition

1 Introduction

Head-Mounted Displays (HMD) allow users' to get visual information without restricting our body movement. HMD enables us to see the computer graphics both indoor and outdoor which can support our everyday life, for example, showing the map when walking outside. Recently, applications that overlaps computer graphics to the actual view are released for entertainment use which are suitable for HMD. Therefore, the need of HMD is increasing.

As a fundamental function of the HMD, visual information is presented through a transmissive display fixed in front of the user's sight. Manipulation of HMD is usually performed by mobile devices when using it outdoor. However, when using mobile device, the user must look at the device, which removes the user's sight from the display. Also, it is necessary to carry the HMD and the controlling device separately. Therefore, new type of input method is required. There are input methods that attach sensors to the back of the hands or arms use the surface of the skin as touch surface [1]. In this way, user can input information without changing the gaze direction, but this does not solve the problem of carrying additional device.

We propose a new interaction technique by touching the forehead, which enables user to input information without removing the sight from the display In this technique, we attach light sensors to the frame of the HMD and measure the shape deformation of the skin caused by the user touching forehead with the finger (Fig. 1). Using the acquired sensor data, the directions of the touch on the forehead can be recognized. The sensors

© IFIP International Federation for Information Processing 2017
Published by Springer International Publishing AG 2017. All Rights Reserved
N. Munekata et al. (Eds.): ICEC 2017, LNCS 10507, pp. 481–484, 2017.
DOI: 10.1007/978-3-319-66715-7_68

are attached to the HMD itself; therefore, additional controlling device is unnecessary. There are also research that utilize forehead skin deformation as an input [2], by moving the muscles of the eyebrows. Our research differs from this research as our method uses deformation of the skin caused by the touch of forehead with fingers.

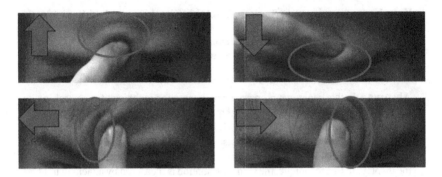

Fig. 1. The deformation of the skin on the forehead.

2   DecoTouch

2.1   Principle

In our studies, we measure the deformation of the skin with some light sensors on the frame of the HMD. This light sensor, called Photo reflective sensor, consists of Infrared LED and phototransistor. This sensor is generally used for measuring the distance from the sensor to the object. We attached the sensors to the frame of the HMD in front of the forehead and measure the distance from the HMD to the forehead. When the user touches the forehead, the deformation of the skin is occurred. As a result, the distance from the sensor to the forehead is changed, and touch gesture can be recognized (Fig. 2).

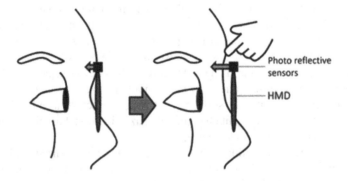

Fig. 2. The principle of the DecoTouch

2.2   Implementation

Hardware

For our recognition system, we attached some light sensors to the front frame of the MOVERIO BT-300 made by EPSON (Fig. 3). In order to get vertical and horizontal deformation of the forehead, we fixed light sensors over two rows. We adopted SG-105 of Codency as a light sensor. Light sensors is connected to the Micro Controller (Arduino Pro Mini, 3.3 V), and sensor data is transmitted to the PC through XBee.

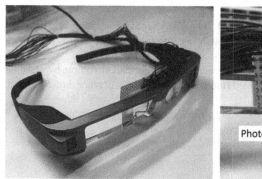 

Fig. 3. The appearance of the DecoTouch

Recognition

Our system performs gesture recognition using the acquired sensor data. We used Support Vector Machine (SVM) which is one of supervised machine learning as gesture recognition. In addition, PSVM: Support Vector Machine for Processing (PSVM) library was used for implementation [3]. This also outputs the result as a probability. Before gesture recognition, we prepare a gesture data set. Our system starts accumulating the learning data by recording the sensor data when the forehead is pulled to the direction of up, down, right or left, and also recording the sensor data when the forehead is not pulled. After collecting sensor data 20 times for each direction, it becomes possible to recognize the gesture that pulls the forehead up, down, left or right, and also the gesture of no touch.

User Trial

We conducted a user study to evaluate the precision accuracy of our system. The participants were instructed to perform the following 5 gestures: 1. No touch, 2. Up pull, 3. Left pull, 4. Right pull, 5. Down pull. We gathered training data 20 times as sensor data for each state and performed ten-fold cross validation for gesture recognition. The participants included 5 men in their 20s. The average accuracy was 80% (standard deviation was 12.5%). In particular, there are a lot of misrecognition about the gesture 1 (No touch) and the gesture 2 (Up pull), and the gesture 1 (No touch) and the gesture 5 (Down pull), which is considered to be caused by the lack in the number of sensors. Adding another sensor row would increase accuracy of the recognition.

3   Conclusion

In this paper, we proposed a new input method for HMD by using forehead as a touch surface. The light sensors attached to the HMD measure the deformation of the forehead when touched with finger. In the user study, we recognized five directional gestures with 80% accuracy (standard deviation was 12.5%).

References

1. Ogata, M., Sugiura, Y., Makino, Y., Inami, M., Imai, M.: SenSkin: adapting skin as a soft interface. In: Proceedings of the 26th Annual ACM Symposium on User Interface Software and Technology, pp. 539–544. ACM (2013)
2. Nakamura, H., Miyashita, H.: Control of augmented reality information volume by glabellar fader. In: Proceedings of the 1st Augmented Human International Conference, article 20, 3 p. ACM (2010)
3. PSVM: Support Vector Machine for Processing. http://makematics.com/code/psvm/

Workshops and Tutorials

An Analysis of Sales Promotion 'Discount' Using Game Refinement Measurement

Long Zuo[✉] and Hiroyuki Iida

Japan Advanced Institute of Science and Technology,
1-1 Asahidai, Nomi, Ishikawa 923-1211, Japan
{zuolong,iida}@jaist.ac.jp

Abstract. This paper explores a promising rate of discount as sales promotion, whereas game refinement measurement is employed for the assessment. Computer simulation was performed to collect data for the analysis, and real data from well known companies such as Amazon JP was used. The results indicate that a reasonable discount zone from the customer's point of view is ranged from 49% to 64% off.

Keywords: Sales promotion · Discount · Game refinement measurement

1 Using Game Refinement Theory to Analyze Discount

Classical game theory originated with the idea of the existence of mixed-strategy equilibrium in zero-sum game. It has been widely applied as a useful tool in many domains such as political science, economics and computer science [1]. Game refinement theory is another theory focusing on the attractiveness and sophistication of a game based on the game outcome uncertainty. Many efforts have been made to the study of the attractiveness in the domain of board games, sports and video games [3], which indicates that measurement for game refinement of sophisticated games is located somewhere between 0.07 and 0.08 regardless of different types of games, as shown in Table 1.

The next challenge is to apply the game refinement measurement to serious game domains such as education and business. In this study we have chosen 'discount' as sales promotion in the business domain. If the rate of discount is reasonable from the perspective of customers, the game of discount would have a comfortable zone value of game refinement like sophisticated boardgames and sports.

Published by Springer International Publishing AG 2017. All Rights Reserved
N. Munekata et al. (Eds.): ICEC 2017, LNCS 10507, pp. 487–491, 2017.
DOI: 10.1007/978-3-319-66715-7_69

Table 1. Measures of game refinement for sophisticated boardgames and sports

Boardgames/Sports	GR
Chess [2]	0.074
Go [2]	0.076
Basketball [3]	0.073
Soccer [3]	0.073

2   Mathematical Model and Data Analysis

Usually customers have little knowledge about the cost of a product of interest [4]. It implies that the cost may be not so essential for customers. They would care about the price of the product, i.e., how much money can be saved by the discounting. Thus, the money saved by the sales promotion 'discount' is considered as the benefit for customers. The total benefit of the shopping activity for customers in a certain time is predictable. The game progress [3] can be constructed by two factors: the total benefit of a certain product (say B) and the total normal price without discount (say P). However, the game information progress is unknown during the in-game period. The presence of uncertainty during the game, often until the final moments of a game, renders exponential game progress. Hence, a realistic model of game information progress is given by Eq. (1).

$$x(t) = B(\frac{t}{P})^n \tag{1}$$

Here n stands for a constant parameter which is given based on the perspective of an observer in the game considered. Then acceleration of game information progress is obtained by deriving Eq. (1) twice. Solving it at $t = P$, the equation becomes

$$x''(P) = \frac{Bn(n-1)}{P^n}P^{n-2} = \frac{B}{P^2}n(n-1) \tag{2}$$

Hence, it is reasonably expected that the larger the value $\frac{B}{P^2}$ is, the more the game becomes exciting due to the uncertainty of game outcome. Thus, we use its root square, $\frac{\sqrt{B}}{P}$, as a game refinement measure for the discount. To normalize this model, we assume that the benefit of a product is ranged from 0 to 100 and the normal price is 100. When there exits a percentage off of discount, there also exists a 100 normal price in our mind since it is expressed as a percentage. Then the game refinement measurement for customers can be shown in Eq. (3) and we get the GR_c of different extent of discount for customers, as shown in Table 2. Here d stands for the discount coefficient. For example, if the discount is 10% off, the discount coefficient is 0.9.

$$GR_c = \frac{\sqrt{B}}{P} = \frac{\sqrt{100(1-d)}}{100} \tag{3}$$

Table 2 shows that GR_c values are ranged from 0 to 1. However, it is important to identify a reasonable discount zone for customers. It is expected that

Table 2. GR_c

Discount	GR_c
0% off	0
10% off	0.032
20% off	0.045
30% off	0.055
40% off	0.063
50% off	0.071
60% off	0.077
70% off	0.084
80% off	0.089
90% off	0.095
100% off	0.1

Table 3. Simulation

Ranking	Discount
1	39% off
2	36% off
3	35% off
4	29% off
5	31% off
6	27% off
7	31% off
8	26% off
9	21% off
10	37% off

Table 4. Amazon JP

Ranking	Discount
1	53% off
2	53% off
3	42% off
4	59% off
5	56% off
6	58% off
7	58% off
8	59% off
9	50% off
10	56% off

lower GR would be less attractive for customers, whereas higher GR would be of some concern about quality and hard for the sustainability of seller. To identify the reasonable discount zone, we need to apply the data for the analysis. The data are collected in two ways. One is to optimize the seller's total profit within a certain time with the genetic algorithm by computer simulation, which is performed from the seller's point of view with the maximum total sales volume. Another way is to collect the data from the real business, via the on-line retailers to find the most popular product, where this data collection considers from the customer's point of view [5]. We observed all the category of the best seller and selected the Bento Boxes & Water Bottles. The reason we select this category is that all the top 10 products have a relatively high level of discount and we would like to see the ranking if there exists a higher discount. Then, we set a fictitious market which intends to sell 10,000 products within a year. The total amount sale is determined by two factors: quantity and price. The discount coefficient will be changed every week and range from 0 to 1. The demand of product follows the F distribution and the customers follow the Poisson distribution. So we put the discount coefficient into each room of chromosome. After crossover(0.8), mutation(0.2) and over 500 times iteration, the best solution was found. We show, in Tables 3 and 4, the discount rate by simulation and real data of Amazon JP, respectively. The discount rate of simulation is ranged from 21% off to 39% off, whereas the top sales product of Amazon JP is ranged from 42% off to 59% off. We should note that the results of simulation must be the best solution for the seller but considers little about customers. However, GR_c of Amazon JP is ranged from 0.065 to 0.077, which is located in the zone value. Thus, we see that simulation concerns about sustainability of the game and Amazon JP concerns about popularity of the game under the assumption that the sales promotion 'discount' is a fascinating game.

Table 5. Discount rate and measures of game renement (GRc) for Amazon JP, Simulation and Recommend

	Discount rate	GR_c
Amazon JP	42% off–59% off	0.065–0.077
Simulation	21% off–39% off	0.046–0.062
Recommend	49% off–64% off	0.07–0.08

3   Finding Comfortable Discount Zone

The attractiveness of games often comes with approximately 0.07 to 0.08 GR values and its corresponding discount zone is ranged from 49% off to 64% off, as shown in Table 5. The essence of game refinement theory is to find a comfortable acceleration (the sense of thrill) for game players. Hence, the discount rate should not be too high. For example, too high GR_c may also cause some concern such as quality of a product of interest. This is why some shopping festivals like "Black Friday" in America and "1111 shopping festival in China both set their discount rate 50% off since this discount rate falls on the comfortable zone in the sense of game sophistication. Higher GR_c means higher entertaining impact and more popular which would be able to highly motivate customers to buy more.

We evaluated the game refinement values of different extent of discount which is considered as the game of sales promotion in business, while using the game refinement measurement derived from the game information progress model. This is because the acceleration of game information progress is related to the emotional impact such as entertainment and engagement which may correspond to the force in our mind. In the business domain, the seller sets the discount rate and the customers will be encouraged to buy more due to the attractiveness. Thus, this study quantified the game refinement value of discounting and recommended the seller to set the discount rate which is ranged from 49% off to 64% off. According to the proposed discount zone, the seller may select its own discount strategy, i.e., the dynamics of discounting.

This paper provides a perspective that discount as sales promotion can be considered as entertainment. Thus, in this paper, we only focused on the attractiveness of discount without considering the cost, the value of item and the motivation of customer. The essential idea of this paper is to offer an appropriate discount zone based on the previous knowledge from the well refined game as we consider that discounting is a kind of game thinking in the business domain. This is the first attempt to apply game refinement theory to the domain of business with a focus on sales promotion 'discount'. Future works may consider other sales promotions such as coupon and freebie.

References

1. Sadrian, A., Yoon, Y.: Business volume discount: a new perspective on discount pricing strategy. Int. J. Purch. Mater. Manag. **28**(2), 43–46 (1992)
2. Iida, H., Takeshita, N., Yoshimura, J.: A metric for entertainment of boardgames: its implication for evolution of chess variants. In: Nakatsu, R., Hoshino, J. (eds.) Entertainment Computing. ITIFIP, vol. 112, pp. 65–72. Springer, Boston, MA (2003). doi:10.1007/978-0-387-35660-0_8
3. Sutiono, A.P., Ramadan, R., Jarukasetporn, P., Takeuchi, J., Purwarianti, A., Iida, H.: A mathematical model of game refinement and its applications to sports games. EAI Endorsed Trans. Creat. Technol. **2**(5), 1–7 (2015)
4. Dada, M., Srikanth, K.N.: Pricing policies for quantity discounts. Manage. Sci. **33**(10), 1247–1252 (1987)
5. url:https://www.amazon.co.jp/gp/bestsellers

Word Recognition by Combining Outline Emphasis and Synthesize Background

Yukihiro Achiha[1]([✉]), Takayoshi Yamashita[1], Mitsuru Nakazawa[2],
Soh Masuko[2], Yuji Yamauchi[1], and Hironobu Fujiyoshi[1]

[1] Chubu University, Kasuga, Japan
yukihiro@vision.cs.chubu.ac.jp
[2] Rakuten Institute of Technology, Rakuten, Inc., Tokyo, Japan

Abstract. Character recognition collects item keywords from images from e-commerce websites; however, it requires a huge amount of training data. In this paper, we propose an efficient method to collect the training data by generating synthesis images and emphasizing outlines to obtain realistic images. The proposed method improves recognition accuracy on both generated images and real images from e-commerce websites.

Keywords: Character recognition · Synthesis image · CNN

1 Introduction

Deep Convolutional Neural Network (DCNN) is a common approach in character recognition of handwritten characters and signs in scenes. Character recognition in scene images consists of two parts: character detection and recognition [4]. This technique can be applied to item images from e-commerce websites to collect the item's information. DCNN requires a huge amount of training data in order to obtain high accuracy [3,5]. Although public datasets are available, the range of fonts in these datasets is too small. In order to address this problem, a character synthesis method was proposed to reduce the image collection cost [1], which generates synthesis images by using font data and background images. However, it assumes English characters on a simple background. In this paper, we propose a method to generate synthesis characters and word images using Japanese font data and complex background images for item images from e-commerce websites. In addition, we introduce an approach to emphasize the outline of characters. Our method trained with synthesized images, which include both with and without outline emphasis, improves recognition accuracy.

2 Proposed Method

The proposed method consists of three steps: generation of character images, addition of margins and emphasis of outlines, and synthesis of the characters with a complex background. Figure 1 shows the flow of character image generation.

© IFIP International Federation for Information Processing 2017
Published by Springer International Publishing AG 2017. All Rights Reserved
N. Munekata et al. (Eds.): ICEC 2017, LNCS 10507, pp. 492–496, 2017.
DOI: 10.1007/978-3-319-66715-7_70

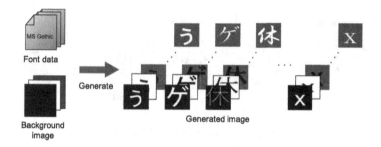

Fig. 1. The flow of character image generation

Fig. 2. Addition of margins and emphasis of outline

Fig. 3. Synthesis of background image (Color figure online)

First, character images are generated from character lists with font data; these images are then synthesized with a background image. We prepared 22 fonts commonly used in e-commerce websites such as MS Mincho and Yuri Gothic.

Character images on complex backgrounds of e-commerce images are sometimes decorated, for example with borders. In order to improve recognition accuracy of such characters, outline emphasis of characters is introduced during character generation. First, a margin is added to the generated image. Then, an outline is added to emphasize characters in the image. At that time, two types of images are generated with different outline thicknesses. Figure 2 shows the flow of the addition of margins to the character image, followed by outline emphasis.

The background region is replaced with a complex background such as an item image. As shown in Fig. 3, the color of the background is green, and the color of the character and the outline are different. The background image is cropped randomly from a banner image of an e-commerce store.

The DCNN is trained by using the synthesis character images. To test the effectiveness of the method, we also applied the proposed method to word synthesis. The word images are generated based on a word list and synthesized with complex backgrounds.

2.1 Structure of DCNN

Figure 4 shows the DCNN network structure. The network consists of 4 layers: 3 convolution layers and 1 fully connected layer. The filter size of each layer

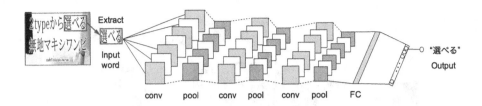

Fig. 4. The structure of DCNN

is 5 × 5. Max pooling is employed for the pooling layer. The fully connected layer has 4,096 units and it employs Dropout [7] during the learning phase. The activation function of each layer is ReLU [6]. The output units have 1,253 classes for character recognition and 241 classes for word recognition. The input image size is 32 × 32 for character recognition and 96 × 96 for word recognition, respectively. AdaGrad [8] is used for the optimization method. The mini batch size is 32 and the epoch number is 50.

3   Evaluation

First, we evaluate the effectiveness of outline emphasis and synthesis with background images using top 5 accuracy. We trained 1,253 characters using 145 images for each (Fig. 5). For evaluation, 227 images collected from e-commerce websites were used. Table 1 shows the result for synthesis images. The method with emphasis and synthesis achieves best performance on top 1 accuracy.

The evaluation results of character recognition and word recognition on real images of e-commerce are shown in Tables 2 and 3, respectively. From Table 2, the method with emphasis performs 12.4% better than baseline, which is without emphasis and synthesis, on top 1 accuracy. On the other hand, the method with synthesis also improves 13.8% than baseline on top 1 accuracy. The combination

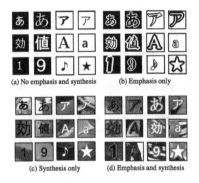

Fig. 5. Example of synthesis images

Table 1. The comparison of character recognition on synthesis images [%]

Outline	Background	Top1	Top2	Top3	Top4	Top5
–	–	99.4	99.8	99.8	99.8	99.9
x	–	96.0	97.7	98.2	98.6	98.8
–	x	99.1	99.6	99.8	99.9	99.9
x	x	99.6	99.9	99.9	99.9	99.9

Table 2. Comparison of character recognition on real images [%]

Outline	Background	Top1	Top2	Top3	Top4	Top5
–	–	50.3	62.0	66.2	69.6	71.5
x	–	62.7	72.5	75.8	77.5	78.7
–	x	64.1	73.1	76.9	79.4	80.9
x	x	64.3	74.4	78.2	80.2	81.4

Table 3. Comparison of word recognition on real images [%]

Outline	Background	Top1	Top2	Top3	Top4	Top5
–	–	27.6	34.1	36.8	40.2	42.1
x	–	48.0	56.0	58.8	60.7	61.9
–	x	52.0	58.5	60.7	63.8	64.4
x	x	62.8	69.3	70.9	73.4	76.2

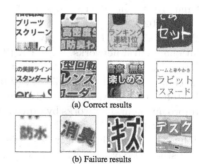

(a) Correct results

(b) Failure results

Fig. 6. Examples of recognition results

of emphasis and synthesis achieves best performance with an improvement of 14.0%. The results of word recognition on real images are shown in Table 3. The method with emphasis improves about 20.4% and 19.8% than baseline on top 1 and top 5, respectively. Synthesis is also effective for real images; it improves accuracy by 24.4% and 22.3% than baseline on top 1 and top 5, respectively. The combination of emphasis and synthesis achieves best performance. Figure 6 shows recognition results. It recognizes words correctly even when the number of characters is different. However, recognition fails when the characters are blurred or rotated.

4   Conclusion

In this paper, we proposed a method to generate outline emphasis of word images and synthesize them with complex background images. The DCNN trained with generated images obtained high accuracy on both synthesized images and real images from e-commerce websites.

References

1. Jaderberg, M., Simonyan, K., Vedaldi, A., Zisserman, A.: Synthetic data and artificial neural networks for natural scene text recognition. In: NIPS Deep Learning Workshop, arXiv 2014 (2014)
2. Kobayashi, T., Nakagawa, M.: A pattern classification method of linear-time learning and constant-time classification. IEICE **89**(11), 981–992 (2006)
3. LeCun, Y., Bottou, L., Bengio, Y., Haffner, P.: Gradient-based learning applied to document recognition. Proc. IEEE **86**(11), 2278–2324 (1998)

4. Liu, C.-L., Koga, M., Fujisawa, H.: Lexicon-driven segmentation and recognition of handwritten character strings for Japanese address reading. TPAMI **24**(11), 1425–1437 (2002)
5. Wang, T., Wu, D.J., Coates, A., Ng, A.Y.: End-to-end text recognition with convolutional neural networks. In: ICPR (2012)
6. Nair, V., Hinton, G.E.: Rectified linear units improve restricted boltzmann machines. In: ICML, pp. 807–814 (2010)
7. Hinton, G.E., Srivastava, N., Krizhevsky, A., Sutskever, I., Salakhutdinov, R.R.: Improving neural networks by preventing co-adaptation of feature detectors. Clinical Orthopaedics and Related Research, abs/1207.0850 (2012)
8. John, D., Hazan, E., Singer, Y.: Adaptive subgradient methods for online learning and stochastic optimization. J. Mach. Learn. Res. **12**, 2121–2159 (2011)

Shaping Attitudes Across Realities.
Exploring Strategies for the Design of Persuasive Virtual, Augmented and Mixed Reality Games

Martijn J.L. Kors[1,2(✉)], Karel Millenaar[2], Erik D. van der Spek[1], Gabriele Ferri[2], Ben A.M. Schouten[1,2], and Tim Marsh[3]

[1] Industrial Design, Eindhoven University of Technology, Eindhoven, The Netherlands
{m.j.l.kors,e.d.vanderspek,bschouten}@tue.nl
[2] Play and Civic Media, Amsterdam University of Applied Sciences,
Amsterdam, The Netherlands
{m.j.l.kors,k.millenaar,g.ferri,b.a.m.schouten}@hva.nl
[3] Griffith Film School, Queensland College of Art, South Brisbane, Australia
t.marsh@griffith.edu.au

Abstract. Virtual, Augmented and Mixed Reality technologies are embraced by designers, scholars and charities alike, some primarily for their entertaining properties, others also for the opportunities in education, motivation or persuasion. Applications with the latter objective, that of persuasion, are designed not only to be entertaining, but are also designed (or framed) to shape how players think and feel about issues in reality. However, despite the growing interest in the persuasive opportunities of these immersive technologies, we still lack the design strategies and best-practices that could support in the design of these 'immersive persuasive games'. To address this still-unexplored and fragmented design space, we organize a design-oriented workshop that brings together academia and industry. The workshop is informed by a Research through Design approach in which the primary focus is to generate knowledge through designing. Participants design and evaluate ideas on-the-spot in an iterative manner using low-fidelity, life-size, prototyping and role-playing techniques, thereby mimicking an embodied interactive immersive environment. By reflecting on design practices and player experiences, we construct a body of knowledge, built exemplar work and distil best-practices to formulate design strategies for the design of immersive persuasive games.

1 Towards Immersive Persuasive Games

It took well over two decades for Virtual Reality to make a commercial comeback after its backlash in the late eighties/early nineties. And even though its future is still uncertain, many have already embraced the new wave of Virtual Reality technologies for various objectives, among which persuasion. Similarly uncertain in its outlook, but not less interesting, we see an increasing proliferation of consumer-grade Augmented Reality devices, such as mobile phones, Google Glass and Microsoft HoloLens.

© IFIP International Federation for Information Processing 2017
Published by Springer International Publishing AG 2017. All Rights Reserved
N. Munekata et al. (Eds.): ICEC 2017, LNCS 10507, pp. 497–501, 2017.
DOI: 10.1007/978-3-319-66715-7_71

Together, these new or resurgent technologies blur the boundaries of the magic circle. They place you virtually inside the body of another person, or change the world around you to reflect another person (or fictional character)'s reality. The experiences in these alternate reality devices can be designed not only to be entertaining, but also hold the intent to shape how players think and feel about issues in their own reality [6].

As we playfully interact with this alternate reality, thus we engage in gameplay, experientially gleaning meaning from this digitally enhanced virtual or augmented world. Bogost pointed at the unique persuasive properties of digital games in general, coining the term 'procedural rhetoric'. Procedural rhetoric, in Bogost's words, is seen as *"the art of persuasion through rule-based representations and interactions rather than the spoken word, writing, images or moving pictures"* [1]. Through rules and procedures, the way simulations play out, games can covertly present players with enthymemes framed to tell something about issues in their own reality. A classic example of such a Persuasive Game is 'Darfur is Dying', a game that *"was created in 2006 to put you* [the player] *in the shoes of a displaced Darfurian refugee"* [10] to have the player experience 'what it feels like' to be a refugee, shape her attitudes, and hope-fully stimulate to take action in the real world. Looking at the contemporary media landscape, there is probably no other field in which questions of empathy and persuasion play a more vibrant role than in that of immersive technologies. Through these tech-nologies it has become significantly easier to immerse the player in a virtual world, creating a sense of presence, and have her stand in someone else's shoes [4, 6]. Artists like Milk have already dubbed Virtual Reality the *"ultimate empathy machine"* [8], and the salience of this topic is further illustrated by recent Virtual and Mixed Reality projects like Project Syria, DeathTolls Experience, and one of our own projects, A Breathtaking Journey [6]. These projects are all designed with the intent to, just like 'Darfur is Dying' over a decade ago, raise empathy and shape attitudes towards refugees by placing the player in their shoes. The idea of placing the player in someone else's shoes relates to the concept of role-playing, perspective taking and direct-experience, which have shown to support persuasion [7]. However, despite the captivating persua-sive potential of immersive technologies [2], we unfortunately still lack the design know-how to advance the design of these immersive persuasive games. This workshop is organized to address this gap in design knowledge. Through a Research through Design inspired approach [13], participants design and evaluate ideas on-the-spot in an iterative manner [3]. We focus on low-fidelity, life-size, prototyping and role-playing techniques, thereby mimicking a Mixed Reality environment without having to rely on technical implementation during the workshop. By reflecting on design practices and player expe-riences we construct a body of knowledge, collect exemplar work and distil best-prac-tices that to help in formulating design strategies.

2   Workshop Planning

The workshop will be held as a single-day event and is expected to host approximately 12 participants. We will distribute the call for papers through social media, industry platforms, mailing lists, special interest groups and the workshop's website. We will also invite experts of exemplar work to join and share their perspective. The following table presents a preliminary planning for the workshop.

Time	Activity
09:00–10:30	**PechaKucha.** After a short introduction by the organizers, we ask each participant to present their PechaKucha presentation [5] based on their submitted abstract, with particular focus on design related factors. After each presentation, we will shortly recap the highlighted design opportunities or issues, which will serve as input for the initial ideation and prototyping session
10:30–11:30	**Initial Ideation.** After dividing the group into teams of 3–4 participants we will explain the persuasive message as starting point for their game; including several background stories and a persuasive game design toolkit. Teams then explore the topic, draft possible arguments, set player experience goals [3] and have a first through about suitable gameplay possibilities
11:30–12:00	**Lunch Break.**
12:00–16:00	**Prototyping.** In the third session each team will have four hours to iteratively [3] work on their prototype using techniques like Bodystorming [11]. Each teams is asked to create a low-fidelity, life-size, prototype using the provided material and tools. This setup will mimic an immersive and embodied interactive Mixed Reality environment, without the need to rely on technical implementation. Throughout we will intervene with Role-playing techniques [12] to evaluate player experience. During these interventions, the team will act as the game's mechanics, while someone from another team acts as the player. As informed by a Research through Design approach [13] we will discuss and document interesting, unexpected and valuable insights throughout the design process for later reflection
16:00–17:00	**Formulating Design Insights.** In the fourth session, we will discuss the insights and formulate possible strategies, techniques and best-practices that were supportive for the ideation and prototyping processes

3   Expected Workshop Outcomes

All accepted submission will be included in the workshop proceedings that are accessible through the workshop's website. After the workshop we will share a summary of the workshop; including a collection of the formulated design strategies and best-practices for later reference, as well as an overview of the prototypes that can serve as exemplar work. After the workshop we also invite authors to submit a case-based design-oriented abstract for review to be included in the Persuasive Gaming in Context book, funded by the Netherlands Organization for Scientific Research [9].

4 Main Workshop Organizers

Martijn J.L. Kors is a doctoral candidate and game designer at the Eindhoven University and Amsterdam University of Applied Sciences. In his design-research he studies the design of immersive interactive entertainment with persuasive intent.

Karel Millenaar is a game designer who supports research at the Amsterdam University of Applied Sciences. He also founded FourceLabs, a company that designs serious games for attitude and behavior change.

5 Submissions

Abstracts should have a maximum of 500 words and include the name of the participant(s), affiliation, background, motivation for joining the workshop, and ideas for persuasive game design. An affinity with one of the following topics is recommended:

- Design or analysis of immersive, persuasive games, techniques and prototypes.
- Persuasive game design strategies, approaches, techniques or best-practices.
- Interviews or ethnographic studies on the development of persuasive games.

Abstracts will be reviewed based on their relevance, quality, and contribution to the workshop.

Acknowledgement. This research is part of the project "Persuasive gaming. From theory-based design to validation and back", funded by the Netherlands Organization for Scientific Research.

References

1. Bogost, I.: Persuasive Games: The Expressive Power of Videogames. Mit Press, Cambridge (2007)
2. Carpenter, J.M., Green, M.C.: Flying with Icarus: narrative transportation and the persuasiveness of entertainment. In: Psychology of Entertainment Media, 2nd edn., pp. 169–194. Routledge, Florence (2012)
3. Fullerton, T.: Game Design Workshop: A Playcentric Approach to Creating Innovative Games. CRC Press, Boca Raton (2008)
4. Grigorovici, D.: Persuasive effects of presence in immersive virtual environments. In: Riva, G., Davide, F., IJsselsteijn, W. (eds.) Being There: Concepts, Effects and Measurement of Presence in Synthetic Environments (2003)
5. Klein, A., Dytham, M.: PechaKucha 20x20. http://www.pechakucha.org
6. Kors, M.J.L., et al.: A breathtaking journey. On the design of an empathy-arousing mixed-reality game. In: Proceedings of the 2016 Annual Symposium on Computer-Human Interaction in Play, pp. 91–104. ACM (2016)
7. Maio, G., Haddock, G.: The Psychology of Attitudes and Attitude Change. Sage, Thousand Oaks (2009)
8. Milk, C.: How virtual reality can create the ultimate empathy machine. TED (2015)

9. Netherlands Organisation for Scientific Research: Persuasive gaming. From theory-based design to validation and back. http://www.nwo.nl/en/research-and-results/research-projects/i/76/10476.html
10. Ruiz, S., et al.: Darfur is dying (2006)
11. Schleicher, D., et al.: Bodystorming as embodied designing. Interactions **17**(6), 47–51 (2010)
12. Simsarian, K.T.: Take it to the next stage: the roles of role playing in the design process. In: CHI 2003 Extended Abstracts on Human Factors in Computing Systems, pp. 1012–1013. ACM, New York (2003)
13. Zimmerman, J., et al.: Research through design as a method for interaction design research in HCI. In: Proceedings of the SIGCHI Conference on Human Factors in Computing Systems, pp. 493–502. ACM (2007)

ECEC2017: The Workshop on E-Commerce and Entertainment Computing

Mitsuru Nakazawa[1]([✉]), Masahumi Muta[1], Kazuki Ookawara[2], and Soh Masuko[1]

[1] Rakuten Institute of Technology, Rakuten, Inc., Setagaya-ku, Japan
{mitsuru.nakazawa,masafumi.muta,so.masuko}@rakuten.com
[2] University of Tsukuba, Tsukuba, Japan
okawara.kazuki@entcomp.esys.tsukuba.ac.jp

Abstract. Online e-commerce has been growing continuously. According to eMarketers latest forecasts, worldwide retail e-commerce sales will reach $4 trillion USD by 2020. In addition, using cutting-edge technologies such as augmented reality (AR), virtual reality (VR), mixed reality (MR), sensing technology, image processing, robotics and online payment technology, new shopping experiences that enhance offline or online shopping, or integrate the two types of shopping experiences are being introduced. In this workshop, new concepts and recent progress in shopping experiences are discussed from various perspectives. The workshop will include invited talk sessions by world-leading innovators, and interactive poster and demonstration presentations of submitted papers and abstracts.

Keywords: E-Commerce · Entertainment computing · Workshop

1 Introduction

Before the emergence of the Internet, shopping was limited to brick-and-mortar stores, where consumers went to see, touch and purchase physical items (offline shopping). However, after the Internet emerged, it became possible for consumers to engage in a new shopping experience, i.e., online shopping. Online shopping has profoundly changed how we purchase goods. Now we can view and purchase products from a large number of online stores anytime from anywhere. According to eMarketers latest forecasts [1], worldwide retail e-commerce sales will reach $4 trillion USD by 2020.

Recently, many cutting-edge technologies such as augmented reality (AR), virtual reality (VR), mixed reality (MR), sensing technology, image processing, robotics and online payment technology have been rapidly refined. Using these technologies, novel services that enhance conventional offline or online shopping have been introduced, e.g., robot reception in a store [2] and AR furniture shopping [3,4]. Moreover, for better coordination of the two types of shopping

N. Munekata et al. (Eds.): ICEC 2017, LNCS 10507, pp. 502–506, 2017.
DOI: 10.1007/978-3-319-66715-7_72

experiences, there have been some attempts to encourage online shopping in an offline store and vice versa, i.e., Offline-to-Online and Online-to-Offline (O2O). In the near future, it is expected that consumers will not be conscious of the difference of the two, which look like smoothly integrated [5].

2 Related Work

In this section, we introduce related work of enhanced offline and online shopping, and O2O services. Figure 1 represents the overview of related work.

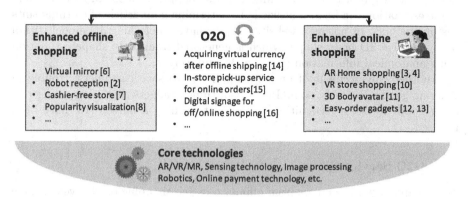

Fig. 1. Overview of enhanced offline and online shopping, and O2O services

2.1 Enhanced Offline Shopping

To make offline shopping more convenient or entertaining, various attempts have been made in an physical store by using cutting-edge technologies. In a fashion store, a virtual mirror was installed by using AR technology so that a customer can try on as many items as they want without putting off their clothes [6]. In an electronics retail store, intelligent movable robots were assigned to eliminate the shortage of professional explainers who have much knowledge of its products [2]. In a grocery store, [7] proposed a cashier-free system by making the best use of vision sensing and pattern recognition technology to realize a store with no lines and no check out. In a sales event of a department store, to easily understand the popularity of each event store, 3D-animated human-shaped icons appeared on a paper map representation in a large display monitor based on hourly point of sales (PoS) data [8]. Purchasing behavior data such as PoS data and a customer flow map are valuable for not only customers but also retailers who hope to optimize their store layout [9].

2.2   Enhanced Online Shopping

Although even conventional online shopping is convenient in term of anytime anywhere shopping, it is originally less sense of reality because an intangible product is displayed in not actual size on a 2D web browser. To solve such lack of reality, AR technology has been often employed. For example, [3, 4] proposed an AR home shopping experience where actual size furniture appears on a smartphone display. VR technology, which allows a user to secure a higher immersion feeling, is another approach to put more reality in online shopping. [10] developed a VR showroom that enables a user to dive into a virtual store that looks exactly like a physical one. In online clothes shopping, technology of 3D body shape estimation can be also utilized. To determine if an article of clothing suits customer's body or not on a website, [11] displayed a clothing 3D model with a representative 3D body shape, which is generated from body shape estimation using anatomical information (e.g., height and weight).

Another enhancement of online shopping is to save customer's trouble in ordering goods. Recently, some Internet-of-things gadgets that allow an user to order goods by voice recognition [12] or just pushing a button [13] have been released.

2.3   O2O Services

To draw potential customers from offline to online shopping or vice versa, some O2O services have been launched. For examples, [15] started in-store pick-up service for online orders. In [14], an user got rewarded with virtual currency that can be used in online shopping after offline shopping. [16] released a digital signage display that can order goods on-line in case of that they are sold out in the physical store.

3   Overview of ECEC2017

Although many services beyond conventional offline and online shopping have already been proposed as described in Sect. 2, we believe that shopping experiences will keep evolving based on upcoming new technologies. Therefore, to discuss new concepts and current progress in shopping experiences, we will hold this workshop. It will include invited talk sessions and an interactive poster and demonstration session. In the invited talk sessions, world-leading innovators will give a talk about their specialized fields of VR shopping [17], Retail analysis [9], Image processing for e-commerce [18] and Drone business [19]. The interactive poster and demonstration session will cover the following topics:

- Gamification of shopping experiences
- Entertainment psychology and shopping experiences
- Shopping attractions
- Online-to-offline, Omni channel with entertainment
- Use of wearable/smart devices for shopping

- Physical shopping interfaces
- Augmenting real-world shopping experiences using VR/AR/MR technologies
- Image/Video processing for e-commerce
- Best practices in e-commerce and entertainment

We look forward to discussion with you toward future shopping at ECEC2017.

References

1. eMarketer: Worldwide Retail Ecommerce Sales Will Reach $1.915 Trillion this Year. https://www.emarketer.com/Article/Worldwide-Retail-Ecommerce-Sales-Will-Reach-1915-Trillion-This-Year/1014369. Accessed 19 June 2017
2. Nestle: Nestle to use humanoid robot to sell Nescafe in Japan. http://www.nestle.com/media/news/nestle-humanoid-robot-nescafe-japan. Accessed 19 June 2017
3. CNET: iPhone's futuristic AR dream starts with Ikea. https://www.cnet.com/news/ikea-ar-app-apple-arkit-report/. Accessed 19 June 2017
4. Murakami, S., Mukasa, T., Tung, T.: Mobile virtual interior stylization from scale estimation. In: ACM SIGGRAPH 2016 Posters, pp. 14:1–14:2 (2016)
5. Bandara, U., Chen, J.: Ubira: a mobile platform for an integrated online/offline shopping experience. In: Proceedings of the 13th International Conference on Ubiquitous Computing, UbiComp 2011, pp. 547–548 (2011)
6. Fitnect: 3D Virtual fitting dressing room/mirror. http://www.fitnect.hu/. Accessed 19 June 2017
7. Amazon: Amazon Go. https://www.amazon.com/b?node=16008589011. Accessed 19 June 2017
8. Masuko, S., Kuroki, R.: AR-HITOKE: Visualizing popularity of brick and mortar shops to support purchase decisions. In: Proceedings of the 6th Augmented Human International Conference, AH 2015, pp. 185–186 (2015)
9. ABEJA: ABEJA PLATFORM for Retail. https://service.abeja.asia/. Accessed 19 June 2017
10. Trillenium: Trillenium VR showroom. http://www.trillenium.com/vr-showroom.html. Accessed 19 June 2017
11. Fits.me: Fits.me. https://fits.me/. Accessed 19 June 2017
12. Google: Start shopping with the Google Assistant on Google Home. https://blog.google/products/home/start-shopping-google-assistant-google-home/. Accessed 19 June 2017
13. Amazon: Amazon Dash Button. https://www.amazon.com/Dash-Buttons/b?node=10667898011. Accessed 19 June 2017
14. Rakuten: McDonalds and Rakuten Announce Rakuten Point Card Partnership to Improve Customer Convenience. https://global.rakuten.com/corp/news/press/2017/0526_01.html. Accessed 19 June 2017
15. Rakuten: Rakuten and Lawson to Collaborate to Launch Convenience Store Pickup Service. https://global.rakuten.com/corp/news/press/2015/0825_01.html. Accessed 19 June 2017
16. Digital Signage Today: Interactive Kiosks Draw in O2O Sales for Department Stores. https://www.digitalsignagetoday.com/press-releases/interactive-kiosks-draw-in-o2o-sales-for-department-stores/. Accessed 19 June 2017

17. Rakuten.today: Getting Real About VR in e-commerce: Rakuten Virtual Boutique. https://rakuten.today/blog/vr-e-commerce-virtual-boutique.html. Accessed 19 June 2017

18. Simo-Serra, E.: Research. http://hi.cs.waseda.ac.jp/esimo/en/research/. Accessed 19 June 2017

19. Rakuten: SoraRaku: Drone Delivery. https://soraraku.rakuten.co.jp/en/. Accessed 19 June 2017

Erratum to: Evaluating a Serious Game for Cognitive Stimulation and Assessment with Older Adults: The Sorting Sheep Game

Helio C. Silva Neto, Joaquim Cerejeira, and Licinio Roque

Erratum to:
Chapter "Evaluating a Serious Game for Cognitive
Stimulation and Assessment with Older Adults:
The Sorting Sheep Game" in: N. Munekata et al. (Eds.):
Entertainment Computing – ICEC 2017, **LNCS 10507,**
https://doi.org/10.1007/978-3-319-66715-7_13

In the original version of this paper, a reference to an earlier paper by the same authors was omitted. This has now been rectified and the reference has been added.

The updated online version of this chapter can be found at
https://doi.org/10.1007/978-3-319-66715-7_13

Gamifying Experiences Using a Peer Learning Assessment System: Combining Two Separate Research Traditions to Promote Student Learning (Poster and Interactive Session)

Audun Grom[✉], Gabrielle Hansen, and George Adrian Stoica

Norwegian University of Science and Technology, Høgskoleringen 1,
7491 Trondheim, Norway
{audun.grom,gabrielle.hansen,george.a.stoica}@ntnu.no

Abstract. This demonstration presents a gamifying use of a new assessment technology, the Peer Learning Assessment System (PeLe), in higher education. By implementing key elements from gaming in a traditional assessment practice, using new technology, students can gain a new understanding of what assessment in higher education could look like: engaging, exciting, interactive, fun and rewarding in terms of new learning experiences. Students will assume the role of players in small teams and acquire a sense of competing against other's teams through quiz-based testing. The students will respond to the quizzes using their own mobile devices. The students will automatically be rewarded points for correct answers and deducted points for wrong answers. Upon completion of the test, the results will be reviewed in a plenary session, where the teams will have the opportunity to close the gap between attained and desired achievements. The overall purpose is to combine the best from two separate research traditions, gaming and assessment, and facilitate more engaging assessment in higher education.

Keywords: Gamifying experiences · Gamification · Assessments · Quiz · Learning

1 Introduction

Gamification, defined as "the use of video game elements in non-gaming systems to improve user experience and engagement" [1], has become a popular technique used in a variety of contexts to motivate people to engage in particular targeted behaviours [2]. In education and employee training, for example, the use of individual game elements is also becoming increasingly popular [2]. The overall purpose is often to provide users with a gamified experience. However, gamified experiences have yet to be accommodated in all parts of the education system. A highly traditional part of this system is assessment practices within higher education. At this educational level, assessment is still considered to be a transmission process in which teachers "give" students feedback on their academic strengths and weaknesses, which students are then supposed to

N. Munekata et al. (Eds.): ICEC 2017, LNCS 10507, pp. 507–509, 2017.
DOI: 10.1007/978-3-319-66715-7

somehow "decode" and convert into concrete actions to improve their understanding and academic progress [3]. There are few, if any, examples of gamifying experiences to increase students' engagement. Nonetheless, learning is at its best when it is active, goal-oriented, contextualized and interesting. Instructional environments should thus be interactive, provide ongoing feedback, grab and sustain attention and have appropriate and adaptive levels of challenge — in other words, have the features of good games [4].

2 Peer Learning Assessment System

One2act PeLe (Peer Learning Assessment System) comprises three main components: a central REST service that deals with all the requests from the users, a student client account that allows the students to participate using their (own) devices and a teacher client account that allows the teacher to create and control sessions. Typically, the teacher will prepare a set of questions (i.e. an assessment) and will define the correct answer and the scores awarded for each of them. The scoring model in PeLe is quite flexible allowing for both simple and advanced operation. The teacher can monitor the status of the classroom as the students answer and is therefore able to prepare the feedback/discussion/competition phase. The teacher can then show the aggregated results for all or a subset of the questions and discuss the results in a plenary review session. PeLe supports discussion through interactive visualization. Furthermore, it supports re-voting questions from the defined set and creation of new questions as required by the discussion.

3 Gamifying Experiences Using PeLe

The students are placed in random teams of three to four players. Each team is given a test with varied quiz questions. First, each player works on the questions individually. This allows the players to process the questions and think through possible arguments for different response options, and thus prepares them for team participation. Then the players will act as a team. Each team must reach an agreement internally within the group before submitting their responses. This is done to emphasize the value of peer collaboration. The teams will be awarded points automatically for correct answers and deducted points for wrong answers. The teacher will have full live coverage of this process.

When the teams have submitted their responses the players will have a short break before they return to the classroom and start a plenary session to review the results. Since the teacher has a clear overview of how each team has performed, he or she can easily identify which areas the students are struggling with and which ones they master, and can then use this information as a guide during the plenary review session. From the students' point of view, this is when the game really begins. During the review, the players will be given several opportunities to re-vote. In other words, they will have an opportunity to change their original, submitted response. They will be awarded double or triple points compared to what they could gain in the original test. This means that those with the lowest score still have the opportunity to win. The teacher chooses the questions he or she wants the players to answer again. It could be questions that the teacher knows the players are struggling with, or questions he or she knows they master. The teacher can also show the players how the different teams have responded as a whole. This would obviously be done without revealing what alternative is correct. Furthermore, the teacher can give the players an academic hint or guidance and ask them to discuss the questions within the teams before re-voting. Each team must now evaluate their original response and discuss whether this was actually correct or not, and whether they are willing to change their original response.

After each re-vote, it is critically important that the teacher goes through the quiz questions and explains why the different alternatives are right or wrong, include the teams and their ways of thinking and thus facilitates student participation and learning experiences. At the end of the plenary review session, the teacher announces the winning team, which is the team with the highest score. From a pedagogical point of view, the gamifying elements have been included to engage the students, and the real winners are those who learned through immediate feedback, teachers' guidance, collaboration and increased engagement.

References

1. Deterding, S., Sicart, M., Nacke, L., O'Hara, K., Dixon, D.: Gamification: Toward a definition. In: Proceedings of the CHI 2011 Gamification Workshop, p. 1, Vancouver, British Columbia, Canada (2011)
2. Landers, R.N.: Developing a theory of gamified learning: linking serious games and gamification of learning. Simul. Gaming, 1–17 (2015)
3. Nicol, D.J., Macfarlane-Dick, D.: Formative assessment and self-regulated learning: a model and seven principles of good feedback practice. Stud. High.Edu. **31**, 199–218 (2006)
4. Shute, V.J.: Stealth assessment in computer-based games to support learning. In: Tobias, S., Fletcher, J.D. (eds.) Computer Games and Instructions, pp. 503–523. Age Publishing Inc. (2011)

Women and Computer Games
(Workshops and Tutorials)

Letizia Jaccheri[1(✉)], Alf Inge Wang[1], Kristine Ask[2],
Sobah Abbas Petersen[3], and Kristina Brend[4]

[1] Department of Computer Science, Norwegian University of Science
and Technology (NTNU), Trondheim, Norway
{letizia.jaccheri,alf.inge.wang}@ntnu.no
[2] Department of Interdisciplinary Studies of Culture, NTNU,
Trondheim, Norway
kristine.ask@ntnu.no
[3] NTNU and SINTEF, Trondheim, Norway
sobah.petersen@sintef.no
[4] NxtMedia, Trondheim, Norway
kristina.brend@gmail.com

Abstract. This full day workshop welcomes contributions that enhance the state of the knowledge about the relation between women and computer games. Women have often been seen as consumers of computer games. The current landscape of computer games show an increasing number of both game designers and players. This workshop aims to bring together game designers, developers and players in engaging discussions about women and computer games. We look for theoretical contributions, specific aspects and examples, and pedagogical frameworks. The workshop is organized as discussions and group work.

Keywords: Computer games · Gender issues

1 Introduction

Gender issues in computer games have been a hot topic the last few years. In the wake of the Gamergate harassment campaign of 2014 that targeted women players and designers, the gendered aspects of play has warranted attention [7]. While research on gender and computer games has been going on since the 1990s [5], it is no longer a topic reserved for the 'ivory tower' [2, 3]. Major news outlets across the world is covering how computer games persists as 'boy's toys', and the women gamers demanding equal treatment [6]. Even though women make up half of the total gaming population, their place and role in gaming culture and industry is still contested. This is visible in both how AAA titles are targeted at male audiences, and in how female gamers and developers are being disproportionally targeted for harassment [1, 5, 9]. As games are increasingly being brought into education, the need for gender inclusive games is also becoming more urgent.

© IFIP International Federation for Information Processing 2017
Published by Springer International Publishing AG 2017. All Rights Reserved
N. Munekata et al. (Eds.): ICEC 2017, LNCS 10507, pp. 510–512, 2017.
DOI: 10.1007/978-3-319-66715-7

A key step in bridging the digital divide in games is to empower women as game designers, and to develop methods for inclusive game design. Informal discussions among game designers highlight differences between female game designers and male designers; e.g. male designers are more interested in the technical aspects of the design while the female designers are interested in the aesthetic aspects. While it may not be easy to generalize on such observations, there is a need to explore the landscape of game design to identify the strengths and creative designs that female designers could contribute. More importantly, inclusive game design methods could leverage on the benefits of females designers' contributions. For this, we need qualified research on gendered aspect of design and play, and ways to disrupt existing design methods and paradigms.

In this workshop, we will look specifically at design processes and research processes of computer games, and how games can be designed for inclusion [4]. The topics for discussions include, but are not limited to:

1. Theoretical contributions, such as analysis of Self Determination Theory and how the different aspects are implemented differently by female designers.
2. Pedagogical frameworks for teaching and learning computer game design related gender issues.
3. Specific aspects of gendered play, like sexual harassment and stereotype threat, but also gamer identity and role in gamer communities. Of particular interests are ways to combat and disrupt discriminatory practices [10].
4. Examples of games for learning, designed and developed by women
5. Examples of inclusive game design or processes of inclusive design [8].

The workshop will ideally server as an arena for networking among researchers interested in women and games, and for seeding ideas and discussions for future research. The organizers anticipate a special issue of the Elsevier Entertainment Computing Journal that is related to this topic, Participants of the workshop will be invited to contribute articles for the special issue.

The Workshop will be held 18th September 2017 in connection with IFIP ICEC. Workshop participants will be invited to present their ideas and there will be room for discussions and creative reflection work.

References

1. Ask, K., Svendsen, S.H.B., Karlstrøm, H.: Når jentene må i skapet: Seksuell trakassering og kjønnsfrihet i online dataspill. Norsk Medietidsskrift 1(1) (2016)
2. Kafai, Y.B., Richard, G.T., Tynes, B.M.: Diversifying Barbie and Mortal, Pittsburgh, Carnegie Mellon. ETC Press (2016)
3. Giannakos M.N., Chorianopoulos K., Jaccheri L., Chrisochoides N.: "This Game Is Girly!" perceived enjoyment and student acceptance of edutainment. In: Göbel, S., Müller, W., Urban, B., Wiemeyer, J. (eds.) E-Learning and Games for Training, Education, Health and Sports. LNCS, vol. 7516, pp. 89–98. Springer, Heidelberg (2012)
4. Hartmann, T., Klimmt, C.: Gender and computer games: exploring females' dislikes. J. Comput.-Mediat. Commun. 11(4), 910–931 (2006)

5. Jenson, J., Castell, S.: Online games, gender and feminism. In: The International Encyclopedia of Digital Communication and Society (2015)
6. Kircher, H.: Closing the Gender Gap, One E-Battle at the Time, New York Times (2016). https://www.nytimes.com/2016/06/26/fashion/league-of-legends-women-video-games.html?_r=0. Accessed 24 June 2016
7. Mortensen, T.E.: Anger, Fear, and Games. Games and Culture, 1555412016640408 (2016). http://doi.org/10.1177/1555412016640408
8. Ray, S.G.: Gender Inclusive Game Design. Charles River Media (2004)
9. Salter, A., Blodgett, B.: Hypermasculinity & dickwolves: the contentious role of women in the new gaming public. J. Broadcast. Electron. Media **56**(3), 401–416 (2012). http://doi.org/10.1080/08838151.2012.705199
10. Chess, S., Shaw, A.: A conspiracy of fishes, or, how we learned to stop worrying about gamergate and embrace hegemonic masculinity. J. Broadcast. Electron. Media **59**(1), 208–220 (2015)

Author Index

Printed in the United States
By Bookmasters